ANDROID

Programming
Concepts

TRISH CORNEZ
UNIVERSITY OF REDLANDS

RICHARD CORNEZ
UNIVERSITY OF REDLANDS

JONES & BARTLETT
LEARNING

World Headquarters
Jones & Bartlett Learning
5 Wall Street
Burlington, MA 01803
978-443-5000
info@jblearning.com
www.jblearning.com

Jones & Bartlett Learning books and products are available through most bookstores and online booksellers. To contact Jones & Bartlett Learning directly, call 800-832-0034, fax 978-443-8000, or visit our website, www.jblearning.com.

07915-9

Production Credits

VP, Executive Publisher: David D. Cella
Publisher: Cathy L. Esperti
Acquisitions Editor: Laura Pagluica
Editorial Assistant: Taylor Ferracane
Production Editor: Sara Kelly
Senior Marketing Manager: Andrea DeFronzo
VP, Manufacturing and Inventory Control: Therese Connell

Composition: S4Carlisle Publishing Services
Cover Design: Kristin E. Parker
Rights and Media Research Coordinator: Abigail Reip
Media Development Assistant: Shannon Sheehan
Cover Image: © Involved Channel/Shutterstock
Printing and Binding: RR Donnelley
Cover Printing: RR Donnelley

Library of Congress Cataloging-in-Publication Data
Cornez, Trish.
Android programming concepts/Trish Cornez, University of Redlands, Redlands, California, [and] Richard Cornez, University of Redlands, Redlands, California.
    pages ; cm
Includes bibliographical references and index.
ISBN 978-1-284-07070-5 (pbk.)
1. Android (Electronic resource) 2. Application software—Development. 3. Tablet computers—Programming.
4. Smartphones—Programming. I. Cornez, Richard. II. Title.

QA76.774.A53C67 2017
005.26'8—dc23

2015008371

6048

Printed in the United States of America
19 18 17 16 15   10 9 8 7 6 5 4 3 2 1

Dedication

For Bob

Contents

Preface

Mobile device users experience their environments through a variety of computing screens. The devices most often used are computers, tablets, and phones. Users today increasingly expect a conncctcd and highly personalized experience that is seamless across all connected devices, including television, home automation gadgets, wearable computers, and cars. Android is the operating system that powers many of these connected devices. As of early 2015, Android is the largest installed base of any mobile platform.

Initially created by Android Inc. by a team led by Andy Rubin, the Android operating system was acquired by Google in 2005. The first commercial version of Android was released in 2008 on an HTC phone named Dream; also known as the T-Mobile G1. Since its initial release, the operating system has undergone an extreme metamorphosis, evolving quickly and frequently, with new and updated versions released at an unprecedented rate.

As a Linux-based system, Android is run as an open source project; this means that anyone can adapt the code for his or her own purposes. This permissive model makes Android unique in that it allows companies and developers to modify and distribute the software freely. Device manufacturers creating phones and tablets often customize the Android operating system to the specific needs of their particular mobile devices.

In this text, readers will learn how to design and implement applications that will run on a variety of Android-driven devices. Building sophisticated applications that are optimized, responsive, and able to perform complex interactions at fast speeds requires patience, skill, and practice. The concepts and techniques you will learn in this text will provide you with the building blocks needed to master the art of mobile programming.

Text Objectives

This text was conceived with two types of individuals in mind: programming students and professional software developers who wish to broaden their expertise. It is essential that readers know how to program in an OOP language, preferably Java, before using this text. For non-Java programmers, familiarization with the Java API is recommended.

This text is intended as a textbook, not as a tutorial. We have designed the text, using an easy-to-understand and straightforward approach, to integrate key concepts relating to application development that students see daily on Android devices. Each chapter presents Android concepts and methodologies with complete abbreviated application examples that are relevant to current platforms.

How to Use This Text

The first three chapters provide an introduction to the foundation of application development. Chapter 1 incorporates two step-by-step tutorials to help readers get started in creating basic applications. Chapters 2 and 3 provide key core concepts for building well-designed applications. It is important that readers are comfortable with these early chapters before proceeding.

After reading the first three chapters, Chapters 4 through 9 do not need to be read in sequential order. Readers wishing to acquire the most invaluable concepts first should start with Chapter 4 and proceed to Chapters 7, 8, and 9; however, multithreading concepts (discussed in Chapter 6) are a prerequisite for the last three chapters. A detailed reading of Chapter 5 is not required for Chapter 6.

Instructor and Student Resource Material

The following ancillary materials are available on the text website:

go.jblearning.com/CornezAndroid

- Source code files for lab examples
- Instructor's Manual containing solutions to end-of-chapter exercises
- Lecture Slides in PowerPoint format
- Test bank

Acknowledgments

We have received invaluable support from friends, students, and colleagues in the preparation of the text. The University of Redlands has provided the resources and means for us to complete the project. Jones & Bartlett Learning offered an excellent team of professionals who handled the book from manuscript to final production. We especially want to thank Laura Pagluica, Taylor Ferracane, Sara Kelly, and Abby Reip.

We are thankful to Jordan Vega and Sam Marrs for many useful suggestions. We are indebted to Jim Bentley and Pani Chakrapani for giving us the opportunity to schedule several mobile programming classes that allowed us to classroom-test portions of our text. Jim Bentley was kind enough to offer department funds for devices for some of our students, who might not otherwise have been able to participate.

We would like to thank the following reviewers, who offered us indispensable pedagogical and content guidance for revision:

Sonia Arteaga
Hartnell College

Jeremy Blum, DSc
Associate Professor of Computer Science
Penn State Harrisburg

Georgia Brown, MS
Instructor
Northern Illinois University

George Dudas
Instructor in Computer Science and Software Engineering
Penn State Erie, The Behrend College

Shane Schartz
Informatics
Fort Hays State University

Robert Steinhoff, PhD
Florida Memorial University

Michael Ziray
Boise State University

Last but not least, thanks to our many students whose struggles, challenges, and successes gave us all the evidence we needed to improve the text.

1

Introduction

Chapter Objectives

In this chapter you will:

- Understand the features of Android.
- Learn the differences between Java and Android Java.
- Examine the Android project structure.
- Build a basic application using Android Studio.
- Learn about the Model-View-Controller design.

■ 1.1 Android Platforms

When the first-generation Android phones were released in 2008, they did not include many of the features that users are familiar with today. For example, the first commercial version of Android seen on the HTC Dream did not incorporate multitouch capabilities or even a virtual onscreen keyboard. Since 2008, Android has been enhanced in a multitude of ways, improving its performance, the user interface design, and adding many features, such as voice searching. By October 2014, Google released a version of Android comprising a powerful core of set standards that work on virtually every device, along with a refined visual component. By 2015, Android applications were including fluid animations, bold color palettes, and sophisticated multitasking menus that featured voice interactions.

Table 1-1 shows the evolution of Android, beginning with Android 1.0, the first commercial version used on the HTC Dream. With each subsequent version of Android, features from previous versions were improved and enhancements were made that targeted overall performance.

As each major version of Android is released, it is identified by a code name, organized in alphabetical order; all of the code names are the names of desserts. The first publicly code-named version of Android appeared in 2009 and was given the name **Cupcake**. In addition to the code name, each version of Android is given an API (application program interface) number and platform version number. Updates

TABLE 1-1 Common Android Platforms

Platform Version	API Level(s)	Year	Version Name	Important Features
5.0	23	2014	Lollipop	Tuned to work on devices with 64-bit ARM, Intel, and MIPS processors
4.4	19	2013	KitKat	Optimized to run with a minimum of 512 MB of RAM
4.3 4.2 4.1	18 17 16	2013, 2012	Jelly Bean	Efficient and refined user interface Google Voice Search
4.0.4, 4.0.3, 4.0.2, 4.0.1, 4.0	15 14	2012 2011	Ice Cream Sandwich	Compatibility with most Android 2.3.x API fixes and refinements
3.2 3.1 3.0	13 12 11	2011	Honeycomb	Tablet-only support
2.3.4, 2.3.3, 2.3.2, 2.3.1, 2.3	10 9	2011 2011	Gingerbread	Enhancements for game developers Support for multicore processors
2.2	8	2010	Froyo	Android Cloud support
2.1 2.0.1 2.0	7 6 5	2010	Eclair	Google Maps Navigation New camera features Bluetooth Speech-to-text
1.6	4	2009	Donut	Integrated camera and camcorder Expanded gestures Introduction of Quick Search Box
1.5	3	2009	Cupcake	Soft keyboard Copy and paste Video recording
1.1	2	2009		Bug fixes to Android 1.0
1.0	1	2008		Gmail Notifications Widgets

are designed so that a new API remains compatible with earlier versions of the API. The API identification is important to developers, as well as to Google Play, because it allows the Google Play store to filter applications so that users can easily download applications that are compatible with their devices. New versions of Android also bring a collection of new APIs for developers, such as notification controls or aids to make applications more memory efficient.

Google services have been integrated into the Android operating system since the first installment. Two of the most substantial inclusions of Android 1.0 were **Google Maps** and **Notifications**, which supported a pull-down window that revealed announcements and messages. The **Notifications feature** remains an important part of the Android user interface. In current releases of Android, this feature has been refined to include chat messages and calendar events that support synchronization across all Android devices, as shown in Figure 1-1.

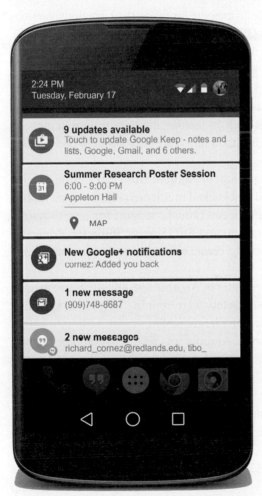

| FIGURE 1-1 Android Lollipop Notifications.

By the time **Cupcake** appeared in 2009, such refinements as the inclusion of self-refreshing widgets and copy-and-paste had been implemented. One of the most significant features that emerged with **Cupcake** was the introduction of a soft keyboard, which also brought the first forms of keyboard skins. Created by third-party developers, keyboard skins provide enhancements to an existing soft keyboard. Unique to Android, skins allow users to personalize their keyboards, for example, by choosing a background texture, an icon set, and a color palette. When Google releases its latest version of Android, device manufacturers typically customize that software for their brand of phone and tablets. Skins have evolved alongside Android and have shifted beyond basic appearance and into more extensive behavior than originally seen in Cupcake. Today, Android device manufacturers regularly offer skins that enhance the user experience by adding functionality to the design.

Created in 2010, Android 2.2 was able to execute far faster than previous versions because of the new Dalvik Just-In-Time (JIT) compiler, first seen on **Froyo**. Dalvik, which will be discussed in more detail in the next section, allowed for better CPU performance, which significantly enhanced processing power. Along with the bolstered speed, Froyo's browser came with a new JavaScript engine, making Internet browsing nearly three times faster than the previously released version of Android. **Froyo** also brought native support for tethering. This built-in feature, along with mobile hotspot support, gave users the ability to turn their phone into a wireless modem and a Wi-Fi hotspot for the first time.

Gingerbread became the prevailing version of Android from 2011 through most of 2012. It was the first version of Android that backed multicore processing on mobile devices. For application developers, **Gingerbread** brought support for new technologies, such as NFC (Near Field Communication) and SIP (Session Initiation Protocol). The SIP API provides developers with tools to create applications that perform video conferencing and instant messaging.

Honeycomb was released as the first version of Android specifically implemented for tablets. Prior to **Honeycomb**, Android tablets were running on phone operating systems that were stretched to fit the screen of a larger tablet.

With the release of **Ice Cream Sandwich**, Android was rebuilt to combine the best characteristics of **Gingerbread** and **Honeycomb** into a single operating system that would work for tablets and phones. **Ice Cream Sandwich** was able to bring many of the design elements of **Honeycomb** to smartphones, while refining the Android experience. The UI was notably more refined and stylish. In addition, navigation buttons became available as soft keys, and the voice input engine provided an open-microphone experience.

When **Jelly Bean** was released in 2012, it was the fastest and smoothest of all the Android versions. Along with its Google Voice Search feature, **Jelly Bean** was a jump in magnitude of performance. This version of Android was often referred to as a turning point for Android, where services and customization options met responsive design guidelines. **KitKat** looked similar to **Jelly Bean**; however, because of its size of 512 MB, it was able to run on a much larger array of devices. Previously, Android required 1 GB to 3 GBs to run.

As of early 2015, **Lollipop** is the latest version of Android used by developers. Lollipop and 64-bit chips provide enhanced performance with graphics, decoding and encoding of high-resolution video, and algorithms for facial recognition and speech interaction.

With so many versions of Android currently being supported, it is often difficult to choose the appropriate target version for which to compile an application. In fact, the latest version of Android is not always the most common version installed on Android phones and tablets. The ability to build an application that runs on multiple versions of Android is an important requirement for developers. For example, in early 2015, the most common version of Android was **Jelly Bean**, with **KitKat** a close second. However, **Ice Cream Sandwich** and **Gingerbread** were still being used on a small, but significant, number of the mobile devices worldwide. Targeting popular earlier versions of Android therefore allows developers to reach a larger number of users, but there can be tradeoffs. An application may require functionality that an older platform cannot support. In this case, an application developer should target a newer platform when building an application.

■ 1.2 Java vs. Android Java

Java is the recommended language for developing Android applications. In this textbook, all Android apps will be developed with Java. It is essential that readers know how to program and have a familiarity with Java libraries before continuing. A large number of Java libraries are available in the Android platform. As any Java programmer knows, Java comes with a library of classes providing a collection of utility functions that most Java programs cannot do without. This class library, called the Java API, has several thousand classes, with tens of thousands of methods that can be used in Android programs.

Android applications use Java, along with the extension libraries that Android provides in the Android software development kit (SDK). The SDK includes a comprehensive set of development tools, including a debugger, software libraries, and an emulator for an Android device.

Important differences distinguish the Java API from the Android API. To understand Android Java, we first need to understand what characterizes Java. Java differs from other programming languages in several noteworthy ways; the crucial difference is platform independence. One reason Java is so popular is that Java programs can be run on any computer with an installed Java Runtime Environment (JRE). Figure 1-2 illustrates Java's platform independence. Java files are compiled to an intermediate representation rather than directly to a platform-specific machine code. This intermediate representation, Java bytecode, is analogous to machine code. The major difference between bytecode and machine code is that bytecode instructions are interpreted by a virtual machine (VM) written specifically for the host hardware. A virtual machine is a software implementation of a machine (i.e., a computer) that executes programs like a physical machine.

To run non-Android Java programs, a Java compiler must translate the source code files into class files. These files can then be executed on a Java virtual machine (JVM), which interprets the intermediate language on a target computer. By preparing a JVM for each platform, a program translated into the intermediate language can be run on many different computers. The Java virtual machine is called "virtual" because it is an abstract computer defined by a specification. Each Java application runs inside a runtime instance of some concrete implementation of the abstract specification of the JVM. The JVM runs on all kinds of hardware executing the Java bytecode without changing the Java execution code. Java bytecode runs in a JRE, which is composed of the Java API and the JVM.

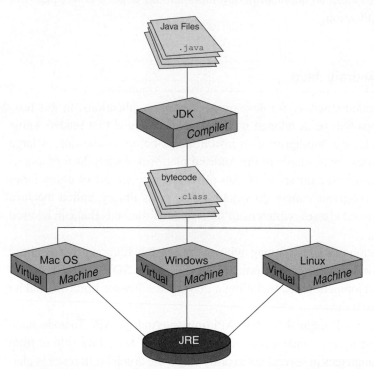

▌ FIGURE 1-2 Java programs are compiled into bytecode and run in Java Runtime Environments.

There is no Java virtual machine in the Android platform; instead, there is Dalvik, which is a specialized virtual machine. Once Java has been compiled into bytecode by the Java compiler, it is compiled again into a proprietary bytecode, as illustrated in Figure 1-3. The bytecode loaded by the Dalvik virtual machine should not be confused with Java bytecode. The dex bytecode is a compact Dalvik executable format designed for Android systems, which are constrained in terms of memory and processor speed. The Android Software Development Kit includes the Dalvik dx tool, used to translate Java bytecode into Dalvik bytecode.

Dalvik is referred to a JIT (Just-In-Time) engine because it compiles bytecode in real time. A new Android Run Time (ART) was introduced in 2014 that takes advantage of current hardware advances. ART relies on an AOT (Ahead of Time) compiler, which compiles bytecode before execution. The ART virtual machine is the default of **Lollipop** and compiles an application to native machine code when installed on a user's device. ART is designed to be fully compatible with Dalvik's existing bytecode format.

Dalvik and ART do not align to all Java class library profiles. Specifically, `Abstract Window Toolkit` and `Swing` are not supported by Dalvik and ART. Instead, Android user interfaces are built using the `View` framework, which is similar to `Swing`. This framework will be discussed in detail in Chapter 2.

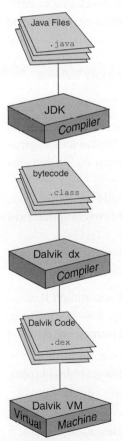

❘ FIGURE 1-3 Java bytecode is compiled into Dalvik bytecode and executed on a Dalvik VM.

■ 1.3 Android Studio IDE

Android applications are often built to take several forms, such as phone, tablet, Wear, and Google Glass. In addition, the project structure of an application consists of many moveable pieces. These factors lead to a complex project structure. To make the development process easier, it is recommended that developers use an integrated development environment (IDE) to build applications. This textbook relies on **Android Studio**.

Based on IntelliJ, **Android Studio** is the official IDE for building Android applications. Developed by Google, this environment focuses exclusively on Android development and comes bundled with the Android Software Development Kit (SDK). The SDK provides developers with a packaged set of developer tools and API libraries for building complete applications, testing them on virtual devices, and performing debugging and optimization.

For readers intent on finding an alternative to Android Studio, it is possible to install a stand-alone SDK tool set that does not include a complete development environment. This option allows developers to access the core SDK tools from a command line or possibly from another IDE, such as Eclipse. This approach is not recommended for first-time developers.

Android Studio is available for download from Android's developer website:

developer.android.com/sdk/installing/studio.html

Updates and improvements are made frequently to Android Studio, as well as to the required plug-ins. You may find that your version of Android Studio looks somewhat different from the images you will see in this text. The core functionality remains the same.

Android Studio requires the Java Development Kit (JDK) for building applications and components. One of the most important tools in the JDK is the Java compiler. Java code featured in this textbook has been compiled with JDK 7.

The following development components are included in Android Studio, or must be added, just as newly released versions of an SDK should be added:

Java Editor	The Java programming language editor contains common IDE features, such as compile-time syntax checking, auto-completion, and integrated documentation for the Android framework APIs.
Layout Editor	Android Studio includes a graphical layout editor for building and editing user interface files. Specifically, this graphical layout editor allows for easy drag-and-drop functionality for designing and previewing user interfaces.
Android SDK	The Android SDK is a collection of API libraries, tools, scripts, and documentation. The SDK separates tools, platforms, and

other components into packages that can be downloaded as needed. As new SDK versions and tools become available, they should be added to Android Studio.

The Android SDK archive initially contains the basic SDK tools. It does not contain an Android platform or third-party libraries. In order to start developing applications, you must install the platform tools and at least one version of the Android platform, using the SDK Manager. Platform tools contain build tools that are periodically updated to support new features in the Android platform.

AVD   To run the Android Emulator, an Android Virtual Device (AVD) is constructed to define the characteristics of the device on which an application can be tested. This includes the system image and screen size, the hardware, data storage, etc. To test an application on multiple Android devices, a unique AVD device must be created for emulation. In Tutorial 1 of this chapter, you will create an AVD to test a simple application.

Gradle   Gradle is the build system used by Android Studio. Provided as a plug-in to Android Studio, it can also be used to build Android apps from the command line. The build configuration of a given Android project is defined inside simple text files that use options from Gradle.

■ 1.4 The Basics of App Design

In the early days of mobile devices, very few apps existed. A mildly interesting and useful application had a fairly decent chance of becoming successful during the first years of Android devices. Today, the competition is far more intense. It is not enough to produce an interesting and useful app, particularly if similar apps are on the market. In addition to a good idea, a promising Android application must perform well, be more interesting than a competing application, and offer a user experience that is highly appealing.

Designing an outstanding application involves considerable thought and analysis of usability and user interface design. These two elements require attention both before and during the development process. In addition to performance, usability and the user experience can often be indicators of the success or failure of an application.

The process for building an application, as depicted in Figure 1-4, begins with an initial idea. Sometimes, research follows to determine the value and demand of an app idea. The initial concept for an application can be somewhat vague at the beginning stage, even if some specifications have been outlined. To evolve design concepts into a workable model, it is advisable to generate a user narrative that recreates a user's experience, given the technical constraints of the application.

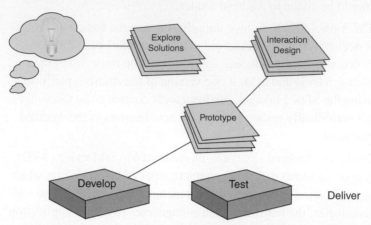

FIGURE 1-4 The process for building begins with an idea and ends with delivery.

Design ideas are generated from the exploration of user experiences. Ideas can start with a simple sketch on paper and evolve into cutout prototypes. Sketches can include design usage scenarios to explore ideas for structuring a navigation system related to the aesthetic qualities of interaction. Cutout prototypes, as shown in Figure 1-5, can serve as micro experiments to explore strengths and weaknesses that involve actual tactile handling. These can also influence technical decisions.

FIGURE 1-5 Use of physical mockups can make application user experiences better understood.

■ 1.5 The Anatomy of an Android Project

A certain amount of technical machinery is necessary in Android to write even the simplest applications. As you learn to develop apps, we will sometimes give you a preliminary explanation and you will have to wait for more complete detail in a later chapter.

The Android SDK tools expect that your project will follow a specific structure so it can compile and package the application correctly. Gradle is at the foundation of the Android SDK build system and is used to automate the building, testing, publishing, and deployment of Android apps.

A project built in Android Studio will be structured similarly to Figure 1-6. The project structure is organized by source code, the application's resources, manifest settings, and build files. All of these files are eventually packaged into an `apk` (Android application package) file, which represents the final application that will be installed and then run on an Android-powered device.

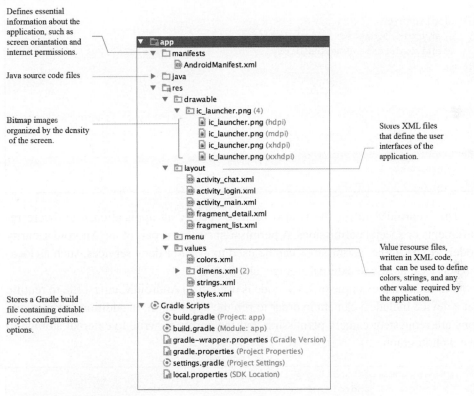

| FIGURE 1-6 Sample Android App Project Structure.

Many of the application files and directories shown in Figure 1-6 are automatically generated and contain default content. Additional files have been generated and hidden from view. At this early stage, it is important that we understand the following six components found in the project structure. Once we understand the purpose of these files, the development process will fit into a more comprehensible context and will be easier to implement.

1.5.1 Android Manifest File

An `AndroidManifest.xml`, is required for every Android application. This file uses XML code to define specific application information. The information can include general application-wide settings, such as the application's style and launch icon. In the example `AndroidManifest.xml` code shown below, Line 6 sets the launch icon to a graphic image stored in the `drawable` folder. Line 7 sets the style of the application so that it has a black background and utilizes a full screen.

```
1  <?xml version="1.0" encoding="utf-8"?>
2  <manifest xmlns:android="http://schemas.android.com/apk/res/android"
3    package="com.cornez.magicjourney" >
4
5  <application
6    android:icon="@drawable/icon"
7    android:theme="@android:style/Theme.Black.NoTitleBar.Fullscreen"
8  >
9  .
10 .
11 .
12
13 </application>
14
15 </manifest>
16
```

The AndroidManifest file is also used to specify an application's hardware requirements or special permissions. A permission system is part of the Android security model. For example, permissions can be used to grant or deny services, such as location services, access to external storage, and SMS.

The following example of XML code is used in an AndroidManifest file to require that a device include a camera in order to run the application. In addition, two permissions are requested: camera permission and the ability to write to external storage to save a photograph.

```
1      <uses-feature
2          android:name="android.hardware.Camera"/>
3          android:required="true" />
4
5      <uses-permission
6          android:name="android.permission.CAMERA"/>
7      <uses-permission
8          android:name=
9              "android.permission.WRITE_EXTERNAL_STORAGE"/>
10
11
12
```

1.5.2 Java Source Code and Activity Class Files

The Java source code of an application is placed in the `java` directory of the project structure. A main file, often named `MainActivity` or sometimes `MyActivity`, is a Java file that is auto-generated when the project is first built. It may have a different name, depending on the Android Studio version you are using. This Java file represents an application activity and is important because it controls the behavior of the application when it is first launched. An Android activity corresponds with a single, focused activity that the user can perform. Applications are made up of one or more Activities. For example, consider a `banking` application that requires the user to log into the account securely before it is possible to access the account information. The login screen would be represented by one activity, while the account overview would be represented by a separate activity.

Each Activity is represented by a visual interface to the user, called a layout, along with source code, such as `MainActivity.java`, that drives it.

Activities are essentially defined using two types of files:

- Java class determines the behavior of the activity.
- Layout determines the visual layout of the activity.

When an application is designed with multiple activities, one activity must be designated as the main activity when the application is launched for the first time. By default, this activity is the one first created and named when the application project is first set up.

1.5.3 Drawable Resources

The drawable folder is located in the `res` directory, which contains the application resources. Drawable resources are image files, such as application icons, buttons, and background textures. Mobile applications typically require many visual elements, which are often managed as drawable resources. For example, in a chess game application, the chess pieces are drawable image files imported into the application project. The most common drawable resource used in an application is a PNG file. Android recommends the use of graphics that are not interlaced and are stored with a 24-bit depth. Images and icons do not need to be restricted to web-safe colors.

Android runs on a variety of devices, ranging from low-density small screens to high-density large screens. A density-independent pixel (dp) is a virtual pixel unit that is equivalent to one physical pixel on a 160-dpi (dots per inch) screen. This is the baseline density assumed by the system for a medium-density screen. The conversion of dp units to screen pixels (px) is:

$$px = dp \times (dpi/160)$$

For example, on a 240-dpi screen, 1 dp equals 1.5 physical pixels.

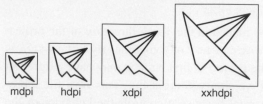

I FIGURE 1-7 Pixel density of graphic images ranges from medium to extra-high density.

Because of the diversity in Android devices, it can be a challenge to construct perfect-looking drawables for all existing Android-powered devices. When creating drawables, it is highly common for app designers to give strong consideration to screen density. For example, developers often create three to five images for the following generalized screen sizes:

extra-large screens are at least 960 dp × 720 dp

large screens are at least 640 dp × 480 dp

normal screens are at least 470 dp × 320 dp

small screens are at least 426 dp × 320 dp

To achieve a high level of graphics quality on all screen densities, developers should provide bitmap resources that are properly scaled to each of the generalized density buckets: low, medium, high, and extra-high density. Figure 1-7 illustrates screen densities created for an application launch icon.

To properly scale application images, it is best to start with a raw resource in vector format and generate the images for each density using the following size scale:

xxhdpi: 3.0

xhdpi: 2.0

hdpi: 1.5

mdpi: 1.0 (baseline)

This means that if a 300 × 300 image is built for xxhdpi devices, the same drawable image should be built in 200 × 200 image for xhdpi, 150 × 150 for hdpi, and 100 × 100 for the mdpi devices. It should be noted that this textbook features a collection of apps designed for exploration. To keep the focus on concepts, we have minimized the time required to build the lab applications. This means that with the exception of Chapter 1, only baseline drawable images are made available for lab applications.

1.5.4 Layout XML Files

In an Android application, the user interface screens are visually designed and coded as XML layout files. An application can have many screen designs, as illustrated in Figure 1-6. These files are stored in the `res/layout` directory of the project structure. A layout is the visual representation of a given interface screen containing all the visual objects on display. As shown in Figure 1-8, the design and arrangement of the elements on the screen are implemented using XML code in a layout file.

When a layout appears on the screen, it is managed by an Activity. An Activity is a Java class that drives the actions and movements that will occur on the screen. Chapter 2 will explore techniques for designing various screen layouts.

I FIGURE 1-8 The User Interface of an application is defined by an XML file.

1.5.5 Value Resources

The `res/values` directory within an Android project is used to manage value resources for the application. This includes strings, colors, dimensions, and styles used by the application. Value resources are implemented as XML files.

Android encourages the separation of functionality and resources. This philosophy of keeping values separate from functions can be very helpful for developers. For example, when developing an application that will be translated into multiple foreign languages, string values can be changed without affecting the deployment of the app. The application can be translated from the first language to a second language by recustomizing the `strings.xml` file. In this way, the application `apk` can remain intact.

Value resource files are organized by the various types of data they contain. A collection of text strings is stored as `strings.xml`, while color definitions can be stored in `colors.xml`.

1.5.6 Gradle Scripts

The Gradle Scripts directory stores the application's build files. These files allow developers to configure build settings, override, edit, and add custom build options.

For example, the following build.gradle project file is used to configure the build settings of an app named Test Application. The minimum SDK version is set to an API level of 16, corresponding to JellyBean. As the name suggests, the minimum API level defines the minimum version of Android on which the application can function. This definition is also used by Play Store to detect if the application is compatible with the user's device.

The target SDK version is specified as API level 23, Lollipop. This is the build target against which Android Studio will build. When building against API level 23, the application will still be able to run on API level 16, as long as the source code does not rely on any APIs that are not available on API level 16.

The build system can also generate multiple apk files with different build configurations for the same module. This is used to build different versions of an application.

```
1   apply plugin: 'com.android.application'
2
3   android {
4       compileSdkVersion 23
5       buildToolsVersion "21.1.1"
6
7       defaultConfig {
8           applicationId "com.cornez.testapplication"
9           minSdkVersion 16
10          targetSdkVersion 23
11          versionCode 1
12          versionName "1.0"
13      }
14  buildTypes {
15      release {
16          minifyEnabled false
17          proguardFiles
18              getDefaultProguardFile('proguard-android.txt'),
19              'proguard-rules.pro'
20      }
21    }
22  }
23
24  dependencies {
25      compile fileTree(dir: 'libs', include: ['*.jar'])
26      compile 'com.android.support:appcompat-v7:21.0.2'
27  }
```

■ 1.6 Building Basic Applications in Android Studio

When Android Studio is launched for the first time, the Setup Wizard, as shown in Figure 1-9, will install a current Android SDK and configure the development environment settings. In addition, an optimized emulator will be created for testing applications.

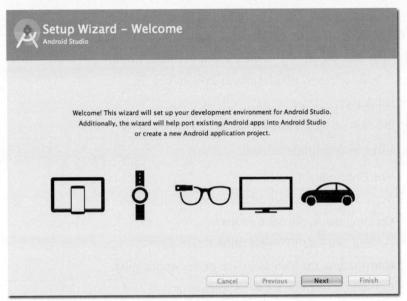

▌ FIGURE 1-9 Android Studio Setup Wizard will install the latest Android SDK.

When building a first application in Android Studio, a certain amount of step-by-step guidance is useful. The following two tutorials will demonstrate the basics of getting started and creating simple applications. Read both tutorials thoroughly to help you understand the anatomy of an application and get acclimated to the development process. In addition, the tutorials will help you with future lab work by providing an important sense of how much background information is assumed about the development process.

■ Tutorial 1: Hello World

Since 1974, it has been a tradition for budding programmers to write an introductory program that displays the greeting "Hello World." Even though Android programmers are not budding programmers, we will preserve that tradition in this step-by-step tutorial with a slight modification. We will create an interactive greeting application named `Hello Goodbye`. As shown in Figure 1-10, the user will be presented with a single button, "Exclamation." When the user clicks the button, the app will respond by displaying the "Hello" greeting in a text field. When the user clicks a second time, the app will respond with "Goodbye." Each subsequent click will toggle the displayed output between "Hello" and "Goodbye."

This first tutorial provides an opportunity to explore the basics for constructing an application using Android Studio. The specific objectives for this tutorial are as follows:

1. Illustrate the process of constructing a simple Android app from beginning to end.
2. Discuss the idea and importance of the Layout Manager Editor.
3. Introduce the basic anatomy of an Android Java source file.
4. Build a virtual device.
5. Test the application on a physical device and a virtual device.

The tutorial is broken into multiple sections:

Part 1:   The Conceptual Design
Part 2:   Verifying the Required SDKs for Android Studio
Part 3:   Creating the Application Project
Part 4:   Adding and Editing Application Resources
Part 5:   Constructing the User Interface of the Application
Part 6:   Coding the Activity for the Application
Part 7:   Packaging the App and Running on a Physical Device
Part 8:   Building an Android Virtual Device
Part 9:   Testing the Application on an Emulator
Part 10:   Optimizing and Improving a Project

Part 1: The Conceptual Design

The storyboard for the `Hello Goodbye` application highlights the user experience, as shown in Figure 1-10. This conceptual design consists of a rough sketch of the user interface and illustrates the user's interactive experience after each click of the button. In addition to the interface elements on the screen, the rough sketch also provides specific design attributes, such as color choices, font sizes, and graphic images.

At its most basic, a project storyboard provides a blueprint outlining three elements that will be considered in the final project:

1. Output
2. UI Interaction
3. Design requirements

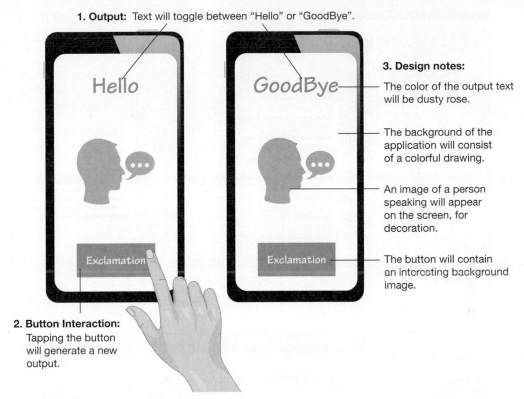

FIGURE 1-10 The storyboard for the `Hello Goodbye` application.

Part 2: Verifying the Required SDKs for Android Studio

Android Studio requires SDKs to develop an application. SDK tools and packages are often updated or new versions are released. To properly configure an Android project, Android Studio may need to install these tools and packages. In this part of the tutorial, the SDK manager will be used to verify the installation of the required SDKs.

Step 1:   Launch **Android Studio**.

A window similar to Figure 1-11 should appear.

Step 2:   Select **Configure** from the **Quick Start** window.

The Configure window allows you to perform a variety of configurations in addition to installing SDKs. For this application, readers can verify the Java compiler version in **Preferences**. The compiler version used by this text is Javac 1.7. Plug-ins—such as an embedded terminal, GitHub, and Google Cloud—are not required for this application, but they can be useful for future lab examples.

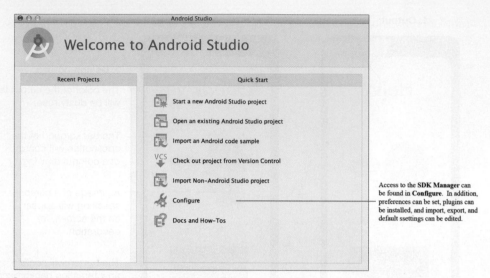

Access to the **SDK Manager** can be found in **Configure**. In addition, preferences can be set, plugins can be installed, and import, export, and default settings can be edited.

▌ FIGURE 1-11 Android Studio provides quick starts to new projects.

Android tools and packages can be installed using the **SDK Manager.**

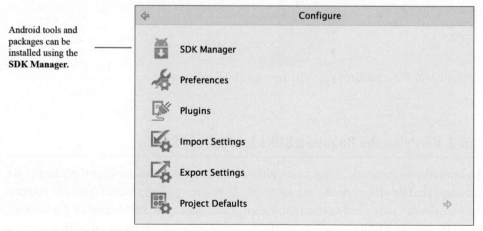

▌ FIGURE 1-12 The SDK Manager can be used to update and install Android tools and packages.

The SDK Manager can be used at any time to update and install tools and packages.

Step 3:   Select **SDK Manager** from the **Configure** window, shown in Figure 1-12.

The SDK manager categorizes tools, platforms, and other components into packages. For example, all the Android SDK build tools are stored in the Tools folder. The Android platform components are stored in folders labeled with the version and API number of the platform.

Step 4:   Verify that the elements shown in Figure 1-13 have been installed, specifically API versions 16 through 23. We strongly recommend installing the most recent version available.

Once the SDKs have been installed, return to the Quick Start window shown in Figure 1-11.

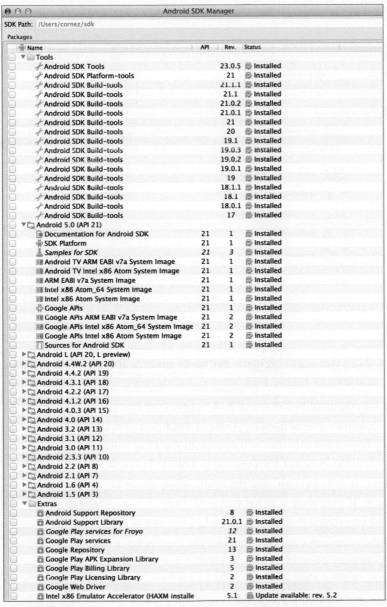

▌ FIGURE 1-13 The SDK Manager categorizes tools and platforms into packages.

Part 3: Creating the Application Project

The application project will have an initial structure. In this part of the tutorial, the preliminary settings and structure for the `Hello Goodbye` application will be specified.

Step 1:   Select **Start a new Android Studio project** from the Android Studio **Quick Start** panel, shown in Figure 1-14.

FIGURE 1-14

In Steps 2–3, you will configure the name and location of your Android project, as shown in Figure 1-15.

Step 2:   Specify the application name as `Hello Goodbye`.

The application name is used by Android Studio to give it a unique identification. It is also the title that will appear in the Play Store and is the title of your application launcher icon once it is installed on a device.

In general, it is important that the application name be unique within the workspace. If you enter a name that is already in use, Android Studio will simply add a version number to the end of the name.

Step 3:   Specify the company domain name. All the applications built in this text will use the company domain `com.cornez`.

By default, Android Studio constructs a package name based on the application name and the company domain.

This package name is the namespace for your application's code files and is added as the package attribute in your application's Android manifest file. This manifest value serves as the unique identifier for your application app when you distribute it to users. The package name follows the same rules as packages in the Java programming language. The name is the reverse domain name of your company, in addition to any identifiers.

Step 4: Set a new location, or use the default location, of your Android project. Click **Next**.

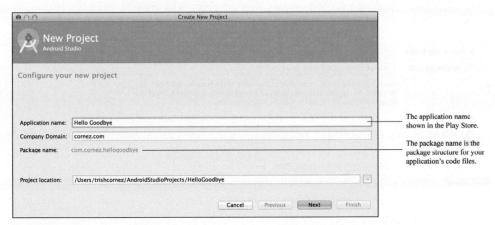

| FIGURE 1-15

In Steps 5–6, you will specify the Android form your application will run on, such as a phone or tablet, a wearable, Google Glass, or TV. In addition, a minimum SDK platform is identified prior to creating the Android project shell.

When developing applications, developers often want to target as many devices as possible. Specifying the lowest possible version of Android will achieve the most number of devices. For example, by specifying Froyo 2.2, API 8, as the minimum SDK, an application will run on almost all devices on the market. However, there are some disadvantages to specifying a low API version, such as a lack of critical features supported by an older platform. The choice of a minimum SDK level should be one that supports the features your application needs, while also trying to reach as many users as possible. The **Help me choose** link, shown in Figure 1-16, provides a cumulative distribution chart of the current API market.

Step 5: Specify Phone and Tablet as the device form, as shown in Figure 1-16.

Step 6: Specify API 16, Android 4.1 (Jelly Bean) as the minimum required SDK. Click **Next**.

Choose the lowest version
of Android that your
application will support.

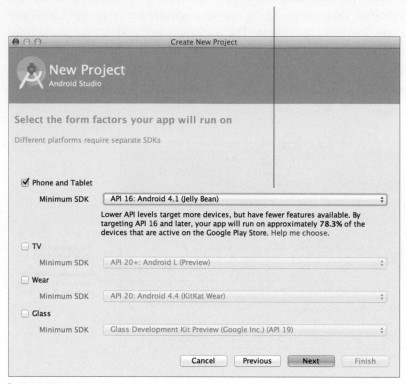

■ FIGURE 1-16

Application templates can be used to create various Android applications, as shown in the template image models in Figure 1-17. These templates are available when a new Android project is created. You can also apply these templates to a new activity that is being added to an existing project.

The **Blank Activity** application template is a simple application template that follows Android Design guidelines. This template design is used when a basic, minimal application is the starting point for an Android project. Other common templates are **Google Maps Activity**, **FullScreen Activity**, and **Master/Detail Flow**.

FullScreen Activity is a template that provides an implementation of an activity, which alternates between a primary, full-screen view and a view with standard user interface controls. User interface controls can include a notification bar and application title bar. The full-screen view is the default for this template. The user can activate the standard view simply by tapping the touchscreen.

The **Master/Detail Flow** template is primarily used for data-driven applications. This template creates a responsive layout for a collection of items, the master list, and the details of each item on the list.

Step 7:   Choose **Blank Activity** from the **Create New Project** window.
Click **Next**.

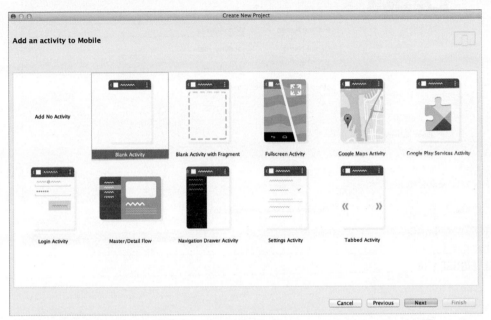

| FIGURE 1-17 The project configuration dialog box.

The **Blank Activity** template creates a blank Activity, which is implemented as a Java source file. This Activity is the main activity for the application and is immediately launched when the user first opens the application. The main activity of the application is linked by default to an XML layout file, which implements the Activity's visual appearance on the screen. The names for each of these files are specified in Steps 9–11, as shown in Figure 1-18.

Step 8:   The activity name is set to `MainActivity`.

Step 9:   The layout name is set to `activity_main`.

Step 10:   **Title** and `Menu Resource Name` should be left to the default settings.
Click **Finish**.

Once the project is created, its structure is generated. For a **Blank Activity** application, the structure will look similar to the one shown in Figure 1-19. Default versions of required files are automatically generated. The collection of related files will eventually be built into an apk file that you install onto a device.

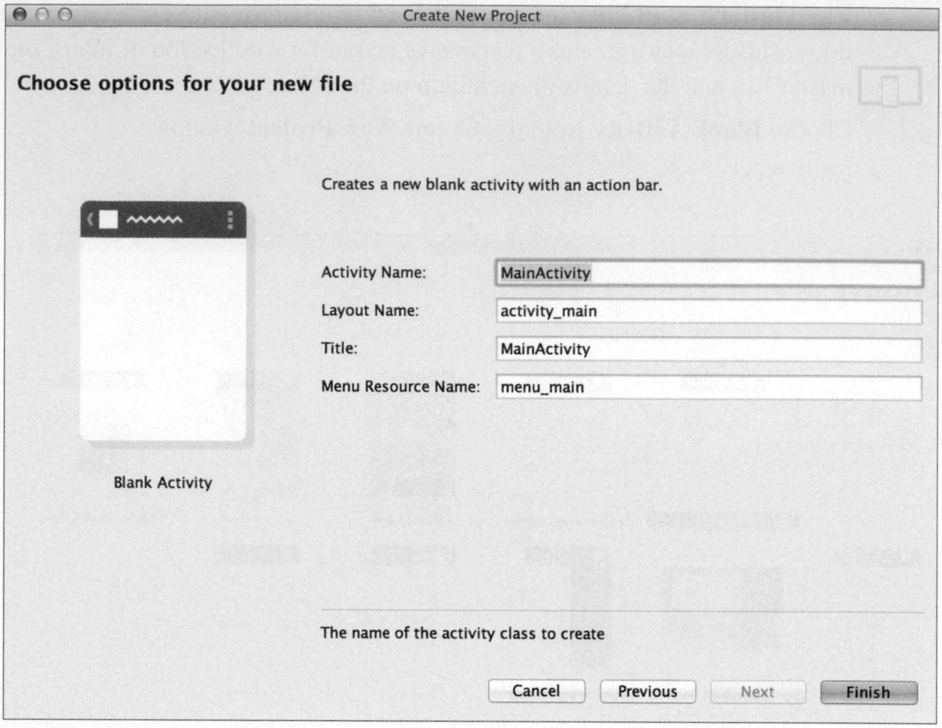

FIGURE 1-18

The `java` folder contains the main Activity Java file, `MainActivity.`
`java`. In general, all Java source code files will be placed in this folder. The
`res` folder stores the application resources categorized by drawable, layout,
menu, and values.

The graphic named `ic_launcher.png` is automatically generated as the
default launch icon for all Android applications. This graphic, shown in Figure 1-20, can be replaced by a new imported drawable. When an application
has been installed on an Android device, its launch icon will appear with all
other installed apps in the launcher. Android runs on a wide variety of devices that have different screen sizes and resolutions. To ensure that a launch
icon is displayed accurately on all devices, multiple versions of each image
are typically provided. Android will automatically choose the correct image
based on the screen's resolution.

The `manifests` folder contains `AndroidManifest.xml`, which describes the attributes of the application. When an Android application is first
built, a default version of this file is automatically generated. Every application must have an `AndroidManifest.xml` file.

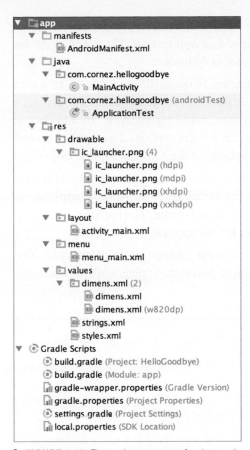

```
▼ 🗀 app
  ▼ 🗀 manifests
      🗋 AndroidManifest.xml
  ▼ 🗀 java
    ▼ 🗀 com.cornez.hellogoodbye
        ©  MainActivity
    ▼ 🗀 com.cornez.hellogoodbye (androidTest)
        ©  ApplicationTest
  ▼ 🗀 res
    ▼ 🗀 drawable
      ▼ 🗀 ic_launcher.png (4)
          🖼 ic_launcher.png (hdpi)
          🖼 ic_launcher.png (mdpi)
          🖼 ic_launcher.png (xhdpi)
          🖼 ic_launcher.png (xxhdpi)
    ▼ 🗀 layout
        🗋 activity_main.xml
    ▼ 🗀 menu
        🗋 menu_main.xml
    ▼ 🗀 values
      ▼ 🗀 dimens.xml (2)
          🗋 dimens.xml
          🗋 dimens.xml (w820dp)
        🗋 strings.xml
        🗋 styles.xml
▼ ⊙ Gradle Scripts
    ⊙ build.gradle (Project: HelloGoodbye)
    ⊙ build.gradle (Module: app)
    📄 gradle-wrapper.properties (Gradle Version)
    📄 gradle.properties (Project Properties)
    ⊙ settings.gradle (Project Settings)
    📄 local.properties (SDK Location)
```

❚ FIGURE 1-19 The project structure for the newly created `Hello Goodbye` project.

❚ FIGURE 1-20 `ic_launch.png` is automatically generated as the default launch icon.
The Android robot is reproduced or modified from work created and shared by Google and used according to terms described in the Creative Commons 3.0 Attribution License.

Step 11:   Examine `AndroidManifest.xml`.

This file will not be altered for this first application. The XML code for `AndroidManifest.xml` is shown as follows.

Lines 2–3:   The Android Application Manifest file is made up of a root manifest tag with a package attribute set to the project's package, `com.cornez.hellogoodbye`. In addition, it includes an `xmlns:android` attribute that supplies several system attributes used within the Android application.

Lines 5–20:   A manifest can contain only one application node. This uses attributes to specify the metadata for the Android application, such as title, launch icon, and theme. The application tag also serves as a container for the application's activities.

Lines 10–19:   A manifest can contain many activity nodes. The `MainActivity` is specified as the application's main activity.

AndroidManifest.xml

```
1   <?xml version="1.0" encoding="utf-8"?>
2   <manifest xmlns:android="http://schemas.android.com/apk/res/android"
3      package="com.cornez.hellogoodbye" >
4
5      <application
6         android:allowBackup="true"
7         android:icon="@drawable/ic_launcher"
8         android:label="@string/app_name"
9         android:theme="@style/AppTheme" >
10        <activity
11           android:name="com.cornez.hellogoodbye.MainActivity"
12           android:label="@string/app_name" >
13           <intent-filter>
14              <action android:name="android.intent.action.MAIN" />
15
16              <category
17                 android:name="android.intent.category.LAUNCHER" />
18           </intent-filter>
19        </activity>
20     </application>
21
22  </manifest>
```

Part 4: Adding and Editing Application Resources

Before we can build a user interface and code the application, we need to add the required resources to the project structure. The resources for a basic application will typically consist of text values, graphic files, data values, and color definitions. All resources should be identified during the conceptual design phase of the application, such as the one we will use from Figure 1-6.

This `Hello Goodbye` application will require three types of resources as follows:

Drawables: Three graphic files will be added to the project structure to enhance the application visually.

String values: Text strings will be used to store the exclamations ("hello" and "goodbye") and the text that appears on the button.

Color values: A color definition that will be used to color the "Hello" and "Goodbye" text generated and displayed by the application.

Step 1: Assemble the drawable resources to be used in the application.

Before constructing the application project, make sure that you have all necessary external application elements. For this tutorial, there will be three image files used in the application: a background image, a button image, and a small graphic for decoration. These elements, shown in Figure 1-21, can be found in the textbook resources. All image file names must contain only lowercase letters.

Within the `drawable` folder for Tutorial 1, you will find three folders holding the `background.png`, `greetimage.png` and `exclamation-btn.png` image files. The `png` files located in these folders have been customized for the screen pixel density specified in the directory's name. In production value applications, it is important to provide images for the different screen pixel densities in your projects.

xxhdpi   extra-extra-high-density screens   (approximately 320 dpi)

xhdpi   extra-high-density screens   (approximately 240 dpi)

Providing different images will reduce artifacts from images being scaled up and down. All of the images in your project will be installed with your app, and the operating system will choose the best one for that specific device.

Step 2: Drag the xxhdpi version of `greetimage.png` to the `drawable` folder in the project structure, as shown in Figure 1-22.

If the file cannot be dragged, perform a copy/paste.

Step 3: Select the xxhdpi destination directory, as shown in Figure 1-23.

Step 4: Choose the name of the file, as shown in Figure 1-24.

Step 5: Verify `greetimage.png` appears in the `drawable` folder, as shown in Figure 1-25.

Step 6: Add the xhdpi version of `greetimage.png` to the `drawable` folder. Use the same method from Step 4.

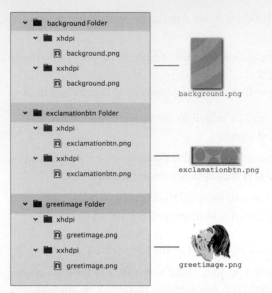

FIGURE 1-21

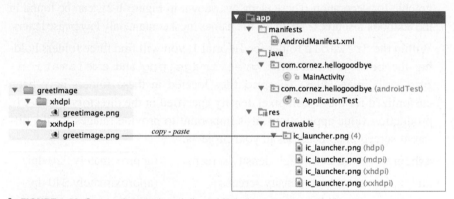

FIGURE 1-22 Copy-and-paste the xxhdi graphic to the `drawable` folder.

FIGURE 1-23

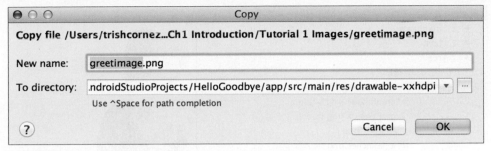

| FIGURE 1-24

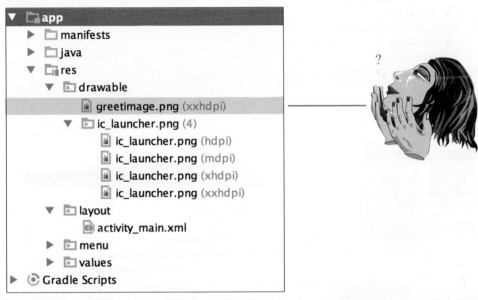

| FIGURE 1-25

Once two versions of the same image are added to the `drawable` folder, Android Studio generates a separate folder with the name of the image. Verify the folder has been created and contains both copied versions of greetimage.png, as shown in Figure 1-26.

Step 7:   Add the xhdpi and xxhdpi versions `background.png` and `exclamation.png` to the `drawable` folder in the project structure.

The complete `drawable` structure should look similar to Figure 1-27.

Strings are important components in every Android application. The external file strings.xml is automatically constructed at the start of a new application and routinely stores the text strings for the application name, action settings, and hello world.

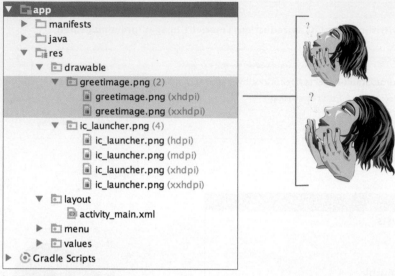

FIGURE 1-26

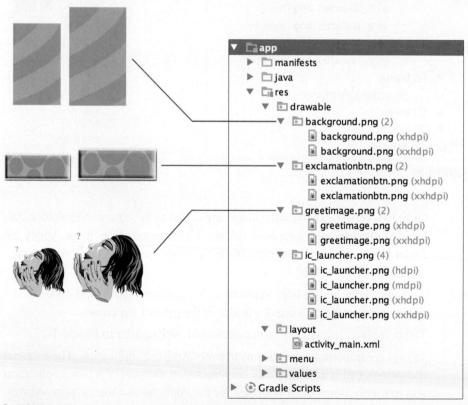

FIGURE 1-27 The tutorial app requires three image files.

As a value resource file, `strings.xml` is always located in the value directory within the res folder, as shown in Figure 1-28.

Step 8: Open `strings.xml` within the `res/values` folder.

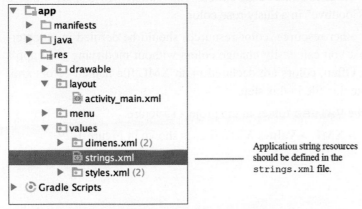

Application string resources should be defined in the strings.xml file.

FIGURE 1-28 Strings are static resources that are stored in an external file.

We will leave the existing text strings intact and simply add the four additional strings our application will require.

String values are entered as key/value pairs. This can be done using the **Translation Editor** feature or entering the XML code. The authors prefer entering resources in the XML code, but you may choose either method.

Step 9: Use the following XML code listing as a guide and enter the string values shown on Lines 8–16.

Save the file.

```
strings.xml
1   <?xml version="1.0" encoding="utf-8"?>
2   <resources>
3
4     <string name="app_name">Hello Goodbye</string>
5     <string name="hello_world">Hello world!</string>
6     <string name="action_settings">Settings</string>
7
8     <!-- STRING USED FOR THE BUTTON -->
9     <string name="exclaim_btn">Exclamation</string>
10
11    <!-- STRINGS USED FOR OUTPUT -->
12    <string name="hello">Hello</string>
13    <string name="goodbye">Goodbye!</string>
14
15    <!-- DESCRIPTION OF THE IMAGE OF THE GIRL -->
16    <string name="exclaim_img">Exclamation image</string>
17
18  </resources>
```

It is often necessary and practical to create additional resource files that contain values that the application will use. Color is such a file. Our application will use a color, called dusty rose, for the exclamations generated when the user hits the Exclamation button. This button will display either a "Hello" or "Goodbye" in a dusty rose color.

As with any other resource, color resources should be defined in an external file so that you can easily change colors without modifying your app's source code. Often, colors are declared in an XML file named colors.xml. We will create this file in this step.

Step 10:   Right-click the Values folder in the project structure.

Choose **New > XML > Values XML file**, as shown in Figure 1-29.

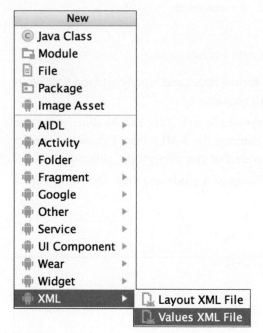

| FIGURE 1-29

Step 11:   Specify the name of the values file as colors.xml, as shown in Figure 1-30.

Click **Finish** to create the file.

Android Studio will open the new file in the XML view. Verify colors.xml appears in the project structure in the values folder, as shown in Figure 1-31.

Step 12:   Use the following XML code listing as a guide to add color for "dusty_rose," shown on Line 3.

Save the file.

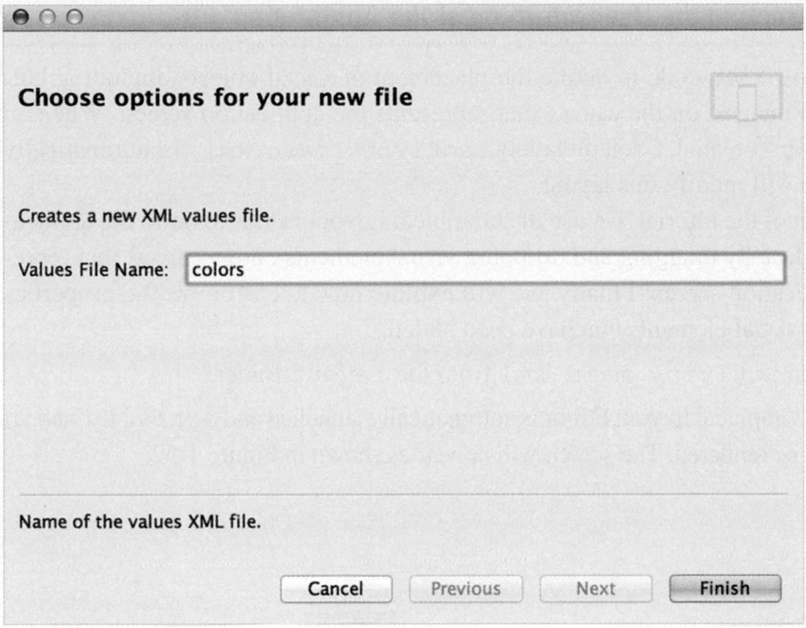

Choose options for your new file

Creates a new XML values file.

Values File Name: colors

Name of the values XML file.

Cancel   Previous   Next   **Finish**

FIGURE 1-30 A color.xml file is a resource file that stores colors used by the application.

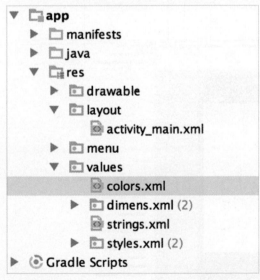

▼ ▢ **app**
　▶ ▢ **manifests**
　▶ ▢ **java**
　▼ ▢ **res**
　　▶ ▢ **drawable**
　　▼ ▢ **layout**
　　　▣ **activity_main.xml**
　　▶ ▢ **menu**
　　▼ ▢ **values**
　　　▣ **colors.xml**
　　　▶ ▢ **dimens.xml** (2)
　　　▣ **strings.xml**
　　　▶ ▢ **styles.xml** (2)
▶ ⊙ **Gradle Scripts**

FIGURE 1-31

```
colors.xml
1  <?xml version="1.0" encoding="utf-8"?>
2  <resources>
3    <color name="dusty_rose">#B530BD</color>
4  </resources>
```

Part 5: Constructing the User Interface of the Application

Layout files use XML code to define the placement of visual objects, including buttons, text, and images, on the canvas that represents the application screen. When an application is first created, a default layout, `activity_main.xml`, is automatically generated. We will modify this layout.

    In this part of the tutorial, we use the Graphical Layout Editor to build the application user interface by dragging and dropping visual elements onto a canvas that represents our application screen. Finally, we will explore how to customize the properties of each of the visual elements that have been added.

Step 1:   Open `activity_main.xml` from the `layout` folder.

         The Graphical Layout Editor is automatically launched and `activity_main` will be rendered. The screen will appear as shown in Figure 1-32.

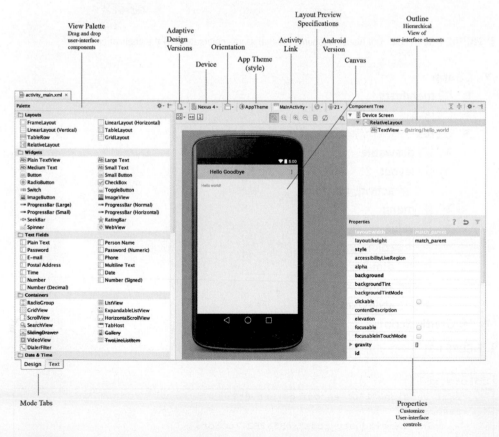

FIGURE 1-32 The Graphical Layout Editor is launched when a layout is activated.

The Graphical Layout Editor provides the following features for building the layout. It is important to become familiar with these features before continuing.

Canvas
The canvas represents the screen that will eventually hold visual elements. The canvas is the area where you can drag and drop display objects, such as user interface components, to design a layout.

Palette
The Palette contains icons representing visual elements that can be added (dragged/dropped) to the canvas. Icons are organized into categories, such as Form Widgets, Text Fields, and Images & Media.

Android Version
An Android version can be specified for rendering layouts in Eclipse.

Device
A device configuration can be specified by name, such as Galaxy Nexus or Nexus One, or by dimensions. Each of the devices listed in this drop-down menu has its own look and feel. The canvas renders the appropriate look based on the device setting, along with the Android version.

Orientation
The orientation of the application can be configured by selecting portrait or landscape. It is also possible to choose a UI Mode, such as Television or Car Dock.

AppTheme
The configuration theme of an application is a specification of style. For example, an application screen can be all black or occupy the full screen with no title. Each theme has a unique identifying name, which can be selected from a menu listing from AppTheme.

Outline
The Outline panel provides a hierarchical list of the visual elements placed on the layout file. This ordered structure is very useful when inspecting the structure of the design and selecting specific components. At the moment, the root element, a RelativeLayout container, is the only object in the file. These containers will be explored in Chapter 2.

Properties
Each visual object placed on the canvas has a collection of context-sensitive properties that can be set. For example, the color of a text field can be set to dusty_rose or the width of a button can be adjusted.

Mode Tabs   The two modes for building the user interface of a given layout are Graphical Layout and the XML code. Click one of the mode tabs to be able to toggle between these two modes.

When building user interface screens, you may use a variety of approaches. A good approach is to use the Graphical Layout Editor to drag and drop visual elements to the screen and then fine-tune the attributes within the XML code file.

In Step 2, we will add a textured background to our user interface screen.

Step 2:   Select RelativeLayout in the **Component Tree** panel of the **Layout Editor**, as shown in Figure 1-33.

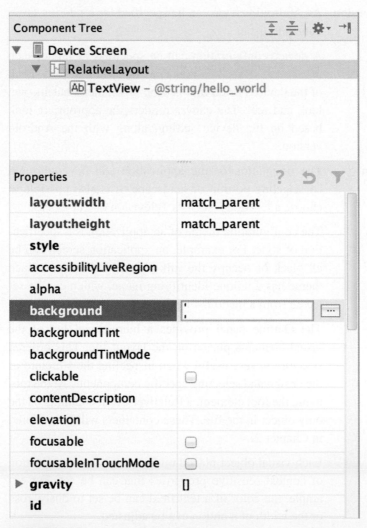

FIGURE 1-33

`RelativeLayout` is a type of container that is used to hold UI components. It serves as the root container for the user interface of our application. At the moment, it holds a text field containing the string "Hello World," which will eventually be deleted. In its final form, `RelativeLayout` will store all of the visual elements of the application.

Once `RelativeLayout` has been selected, its set of properties will appear in the **Properties** panel.

Many of the visual elements located on the canvas, including the `Relative-Layout` container, can be set with an interesting background image. In Step 3 we will explore how to set the **background** property of the layout root element.

Step 3: Locate the **background** within the **Properties** panel, shown in Figure 1-33. Briefly familiarize yourself with the set of properties that can be applied to a visual object on the screen. This can be done with a quick scroll through the other properties in the list.

Step 4: From the **background** property, click in the box to the right of the divider and select the ⋯ button.

Step 5: When the **Resources** chooser window appears, as shown in Figure 1-34, locate and select the file named `background` from the `Drawable` folder. Click **OK**.

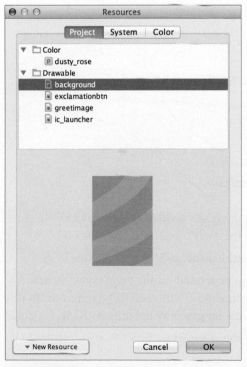

| **FIGURE 1-34**

The value stored in the background property for the root `Relative-Layout` should now appear as `@drawable/background`. Verify that a green graphic fills the canvas, as shown in Figure 1-35.

When you double-click a specific item on the canvas or in the **Component Tree** panel, a context-sensitive selection of properties will appear in an independent window. This method can also be used to set properties.

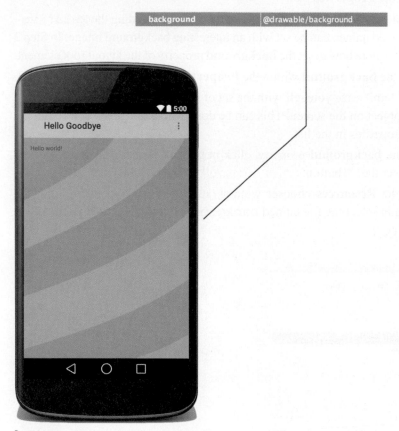

| background | @drawable/background |

▌ FIGURE 1-35 A background image is added to the application.

In Steps 6 and 7 we will examine the XML code of the `activity_main.xml` layout file and edit it within the **Text** mode.

Step 6: Select the **Text** mode in the **Layout Editor**, as shown in Figure 1-36.

The "Hello World" string is always generated for the main layout in new Android projects. As a throwaway element, it will need to be removed. In this next step, we will remove it from the interface by deleting its XML tag code.

Step 7: As shown in Figure 1-36, select the complete `<TextView>` element and delete it.

Step 8:   Return to the **Design** mode of the **Layout Editor** and verify that "Hello World" has been removed.

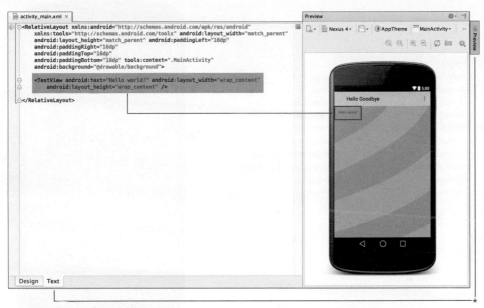

❙ FIGURE 1-36 The `TextView` element is removed in the XML code.

The purpose of this application is to generate a "hello" or a "goodbye" exclamation when the user taps a button on the screen. A text field element is required for displaying this text.

`TextViews` are text field Widgets. They are used to display text, such as static title elements or text that is dynamically output during runtime.

In Steps 9–12, we will add a `TextView` Widget to the canvas. We can then initialize its text value and set its color and text size.

Step 9:   Drag the **Large Text** element from the Widgets palette to the canvas. Drop it so that it is centered horizontally (see centerHorizontal) at the top of the canvas, as shown in Figure 1-37.

Once the `TextView` appears on the canvas, it will also appear in the **Component Tree** panel under the name `textView`. This name is a unique identifier, which will be used in our application source code to reset its value during runtime.

Step 10:   Double-click the **Large Text** element that was just added to the canvas.

The **text/id** dialog box, shown at the top of Figure 1-38, will appear on the screen.

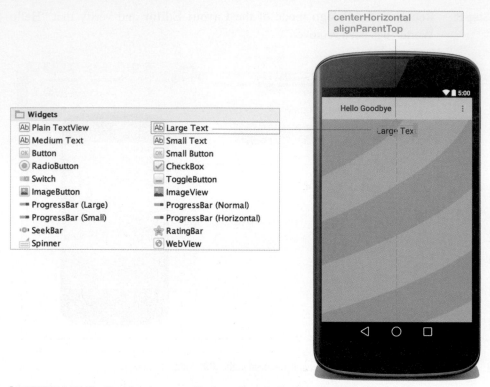

I FIGURE 1-37 The TextView is centered horizontally and aligned at the top.

Step 11: Click the ⋯ button to set the text property.

The **Resources** chooser window will appear, as shown in Figure 1-38.

Step 12: Locate and select the `hello` string resource as shown in Figure 1-38.

Click **OK**.

The value stored in the text property for the `textView` component is now `@string/hello (Hello)`. Verify that "Hello" appears on the canvas.

In Steps 13–15, we will edit the color of `textView` on the canvas.

Step 13: Select `textView` and locate the **textColor** property in the Property panel.

Step 14: Click in the box to the right of the divider and click the ⋯ button.

The color Resources chooser window will appear.

Step 15: Locate and select `dusty_rose,` as shown in Figure 1-39.

Click **OK**.

Colors can also be selected from a set of system values or the color palette provided by Android Studio.

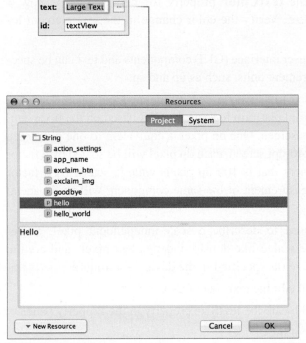

FIGURE 1-38 String values can be selected for TextView objects placed on the canvas.

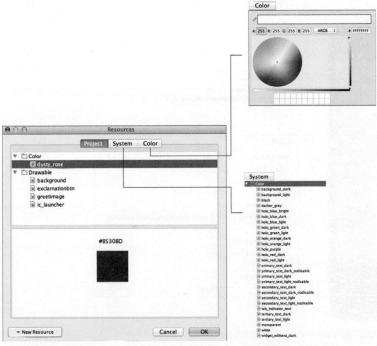

FIGURE 1-39 Color can be selected from the Color XML file.

The value stored in the **textColor** property for `textView` is now @ `color/dusty_rose`. Verify the color change in the text element located on the canvas.

The sizes of graphical user interface (GUI) components and text can be specified in various measurement units, such as dp and sp.

The notation dp is used to specify a density-independent pixel. Defining GUIs enables the Android platform to scale the GUI based on the pixel density of a given device's screen. One dp pixel is equivalent to one pixel on a 160-dpi screen. On a 240-dpi screen, each dp pixel will be scaled by a factor of 240/160. A component that is 100 dp pixels wide is scaled by a factor of 120/160. The sp measurement of the same component will be 75 actual pixels wide.

The notation sp is used to describe a scale-independent pixel. Scale-independent pixels are scaled like density-independent pixels and are the user's preferred font size (as specified in the device's settings).

In Steps 16–17, we will edit the text size of `textView`.

Step 16:   Select `textView` and locate the **textSize** property in the Property panel.

Step 17:   Enter 60sp to the right of the divider.

At this point, `activity_main.xml` should look similar to Figure 1-40.

▌ FIGURE 1-40 The output TextView will appear on the canvas.

In Steps 18–25, we will add a decorative image element to the canvas. The main purpose of adding this element is to illustrate how it is done and to add interest to the application screen.

Step 18: Unselect any canvas elements that are currently selected.

Step 19: Locate the **ImageView** component in the Widgets palette.

Step 20: Drag and drop the ImageView to the center of the canvas, as shown in Figure 1-41. Note the centerHorizontal and centerVertical location indicators that appear.

A small nub will appear on the canvas.

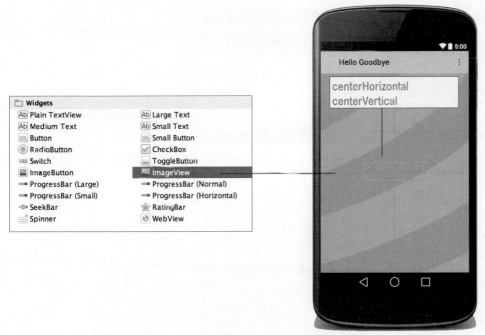

FIGURE 1-41 An ImageView is placed in the center of the canvas.

Step 21: Double-click the nub that appears on the canvas and click the ⊡ button next to src, as shown in Figure 1-42.

The Resources chooser window will appear with a list of drawable elements to choose from.

Step 22: Locate and select `greetimage` from the Drawable folder, as shown in Figure 1-43.

Click **OK**.

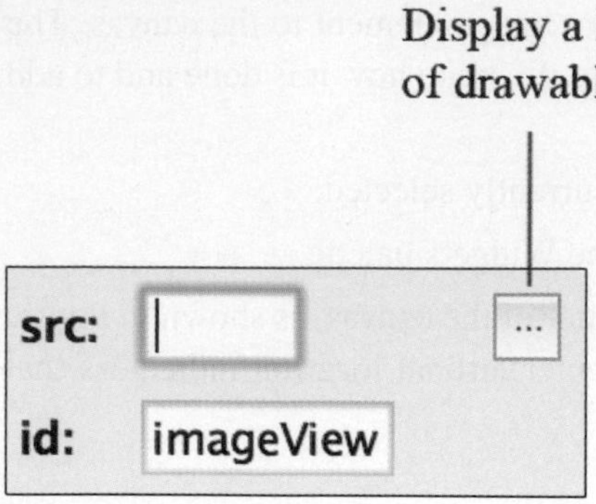

Display a list
of drawables.

src:

id: imageView

▌ FIGURE 1-42

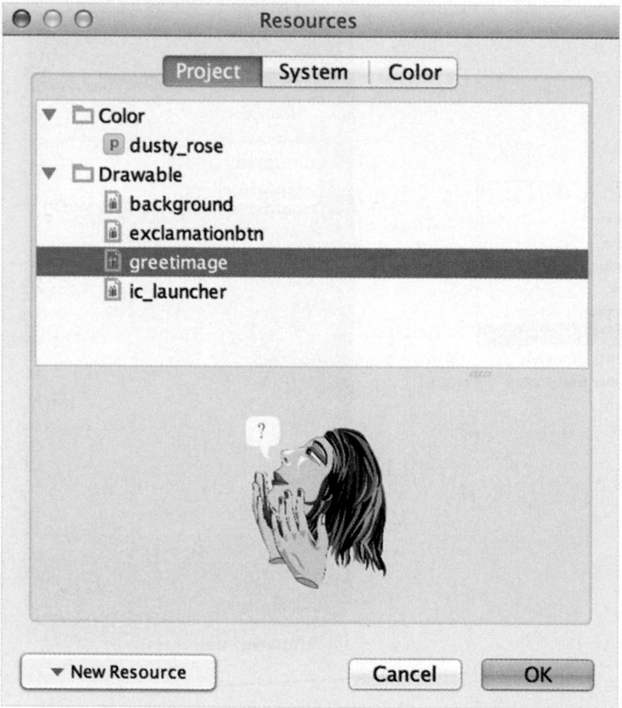

Resources

Project System Color

▼ ☐ Color
    Ⓟ dusty_rose
▼ ☐ Drawable
    🖼 background
    🖼 exclamationbtn
    🖼 greetimage
    🖼 ic_launcher

▼ New Resource   Cancel   OK

▌ FIGURE 1-43 The ImageView container is set to hold `greetimage.png`.

Your layout will look similar to Figure 1-44. Once the **ImageView** object appears on the canvas, it will also appear in the **Component Tree** panel. As with all objects added to the canvas, it will be given a unique identifying name. In this instance, the unique id is `imageView`.

Image components added to the canvas should have a content description describing the content of an image. A warning, in the form of a small yield symbol, will appear until this task is performed.

Step 23: With `imageView` selected on the canvas, locate the **contentDescription** property in the Property palette.

Step 24: Click the ⬚ button.

Step 25: When the **Resource** chooser window appears, select `exclaim_img` from the **Strings** folder.

Click **OK**.

The property settings for `imageView` are shown in Figure 1-44.

▌ **FIGURE 1-44**

In Steps 26–30, we will add a button to the canvas and customize it. When the user taps the button, a toggle string will appear in `textView`.

Step 26: Locate **Button** from the **Widgets** palette and drag and drop it onto the canvas, as shown in Figure 1-45.

Once the button appears on the canvas, it will also appear in the **Component Tree** panel with a unique identifying name, `button`.

Step 27: Locate and select the **text** property for `button`. Click the ⬚ symbol.

Step 28: When the **Resources** chooser window appears, select `exclaim_btn`. Click **OK**.

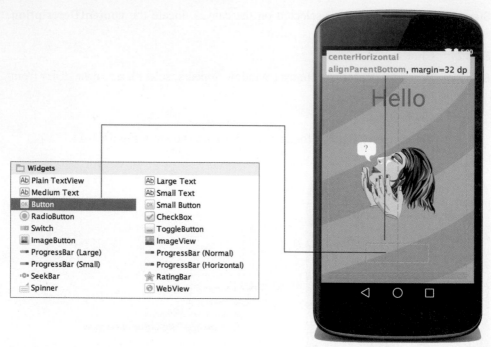

FIGURE 1-45 The Button widget is given an identifying name, `button`.

The value stored in the **text** property for `button` will appear as `@string/exclaim_btn (Exclamation)`.

Verify that "Exclamation" appears as the label for the button on the canvas.

Buttons can be configured with background images, colors, and styles. In Step 29, we will set a new button background.

Step 29: Locate and select the **background** property for `button`. Click the ⋯ symbol.

Step 30: When the **Resources** chooser window appears, select `exclamationBtn.`, as shown in Figure 1-46.

Click **OK**.

The final property settings for button are shown in Figure 1-47.

The authors encourage readers to browse the list of properties associated with `button`, and note the `onClick` property. `onClick` is often added to button components to set an event handler that responds to a click event. We will discuss the `onClick` property in the next tutorial. For this tutorial, we will explore the concept of registering a listener event for a button in Part 6.

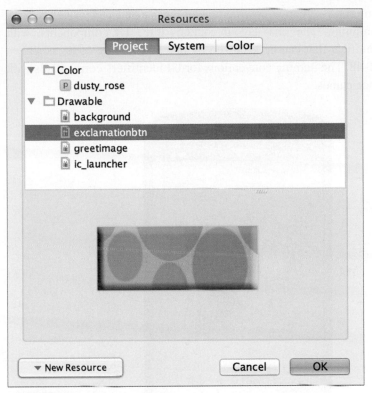

FIGURE 1-46

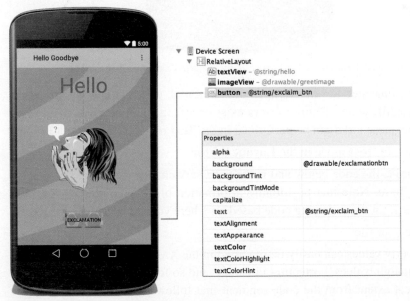

FIGURE 1-47 Final property settings for `button`.

The user interface screen is now complete. Save `activity_main.xml` before continuing. The final layout contains three UI components, with unique identifiers that can be accessed by our Java source code, as shown in Figure 1-48. The naming conventions for UI identifiers corresponds with Java instance names.

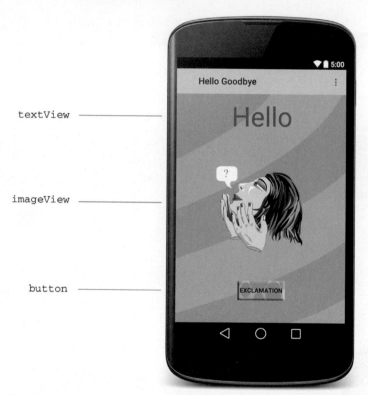

textView

imageView

button

▌ FIGURE 1-48 The completed layout contains `textView`, `imageView`, and `button1`.

In the final step for this segment of the tutorial, we will examine the generated XML code. If minor errors exist or arrangement changes need to be made, these tasks can be performed in the **Text** mode of the Layout Editor.

Step 31: Select the **Text** mode in the **Layout Editor**.

Step 32: Examine the code below and make necessary changes to fix any errors you may have. Note that positioning information of your graphic images will differ from the following code based on where your objects were placed.

Save your file.

Property values can easily be modified in the XML mode, such as changing the margin values, correcting id names, and so forth. If your code differs to a great extent from the code segment that follows, it is important that you make the necessary changes.

Many of the XML tags are self explanatory. Tags related to Android will be discussed in Chapter 2. To study XML in more detail, you may want to consult an XML reference source.

```
activity_main.xml
1   <RelativeLayout
2   xmlns:android="http://schemas.android.com/apk/res/android"
3   xmlns:tools="http://schemas.android.com/tools"
4
5   android:layout_width="match_parent"
6   android:layout_height="match_parent"
7   android:paddingLeft="@dimen/activity_horizontal_margin"
8   android:paddingRight="@dimen/activity_horizontal_margin"
9   android:paddingTop="@dimen/activity_vertical_margin"
10  android:paddingBottom="@dimen/activity_vertical_margin"
11  tools:context=".MainActivity"
12  android:background="@drawable/background">
13
14  <TextView
15     android:layout_width="wrap_content"
16     android:layout_height="wrap_content"
17     android:textAppearance="?android:attr/textAppearanceLarge"
18     android:text="@string/hello"
19     android:id="@+id/textView"
20     android:layout_alignParentTop="true"
21     android:layout_centerHorizontal="true"
22     android:textColor="@color/dusty_rose"
23     android:textSize="60sp"/>
24
25  <ImageView
26     android:layout_width="wrap_content"
27     android:layout_height="wrap_content"
28     android:id="@+id/imageView"
29     android:layout_centerVertical="true"
30     android:layout_centerHorizontal="true"
31     android:src="@drawable/greetimage"
32     android:contentDescription="@string/exclaim_img" />
33
34  <Button
35     android:layout_width="wrap_content"
36     android:layout_height="wrap_content"
37     android:text="@string/exclaim_btn"
38     android:id="@+id/button"
39     android:layout_alignParentBottom="true"
40     android:layout_centerHorizontal="true"
41     android:layout_marginBottom="32dp"
42     android:background="@drawable/exclamationbtn"
43     android:focusableInTouchMode="false" />
44  </RelativeLayout>
```

Part 6: Coding the Activity for the Application

Once the application resources have been added and the user interface screen has been built, the Java source code can be written. In this tutorial, the controller element of the application will be implemented as an Android Activity. The Activity class will be explored in more detail in Chapters 3 and 4.

The two objectives for the main Activity in this example are:

1. Inflate the user interface layout.
2. Control and respond to the UI elements located on the user interface layout.

Step 1: Open the `MainActivity` file located in `java.com.cornez. hellogoodbye`.

`MainActivity.java`, is the `Activity` class that was automatically generated when the application project was created in Part 2 of the tutorial. This default class represents the main Java class that will be executed when the application is launched for the first time on the device. At its inception, `MainActivity.java` contains default content that is trivial and therefore will need to be modified.

To gain a better understanding of the anatomy of our application activity source file, we will examine the code file.

Step 2: Edit the file from its original content using the code outline below.

Lines 3–6:   Import statements for Activity, Bundle, Menu, and MenuItem will be needed for this application. `MainActivity.java` is an extension of the `Activity` class. Android.os.Bundle is a utility class that stores the last state of the application. For example, the Bundle object can be used to store a series of state variables, such as the last greeting displayed to the user. This greeting will then appear when the user relaunches the application. Menus are typically used in applications, and a shell is generated as a default. In this example, the menu component will not be altered.

Lines 7–9:   A `View` is the base class of all user interface components, such as buttons and text fields. For this application, the `View` import is required for registering a button click listener and handling the event.

The `Button` and `TextView` widgets require import libraries.

Line 11:   `MainActivity` is the entry point to this application. When Android runs the Hello Goodbye application, this is the first file that executes.

This line defines `MainActivity` as an extension of the `Activity` class. As a subclass of `Activity`, `MainActivity` inherits method callbacks (methods that are automatically called) when the activity is created, paused, stopped, resumed, and destroyed during various phases of the application. These callback methods will be discussed in detail in Chapter 3.

Line 14:   A `TextView` object, `greetingTextView`, is declared to reference the `textview` element located on the layout.

Lines 19–34:   As the name suggests, `onCreate()` is a callback method that is automatically called when the activity is created. The `onCreate()` method is often used to initialize the activity. For simple applications, this involves setting up the user interface and initializing state-related variables.

Line 23:   The `setContentView()` inflates the user interface layout to appear on the screen. This layout is the `activity_main.xml` file built previously in the tutorial. The argument `R.layout.activity_main` refers to the referenced item in a generated resource file named `R`.

Line 26:   A reference to `textView`, the output UI component, is established. Once this reference has been made, we can access it in the source code. The argument that refers to this component is R.id.textView.

Lines 32–33:   A `Button` object, `exclaimBtn`, is declared to the reference `button` located on the layout.

An `onClick` listener event is registered to the button. This listener event will be used to detect when the user has tapped the button. When this event does occur, it will trigger the event handler `toggleGreeting()`.

Lines 36–49:   It is not uncommon to implement listener classes as inner classes. There are two advantages to this. First, listener classes tend to be short; therefore, it is highly readable to locate them where they are needed. This is an inner class because it is declared inside another class. Second, inner classes have access to instance variables and methods of the surrounding class. As an inner class, we do not have to pass the constructor or method arguments for them to perform their jobs. This is very convenient.

When the user taps on the button, an `onClick` event occurs. To handle the event, we arrange for the appropriate task to be carried out. Detecting the event and carrying out the required task is called handling the event. Detecting the event requires a listener event, such as `OnClickListener()` on Line 33. Simply stated, this listener cycles in a loop, waiting for a specific event.

Lines 43 and 46 set the text of the `TextView`, referenced by `greetingTextView`, using the stored strings in `strings.xml`. `R.string.goodbye` is the argument for accessing a string resource file element named `hello`.

```
MainActivity.java
1   package com.cornez.hellogoodbye;
2
3   import android.app.Activity;
4   import android.os.Bundle;
5   import android.view.Menu;
6   import android.view.MenuItem;
7   import android.view.View;
8   import android.widget.Button;
9   import android.widget.TextView;
10
11  public class MainActivity extends Activity {
12
13      //DECLARE TEXT REFERENCE TO THE INTERFACE LAYOUT COMPONENT
14      private TextView greetingTextView;
15
16    //INDICATES HELLO IS CURRENTLY DISPLAYED
17      private boolean isHello;
18
19      @Override
20      protected void onCreate(Bundle savedInstanceState) {
21          //TASK 1: INFLATE THE MAIN SCREEN LAYOUT USED BY THE APP
22          super.onCreate(savedInstanceState);
23          setContentView(R.layout.activity_main);
24
25          //TASK 2: ESTABLISH REFERENCES TO THE TEXTVIEW AND BUTTON
26          greetingTextView = (TextView) findViewById(R.id.textView);
27
28          //TASK 3: INITIALIZE GREETINGS
29          initializeGreeting();
30
31          //TASK 4: REGISTER THE LISTENER EVENT FOR THE BUTTON
32          Button exclaimBtn = (Button) findViewById(R.id.button);
33          exclaimBtn.setOnClickListener(toggleGreeting);
34      }
35
36      private final View.OnClickListener toggleGreeting =
```

```
37      new View.OnClickListener() {
38
39        public void onClick(View btn) {
40          //TASK: CONSTRUCT THE TOGGLE GREETING
41          if (isHello) {
42            isHello = false;
43            greetingTextView.setText(R.string.goodbye);
44          } else {
45            isHello = true;
46            greetingTextView.setText(R.string.hello);
47          }
48        }
49      };
50
51    private void initializeGreeting() {
52      isHello = true;
53    }
54
55    @Override
56    public boolean onCreateOptionsMenu(Menu menu) {
57      // Inflate the menu;
58      // this adds items to the action bar if it is present.
59      getMenuInflater().inflate(R.menu.menu_main, menu);
60      return true;
61    }
62
63    @Override
64    public boolean onOptionsItemSelected(MenuItem item) {
65      // Handle action bar item clicks here. The action bar will
66      // automatically handle clicks on the Home/Up button, so long
67      // as you specify a parent activity in AndroidManifest.xml.
68      int id = item.getItemId();
69
70      //noinspection SimplifiableIfStatement
71      if (id == R.id.action_settings) {
72        return true;
73      }
74
75      return super.onOptionsItemSelected(item);
76    }
  }
```

Part 7: Packaging the App and Running on a Physical Device

Testing your applications on physical devices is an important part of application development. In this part of the tutorial, you will set up your device to run the Hello Goodbye application.

Step 1:   Configure your device for development.

To test your application on a physical device, you will need to enable it for development. This will allow it to accept applications that are not from Google Play.

On devices running Android 4.1 or earlier, open the device's **Settings** and go to **Applications**. Make sure that Unknown sources is checked.

On devices running Android 4.2 or later, go to **Settings > Security** to find the Unknown sources options.

Step 2:   Enable USB debugging on the device.

On devices running versions below Android 4.0, go to **Settings > Applications > Development**. Find the option to enable USB debugging.

On devices running Android 4.0 or 4.1, go to **Settings > Developer options**. Enable USB debugging.

On devices running 4.2 or later, **Developer options** may not be visible. To enable this option, go to **Settings > about Table/Phone** and press **Build** seven times. Developer options should now be visible. Locate the option to enable USB debugging.

Step 3:   In Android Studio choose **Build > Rebuild Project**.

During the build process, your Android project is compiled and then packaged into an .apk file. This .apk file contains all of the information necessary to run your application, such as compiled .dex files (.class files converted to Dalvik byte code), a binary version of the AndroidManifest.xml file, compiled resources and un-compiled resource files for your application.

| FIGURE 1-49

The components involved in building and running an application are shown in Figure 1-49. To run an application on an emulator or physical device, the application must be signed. A debug keystore will allow you to sign an `apk` that will run on any device. In development, Android Studio signs the application for you when you are in debug mode. The steps for this process will be examined in Tutorial 2. When you are ready to release the app to Google Play, you must sign the application in release mode, using your own private key.

In this tutorial, we will rely on an .apk file that is automatically output to the bin folder of the project. You do not have to do anything extra to generate the `apk`. By default, the `apk` will be concealed until a private key has been obtained.

The build process requires a collection of tools to generate intermediate files that will be packaged into the `apk`.

`build.gradle`, located in the Gradle Scripts directory of the project structure, is a Gradle build script that provides the locations of the application's manifest, source, resources, and assets. The Android Asset Packaging Tool (aapt) collects all resource XML files, such as Android-`Manifest.xml`, `activity_main.xml`, and `strings.xml`, and compiles them into a Java file, `R.java`. The `R.java` provides the complete reference to resources.

Java files are then compiled by the Java compiler to produce .class files. The dex tool converts the .class files to Dalvik bytecode. Any third-party libraries and .class files are also converted into dex files. The compiled dex resources and the noncompiled resources, such as drawables, are sent to an apkbuilder tool, which packages them into the final .apk file.

Step 4:   Connect the Android device to your system.

Step 5:   Choose **Run > Run 'app'**.

If you are developing on a Mac, your system should recognize the device right away. On Windows, you may need to install the ABD (Android Debug Bridge) driver. If Windows cannot find the ABD driver, then download one from your device's manufacturer website.

When your device is recognized, it will appear in the **Choose Device** window, as shown in Figure 1-50.

Step 6:   Select the device.

       Click **OK**.

If code errors do not exist, the `Hello Goodbye` application will launch on the connected device.

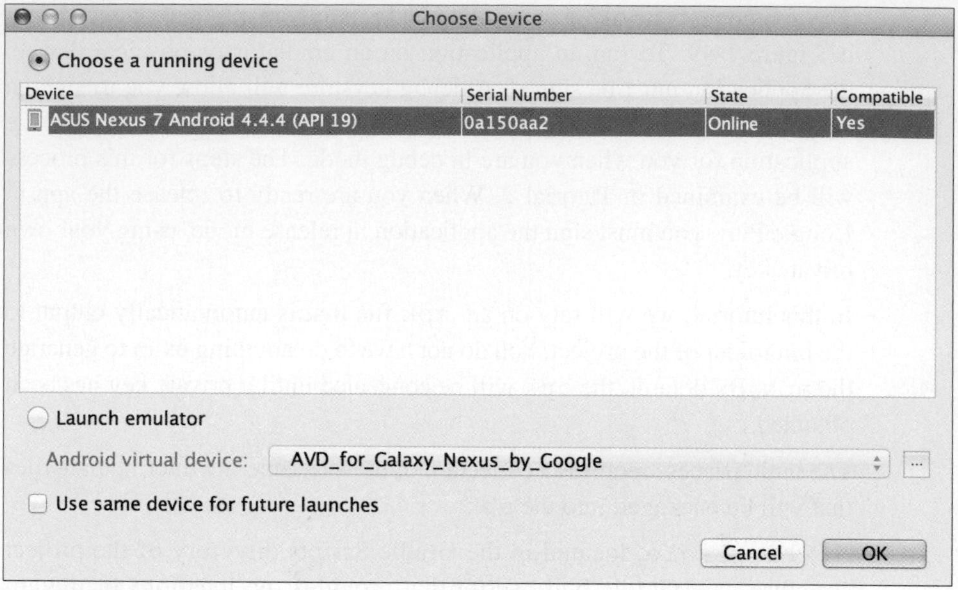

FIGURE 1-50

Part 8: Building an Android Virtual Device

Testing on as many unique physical devices as possible is often advisable during the development of an application. It is impossible to test on all devices. The advantage of an emulator is the ability to construct a variety of virtual devices, particularly non-mainstream devices, on which to test applications. For example, Figure 1-51 shows a virtual device containing a physical keyboard. This Android virtual device emulates one of the few QWERTY devices released for Android.

Before you can run your application on the Android Emulator, you must create an Android Virtual Device, called an AVD. The Android SDK includes a virtual mobile device emulator that runs on your computer. The emulator lets you prototype, develop, and test Android applications without using a physical device. In this part of the tutorial, you will use the AVD Manager to build a very basic AVD.

The Android emulator mimics all of the hardware and software features of a typical mobile device, except that it cannot place actual phone calls. It can be configured in multiple ways to provide navigation and control. Touchscreens are emulated using your mouse or keyboard to generate events for your application. In addition to your application, the emulator screen can display other active Android applications.

Step 1:   Choose **Tools > Android > AVD Manager**, as shown in Figure 1-52.

The AVD Manager provides an easy-to-use user interface to manage your AVD configurations.

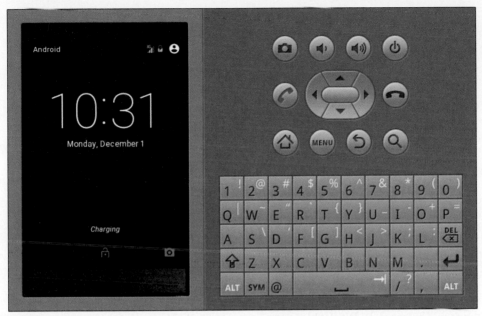

I FIGURE 1-51 An AVD lets developers emulate a physical device.

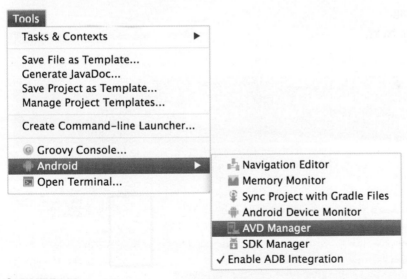

I FIGURE 1-52

Step 2: Select **Create Virtual Device** from the AVD Manager, as shown in Figure 1-53.

Step 3: Choose **Phone** from **Category**.

A set of standard Android devices can be emulated. These are listed in the Virtual Device Configuration window, as shown in Figure 1-54. Each of

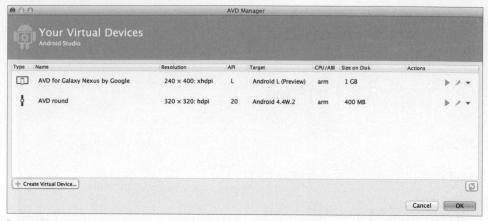

FIGURE 1-53

these device types can be further configured. In this tutorial, the most basic emulator will be built.

Step 4: Choose **3.3" WQVGA** as shown in Figure 1-54.

This small 3.3-inch device has a resolution of 240 × 400 with a low-density setting.

Click **Next**.

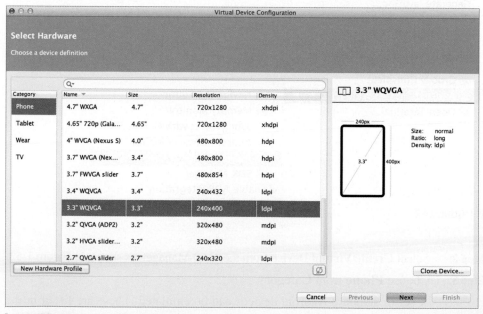

FIGURE 1-54

Step 5: Choose **API 19 KitKat Android 4.4.2 armeabi-v7a**, as shown in Figure 1-55.

The AVD must have an API level equal to or greater than the API level that your application compiles against. Android can run on several different computer architectures. EABI is an embedded-application binary interface. The armeabi-v7a refers to a device that uses ARM architecture and conventions supported by EABI. The v7a specifies support for hardware floating point operations. Click **Next**.

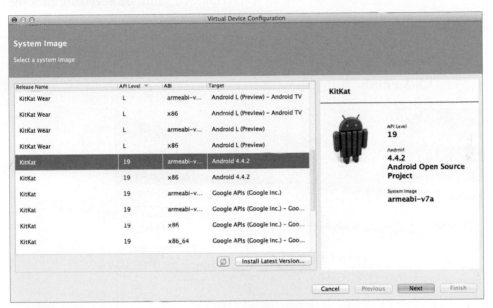

FIGURE 1-55 Android Virtual Devices range from size 2.7–10.1.

Step 6: Provide the identifying name for the **AVD** as **Galaxy_Nexus_3.3**.

Not all devices have the same natural orientation. This can be configured in an AVD.

Step 7: Specify the orientation of the device as **Portrait**.

Step 8: Set the Host GPU for the emulated performance.

A Snapshot will resume the execution of a previous application when the AVD is relaunched. This can lead to a faster load.

Step 9: Select Advanced Settings and make the following edits:

Custom skin definition: No Skin

Each Android platform has its own set of skins. For emulators that have performance issues, it is recommended that default skins, rather than custom skin definitions, be used.

RAM:	512 MB
VM heap:	16 MB
Internal Storage:	200 MB
Camera Front:	None
Camera Back:	None
Keyboard:	To not enable keyboard input.
	If an AVD requires a hardware keyboard, click the Keyboard option on.
Network Speed:	Full
Network Latency:	None

Click **Finish**.

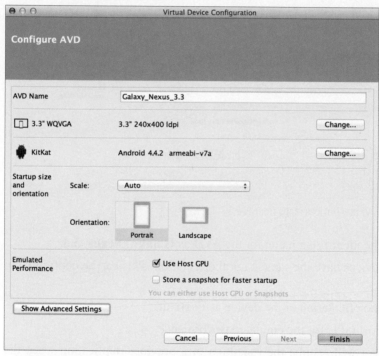

| FIGURE 1-56 The Galaxy_Nexus_3.3 AVD is configured.

Part 9: Testing the Application on an Emulator

In this part of the tutorial, we will run the Hello Goodbye application on the previously defined AVD. In the course of developing an Android application, it will be necessary to compile and run an application multiple times on many AVDs. Each AVD functions as an independent device, with its own private storage for user data, SD card, and so on. When you launch the emulator with an AVD configuration, it automatically loads the user data and SD card data from the AVD directory. By default, the emulator stores the user data, SD card data, and cache in the AVD directory.

It should be noted that an emulator can be useful, but testing on a real device provides developers with more accurate results.

Step 1:   Select **Run > Run 'app'**.

A list of devices identified as compatible configurations for the application will appear.

Step 2:   Choose **Galaxy_Nexus_3.3**, as shown in Figure 1-57.

The first time the emulator launches, it can load rather slowly. It is useful to keep the emulator running between tests rather than quitting and relaunching the virtual device.

Once your application is running on the emulator, it can use the services of the Android platform to invoke other applications, access the network, play audio and video, store and retrieve data, notify the user, and render graphical transitions and themes.

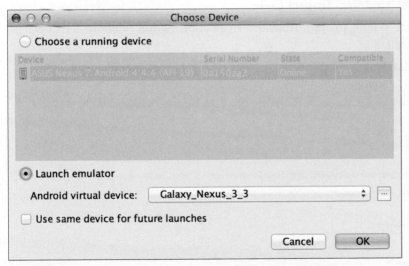

I FIGURE 1-57 An AVD can be selected from the Choose Device window.

Step 3:   Test the application by tapping the Exclamation button.

Several screens produced by the AVD are illustrated in Figure 1-58. The emulator also includes a variety of debug capabilities, which will be discussed in the next part of the tutorial. Multiple AVDs should be constructed to test applications. For example, an AVD can be built for each platform and screen type with which your application is compatible.

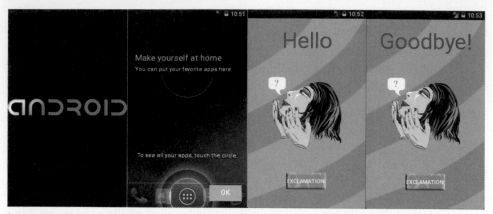

I FIGURE 1-58

Part 10: Optimizing and Improving a Project

In this part of the tutorial, we will use an Android Studio analysis tool to inspect the project and analyze performance. In addition to testing your Android application, it is important to ensure that your project is structurally sound and it runs as efficiently as possible.

Step 1:   Select **Analyze > Inspect Code**.

Step 2:   Select **Whole project** from the **Inspection Scope** window, as shown in Figure 1-59.

Click **OK**.

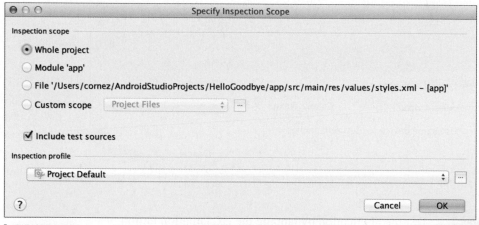

I FIGURE 1-59

The inspection results appear in the Inspection Profile window. Android Lint is a code analysis tool that checks project source files for possible structural flaws. Lint can be used to provide suggestions for a specific issue. For example, it is possible to restrict the issues by checking and assigning a severity level for those issues. Lint can be configured to check for issues for an entire project or for specific elements such as a project module, file, Java class, method, and so forth.

In addition to detecting flaws, Lint will also provide suggestions on how to improve optimization or fix structural problems. This tool has a command-line interface, which allows it to integrate easily into automated testing.

Step 3: Open the items in **Android Lint**, as shown in Figure 1-60.

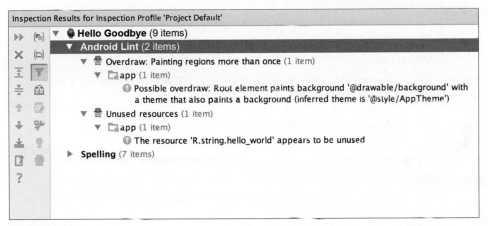

Android Lint detects two issues associated with the Hello Goodbye application. The first issue identifies a potential "overdraw" weakness in the project. An overdraw occurs when an element has been painted with a graphic element more than once. For example, the root view in activity_main.xml was painted with a background drawable, from Part 2 of the tutorial. An overdraw was caused because the theme that was applied to the activity of the application also contains a painted background. This is not an error, and it can sometimes be an intentional design objective. However, in this case, Lint suggests that performance will be improved by reducing the excessive painting. We can eliminate the "overdraw" by customizing the application theme background in style.xml so that it uses the graphic background we applied to the root view. This will allow us to remove the background drawable from the root view in activity_main.xml.

Step 4: Open the file style.xml, located in res/values.

Step 5: Modify the XML code by adding Lines 5–6, as shown below.

Lines 5–6 show a custom windowBackground containing background.png.

```
style.xml
1   <resources>
2
3       <style name="AppTheme"
4           parent="android:Theme.Holo.Light.DarkActionBar">
5           <item name="android:windowBackground">
6               @drawable/background</item>
7       </style>
8
9   </resources>
```

The drawable `background.png` can be eliminated from `activity_main.xml`.

Step 6:   Open `activity_main.xml` and delete the instruction on Line 12, as shown in the code below.

```
activity_main.xml
1   <RelativeLayout
2       xmlns:android="http://schemas.android.com/apk/res/android"
3       xmlns:tools="http://schemas.android.com/tools"
4
5       android:layout_width="match_parent"
6       android:layout_height="match_parent"
7       android:paddingLeft="@dimen/activity_horizontal_margin"
8       android:paddingRight="@dimen/activity_horizontal_margin"
9       android:paddingTop="@dimen/activity_vertical_margin"
10      android:paddingBottom="@dimen/activity_vertical_margin"
11      tools:context=".MainActivity"
12      android:background="@drawable/background">
    .
    .
    .
```

The second issue detected by Lint is an unused resource in the `Hello Goodbye` application. Specifically, the string resource `hello_world`, which was automatically generated when the project was first created, is never used. This string can be deleted from `strings.xml`.

Step 7:   Open `strings.xml` and delete the key-value pair on Line 4, as shown in the code below.

In general, unused resources can make applications larger and will often slow down builds.

```
strings.xml
1   <?xml version="1.0" encoding="utf-8"?>
2   <resources>
3
4       <string name="app_name">Hello Goodbye</string>
5       <string name="hello_world">Hello world!</string>
6       <string name="action_settings">Settings</string>
    .
    .
    .
```

■ 1.7 Model-View-Controller

Android applications tend to rely on the Model-View-Controller design architecture. This architecture assigns one of three roles that objects can play in an application. For example, an object can be a Model, View, or Controller. By establishing their specific purpose, given these assigned roles, it is easier to define how they will communicate with each other.

Model objects are used to encapsulate the data in an application. They can also define the logic and computation that manipulate and process that data. For example, a model object might represent the data associated with a character in a game. A Model object should have no explicit connection to the View object, which visually presents its data and allows the user to interact with that data. This means that Model objects should not be concerned with user-interface and presentation issues.

View objects are visual display objects. These are objects that users can see and will often use interactively. For example, a `TextView` element is a View object that displays text on the screen. A `Button` element is a View object that can respond to user actions.

A Controller object acts as an intermediary between one or more of an application's View objects and one or more of its Model objects. For example, an `Activity` is a controller object in an Android application. In Tutorial 1, `MainActivity` was used to respond to user actions made on a View object, specifically the clicking of a button.

In a Model-View-Controller design architecture, the Controller communicates new or changed data to the Model object. When a Model object changes, a controller object communicates that new data to the View objects so that they can display it. View objects are always notified about changes in Model data through the application's controller objects.

Figure 1-61 illustrates the lines of communication between the Controller, Model, and View objects. The Controller receives user-initiated actions, such as clicking a button or entering text into a text field. The controller then updates data in the Model. The Controller also receives notification of processed data from the Model and responds by updating a View object to the results.

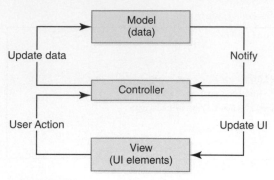

▌ FIGURE 1-61

▪ Tutorial 2: The Tap Button Counter App

Tutorial 2 explores the construction of an application that uses the Controller-View-Model design architecture. In addition, this tutorial will provide an introduction to common features that were not demonstrated in Tutorial 1.

Part 1: The Design

A button tap counter is the application that will be built in this tutorial. The application storyboard, illustrating the user experience, is shown in Figure 1-62. At first launch, the application user interface will appear in landscape orientation. This orientation will be enforced during the entire execution of the application.

The interface screen will display a "Tap" button and a count number, which is initialized to 0. The objective of the app is to count how many times the user taps the button. The count result will be displayed in a text field and updated after each tap on the button. When the user exits the application and then relaunches it, the last count value will appear on the screen. The number can never be reset back to 0.

The objectives for this tutorial are as follows:

1. Add an orientation attribute to the Manifest file.
2. Construct a new user interface file.
3. Use the `onClick` property for a button in the layout file.
4. Employ the Model-View-Controller architecture.

The final project structure for the Tap Button Counter app is shown in Figure 1-63. The Java source file named `Counter` will serve as the **Model** blueprint of the application. A `Counter` object will represent the data related to the count of taps on the button. The `main_layout.xml` file is the layout file that contains the **View** objects of the application. These objects are the visual display objects: the interactive button and the text field showing the number of counts.

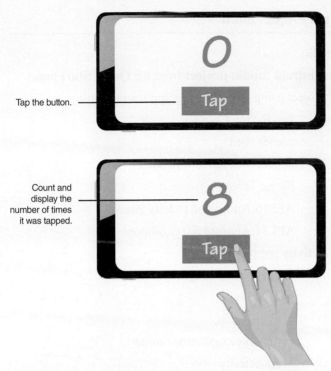

Tap the button.

Count and display the number of times it was tapped.

FIGURE 1-62 An application for exploring basic touch events.

`MainActivity` is the **Controller** acting as the conduit between the `Counter` object and the visual display objects of the user interface. The **Controller** will intercept button actions, communicate the new count data to the `Counter` object, and update the text field in the user interface.

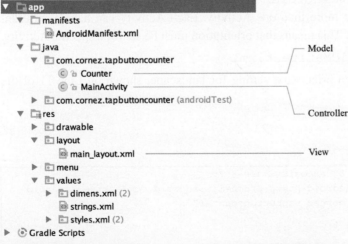

FIGURE 1-63 The final project structure for the Tap Button Counter app.

Part 2: Creating the Android Project Shell

Step 1: Launch Android Studio.

Step 2: Select **Start a new Android Studio project** from the **Quick Start** panel.

Step 3: Configure the new project using the following application settings.

Application Name:	Tap Button Counter
Company Domain:	cornez.com
Package Name:	com.cornez.tapbuttoncounter
Form:	Phone Tablet
Minimum SDK:	API 16:Android 4.1 (Jelly Bean)
Compile with:	API 21:Android 5.0 (Lollipop)

Step 4: Choose the **Blank Activity** template.

Step 5: Specify the following file name options:

Activity Name:	MainActivity
Layout Name:	activity_main
Package Name:	com.cornez.tapbuttoncounter
Title:	MainActivity
Menu Resource Name:	*Leave as the default value.*

Part 3: Edit the Manifest and Add the String Value Resources

The Tap Button Counter application will be restricted to a landscape orientation. When the user rotates the screen, the orientation will remain in landscape mode. This setting can be enforced within the `AndroidManifest.xml` file. As mentioned previously, an application can have more than one Activity. Each Activity can have a different orientation requirement. This means that orientation must be set for a specific Activity.

Step 1: Open `AndroidManifest.xml`.

Step 2: Add the screen orientation setting for landscape, shown on Line 11 of the code below.

Save the file.

```
AndroidManifest.xml
1   <?xml version="1.0" encoding="utf-8"?>
2   <manifest xmlns:android="http://schemas.android.com/apk/res/android"
3       package="com.cornez.tapbuttoncounter" >
4
5       <application
6           android:allowBackup="true"
```

```
 7        android:icon="@drawable/ic_launcher"
 8        android:label="@string/app_name"
 9        android:theme="@style/AppTheme" >
10        <activity
11            android:screenOrientation="landscape"
12            android:name=".MainActivity"
13            android:label="@string/app_name" >
14            <intent-filter>
15                <action android:name="android.intent.action.MAIN" />
16
17                <category
18                    android:name="android.intent.category.LAUNCHER" />
19            </intent-filter>
20        </activity>
21    </application>
22
23 </manifest>
```

The only value resources that will be used by the application are strings. As shown in the storyboard sketch of the application, two text elements will appear on the user interface. The button contains the string "Tap" and the initial count value, 0. Both of these strings will be added to `strings.xml`.

Step 3:   Open `strings.xml`.

Step 4:   Use the following XML code listing as a guide, and add the strings shown on Lines 8–9.

```
strings.xml
 1 <?xml version="1.0" encoding="utf-8"?>
 2 <resources>
 3
 4     <string name="app_name">Tap Button Counter</string>
 5     <string name="hello_world">Hello world!</string>
 6     <string name="action_settings">Settings</string>
 7
 8     <string name="tap_btn">TAP</string>
 9     <string name="zero">0</string>
10
11 </resources>
```

Part 4: Constructing the User Interface of the App

In this part of the tutorial, we will construct a new layout file, `main_layout.xml`, rather that altering the existing `activity_main.xml` file. We are creating this new layout file simply for demonstration. It will be necessary for readers to build multiple layout files in future applications.

Step 1:   Right-click the `res/layout` folder.

All layout files are resources and must be located in the `layout` folder inside the `res` directory of the project structure.

Step 2:   Choose **New** > **XML** > Layout XML file, as shown in Figure 1-64.

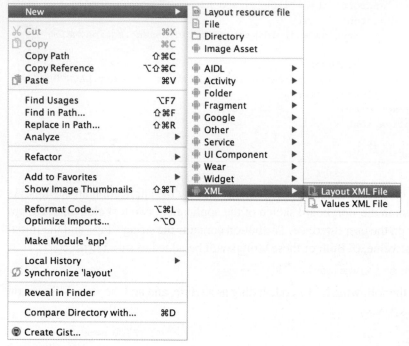

| FIGURE 1-64

`main_layout.xml` serves as the visual entry point for the Tap Button Counter application. The word "main" is used to reflect this.

Step 3:   Enter `main_layout` for the file name.

The root tag of a layout file describes the type of container that will hold the UI elements on the screen. In this application, a `RelativeLayout` will be the root container. This container will eventually hold the text element and the button. `RelativeLayout`, along with the other types of view containers, will be discussed in depth in the next chapter.

Step 4:   Enter `RelativeLayout` for the root tag, as shown in Figure 1-65.

Click **Finish**.

A blank layout will be rendered in the Graphical Layout Editor.

In a previous step, the `AndroidManifest` file was set to restrict the screen to landscape mode when the application runs on a device. It is a good idea to make the Graphical Layout Editor consistent with this altered orientation.

● ○ ○

Choose options for your new file

Creates a new XML layout file.

Layout File Name: | main_layout |

Root Tag: | RelativeLayout |

The root XML tag for the new file

| Cancel | Previous | Next | **Finish** |

| FIGURE 1-65

Step 5:   Select **Design** mode in the Graphical Layout Editor.

Step 6:   Use the **Orientation** icon to set the device orientation to a landscape appearance.

Verify the change in the generated image of the device.

In Step 7, the user interface for `main_layout` will need to be constructed as shown in Figure 1-65. This requires the addition and arrangement of a `Button` and `TextView`.

Step 7:   Use Figure 1-66 as a guide for placing a **Plain TextView Widget** and a **Button Widget** on the layout. Configure these elements using the skills you learned in Tutorial 1. The text and id for both elements must be set as shown in the figure. It is important to be able to perform these tasks on your own before continuing.

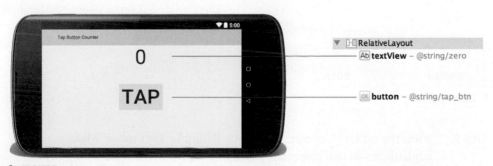

| FIGURE 1-66

Step 8:   Button must be given the onClick property settings shown in Figure 1-67. Type in "countTap" to the right of the divider of the onClick property in the button properties panel.

The onClick property is a useful method for registering a listener event and specifying the event handler. The Java method that handles the button click event, countTap(), will be implemented in MainActivity. In high-performance contexts, this method is preferred to the approach illustrated in Tutorial 1.

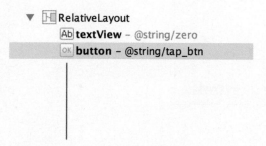

Properties

onClick	m countTap
outlineProvider	
▶ padding	[]
paddingEnd	
paddingStart	
shadowColor	
singleLine	
stateListAnimator	
text	**@string/tap_btn**
textAlignment	
textAppearance	
textColor	
textColorHighlight	
textColorHint	
textColorLink	
textSize	**60sp**

❘ FIGURE 1-67

Step 9:   View the main_layout.xml code listing in **Text** mode. Make necessary adjustments so that it appears exactly as shown in the code listing below.

The user interface screen is now completed. Save your file.

```
main_layout.xml
1   <?xml version="1.0" encoding="utf-8"?>
2   <RelativeLayout
3       xmlns:android="http://schemas.android.com/apk/res/android"
4       android:layout_width="match_parent"
5       android:layout_height="match_parent">
6
7       <TextView
8           android:layout_width="wrap_content"
9           android:layout_height="wrap_content"
10          android:textAppearance="?android:attr/textAppearanceLarge"
11          android:text="@string/zero"
12          android:id="@+id/textView"
13          android:layout_alignParentTop="true"
14          android:layout_centerHorizontal="true"
15          android:textSize="60sp" />
16
17      <Button
18          android:layout_width="wrap_content"
19          android:layout_height="wrap_content"
20          android:text="@string/tap_btn"
21          android:id="@+id/button"
22          android:layout_centerVertical="true"
23          android:layout_centerHorizontal="true"
24          android:textSize="60sp"
25          android:onClick="countTap" />
26  </RelativeLayout>
```

Part 5: Coding the Application

Applications designed for Android are best modeled after the Model-View-Controller architecture. The Model blueprint in this application is the Counter class.

Step 1:   Add the Counter class to the Java directory, as shown in the project structure in Figure 1-68.

This class contains a single data member, mCount, for storing the tap counts of the button. Access to this data element is provided by public methods addCount() and getCount().

The Java code listing for Counter is shown as follows:

The controller used by the application is MainActivity.java. The code listing for this file is shown as follows:

```
Counter.java
1   package com.cornez.tapbuttoncounter;
2
3   class Counter {
4       private int mCount;
```

```
5
6      public Counter(){
7          mCount = 0;
8      }
9
10     public void addCount(){
11         mCount++;
12     }
13
14     public Integer getCount() {
15         return mCount;
16     }
17
18  }
```

Step 2:   Edit `MainActivity.java`.

Line 21:   `main_layout` is set as the user interface screen (content view) for this application activity.

Line 24:   `countView` is the display object that references the Text-View located on the user interface screen, `main_layout`.

Lines 27–30:   The `countTap()` method is called when the user taps on the button. This `onClick` property value was previously set for `button` in `main_layout`. Once this method is triggered, it will produce text output indicating the number of tap counts.

`MainActivity.java`

```
1   package com.cornez.tapbuttoncounter;
2
3   import android.app.Activity;
4   import android.os.Bundle;
5   import android.view.Menu;
6   import android.view.MenuItem;
7   import android.view.View;
8   import android.widget.TextView;
9
10  public class MainActivity extends Activity {
11
12      //MODEL
13      private Counter count;
14
15      //VIEW
16      private TextView countView;
17
18      @Override
19      protected void onCreate(Bundle savedInstanceState) {
```

```
20        super.onCreate(savedInstanceState);
21        setContentView(R.layout.main_layout);
22
23        count = new Counter();
24        countView = (TextView) findViewById(R.id.textView);
25    }
26
27    public void countTap(View view){
28        count.addCount();
29        countView.setText(count.getCount().toString());
30    }
31
32    @Override
33    public boolean onCreateOptionsMenu(Menu menu) {
34        // Inflate the menu;
35        // this adds items to the action bar if it is present.
36        getMenuInflater().inflate(R.menu.menu_main, menu);
37        return true;
38    }
39
40    @Override
41    public boolean onOptionsItemSelected(MenuItem item) {
42        // Handle action bar item clicks here. The action bar will
43        // automatically handle clicks on the Home/Up button, so long
44        // as you specify a parent activity in AndroidManifest.xml.
45        int id = item.getItemId();
46
47        //noinspection SimplifiableIfStatement
48        if (id == R.id.action_settings) {
49            return true;
40        }
41
42        return super.onOptionsItemSelected(item);
43    }
44 }
```

Step 3:   Build and run the project.

Step 4:   Test the application on an AVD or physical device.

■ 1.8 Debugging Android Applications

Debugging an application, as well as ensuring that it performs well, is a crucial part of development. Android Studio and the Android SDK provide a collection of features and tools for debugging and optimizing applications. In addition to the Lint tool, which analyzes an application to test for structural problems, Android Studio enables a debugging mode.

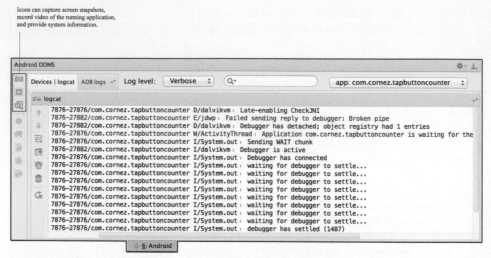

Icons can capture screen snapshots,
record video of the running application,
and provide system information.

│ FIGURE 1-68 The Android DDMS panel debugging and testing features.

An application must be running on a physical device or in an emulator to be debugged. An adb device daemon runs on the device or emulator and provides a means for the adb host daemon to communicate with the device or emulator. The DDMS (Dalvik Debug Monitor Service), shown in Figure 1-68, interacts with the debugger and communicates with the physical device, or emulator, through adb. DDMS is an invaluable tool for development because it can capture screenshots and record video of an application currently running; it can also provide state information, such as memory usage and package information.

When an Android application is running while connected through abd, various system messages are generated and provide output to a real-time system log. For developers, this log information can be useful for detecting bugs. The abd logcat is a feature that provides functionality by filtering the system log messages based on priority.

In Android Studio, logcat is integrated into DDMS. Log messages are obtained using the `android.util.Log` class, which sends log messages to a shared system-level log system. Messages can range from debug builds to stack traces produced by throw exceptions. Figure 1-68 shows log messages produced from the Tap Button Counter application. These messages were output during the application execution while connected to the development machine via USB cable.

Sending output to logcat is as simple as calling the corresponding Log method. The logging facilities provide the following five distinct levels of logging:

Log.e():   e() is error-level logging that is used when something fatal
                has happened. This includes occurrences that will have user-
                visible consequences and cannot be recovered without explicitly

deleting data. This level is always logged. Issues produced at this level should be considered for reporting to a statistics-gathering server.

Log.w():   w() is warning-level logging. Warning-level errors are recoverable error-type logs that do not produce data loss. This level is always logged.

Log.i():   i() is informative-level logging and is used to inform of a high-impact condition. For example, an application that has successfully connected to a server will report this condition as an information-level log.

Log.d():   d() is debug logging. This type of log is used to report unexpected behaviors. This level will be logged, even on applications that are released on the Play Store.

Log.v():   v() is verbose logging, recording more information than usual, and should be used for all other types of logging. This level will only be logged on applications in debug builds.

While logging reports are helpful to developers, they can have a negative impact on performance and quickly lose their usefulness if messages are not kept reasonably concise. Wherever possible, messages should be restricted to a single line. Line lengths up to 80–100 characters are perfectly acceptable, but lengths longer than 130–160 characters should be avoided if possible.

In addition to DDMS, Android Studio provides a Debugging mode that can be applied to an application executing on an emulator or a physical device. Debugging mode can be activated by selecting **Debug 'app'** from the **Run** menu. The Debug icon will appear during the duration of application execution. Figure 1-69 shows the Debug pane displaying thread information for the Tap Button Counter application.

A **Gradle console** tool is available in Android Studio for viewing information about Gradle build tasks as they are executed. This information provides the details about the success or failure of a build. Figure 1-70 shows the complete **Gradle Console** output after Tap Button Counter was successfully built. This information is produced when **Rebuild Project** is selected from **Run**.

A command line, **Terminal**, is integrated within Android Studio, as shown in Figure 1-71. **Terminal** makes it easy to launch specific tasks from a Command Prompt or Mac OS Terminal interface. To display information about the built-in list of shell commands, type **help**. Multiple terminals can be launched to execute different commands.

The **Memory Monitor** tool, shown in Figure 1-72, allows developers to monitor the memory usage of a running app over time. For example, the memory use of the Tap Button Counter application developed in Tutorial 1 remains at a fixed memory use of 8 MB, as shown in Figure 1-71. This information is useful in tracking heap (memory

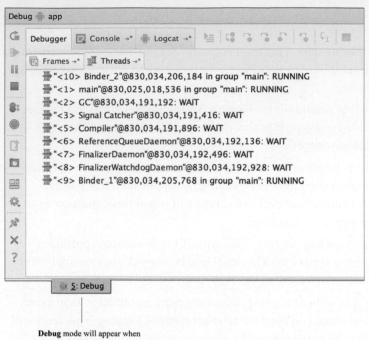

Debug app
Debugger
Console
Logcat
Frames
Threads
"<10> Binder_2"@830,034,206,184 in group "main": RUNNING
"<1> main"@830,025,018,536 in group "main": RUNNING
"<2> GC"@830,034,191,192: WAIT
"<3> Signal Catcher"@830,034,191,416: WAIT
"<5> Compiler"@830,034,191,896: WAIT
"<6> ReferenceQueueDaemon"@830,034,192,136: WAIT
"<7> FinalizerDaemon"@830,034,192,496: WAIT
"<8> FinalizerWatchdogDaemon"@830,034,192,928: WAIT
"<9> Binder_1"@830,034,205,768 in group "main": RUNNING
5: Debug
Debug mode will appear when
when Debug 'app'
is selected from the Run menu.

FIGURE 1-69

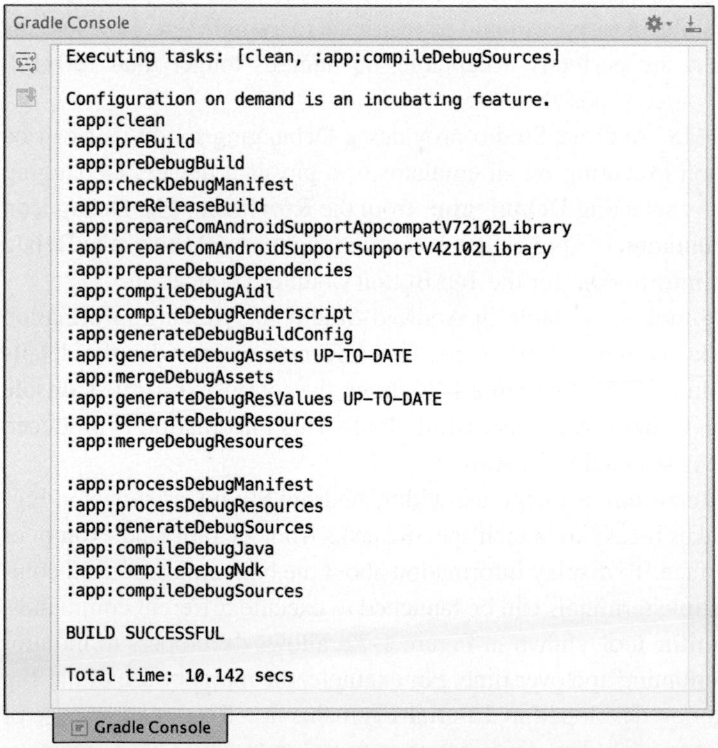

Gradle Console
Executing tasks: [clean, :app:compileDebugSources]
Configuration on demand is an incubating feature.
:app:clean
:app:preBuild
:app:preDebugBuild
:app:checkDebugManifest
:app:preReleaseBuild
:app:prepareComAndroidSupportAppcompatV72102Library
:app:prepareComAndroidSupportSupportV42102Library
:app:prepareDebugDependencies
:app:compileDebugAidl
:app:compileDebugRenderscript
:app:generateDebugBuildConfig
:app:generateDebugAssets UP-TO-DATE
:app:mergeDebugAssets
:app:generateDebugResValues UP-TO-DATE
:app:generateDebugResources
:app:mergeDebugResources
:app:processDebugManifest
:app:processDebugResources
:app:generateDebugSources
:app:compileDebugJava
:app:compileDebugNdk
:app:compileDebugSources
BUILD SUCCESSFUL
Total time: 10.142 secs
Gradle Console

FIGURE 1-70

Launch multiple
Terminal windows.

```
Terminal                                                          ☼ ·  ⤓
  +    variables - Some variable names an wait [n]
       while COMMANDS; do COMMANDS; done  { COMMANDS ; }
  ✕  trishs-mbp:app trishcornez$ ls
     app-debug.apk                    libs
     app-release.apk                  manifest-merger-debug-report.txt
     app.iml                          manifest-merger-release-report.txt
     build                            proguard-rules.pro
     build.gradle                     src
     trishs-mbp:app trishcornez$ █
```
                        ▣ Terminal

❙ FIGURE 1-71

reserved for data created at runtime) usage at a certain point in time during the execution of your app. Additional memory-profiling features are planned for Android Studio
in future releases.

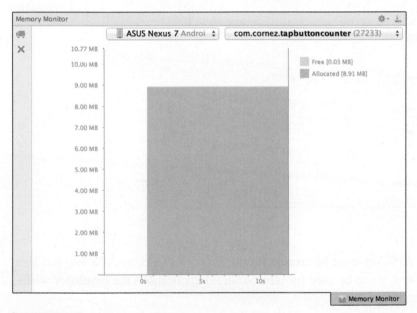

❙ FIGURE 1-72

▪ 1.9 Sharing Your Android Applications

To share applications you have built, or to place them on Google Play, Android requires
that the application be digitally signed with a certificate. Android uses this certificate
to identify the author. Android apps typically use self-signed certificates in which the
app developer holds the certificate's private key.

Developers can sign an application in debug mode or in release mode. During development, an app is signed in debug mode. Android Studio signs your app in debug mode automatically when you run or debug your project. Once the application is ready to be distributed to users, it must be signed in release mode. The Android SDK generates a certificate to sign apps in debug mode. To sign the final product in release mode, developers will need to generate their own certificate.

The following steps outline the process for signing an application for the first time. Once the app has been signed, it can be emailed or shared with others. To follow these steps, you must be using Android Studio and working on the development of an application, such as Tap Button Counter from Tutorial 2.

Step 1:   Choose **Build** > **Generate Signed APK** . . .

Step 2:   Select **app** from **Module**, as shown in Figure 1-73.

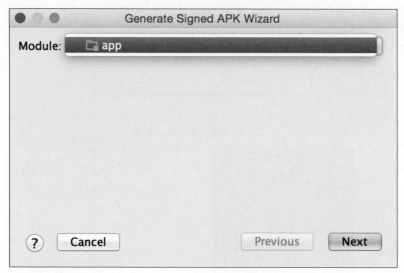

FIGURE 1-73

An APK key must be created for the first time. Once an APK key has been created, it can be used for other Android applications the developer wishes to build.

Step 3:   Click **Create new** . . . from the APK Wizard, shown in Figure 1-74.

The keystore creates a certificate with a private key and a password. You can run and debug your application without entering the password every time you make a change to your project. A keystore is a binary file that contains a set of private keys. A private key represents the entity, such as a person or a company, to be identified with the application.

Click **Create new ...** to create a new keystore.
Once a key is generated, it can be used to update
apps for many years.

Generate Signed APK Wizard

Key store path:

Create new...   Choose existing...

Key store password:

Key alias:

Key password:

☐ Remember password

? Cancel   Previous   Next

I FIGURE 1-74

Step 4:   Enter the required information as shown in Figure 1-75.

Once a key is created, it can be used to sign app updates. The same key can
be used throughout the lifespan of the application.

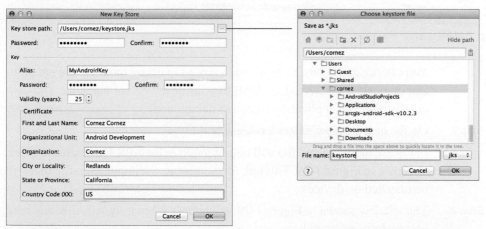

I FIGURE 1-75 A keystore password, an alias, and a key password must be provided before a Signed APK
certificate can be generated.

Step 5:   Enter the required information in the Generate Signed APK Wizard window, as shown in Figure 1-76.

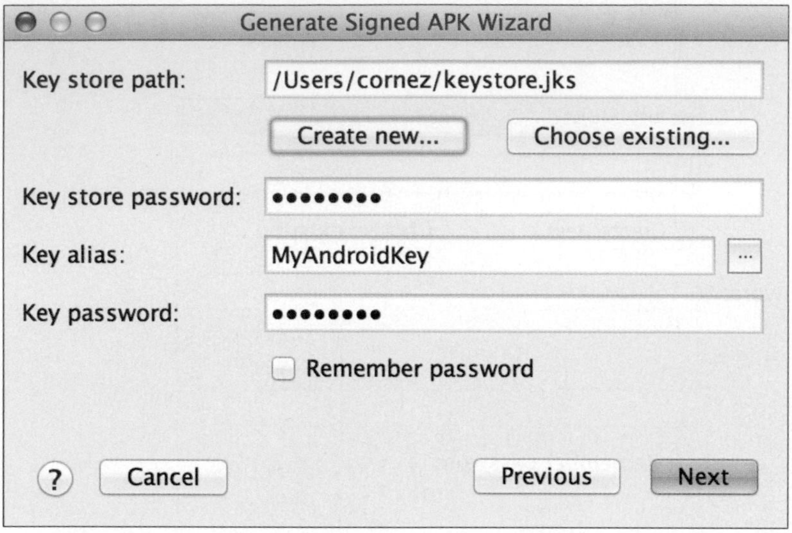

| FIGURE 1-76

Step 6:   Enter a master password, as shown in Figure 1-77.

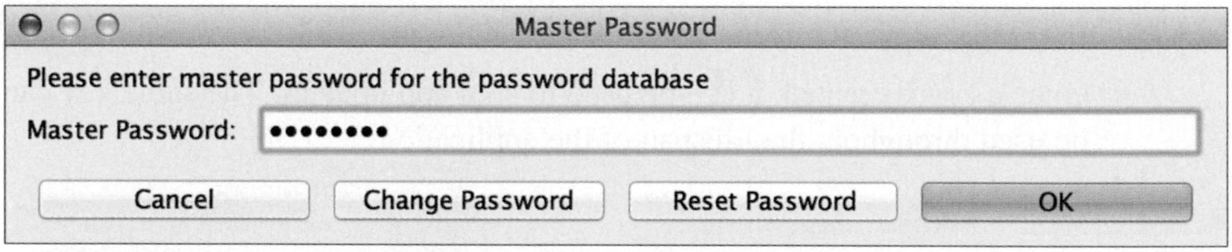

| FIGURE 1-77

You can run and debug an application signed in debug mode on the emulator and on devices connected via USB to your development machine. You cannot distribute an application signed in debug mode.

Step 7:   On the next window, select a **release** build type.

In release mode, an apk file will be generated in the APK Destination Folder, as shown in Figure 1-78. This apk file represents the application file that will be installed on devices.

Step 8:   The window shown in Figure 1-79 will appear when a signed APK has been successfully generated.

Once the apk file has been packaged for distribution, it will appear in the app folder of the application, as shown in Figure 1-80. This file can be shared with users without requiring them to connect to the development machine via USB.

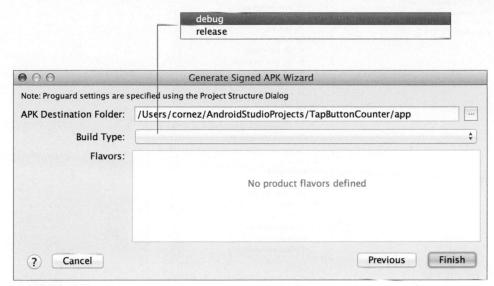

FIGURE 1-78

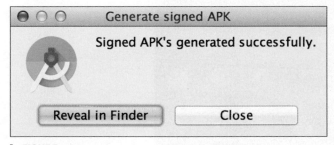

FIGURE 1-79

It is not uncommon to send applications through email as an attachment.

Step 9:   Send an email containing the `app-release.apk` file as an attachment. This email should be received on an Android device running the correct platform.

In order for an Android device to download and install an Android application from a source other than the Play Store, the Device Administrator must be set to **Unknown sources**.

Step 10:   Using the physical device, select **Settings > Security**.

Make sure to check **Unknown sources** to allow the installation of applications from sources outside of the Play Store.

Step 11:   Select the attachment from your email app or mobile browser.

Step 12:   Choose the **Downloads** widget (shown in Figure 1-81) to download and install the app.

The window shown in Figure 1-82 will appear when a signed application has been successfully installed. Its launch icon can be activated.

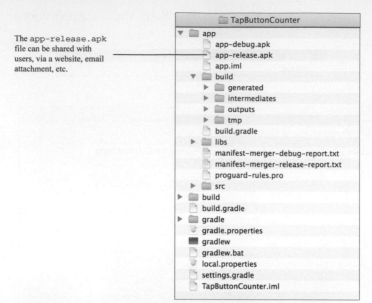

The `app-release.apk` file can be shared with users, via a website, email attachment, etc.

| FIGURE 1-80

Download apps and install outside Google Play Store

| FIGURE 1-81

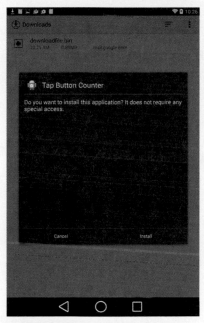
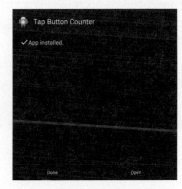

FIGURE 1-82

Exercises

1.1 Dalvik code is produced by the _____.

1.2 Dalvik is a(n) _____ engine.

1.3 What is KitKat's most notable feature?

1.4 Name two Android development environments.

1.5 List the important Android development components.

1.6 What is a drawable?

1.7 The role of the JVM is to read the Java application through the _____.

1.8 True or False: ADT Bundle is a streamlined development version of Eclipse IDE.

1.9 True or False: You can generate App design ideas by exploring interaction designs using specific usage scenarios.

1.10 What is the conversion of dp units to screen pixels?

1.11 Identify the basic components of an Android application.

1.12 Describe the Model-View-Controller pattern design.

1.13 Bytecode is interpreted by a _____.

1.14 Java programs can run on any computer with an Installed _____.

1.15 JVM stands for _____.

1.16 Identify the Android platforms.

1.17 Briefly describe the differences between KitKat and Jelly Bean.

1.18 ADT stands for _____.

1.19 An application file is represented as a(n) _____ file and can be installed on an Android device.

1.20 A density-independent pixel (dp) is a virtual pixel unit that is equivalent to one physical pixel on a(n) _____ dpi screen.

1.21 True or False: The Abstract Window Toolkit and Swing are not supported in Dalvik.

1.22 True or False: For Android, the dex compiler recompiles Java bytecode into proprietary Dalvik bytecode.

1.23 True or False: There is a virtual machine in the Android platform.

2 Building User Interfaces and Basic Applications

Chapter Objectives

In this chapter you will:

- Become familiar with Android's user interface (UI) structure.
- Learn about text input widgets and how to configure the soft keyboard.
- Understand `Views`, widgets, and how the `R.java` class is constructed.
- Implement applications that require various User Interface Controls.
- Examine Adaptive Design Concepts.
- Learn how to organize screen content using `ViewGroup` containers.
- Learn how to use Adapters to create sophisticated user interfaces.

■ 2.1 Android User Interface

A user interface is essentially a collection of visual objects arranged on the screen; the user can see them and interact with them. Every Android application requires a user interface that can be built in one of two ways: The visual objects can either be created in Java code or in an external XML layout file. When using Android Studio to build an app, the Graphical Layout tool is used interactively to build the external XML layout file.

The graphical user interface for an Android app is built using a hierarchy of `View` and `ViewGroup` objects. View objects are usually UI widgets, such as buttons or text fields, and `ViewGroup` objects are invisible view containers that define how the child views are laid out, such as in a grid or a vertical list.

Android provides an XML vocabulary that corresponds to the subclasses of `View` and `ViewGroup` so you can define your UI in XML using a hierarchy of UI elements. Android applications use a range of standard platform resources for designing and programming user interfaces. An application's user interface is everything that the user can see and interact with on a given screen. This includes user interface control components, menus, output notifications, and dialogs. Android development relies on the Java framework; however, common Java libraries used for graphical user interfaces, such as Swing, are not supported in Android. Instead, Android applications use classes in the Java language, along with a core set of Android packages and classes, to implement various aspects of Graphical User Interface (GUI) functionality. Developers can use XML data to declare screen layouts and create Java and Android classes to define behavior.

Each screen in an Android app is identified as a layout resource. Typically, an activity instructs the user's device to treat the launch of the activity as a screen that represents the user interface for that activity. For example, in the following onCreate() method for an Activity, the instruction on Line 3 specifies an external layout file named activity_my.xml to represent the visual interface for this Activity. This layout file will be inflated on the screen when the Activity is created.

```
1   protected void onCreate(Bundle savedInstanceState) {
2         super.onCreate(savedInstanceState);
3         setContentView(R.layout.activity_my);
4       }
```

Activities can reference various visual and interactive elements stored on a layout file and can implement event handlers, such as handlers to deal with users pressing buttons and selecting menu items. Android developers can use Java and XML code to define the layouts for each Activity in an application. A Layout is simply the visual implementation of the Android application screen. It consists of a collection of UI elements for input, output, and interactions. This chapter explores Android layout concepts and basic interactions.

■ 2.2 Layouts

Visual interfaces in an Android application can be defined by one or more layout files, which specifically outline the placement of UI control elements displayed on a given screen. The term "layout" denotes the visual architecture of the application; it defines the visual display object that the user sees and interacts with on the screen. Android app developers can use Java and XML code to define the layouts for each Activity in an application. Developers typically construct a single XML layout file for each Activity class in an application. Layout XML files often contain other layout XML files allowing the reuse of screen elements for multiple locations.

The application resources folder within the project holds the XML layout files as well as graphics for the GUI. All layout files are configured in a hierarchical tree structure, with a root layout element at the highest position in the structure. The root layout is a container that holds the UI elements within the layout file. The Android platform provides a range of standard root layouts developers can use, determining

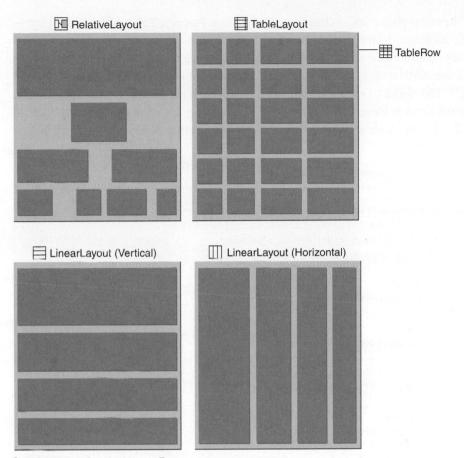

| FIGURE 2-1 Standard Layout Types.

the positioning of each visible element in the layout file. There are six standard root layouts as follows:

1. `RelativeLayout`
2. `LinearLayout`
3. `TableLayout`
4. `RowLayout`
5. `GridLayout`
6. `FrameLayout`

A `RelativeLayout` is used for screen designs that require control elements to be positioned in relation to one another. The example XML code file that follows relies on a `RelativeLayout` to arrange a set of generic text and button control elements on a screen. The screen display that results from this code is shown in Figure 2-2.

Alignment properties, such as layout_alignParentTop, layout_align-Left, layout_toRightOf, and layout_marginTop, are used to position individual control elements within the context of existing elements. For example, Lines 16–22 use XML code to define a TextView element identified by the name @+id/text2. This TextView element is positioned below and aligned along the left margin of the element named @+id/text1. The property layout_marginTop, from Line 22, has been set to position the TextView so that it is exactly 51 dps below @+id/text1.

```
1   <RelativeLayout
2   xmlns:android="http://schemas.android.com/apk/res/android"
3       xmlns:tools="http://schemas.android.com/tools"
4       android:layout_width="match_parent"
5       android:layout_height="match_parent">
6
7       <TextView
8           android:text="Text 1"
9           android:id="@+id/text1"
10          android:layout_alignParentTop="true"
11          android:layout_alignParentLeft="true"
12          android:layout_alignParentStart="true"
13          android:layout_marginLeft="65dp"
14          android:layout_marginTop="86dp" />
15
16      <TextView
17          android:text="Text 2"
18          android:id="@+id/text2"
19          android:layout_below="@+id/text1"
20          android:layout_alignLeft="@+id/text1"
21          android:layout_alignStart="@+id/text1"
22          android:layout_marginTop="51dp" />
23
24      <Button
25          android:text="Button"
26          android:id="@+id/button"
27          android:layout_alignBottom="@+id/text2"
28          android:layout_toRightOf="@+id/text2"
29          android:layout_marginLeft="95dp" />
30
31      <TextView
32          android:text="Text 3"
33          android:id="@+id/text3"
34          android:layout_below="@+id/button"
35          android:layout_alignLeft="@+id/button"
36          android:layout_alignStart="@+id/button"
37          android:layout_marginTop="57dp" />
38  </RelativeLayout>
```

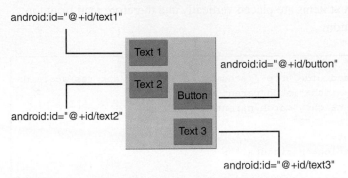

Relative Layout

android:id="@+id/text1"

Text 1

android:id="@+id/button"

Text 2

Button

android:id="@+id/text2"

Text 3

android:id="@+id/text3"

❙ FIGURE 2-2 RelativeLayout elements are positioned relative to each other.

A `LinearLayout` is used for simple arrangments that require elements to be displayed along either a horizontal or vertical line. In the case of a vertical orientation, each element is placed within the layout below the last. A horizontal layout adds elements left to right. The layout fills the available space both horizontally and vertically using the "layout_width" and "layout_height" attributes. It should be noted that the term "layout attribute" can also be referred to as "layout parameter" or "alignment property." The visual structure of a horizontally and vertically oriented `LinearLayout` is shown in Figure 2-3.

A `TableLayout`, as the name suggests, is used to arrange elements into tabular rows and columns. A `TableLayout` can be used to align screen content in a way that is similar to an HTML table on a webpage. It organizes its contained elements into neatly defined rows and columns. A `TableRow`, also a layout root element, is simply a layout that is used by a `TableLayout` to store individual table rows. The idea of adding a `TableRow` to a layout is important when creating dynamic screens and will be explored further in subsequent chapters. A `Gridlayout` works with a flat-view hierarchy. Child objects can be placed into a `Gridlayout` using a horizontal or vertical orientation.

In following code example, XML is used to define a layout that utilizes a `Gridlayout` as the root element.

Line 5:	The number of columns is set to 2.
Line 6:	The number of rows is set to 2.
Line 7:	Orientation determines the order in which the cells will be populated. A horizontal orientation will populate cells row by row, filling in values moving from left to right. The result is a layout that contains four items grouped into two rows and two columns that read from left to right. The screenshot for this layout is shown on the left in Figure 2-3. The right-hand image, shows the screenshot

when the orientation on Line 6 is set to a "vertical" orientation. The text items are placed vertically and therefore read from top to bottom.

```
1   <?xml version="1.0" encoding="utf-8"?>
2   <GridLayout xmlns:android="http://schemas.android.com/apk/res/android"
3       android:layout_width="match_parent"
4       android:layout_height="match_parent"
5       android:columnCount="2"
6       android:rowCount="2"
7       android:orientation="horizontal" >
8
9       <TextView
10          android:text="Text 1" />
11
12      <TextView
13          android:text="Text 2" />
14
15      <TextView
16          android:text="Text 3" />
17
18      <TextView
19          android:text="Text 4" />
20
21  </GridLayout>
```

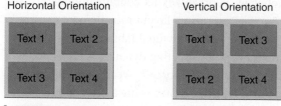

GridLayout - Flat-view hierarchy

I FIGURE 2-3 A GridLayout has two orientations.

Child elements can be added to a GridLayout in a controlled way. By specifying a row-and-column location within the grid, using the layout_row and layout_column attributes, the GridLayout can quickly position components in the grid without requiring a table. The main purpose of a GridLayout is to display tabular data from an Adapter. Adapter-based elements are primarily used when there is a significant amount of data for the user to navigate by scrolling. This topic will be explored in later chapters.

The last root layout type provided by Android is the FrameLayout. A FrameLayout is generally used to display a single element. Figure 2-4 shows two examples of a FrameLayout. The top image shows a FrameLayout that contains a drawable canvas. The bottom image of Figure 2-4 shows a FrameLayout for

☐ **FrameLayout**

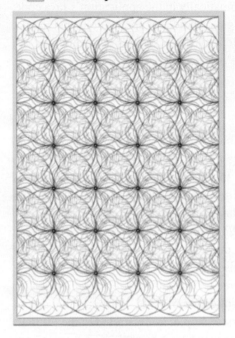

A **FrameLayout**
containing
a drawing
canvas.

☐ **FrameLayout**

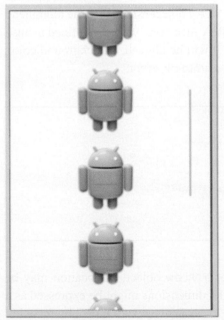

A **FrameLayout**
containing
a scrollable
list.

❙ FIGURE 2-4 FrameLayouts contain a single control object, such as a canvas or list.

storing a scrollable control element. A `FrameLayout` can be defined within XML layout resources, but it is often created programmatically in the application's Java code. The flexibility of a `FrameLayout` makes it a good choice for applications that require dynamic behavior, such as updates from the cloud or game screens with canvases. We will explore the programmatic creation and use of `FrameLayout` in future chapters.

■ 2.3 The `View` Class

An Android user interface is built around an object called a `View`. A `View` describes every interactive visual control object that appears on an application screen. This means that every control object in an Android user interface is a subclass of the Android `View` class, or more precisely, `android.view.View`. The Android SDK provides developers with a set of primitive `View` subclasses for building control objects, such as buttons, input and output text elements, radio buttons, and checkboxes. The layout files of an application are merely a collection of these `View` objects arranged on the screen and translated into an XML file for Android to use.

When a `View` object is placed on the screen, it occupies a rectangular area. In addition, its appearance is characterized by a collection of XML attributes that can be customized to alter how it will look to users. For example, as illustrated in the tutorials of Chapter 1, a `TextView` object has attributes such as `textSize`, `textColor`, and `gravity`. The values for these attributes can be edited to modify the appearance of a `TextView` object. If `textSize` is incremented, the size of the text will increase in pixels. The `gravity` attribute for the `TextView` object establishes the alignment.

Consider the following XML code segment. A `Button View` is defined using a set of attributes, such as as width, height, how it will be aligned, a background color, and the handler method that will respond to an `onClick` event.

```
1    <Button
2        android:id="@+id/button1"
3        android:layout_width="wrap_content"
4        android:layout_height="20dp"
5        android:layout_alignParentTop="true"
6        android:layout_centerHorizontal="true"
7        android:onClick="goTap"
8        android:background="blue"
9        android:text="Button" />
```

As a result of the rectangular geometry of a `View` object, its location may be expressed as a pair of left and top coordinates. Its dimensions might be expressed as a width and a height. It is possible to retrieve the location of a `View` object by invoking the methods `getLeft()` and `getTop()`. The width and height can be obtained by calling the methods `getWidth()` and `getHeight()`; they can be set by calling them `setWidth()` and `setHeight()`.

The user interface for your application can be built in one of two ways: (1) constructing it as a layout using XML code, or (2) building the entire layout, or pieces of the layout, programmatically at runtime. Declaring user interface elements using XML is a straightforward process. Android provides the XML vocabulary that easily corresponds to View classes and subclasses.

The Android framework gives you the flexibility to use either or both of these methods for declaring and managing your application's View objects. For example, you could declare your application's default layouts in XML, including the screen elements that will appear in them and their properties. You could then add code in your application that would modify the state of the screen objects at runtime, including those declared in XML.

The advantage to declaring your UI in XML is that it provides you with a better way to separate the presentation of your application from the code that controls its behavior. Your UI descriptions are external to your application code, which means that you can modify or adapt it without having to modify your source code and recompile. For example, you can create XML layouts for different screen orientations, different device screen sizes, and different languages. Additionally, declaring the layout in XML makes it easier to visualize the `View` structure of your UI and, therefore, easier to debug.

■ 2.4 Text Input and Output

Android provides two categories for text input and text output. `TextView` and `EditText` are the two Android text field classes, both derived from the `View` superclass. These two classes are used to represent textual control objects and will inherit the characteristics and functionality passed on from the `View` class.

`TextView` is used primarily for text output, as well as any textual elements that are static, such as labels and titles. Text fields that are used as input controls by the app are most often represented by `EditTexts`.

The `EditText` (`android.widget.EditText`) class is actually a `TextView`, but it has been reconfigured to allow text input and editing by the user. It should be noted that there is some flexibility in the `TextView` class that makes it possible for a `TextView` object to behave as an input text field. This textbook adopts the `EditText` class solely for the purpose of input text fields and the `TextView` class for output and static textual elements.

When the user taps an `EditText` object on a user interface, a cursor will automatically appear within the text field and a soft keyboard will be displayed in the lower part of the screen for immediate input. `EditText` provides a complete text editor, allowing the user to perform tasks such as text selection, data entry with auto-completion, cut, copy, and paste. `EditTexts` can also be configured for single line or multiline data input.

Attributes must be applied to an `EditText` object to customize the type of data that can be input. `EditText` controls can have a range of input types, such as number, date, password, or email address. Input within an `EditText` can be further refined by setting multiple `InputType` properties. A small subset of these `InputType` properties are:

```
textCapCharacters

textAutoCorrect

textAutoComplete

textNoSuggestions
```

`InputType` properties will be used to reconfigure the soft keyboard by adjusting its keys, thereby controlling the kind of characters allowed inside the `EditText` field. Consider an `EditText` field that requires the user to input a person's complete name. Let us assume the first letter of each name must be capitalized.

Figure 2-5 captures three snapshots of a screen containing an `EditText` object for the input of a person's name. The first image shows the screen as it looks prior to the user entering the person's name. Note that a hint appears in the `EditText` field, and an uppercase keyboard is activated when entering the first letter of a first name. The second image shows the screen as the user is in the process of completing the input of the first name. Note the appearance of lowercase keys in the keyboard. The last image shows the screen, with the keyboard reverting back to uppercase keys as the user begins inputing the second name.

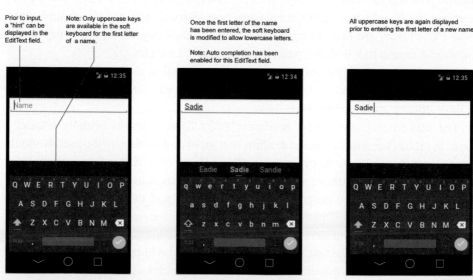

FIGURE 2-5 Soft keyboards can be altered during stages of input.

The XML code for the layout that produces the soft keyboards from Figure 2-5 is listed below.

Line 10:   The `EditText` widget is given a unique name using the id property. This identifier will be used to retrieve the value of this control programmatically.

Line 11:   An input hint is provided to the user. The `hint` property is helpful in a user interface because it provides a prompt when the user is required to add data in a text field. When the user begins entering input into this control, the hint is overwritten.

Line 12:   The property `inputType` is used to configure the attributes for the type of input. Multiple configurations can be applied, such as a person's name with the first letter of the first and last name capitalized. This property is discussed further in the next section of this chapter.

```
1   <?xml version="1.0" encoding="utf-8"?>
2   <LinearLayout xmlns:android="http://schemas.android.com/apk/res/android"
3       android:orientation="vertical"
4       android:layout_width="match_parent"
5       android:layout_height="match_parent">
6
7       <EditText
8           android:layout_width="match_parent"
9           android:layout_height="wrap_content"
10          android:id="@+id/editText"
11          android:hint="Name"
12          android:inputType="textCapWords|textPersonName" />
13
14  </LinearLayout>
```

`EditText` objects are normally added to a layout file using XML. Because the `EditText` class is derived from the `TextView` class, most static `TextView` control attributes (and related methods) still apply. For example, it is possible to set attributes that adjust the control's appearance, such as the text size, color, font or other style settings.

To retrieve the value of an `EditText` control from within an activity, you can use the `getText ()` method of the `EditText` class. For example, the following code retrieves a handler to the `EditText` control defined as `messageEt`.

```
1   EditText messageET = (EditText) findViewById(R.id. messageET);
2   String strValue = messageEt.getText().toString();
```

Flexibility can be built into `EditText` controls, as well as other input controls, by using Android view control listeners. A view control listener will listen for an event that occurs on an attached `View`. For example, in Tutorial 1 of Chapter 1, we saw how a view control listener was attached to a button to listen for an `onClick` event. An `onClick` event indicates the user tapped a finger on a button to activate it. Similarly, a `TextWatcher` is a view control listener that listens for input changes in an `EditText` control. We will explore a `TextWatcher` firsthand in the first lab of this chapter.

In addition to the `TextWatcher`, the `setOnFocusChangeListener` () method is useful for identifying when the user changes focus to or from a control. For example, the following code segment declares an `EditText` control object named `mEditText` that is linked to the resource "editText1." The listener event "setOnFocusChangeListener" is applied to the control object. When the control first gets focus, an `onFocusChange` event will occur. Once the user moves focus away from this control, an `onFocusChange` event will occur again.

```
1  EditText mEditText = (EditText) findViewById(R.id.editText1);
2  mEditText.setOnFocusChangeListener(new OnFocusChangeListener() {
3      public void onFocusChange(View v, boolean hasFocus) {
4          String strValue = mEditText.getText().toString();
5      }
6  });
```

■ 2.5 Soft Keyboards

When a user begins the process of inputing data into an `EditText` control, the Android system displays an onscreen keyboard. This keyboard is called a soft keyboard, as opposed to a physical keyboard, because it can instantly generate a specific configuration that precisely fits the needs of an `EditText` once it receives focus. Android provides flexible soft keyboards that can easily be adapted to a specific user experience for an application. As a developer, you can set the characteristics that represent the type of input you expect for a text file (such as whether it's a password, phone number, or email address) and how the input method should behave (such as whether it performs autocorrect for spelling mistakes).

The type of input for a text field is used to determine the kind of characters allowed within the text field. For example, an email address requires the @ symbol to be embedded in an address. When inputting an email address, it's important that the keyboard display normal text keys along with the @ symbol prominently, as shown in Figure 2-6.

When an application requires that a password be entered into a text field, the soft keyboard should hold a normal set of keys, including uppercase and lowercase text keys, numbers, and some special characters, such as underscore. In addition, the behavior of input must be altered. For example, characters within the password will be masked as a security measure. As shown in Figure 2-7, the characters are turned into dots once they have been typed.

FIGURE 2-6 A soft keyboard configured for the input of an email address.

FIGURE 2-7 A soft keyboard configured for password input.

By default, the soft keyboard for input within a simple `EditText` control is a basic keyboard with plain keys. This type of text input is called plain text. To facilitate input of different types of text, a standard soft keyboard can be configured by setting the `android:inputType` attribute of the text field. For example, if you want the user to input an email address, the `inputType` attribute of the `EditText` control object can be initialized to `textEmailAddress`, as shown on Line 6 of the following XML code.

```
1   <EditText
2       android:id="@+id/editText1"
3       android:layout_width="fill_parent"
4       android:layout_height="wrap_content"
5       android:hint="email address"
6       android:inputType="textEmailAddress" />
```

A variety of input types can constrain text input to a specific type. Android provides a set of Text Field input-type properties that can be used to restrict input by reconfiguring the soft keyboard. These Text Fields, which can be placed on a layout file in the graphic layout editor, are listed in Table 2-1. To allow generic plain text to be input into a text field, the inputType property can be set to "none" or can be left out of the `EditText` XML definition in the layout.

The soft keyboards that these controls generate are shown in Figure 2-8. In some cases, there are very small differences in the keys provided. You can add further input

TABLE 2-1 Text Fields that Define the EditView Controls.

Text Field	`inputType` Property Value
Plain Text	`none`
Person Name	`textPersonName`
Password	`textPassword`
Password (Numeric)	`numberPassword`
Email	`textEmailAddress`
Phone	`phone`
Postal Address	`textPostalAddress`
Multiline Text	`textMultiLine`
Time	`time`
Date	`date`
Number	`number`
Number (Signed)	`numberSigned`
Number (Decimal)	`numberDecimal`

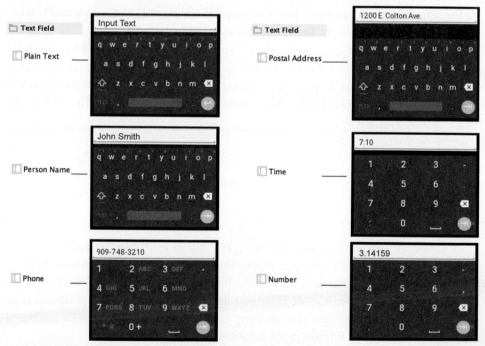

FIGURE 2-8 Android supports multiple soft keyboard configurations.

restrictions for a text field by specifying more input requirements in the `inputType` attribute of the `View` control object. You can also place these specifications in the XML code from the Properties Tab.

You can combine properties in the `android:inputType` attribute for a text field to specify, not only the input method, but also additional behaviors. For example, a password text field might require solely capital letters.

By specifying both of these properties in the `android:inputType` attribute, you will be able to generate a specific type of soft keyboard and specify various behaviors for the input method.

In the XML code segment below, the `EditText` object is configured to hold multiple lines of plain text, the first letter of a given sentence is capitalized, and text input, as shown in Figure 2-9, is flagged for autocompletion and autocorrection.

```
1  <EditText
2      android:layout_width="match_parent"
3      android:layout_height="wrap_content"
4      android:inputType=
5      "textMultiLine|textCapSentences
6                    |textAutoComplete|textAutoCorrect"
7      android:id="@+id/editText1" />
```

I FIGURE 2-9 Text `AutoComplete` will produce dictionary-based suggestions during input.

In addition to the inputType properties outlined in Table 2-1, further attributes can be applied to text input controls. These attributes are listed as follows.

textCapSentences	Normal text keyboard that capitalizes the first letter for each new sentence.
textCapCharacters	Uppercase keyboard that capitalizes all characters.
textCapWords	Normal text keyboard that capitalizes the first letter of every word. Good for titles or names.
textImeMultiLine	Normal text keyboard that capitalizes every word. Good for titles or person names.
textAutoCorrect	Text editor corrects commonly misspelled words.
textAutoComplete	The text editor (which means the application) is performing autocompletion of the text being entered based on its own semantics, which is presented to the user as they type.
textNoSuggestions	Flags the input method to prevent display of any dictionary-based candidates.
textUri	Normal text keyboard with the / character. Used for entering a URI.
textShortMessage	Entering a short, possibly informal, message such as an instant message or a text message.
textLongMessage	Text field inputType for entering the content of a long, possibly formal, message such as the body of an email.
textWebEditText	Entering text inside a web form.
textFilter	Text to filter contents, such as of a list.
textPhonetic	Entering text for phonetic pronunciation, such as a phonetic name field in contacts.

By default, the cursor for text input controls is automatically displayed during input. You can hide the cursor by setting the cursorVisible property to false, as shown in Line 5 of the following EditText definition.

```
1   <EditText
2         android:layout_width="match_parent"
3         android:layout_height="wrap_content"
4         android:inputType="textMultiLine"
5         android:cursorVisible="false"
6         android:id="@+id/editText1" />
```

Most soft input methods provide a user action button in the bottom corner that's appropriate for the current text field. By default, the system uses this button for either a `Next` or `Done` action unless your text field allows multiline text (such as with `android:inputType="textMultiLine"`), in which case the action button is a carriage return. However, you can specify additional actions that might be more appropriate for your text field, such as `Send`, `Done`, and `Go`.

To specify the keyboard action button, use the `android:imeOptions` attribute with an action value such as "actionSend" or "actionSearch." For example, the code segment that follows produces a keyboard with a search icon, as shown in Figure 2-10.

```
1  <EditText
2      android:id="@+id/editText"
3      android:layout_width="fill_parent"
4      android:layout_height="wrap_content"
5      android:hint="@string/search_hint"
6      android:inputType="text"
7      android:imeOptions="actionSearch" />
```

——Search Icon

❙ FIGURE 2-10 The Search icon appears when you declare android:imeOptions="actionSearch."

The following Android `imeOptions` property can be assigned a range of values to produce keyboard icons.

`actionSend`

`actionDone`

`actionGo`

`actionNext`

`actionPrevious`

Furthermore, listener events can be registered to an action button, which is done by applying a `setOnEditorActionListener` to the `EditText` object. For example, in the code segment below, a listener is used to respond to the appropriate IME action `EditorInfo`. These actions are defined in the `EditorInfo` class, such as `IME_ACTION_SEARCH`.

```
1   EditText nameEditText = (EditText) findViewById(R.id.editText);
2   nameEditText.setOnEditorActionListener(new OnEditorActionListener() {
3       @Override
4       public boolean onEditorAction(TextView v,
5                                     int actionId,
6                                     KeyEvent event) {
7           boolean handled = false;
8           if (actionId == EditorInfo.IME_ACTION_SEARCH) {
9               searchName();
10              handled = true;
11          }
12          return handled;
13      }
14  });
```

▮ Lab Example 2-1: Basic Input and the Shipping Calculator

The first app of this chapter examines basic layout construction and data input without the use of a button to trigger a computation. The Shipping Cost Calculator is a simple app that will be used to illustrate the input of data via a soft keyboard within an `EditView` object. The user will input the weight, in ounces, of an item to be shipped. As the user inputs a shipping value, the base cost, added cost, and total cost of shipping will be directly computed and then displayed in a collection of `TextView` objects.

Part 1: Conceptual Design

The conceptual design for this application begins with a rough sketch that outlines the user interface elements, along with their placement on the screen. The initial visual design for this app, along with the final view of the app running, is shown in

Figure 2-11. The design takes into consideration the amount of screen space the soft keyboard requires. `View` objects are arranged so that all views are easily within view. In addition, the alignment of numeric values and labels further enhances the readability of the design. Padding around these `View` objects will help position them on the screen.

In a user interface, we use buttons as a practical solution to many applications. Buttons can be and have been enormously helpful with interactions; however, they may not always be the best choice for an application that needs a more intuitive interaction. When looking at efficiency and effectiveness, a button may be a wasteful form of user interaction in that it requires extra gestures that can be eliminated. The shipping cost application shown in Figure 2-11 will not use a button to trigger a computation. Instead, the application will "listen" for input and respond immediately.

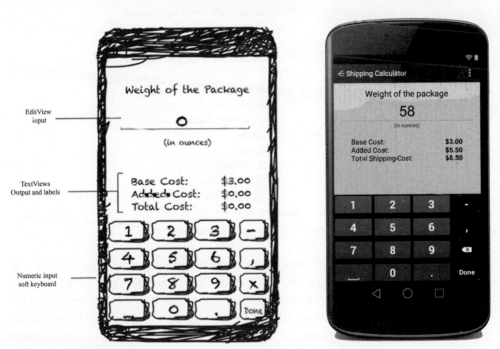

FIGURE 2-11 The Shipping Cost Calculator is partially conceptualized in a sketched prototype.

Part 2: Application Structure and Setup

The settings for the application are as follows:

- Application Name: Shipping Calculator
- Package Name: com.cornez.shippingcalculator
- Android Form: Phone and Tablet
- Minimum SDK: API 18: Android 4.3 (Jelly Bean)

- Target SDK: API 21: Android 5.0 (Lollipop)
- Compile with: API 21: Android 5.0 (Lollipop)
- Activity Name: `MyActivity`
- Layout Name: `activity_my`

The final project structure for this application is shown in Figure 2-12. It includes two drawable elements: the background image and the launch icon. In addition, a blank activity and a layout are automatically generated with the default names `MyActivity` and `activity_my`.

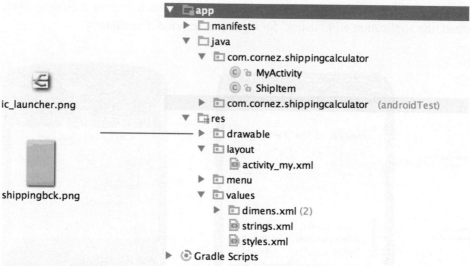

FIGURE 2-12 The final project structure for the Shipping Calculator app.

The configuration options specified for this shipping calculator application can be altered within the `build.gradle` file, found in the src directory of the project. Keep in mind that gradle overrides the manifest values found in the `AndroidManifest.xml file`. For developers using Android Studio, it is preferable to update the `build.gradle` file rather than the manifest, which, in Eclipse, is used to contain package name, version code, version name, target SDK, and many other specifictions. If you wish to change the minimum SDK, it should be done via `build.gradle`.

```
build.gradle
1  apply plugin: 'com.android.application'
2
3  android {
4      compileSdkVersion 20
5      buildToolsVersion "20.0.0"
6
```

```
 7        defaultConfig {
 8            applicationId "com.cornez.shippingcalculator"
 9            minSdkVersion 18
10            targetSdkVersion 20
11            versionCode 1
12            versionName "1.0"
13        }
14        buildTypes {
15            release {
16                runProguard false
17                proguardFiles getDefaultProguardFile(
18                    'proguard-android.txt'), 'proguard-rules.pro'
19            }
20        }
21    }
22
23    dependencies {
24        compile fileTree(dir: 'libs', include: ['*.jar'])
25    }
```

Part 3: External Value Resources

The value resources for this application revolve around dimensions and strings. Because we will consistently be using the same padding dimension in many of the display views, a dimension definition will be added to the dimens.xml file. The definition, shown on Line 5, is given the name output_margin_buffer and is set to 30.

```
dimens.xml
1    <resources>
2        <!-- Default screen margins, per the Android Design guidelines. -->
3        <dimen name="activity_horizontal_margin">16dp</dimen>
4        <dimen name="activity_vertical_margin">16dp</dimen>
5        <dimen name="output_margin_buffer">30</dimen>
6    </resources>
```

The additional string values for this application are defined on Lines 8–14 of the strings.xml file. These strings will be used primarily to label the output values the calculator produces.

```
strings.xml
1    <?xml version="1.0" encoding="utf-8"?>
2    <resources>
3
4        <string name="app_name">Shipping Calculator</string>
5        <string name="hello_world">Hello world!</string>
6        <string name="action_settings">Settings</string>
7
```

```
 8        <string name="weightLBL">Enter the weight of\nyour package</string>
 9        <string name="ouncesLBL">(in ounces)</string>
10        <string name="baseLBL">Base Cost:</string>
11        <string name="addCostLBL">Added Cost:</string>
12        <string name="totalLBL">Total Shipping Cost:</string>
13        <string name="zeroDec">$0.00</string>
14        <string name="zero">0</string>
15
16   </resources>
```

Part 4: The User Interface as a Layout XML File

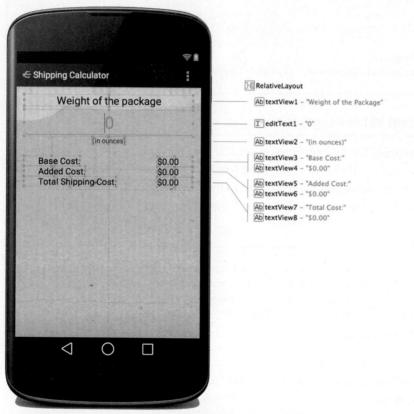

FIGURE 2-13 View objects arranged in the Layout Editor's Design mode.

The XML code for the `activity_my.xml` layout file contains a `RelativeLay-out View` as the root element. Figure 2-13 shows the arrangement of the View objects. The input control for weight entry by the user will be an `EditText` object. This `EditText` is defined on Lines 25–40.

Line 34:   The input type for this `EditText` view is specified as a number, which will generate a numeric soft keyboard.

Line 35: The `selectAllOnFocus` option selects the view when the view takes focus. This option is available only for selectable views.

Line 37: Hint text will be displayed when the `EditText` view is empty.

Line 39: When the activity starts, the focus will go to the input `EditText`, and the soft keyboard will immediately appear. Any element representing a `View` object can include this specification, which gives its parent initial focus on the screen. You can have only one of these elements per layout file.

```
activity_my.xml
1   <RelativeLayout
2   xmlns:android="http://schemas.android.com/apk/res/android"
3       xmlns:tools="http://schemas.android.com/tools"
4       android:layout_width="match_parent"
5       android:layout_height="match_parent"
6       android:paddingLeft="@dimen/activity_horizontal_margin"
7       android:paddingRight="@dimen/activity_horizontal_margin"
8       android:paddingTop="@dimen/activity_vertical_margin"
9       android:paddingBottom="@dimen/activity_vertical_margin"
10      android:background="@drawable/shippingbck"
11      tools:context=".MyActivity">
12
13      <!-- WEIGHT INPUT SECTION -->
14      <TextView
15          android:id="@+id/textView1"
16          android:layout_width="fill_parent"
17          android:layout_height="wrap_content"
18          android:layout_alignParentTop="true"
19          android:layout_centerHorizontal="true"
20          android:text="@string/weightLBL"
21          android:textAppearance="?android:attr/textAppearanceLarge"
22          android:gravity="center_horizontal" />
23
24      <!-- WEIGHT INPUT EDIT TEXT FIELD RECEIVES FOCUS -->
25      <EditText
26          android:id="@+id/editText1"
27          android:layout_width="wrap_content"
28          android:layout_height="wrap_content"
29          android:layout_below="@+id/textView1"
30          android:layout_centerHorizontal="true"
31          android:layout_marginTop="5dp"
32          android:ems="10"
33          android:gravity="center_vertical|center_horizontal"
34          android:inputType="number"
35          android:selectAllOnFocus="true"
36          android:textSize="35sp"
37          android:hint="@string/zero">
38
```

```
39          <requestFocus />
40      </EditText>
41
42
43      <TextView
44          android:id="@+id/textView2"
45          android:layout_width="wrap_content"
46          android:layout_height="wrap_content"
47          android:layout_below="@+id/editText1"
48          android:layout_centerHorizontal="true"
48          android:text="@string/ouncesLBL"
50          android:textAppearance="?android:attr/textAppearanceSmall" />
```

The remaining TextView objects within this layout will be used to represent the computed shipping calculations and the labels that identify them to the user. Note that all of them rely on the padding dimension defined in the dimens.xml file.

activity_my.xml   *Continued*

```
51      <!-- TEXTVIEWS FOR BASE COST LABEL AND COMPUTATION  -->
52      <TextView
53          android:id="@+id/textView3"
54          android:layout_width="wrap_content"
55          android:layout_height="wrap_content"
56          android:layout_alignParentLeft="true"
57          android:layout_below="@+id/editText1"
58          android:layout_marginTop="40dp"
59          android:paddingLeft="@dimen/output_margin_buffer"
60          android:text="@string/baseLBL"
61          android:textAppearance="?android:attr/textAppearanceMedium" />
62
63      <TextView
64          android:id="@+id/textView4"
65          android:layout_width="wrap_content"
66          android:layout_height="wrap_content"
67          android:layout_alignBaseline="@+id/textView3"
68          android:layout_alignBottom="@+id/textView3"
69          android:layout_alignParentRight="true"
70          android:paddingRight="@dimen/output_margin_buffer"
71          android:text="@string/zeroDec"
72          android:textAppearance="?android:attr/textAppearanceMedium" />
73
74      <!-- TEXTVIEWS FOR ADDED COST LABEL AND COMPUTATION  -->
75      <TextView
76          android:id="@+id/textView5"
77          android:layout_width="wrap_content"
78          android:layout_height="wrap_content"
79          android:layout_alignParentLeft="true"
80          android:layout_below="@+id/textView3"
```

```
81          android:paddingLeft="@dimen/output_margin_buffer"
82          android:text="@string/addCostLBL"
83          android:textAppearance="?android:attr/textAppearanceMedium" />
84
85      <TextView
86          android:id="@+id/textView6"
87          android:layout_width="wrap_content"
88          android:layout_height="wrap_content"
89          android:layout_alignBaseline="@+id/textView5"
90          android:layout_alignBottom="@+id/textView5"
91          android:layout_alignParentRight="true"
92          android:paddingRight="@dimen/output_margin_buffer"
93          android:text="@string/zeroDec"
94          android:textAppearance="?android:attr/textAppearanceMedium" />
95
96
97      <!-- TEXTVIEWS FOR THE TOTAL COST LABEL AND COMPUTATION  -->
98      <TextView
99          android:id="@+id/textView7"
100         android:layout_width="wrap_content"
101         android:layout_height="wrap_content"
102         android:layout_alignParentLeft="true"
103         android:layout_below="@+id/textView5"
104         android:paddingLeft="@dimen/output_margin_buffer"
105         android:text="@string/totalLBL"
106         android:textAppearance="?android:attr/textAppearanceMedium" />
107
108     <TextView
109         android:id="@+id/textView8"
110         android:layout_width="wrap_content"
111         android:layout_height="wrap_content"
112         android:layout_alignBaseline="@+id/textView7"
113         android:layout_alignBottom="@+id/textView7"
114         android:layout_alignParentRight="true"
115         android:paddingRight="@dimen/output_margin_buffer"
116         android:text="@string/zeroDec"
117         android:textAppearance="?android:attr/textAppearanceMedium" />
118
119 </RelativeLayout>
```

Part 5: Source Code for Application

The Shipping Calculator app will rely on two Java files: `ShipItem` and `MyActivity`. The first Java file, `ShipItem.java`, is the class that represents an item to be shipped. All items to be shipped will have a base cost of $3.00 for the first 16 ounces. All items weighing more than 30 ounces will have a base cost of $4.00.

In addition, items weighing more than 16 ounces will have an added charge of $.50 for each additional four ounces. For example, an item weighing more than 16, but no more than 20, ounces will cost $3.50 to deliver. An item weighing more than 20, but no more than 24, ounces will cost $4.00 to deliver. Therefore, it will cost the same amount to deliver an item that weighs 24 ounces as an item that weighs more than 30 ounces. All shipped item costs are computed in the method computeCosts ().

ShipItem.java

```
1   package com.cornez.shippingcalculator;
2
3   public class ShipItem {
4
5       // SHIPPING CONSTANTS
6       static final Double BASE = 3.00;
7       static final Double ADDED = .50;
8       static final int BASE_WEIGHT = 16;
9       static final double EXTRA_OUNCES = 4.0;
10
11      // DATA MEMBERS
12      private Integer mWeight;
13      private Double mBaseCost;
14      private Double mAddedCost;
15      private Double mTotalCost;
16
17      public ShipItem() {
18          mWeight = 0;
19          mAddedCost = 0.0;
20          mBaseCost = BASE;
21          mTotalCost = 0.0;
22      }
23
24      public void setWeight (int weight){
25          mWeight = weight;
26          computeCosts();
27      }
28
29      private void computeCosts() {
30          mAddedCost = 0.0;
31          mBaseCost = BASE;
32
33          if (mWeight <= 0)
34              mBaseCost = 0.0;
35          else if (mWeight > BASE_WEIGHT)
36              mAddedCost = Math.ceil((double)
37                  (mWeight - BASE_WEIGHT) / EXTRA_OUNCES) * ADDED;
38
39          mTotalCost = mBaseCost + mAddedCost;
40      }
41
42      public Double getBaseCost() {
43          return mBaseCost;
```

```
44          }
45
46          public Double getAddedCost() {
47              return mAddedCost;
48          }
49
50          public Double getTotalCost() {
51              return mTotalCost;
52          }
53
54  }
```

MyActivity is the controller of the application. Whenever the user inputs a weight, this class calls the setWeight() method in the ShipItem class to tell it to change its state appropriately. The listeners specified in the Controller detect an input by the user and call the method computeCosts() in the ShipItem to compute the necessary costs. Finally, this class updates the Views to display the shipping costs to the user.

Lines 3–11:   The first lines of code are used to import the needed libraries. It is customary for libraries to be listed in alphabetical order.

Line 5:   android.text.Editable provides the interface for text in which the content and markup can be changed (as opposed to immutable text like Strings).

Line 6:   TextWatcher is a public interface that will be used with the EditText object to identify when the user has altered input values.

Lines 10–11:   EditText is essentially a TextView. It is important to remember that EditText contains an additional property that reconfigures itself to be editable; TextView doesn't have this feature. This means that both android.widget.EditText and android.widget.TextView are required for this app.

Lines 33–39:   Once the activity content from activity_my.xml has been set, the input and output text fields are referenced with the View objects in the layout.

Line 42:   An addTextChangedListener is registered for the EditText. This adds the TextWatcher interface methods that will be called when the user changes the EditText's input values.

```
MyActivity.java
1  package com.cornez.shippingcalculator;
2
3  import android.app.Activity;
4  import android.os.Bundle;
5  import android.text.Editable;
```

```
 6   import android.text.TextWatcher;
 7
 8   import android.view.Menu;
 9   import android.view.MenuItem;
10   import android.widget.EditText;
11   import android.widget.TextView;
12
13
14   public class MyActivity extends Activity {
15       //DATA MODEL FOR SHIP ITEM
16       private ShipItem shipItem;
17
18       //VIEW OBJECTS FOR LAYOUT UI REFERENCE
19       private EditText weightET;
20       private TextView baseCostTV;
21       private TextView addedCostTV;
22       private TextView totalCostTV;
23
24       @Override
25       protected void onCreate(Bundle savedInstanceState) {
26           //TASK 1: SET ACTIVITY CONTENT
27           super.onCreate(savedInstanceState);
28           setContentView(R.layout.activity_my);
29
30           //TASK 2: CREATE A DATA MODEL FOR STORING AN ITEM TO BE SHIPPED
31           shipItem = new ShipItem();
32
33           //TASK 3: ESTABLISH THE REFERENCES TO INPUT WEIGHT ELEMENT
34           weightET = (EditText) findViewById(R.id.editText1);
35
36           //TASK 4: ESTABLISH THE REFERENCES TO OUTPUT ELEMENTS
37           baseCostTV = (TextView) findViewById(R.id.textView4);
38           addedCostTV = (TextView) findViewById(R.id.textView6);
39           totalCostTV = (TextView) findViewById(R.id.textView8);
40
41           //TASK 5: REGISTER THE LISTENER EVENT FOR WEIGHT INPUT
42           weightET.addTextChangedListener(weightTextWatcher);
43
44       }
```

A TextWatcher requires that three methods are called once an attached `Text-View` has been edited: `onTextChanged()`, `afterTextChanged()`, and `beforeTextChanged()`.

Lines 49–58:   The method `onTextChanged()` is called each time the user types a weight value into EditText. It is important to catch an exception during this input. Even though the soft keyboard has been set to numeric, it is required that any exception for input that is not a number be handled. In this exception, the weight for this shipped item is set to zero. The method displayShipping () in line 57 performs the task of outputting the new shipping charges.

Lines 59–61:   The callback methods afterTextChanged () and before-TextChanged () are required for the TextWatcher interface. However, this app does not use them.

```
MyActivity.java  Continued
45  private TextWatcher weightTextWatcher = new TextWatcher() {
46      //THE INPUT ELEMENT IS ATTACHED TO AN EDITABLE,
47      //THEREFORE THESE METHODS ARE CALLED WHEN THE TEXT IS CHANGED
48
49      public void onTextChanged(CharSequence s,
50                              int start, int before, int count){
51          try {
52              shipItem.setWeight((int)
53                  Double.parseDouble(s.toString()));
54          }catch (NumberFormatException e){
55              shipItem.setWeight(0);
56          }
57          displayShipping();
58      }
59      public void afterTextChanged(Editable s) {}
60      public void beforeTextChanged(CharSequence s,
61                              int start, int count, int after){}
62  };
```

Lines 63–71:   The method displayShipping () is used to display the computed shipping costs to the user. The onCreateOptions-Menu() and onOptionsItemSelected() methods, which were automatically generated, are not used.

```
MyActivity.java  Continued
63  private void displayShipping() {
64      //DISPLAY THE BASE COST, ADDED COST, AND TOTAL COST
65      baseCostTV.setText("$" + String.format("%.02f",
66              shipItem.getBaseCost()));
67      addedCostTV.setText("$" + String.format("%.02f",
68              shipItem.getAddedCost()));
69      totalCostTV.setText("$" + String.format("%.02f",
70              shipItem.getTotalCost()));
71  }
72
73
74
75      @Override
76      public boolean onCreateOptionsMenu(Menu menu) {
```

```
77          // Inflate the menu;
78          getMenuInflater().inflate(R.menu.my, menu);
79          return true;
80      }
81
82      @Override
83      public boolean onOptionsItemSelected(MenuItem item) {
84          // Handle action bar item clicks here. The action bar will
85          // automatically handle clicks on the Home/Up button, so long
86          // as you specify a parent activity in AndroidManifest.xml.
87          int id = item.getItemId();
88          if (id == R.id.action_settings) {
89              return true;
90          }
91          return super.onOptionsItemSelected(item);
92      }
93  }
```

■ 2.6 Android's Form Widgets for User Interfaces

Input controls, such as `EditText` and `Button` Views, are the interactive components in an application's user interface. Android provides a wide set of input controls, also called widgets, to be used in an app's user interface. These built-in widgets, shown in Figure 2-14, are subclasses of the `View` base class, which provides the functionality that is common to all widgets.

Widgets, including seek bars, checkboxes, and switches, can be added easily to XML layout, similar to `Buttons`, `EditTexts`, and `TextViews`. Each widget has a built-in set of properties that can be used to customize the appearance of a widget as seen by the user. For example, a `TextView` widget might be designated as `Large Text`, `Medium Text`, or `Small Text`, but it also contains a numeric textsize property that can be altered further. By editing the `textsize` of a `TextView`, the small, medium, or large designations are no longer relevant.

Each widget control supports a specific set of input events that can be listened for and handled, such as when the user slides the knob on a seek bar or toggles a switch. If an app requires a specific kind of input control, these controls can be customized or even built programmatically.

`TextView`, `EditText`, and `Button` widgets have already been discussed in the previous two sections of this chapter. This section will explore several other widgets from the list in Figure 2-14.

2.6.1 `RadioButton` and `CheckBox`

A radio button is a familiar UI component for programmers. It is specifically used when a single item from a collection of items must be made. If a radio button is already

📁 **Widgets**

Ab Plain TextView	Ab Large Text
Ab Medium Text	Ab Small Text
OK Button	OK Small Button
⦿ RadioButton	☑ CheckBox
▬ Switch	▭ ToggleButton
🖼 ImageButton	🖼 ImageView
▬ ProgressBar (Large)	▬ ProgressBar (Normal)
▬ ProgressBar (Small)	▬ ProgressBar (Horizontal)
⦿ SeekBar	★ RatingBar
▤ Spinner	◉ WebView

FIGURE 2-14 Widgets are subclasses of the `View` base class.

selected, it will be de-selected when another radio button in the collection is selected. The `RadioButton` in Android is specifically a single item in the collection. In Figure 2-15, a `RadioGroup` is used to contain three `RadioButton` widgets.

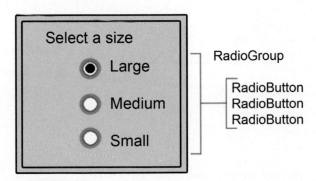

FIGURE 2-15

As with radio buttons, the `CheckBox` widget is also a common UI component for programmers. Specifically, it is a type of two-state button that can either be checked or unchecked.

2.6.2 `ToggleButton`

A toggle button allows the user to change a setting between two states, such as on or off. Android 4.0 (API level 14) introduced another kind of toggle button called a switch that provides a slider control, which you can add with a `Switch` object.

2.6.3 `Switch`

A `Switch` is a two-state toggle switch widget that can select between two options, off and on. The user can drag the "thumb" back and forth to choose the selected option; instead, the user can simply tap to toggle as if it were a checkbox. Figure 2-16 shows two `Switch` widgets and a `ToggleButton` widget. The `Switch` widgets incorporate a label, such as Wi-Fi and Bluetooth, and an easy-to-understand toggle control button. The `ToggleButton` widget is merely the button.

The following XML code segment is used to produce the `Switch` widgets shown in Figure 2-16.

```
1   <Switch
2           android:layout_width="wrap_content"
3           android:layout_height="wrap_content"
4           android:text="@string/wifi"
5           android:id="@+id/wi_fi"
6           android:layout_below="@+id/textView"
7           android:layout_toEndOf="@+id/textView"
8           android:layout_marginTop="104dp"
9           android:checked="false" />
10
11      <Switch
12          android:layout_width="wrap_content"
13          android:layout_height="wrap_content"
14          android:text="@string/bluetooth"
15          android:id="@+id/bluetooth"
16          android:layout_below="@+id/wi_fi"
17          android:layout_alignEnd="@+id/wi_fi" />
```

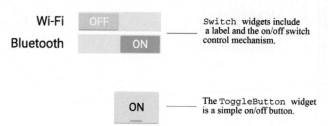

Wi-Fi   OFF   Switch widgets include
                      a label and the on/off switch
Bluetooth   ON   control mechanism.

ON   The ToggleButton widget
            is a simple on/off button.

❙ FIGURE 2-16 `Switch` and `TobbleButton` widgets.

2.6.4 `ProgressBar`

A `ProgressBar` is a visual indicator of progress in a given operation. For example, a `ProgressBar` control can be displayed to the user representing how far an operation has progressed; the application can change the amount of progress (modifying the length of the bar) as it moves forward, such as the buffer level during a streaming playback.

A progress bar can also be made indeterminate. In indeterminate mode, the progress bar shows a cyclic animation without an indication of progress. This mode is used by applications when the length of the task is unknown. The indeterminate progress bar can be either a spinning wheel or a horizontal bar.

2.6.5 `SeekBar`

A `SeekBar` is an extension of `ProgressBar` that adds a draggable thumb. The user can touch the thumb and drag left or right to set the current progress level or use the arrow keys. A Seekbar widget is used in Figure 2-17 to select an amount of chocolate.

FIGURE 2-17 `CheckBox`, `Seekbar`, `Switch`, and `Button` widgets arranged in a `LinearLayout`.

Placing focusable widgets to the left or right of a `SeekBar` is discouraged. Soft keyboards on an Android device cannot decide which input widget to which to send its input events. Input events are sent to the view that has focus. Clients of the `SeekBar` can attach a `SeekBar.OnSeekBarChangeListener` to be notified of the user's input actions.

2.6.6 `RatingBar`

A `RatingBar` is an extension of `SeekBar` and `ProgressBar` that shows a rating in stars. The user can touch/drag or use arrow keys to set the rating when using the default size `RatingBar`. The smaller `RatingBar` style (`ratingBarStyleSmall`) and the larger indicator-only style (`ratingBarStyleIndicator`) do not support user interaction and should be used only as indicators.

When using a `RatingBar` that supports user interaction, placing widgets to the left or right of the `RatingBar` is discouraged. The number of stars set (via `setNumStars`(int) or in an XML layout) will be shown when the layout width is set to wrap content; if another layout width is set, the results may be unpredictable.

2.6.7 `Spinner`

`Spinner`s provide a quick way to select one value from a set of values. For example, in Figure 2-18 an individual contact can be selected from a set of contacts. In the default state, a spinner shows its currently selected value—or in this case, none. Touching the spinner, Contacts displays a drop-down menu containing the complete set of contacts from which to choose. The user can then select one.

❘ FIGURE 2-18 A Spinner widget displays values from a set.

The choices you provide for the spinner can come from any source, but they most often will originate from a database. In the example, the available contact choices are predetermined, provided by a string array defined in a value string resource file. This file would be located in the res/values directory of the project.

```
1   <?xml version="1.0" encoding="utf-8"?>
2   <resources>
3       <string-array name="key_contacts">
4           <item>Jesse</item>
5           <item>Sally</item>
6           <item>Alan</item>
7           <item>Jordan</item>
8       </string-array>
9   </resources>
```

Loading the Spinner with the contact names is done with Java code, such as the segment shown in the code below. Spinners rely on Adapters, or an Array-Adapter such as the one declared in Line 5. The Adapter object acts as a bridge between a Spinner and the underlying data for that Spinner. The Adapter provides access to the contact items.

```
1   //TASK 1: REFERENCE THE SPINNER
2   Spinner mSpinner = (Spinner) findViewById(R.id.spinner);
3
4   //TASK 2: USE AN ADAPATER TO BUILD THE LIST
5   ArrayAdapter<CharSequence> adapter =
6   ArrayAdapter.createFromResource(this,
7          R.array.key_contacts, android.R.layout.simple_spinner_item);
8   //TASK 3: SET A DROP DOWN VIEW RESOURCE
9   adapter.setDropDownViewResource(android.R.activity_my.spinner1);
10
11  //TASK 4: APPLY THE ADAPTER TO THE SPINNER
12  mSpinner.setAdapter(adapter);
```

■ 2.7 Unique ID of a View Object and the R Class

Some attributes are common to all `View` objects, because they are inherited from the `View` base class. As with all Java classes, these attributes are inherited by objects that extend the class. One of the most important `View` attributes is the `id` attribute. Every `View` object shares this attribute.

When an app has been compiled, all of its View objects are assigned a unique integer that identifies them. The file named `R.java`, which is an auto-generated file when you build an Android application, categorizes these unique identifiers (normally 32-bit numbers) into groupings for drawables, strings, layout elements, and so on. The main purpose of the `R.java` file is rapid accessibility of resources in the project. As resources are deleted and added to an Android project, the `R.java` file is updated automatically. The generated R class, located in the build folder in an Android Studio project, will be constructed with final 32-bit values.

In addition to the `R.java` listing of unique integer identifiers, the `View` class provides an XML attribute for defining a unique string id for referencing the View object. String identifications are readable and easy to work with when writing code. In the following example XML instruction, a `Button View` object is constructed. The syntax for the button ID, inside the XML tag, is shown on Line 2.

```
1       <Button
2           android:id="@+id/go_button"
3           android:layout_width="wrap_content"
4           android:layout_height="wrap_content"
5           android:onClick="goGet"
6           android:text="Button" />
```

The at-symbol (@) at the beginning of the string indicates that the XML parser should parse and expand the rest of the ID string and identify it as an ID resource. The plus-symbol (+) means that this is a new resource name that must be created and added to the resources (in the `R.java file`).

Once a `View` can be uniquely identified, it can be referenced in Java source code. For example, the `Button` object, defined in the XML code above, was given the string id of "go_button." In the Java instruction below, this button is referenced using `findViewById()`. `findViewById()` locates a view that was identified by the id attribute from the XML code.

```
1   Button goBtn = (Button) findViewById(R.id. go_button);
```

It is also possible to use other ID resources that are offered by the Android framework. When referencing an Android resource ID, you do not need the plus-symbol, but you must add the android package namespace:

android:id="@android:id/empty"

Resources include all the external resources for the application and include elements such as the layouts, layout control elements, strings, and drawables. All resource elements are defined and compiled into the file `R.java`, stored in the `app/build/generated/` subdirectory. An example of the generated file is shown as follows:

```
1   public final class R {
2       public static final class dimen {
3           public static final int activity_horizontal_margin=0x7f040000;
4           public static final int activity_vertical_margin=0x7f040001;
5       }
6       public static final class drawable {
7           public static final int ic_launcher=0x7f020000;
8       }
9       public static final class id {
10          public static final int button1=0x7f080004;
11          public static final int checkBox1=0x7f080000;
12          public static final int seekBar1=0x7f080001;
13          public static final int switch1=0x7f080003;
14          public static final int textView1=0x7f080002;
15      }
16      public static final class layout {
17          public static final int activity_my=0x7f030000;
18      }
19  public static final class string {
20          public static final int action_settings=0x7f050000;
21          public static final int app_name=0x7f050001;
22          public static final int btn_settings=0x7f050002;
23          public static final int _world=0x7f050003;
24          public static final int txt_settings=0x7f050004;
25      }
26      public static final class style {
27
28          public static final int AppTheme=0x7f060000;
29      }
30  }
```

■ 2.8 The `ViewGroup`

The user interface of an app is defined using a hierarchy of `View` and `ViewGroup` objects. A `ViewGroup` is a container of `View` objects. The distinction between `View` and `ViewGroup` can sometimes be confusing because all `ViewGroup` are also `View` objects.

As the term implies, a `ViewGroup` is a special type of `View` that is designed to hold groups of `Views`. Each `ViewGroup` is an invisible container that organizes child `Views`. The child views may be input controls or other widgets that draw some part of the UI. The `ViewGroup` subclass is the base class for all containers.

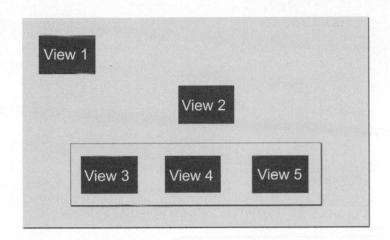

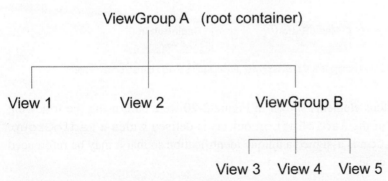

FIGURE 2-19 `View` objects can be organized in `ViewGroup` containers.

As shown in Figure 2-19, a `ViewGroup` is used as the root container for storing all `View` objects. One of the `View` objects, `ViewGroup B`, is a `ViewGroup` containing its own set of `View` objects. A `ViewGroup` hierarchy tree can be as simple or as complex as needed, with `ViewGroups` nested into many levels. Be judicious in how you design `ViewGroups`, because simplicity is best for performance.

2.8.1 `RadioGroup`

A `RadioGroup` object is a `ViewGroup` container. As a `ViewGroup`, the `Radio-Group` is used to group together a related set of RadioButtons, as illustrated in Figure 2-20. More specifically, a `RadioGroup` establishes a multiple-exclusion scope for its contained set of radio buttons.

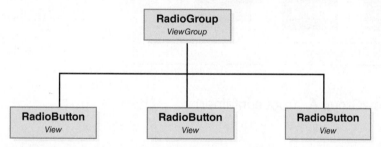

FIGURE 2-20 A `RadioGroup` is a `ViewGroup` that contains `RadioButton` widgets.

The radio buttons elements shown in Figure 2-20 were built using the following XML code. Each of the `RadioButton` objects is defined within a `RadioGroup`. Each `RadioButton` is assigned a unique identification so that it may be referenced in the Java source code.

```
1    <RadioGroup
2        android:layout_width="fill_parent"
3        android:layout_height="fill_parent"
4        android:layout_alignParentTop="true"
5        android:layout_centerHorizontal="true"
```

```
6            android:layout_marginTop="35dp"
7            android:gravity="right"
8            android:paddingRight="50dp">
9
10           <RadioButton
11               android:layout_width="wrap_content"
12               android:layout_height="wrap_content"
13               android:text="Cupcake"
14               android:id="@+id/radioButton1" />
15
16           <RadioButton
17               android:layout_width="wrap_content"
18               android:layout_height="wrap_content"
19               android:text="Froyo"
20               android:id="@+id/radioButton2" />
21
22           <RadioButton
23               android:layout_width="wrap_content"
24               android:layout_height="wrap_content"
25               android:text="Ice Cream Sandwich"
26               android:id="@+id/radioButton3" />
27       </RadioGroup>
```

Every `ViewGroup` class implements a nested class that extends `View-Group.LayoutParams`. This subclass contains property types that define the size and position for each child view, as appropriate for the `ViewGroup`. The parent `ViewGroup` defines layout parameters for each child view. In the preceding XML code, Lines 7 and 8 set `paddingRight` and the gravity to a right alignment for the `RadioGroup`. These are automatically applied to the child views, as shown in Figure 2-20.

Each layout file must contain exactly one root element, which must be a `View` or `ViewGroup` object. Once a root element has been defined, additional layout objects or widgets can be added as child elements to gradually build a `View` hierarchy that defines a layout.

■ Lab Example 2-2: Burger Calorie Calculator App

The Burger Calorie Calculator App explores the use of various UI controls and widgets in a user interface. This lab looks at the construction of a calorie counter for a restaurant that serves gourmet hamburgers. A screen interface allows the user to select various burger choices. `ViewGroup` containing widgets, such as `RadioButtons`, a `Checkbox`, and a `SeekBar`, will be used to organize user input controls. Upon selecting an option from the burger menu, the user will see the number of calories of each choice. Listener events will be attached to the input controls for the immediate computation and display of calories. Figure 2-21 shows the final Burger Calorie Calculator App with its `ViewGroup` and `View` hierarchy of UI controls.

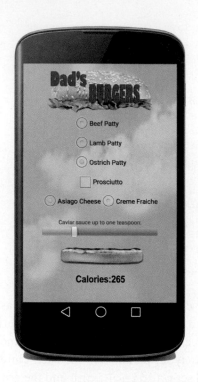

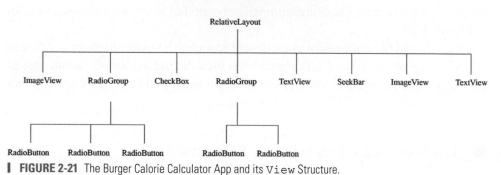

❙ FIGURE 2-21 The Burger Calorie Calculator App and its `View` Structure.

Part 1: Application Structure and Setup

The settings for the application were set as follows:

- Application Name: Burger Calorie Counter
- Project Name: BurgerCalorieCounter

- Package Name: com.cornez.burgercaloriecounter
- Android Form: Phone and Tablet
- Minimum SDK: API 18: Android 4.3 (Jelly Bean)
- Target SDK: API 21: Android 5.0 (Lollipop)
- Compile with: API 21: Android 5.0 (Lollipop)
- Activity Name: `MyActivity`
- Layout Name: `activity_my`

The final project structure for this app appears in Figure 2-22. The drawable folders in the res/ directory contain bitmap PNG files to make the app more interesting visually. These files can be found in the textbook resources. The launcher icon is set to the Android default `ic_launcher.png` file.

The activity for the application is set to the default name `MyActivity`, and the layout file that displays the visual elements for the activity is given the name `activity_my`.

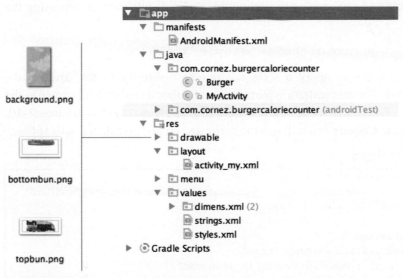

FIGURE 2-22 The final project structure for the Burger Calorie Counter app.

Part 2: The Theme of the Application

The theme of an application describes the look and feel of the app through the user's perspective. A theme is a set of styles, often defined in a separate XML file named `styles.xml`.

By default, Android comes with many themes that we can directly use. It is also possible to create our own themes, which typically remain consistent throughout the execution of the app.

The `AndroidManifest.xml` file is used to apply the theme defined by the `style.xml` file. The `styles.xml` file is located in res/values/ directory. The default style defined for the app is shown in the following code segment. The name of this style is `AppTheme`, and it consists of a `Holo.LightDarkActionBar`. This particular style uses a light theme for the content area and has a solid opaque action bar in an inverse color that makes it stand out against the light content.

```
styles.xml
1  <resources>
2
3      <!-- BASE APPLICATION THEME -->
4      <style name="AppTheme"
5             parent="android:Theme.Holo.Light.DarkActionBar">
6      </style>
7
8  </resources>
9
```

`AndroidManifest.xml` file applied this defined style to your app using the instruction:

<code>android:theme="@style/AppTheme"</code>

It is also possible to apply a style configuration directly to the `android-Manifest.xml`. For demonstration purposes, we applied a new style as shown in the `AndroidManifext.xml` code below. By altering the theme, as seen in Lines 9–10, the Burger Calorie Counter app will use the entire screen and no title bar will appear.

```
AndroidManifest.xml
1   <?xml version="1.0" encoding="utf-8"?>
2   <manifest xmlns:android="http://schemas.android.com/apk/res/android"
3       package="com.cornez.burgercaloriecounter" >
4
5       <application
6           android:allowBackup="true"
7           android:icon="@drawable/ic_launcher"
8           android:label="@string/app_name"
9           android:theme=
10              "@android:style/Theme.Light.NoTitleBar.Fullscreen">
11          <activity
12              android:name=".MyActivity"
13              android:label="@string/app_name" >
14          <intent-filter>
15              <action android:name="android.intent.action.MAIN" />
16
17              <category
18                  android:name="android.intent.category.LAUNCHER" />
19          </intent-filter>
```

```
20        </activity>
21      </application>
22
23  </manifest>
```

Part 3: External Value Resources

Other than the `styles.xml` file, strings is the only other value resource on which this app depends. The strings shown in the `strings.xml` code below represent the labels that will identify the user interface controls.

```
strings.xml
    <?xml version="1.0" encoding="utf-8"?>
1   <resources>
2
3       <string name="app_name">Burger Calorie Counter</string>
4       <string name="hello_world">Hello world!</string>
5       <string name="action_settings">Settings</string>
6
7       <string name="one">Beef Patty</string>
8       <string name="two">Lamb Patty</string>
9       <string name="three">Ostrich Patty</string>
10
11      <string name="prosciutto">Prosciutto</string>
12      <string name="cheddar">Asiago Cheese</string>
13      <string name="provolone">Creme Fraiche</string>
14
15      <string name="sauce">Caviar sauce up to one teaspoon:</string>
16      <string name="calorie">Calories?</string>
17
18      <string name="bun_img">bun</string>
19
20  </resources>
```

Part 4: The User Interface as a Layout XML File

The final design for the layout, `activity_my.xml`, of this application is shown in Figure 2-23. It uses a `RelativeLayout` as the root element. A `RelativeLayout` is also a `ViewGroup`. Within the `RelativeLayout` is a collection of `ImageViews`, `TextViews`, `RadioGroups` (containing `RadioButtons`), a `SeekBar`, and a `CheckBox`.

The first segment of `activity_my` is used to define a `RelativeLayout` as the root `ViewGroup`, set images, and define the first `RadioGroup`.

Line 11:   For visual interest, the background of the `RelativeLayout` is set to `background.png`.

│ FIGURE 2-23 `activity_my.xml` layout design.

Lines 14–21:   The logo of the application, a top bun with the restaurant name, is placed directly on the layout.

Lines 32–50:   A `RadioGroup` for hamburger meat choices is defined and given the name `radioGroup1`. Three `RadioButton Views` are added to the `RadioGroup`, and each is given a unique name: `radio0`, `radio1`, and `radio2`.

```
activity_my.xml
1   <RelativeLayout
2   xmlns:android="http://schemas.android.com/apk/res/android"
3       xmlns:tools="http://schemas.android.com/tools"
4       android:layout_width="match_parent"
5       android:layout_height="match_parent"
6       android:paddingLeft="@dimen/activity_horizontal_margin"
7       android:paddingRight="@dimen/activity_horizontal_margin"
8       android:paddingTop="@dimen/activity_vertical_margin"
9       android:paddingBottom="@dimen/activity_vertical_margin"
10      tools:context=".MyActivity"
11      android:background="@drawable/background">
12
```

```
13      <!-- BURGER WITH TITLE -->
14      <ImageView
15          android:id="@+id/imageView1"
16          android:layout_width="wrap_content"
17          android:layout_height="wrap_content"
18          android:layout_alignParentTop="true"
19          android:layout_centerHorizontal="true"
20          android:src="@drawable/topbun"
21          android:contentDescription="@string/app_name" />
22
23      <!-- RADIO GROUP CONTAINING -->
24      <!-- RADIO BUTTONS FOR BURGER PATTY TYPES -->
25      <RadioGroup
26          android:id="@+id/radioGroup1"
27          android:layout_width="wrap_content"
28          android:layout_height="wrap_content"
29          android:layout_below="@+id/imageView1"
30          android:layout_centerHorizontal="true" >
31
32          <RadioButton
33              android:id="@+id/radio0"
34              android:layout_width="wrap_content"
35              android:layout_height="wrap_content"
36              android:checked="true"
37              android:text="@string/one" />
38
39          <RadioButton
40              android:id="@+id/radio1"
41              android:layout_width="wrap_content"
42              android:layout_height="wrap_content"
43              android:text="@string/two" />
44
45          <RadioButton
46              android:id="@+id/radio2"
47              android:layout_width="wrap_content"
48              android:layout_height="wrap_content"
49              android:text="@string/three" />
50      </RadioGroup>
```

The second segment of `activity_my` will define the CheckBox widget and the second RadioGroup.

Lines 51–58:   The CheckBox is defined, centered horizontally, assigned the text "Prosciutto," and given the identifier name checkBox1.

Lines 60–82:   The second RadioGroup, used to provide the user with cheese selections, is defined. This ViewGroup is given the name radioGroup1. Two RadioButton Views are added to the

RadioGroup, and each is given a unique name: radio3 and radio4. Note that these names differ from the first set of RadioButtons. The Java code will identify RadioButtons by their name, not by the RadioGroups to which they belong.

```
activity_my.xml  Continued
51      <!-- CHECKBOX FOR PROSCIUTTO -->
52      <CheckBox
53          android:id="@+id/checkBox1"
54          android:layout_width="wrap_content"
55          android:layout_height="wrap_content"
56          android:layout_below="@+id/radioGroup1"
57          android:layout_centerHorizontal="true"
58          android:text="@string/prosciutto" />
59
60      <!-- RADIO GROUP CONTAINING -->
61      <!-- RADIO BUTTONS FOR CHEESE  TYPES -->
62      <RadioGroup
63          android:id="@+id/radioGroup2"
64          android:layout_width="wrap_content"
65          android:layout_height="wrap_content"
66          android:layout_below="@+id/checkBox1"
67          android:layout_centerHorizontal="true"
68          android:orientation="horizontal" >
69
70          <RadioButton
71              android:id="@+id/radio3"
72              android:layout_width="wrap_content"
73              android:layout_height="wrap_content"
74              android:checked="true"
75              android:text="@string/cheddar" />
76
77          <RadioButton
78              android:id="@+id/radio4"
79              android:layout_width="wrap_content"
80              android:layout_height="wrap_content"
81              android:text="@string/provolone" />
82      </RadioGroup>
```

The final XML code segment of activity_my defines the SeekBar UI control for selecting the amount of caviar added to the burger. A final SeekBar and an output TextView for displaying the calories to the user are also defined.

Lines 83–103:   The label for the caviar SeekBar and the SeekBar itself are defined. The SeekBar is given the identifier name seekBar1.

Lines 105–113:   For visual interest, an ImageView displays the bottom bun of a hamburger.

Lines 115–124:   The calorie computation will be displayed in a `TextView`. This `TextView` is given the identifier name `textView2`.

Line 126:   The `RelativeLayout`, the root container of this layout, is closed.

```
activity_my.xml  Continued
83      <!-- CAVIAR SAUCE SEGMENT -->
84      <!-- CAVIAR LABEL -->
85      <TextView
86          android:id="@+id/textView1"
87          android:layout_width="wrap_content"
88          android:layout_height="wrap_content"
89          android:layout_below="@+id/radioGroup2"
90          android:layout_centerHorizontal="true"
91          android:layout_marginTop="20dp"
92          android:text="@string/sauce"
93          android:textAppearance="?android:attr/textAppearanceSmall" />
94
95      <!-- CAVIAR SEEKBAR -->
96      <SeekBar
97          android:id="@+id/seekBar1"
98          android:layout_width="match_parent"
99          android:layout_height="wrap_content"
100         android:layout_alignLeft="@+id/radioGroup2"
101         android:layout_alignRight="@+id/radioGroup2"
102         android:layout_below="@+id/textView1" />
103
104     <!-- BURGER BUN BOTTOM -->
105     <ImageView
106         android:id="@+id/imageView2"
107         android:layout_width="wrap_content"
108         android:layout_height="wrap_content"
109         android:layout_below="@+id/seekBar1"
110         android:layout_centerHorizontal="true"
111         android:layout_marginTop="20dp"
112         android:src="@drawable/bottombun"
113         android:contentDescription="@string/app_name" />
114
115     <!-- CALORIE OUTPUT TEXTVIEW -->
116     <TextView
117         android:id="@+id/textView2"
118         android:layout_width="wrap_content"
119         android:layout_height="wrap_content"
120         android:layout_alignParentBottom="true"
121         android:layout_centerHorizontal="true"
122         android:layout_marginBottom="29dp"
123         android:text="@string/calorie"
124         android:textAppearance="?android:attr/textAppearanceLarge" />
125
126 </RelativeLayout>
```

Part 5: Source Code for Application

The two Java class files for this application are `Burger.java` and `MyActivity.java`. The Burger class provides the data for the application. `MyActivity` is launched when the application loads. This class serves as the controller of the application.

| Lines 4–9: | To keep things simple, constant calories are assigned within the Burger class. |
| Lines 16–21: | The constructor sets the initial ingredients to a beef patty with asiago cheese. No condiments are added to the initial burger. |

The remaining instruction for this class will set and get the values for the data members.

`Burger.java`

```java
1   package com.cornez.burgercaloriecounter;
2
3   public class Burger {
4       static final int BEEF = 100;
5       static final int LAMB = 170;
6       static final int OSTRICH = 150;
7       static final int ASIAGO = 90;
8       static final int CREME_FRAICHE = 120;
9       static final int PROSCIUTTO = 115;
10
11      private int mPattyCal;
12      private int mCheeseCal;
13      private int mProsciuttoCal;
14      private int mSauceCal;
15
16      public Burger() {
17          mPattyCal = BEEF;
18          mCheeseCal = ASIAGO;
19          mProsciuttoCal = 0;
20          mSauceCal = 0;
21      }
22
23      public void setPattyCalories(int calories){
24          mPattyCal = calories;
25      }
26
27      public void setCheeseCalories(int calories){
28          mCheeseCal = calories;
29      }
30      public void setProsciuttoCalories (int calories){
31          mProsciuttoCal = calories;
32      }
```

```
33      public void clearProsciuttoCalories (){
34          mProsciuttoCal = 0;
35      }
36      public void setSauceCalories(int calories){
37          mSauceCal = calories;
38      }
39
40      public int getTotalCalories() {
41          return mPattyCal + mCheeseCal + mProsciuttoCal + mSauceCal;
42      }
43
44  }
```

MyActivity.java will serve as the controller of the application.

Lines 3–15:   The import statements enable the use of View, various widgets, and listeners. OnCheckedChangeListener provides the interface definition for callbacks to be invoked when a CheckBox or a RadioButton has been selected or unselected. OnSeek-BarChangeListener is similar to OnCheckedChange-Listener, except that it is applied to changes in a SeekBar.

Lines 19–24:   All input controls defined within a layout must be referenced in order for MyActivity to retrieve their data. Acronyms have been used to identify the type of widget referenced more clearly. For example, pattyRG is the hamburger patty RadioGroup, and the object sauceSBR is the sauce SeekBar.

Lines 55–60:   Change listeners are registered for all of the input controls. When a change is triggered in an input control, the listener event is called. The listener event for pattyRG and cheeseRG is handled by the same change listener, foodListener().

MyActivity.java

```
1   package com.cornez.burgercaloriecounter;
2
3   import android.app.Activity;
4   import android.os.Bundle;
5   import android.view.Menu;
6   import android.view.MenuItem;
7
8   import android.view.View;
9   import android.view.View.OnClickListener;
10  import android.widget.CheckBox;
11  import android.widget.RadioGroup;
12  import android.widget.RadioGroup.OnCheckedChangeListener;
13  import android.widget.SeekBar;
```

```
14  import android.widget.SeekBar.OnSeekBarChangeListener;
15  import android.widget.TextView;
16
17  public class MyActivity extends Activity {
18
19      // TASK 1: DECLARE UI OBJECTS TO BE REFERENCED
20      private RadioGroup pattyRG;
21      private CheckBox prosciuttoCBX;
22      private RadioGroup cheeseRG;
23      private SeekBar sauceSBR;
24      private TextView caloriesTV;
25
26      // TASK 2: DECLARE VARIABLES FOR COMPUTING CALORIES
27      private Burger burger;
28
29
30      @Override
31      protected void onCreate(Bundle savedInstanceState) {
32          super.onCreate(savedInstanceState);
33          setContentView(R.layout.activity_my);
34
35          // TASK 4: INITIALIZE UI OBJECTS AND VARIABLES
36          burger = new Burger();
37          initialize();
38
39          // TASK 5: REGISTER CHANGE LISTENERS
40          registerChangeListener();
41
42      }
43
44      private void initialize() {
45          // TASK 5: GET REFERENCE TO EACH OF THE UI COMPONENTS
46          pattyRG = (RadioGroup) findViewById(R.id.radioGroup1);
47          prosciuttoCBX = (CheckBox) findViewById(R.id.checkBox1);
48          cheeseRG = (RadioGroup) findViewById(R.id.radioGroup2);
49          sauceSBR = (SeekBar) findViewById(R.id.seekBar1);
50          caloriesTV = (TextView) findViewById(R.id.textView2);
51
52          displayCalories();
53      }
54
55      private void registerChangeListener() {
56          pattyRG.setOnCheckedChangeListener(foodListener);
57          prosciuttoCBX.setOnClickListener(baconListener);
58          cheeseRG.setOnCheckedChangeListener(foodListener);
59          sauceSBR.setOnSeekBarChangeListener(sauceListener);
60      }
```

MyActivity.java will use an anonymous inner class that extends On-CheckedChangeListener to respond to the user's selection of certain food items. foodListener() listens for changes in the RadioGroup for the patty and cheese selections the user makes.

Lines 61–63:   OnCheckedChange() is called when the user selects one of the RadioButton widgets. This callback requires two parameters, RadioGroup and radioId. radioId is the object that allows us to identify which RadioButton the user has just selected.

Lines 65–79:   For demonstration purposes, and to provide you with firsthand experience using the hex resource identifiers, this application will rely on the generated R.java. This file is located in the following directory:

app/build/generated/source/r/degug/com/com.cornez.burgercaloriecounter.

Calories are set for the selected burger item identified by the hex value associated with the appropriate RadioButton. The case statements in this segment of code use the resource constant values taken directly from the R.java, as shown in Figure 2-24.

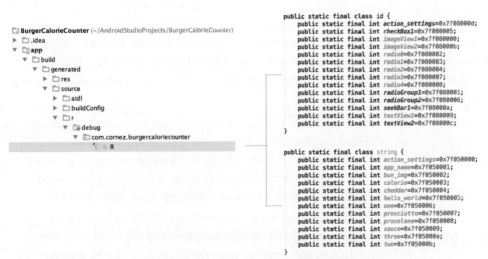

| **FIGURE 2-24** Sample contents of R.java showing generated-resource identifiers.

Line 80:   Calories are redisplayed with a call to displayCalories(), following any changes made to the RadioButtons.

```
MyActivity.java  Continued
61      private OnCheckedChangeListener foodListener = new
62          OnCheckedChangeListener() {
63      public void onCheckedChanged(RadioGroup rbGroup, int radioId) {
64          switch (radioId) {
65              case 0x7f080002: // BEEF PATTY
66                  burger.setPattyCalories(Burger.BEEF);
67                  break;
68              case 0x7f080003: // LAMB PATTY
69                  burger.setPattyCalories(Burger.LAMB);
70                  break;
71              case 0x7f080004: // OSTRICH PATTY
72                  burger.setPattyCalories(Burger.OSTRICH);
73                  break;
74              case 0x7f080007: // ASIAGO CHEESE
75                  burger.setCheeseCalories(Burger.ASIAGO);
76                  break;
77              case 0x7f080008: // CREME FRAICHE
78                  burger.setCheeseCalories(Burger.CREME_FRAICHE);
79          }
80          displayCalories();
81      }
82  };
```

The CheckBox (the Proscuitto selection) and the SeekBar (the amount of caviar added to the burger) had listener events registered to them so that calories could be computed immediately if the user altered either of these selections. This segment of code defines the anonymous inner class that extends OnClickListener and OnSeekBarChangeListener.

Lines 85–93:   A CheckBox is a specific type of two-states button that can either be checked or unchecked. This segment of instructions creates an OnClickListener named baconListener to respond to an onClick() event. onClick() is called when the user checks or unchecks the CheckBox button.

Lines 95–109:   An OnSeekBarChangeListener named sauceListener is created to respond directly to changes in the SeekBar, which is used to add specified amounts of caviar to the hamburger. Changes in a SeekBar are monitored in several ways. The three notification callbacks are as follows:

onProgressChanged: The SeekBar progress is actively being changed. This callback is our sole concern, as it indicates the advancement of the bar.

| onStartTrackingTouch: | The user has just touched the SeekBar. We will not respond to this callback. |
| onStopTrackingTouch: | The user has just touched the SeekBar. As with the previous callback, this callback will be left empty. |

MyActivity.java *Continued*

```
84      private OnClickListener baconListener = new OnClickListener() {
85          public void onClick(View v) {
86              if (((CheckBox) v).isChecked())
87                  burger.setProsciuttoCalories(Burger.PROSCIUTTO);
88              else
89                  burger.clearProsciuttoCalories();
90
91              displayCalories();
92          }
93      };
94
95      private OnSeekBarChangeListener sauceListener = new
96              OnSeekBarChangeListener() {
97          public void onProgressChanged(SeekBar seekBar, int progress,
98                                      boolean fromUser) {
99              burger.setSauceCalories(seekBar.getProgress());
100             displayCalories();
101         }
102
103         public void onStartTrackingTouch(SeekBar seekBar) {
104         }
105
106         public void onStopTrackingTouch(SeekBar seekBar) {
107         }
108     };
```

The remaining instructions in MyActivity.java display the computed calories.

MyActivity.java *Continued*

```
109     private void displayCalories() {
110
111         // CONSTRUCT AN OUTPUT STRING AND DISPLAY IN THE TEXTVIEW
112         String calorieText = "Calories: " + burger.getTotalCalories();
113         caloriesTV.setText(calorieText);
114     }
115
116     @Override
117     public boolean onCreateOptionsMenu(Menu menu) {
```

```
121        // Inflate the menu;
122        getMenuInflater().inflate(R.menu.my, menu);
123        return true;
124    }
125
126    @Override
127    public boolean onOptionsItemSelected(MenuItem item) {
128        // Handle action bar item clicks here. The action bar will
129        // automatically handle clicks on the Home/Up button, so long
130        // as you specify a parent activity in AndroidManifest.xml.
131        int id = item.getItemId();
132        if (id == R.id.action_settings) {
133            return true;
134        }
        return super.onOptionsItemSelected(item);
    }
}
```

■ 2.9 Adaptive Design Concepts—Screens and Orientations

Android apps can be difficult to design and build because of the many variations in screen sizes available on the market at any given time. Forcing a single design for an app that is expected to fit on a wide range of screen sizes can often result in an ineffective and inefficient user interface. Adaptive Design is so important to Android because it supports flexibility when designing an app that can work on multiple devices. Another method for dealing with Android device variations, called Responsive Design, will be introduced in Chapter 4.

Adaptive Design refers to the adaptation of a layout design that fits an individual screen size and or orientation. Designing for a device's size or orientation makes it possible to make better use of the opportunities each one offers. For example, when building an app for a Nexus phone that has a screen size of 4.7", the layout can be constructed to comply specifically with the standards of that screen. The layout of the application might also need to have a separate design for a landscape orientation. Figure 2-25 shows six different general screen sizes for Android. Depending on the screen size, a different, yet similar, background has been applied.

Android applications need to adapt to a number of different types of devices. These devices can range from wearables to 3" phones to 10" tablets. Adaptive Design models a layout for general sizes, which means that designs are structured around approximations. For example, a screen size between 3 and 5 inches is generally suitable for showing content in a vertical manner. Larger screens, such as those found on tablets and TVs, on the other hand, generally have much more available screen space and are able to present content in less restrictive ways.

Android screen designs can be categorized using two general properties: size and density. Users are accustomed to seeing a variety of different screens and are accepting

FIGURE 2-25 Adaptive Design is used to display different content for different screens.

of different presentations, as long as they are well designed. Problems can arise when a user interface designed for a large layout is moved to a smaller one. Developers should expect their applications to be installed on devices with screens that range in both size and density.

Screen orientation is also considered a variation of screen size. Apps should revise layouts to optimize the user experience in each orientation: landscape or portrait.

A unique layout XML file can be created for each screen size on which the app might be launched. Four generalized sizes can be targed: small, normal, large, and xlarge. Each layout should be saved into the appropriate resources directory, named with a `-<screen_size>` suffix. Figure 2-26 shows four different versions of the layout named `activity_my.xml`, saved to the appropriate layout directory. The layout version that will be used for the large tablet is saved under `res/layout-xlarge/`.

As you have already experienced, Android automatically scales a layout so that it properly fits the device on which it is launched. Thus, do not worry about the absolute size of UI elements; focus instead on the layout structure that affects the user experience (such as the size or position of important views relative to sibling views). The system loads the layout file from the appropriate layout directory based on the screen size of the device on which your app is running.

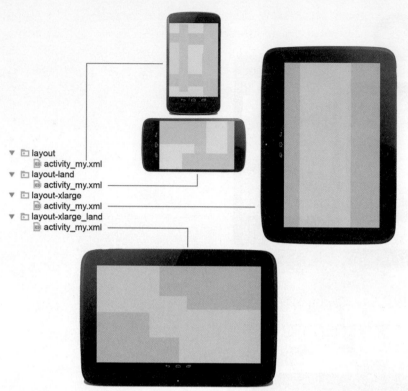

I FIGURE 2-26 Many versions of `activity_my.xml` can be used by an application.

Designing for screen size approximations produces better-quality user interfaces because they can be targeted more specifically. This method, however, is not without its flaws. Beware that an intended design could deviate in small measure from the targeted size. Sizes are generalized rather than exact.

■ Lab Example 2-3: Shipping Cost Calculator II—Adaptive Design

The Shipping Cost Calculator, produced in Lab 2-1, did not adapt well to changes in screen orientation. For example, the user could clearly see the input and output elements when using a small device held in portrait orientation. If the small device were tilted to a landscape orientation, however, the output elements would be cut off. This would not impede the performance of the app because the user could always take the extra action of pressing the "Done" key. However, it is clear that this one-size-fits-all approach does not produce the best possible experience for the user. The solution to this problem is to create layouts with adaptive design methods.

In this lab, we will revise the layout used from Lab 2-1 and add an alternate version of the layout to be used for a landscape orientation. When the user is holding the device in portrait orientation, the first layout shown on the left in Figure 2-27 will appear on the screen. When the user rotates the device, the screen display will automatically change to the second layout, shown to the right in Figure 2-27.

In addition, this lab will explore the use of `ViewGroups` for categorizing elements on the screen. `ViewGroups` can be highly effective in screen design because they allow an easy grouping of related controls. For example, in the portrait layout, a `RelativeLayout` is used to group together all output widgets, including the labels used to identify the output values.

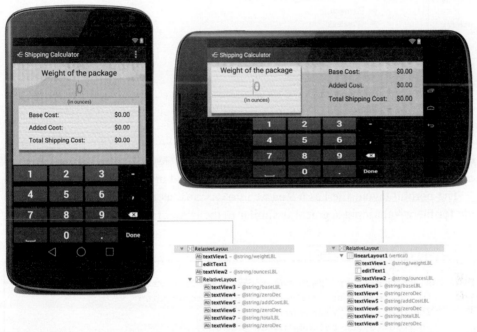

I FIGURE 2-27 The Shipping Cost app reconceptualized in portrait and landscape orientations.

Part 1: Project Structure

A bitmap representing a small piece of paper is placed on both layouts for this application. This will provide the user with a visual cue. This graphic needs to be added to the drawable folder within the project.

The final project structure, shown in Figure 2-28, uses two layout directories. Both of these directories store a layout file named `activity_my.xml`. This file represents the user interface for `MyActivity`. The first version of `activity_my.xml` is stored in `res/layout`, which is the default portrait orientation. The layout stored in `res/layout-land` will be used for a landscape orientation.

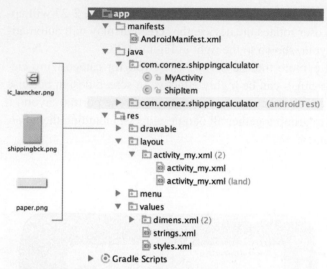

ic_launcher.png

shippingbck.png

paper.png

▌ FIGURE 2-28 Additional layout directories can be used to store different configurations of a user interface.

Part 2: Portrait Layout—the Default

The portrait layout for this application is the default layout and retains the name `activity_my.xml`. As the default layout, it is stored in `res/layout`.

The portrait layout file has a `RelativeLayout` as its root element. The XML code for the weight input segment is similar to the layout from Lab 1 of this chapter.

```
res/layout/activity_my.xml
 1   <RelativeLayout
 2   xmlns:android="http://schemas.android.com/apk/res/android"
 3       xmlns:tools="http://schemas.android.com/tools"
 4       android:layout_width="match_parent"
 5       android:layout_height="match_parent"
 6       android:paddingLeft="@dimen/activity_horizontal_margin"
 7       android:paddingRight="@dimen/activity_horizontal_margin"
 8       android:paddingTop="@dimen/activity_vertical_margin"
 9       android:paddingBottom="@dimen/activity_vertical_margin"
10       android:background="@drawable/shippingbck"
11       tools:context=".MyActivity">
12
13       <!-- WEIGHT INPUT SECTION -->
14       <TextView
15           android:id="@+id/textView1"
16           android:layout_width="fill_parent"
17           android:layout_height="wrap_content"
18           android:layout_alignParentTop="true"
19           android:layout_centerHorizontal="true"
20           android:text="@string/weightLBL"
```

```
21          android:textAppearance="?android:attr/textAppearanceLarge"
22          android:gravity="center_horizontal" />
23
24      <!-- WEIGHT INPUT EDIT TEXT FIELD RECEIVES FOCUS -->
25      <EditText
26          android:id="@+id/editText1"
27          android:layout_width="wrap_content"
28          android:layout_height="wrap_content"
29          android:layout_below="@+id/textView1"
30          android:layout_centerHorizontal="true"
31          android:layout_marginTop="5dp"
32          android:ems="10"
33          android:gravity="center_vertical|center_horizontal"
34          android:inputType="number"
35          android:selectAllOnFocus="true"
36          android:textSize="35sp"
37          android:hint="@string/zero">
38
39          <requestFocus />
40      </EditText>
41
42      <TextView
43          android:id="@+id/textView2"
44          android:layout_width="wrap_content"
45          android:layout_height="wrap_content"
46          android:layout_below="@+id/editText1"
47          android:layout_centerHorizontal="true"
48          android:text="@string/ouncesLBL"
49          android:textAppearance="?android:attr/textAppearanceSmall" />
```

Contained within this layout is another `RelativeLayout`, as shown in Figure 2-29. This nested `ViewGroup` allows us to group the related cost calculations the user needs to see for the item that will be shipped. The code for the nested `RelativeLayout` element appears in Lines 50–138. A paper graphic has been applied to the nested `ViewGroup` in Line 57.

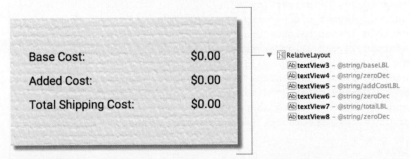

FIGURE 2-29 Computed output values are organized in a separate `ViewGroup` container in `res/layout/activity_my.xml`.

Res/layout/activity_my.xml *Continued*

```
50  <!-- VIEWGROUP CONTAINER FOR DISPLAYING SHIPPING CALCULATIONS   -->
51
52      <RelativeLayout
53          android:layout_width="wrap_content"
54          android:layout_height="wrap_content"
55          android:layout_below="@+id/textView2"
56          android:layout_centerHorizontal="true"
57          android:background="@drawable/paper">
58
59
60
61          <!-- TEXTVIEWS FOR BASE COST LABEL AND COMPUTATION   -->
62          <TextView
63              android:id="@+id/textView3"
64              android:layout_width="wrap_content"
65              android:layout_height="wrap_content"
66              android:layout_alignParentLeft="true"
67              android:layout_alignParentTop="true"
68              android:layout_marginTop="50dp"
69              android:paddingLeft="@dimen/output_margin_buffer"
70              android:text="@string/baseLBL"
71              android:textAppearance="?android:attr/textAppearanceMedium" />
72
73          <TextView
74              android:id="@+id/textView4"
75              android:layout_width="wrap_content"
76              android:layout_height="wrap_content"
77              android:layout_alignBaseline="@+id/textView3"
78              android:layout_alignBottom="@+id/textView3"
79              android:layout_alignParentRight="true"
80              android:paddingRight="@dimen/output_margin_buffer"
81              android:text="@string/zeroDec"
82              android:textAppearance="?android:attr/textAppearanceMedium" />
83
84          <!-- TEXTVIEWS FOR ADDED COST LABEL AND COMPUTATION   -->
85          <TextView
86              android:id="@+id/textView5"
87              android:layout_width="wrap_content"
88              android:layout_height="wrap_content"
89              android:layout_alignParentLeft="true"
90              android:layout_below="@+id/textView3"
91              android:layout_marginTop="15dp"
92              android:paddingLeft="@dimen/output_margin_buffer"
93              android:text="@string/addCostLBL"
94              android:textAppearance="?android:attr/textAppearanceMedium" />
95
96          <TextView
97              android:id="@+id/textView6"
98              android:layout_width="wrap_content"
```

```
 99              android:layout_height="wrap_content"
100              android:layout_alignBaseline="@+id/textView5"
101              android:layout_alignBottom="@+id/textView5"
102              android:layout_alignParentRight="true"
103              android:paddingRight="@dimen/output_margin_buffer"
104              android:text="@string/zeroDec"
105              android:textAppearance="?android:attr/textAppearanceMedium" />
106
107
108          <!-- TEXTVIEWS FOR THE TOTAL COST LABEL AND COMPUTATION   -->
109          <TextView
110              android:id="@+id/textView7"
111              android:layout_width="wrap_content"
112              android:layout_height="wrap_content"
113              android:layout_alignParentLeft="true"
114              android:layout_below="@+id/textView5"
115              android:layout_marginTop="15dp"
116              android:paddingLeft="@dimen/output_margin_buffer"
117              android:text-"@string/totalLBL"
118              android:textAppearance="?android:attr/textAppearanceMedium" />
119
120          <TextView
121              android:id="@+id/textView8"
122              android:layout_width="wrap_content"
123              android:layout_height="wrap_content"
124              android:layout_alignBaseline="@+id/textView7"
125              android:layout_alignBottom="@+id/textView7"
126              android:layout_alignParentRight="true"
127              android:paddingRight="@dimen/output_margin_buffer"
128              android:text="@string/zeroDec"
129              android:textAppearance="?android:attr/textAppearanceMedium" />
130
131
132      </RelativeLayout>
133
134  </RelativeLayout>
135
136
137
138
139
140
```

Part 3: Landscape Layout

The landscape version of the layout is also named `activity_my.xml`. In order to differentiate between the two layouts, the landscape layout is stored in a separate folder, `res/layout-land`. The easiest way to create this folder is to choose `Create Land-scape Variation` from the `Configuration Icon` ⬛▾ in the Graphical Layout

Editor in the Design mode. The landscape layout uses a `RelativeLayout` as the root element. It differs from the default layout in that it incorporates a `ViewGroup`, the `LinearLayout`, to group the controls that are related to input, as shown in Figure 2-30.

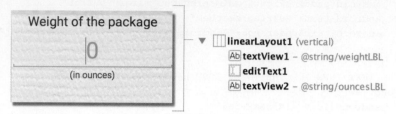

FIGURE 2-30 A `LinearLayout` is added to `res/layout-land/activity_my.xml` to group elements related to weight input.

The XML code for the landscape layout resource file is shown as follows:

```
res/layout-land/activity_my.xml
1   <?xml version="1.0" encoding="utf-8"?>
2   <RelativeLayout
3   xmlns:android="http://schemas.android.com/apk/res/android"
4       android:layout_width="match_parent"
5       android:layout_height="match_parent"
6       android:background="@drawable/shippingbck">
7
8       <LinearLayout
9           android:id="@+id/linearLayout1"
10          android:layout_width="250dp"
11          android:layout_height="wrap_content"
12          android:layout_alignParentLeft="true"
13          android:layout_alignParentTop="true"
14          android:layout_marginLeft="10dp"
15          android:layout_marginTop="10dp"
16
17          android:orientation="vertical"
18          android:background="@drawable/paper">
19
20          <!-- WEIGHT INPUT SECTION -->
21
22          <TextView
23              android:id="@+id/textView1"
24              android:layout_width="match_parent"
25              android:layout_height="match_parent"
26              android:gravity="center_horizontal"
27              android:text="@string/weightLBL"
28              android:textAppearance="?android:attr/textAppearanceLarge"
29
30              android:textSize="20sp" />
31
```

```
32          <!-- WEIGHT INPUT EDIT TEXT FIELD RECEIVES FOCUS -->
33
34          <EditText
35              android:id="@+id/editText1"
36              android:layout_width="match_parent"
37              android:layout_height="match_parent"
38              android:layout_marginTop="5dp"
39              android:ems="10"
40              android:gravity="center_vertical|center_horizontal"
41              android:inputType="number"
42              android:selectAllOnFocus="true"
43              android:textSize="35sp"
44              android:hint="@string/zero">
45
46              <requestFocus />
47          </EditText>
48
49          <TextView
50              android:id="@+id/textView2"
51              android:layout_width="match_parent"
52              android:layout_height="wrap_content"
53              android:gravity="center_horizontal"
54              android:text="@string/ouncesLBL"
55              android:textAppearance="?android:attr/textAppearanceSmall"
56               />
57
58      </LinearLayout>
59
60      <!-- TEXTVIEWS FOR BASE COST LABEL AND COMPUTATION  -->
61      <TextView
62          android:id="@+id/textView3"
63          android:layout_width="wrap_content"
64          android:layout_height="wrap_content"
65          android:layout_alignParentTop="true"
66          android:layout_marginLeft="44dp"
67          android:layout_marginTop="16dp"
68          android:layout_toRightOf="@+id/linearLayout1"
69          android:text="@string/baseLBL"
70          android:textAppearance="?android:attr/textAppearanceMedium"
71          android:paddingLeft="@dimen/output_margin_buffer" />
72
73      <TextView
74          android:id="@+id/textView4"
75          android:layout_width="wrap_content"
76          android:layout_height="wrap_content"
77          android:layout_alignBaseline="@+id/textView3"
78          android:layout_alignBottom="@+id/textView3"
79
80          android:layout_alignParentRight="true"
81          android:paddingRight="@dimen/output_margin_buffer"
```

```
82
83            android:text="@string/zeroDec"
84            android:textAppearance="?android:attr/textAppearanceMedium" />
85
86        <!-- TEXTVIEWS FOR ADDED COST LABEL AND COMPUTATION  -->
87        <TextView
88            android:id="@+id/textView5"
89            android:layout_width="wrap_content"
90            android:layout_height="wrap_content"
91            android:layout_alignLeft="@+id/textView3"
92            android:layout_below="@+id/textView3"
93            android:layout_marginTop="16dp"
94            android:text="@string/addCostLBL"
95            android:textAppearance="?android:attr/textAppearanceMedium"
96            android:paddingLeft="@dimen/output_margin_buffer" />
97
98        <TextView
99            android:id="@+id/textView6"
100           android:layout_width="wrap_content"
101           android:layout_height="wrap_content"
102           android:layout_alignBaseline="@+id/textView5"
103           android:layout_alignBottom="@+id/textView5"
104           android:layout_alignParentRight="true"
105           android:paddingRight="@dimen/output_margin_buffer"
106
107
108           android:text="@string/zeroDec"
109           android:textAppearance="?android:attr/textAppearanceMedium"
110           />
111
112       <!-- TEXTVIEWS FOR THE TOTAL COST LABEL AND COMPUTATION  -->
113       <TextView
114           android:id="@+id/textView7"
115           android:layout_width="wrap_content"
116           android:layout_height="wrap_content"
117           android:layout_alignLeft="@+id/textView5"
118           android:layout_below="@+id/textView5"
119           android:layout_marginTop="16dp"
120           android:text="@string/totalLBL"
121           android:textAppearance="?android:attr/textAppearanceMedium"
122           android:paddingLeft="@dimen/output_margin_buffer" />
123
124       <TextView
125           android:id="@+id/textView8"
126
127           android:layout_width="wrap_content"
128           android:layout_height="wrap_content"
129           android:layout_alignBaseline="@+id/textView7"
```

```
130    android:layout_alignBottom="@+id/textView7"
131    android:layout_alignParentRight="true"
132    android:paddingRight="@dimen/output_margin_buffer"
133
134    android:text="@string/zeroDec"
135    android:textAppearance="?android:attr/textAppearanceMedium" />
136
137  <TableLayout
138    android:layout_width="fill_parent"
139    android:layout_height="fill_parent"
140    android:layout_alignParentTop="true"
141    android:layout_alignStart="@+id/linearLayout1"
142    android:layout_marginLeft="26dp"
143    android:layout_marginTop="88dp"></TableLayout>
144
145  </RelativeLayout>
```

■ 2.10 `TableLayout` **and** `TableRow`

In Android, `TableLayouts` are often used to organize data content into tabular form. This `ViewGroup` is highly effective in layout designs that require a neat alignment of user interface controls arranged into rows and columns. When used correctly, `TableLayouts` can be a powerful layout paradigm, which apps can use to display a variety of elements.

Tables can be added to a layout file using the Graphical Layout Editor or programmatically using Java. However the layout is constructed, the build rules will be the same. The number of columns within a table automatically matches the number of columns in the row with the most columns. The width of each column is defined as the width of the widest content in the column. The `TableLayout`'s child rows and cells `layout_width` attributes are always `MATCH_PARENT`; although they can be put in an XML file, the actual value cannot be overridden. The `TableLayout`'s `layout_height` of a cell can be defined, but a `TableRow` attribute for `layout_height` is always `WRAP_CONTENT`.

Java requires two class imports for this purpose: `android.widget.TableLayout` and `android.widget.TableRow`. The following code segment uses Java code to generate a layout screen consisting of a table. This table contains two rows and two columns. Each cell in the table will store a `TextView` element.

Line 1:   A `TableLayout` is instantiated for the given context. Since the goal is to generate a layout and set the app content to this view, the context will be the application environment.

Lines 3–4:   Columns can be marked as stretchable, which means that the width can expand to the size of the parent container. Columns can also be marked as shrinkable, which means that they can be reduced in width so the whole row fits in the space provided by the parent container. You can also collapse an entire column.

It should be noted that a table cell can span multiple columns, but not rows. This is done through the layout_span attribute of the child view of a TableRow. A cell is a single child view within a TableRow. If you want a more complex cell with multiple views, use a layout view to encapsulate the other views.

Lines 6–22:   The first TableRow, row1, is constructed and two TextView elements are added using the addView() method. The second TableRow is constructed in the same manner.

Line 24:   The layout for this given application is set to the table that was just constructed. The screen for this application will look similar to the one shown in Figure 2-31.

```
1      TableLayout table = new TableLayout(this);
2
3      table.setStretchAllColumns(true);
4      table.setShrinkAllColumns(true);
5
6      TableRow row1 = new TableRow(this);
7      TextView fruit1 = new TextView(this);
8      fruit1.setText("Apple");
9      TextView fruit2 = new TextView(this);
10     fruit2.setText("Banana");
11     row1.addView(fruit1);
12     row1.addView(fruit2);
13
14     TableRow row2 = new TableRow(this);
15     TextView fruit3 = new TextView(this);
16     fruit3.setText("Cherry");
17     TextView fruit4 = new TextView(this);
18     fruit4.setText("Strawberry");
19     row2.addView(fruit3);
20     row2.addView(fruit4);
21     table.addView(row1);
22     table.addView(row2);
23
24     setContentView(table);
```

Although it is possible for TableLayouts to be used to design entire user interfaces, they are often combined with other layout Views. As a derivative of a LinearLayout, the TableLayout is little more than an organized set of nested

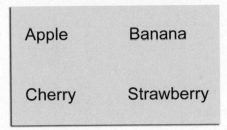

FIGURE 2-31 A `TableLayout` built in Java.

`LinearLayouts`. Nesting layouts too deeply is generally discouraged for performance concerns.

■ Lab Example 2-4: Simple Calculator App and the `TableLayout`

The purpose of this lab is to illustrate how a `TableLayout` `ViewGroup` can be used to design a user interface containing table cells that are customized. The Calculator app takes advantage of table structure for organizing the control elements. The final app is shown in Figure 2-32.

FIGURE 2-32 The Calculator running in an AVD designed for a small device.

Part 1: Application Structure and Setup

The settings for the application are as follows:

- Application Name: Calculator
- Project Name: Calculator
- Package Name: com.cornez.calculator
- Android Form: Phone and Tablet
- Minimum SDK: API 18: Android 4.3 (Jelly Bean)
- Target SDK: API 21: Android 5.0 (Lollipop)
- Compile with: API 21: Android 5.0 (Lollipop)
- Activity Name: `MyActivity`
- Layout Name: `activity_my`

No bitmap elements are required for the design of this app. The launcher icon will remain as the default bitmap, `ic_launcher.png`. The final structure will resemble the one shown in Figure 2-33.

| FIGURE 2-33 The project structure for the Calculator application.

For more control over the visual presentation of the calculator, the orientation is fixed in portrait mode. When the user rotates the device to a landscape orientation, the application remains fixed in portrait mode. A quick and easy method for fixing orientation is to set the `screenOrientation` property of the activity within `AndroidManifest.xml`.

Line 12:   Screen orientation is fixed in portrait mode.

The `screenOrientation` property applies solely to activities and not to an application. If an app contains multiple activities, the `screenOrientation` property can be set for each one individually. If an orientation is not specified for an activity, it will run in the current preferred orientation of the screen.

In addition to portrait, `screenOrientation` can be set to the following values: `landscape`, `locked`, `reverseLandscape`, and `reversePortrait`. This value list is not complete. Refer to Android documentation for the full list.

AndroidManifest.xml

```
1   <?xml version="1.0" encoding="utf-8"?>
2   <manifest xmlns:android="http://schemas.android.com/apk/res/android"
3       package="com.cornez.calculator" >
4
5       <application
6           android:allowBackup="true"
7           android:icon="@drawable/ic_launcher"
8           android:label="@string/app_name"
9           android:theme="@style/AppTheme" >
10          <activity
11              android:name=".MyActivity"
12              android:screenOrientation="portrait"
13              android:label="@string/app_name" >
14              <intent-filter>
15                  <action android:name="android.intent.action.MAIN" />
16
17                  <category android:name="android.intent.category.LAUNCHER" />
18              </intent-filter>
19          </activity>
20      </application>
21
22  </manifest>
23
```

Part 2: External Value Resources

Two value resource files are required for the Calculator app. The first is the `string.xml` file, which stores the text on display within the keypad holding the numbers, operators, and accumulator key (AC).

The second value resource file is the `color.xml` file. Color is used make the calculator easier to navigate. Colors are applied to certain keys and to the display component of the calculator. `orange_cream` is used for the display, `grey` is used for the numeric keys and operators, and `dusk_blue` is used for "=" and AC. Note that both `dusk_blue` keys on the calculator span two regular keys, two columns. The display component spans across four columns in the table structure.

The XML code for `strings.xml` and `color.xml` are listed as follows.

strings.xml

```xml
1   <?xml version="1.0" encoding="utf-8"?>
2   <resources>
3
4       <string name="app_name">Calculator</string>
5       <string name="hello_world">Hello world!</string>
6       <string name="action_settings">Settings</string>
7
8       <string name="one">1</string>
9       <string name="two">2</string>
10      <string name="three">3</string>
11      <string name="four">4</string>
12      <string name="five">5</string>
13      <string name="six">6</string>
14      <string name="seven">7</string>
15      <string name="eight">8</string>
16      <string name="nine">9</string>
17      <string name="zero">0</string>
18
19      <string name="ac">AC</string>
20      <string name="sign">+/-</string>
21      <string name="percent">%</string>
22      <string name="div">/</string>
23      <string name="mult">x</string>
24      <string name="subtract">-</string>
25      <string name="add">+</string>
26      <string name="equal">=</string>
27      <string name="decimal">.</string>
28
29  </resources>
```

color.xml

```xml
1   <?xml version="1.0" encoding="utf-8"?>
2   <resources>
3       <color name="orange_cream">#00FF00</color>
4       <color name="grey">#EDBA69</color>
5       <color name="dusk_blue">#8BADCA</color>
6   </resources>
```

Part 3: The User Interface as a Layout XML File

The root element of the layout file for the main activity of this application is a `Table-Layout`. The `TableLayout` contains exactly six `TableRows`, named `tableRow1`, `tableRow2`, and so on. The design for this layout is shown in Figure 2-34.

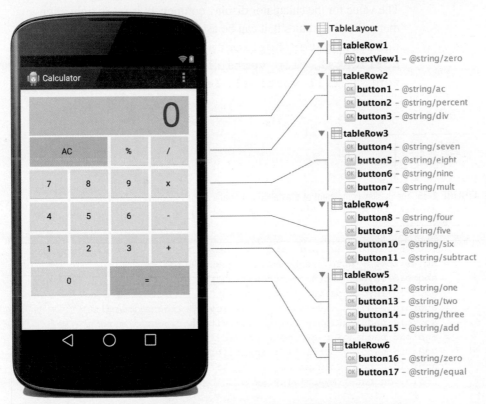

❚ FIGURE 2-34 The Layout design, `activity_my.xml`, for the Calculator application.

The XML code for `activity_my.xml` appears below. The first 28 lines of this file define the configuration of the `TableLayout` and the display component located at the top of the calculator.

Line 9:   The `TableLayout` columns to stretch are set to indexes 0, 1, 2, and 3. When listing the columns that will be stretched, the numeric indices must be used and separated by a comma. It is possible to stretch all columns by using the value "*" instead of specifying specific columns.

Lines 13–17:   A first row is defined as `tableRow1`.

Lines 18–28:   The display component of the Calculator is defined as a `Text-View` named `textView1`. It is placed within `tableRow1`.

Line 22:   The Calculator will display computed values in a display component, textView1, defined to occupy an entire row of TableLayout. This row spans four cells/ columns, as shown in Figure 2-35.

Line 24:   The gravity property is used to specify text alignment along textView1's x- and/or y-axis when the text is smaller than the view. The value for the calculator display component is set to right alignment. Possible values that can be assigned to gravity are: bottom, center, center_horizontal, center_vertical, clip_horizontal, clip_vertical, end, fill, fill_horizontal, fill_vertical, left, right, start, and top.

tableRow1: Spans 4 cells

FIGURE 2-35 The display component of the calculator spans across four cells.

```
activity_my.xml
1   <TableLayout xmlns:android="http://schemas.android.com/apk/res/android"
2       xmlns:tools="http://schemas.android.com/tools"
3       android:layout_width="match_parent"
4       android:layout_height="match_parent"
5       android:paddingLeft="@dimen/activity_horizontal_margin"
6       android:paddingRight="@dimen/activity_horizontal_margin"
7       android:paddingTop="@dimen/activity_vertical_margin"
8       android:paddingBottom="@dimen/activity_vertical_margin"
9       android:stretchColumns="0, 1, 2, 3"
10      tools:context=".MyActivity">
11
12
13      <TableRow
14          android:id="@+id/tableRow1"
15          android:layout_width="wrap_content"
16          android:layout_height="wrap_content" >
17
18          <TextView
19              android:id="@+id/textView1"
20              android:layout_width="match_parent"
21              android:layout_height="wrap_content"
22              android:layout_span="4"
23              android:background="@color/orange_cream "
24              android:gravity="right"
25              android:text="@string/zero"
26              android:textSize="70sp" />
27
28      </TableRow>
```

Lincs 29–63 of `activity_my.xml` code are used to define the second row of the `TableLayout`, as shown in Figure 2-36. The second row of the calculator contains three buttons.

Line 38:   The button representing the AC control is set to span two cells. Not specifying the span of the other two buttons results in a default span of one cell/ column.

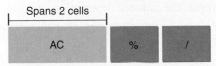

I FIGURE 2-36 The second row of the Calculator contains the AC, %, and / buttons.

```
activity_my.xml  Continued
29   <TableRow
30           android:id="@+id/tableRow2"
31           android:layout_width="wrap_content"
32           android:layout_height="wrap_content">
33
34       <Button
35           android:id="@+id/button1"
36           android:layout_width="wrap_content"
37           android:layout_height="wrap_content"
38           android:layout_span="2"
39           android:background="@color/dusk_blue"
40           android:contentDescription="@string/ac"
41           android:minHeight="70dip"
42           android:onClick="goAC"
43           android:text="@string/ac" />
44
45       <Button
46           android:id="@+id/button2"
47           android:layout_width="wrap_content"
48           android:layout_height="wrap_content"
49           android:minHeight="70dip"
50           android:contentDescription="@string/percent"
51           android:onClick="goOperator"
52           android:text="@string/percent" />
53
54       <Button
55           android:id="@+id/button3"
56           android:layout_width="wrap_content"
57           android:layout_height="wrap_content"
58           android:minHeight="70dip"
59           android:contentDescription="@string/div"
60           android:onClick="goOperator"
61           android:text="@string/div" />
62
63       </TableRow>
```

Line 63–193:   TableRows 3, 4, and 5 are added to the `TableLayout`. As shown in Figure 2-37, these cells are displayed with equal size.

Lines 72, 83, 92, 101, 116, 127, 136, 145:

The `android:contentDescription` is required for the buttons occupying the 3rd, 4th, and 5th rows. `MyActivity.java` uses these description values to uniquely identify which key the user tapped. For example, the content description of `button4` is set to the string "seven," which represents value 7. As shown in Figure 2-37, each button is of equal size and spans a single column in the table row.

Table cells of equal size

FIGURE 2-37 The buttons in the 3rd , 4th, and 5th rows are of equal size.

```
activity_my.xml  Continued
63   <TableRow
64          android:id="@+id/tableRow3"
65          android:layout_width="wrap_content"
66          android:layout_height="wrap_content">
67
68          <Button
69              android:id="@+id/button4"
70              android:layout_width="wrap_content"
71              android:layout_height="wrap_content"
72              android:contentDescription="@string/seven"
73              android:minHeight="70dip"
74              android:minWidth="70dp"
75              android:onClick="goOperand"
76              android:text="@string/seven" />
77
78          <Button
79              android:id="@+id/button5"
80              android:layout_width="wrap_content"
81              android:layout_height="wrap_content"
82              android:minHeight="70dip"
83              android:contentDescription="@string/eight"
```

```
84              android:onClick="goOperand"
85              android:text="@string/eight" />
86
87          <Button
88              android:id="@+id/button6"
89              android:layout_width="wrap_content"
90              android:layout_height="wrap_content"
91              android:minHeight="70dip"
92              android:contentDescription="@string/nine"
93              android:onClick="goOperand"
94              android:text="@string/nine" />
95
96          <Button
97              android:id="@+id/button7"
98              android:layout_width="wrap_content"
99              android:layout_height="wrap_content"
100             android:minHeight-"70dip"
101             android:contentDescription="@string/mult"
102             android:onClick="goOperator"
103             android:text="@string/mult" />
104
105     </TableRow>
106
107     <TableRow
108         android:id="@+id/tableRow4"
109         android:layout_width="wrap_content"
110         android:layout_height="wrap_content">
111
112         <Button
113             android:id="@+id/button8"
114             android:layout_width="wrap_content"
115             android:layout_height="wrap_content"
116             android:contentDescription="@string/four"
117             android:minHeight="70dip"
118             android:minWidth="70dp"
119             android:onClick="goOperand"
120             android:text="@string/four" />
121
122         <Button
123             android:id="@+id/button9"
124             android:layout_width="wrap_content"
125             android:layout_height="wrap_content"
126             android:minHeight="70dip"
127             android:contentDescription="@string/five"
128             android:onClick="goOperand"
129             android:text="@string/five" />
130
131         <Button
132             android:id="@+id/button10"
133             android:layout_width="wrap_content"
134             android:layout_height="wrap_content"
```

```
135                android:minHeight="70dip"
136                android:contentDescription="@string/six"
137                android:onClick="goOperand"
138                android:text="@string/six" />
139
140           <Button
141                android:id="@+id/button11"
142                android:layout_width="wrap_content"
143                android:layout_height="wrap_content"
144                android:minHeight="70dip"
145                android:contentDescription="@string/subtract"
146                android:onClick="goOperator"
147                android:text="@string/subtract" />
148
149        </TableRow>
150
151        <TableRow
152            android:id="@+id/tableRow5"
153            android:layout_width="wrap_content"
154            android:layout_height="wrap_content" >
155
156           <Button
157                android:id="@+id/button12"
158                android:layout_width="wrap_content"
159                android:layout_height="wrap_content"
160                android:contentDescription="@string/one"
161                android:minHeight="70dip"
162                android:minWidth="70dp"
163                android:onClick="goOperand"
164                android:text="@string/one" />
165
166           <Button
167                android:id="@+id/button13"
168                android:layout_width="wrap_content"
169                android:layout_height="wrap_content"
170                android:minHeight="70dip"
171                android:contentDescription="@string/two"
172                android:onClick="goOperand"
173                android:text="@string/two" />
174
175           <Button
176                android:id="@+id/button14"
177                android:layout_width="wrap_content"
178                android:layout_height="wrap_content"
179                android:minHeight="70dip"
180                android:contentDescription="@string/three"
181                android:onClick="goOperand"
182                android:text="@string/three" />
183
184           <Button
185                android:id="@+id/button15"
```

```
186          android:layout_width="wrap_content"
187          android:layout_height="wrap_content"
188          android:minHeight="70dip"
189          android:contentDescription="@string/add"
190          android:onClick="goOperator"
191          android:text="@string/add" />
192
193      </TableRow>
```

Lines 194–220:   The final row of the table, `tableRow6`, is defined. As shown
in Figure 2-38, `tableRow6` contains two buttons.

Lines 204, 213:   `button16` and `button17` spans two row cells.

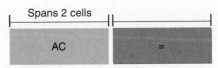

FIGURE 2-38 The final `TableRow` of the `TableLayout` contains two `Buttons`.

```
activity_my.xml  Continued
194  <TableRow
195          android:id="@+id/tableRow6"
196          android:layout_width="wrap_content"
197          android:layout_height="wrap_content" >
198
199      <Button
200          android:id="@+id/button16"
201          android:layout_width="wrap_content"
202          android:layout_height="wrap_content"
203          android:minHeight="70dip"
204          android:layout_span="2"
205          android:contentDescription="@string/zero"
206          android:onClick="goOperand"
207          android:text="@string/zero" />
208
209      <Button
210          android:id="@+id/button17"
211          android:layout_width="wrap_content"
212          android:layout_height="wrap_content"
213          android:layout_span="2"
214          android:background="@color/dusk_blue"
215          android:contentDescription="@string/equal"
216          android:minHeight="70dip"
217          android:onClick="goCompute"
218          android:text="@string/equal" />
219
220      </TableRow>
221
222  </TableLayout>
```

Part 4: Source Code for Application

MyActivity controls all activity, while the data model for a calculator expression is SimpleExpression.

The class SimpleExpression.java models a basic expression involving integers as operators.

Lines 4–7: The data members for this class define the operator, two operands, and the computed value. A SimpleExpression is shown in Figure 2-39.

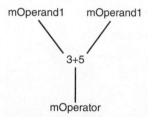

I FIGURE 2-39 A SimpleExpression object is defined by two operands and an operator.

```
SimpleExpression.java
1   package com.cornez.calculator;
2
3   public class SimpleExpression {
4       private Integer mOperand1;
5       private Integer mOperand2;
6       private String mOperator;
7       private Integer mValue;
8
9       public SimpleExpression() {
10          mOperand1 = 0;
11          mOperand2 = 0;
12          mOperator = "+";
13          mValue = 0;
14      }
15
16      public void setOperand1(int v) {
17          mOperand1 = v;
18      }
19
20      public int getOperand1() {
21          return mOperand1;
22      }
23
24      public void setOperand2(int v) {
25          mOperand2 = v;
26      }
27
28      public int getOperand2() {
29          return mOperand2;
30      }
```

```
31
32        public void setOperator(String s) {
33            mOperator = s;
34        }
35
36        public String getOperator() {
37            return mOperator;
38        }
39
40        public Integer getValue() {
41            computeValue();
42            return mValue;
43        }
44
45        /*
46         * Clears the operands within an expression
47         */
48        public void clearOperands() {
49            mOperand1 = 0;
50            mOperand2 = 0;
51        }
52
53        /*
54         * Computes the integer value of the expression.
55         */
56        private void computeValue() {
57            mValue = 0;
58            if (mOperator.contentEquals("+"))
59                mValue = mOperand1 + mOperand2;
60            else if (mOperator.contentEquals("-"))
61                mValue = mOperand1 - mOperand2;
62            else if (mOperator.contentEquals("x"))
63                mValue = mOperand1 * mOperand2;
64            else if (mOperator.contentEquals("/") && mOperand2 != 0)
65                mValue = mOperand1 / mOperand2;
66            else
67                mValue = mOperand1 % mOperand2;
68        }
69
70    }
```

As the controller of the application, the class `MyActivity.java` will implement the interface listener events to reference the layout, `activity_my.xml`, and `update` will update the calculator as the user enters expressions to be computed.

Lines 13–14:   The calculator display, `mNumberDisplay`, and the expression to be computed by the calculator, `mExpression`, are defined.

Line 20:   A reference to the layout `TextView` is established for the calculator display component.

Lines 25–38:   The handlers for the onClick listener events are implemented,
               goAC()   and goOperand(). Recall that onClick events
               were established in the layout.

Line 32:   The operand key, activated by the user, can be identified by its
               android:contentDescription property.

```
MyActivity.java
 1   package com.cornez.calculator;
 2
 3   import android.app.Activity;
 4   import android.os.Bundle;
 5   import android.view.Menu;
 6   import android.view.MenuItem;
 7   import android.view.View;
 8   import android.widget.TextView;
 9
10
11   public class MyActivity extends Activity {
12
13       private TextView mNumberDisplay;
14       private SimpleExpression mExpression;
15
16       @Override
17       protected void onCreate(Bundle savedInstanceState) {
18           super.onCreate(savedInstanceState);
19           setContentView(R.layout.activity_my);
20           mNumberDisplay = (TextView) findViewById(R.id.textView1);
21
22           mExpression = new SimpleExpression();
23       }
24
25       public void goAC (View view){
26           mExpression.clearOperands();
27           mNumberDisplay.setText("0");
28       }
29
30       public void goOperand (View view) {
31           String val = (String) mNumberDisplay.getText();
32           String digit = (String) view.getContentDescription();
33           if (val.charAt(0) == '0')
34               mNumberDisplay.setText(digit);
35           else
36               mNumberDisplay.setText((String) mNumberDisplay.getText()
37                       + digit.charAt(0));
38       }
```

Lines 25–38:   The handler for the onClick listener event goOperator() is
               implemented.

Lines 41–49:   Once the user touches an operator key, the first operand of the expression is set to the integer value found in the display component of the calculator. A `try`/`catch` statement is used to ensure the user has correctly entered integers.

Line 44:   Recall that the method `parseInt()`, from the wrapper class `Integer`, is used to parse a string as a signed decimal integer value.

Lines 55–65:   The handler for the `onClick` listener event `goCompute()` is implemented. This handler is triggered when the user taps the "=" button. The value for the existing expression is computed and displayed. A `try`/`catch` statement is used to ensure the expression is valid.

```
MyActivity.java  Continued
39  public void goOperator (View view) {
40       String operator = (String) view.getContentDescription();
41       try {
42           String val = (String) mNumberDisplay.getText();
43           mExpression.setOperand1((int)
44               Integer.parseInt(val.toString()));
45       }
46       catch (NumberFormatException e){
47           mExpression.setOperand1(0);
48       }
49       mNumberDisplay.setText("0");
50       mExpression.setOperator(operator);
51  }
52
53
54       //WHEN THE = BUTTON IS CLICKED, COMPUTE AND DISPLAY THE VALUE
55       public void goCompute (View view){
56           try {
57               String val = (String) mNumberDisplay.getText();
58               mExpression.setOperand2((int)
59                   Integer.parseInt(val.toString()));
60           }
61           catch (NumberFormatException e){
62               mExpression.setOperand2(0);
63           }
64           mNumberDisplay.setText(mExpression.getValue().toString());
65       }
66
67
68       @Override
69       public boolean onCreateOptionsMenu(Menu menu) {
70           // Inflate the menu
71           getMenuInflater().inflate(R.menu.my, menu);
```

```
72          return true;
73      }
74
75      @Override
76      public boolean onOptionsItemSelected(MenuItem item) {
77          // Handle action bar item clicks here. The action bar will
78          // automatically handle clicks on the Home/Up button, so long
79          // as you specify a parent activity in AndroidManifest.xml.
80          int id = item.getItemId();
81          if (id == R.id.action_settings) {
82              return true;
83          }
84          return super.onOptionsItemSelected(item);
85      }
86  }
```

■ 2.11 Container Views

Container Views are simply `ViewGroups`, which are `Views`. Figure 2-40 shows a collection of Containers. Android categorizes this group of Views as "containers" because its sole function is to act as containers for other views. Any object that provides access to container values is referred to as a Container.

▢ **Containers**

  ▨ RadioGroup   ▤ ListView

  ▦ GridView   ▥ ExpandableListView

  ↕ ScrollView   ↔ HorizontalScrollView

  🔍 SearchView   ▶ VideoView

❙ **FIGURE 2-40** `ViewGroup` Containers.

Once a container is created, it can be queried for values. The method for accessing values from a container will depend on the type of container being used. Typically containers are used with `Adapters`, which map data to a `View`. `Adapters` are explored in more detail in the next section of the chapter, as well as in subsequent chapters. For now, it is easiest to think of an `Adapter` as an object that acts as a bridge between the container and the data items with which it will be populated. The container `Views` that are used with `Adapters` are subclasses of the `AdapterView` class.

When the content of an application is dynamic or not predetermined, an `Adapter` is used to populate the layout with `Views` at runtime. Containers and `Adapters` provide the mechanism for grouping elements and presenting content in a more intuitive and device-sensitive manner.

2.11.1 `ListView`, `GridView`, and `ExpandableListView`

The `ListView`, `GridView`, and `ExpandableListView` are all `Adapter-Views`. This means they are populated with `Views` that are identified by an `Adapter`.

A `ListView` object displays items in a vertically scrolling list. The list items are automatically inserted into the list using an `Adapter` that pulls content from a source, such as an array or database query, and converts each item result into a view that's placed into the list.

A `GridView` object is similar to a `ListView`, except that displays contain items in a two-dimensional scrolling grid. The items in the grid are inserted using an `Adapter`.

A `ExpandableListView` is an extension of a `ListView`. This type of container displays items in a vertically scrolling list that supports two levels. For example, the top level contains a group of items that can be individually expanded to show its child `Views`.

2.11.2 `ScrollView` and `HorizontalScrollView`

The `ScrollView` and the `HorizontalScrollView` are containers specifically designed to support scrolling by the user. `ScrollView` supports only vertical scrolling, and `HorizontalScrollView` should always be used for horizontal scrolling.

Both of these containers are extensions of the `FrameLayout`, which means they should contain a single `View`. Once a `View` has been placed in either of these containers, the view can be made scrollable. For example, a `LinearLayout` that contains a large number of items can be inserted into a `ScrollView` that the user can scroll through when the list is larger than the physical display.

Optimization should be considered when using containers that scroll. For example, it is not advisable to use a `ScrollView` with a `ListView`, because `ListView` already supports scrolling. Most important, doing this defeats optimizations found in `ListView` when dealing with large lists.

2.11.3 `SearchView`

The `SearchView` is one of the most useful UI controls to be introduced into the Android framework. This `View`, which we regarded as more of a widget than a container, is typically added to the menu and provides an easy way to incorporate a standard search into the header of any activity.

It should be pointed out that by default, the Android system controls all search events. When the user submits a query, the system delivers the query to the activity that you specify to handle searches. This system default can be overridden with various callback methods and listeners.

A `SearchView` object can be placed anywhere in your layout and will function like a standard `EditText` `View`.

2.11.4 `VideoView`

A `VideoView` is an extension of a `SurfaceView`, which will be discussed in Chapter 6. More simply stated, this container is used to display a video file. It is designed as an implementation of Android's `MediaController.MediaPlayerControl` class. This means that it can load images from various sources (such as resources or content providers), and it provides various display options, such as scaling and tinting.

2.12 Using an Adapter

In Android, an `Adapter` provides a common interface to the data model behind an `AdapterView`, such as a `ListView` object. An `Adapter` is the control that is responsible for accessing the data to be supplied to a container widget and converting the individual elements of data into a specific `View` to be added to and displayed inside the `AdapterView`.

The `Adapter` behaves as a middleman between the data source and the `AdapterView` layout. The `Adapter` retrieves the data (from a source such as an array or a database query) and converts each entry into a `View` that can be added into the `AdapterView`.

It is typical to populate an `AdapterView` by binding it to an `Adapter`. The following code segment illustrates this process. The `ListView` named `mListView` is referenced from the layout XML file. The method `setAdapter()` is called on `mListView` to bind the data.

```
1   ListView mListView;
2   mListView = (ListView) findViewById(R.id.listview);
3   mListView.setAdapter(adapter);
```

Android provides several subclasses of `Adapters` that are useful for retrieving different kinds of data and building views for an `AdapterView`. A common `Adapter` is the `ArrayAdapter`.

`ArrayAdapter` is used when the data source is an array. By default, an `ArrayAdapter` creates a view for each array item by calling `toString()` on each item and placing the contents in a `TextView`.

For example, if an array of strings needs to be displayed in a `ListView`, a new `ArrayAdapter` can be initialized using a constructor to specify the layout for each string and the string array.

Consider the code segment below.

Line 1:   A data source is constructed as an `ArrayList` that contains an array of contact elements.

Line 3:   An `ArrayAdapter is` created that will convert the array of contacts into `Views` on a layout.

Lines 5–6: The `ArrayAdapter` is attached to the `ListView` named `mListView`.

```
1   ArrayList<Contact> arrayOfContacts = new ArrayList<Contact>();
2
3   ArrayAdapter mArrayAdapter = new ArrayAdapter(this, arrayOfContacts);
4
5   ListView mListView = (ListView) findViewById(R.id. listView);
6   mListView.setAdapter(mArrayAdapter);
```

■ Lab Example 2-5: Renaissance Paintings App

A common design in mobile applications is a scrollable list of items, such as text elements and images. This design pattern can be constructed using a `ViewGroup` populated with elements. The `ViewGroup` can then be made scrollable by storing it in a `ScrollView`. The Renaissance Paintings App, seen in Figure 2-41, uses a `HorizontalScrollView` to achieve a scrollable list of paintings by Renaissance artists.

Part 1: Design

The user is presented with a scrollable gallery of paintings from the Renaissance period, which can revolve horizontally with a simple swipe of a finger. Each of the paintings in the gallery is touch-sensitive. When the user touches a specific painting within the scrollable gallery, information about that painting appears for a brief moment in the form of a Toast.

A `HorizontalScrollView` has been chosen for this design because, not only is it a `Scrollview`, but it also uses a horizontal orientation. `ScrollViews` and `HorizontalScrollViews` can be used on an entire screen in which all elements can be scrolled up or down. It can also be used on smaller segments of the screen, allowing intended static screen elements to remain stable while the container elements scroll. In this design, we will use a stable title with the `HorizontalScrollView` positioned below it.

A `HorizontalScrollView` is used to hold a `LinearLayout` containing a gallery of paintings.

Each painting is touch-sensitive and will produce a Toast "popup" when tapped.

❙ FIGURE 2-41 The Renaissance Paintings App contains clickable paintings that scroll horizontally.

Part 2: Application Structure and Setup

The settings for the application are as follows:

- Application Name: Renaissance Paintings
- Project Name: RenaissancePaintings
- Package Name: com.cornez.renaissancepaintings
- Android Form: Phone and Tablet
- Minimum SDK: API 18: Android 4.3 (Jelly Bean)
- Target SDK: API 21: Android 5.0 (Lollipop)
- Compile with: API 21: Android 5.0 (Lollipop)
- Activity Name: `MyActivity`
- Layout Name: `activity_my`

The launcher is set to the Android default `ic_launcher.png` file. The drawables, in res directory, contain a sample of six Renaissance paintings. In addition to the paintings, two decorative graphics have been added to provide interest to the application: a textured background graphic and a graphic for the application title. The final project structure for the completed app appears in Figure 2-42.

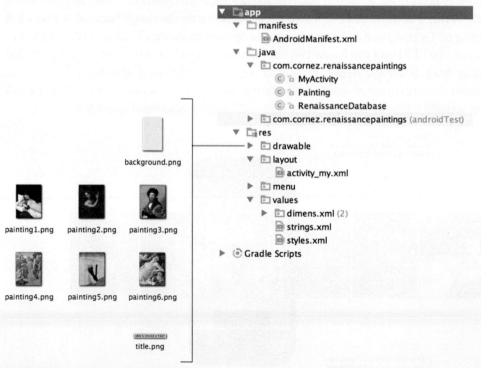

I FIGURE 2-42 Project Structure for the Renaissance application.

The `AndroidManifest.xml` file will set the `screenOrientation` so that it will be fixed in portrait mode, Line 12.

```
AndroidManifest.xml
1   <?xml version="1.0" encoding="utf-8"?>
2   <manifest xmlns:android="http://schemas.android.com/apk/res/android"
3       package="com.cornez.renaissancepaintings" >
4
5       <application
6           android:allowBackup="true"
7           android:icon="@drawable/ic_launcher"
8           android:label="@string/app_name"
9           android:theme="@style/AppTheme" >
10          <activity
11              android:name=".MyActivity"
12              android:screenOrientation="portrait"
13              android:label="@string/app_name" >
14              <intent-filter>
15                  <action android:name="android.intent.action.MAIN" />
16                  <category
17                      android:name="android.intent.category.LAUNCHER" />
18              </intent-filter>
19          </activity>
20      </application>
21
22  </manifest>
```

Part 3: External Value Resources

The style of the app is set within `styles.xml`. The default setting, `Holo.Light.DarkActionBar`, has been eliminated.

Line 6:   The new `Theme` for the application does not specify `Holo`, `Light`, or `Dark`. The result will be a black screen. This provides a nice canvas in which to place a gallery of paintings.

```
styles.xml
1   <resources>
2
3       <!-- Base application theme. -->
4       <style
5           name="AppTheme"
6           parent="android:Theme.NoTitleBar.Fullscreen">
7       </style>
8
9   </resources>
```

Part 4: The User Interface Layout XML File

`activity_my.xml` is the layout file that this application uses. It will serve as the user interface file associated with `MyActivity`. As shown in Figure 2-43, the root element is a `RelativeLayout` containing two `View` objects: an `ImageView` and a `HorizontalScrollView`.

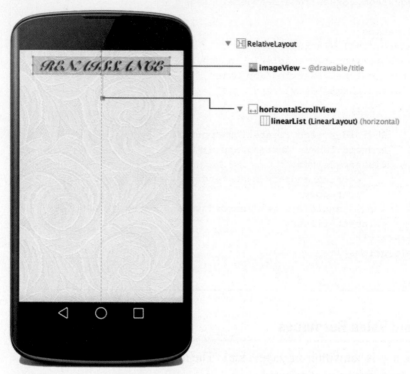

FIGURE 2-43 The layout structure for `activity_my.xml`.

Line 6:   The background of the root element is set to display the textured background graphic.

Lines 7–10: Padding is added to provide a buffer to make the screen more readable, as well as to improve the look of the application.

Line 13–20: The `ImageView` to display a static title is defined.

Line 19:   Content description for the title image is provided.

Note:

Android Studio will display a warning to ensure that image `Views` provide a `contentDescription`.

The `contentDescription` defines text that briefly describes content of the `View`. This property is used primarily for accessibility. Because some views do not have textual representation, this attribute can be used for providing such representation.

Nontextual widgets like `ImageViews` and `ImageButtons` should use the `contentDescription` attribute to specify a textual description of the widget such that screen readers and other accessibility tools can adequately describe the user interface. Many Android users have disabilities that require them to interact with their Android devices in different ways. These include users who have visual, physical, or age-related disabilities that prevent them from fully seeing or using a touchscreen. Android provides accessibility features and services for helping these users navigate their devices more easily, including text-to-speech features that augment their experience. Android application developers can take advantage of these services to make their applications more accessible by adding descriptive text to user interface controls. These descriptions are applied to the `android:contentDescription` attribute for widgets, such as `ImageView`, `ImageButtons`, and `CheckBoxes`.

```
activity_my.xml
1   <RelativeLayout
2   xmlns:android="http://schemas.android.com/apk/res/android"
3       xmlns:tools="http://schemas.android.com/tools"
4       android:layout_width="fill_parent"
5       android:layout_height="match_parent"
6       android:background="@drawable/background"
7       android:paddingBottom="@dimen/activity_vertical_margin"
8       android:paddingLeft="@dimen/activity_horizontal_margin"
9       android:paddingRight="@dimen/activity_horizontal_margin"
10      android:paddingTop="@dimen/activity_vertical_margin"
11      tools:context=".MyActivity">
12
13      <ImageView
14          android:id="@+id/imageView"
15          android:layout_width="wrap_content"
16          android:layout_height="wrap_content"
17          android:layout_alignParentTop="true"
18          android:layout_centerHorizontal="true"
19          android:contentDescription="@string/app_name"
20          android:src="@drawable/title" />
```

Line 21:   A `HorizontalScrollView` is defined as the Layout container that will supply scrollability to the `View` it contains.

Lines 29–34:   A `LinearLayout` is added to the `HorizontalScrollView`. This layout will hold the Renaissance paintings.

Line 33:   The orientation of both the `LinearLayout` and the `Scroll-View` will be in horizontal mode.

```
activity_my.xml   Continued
21  <HorizontalScrollView
22          android:id="@+id/horizontalScrollView"
23          android:layout_width="wrap_content"
24          android:layout_height="wrap_content"
25          android:layout_below="@+id/imageView"
26          android:layout_centerHorizontal="true"
27          android:layout_marginTop="51dp">
28
29          <LinearLayout
30              android:id="@+id/linearLayout"
31              android:layout_width="wrap_content"
32              android:layout_height="fill_parent"
33              android:orientation="horizontal">
34          </LinearLayout>
35      </HorizontalScrollView>
36  </RelativeLayout>
```

Part 5: Source Code for Application

Each of the paintings in the gallery has information that the user will see after tapping his or her finger on a specific painting. The data source for this information is the Java file `RenaissanceDatabase`.

Lines 5–11:   The array named `description` will hold a collection of strings that provide all textual information about each painting. This includes:

Name of the painting

Artist

Year

Lines 13–20:   The painting images, stored in the `Drawable` folder, have each been assigned unique integer identifications, which are stored in `R.java`. These id values are placed in the array named `id`. This array will be used for painting identification purposes, establishing which painting the user has selected.

```
RenaissanceDatabase.java
1   package com.cornez.renaissancepaintings;
2
3   public class RenaissanceDatabase {
4
5       public static String description[] = {
6               "Venus of Urbino\nTitan, 1538",
7               "St. John the Baptist\nLeonardo da Vinci, 1516",
```

```
8              "Protrait of Baldassare Castiglione\nRaphael, 1515",
9              "The Entombent of Christ\nCaravaqqio, 1603",
10             "Coronation of the Virgin\nFra Angelico, 1435",
11             "Mars and Venus\n Sandro Bottcelli, 1483"};
12
13      public static int id[] = {
14             R.drawable.painting1, // VENUS OF URBINO
15             R.drawable.painting2, // ST.JOHN BAPTIST
16             R.drawable.painting3, // BALDASSARE
17             R.drawable.painting4, // ENTOMBENT OF CHRIST
18             R.drawable.painting5, // CORONOATION
19             R.drawable.painting6  // MARS AND VENUS
20      };
21  }
```

Each of the paintings in the gallery is a member of the Painting class. The data for this class specify the painting description and its unique drawable identification from the generated R.java file.

Painting.java
```
1   package com.cornez.renaissancepaintings;
2
3   /**
4    * Data Model for a single painting
5    */
6   public class Painting {
7
8       private String mDescription;
9       private int mId;   //DRAWABLE IDENTIFICATION
10
11      public Painting (String description, int id){
12          mDescription = description;
13          mId = id;
14      }
15
16      public String getDescription() {
17          return mDescription;
18      }
19      public void setDescription(String description){
20          mDescription = description;
21      }
22
23      public int getId() {
24          return mId;
25      }
26      public void setId(int id){
27          mId = id;
28      }
29
30  }
```

MyActivity.java is launched when the application launches. This java source file drives the application.

Lines 3–10:   Notice that a HorizontalScrollView import is not required for the app. This is because AdapterView is being used solely as an invisible container to provide scrollability to the LinearLayout.

Line 10:   A Toast object is a View object. Since we are creating and displaying Toasts continually as the user taps paintings, this class must be imported into the project.

Line 16:   mLinearLayout serves as the gallery of paintings. mLinearLayout is defined here and referenced on line 25 so that Renaissance paintings can be added to it later.

Lines 32–61: The LinearLayout is populated with all the paintings from the Renaissance database.

Lines 36–41: Each of the paintings is constructed as an ImageButton. The instruction getResources() is used to return a resource instance.

Line 51:   The setContentDescription () method has been called to populate all ImageButton items with relevant painting information. This will allow a future Toast method to access the painting information and display it to the user.

Line 59:   The setOnClickListener event is applied to all constructed ImageButtons.

Line 62:   The ImageButton item is added to the LinearLayout.

```
MyActivity.java
1   package com.cornez.renaissancepaintings;
2
3   import android.app.Activity;
4   import android.os.Bundle;
5   import android.view.Menu;
6   import android.view.MenuItem;
7   import android.view.View;
8   import android.widget.ImageButton;
9   import android.widget.LinearLayout;
10  import android.widget.Toast;
11
12
13  public class MyActivity extends Activity {
14
15      //GALLERY OF PAINTINGS
16      private LinearLayout mLinearLayout;
17
18
```

```
19      @Override
20      protected void onCreate(Bundle savedInstanceState) {
21          super.onCreate(savedInstanceState);
22          setContentView(R.layout.activity_my);
23
24          //REFERENCE THE SCROLLABLE LAYOUT STRUCTURE IN MAIN_SCREEN.XML
25          mLinearLayout = (LinearLayout) findViewById(R.id.linearList);
26
27          //FILL THE SCROLLABLE LAYOUT STRUCTURE WITH PAINTINGS
28          fillPaintingGallery();
29
30      }
31
32      private void fillPaintingGallery () {
33
34          // POPULATE THE LINEARLAYOUT GALLERY
35          // WITH PAINTINGS AND DESCRIPTIONS
36          ImageButton buttonItem;
37
38          for (int i - 0; i < RenaissanceDatabase.description.length;
39              i++) {
40              //STORE THE INDIVIDUAL PAINTINGS AS BUTTONS
41              buttonItem = new ImageButton(this);
42
43
44              Painting painting = new
45                  Painting(RenaissanceDatabase.description[i],
46                  RenaissanceDatabase.id[i]);
47
48              //USE THE CONTENT DESCRIPTION PROPERTY TO STORE
49              //PAINTING DATA
50
51              buttonItem.setContentDescription(painting.getDescription());
52
53              //LOAD THE PAINTING USING ITS UNIQUE ID
54
55              buttonItem.setImageDrawable(getResources().getDrawable(
56                  painting.getId())));
57
58              //SET AN ONCLICK LISTENER FOR THE IMAGE BUTTON
59              buttonItem.setOnClickListener(displayPaintingInformation);
60
61              //ADD THE IMAGE BUTTON TO THE SCROLLABLE LINEAR LIST
62              mLinearLayout.addView(buttonItem);
63          }
64      }
```

Lines 65–75:   The anonymous inner class for a generic `OnClickListener` is defined. The `View` parameter from the `OnClick(View btn)` callback is used to assign the painting description.

Lines 77–82:   A `Toast` contains a quick little message display to the user. When the user sees the `View`, it appears as a floating view over the application. The user will never focus on it; the idea of a `Toast` is to be as unobtrusive as possible. `Toast` will be featured in more lab examples later in the book. The method `makeText ()` requires three parameters: the context, the string to be displayed, and the length of time the `Toast` will appear to the user. The `show ()` method performs the actual display of the `Toast`.

`MyActivity.java` *Continued*

```
65   private View.OnClickListener displayPaintingInformation =
66          new View.OnClickListener() {
67          public void onClick(View btn) {
68              // COLLECT THE INFORMATION STORED ABOUT THE PAINTING
69              String paintingDescription = (String)
70          btn.getContentDescription();
71
72              // MAKE A METHOD CALL TO DISPLAY THE INFORMATION
73              displayToast(paintingDescription);
74          }
75      };
76
77      private void displayToast(String paintingDescription) {
78          // SHOW THE INFORMATION ABOUT THE PAINTING AS
79          // A TOAST WITH A SHORT DISPLAY LIFE
80          Toast.makeText(this, paintingDescription,
81          Toast.LENGTH_SHORT).show();
82      }
83
84
85      @Override
86      public boolean onCreateOptionsMenu(Menu menu) {
87          // Inflate the menu;
88          getMenuInflater().inflate(R.menu.my, menu);
89          return true;
90      }
91
92      @Override
93      public boolean onOptionsItemSelected(MenuItem item) {
94          // Handle action bar item clicks here. The action bar will
95          // automatically handle clicks on the Home/Up button, so long
96          // as you specify a parent activity in AndroidManifest.xml.
97          int id = item.getItemId();
```

```
98          if (id == R.id.action_settings) {
99              return true;
100         }
101         return super.onOptionsItemSelected(item);
102     }
103 }
```

■ EXERCISES

2.1 Name the six standard root layouts provided by Android. Briefly describe each of them.

2.2 Explain the main difference between a `TableLayout` and a `GridLayout`.

2.3 Name three alignment attributes used with `RelativeLayout`.

2.4 Draw the interface produced by the following layout XML code:

```
1   <?xml version="1.0" encoding="utf-8"?>
2   <GridLayout xmlns:android="http://schemas.android.com/apk/res/android"
3       android:layout_width="match_parent"
4       android:layout_height="match_parent"
5       android:columnCount="2"
6       android:orientation="horizontal"
7       android:rowCount="2">
8
9       <TextView
10          android:text="Apple" />
11
12      <TextView
13          android:text="Cherry" />
14
15      <TextView
16          android:text="Banana" />
17
18      <TextView
19          android:text="Peach" />
20
21  </GridLayout>
```

2.5 Explain the importance of the Android's `View` class.

2.6 Describe the similarities between a `TextView` and an `EditText`. Describe the differences between the two.

2.7 Name three `InputType` values that can be used with an `EditText`.

2.8 Describe the input expectation and the soft keyboard configurations produced by the following XML code:

```
1  <?xml version="1.0" encoding="utf-8"?>
2  <LinearLayout xmlns:android="http://schemas.android.com/apk/res/android"
3      android:orientation="vertical"
4      android:layout_width="match_parent"
5      android:layout_height="match_parent">
6
7      <EditText
8          android:layout_width="match_parent"
9          android:layout_height="wrap_content"
10         android:id="@+id/editText1"
11         android:inputType="textCapWords|textPersonName" />
12
13     <EditText
14         android:id="@+id/editText2"
15         android:layout_width="fill_parent"
16         android:layout_height="wrap_content"
17         android:inputType="textEmailAddress|textAutoComplete" />
18
19     <EditText
20         android:id="@+id/editText3"
21         android:layout_width="fill_parent"
22         android:layout_height="wrap_content"
23         android:inputType="textPostalAddress " />
24
25
26  </LinearLayout>
```

2.9 Name the built-in user interface widgets provided by Android. Briefly explain the use of each one.

2.10 What is the difference between a `ToggleButton` and a `Switch`?

2.11 What is the purpose of the `R.java` file? Briefly explain its construction.

2.12 What is the difference between a `ViewGroup` and a `View`?

2.13 Briefly explain the concept of Adaptive Design.

2.14 Explain how `Adapters` are used with `ViewGroups`.

3 | Activities and Intents

Chapter Objectives

In this chapter you will:

- Explore an `Activity`'s lifecycle.
- Learn about saving and restoring an `Activity`.
- Understand `Intents` and how they are used with multiple `Activities`.
- Become familiar with passing data between `Activities`.
- Implement applications that require basic animation `Activity` transitions.
- Study Scene transitions.

■ 3.1 Activity Lifecycle

All Android applications comprise at least one `Activity` class. In most cases, applications will require the use of several activities. Consider a chess game application that allows opponents to play a game and chat during the game. Such an application, as shown in Figure 3-1, might utilize one activity for chess play and a separate activity for reading and sending chat messages. During chess play, a player might be notified of sent messages from an opponent, which informally connects these two activities. Although the activities may work together to form a complete user experience, each one is independent of the other. The application can start and end any one of its activities.

Activities in an application are often loosely connected to each other. Information can be passed from one activity to another, but the activities remain distinct and separate in every other way.

Every application has one activity class that serves as the main activity, which is presented to the user when the application is launched for the first time. For example, in a banking application, users must first log into their accounts before they are given access to their account information and app tools, such as paying bills and transferring money. Each activity can then start another activity in order to perform different actions. Each time a new activity starts, the previous activity is paused and the Android system preserves its status.

FIGURE 3-1 A Chess Game App Showing Two Activities: Game Play and Chatting.

Activities must be declared in the `AndroidManifest.xml` file in order to be accessible to the system. As illustrated in the following `AndroidManifest.xml` code, `Activities` are defined using the `<activity>` tag. An `<activity>` must be added as a child to the `<application>` element. The XML code in the following example defines an application constructed with four activities, all declared within the opening and closing `<application>` tag.

Lines 3–11:   The main activity of the application is defined.

Line 5:   The first activity defined in the `AndroidManifest` file is named `MyActivity`. This statement specifies that the activity implementation will be the Java source file `MyActivity.java`.

Line 7:   The action intent of this activity, referred to by the constant `android.intent.action.MAIN`, designates the activity as the main entry point for the application.

Lines 8–9:   The category of the main activity is specified as the top-level launcher.

Lines 14–32:   Three child activities within the application are defined: `GameActivity`, `ChatActivity`, and
`GameOptionsActivity`. Each one of these `Activities`
is implemented as a Java source file. It is customary for
`Activity` classes to end with the string `Activity`. Note that
the parent `Activity` for all three of these activities is specified
as the top-level launcher, `MyActivity`.

```
AndroidManifest.xml
1   <application>
2
3   <!-- MAIN ACTIVITY -->
4   <activity
5               android:name=".MyActivity" >
6   <intent-filter>
7   <action android:name="android.intent.action.MAIN" />
8   <category
9   android:name="android.intent.category.LAUNCHER" />
10  </intent-filter>
11  </activity>
12
13
14  <!—CHESS GAME ACTIVITY -->
15  <activity
16              android:name=".GameActivity"
17              android:parentActivityName=".MyActivity " >
18  </activity>
19
20
21  <!-- CHAT ACTIVITY -->
22  <activity
23              android:name=".ChatActivity"
24              android:parentActivityName=".MyActivity " >
25  </activity>
26
27
28  <!— SET CHESS GAME OPTIONS ACTIVITY -->
29  <activity
30              android:name=".GameOptionsActivity"
31              android:parentActivityName=".MyActivity " >
32  </activity>
33
34  </application>
35
36  </manifest>
```

The activities in an application are implemented as a subclass of `Activity`. The `Activity` class is an important part of every application's overall lifecycle. The manner in which activities are launched and created is a fundamental part of the platform's application model.

When an application is first loaded, its main activity, specified within the `AndroidManifest`, is immediately created. Once the main activity is started, it is given a window in which to draw its layout. Its layout is its associated user interface screen.

A main activity of the application can start another activity in order to perform different actions. Each activity can start another activity. An `Activity` stack manages the `Activities` in an application. When a new activity is started, it is pushed onto the top of the stack and becomes the running activity.

When an activity is running, it takes user focus. The previous activity remains just below the running activity in the stack, using the Last-In, First-Out mechanism. The previous activity will not come to the foreground again until the top activity above it exits. Each time a new activity starts, the previous activity is stopped and preserved in the stack.

Each activity in an Android application goes through its own lifecycle, illustrated in Figure 3-2. It relies on the implementation of a series of callback methods that the system calls when the activity transitions between various stages of its lifecycle.

The `Activity` class defines the following seven callback methods, beginning with the creation of the `Activity` and ending with its destruction:

1. `onCreate()`
2. `onStart()`
3. `onResume()`
4. `onPause()`
5. `onStop()`
6. `onRestart()`
7. `onDestroy()`

As shown in Figure 3-2, `onCreate ()` is automatically called when an activity is first created. The `onDestroy ()` callback is called when a running activity exits and needs to be destroyed by the system.

The `onCreate ()` method can be used to initialize the activity, such as inflating the layout for the user interface of the activity.

Line 3:   An activity can inflate its user interface layout by calling `setContentView()`.

Line 4:   The user interface controls used in an activity are defined by the specific layout associated with the running activity.

```
1    protected void onCreate(Bundle savedInstanceState) {
2            super.onCreate(savedInstanceState);
3            setContentView(R.layout.activity_my);
4            (TextView) myTextView = (TextView) findViewById
5                                 (R.id.textView);
6
7        }
```

When an activity has been created and becomes visible to the user, the onStart () callback method is called. For the user to begin interacting with the application activity, onResume() is called. Both the onStart() and onResume () callback methods are performed in sequence automatically after onCreate(). Actions such as transition animations, and access to required devices, such as the camera, are often initiated within the onResume() method.

When an activity has been paused because a previous activity was resumed, the onPause() callback method is called. A paused state is the first indication that the user is exiting the activity. A paused activity does not receive user input and cannot execute any code. onPause() is called as part of the activity lifecycle when an activity is going into the background, but it has not been destroyed.

The onPause() callback is most often used for saving a persistent state the activity might be editing. This is useful for presenting an edit-in-place model to the user. An edit-in-place model means maintaining the state so that nothing will be lost, even in the event that not enough resources are available when starting a new activity. onPause() is a good place to stop actions that consume a noticeable amount of CPU in order to make the switch to the next activity as fast as possible. It is also used to close resources that require exclusive access, such as the camera. Once an activity has been paused and a new activity comes into focus, the onStop() method is called.

Android devices have a limited amount of memory. In some situations, the system may require more memory while an application is currently running. In this circumstance, which is not uncommon, the system may kill processes that are on pause in order to reclaim resources. As a precaution, it is useful to design activities to save their current state using onSaveInstanceState(Bundle). For example, if an activity has been shut down, its current state can be stored in a Bundle object. Once the activity is re-initialized after being previously shut down, the Bundle object can be used to resupply the activity with its most recent data. Issues concerning the onSaveInstanceState() method are discussed further in the next section.

If an activity has not been destroyed, it can be restarted once it has been stopped or paused. For example, when the user navigates back to an activity that has been stopped, the activity can be started again by the callback method onRestart() and followed by onStart(). The paused activity can resume interactions using the callback onResume().

If a paused or stopped activity requires destruction due to a system need for more memory, the activity must be recreated. This can be done by calling onCreate().

onStart() should always be called after onRestart(). onRestart() is triggered when an activity has been stopped and then restarted when the user navigates back to the activity.

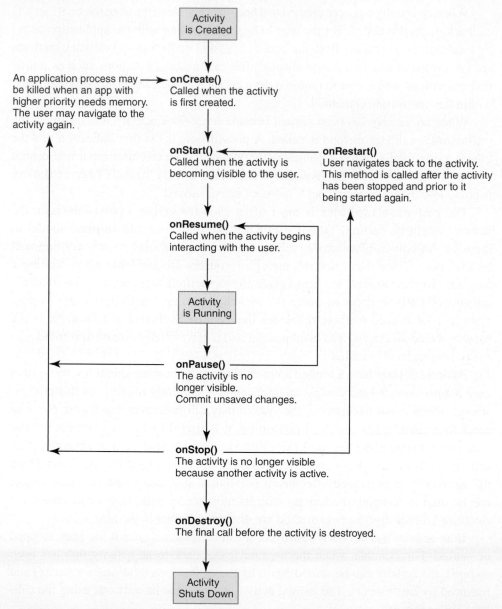

FIGURE 3-2 Activity Lifecycle.

onStop() is called when the activity is no longer visible to the user. The next callbacks in the sequence are usually onRestart() and onDestroy().

onDestroy() performs final cleanup prior to an activity's destruction. OnDestroy() can be triggered in two ways: (1) when the app has ended the activity naturally, and (2) when the system is temporarily destroying this instance of the activity to save space.

When an activity is destroyed, it is always prudent to ensure that it is not leaving unintended resources behind. Remaining activity resources can sometimes cause unexpected interruptions, thereby creating a poor user experience. When an activity is done and needs to be closed, the method finish() can be called. This is usually performed in onDestroy() to free resources, such as Threads, that are linked to the activity.

■ 3.2 Starting, Saving, and Restoring an Activity

When an activity is paused or stopped, the state of the activity is retained. This means that an Activity object is still held in memory, along with all of its information about its data objects. This makes a good user experience. For example, any changes the user has made within the activity will be retained so that when the activity returns to the foreground and resumes running, the user will see the changes intact.

When the system destroys an activity in order to recover memory, the memory for that activity object is also destroyed. This can be a problem because once this memory has been erased, the system cannot simply resume the activity with its state intact.

To safeguard important information about the activity, the state can be preserved by calling the onSaveInstanceState() callback method. This method allows the system to recreate the Activity object so the user can navigate back to an intact Activity state. The system issues a call to onSaveInstanceState() before making the activity vulnerable to destruction.

A Bundle is a container for the activity state information that can be saved. More specifically, a Bundle can save state information about the activity using name-value pairs. A collection of put methods can be used to insert data into the Bundle. The following is an incomplete list of these methods:

putChar()

putString()

putBoolean()

putByte()

putFloat()

putLong()

putShort()

putParcelable() (used for objects that implement Parcelable)

If the system needs to kill an application process and the user navigates back to the activity that was destroyed, the system recreates the activity and passes the `Bundle` to both `onCreate()` and `onRestoreInstanceState()`. Using either of these methods, we can extract a saved state from the `Bundle` and restore the activity state. If there is no state information to restore, the `Bundle` will contain a null value indicating that the activity is being created for the first time.

Consider the Chess Game application described at the beginning of this chapter. A good user experience may require the app to keep track of the user's playing level. The player's level may be defined as an integer from 1 through 10, where 1 is a beginner level and 10 describes a most advanced player. The following segment of code illustrates how this information can be added to a `Bundle` object:

Line 1:   The `Bundle` object stores data in key-value pairs. This first line defines a key that represents the player's level.

Lines 4–8:   The implementation of `onSaveInstanceState()`.

Line 6:   The value in the key-value pair is `mPlayerLevel`.

Line 7:   The superclass is called to save the view hierarchy state.

```
1   static final String CHESS_LEVEL = "playerLevel";
2   private int mPlayerLevel;
3   ...
4   @Override
5   public void onSaveInstanceState(Bundle savedInstanceState) {
6       savedInstanceState.putInt(STATE_LEVEL, mPlayerLevel);
7       super.onSaveInstanceState(savedInstanceState);
8   }
```

When an activity is recreated after it was previously destroyed, you can recover the saved state from the `Bundle` that the system passes to the activity. Both the `onCreate()` and `onRestoreInstanceState()` callback methods receive the same `Bundle` object that contains the instance state information.

Because the `onCreate()` method is called whether the system is creating a new instance of your activity or recreating a previous one, you must check whether the activity's state (stored in the `Bundle` object) is null before you attempt to read it. If it is null, then the system is creating a new instance of the `Activity` class instead of restoring a previous one that was destroyed.

For example, here's how you can restore some state data in `onCreate ()`:

Line 3:   The `onCreate ()` superclass should always be called first.

Lines 4–8:   Before restoring values, check whether the activity is being launched for the first time, which is indicated when the value of `savedInstanceState` is `null`.

If `savedInstanceState` is not a `null` value, the activity was previously destroyed and is now being recreated.

Line 6:   Restore the value of `mPlayerLevel` from previously saved state.

```
1  @Override
2  protected void onCreate(Bundle savedInstanceState) {
3      super.onCreate(savedInstanceState);
4
5      if (savedInstanceState != null) {
6          mPlayerLevel = savedInstanceState.getInt(CHESS_LEVEL);
7      }
8  }
```

Device configurations can change during the execution of an application. For example, during runtime, the user may alter the screen orientation.

When a configuration change occurs, the system will automatically recreate the currently running activity by calling `onDestroy()`, and then immediately calling `onCreate()`. This behavior is designed to help your application adapt to new configurations by automatically reloading your application with alternative resources, such as adaptive layouts for different screen size and orientation.

Properly designed activities are able to handle a restart due to a screen orientation change and restore the activity state as described above. It is always a good idea to test an application's adaptability and resilience when dealing with unexpected events in an `Activity` lifecycle.

■ Lab Example 3-1: Activity Lifecycle Exploration Application

This lab is used for the purpose of exploring Android activities. The main objective of the app for this example is to experience callback methods firsthand. The app will allow you to perform four experiments that illustrate when callbacks occur for the following actions:

1. The system creation of an `Activity`

2. The system launching of an `Activity`

3. An `Activity` running in the foreground

4. An `Activity` paused by another `Activity` running in front of it

5. The `Activity` is no longer visible on the screen

6. An `Activity` is restarted

At the end of this lab, you will be given a set of experiments to try.

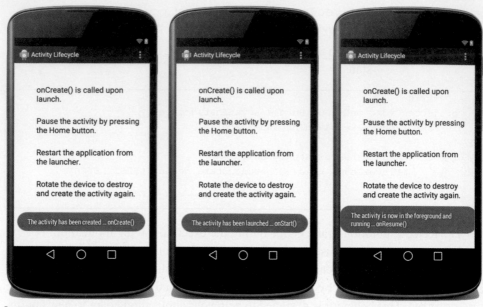

FIGURE 3-3 Activity lifecycle experiment application.

Part 1: Design Features

As an aid to understanding the `Activity` lifecycle and its callback methods, this application is designed as a basic logging tool for performing experiments on the `Activity`. As a logging tool, it will track callback events that happen as a set of tasks is performed. To indicate the state of the `Activity` and that certain `Activity` events have occurred, a descriptive message will appear in the form of a `Toast`. A `Toast` is particularly useful when performing the set of experiments on a physical device. However, `Toasts` cannot leave a trail of messages to scroll through and they can be slow when a series of messages needs to be displayed in rapid sequence. Therefore, in addition to `Toasts`, this application will also display messages to the `LogCat` using `Log.d`.

It is ideal to test this app using a real device. Several of the experiments can be done on an emulator, such as the one shown in Figure 3-3.

Part 2: Application Structure and Setup

The settings for the application are as follows:

- Application Name: Activity Lifecycle
- Project Name: ActivityLifecycle
- Package Name: `com.cornez.activitylifecycle`
- Android Form: Phone and Tablet
- Minimum SDK: API 18: Android 4.3 (Jelly Bean)

- Target SDK: API 21: Android 5.0 (Lollipop)
- Compile with: API 21: Android 5.0 (Lollipop)
- Activity Name: `MyActivity`
- Layout Name: `activity_my`

The launcher is set to the Android default `ic_launcher.png file`. The final structure for this app is shown in Figure 3-4. The three files that will be altered are:

1. `MyActivity.java`
2. `activity_my.xml`
3. `strings.xml`

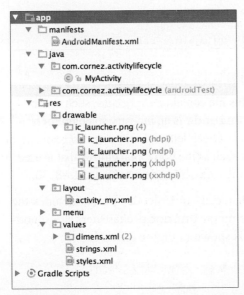

FIGURE 3-4 The project structure of `Activity` Lifecycle Explore application.

Part 3: External Value Resources

All the resource files in the application, with the exception of `strings.xml`, will be left unaltered and will contain their default build content. The `strings.xml` resource file will primarily be used as a message repository. It will store all possible strings pertaining to the actions and callback methods that occur during the lifecycle of the activity.

The first lines of XML code within `strings.xml` list the requisite application name and action settings. These should be left unaltered.

Lines 9–16:   Four experiments are designed to be used with this app. The results of each experiment will appear in a `TextView` in the activity's layout, `activity_my.xml`. The strings defined on these lines are the names of the experiments.

strings.xml

```
1  <?xml version="1.0" encoding="utf-8"?>
2  <resources>
3
4      <string name="app_name">Activity Lifecycle</string>
5      <string name="hello_world">Hello world!</string>
6      <string name="action_settings">Settings</string>
7
8      <!—THE LIST OF EXPERIMENTS -->
9      <string name="experiment1">onCreate() is called
10         upon launch.</string>
11     <string name="experiment2">Pause the activity by
12         pressing the Home button.</string>
13     <string name="experiment3">Restart the application
14         from the launcher.</string>
15     <string name="experiment4">Rotate the device to
16         destroy and create the activity again.</string>
```

Lines 17–29:   String description for all possible activity states.

Line 19:   Several of the strings in this file contain a Unicode, such as the one found on this line. A Unicode is an industry standard for representing characters, such as Greek letters, Latin extensions, or smiley faces. A text character such as the horizontal ellipsis that is used for this app is defined by the Unicode decimal value &#8230.

There are more than 100,000 graphic characters in Unicode, which includes the keyboard characters of many languages. Common Unicode characters are emoticons. The Unicode for a small set of these is shown in Figure 3-5.

😀   😁   😂

😃   😄   😅

FIGURE 3-5 Common Unicodes.

```
strings.xml    continued
17   <!-- MESSAGES DISPLAYED FOR ACTIVITY EVENTS -->
18   <string name="create_message">The activity has been
19          created  &#8230; onCreate()</string>
20   <string name="start_message">The activity has been
21          launched &#8230; onStart()</string>
22   <string name="resume_message">The activity is now
23          in the foreground and running &#8230; onResume()</string>
24   <string name="pause_message">Another activity is
25          in front of this activity &#8230; onPause()</string>
26   <string name="stop_message">The activity is no
27          longer visible on the screen &#8230; onStop()</string>
28   <string name="restart_message">The activity is
29          restarting after being stopped &#8230; onRestart()</string>
30
31   </resources>
```

❙ FIGURE 3-6 The layout for `Activity` Lifecycle Explorer app is blank with a `RelativeLayout` root.

Part 4: The User Interface

The screen layout for the application, defined by `activity_my.xml` and shown in Figure 3-6, uses a `RelativeLayout` root holding four `TextViews`. The `TextViews` contain the description of the activity experiments. A small amount of room is vacated at the bottom of the layout so that `Toasts` can appear without obscuring the visibility of other elements on the screen.

The XML code for this file appears as follows:

activity_my.xml

```
1   <RelativeLayout xmlns:android="http://schemas.android.com/apk/res/
2   android"
3       xmlns:tools="http://schemas.android.com/tools"
4       android:layout_width="match_parent"
5       android:layout_height="match_parent"
6       android:paddingLeft="@dimen/activity_horizontal_margin"
7       android:paddingRight="@dimen/activity_horizontal_margin"
8       android:paddingTop="@dimen/activity_vertical_margin"
9       android:paddingBottom="@dimen/activity_vertical_margin"
10      tools:context=".MyActivity">
11
12
13  <TextView
14          android:layout_width="wrap_content"
15          android:layout_height="wrap_content"
16          android:textAppearance="?android:attr/textAppearanceLarge"
17          android:text="@string/experiment1"
18          android:id="@+id/textView1"
19          android:layout_alignParentTop="true"
20          android:layout_alignParentStart="true"
21          android:layout_marginLeft="48dp"
22          android:layout_marginTop="48dp" />
23
24  <TextView
25          android:layout_width="wrap_content"
26          android:layout_height="wrap_content"
27          android:textAppearance="?android:attr/textAppearanceLarge"
28          android:text="@string/experiment2"
29          android:id="@+id/textView2"
30          android:layout_below="@+id/textView1"
31          android:layout_alignParentStart="true"
32          android:layout_marginLeft="48dp"
33          android:layout_marginTop="37dp" />
34
35      <TextView
36          android:layout_width="wrap_content"
37          android:layout_height="wrap_content"
38          android:textAppearance="?android:attr/textAppearanceLarge"
39          android:text="@string/experiment3"
40          android:id="@+id/textView3"
41          android:layout_below="@+id/textView2"
42          android:layout_alignParentStart="true"
43          android:layout_marginLeft="48dp"
44          android:layout_marginTop="37dp" />
45
46      <TextView
47          android:layout_width="wrap_content"
48          android:layout_height="wrap_content"
```

```
49              android:textAppearance="?android:attr/textAppearanceLarge"
50 android:text="@string/experiment4"
51              android:id="@+id/textView4"
52              android:layout_below="@+id/textView3"
53              android:layout_alignParentStart="true"
54              android:layout_marginLeft="48dp"
55              android:layout_marginTop="37dp" />
56
57 </RelativeLayout>
```

Part 5: Source Code for Application

The source code for this application is the `MyActivity` class.

Line 3:	The class begins with the required imports, including `Activity`, `Bundle`, and `Toast`.
Line 11:	As with all application activities, this class is modified to extend the abstract `Activity` class.
Lines 13–18:	Variables are declared to store preloaded experiment messages.
Lines 32–45:	Messages are preloaded into the appropriate string variables and will be displayed when a callback method occurs. Strings for these message variables are found in the `strings.xml` file.
Lines 27–28:	The first `Toast` and `Log.d` displays occur with the callback `onCreate` (). Note that the `onCreate` () method has been overridden.

```
MyActivity.java
1  package com.cornez.activitylifecycle;
2
3  import android.app.Activity;
4  import android.os.Bundle;
5  import android.util.Log;
6  import android.view.Menu;
7  import android.view.MenuItem;
8  import android.widget.Toast;
9
10
11 public class MyActivity extends Activity {
12
13     private String createMsg;
14     private String startMsg;
15     private String resumeMsg;
16     private String pauseMsg;
17     private String stopMsg;
18     private String restartMsg;
19
```

```
20      @Override
21      protected void onCreate(Bundle savedInstanceState) {
22          super.onCreate(savedInstanceState);
23          setContentView(R.layout.activity_my);
24
25          initializeMessages();
26
27          Toast.makeText(this, createMsg, Toast.LENGTH_LONG).show();
28          Log.d(msg, createMsg);
29
30      }
31
32      private void initializeMessages(){
33          createMsg = (String)
34              getResources().getText(R.string.create_message);
35          startMsg = (String)
36              getResources().getText(R.string.start_message);
37          resumeMsg = (String)
38              getResources().getText(R.string.resume_message);
39          pauseMsg = (String)
40              getResources().getText(R.string.pause_message);
41          stopMsg = (String)
42              getResources().getText(R.string.stop_message);
43          restartMsg = (String)
44              getResources().getText(R.string.restart_message);
45      }
```

Each of the Activity callback methods is overridden so that the appropriate Toast and Log.d can be displayed.

Line 48:   The superclass of the callback is called to perform its own explicit tasks.

Line 49:   An activity is displayed with a long delay.

MyActivity.java   continued

```
46      @Override
47      protected void onStart(){
48          super.onStart();
49          Toast.makeText(this, startMsg, Toast.LENGTH_LONG).show();
50          Log.d(msg, startMsg);
51
52      }
53      @Override
54      protected void onResume(){
55          super.onResume();
56          Toast.makeText(this, resumeMsg, Toast.LENGTH_LONG).show();
57          Log.d(msg, resumeMsg);
58      }
59
```

```
60      @Override
61      protected void onPause(){
62          super.onPause();
63          Toast.makeText(this, pauseMsg, Toast.LENGTH_LONG).show();
64          Log.d(msg, pauseMsg);
65      }
66
67      @Override
68      protected void onStop(){
69          super.onStop();
70          Toast.makeText(this, stopMsg, Toast.LENGTH_LONG).show();
71          Log.d(msg, stopMsg);
72      }
73
74      @Override
75      protected void onRestart(){
76          super.onRestart();
77          Toast.makeText(this, restartMsg, Toast.LENGTH_LONG).show();
78          Log.d(msg, restartMsg);
79      }
80
81
82      @Override
83      public boolean onCreateOptionsMenu(Menu menu) {
84          // Inflate the menu;
85          getMenuInflater().inflate(R.menu.my, menu);
86          return true;
87      }
88
89      @Override
90      public boolean onOptionsItemSelected(MenuItem item) {
91          // Handle action bar item clicks here. The action bar will
92          // automatically handle clicks on the Home/Up button, so long
93          // as you specify a parent activity in AndroidManifest.xml.
94          int id = item.getItemId();
95          if (id == R.id.action_settings) {
96              return true;
97          }
98          return super.onOptionsItemSelected(item);
99      }
100 }
```

Execute the following actions to initiate the creation, pausing, stopping, and other stages of the activity for this app.

Experiment 1:

> Launch the application from a physical device or the emulator. The first experiment tests the beginning of the Activity

lifecycle. An activity begins by launching the application. The callback methods you should see are onCreate(), followed by onStart(), followed by onResume().

Experiment 2:

Pause the activity by pressing the Home button. This can be done in the emulator or on a physical device. The callback methods you should see are onPause() and onStop().

Experiment 3:

Restart the application from the launcher. Both the emulator and the physical device can be used for this test. The callback methods you will see are restart(), onStart(), and onResume().

Experiment 4:

This last experiment must be done using a physical device. An activity is destroyed when the screen of a device, not fixed to a particular orientation, is rotated. Once the activity is destroyed, it is created again. The callback methods you will see are onPause(), onStop(), onCreate(), onStart(), and finally onResume().

3.3 Multiple Activities and the Intent Class

Applications that are built with multiple activities need to utilize the Intent class. This class provides the framework for the navigation from one screen to another. In simple terms, an Intent object is a message from one component to another component, either within the application or outside the application. For example, consider ActivityA, which needs to start another activity, ActivityB. ActivityA can communicate this intention to ActivityB, using an Intent object. Hence, an Intent is an object carrying an intention to perform a specific action.

Intents are designed to communicate messages between three application core components of Android.

There are separate mechanisms for delivering Intents to these types of component.

Activities: Intents are used to request the launch of another activity. The mechanism for delivering an Intent to an activity is sendActivity().

Broadcast receivers:

A broadcast receiver can be implemented to listen for a specific Intent. For example, a Broadcast Intent can be defined to communicate the notification of a low battery level. An `Intent` object is passed to the method `sendBroadcast()` to deliver a message to all interested `Broadcast` receivers.

Service: A `Service` is a component of the app that is meant to perform long-running operations in the background. These operations do not provide a user interface. For example, a `Service` might handle network transactions, play music, perform file I/O, or interact with a content provider, all from the background. An `Intent` object is passed to the `startService()` method, along with the name of the `Service` it wishes to start.

The `Intent` object is a passive data structure. It holds an abstract description of an operation to be performed. This abstract description involves a collection of data components, some of which are not required. The following is a list of the required components. Optional information about an `Intent` object will be discussed elsewhere in the chapter.

Action: This component describes the action to take upon receiving the `Intent`. `Action` is a crucial part of the `Intent`'s abstract description. This is a required data component for all `Intents`. The value for `Action` is a string identifying the action to be performed. The `Intent` class provides a set of `Action` constants to use for this purpose. The following is a small list of these constants:

ACTION_CALL: An activity will be the target component. The intended action is to initiate a phone call.

ACTION_ANSWER: The target component for this action constant is an activity. The intended action is to handle an incoming phone call.

ACTION_BATTERY_LOW:
The target component for this constant is a `Broadcast`. The intended action is notification when the battery is low.

ACTION_AIRPLANE_MODE_CHANGED:
The target for this constant is a `Broadcast`. The intended action is notification that the user has switched the device into or out of Airplane Mode.

Data: Identifies the data resource. More specifically, it contains the `Uniform Resource Identifier` (URI) of the data. `Data` and `Action` are paired in an `Intent`. For example, if

Action was defined as ACTION_CALL, the Data would contain a telephone number to call.

Category: An Intent object primarily contains an Action and a Data component, based on what it is communicating or going to perform. The category of an Intent is not required, but it can sometimes be useful. A category is specified when it is necessary to define a particular component that will handle the Intent. For example, a category named CATEGORY_APP_CALCULATOR can be used with the action named ACTION_MAIN to launch the calculator application. Standard category constants, such as CATEGORY_APP_CALENDAR and CATEGORY_APP_CONTACTS, are defined within the Intent class. Constants so defined are named containing the starting string CATEGORY_.

Intents are broadly grouped into two categories: explicit and implicit.

3.3.1 Explicit Intents

Explicit Intents use a specific name when starting a component. This name will be the full Java class name of the activity or service. The most common use of an explicit Intent is the launching of a target component with a known name within the currently running application.

The code segment below shows the start of a new activity in response to a user action, such as tapping a button. The launchTargetActivity() method is an onclick handler.

Lines 2–3:   An explicit Intent is constructed. The context of the application is required for the first argument. The second argument is the explicit target name of the activity, TargetActivity.class.

Line 5:   The target activity is started. When you create an explicit Intent to start an activity or service, the system immediately starts the app component specified in the Intent object.

```
Explicit Intent example
1  public void launchTargetActivity (View view) {
2      Intent intent = new Intent(getApplicationContext(),
3          TargetActivity.class);
4
5      startActivity(intent);
6  }
```

3.3.2 Implicit `Intents`

Unlike an explicit `Intent`, an implicit `Intent` does not name a specific component; instead, it declares a general action to perform, which allows a component from another app to handle it. When an implicit `Intent` is created, the system locates the appropriate target component by comparing the contents of the `Intent` to an `Intent filter`. `Intent filters` are declared in the manifest file of other apps located on a given device. When the `Intent` has found a match with the `Intent filter`, the system starts that component and delivers it to the `Intent` objcct.

In some situations, many matches can be found when comparing the contents of a given `Intent` to the application's `Intent filters`. When this happens, the system will display a dialog box to the user so that they may pick the app they want.

The code segment below shows the start of a new activity in response to a user action, such as tapping a button. The `launchTargetActivity()` method is an `onclick` handler.

Lines 1–2:   An implicit `Intent` is created. The first argument is a string describing the action. `ACTION_VIEW` is an `Activity Action` that displays data to the user. It is the generic action that can be used on data, which makes it the most common action performed on data. In this example, it is being used to bring up a window filled with the information supplied by the URI, `www.example.com`.

Line 4:   Starts the implicit activity.

```
Implicit Intent example
1   Intent intent = new Intent(Intent.ACTION_VIEW,
2            Uri.parse("http://www.example.com"));
3
4   startActivity(intent);
```

■ 3.4 Handling Keyboard Visibility in an Activity

Android shows or hides the soft keyboard when input focus moves into or out of an editable text field. The system also makes decisions about how your UI and the text field appear above the keyboard. For example, when the vertical space on the screen is constrained, the text field might fill all space above the keyboard. For most applications, these default behaviors are satisfactory.

In certain situations, more control over the visibility of the soft keyboard is needed. It is possible to specify how you want your layout to appear when the keyboard is visible. Android gives focus to the first `EditText` element in the layout launched by a running activity. It does not immediately display the keyboard. This behavior is appropriate because entering text might not be the primary task in the activity. Sometimes apps require text to be input at the start of an activity. For example, a login screen needs the input of a login or user name followed by a password prior to allowing the user to do anything else.

When text input is required at the start of an activity, it would be a good idea for the keyboard to appear by default. This can be accomplished by adding an input mode property to the AndroidManifest.xml file.

In the example below, the sole activity defined in the application contains the android:windowSoftInputMode attribute. This attribute must be located in the <activity> element. Its value is set to stateVisible.

This attribute can be used to configure the keyboards for multiple activities in an application.

```
1  <application ... >
2  <activity
3          android:windowSoftInputMode="stateVisible" ... >
4          ...
5  </activity>
6      ...
7  </application>
```

It is also possible to request the focus of a View programmatically. The method requestFocus can be called to give focus to a specific View or to one of its descendants. This can be useful in cases when you want to ensure that the keyboard is visible. A View will not actually take focus if it is not focusable.

In the following code segment, the displaySoftKeyboard() method receives a View in which the user should type something. If the View is focusable, an InputMethodManager object is used to give it focus. The InputMethodManager arbitrates interaction between applications and the current input method.

showSoftInput () will explicitly request that the current input method's soft input area be shown to the user.

```
1  public void displaySoftKeyboard(View view) {
2      if (view.requestFocus()) {
3          InputMethodManager inputMM = (InputMethodManager)
4                  getSystemService(Context.INPUT_METHOD_SERVICE);
5          inputMM.showSoftInput(view, InputMethodManager.SHOW_IMPLICIT);
6      }
7  }
```

Once the keyboard is visible, it should not be programmatically hidden. The system hides the keyboard when the user finishes the task in the editable text field. The user can also hide the keyboard with a system control, such as with the Back button.

As we have seen in previous apps created in this textbook, when a keyboard appears on the screen it takes up valuable screen space. The system determines how best to adjust the visible portion of your user interface for a given activity. It is possible to specify the display attributes of your activity.

The following code segment specifies a resize adjustment, `adjustResize`, to ensure that the system resizes your layout to the available space. The result is that all of the layout content will accessible. In some cases, screen content will require scrolling. This attribute must be defined within the `<activity>` element.

```
1  <application ... >
2  <activity
3          android:windowSoftInputMode="adjustResize" ... >
4          ...
5  </activity>
6          ...
7  </application>
```

■ Lab Example 3-2: Navigating Multiple Screens—Paint Calculator App

This lab is a first look at an application that uses multiple screens. The objective for building the Paint Calculator app is to explore the use of multiple activities in an application and to illustrate navigation between them.

Part 1: The Design

The Paint Job Calculator allows a user to calculate how many gallons of paint are required to paint a single room. The number of gallons is based on a single coat of paint covering four walls and the ceiling. The user must provide the dimensions of the room, as well as the number of doors and windows. The input for the dimensions of the room is the length, width, and height of the room. In addition, the user must provide the number of doors and windows in the room; the area of the doors and windows will not be included in the area to be painted. A door has a standard measurement of 7×3 feet. All windows have a standard measurement of 4×4 feet.

The app assumes one gallon of paint covers approximately 275 square feet. The output consists of the number of gallons needed and the computed surface area to be painted. This app includes the following general features:

1. Provide `EditText` widgets for the input of the dimensions of the room and the number of windows and doors.

2. Provide a help button that explains the input requirements and how the number of gallons will be computed.

3. Provide a compute button that performs the calculation and displays the results.

The main activity, the left-hand image screen shown in Figure 3-7, is the input screen for the dimensions of the room and the number of doors and windows. The secondary activity, the right-hand image screen shown in Figure 3-7, is a help screen providing details on how the calculator computes surface area and the number of gallons needed to paint a given room. When the secondary activity is launched, the main activity will pause.

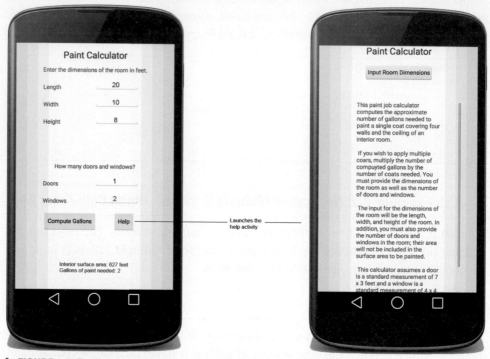

FIGURE 3-7 The Paint Job Calculator uses two screens: input and help.

Part 2: Application Structure and Setup

The settings for the application are as follows:

- Application Name: Paint Calculator
- Project Name: PaintCalculator
- Package Name: `com.cornez.paintcalculator`
- Android Form: Phone and Tablet
- Minimum SDK: API 18: Android 4.3 (Jelly Bean)
- Target SDK: API 21: Android 5.0 (Lollipop)
- Compile with: API 21: Android 5.0 (Lollipop)
- Activity Name: `MyActivity`
- Layout Name: `activity_my`

The launcher is set to the Android default `ic_launcher.png` file. To make the application visually more interesting, a background image has been added to the `drawable` folder.

The final project structure, shown in Figure 3-8, contains three source files and two layout files. The two activity classes are named `MyActivity` and `HelpActivity`. `MyActivity`, the main activity of the application, sets the screen content to `input_layout.xml`, and `HelpActivity` displays the `input_layout` screen content. There is only one `drawable` resource, `paintbackground.png`, which adds visual context to the application. This file can be found in the textbook resources.

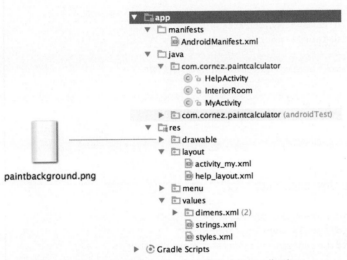

paintbackground.png

▌ FIGURE 3-8 Project structure for the Paint Calculator application.

The theme for this application has been set in the `AndroidManifest` file.

A critical component of the `Intent/Activity` model is the `manifest` file. For the above code to work properly, we need to specify the `Activities` of this application in the manifest file (see `AndroidManifest.xml` for details of how `Activities` are defined). A common error when one is new to the Android framework is to forget to add the activity details in the `manifest` file.

Lines 12–22:   The main activity of the application is declared and named `MyActivity`. `MyActivity` will be implemented in `MyActivity.java`.

Line 25–33:   The secondary activity of the application is declared and named `HelpActivity`. `HelpActivity` will be implemented in `HelpActivity.java`. Note that the parent activity for the secondary activity is `MyActivity`.

```
AndroidManifest.xml
1   <?xml version="1.0" encoding="utf-8"?>
2   <manifest xmlns:android="http://schemas.android.com/apk/res/android"
3       package="com.cornez.paintcalculator" >
4
5   <application
6           android:allowBackup="true"
7           android:icon="@drawable/ic_launcher"
8           android:label="@string/app_name"
9           android:theme="@android:style
10  /Theme.Light.NoTitleBar.Fullscreen" >
11
12  <!- THE MAIN ACTIVITY -->
13  <activity
14          android:name=".MyActivity"
15          android:label="@string/app_name" >
16  <intent-filter>
17  <action android:name="android.intent.action.MAIN" />
18
19  <category
20  android:name="android.intent.category.LAUNCHER" />
21  </intent-filter>
22  </activity>
23
24
25  <!-- HELP ACTIVITY FOR USER HELP -->
26  <activity
27          android:name=".HelpActivity"
28          android:label="@string/app_name"
29          android:parentActivityName=".MyActivity" >
30  <meta-data
31              android:name="android.support.PARENT_ACTIVITY"
32              android:value=".MyActivity" />
33  </activity>
34
35  </application>
36
37  </manifest>
```

Part 3: External Value Resources

The Paint Calculator application uses values from both the strings.xml file and the dimens.xml file. The strings.xml file contains static labels shown on the layout screens. In addition, strings.xml also stores the help text displayed in the help screen. The XML code for this file is as follows:

```
strings.xml
1   <?xml version="1.0" encoding="utf-8"?>
2   <resources>
3
4   <string name="app_name">Paint Calculator</string>
5   <string name="hello_world">Hello world!</string>
6   <string name="action_settings">Settings</string>
7
8   <string name="enter_dimensions">Enter the dimensions of
9           the room in feet.</string>
10  <string name="length">Length</string>
11  <string name="width">Width</string>
12  <string name="height">Height</string>
13
14  <string name="enter_door_window">How many doors
15                   and windows?</string>
16  <string name="doors">Doors</string>
17  <string name="windows">Windows</string>
18
19  <string name="compute_btn">Compute Gallons</string>
20  <string name="help_btn">Help</string>
21
22  <string name="n_gallons">Gallons</string>
23  <string name="return_btn">Input Room Dimensions</string>
24
25  <!-- HELP TEXT -->
26  <string name="help_text">
27          This paint job calculator computes the approximate number
28          of gallons needed to paint a single coat covering four walls
29           and the ceiling of an interior room.
30          \n\n
31          If you wish to apply multiple coats, multiply the number of
32          computed gallons by the number of coats needed. You must
33          provide the dimensions of the room as well as the number of
34           doors and windows.
35          \n\n
36          The input for the dimensions of the room will be the length,
37           width, and height of the room. In addition, you must also
38           provide the number of doors and windows in the room; their
39           area will not be included in the surface area to be painted.
40           \n\n
41          This calculator assumes a door is a standard measurement of
42          7 x 3 feet and a window is a standard measurement of 4 x 4
43          feet.
44          \n\n
45          A gallon of paint will cover approximately 275 square feet.
46  </string>
47
48
    </resources>
```

The `dimens.xml` file is used to store one value, a left margin setting that will be used many times in the layout to align label elements. The XML code for the dimensions is as follows:

```
dimens.xml
1  <resources>
2  <!-- Default screen margins, per the Android Design guidelines. -->
3  <dimen name="activity_horizontal_margin">16dp</dimen>
4  <dimen name="activity_vertical_margin">16dp</dimen>
5
6  <dimen name="label_left_margin">50dp</dimen>
7  </resources>
```

Part 4: The User Interface

There are two activity screen layouts for this application: `input_layout.xml` and `help_layout.xml`. The application uses the background image for both of these activity screens. The input screen is the layout associated with the main activity. This screen layout will appear when the application is first launched. The layout design, shown in Figure 3-9, uses a `RelativeLayout` as the root `View`, with the background property set to `paintbackground.png`.

`TextView` widgets are used for all static labels and titles, and EditTexts are used for all input fields. The last `TextView`, `textView9`, is used as a placeholder for the results of the computation to be displayed.

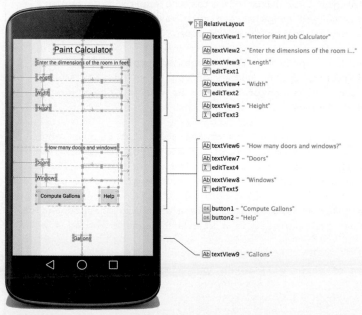

▌ FIGURE 3-9 The layout structure for `input_layout.xml`.

The `Compute Gallons` button is used to compute the number of gallons needed. The `Help` button accesses the help screen, via a secondary activity. Both buttons will be assigned `onClick` methods rather than using listener events in the source code files. The `onClick()` method assigned to compute the number of gallons is `computeGallons()`, and the `onClick` method assigned to display help is `gotoHelp()`.

```
activity_my.xml
1   <RelativeLayout
2   xmlns:android="http://schemas.android.com/apk/res/android"
3       xmlns:tools="http://schemas.android.com/tools"
4       android:layout_width="match_parent"
5       android:layout_height="match_parent"
6       android:paddingLeft="@dimen/activity_horizontal_margin"
7       android:paddingRight="@dimen/activity_horizontal_margin"
8       android:paddingTop="@dimen/activity_vertical_margin"
9       android:paddingBottom="@dimen/activity_vertical_margin"
10      android:background="@drawable/paintbackground"
11      tools:context=".MyActivity">
12
13  <!-- TITLE -->
14  <TextView
15          android:id="@+id/textView1"
16          android:layout_width="wrap_content"
17          android:layout_height="wrap_content"
18          android:layout_alignParentTop="true"
19          android:layout_centerHorizontal="true"
20          android:text="@string/app_name"
21          android:textAppearance="?android:attr/textAppearanceLarge" />
22
23  <!-- ENTER THE DIMENSIONS OF THE ROOM -->
24  <TextView
25          android:id="@+id/textView2"
26          android:layout_width="wrap_content"
27          android:layout_height="wrap_content"
28          android:layout_below="@+id/textView1"
29          android:layout_centerHorizontal="true"
30          android:layout_marginTop="14dp"
31          android:text="@string/enter_dimensions"
32          android:textAppearance="?android:attr/textAppearanceSmall" />
33
34  <!-- LENGTH OF THE ROOM -->
35  <TextView
36          android:id="@+id/textView3"
37          android:layout_width="wrap_content"
38          android:layout_height="wrap_content"
39          android:layout_alignParentLeft="true"
40          android:layout_marginLeft="@dimen/label_left_margin"
```

```
41          android:layout_below="@+id/textView2"
42          android:layout_marginTop="25dp"
43          android:text="@string/length"
44          android:textAppearance="?android:attr/textAppearanceSmall" />
45
46  <EditText
47          android:id="@+id/editText1"
48          android:layout_width="wrap_content"
49          android:layout_height="wrap_content"
50          android:layout_alignBottom="@+id/textView3"
51          android:layout_alignRight="@+id/textView2"
52          android:layout_marginRight="19dp"
53          android:ems="5"
54          android:inputType="number" />
55
56  <!-- WIDTH OF THE ROOM -->
57
58  <TextView
59          android:id="@+id/textView4"
60          android:layout_width="wrap_content"
61          android:layout_height="wrap_content"
62          android:layout_alignParentLeft="true"
63          android:layout_below="@+id/textView3"
64          android:layout_marginLeft="@dimen/label_left_margin"
65          android:layout_marginTop="25dp"
66          android:text="@string/width"
67          android:textAppearance="?android:attr/textAppearanceSmall" />
68
69  <EditText
70          android:id="@+id/editText2"
71          android:layout_width="wrap_content"
72          android:layout_height="wrap_content"
73          android:layout_alignBottom="@+id/textView4"
74          android:layout_alignRight="@+id/textView2"
75          android:layout_marginRight="19dp"
76          android:ems="5"
77          android:inputType="number" />
78
79  <!-- HEIGHT OF THE ROOM -->
80
81  <TextView
82          android:id="@+id/textView5"
83          android:layout_width="wrap_content"
84          android:layout_height="wrap_content"
85          android:layout_alignParentLeft="true"
86          android:layout_below="@+id/textView4"
87          android:layout_marginLeft="@dimen/label_left_margin"
88          android:layout_marginTop="25dp"
89          android:text="@string/height"
```

```
90          android:textAppearance="?android:attr/textAppearanceSmall" />
91
92  <EditText
93          android:id="@+id/editText3"
94          android:layout_width="wrap_content"
95          android:layout_height="wrap_content"
96          android:layout_alignBottom="@+id/textView5"
97          android:layout_alignRight="@+id/textView2"
98          android:layout_marginRight="19dp"
99          android:ems="5"
100         android:inputType="number" />
101
102 <!-- ENTER THE NUMBER OF DOORS AND WINDOWS -->
103
104 <TextView
105         android:id="@+id/textView6"
106         android:layout_width="wrap_content"
107         android:layout_height="wrap_content"
108         android:layout_centerHorizontal="true"
109         android:layout_centerVertical="true"
100         android:text="@string/enter_door_window" />
111
112 <!-- NUMBER OF DOORS -->
113
114 <TextView
115         android:id="@+id/textView7"
116         android:layout_width="wrap_content"
117         android:layout_height="wrap_content"
118         android:layout_alignParentLeft="true"
119         android:layout_below="@+id/textView6"
120         android:layout_marginLeft="@dimen/label_left_margin"
121         android:layout_marginTop="25dp"
122         android:text="@string/doors"
123         android:textAppearance="?android:attr/textAppearanceSmall" />
124
125 <EditText
126         android:id="@+id/editText4"
127         android:layout_width="wrap_content"
128         android:layout_height="wrap_content"
129         android:layout_alignBottom="@+id/textView7"
130         android:layout_alignRight="@+id/textView2"
131         android:layout_marginRight="19dp"
132         android:ems="5"
133         android:inputType="number" />
134
135 <!-- NUMBER OF WINDOWS -->
136
137 <TextView
138         android:id="@+id/textView8"
```

```
139         android:layout_width="wrap_content"
140         android:layout_height="wrap_content"
141         android:layout_alignParentLeft="true"
142         android:layout_below="@+id/textView7"
143         android:layout_marginLeft="@dimen/label_left_margin"
144         android:layout_marginTop="25dp"
145         android:text="@string/windows"
146         android:textAppearance="?android:attr/textAppearanceSmall" />
147
148 <EditText
149         android:id="@+id/editText5"
150         android:layout_width="wrap_content"
151         android:layout_height="wrap_content"
152         android:layout_alignBottom="@+id/textView8"
153         android:layout_alignRight="@+id/textView2"
154         android:layout_marginRight="19dp"
155         android:ems="5"
156         android:inputType="number" />
157
158 <Button
159         android:id="@+id/button1"
160         style="?android:attr/buttonStyleSmall"
161         android:layout_width="wrap_content"
162         android:layout_height="wrap_content"
163         android:layout_alignLeft="@+id/textView8"
164         android:layout_below="@+id/textView8"
165         android:layout_marginTop="17dp"
166         android:text="@string/compute_btn"
167         android:onClick="computeGallons" />
168
169 <Button
170         android:id="@+id/button2"
171         style="?android:attr/buttonStyleSmall"
172         android:layout_width="wrap_content"
173         android:layout_height="wrap_content"
174         android:layout_alignBaseline="@+id/button1"
175         android:layout_alignBottom="@+id/button1"
176         android:layout_alignRight="@+id/textView6"
177         android:text="@string/help_btn"
178         android:onClick="gotoHelp" />
179
180 <TextView
181         android:id="@+id/textView9"
182         android:layout_width="wrap_content"
183         android:layout_height="wrap_content"
184         android:layout_alignParentBottom="true"
185         android:layout_centerHorizontal="true"
186         android:layout_marginBottom="24dp"
187         android:text="@string/n_gallons"
188         android:textAppearance="?android:attr/textAppearanceSmall" />
189 </RelativeLayout>
```

The secondary activity layout file for this application is `help_layout.xml`. This help screen is associated with the `HelpActivity`. The screen layout for `HelpActivity` appears when the user clicks the help button. The layout design, shown in Figure 3-10, uses a `RelativeLayout` as the root `View`, with the background property set to `paintbackground.png`, just as for the input screen.

A `TextView` widget is used to display the static title for the application, and a `Button` widget is used to return to the input layout screen. Help information can often be very long and may not always fit on a small screen. When this happens, the text gets truncated. In this layout, a `ScrollView`, the `ViewGroup` container named `scrollView1`, is used to hold a `TextView`. This allows the text to scroll when the screen cannot accommodate the full text.

`TextViews` are used for all static labels and titles, and `EditTexts` are used for all input fields. The last `TextView`, `textView9`, is used as a placeholder for the results of the computation to be displayed.

❙ FIGURE 3-10 The layout design for `help_layout.xml`.

Lines 18–27:   `button1` is defined. The purpose of this `Button` is to exit help and return to the input screen. `button1` is assigned an `onClick` method `gotoInput()`.

Lines 29–47:   Scrollable text can be built in several ways. For this app, a vertical `ScrollView` will be used as a container to store a `TextView`. This scrollable element will display the help contents of the application.

help_layout.xml

```
1   <?xml version="1.0" encoding="utf-8"?>
2   <RelativeLayout
3   xmlns:android="http://schemas.android.com/apk/res/android"
4       android:layout_width="match_parent"
5       android:layout_height="match_parent"
6       android:background="@drawable/paintbackground">
7
8   <!-- TITLE -->
9   <TextView
10          android:id="@+id/textView1"
11          android:layout_width="wrap_content"
12          android:layout_height="wrap_content"
13          android:layout_alignParentTop="true"
14          android:layout_centerHorizontal="true"
15          android:text="@string/app_name"
16          android:textAppearance="?android:attr/textAppearanceLarge" />
17
18  <Button
19          android:id="@+id/button1"
20          style="?android:attr/buttonStyleSmall"
21          android:layout_width="wrap_content"
22          android:layout_height="wrap_content"
23          android:layout_below="@+id/textView1"
24          android:layout_centerHorizontal="true"
25          android:layout_marginTop="22dp"
26          android:text="@string/return_btn"
27          android:onClick="gotoInput" />
28
29  <ScrollView
30          android:id="@+id/scrollView1"
31          android:layout_width="wrap_content"
32          android:layout_height="wrap_content"
33          android:layout_below="@+id/button1"
34          android:layout_centerHorizontal="true"
35          android:layout_marginTop="50dp"
36          android:scrollbars="vertical" >
37
38  <TextView
39              android:id="@+id/textView2"
40              android:layout_width="300dp"
41              android:layout_height="214dp"
42              android:paddingLeft="@dimen/label_left_margin"
43              android:paddingRight="@dimen/label_left_margin"
44              android:text="@string/help_text" >
45
46  </TextView>
47  </ScrollView>
48
49  </RelativeLayout>
```

Part 5: Source Code for Application

Line 4:   Navigating between activities requires an `Intent` import.

Lines 72-74:   An `Intent` is created and dispatched when the user clicks on the help button, located on the input layout screen. The help button is wired, using the `onClick` attribute in the `xml` file, to respond by calling the method `gotoHelp()`.

To start another activity, the `Intent` needs to know the sender, as well as a receiver. The sender can be specified using `getApplicationContext()`. The sender can also be accessed by the context of the activity, as shown in Line 72. The receiver is the class name `HelpActivity`. Once the `Intent` is created, we dispatch it via the `startActivity()` method. The `startActivity()` method is provided by the Android framework and will handle the starting of the activity specified in the `Intent` message.

As illustrated in this example, an `Intent` object is a task request that matches the `Intent` action with the appropriate activity.

```
MyActivity.java
1   package com.cornez.paintcalculator;
2
3   import android.app.Activity;
4   import android.content.Intent;
5   import android.os.Bundle;
6   import android.view.Menu;
7   import android.view.MenuItem;
8   import android.view.View;
9   import android.widget.EditText;
10  import android.widget.TextView;
11
12
13  public class MyActivity extends Activity {
14
15      //OBJECT THAT REPRESENTS A ROOM TO BE PAINTED
16      private InteriorRoom mRoom;
17
18      //EDIT TEXTS FOR USER INPUT
19      private EditText lengthET;
20      private EditText widthET;
21      private EditText heightET;
22      private EditText nDoorsET;
23      private EditText nWindowsET;
24
25      // TEXT VIEW FOR DISPLAYING THE PAINT JOB CALCULATION
26      private TextView nGallonsV;
27
```

```
28    @Override
29    protected void onCreate(Bundle savedInstanceState) {
30        super.onCreate(savedInstanceState);
31        setContentView(R.layout.activity_my);
32
33        //OBTAIN REFERENCES TO UI ELEMENTS IN THE MAIN LAYOUT
34        referenceUIcomponents();
35
36        //CREATE A ROOM
37        mRoom = new InteriorRoom();
38    }
39
40    private void referenceUIcomponents() {
41        lengthET = (EditText) findViewById(R.id.editText1);
42        widthET = (EditText) findViewById(R.id.editText2);
43        heightET = (EditText) findViewById(R.id.editText3);
44        nDoorsET = (EditText) findViewById(R.id.editText4);
45        nWindowsET = (EditText) findViewById(R.id.editText5);
46        nGallonsV = (TextView) findViewById(R.id.textView9);
47    }
48
49    public void computeGallons (View view) {
50        //TASK 1: SET ROOM DIMENSIONS FROM USER INPUT
51        double l = Double.valueOf(lengthET.getText().toString());
52        double w = Double.valueOf(widthET.getText().toString());
53        double h = Double.valueOf(heightET.getText().toString());
54        mRoom.setLength(l);
55        mRoom.setWidth(w);
56        mRoom.setHeight(h);
57
58        //TASK 2: SET THE NUMBER OF DOORS AND WINDOWS FROM USER INPUT
59        int doors = Integer.valueOf(nDoorsET.getText().toString());
60        int windows = Integer.valueOf(nWindowsET.getText().toString());
61        mRoom.setDoors(doors);
62        mRoom.setWindows(windows);
63
64
65        //TASK 3: DISPLAY THE AREA TO BE PAINTED AND GALLONS NEEDED
66        nGallonsV.setText("Interior surface area: " +
67                mRoom.surfaceArea() + " feet"
68                + "\nGallons needed: " + mRoom.gallons());
69    }
70
71    public void gotoHelp(View view){
72        Intent helpIntent = new Intent (MyActivity.this,
73                                        HelpActivity.class);
74        startActivity(helpIntent);
75    }
76
77
```

```
78      @Override
79      public boolean onCreateOptionsMenu(Menu menu) {
80          // Inflate the menu;
81          getMenuInflater().inflate(R.menu.my, menu);
82          return true;
83      }
84
85      @Override
86      public boolean onOptionsItemSelected(MenuItem item) {
87          // Handle action bar item clicks here. The action bar will
88          // automatically handle clicks on the Home/Up button, so long
89          // as you specify a parent activity in AndroidManifest.xml.
90          int id = item.getItemId();
91          if (id == R.id.action_settings) {
92              return true;
93          }
94          return super.onOptionsItemSelected(item);
        }
    }
```

The `InteriorRoom.java` class is the model for a room to be painted.

InteriorRoom.java

```
1   package com.cornez.paintcalculator;
2
3
4   public class InteriorRoom {
5       //ROOM CONSTANTS
6       static final int WINDOW_AREA = 16;
7       static final int DOOR_AREA = 21;
8       static final int SQR_FEET_PER_GAL = 275;
9
10
11      // DATA MEMBERS FOR ROOM DIMENSIONS
12      private double mLength;
13      private double mWidth;
14      private double mHeight;
15
16      // DATA MEMBERS FOR WINDOWS AND DOORS
17      private int mDoors;
18      private int mWindows;
19
20      public void setWidth(double width){
21          mWidth = width;
22      }
23      public void setHeight(double height){
24          mHeight = height;
25      }
```

```
26        public void setLength(double length){
27            mLength = length;
28        }
29
30        public void setDoors(int doors){
31            mDoors = doors;
32        }
33
34        public void setWindows(int windows){
35            mWindows = windows;
36        }
37
38        public double wallSurface() {
39            return 2*mLength*mHeight + 2*mWidth*mHeight + mLength*mWidth;
40        }
41
42        public int doorWindowArea (){
43            return mDoors*DOOR_AREA + mWindows*WINDOW_AREA;
44        }
45
46        public double surfaceArea() {
47            return wallSurface() - doorWindowArea();
48        }
49
50        public int gallons(){
51            return (int) Math.ceil(surfaceArea()) / SQR_FEET_PER_GAL;
52        }
53  }
```

HelpActivity.java is the activity associated with the help screen for the Paint Calculator app.

Line 7:   HelpActivity is an extension of the Activity class.

Line 11:   The user interface for HelpActivity is set to layout.help_layout.xml file.

Lines 14–16:   The method gotoInput() is the onClick listener event handler that returns the user to the input screen in MyActivity.

Line 15:   The method finish () is called when the activity needs to be closed. The ActivityResult is propagated back to MyActivity, which launched it.

```
HelpActivity.java
1   package com.cornez.paintcalculator;
2
3   import android.app.Activity;
4   import android.os.Bundle;
5   import android.view.View;
6
```

```
 7  public class HelpActivity extends Activity {
 8      @Override
 9      public void onCreate (Bundle savedInstanceState) {
10          super.onCreate(savedInstanceState);
11          setContentView(R.layout.help_layout);
12      }
13
14      public void gotoInput(View view){
15          finish();
16      }
17  }
```

■ 3.5 Passing Data between Activities

Although multiple screens allow for the construction of complex applications, they often require carefully planned data management. In many cases, various data entities must be sent from one activity to another.

The Android framework provides a simple and flexible approach to working with multiple activities. Android also offers an efficient model for passing information between various activities.

Data can be passed as a message object to an activity implemented within the application or outside the applications. For example, a value computed by one activity can be attached to a message and passed to another activity within the application. This message can also be passed on to an activity outside of the application boundary. Because of the potential dangers involved in transferring data between applications, the designers of Android have built a robust security model to ensure that this flexibility and power do not compromise data safety.

When an `Intent` object is constructed, its action is specified. This represents the action we want the `Intent` to trigger. For example, the action `ACTION_SEND` indicates that the `Intent` will be sending data from one activity to another. This action will also send data across process boundaries. Sending and receiving data between applications is most commonly used for social sharing of content.

It is possible to add extended data to a given `Intent`. This is done using the `putExtra()` method. `putExtra()` requires two parameters: a name for the data and a String data value. The data name must include a package prefix. For example an application named `com.android.contacts` might use a name such as "`com.android.contacts.ShowAll`". The `String` data value is the literal data element that will be attached to the `Intent`.

The code segment shown below illustrates a simple `Intent` with attached data:

Line 2:   The action of the created `Intent` is set to `ACTION_SEND`.
               `ACTION_SEND` is used to deliver data to another activity.

Line 3:   The first argument of putExtra () is the name.
                     EXTRA_TEXT, the constant used in this example, is associated
                     with ACTION_SEND. The value of EXTRA_TEXT is simply
                     "android.Intent.extra.TEXT". The second argument is
                     the String value that will be attached to the Intent.

```
1  Intent intent = new Intent();
2  intent.setAction(Intent.ACTION_SEND);
3  intent.putExtra(Intent.EXTRA_TEXT, "Hello World");
4  startActivity(intent);
```

A common use of the ACTION_SEND action is the distribution of text content from one activity to another activity outside the application. For example, a user viewing a webpage from the Android built-in browser app may want to share the URL, as text, with another application. This action is useful for sharing an article or website with friends via email or social networking.

The code segment shown below illustrates a basic Intent with this purpose:

Lines 1–2:   The Intent action is set to ACTION_SEND. ACTION_SEND
                     will be used to deliver data to an activity outside the application.

Line 3:   The first element of extended data is the subject line of a mes-
                     sage. "android.Intent.extra.SUBJECT" is the constant
                     value of EXTRA_SUBJECT.

Line 5:   When the activity is launched using the target Intent, a
                     "chooser" is created. Specifically, the createChooser ()
                     method constructs an ACTION_CHOOSER Intent that wraps
                     itself around the target Intent. If the target Intent has speci-
                     fied read or write permissions, these flags will automatically be
                     set in the returned chooser Intent.

```
1  Intent intent = new Intent();
2  intent.setAction(Intent.ACTION_SEND);
3  intent.putExtra(Intent.EXTRA_SUBJECT, "Sharing URL");
4  intent.putExtra(Intent.EXTRA_TEXT, "http://www.url.com");
5  startActivity(Intent.createChooser(intent, "Share URL"));
```

The manifest file would be modified to include the <Intent-filter> attribute. If, using the filter, an installed application is located that matches ACTION_SEND, the Android system will launch it.

```
1
2  <activity android:name=".MyActivity">
3  <intent-filter>
4  <action android:name="android.intent.action.SEND" />
```

```
5  <category android:name="android.intent.category.DEFAULT" />
6  </intent-filter>
7  </activity>
```

To send multiple elements, the action `ACTION_SEND_MULTIPLE` can be used with a list of URIs that reference to the data content. The receiving application is required to parse and process the data it receives.

Lines 1–3:	An `ArrayList` is used to store two photographs.
Line 6:	The action for the `Intent` specifies multiple data elements will be sent.
Line 7:	`putParcelableArrayListExtra` () adds extended data to the `Intent`. Specifically, this data will be the `ArrayList` data value, `photoUris`.
Line 9:	`createChooser` () enables the user to pick another application, other than the default.

```
1  ArrayList<Uri> photoUris = new ArrayList<Uri>();
2  imageUris.add(photoUri1);
3  imageUris.add(photoUri2);
4
5  Intent intent = new Intent();
6  intent.setAction(Intent.ACTION_SEND_MULTIPLE);
7  intent.putParcelableArrayListExtra(Intent.EXTRA_STREAM, photoUris);
8  intent.setType("image/*");
9  intent (Intent.createChooser(intent, "Share photos"));
```

■ Lab Example 3-3: Automotive Calculator App

In this lab, we will build an app that illustrates how data are passed between activities within the same application.

Part 1: The Design

Tom's Cars is a small car dealership that sells and finances the cars on its lot. Consumers typically want to be informed about the costs involved when purchasing a car. Computing a monthly car loan payment can be a little complicated for many people because it depends on a number of factors, such as the sales tax and interest rates. This app is designed to simplify the process. In addition, it allows users to experiment with a down payment amount and the term agreement before arriving at the dealership, giving them a better understanding of costs prior to making their purchase.

This app makes several assumptions. The sales tax rate in California, where Tom has his dealership, is fixed at 7%. In addition, we assume that Tom charges an interest rate of 9% for all cars purchased from his lot. The input requirements are the cost of the car, the down payment, and the length of the term. The length of the term can be set to one, two, or three years. No more, no less.

The loan calculator app uses two user interface screens. Figure 3-11 shows the completed screens. After entering the car purchase information into the data entry screen, as shown on the left, the user can then generate a loan report to outline the costs. The loan report is displayed in the screen on the right. The user can return to the input screen to enter another set of car purchase values.

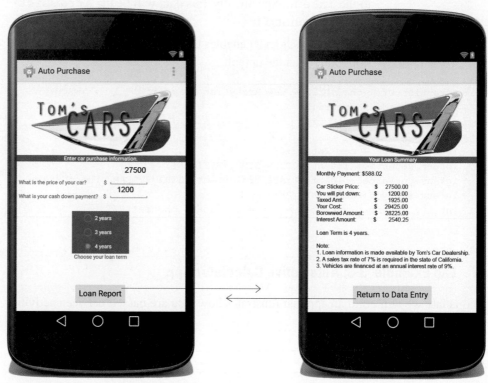

FIGURE 3-11 Auto Purchase application.

Part 2: Application Structure and Setup

The settings for the application are as follows:

- Application Name: Auto Purchase
- Project Name: AutoPurchase

- Package Name: `com.cornez.autopurchase`
- Android Form: Phone and Tablet
- Minimum SDK: API 18: Android 4.3 (Jelly Bean)
- Target SDK: API 21: Android 5.0 (Lollipop)
- Compile with: API 21: Android 5.0 (Lollipop)
- Activity Name: `PurchaseActivity`
- Layout Name: `purchase_layout`

The final project structure can be seen in Figure 3-12. The launcher icon remains set to the Android default `ic_launcher.png` file. In addition to this Android graphic, a logo graphic for Tom's Dealership has been added to the drawable folder.

Three source files are shown in the Java folder. `Auto.java` represents the data model for an automobile. `PurchaseActivity` is the main activity of the application. `PurchaseActivity` is launched when the application is launched for the first time. `LoanSummaryActivity` is a secondary activity and is used to display the generated loan report. When the secondary `LoanSummaryActivity` begins, `PurchaseActivity` will pause while `LoanSummaryActivity` is active.

Two layouts correspond to the two activities of the application. The main activity, `PurchaseActivity`, is visually represented by the layout named `purchase_layout.xml`. This layout displays a screen for the input of car purchase values, such as the price of the car, the down payment, and the terms of the loan. The secondary `LoanSummaryActivity` is visually represented by the layout named `loansummary_layout.xml`.

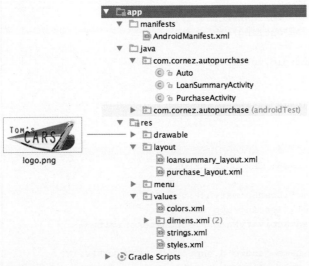

FIGURE 3-12 Project structure for the Auto Purchase application.

The `AndroidManifest.xml` file declares the activities used by this application and sets additional attributes.

Lines 9–10:   The theme for the application, governing all of its activities, is set to use a fullscreen with no titlebar.

Lines 12–22:   The main activity of the application is declared. The class name is `PurchaseActivity`, and it is categorized to launch with the application.

Lines 24–32:   The secondary `LoanSummaryActivity` class of the application is declared. The class name is `LoanSummaryActivity` and it is supported by the parent activity, `PurchaseActivity`.

```
AndroidManifest.xml
1   <?xml version="1.0" encoding="utf-8"?>
2   <manifest xmlns:android="http://schemas.android.com/apk/res/android"
3       package="com.cornez.autopurchase" >
4
5   <application
6           android:allowBackup="true"
7           android:icon="@drawable/ic_launcher"
8           android:label="@string/app_name"
9           android:theme="@android:style/
10              Theme.Light.NoTitleBar.Fullscreen" >
11
12  <!--MAIN ACTIVITY CLASS:  INPUT THE CAR PURCHASE INFORMATION -->
13  <activity
14              android:name=".PurchaseActivity"
15              android:label="@string/app_name" >
16  <intent-filter>
17  <action android:name="android.intent.action.MAIN" />
18
19  <category
20  android:name="android.intent.category.LAUNCHER" />
21  </intent-filter>
22  </activity>
23
24  <!--SECONDARY ACTIVITY CLASS: CAR LOAN REPORT -->
25  <activity
26              android:name=".LoanSummaryActivity"
27              android:label="@string/app_name"
28              android:parentActivityName=".PurchaseActivity" >
29  <meta-data
30                  android:name="android.support.PARENT_ACTIVITY"
31                  android:value=".PurchaseActivity" />
```

```
32  </activity>
33
34  </application>
35
36  </manifest>
```

Part 3: Value Resources

Colors and strings play an important role in this application. The colors are used to provide contrast for input fields, making them easier to see and, thus, navigate for the user. The color resources are defined in the XML file shown below:

```
colors.xml
1  <?xml version="1.0" encoding="utf-8"?>
2  <resources>
3  <color name="steel_blue">#515169</color>
4  <color name="bone_white">#FFFFFF</color>
5  </resources>
```

The static string values have been grouped into categories: input labels and report labels.

```
strings.xml
1  <?xml version="1.0" encoding="utf-8"?>
2  <resources>
3
4  <string name="app_name">Auto Purchase</string>
5  <string name="hello_world">Hello world!</string>
6  <string name="action_settings">Settings</string>
7
8  <!-- INPUT LABELS FOR INPUT FIELDS -->
9  <string name="title_activity_main">Car Dealership</string>
10 <string name="instruction">Enter car purchase information.</string>
11 <string name="dollar_sign">$</string>
12 <string name="car_price">What is the price of your car?</string>
13 <string name="down_payment">What is your cash down payment?</string>
14 <string name="loan_term">Choose your loan term</string>
15 <string name="years2">2 years</string>
16 <string name="years3">3 years</string>
17 <string name="years4">4 years</string>
18 <string name="loan_summary">Your Loan Summary</string>
19 <string name="generate_btn">Loan Report</string>
20 <string name="go_data_entry">Return to Data Entry</string>
21
22 <!-- REPORT LABELS -->
23 <string name="report_line1"> \n\t\t\t<b>Monthly
24 Payment:</b>\t$</string>
```

```
25   <string name="report_line2"> \n\n\nNOTE: </string>
26   <string name="report_line3"> \n1. Loan information is
27   made available by Tom\'s Car Dealership.</string>
28   <string name="report_line4"> \n\n2. A sales tax rate of 7% is
29   required in the state of California.</string>
30   <string name="report_line5"> \n\n3. Vehicles are financed at
31   an annual interest rate of 9%.\n\n</string>
32   <string name="report_line6"> \n\tCar Sticker Price: $</string>
33   <string name="report_line7"> \n\tYou will put down: $</string>
34   <string name="report_line8"> \n\tLoan Term is </string>
35   <string name="report_line9"> \n\tTaxed Amt: $ </string>
36   <string name="report_line10">\n\tYour Cost: $</string>
37   <string name="report_line11">\n\tBorrowed Amount: $</string>
38   <string name="report_line12">\n\tInterest Amount: $</string>
39
40   </resources>
```

Part 4: The User Interface

Based on the design of the application, the two layout structures will be simple. Because all visual objects need to be placed relative to each other, a `RelativeLayout` `ViewGroup` is used as the root element. `TextViews` is used for the static labels of all input text fields.

The design and hierarchy outline for the main layout, `purchase_layout` `.xml`, is shown in Figure 3-13.

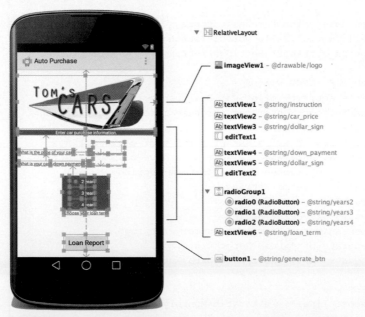

▌ FIGURE 3-13 Graphic layout design for `purchase_layout.xml`.

The XML code for `purchase_layout.xml` is shown below:

Lines 59–73:   An `EditText` is used for inputting the car price amount. The soft keyboard for this `View` is restricted to numeric values. As the first `EditText` of the layout, this `View` requests focus.

Lines 114–151: The term of the loan has fixed options: one, two, or three years. The input control for selecting the appropriate loan term is a `RadioGroup` containing a set of three `RadioButtons`.

Line 170:   The `onClick()` handler for the button is identified as `activateLoanSummary()`. This method will launch the secondary activity.

```
purchase_layout.xml
 1  <RelativeLayout
 2  xmlns:android="http://schemas.android.com/apk/res/android"
 3      xmlns:tools="http://schemas.android.com/tools"
 4      android:layout_width="match_parent"
 5      android:layout_height="match_parent"
 6      android:paddingTop="@dimen/activity_vertical_margin"
 7      android:paddingBottom="@dimen/activity_vertical_margin"
 8      tools:context=".MyActivity">
 9
10  <!-- LOGO AND DATA ENTRY INSTRUCTION -->
11
12  <ImageView
13          android:id="@+id/imageView1"
14          android:layout_width="fill_parent"
15          android:layout_height="wrap_content"
16          android:layout_alignParentTop="true"
17          android:layout_centerHorizontal="true"
18          android:contentDescription="@string/title_activity_main"
19          android:src="@drawable/logo" />
20
21  <TextView
22          android:id="@+id/textView1"
23          android:layout_width="wrap_content"
24          android:layout_height="wrap_content"
25          android:layout_alignParentLeft="true"
26          android:layout_alignRight="@+id/imageView1"
27          android:layout_below="@+id/imageView1"
28          android:background="@color/steel_blue"
29          android:gravity="center_horizontal"
30          android:text="@string/instruction"
31          android:textColor="@color/bone_white"
32          android:textSize="12sp" />
33
```

```
34   <!-- CAR PRICE INPUT SECTION -->
35
36   <TextView
37           android:id="@+id/textView2"
38           android:layout_width="wrap_content"
39           android:layout_height="wrap_content"
40           android:layout_alignParentLeft="true"
41           android:layout_below="@+id/textView1"
42           android:layout_marginLeft="5dp"
43           android:layout_marginTop="40dp"
44           android:text="@string/car_price"
45           android:textColor="@color/steel_blue"
46           android:textSize="12sp" />
47
48   <TextView
49           android:id="@+id/textView3"
50           android:layout_width="wrap_content"
51           android:layout_height="wrap_content"
52           android:layout_alignBottom="@+id/textView2"
53           android:layout_marginLeft="40dp"
54           android:layout_toRightOf="@+id/textView2"
55           android:text="@string/dollar_sign"
56           android:textColor="@color/steel_blue"
57           android:textSize="12sp" />
58
59   <EditText
60           android:id="@+id/editText1"
61           android:layout_width="wrap_content"
62           android:layout_height="wrap_content"
63           android:layout_alignBottom="@+id/textView3"
64           android:layout_marginLeft="5dp"
65           android:layout_toRightOf="@+id/textView3"
66           android:ems="10"
67           android:gravity="right"
68           android:inputType="number"
69           android:textColor="@color/steel_blue"
70           android:width="90dp" >
71
72   <requestFocus />
73   </EditText>
74
75   <!-- DOWN PAYMENT INPUT SECTION -->
76
77   <TextView
78           android:id="@+id/textView4"
79           android:layout_width="wrap_content"
80           android:layout_height="wrap_content"
81           android:layout_alignParentLeft="true"
82           android:layout_below="@+id/textView2"
83           android:layout_marginLeft="5dp"
```

```
84          android:layout_marginTop="17dp"
85          android:text="@string/down_payment"
86          android:textColor="@color/steel_blue"
87          android:textSize="12sp" />
88
89  <TextView
90          android:id="@+id/textView5"
91          android:layout_width="wrap_content"
92          android:layout_height="wrap_content"
93          android:layout_alignBottom="@+id/textView4"
94          android:layout_marginLeft="12dp"
95          android:layout_toRightOf="@+id/textView4"
96          android:text="@string/dollar_sign"
97          android:textColor="@color/steel_blue"
98          android:textSize="12sp" />
99
100 <EditText
101          android:id="@+id/editText2"
102          android:layout_width="wrap_content"
103          android:layout_height="wrap_content"
104          android:layout_alignBottom="@+id/textView5"
105          android:layout_marginLeft="5dp"
106          android:layout_toRightOf="@+id/textView5"
107          android:ems="10"
108          android:gravity="right"
109          android:inputType="number"
110          android:textColor="@color/steel_blue"
111          android:width="90dp" >
112 </EditText>
113
114 <!-- LOAN TERM SELECTION  -->
115 <RadioGroup
116          android:id="@+id/radioGroup1"
117          android:layout_width="wrap_content"
118          android:layout_height="wrap_content"
119          android:layout_below="@+id/textView4"
120          android:layout_centerHorizontal="true"
121          android:layout_marginTop="26dp"
122          android:background="@color/steel_blue"
123          android:paddingRight="40dp"
124          android:paddingLeft="20dp">
125
126 <RadioButton
127              android:id="@+id/radio0"
128              android:layout_width="wrap_content"
129              android:layout_height="wrap_content"
130              android:checked="true"
131              android:text="@string/years2"
132              android:textColor="@color/bone_white"
133              android:textSize="12sp" />
```

```
134
135   <RadioButton
136            android:id="@+id/radio1"
137            android:layout_width="wrap_content"
138            android:layout_height="wrap_content"
139            android:text="@string/years3"
140            android:textColor="@color/bone_white"
141            android:textSize="12sp" />
142
143   <RadioButton
144            android:id="@+id/radio2"
145            android:layout_width="wrap_content"
146            android:layout_height="wrap_content"
147            android:text="@string/years4"
148            android:textColor="@color/bone_white"
149            android:textSize="12sp" />
150
151   </RadioGroup>
152
153   <TextView
154          android:id="@+id/textView6"
155          android:layout_width="wrap_content"
156          android:layout_height="wrap_content"
157          android:layout_below="@+id/radioGroup1"
158          android:layout_centerHorizontal="true"
159          android:text="@string/loan_term"
160          android:textColor="@color/steel_blue"
161          android:textSize="12sp"   />
162
163   <Button
164          android:id="@+id/button1"
165          android:layout_width="wrap_content"
166          android:layout_height="wrap_content"
167          android:layout_alignParentBottom="true"
168          android:layout_centerHorizontal="true"
169          android:text="@string/generate_btn"
170          android:onClick="activateLoanSummary"/>
171
172   </RelativeLayout>
```

The second layout screen, `loansummary_layout.xml`, appears when the activity named `LoanSummaryActivity` is running in the foreground. This layout is used to display a loan summary of the calculated costs for a car purchased from Tom's car lot. The graphic layout design is shown in Figure 3-14.

A set of three `TextViews` is also used for the display of the generated loan report. The XML code for `loansummary_layout.xml` appears below:

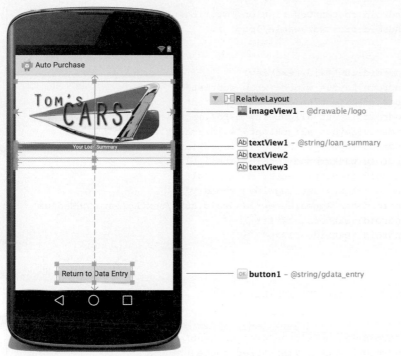

FIGURE 3-14 Layout structure for the `loansummary_layout.xml`.

Line 68: A button is declared to return the user to the input screen for entry of new car purchase information. The `onClick()` handler for this button is identified as `go_data_entry()`. This method will relaunch `PurchaseActivity`.

```
loansummary_layout.xml
1   <?xml version="1.0" encoding="utf-8"?>
2   <RelativeLayout
3   xmlns:android="http://schemas.android.com/apk/res/android"
4       android:layout_width="match_parent"
5       android:layout_height="match_parent"
6       android:paddingTop="@dimen/activity_vertical_margin"
7       android:paddingBottom="@dimen/activity_vertical_margin">
8
9   <!-- LOGO AND INSTRUCTION SECTION -->
10  <ImageView
11          android:id="@+id/imageView1"
12          android:layout_width="fill_parent"
13          android:layout_height="wrap_content"
14          android:layout_alignParentTop="true"
15          android:layout_centerHorizontal="true"
```

```
16              android:contentDescription="@string/title_activity_main"
17              android:src="@drawable/logo" />
18
19     <TextView
20              android:id="@+id/textView1"
21              android:layout_width="wrap_content"
22              android:layout_height="wrap_content"
23              android:layout_alignLeft="@+id/imageView1"
24              android:layout_alignRight="@+id/imageView1"
25              android:layout_below="@+id/imageView1"
26              android:background="@color/steel_blue"
27              android:gravity="center_horizontal"
28              android:text="@string/loan_summary"
29              android:textAppearance="?android:attr/textAppearanceMedium"
30              android:textColor="#fff"
31              android:textSize="12sp" />
32
33
34
35     <!-- TEXTVIEW HOLDING THE MONTHLY PAYMENT -->
36     <TextView
37              android:id="@+id/textView2"
38              android:layout_width="wrap_content"
39              android:layout_height="wrap_content"
40              android:layout_alignLeft="@+id/textView1"
41              android:layout_alignRight="@+id/textView1"
42              android:layout_below="@+id/textView1"
43              android:layout_marginTop="2dp"
44              android:textSize="18sp" />
45
46
47     <!-- TEXTVIEW HOLDING THE CAR LOAN SUMMARY -->
48     <TextView
49              android:id="@+id/textView3"
50              android:layout_width="wrap_content"
51              android:layout_height="wrap_content"
52              android:layout_alignLeft="@+id/textView1"
53              android:layout_alignRight="@+id/textView1"
54              android:layout_below="@+id/textView2"
55              android:layout_marginTop="2dp"
56              android:textSize="16sp"
57              android:typeface="monospace"
58              android:paddingLeft="10dp"
59              android:paddingRight="10dp" />
60
61     <Button
62              android:id="@+id/button1"
63              android:layout_width="wrap_content"
64              android:layout_height="wrap_content"
```

```
65              android:layout_alignParentBottom="true"
66              android:layout_centerHorizontal="true"
67              android:onClick="goDataEntry"
68              android:text="@string/go_data_entry" />
69
70  </RelativeLayout>
```

Part 5: Source Code for Application

The Auto.java source file is the data model for an abstract automobile purchase. The data members for this class are the price, down payment, and the loan term in years. The state tax is fixed at the rate of 7%. The interest rate for a loan is fixed at 9%.

Auto.java
```
1   package com.cornez.autopurchase;
2
3   /**
4    * Data model for an auto
5    */
6   public class Auto {
7       static final double STATE_TAX = .07;
8       static final double INTEREST_RATE = .09;
9
10
11      private double mPrice;
12      private double mDownPayment;
13      private int mLoanTerm;
14
15      public void setPrice(double price) {
16          mPrice = price;
17      }
18
19      public double getPrice() {
20          return mPrice;
21      }
22
23      public void setDownPayment(double down) {
24          mDownPayment = down;
25      }
26
27      public double getDownPayment() {
28          return mDownPayment;
29      }
30
31      public void setLoanTerm(String term) {
32          if (term.contains("2"))
33              mLoanTerm = 2;
```

```
34          else if (term.contains("3"))
35              mLoanTerm = 3;
36          else
37              mLoanTerm = 4;
38      }
39
40      public int getLoanTerm() {
41          return mLoanTerm;
42      }
43
44      public double taxAmount() {
45          return mPrice * STATE_TAX;
46      }
47
48      public double totalCost() {
49          return mPrice + taxAmount();
50      }
51
52      public double borrowedAmount() {
53          return totalCost() - mDownPayment;
54      }
55
56      public double interestAmount() {
57          return borrowedAmount() * INTEREST_RATE;
58      }
59
60      public double monthlyPayment() {
61          return borrowedAmount() / (mLoanTerm * 12);
62      }
63
64  }
```

The Java code for `PurchaseActivity` is shown below:

Lines 23–24:   The two data elements to be attached to an `Intent` are declared.

PurchaseActivity.java

```
1   package com.cornez.autopurchase;
2
3   import android.app.Activity;
4   import android.content.Intent;
5   import android.content.res.Resources;
6   import android.os.Bundle;
7   import android.view.Menu;
8   import android.view.MenuItem;
9   import android.view.View;
10
```

```
11  import android.widget.EditText;
12  import android.widget.RadioButton;
13  import android.widget.RadioGroup;
14
15  //THE APPLICATION'S MAIN ACTIVITY
16  public class PurchaseActivity extends Activity {
17
18      // THE AUTO OBJECT CONTAINS THE INFORMATION
19      //ABOUT THE VEHICLE BEING PURCHASED
20      Auto mAuto;
21
22      // THE DATA TO BE PASSED TO THE LOAN ACTIVITY
23      String loanReport;
24      String monthlyPayment;
25
26      // LAYOUT INPUT REFERENCES
27      private EditText carPriceET;
28      private EditText downPayET;
29      private RadioGroup loanTermRG;
30
31      @Override
32      protected void onCreate(Bundle savedInstanceState) {
33          super.onCreate(savedInstanceState);
34          setContentView(R.layout.purchase_layout);
35
36          //ESTABLISH REFERENCES TO EDITABLE TEXT FIELDS AND RADIO BUTTON
37          carPriceET = (EditText) findViewById(R.id.editText1);
38          downPayET = (EditText) findViewById(R.id.editText2);
39          loanTermRG = (RadioGroup) findViewById(R.id.radioGroup1);
40
41          //CREATE AN AUTOMOBILE OBJECT TO STORE AUTO DATA
42          mAuto = new Auto();
43      }
44
45      private void collectAutoInputData() {
46          // TASK 1: SET THE CAR PRICE
47          mAuto.setPrice ((double) Integer.valueOf(carPriceET.getText()
48                  .toString()));
49
50          //TASK 2: SET THE DOWN PAYMENT
51          mAuto.setDownPayment((double)
52                  Integer.valueOf(downPayET.getText()
53                          .toString()));
54
55          //TASK 3 SET THE LOAN TERM
56          Integer radioId = loanTermRG.getCheckedRadioButtonId();
57          RadioButton term = (RadioButton) findViewById(radioId);
58          mAuto.setLoanTerm(term.getText().toString());
59      }
```

Line 91–108: `activateLoanSummary()` is the `onClick()` handler for the button that activates the loan summary.

Lines 97–98: An `Intent` is instantiated. The context class is the `PurchaseActivity`, specified by `this`. The name of the activity to be launched is `LoanSummaryActivity`.

Lines 103–104: The `Intent` that is used to launch the new activity will be extended with two additional data elements: `loanReport` and `monthlyPayment`. The `putExtra` method will configure the `Intent` to send the data to the next activity.

`putExtra` accepts data as a `KEY-VALUE` pair where `VALUE` is retrieved in the second activity using the `KEY`. Several variants of `putExtra` allow other types of data to be sent. Explore the Android documentation for value types that can be included into the extras of an `Intent`, such as `int`, `int[]`, `Bundle`, and `Parcelable`.

Line 107: The new activity is launched with the `Intent`.

```
PurchaseActivity.java    continued
60  private void buildLoanReport() {
61          // TASK 1: CONSTRUCT THE MONTHLY PAYMENT
62          Resources res = getResources();
63          monthlyPayment = res.getString(R.string.report_line1)
64                  + String.format("%.02f", mAuto.monthlyPayment());
65
66
67          // TASK 2: CONSTRUCT THE LOAN REPORT
68          loanReport = res.getString(R.string.report_line6)
69                  + String.format("%10.02f", mAuto.getPrice());
70          loanReport += res.getString(R.string.report_line7)
71                  + String.format("%10.02f", mAuto.getDownPayment());
72
73          loanReport += res.getString(R.string.report_line9)
74                  + String.format("%18.02f", mAuto.taxAmount());
75          loanReport += res.getString(R.string.report_line10)
76                  + String.format("%18.02f", mAuto.totalCost());
77          loanReport += res.getString(R.string.report_line11)
78                  + String.format("%12.02f", mAuto.borrowedAmount());
79          loanReport += res.getString(R.string.report_line12)
80                  + String.format("%12.02f", mAuto.interestAmount());
81
82          loanReport += "\n\n" + res.getString(R.string.report_line8) +
83              " " + mAuto.getLoanTerm() + " years.";
84
85          loanReport += "\n\n" + res.getString(R.string.report_line2);
```

```
86          loanReport += res.getString(R.string.report_line3);
87          loanReport += res.getString(R.string.report_line4);
88          loanReport += res.getString(R.string.report_line5);
89      }
90
91      public void activateLoanSummary(View view) {
92          //TASK 1: BUILD A LOAN REPORT FROM THE INPUT DATA
93          collectAutoInputData();
94          buildLoanReport();
95
96          //TASK 2: CREATE AN INTENT TO DISPLAY THE LOAN SUMMARY ACTIVITY
97          Intent launchReport = new Intent(this,
98              LoanSummaryActivity.class);
99
100         //TASK 3: PASS THE LOAN SUMMARY ACTIVITY TWO PIECES OF DATA:
101         //      THE LOAN REPORT CONTAINING LOAN DETAILS
102         //      THE MONTHLY PAYMENT
103         launchReport.putExtra("LoanReport", loanReport);
104         launchReport.putExtra("MonthlyPayment", monthlyPayment);
105
106         //TASK 4: START THE LOAN ACTIVITY
107         startActivity(launchReport);
108     }
109
110     @Override
111     public boolean onCreateOptionsMenu(Menu menu) {
112         // Inflate the menu;
113         getMenuInflater().inflate(R.menu.my, menu);
114         return true;
115     }
116
117     @Override
118     public boolean onOptionsItemSelected(MenuItem item) {
119         // Handle action bar item clicks here. The action bar will
120         // automatically handle clicks on the Home/Up button, so long
121         // as you specify a parent activity in AndroidManifest.xml.
122         int id = item.getItemId();
123         if (id == R.id.action_settings) {
124             return true;
125         }
126         return super.onOptionsItemSelected(item);
127     }
128 }
```

The secondary activity for the Car Purchase app is implemented as `Loan-SummaryActivity`, as shown below:

Line 19:   `getIntent()` is used to identify which `Intent` started this
                 activity. This method is typically placed in `onCreate()`, but it
                 is not required.

Lines 21–22:   The `LoanSummaryActivity` receives the data sent by the activity that launched it. `getStringExtra()` returns the value of the item that was previously added with `putExtra ()`. The key-value pairs were initially specified in `PurchaseActivity` as follows:

```
launchReport.putExtra("LoanReport",
    loanReport);
```

```
launchReport.putExtra
    ("MonthlyPayment", monthlyPayment);
```

It should be noted that the method `getExtras()` can also be used to retrieve a map of extended data from an `Intent`.

Lines 30–32:   `finish ()` is called when the user is through with this activity and wishes to return to the input screen. When the input screen is relaunched, this activity must be closed. `finish ()` performs these tasks and relies on `ActivityResult` to propagate back to the activity that launched it.

```
LoanSummaryActivity.java
 1  package com.cornez.autopurchase;
 2
 3  import android.app.Activity;
 4  import android.content.Intent;
 5  import android.os.Bundle;
 6  import android.view.View;
 7  import android.widget.TextView;
 8
 9  public class LoanSummaryActivity extends Activity {
10
11      @Override
12      public void onCreate(Bundle savedInstanceState) {
13          super.onCreate(savedInstanceState);
14          setContentView(R.layout.loansummary_layout);
15          TextView monthlyPayET = (TextView) findViewById(R.id.textView2);
16          TextView loanReportET = (TextView) findViewById(R.id.textView3);
17
18          // PASS DATA
19          Intent intent = getIntent();
20
21          String report;
22          report = intent.getStringExtra("LoanReport");
23
24          String monthlyPay;
25          monthlyPay = intent.getStringExtra("MonthlyPayment");
26          monthlyPayET.setText(monthlyPay);
```

```
27          loanReportET.setText(report);
28      }
29
30      public void goDataEntry(View view) {
31          finish();
32      }
33  }
```

■ 3.6 Basic Transitions between Activities

The quality of an application can depend on several characteristics, such as its content, usability, and design features. Enhancements made to interaction design, through the use of animation, can make a fundamental difference in the usability of an application. Users' experiences and their impression of an app are shaped by a combination of factors, with interaction playing a very large role. There is more to design than simple functionality. The primary reason for this is that user interfaces are not static designs, but rather engaging and dynamic design patterns.

When users fling their fingers across the touchscreen, the result can cause a large change; for example, the current layout can be replaced by an entirely different layout. On the other hand, the change could be so small that it might go unnoticed, such as when elements are rearranged on an existing layout. Users may sometimes find it difficult to know where to focus their attention or even to understand how the screen content got from point A to point B. Transitions in a user interface have been effective in supporting user focus and guiding attention during navigation of an application.

When a new layout appears on the screen featuring different content, the result can be a loss of context for the user. As the screen moves from layout to layout, we can assume that the user expects a linear experience, with each screen building upon the other in context. By enhancing the screen changes with an animated transition, the application can provide a better understanding about the subsequent new screen. Animated transitions primarily serve a functional purpose, but they may also improve the overall beauty of a user experience.

It should be noted that overusing animation transitions or using them at inappropriate moments might detract from the quality of the experience. During the design phase of an application, animation transitions should be analyzed carefully to ensure they will not cause unnecessary delays; they should then be applied judiciously.

Custom transition animations are resources that can be built by methods in XML code. By using the method `overridePendingTransition()`, the custom-built transitions can be explicitly applied to the entering and exiting activities. `overridePendingTransition()` requires two arguments: an enter animation implementation and an exit animation implementation. The enter animation resource will be used for an incoming activity, and the exit animation resource will be used for an exiting activity.

The code segment shown below illustrates overridePendingTransition():

Line 1:   An Intent is instantiated to exit ActivityA and launch ActivityB.

```
ActivityA.java
1   Intent intent = new Intent(ActivityA.this, ActivityB.class);
2    startActivity(intent);
```

Line 2:   onStart () is called when ActivityB is becoming visible to the user.

Lines 4–5:   overridePendingTransition() is called to apply transition_out.xml to the incoming activity and transition_out.xml to the outgoing activity.

```
ActivityB.java
1   @Override
2       protected void onStart() {
3           super.onStart();
4           overridePendingTransition(R.anim.transition_in,
5                                 R.anim.transition_out);
6       }
```

Notice that arguments for overridePendingTransition () use R class identifications for both of the two transition animations. The dynamically generated R.class contains numeric constants that uniquely identify all animation transition XML files, such as those shown on Lines 3 and 4 in the code below. These Android resources are available for usage in Java classes within the app.

```
R.java
1   public final class R {
2       public static final class anim {
3           public static final int transition _in=0x7f040000;
4           public static final int transition _out=0x7f040001;
5   }
6   .
7   .
8   .
```

Animation resource files are defined using XML code. They are stored in an animation folder, typically named anim, within the res directory of the project.

Animation resources can be defined in one of two ways: property animation and View animation. Property animations involve the modification of a View's properties, using an animator, over a set period of time.

A `View` animation uses `tweens` and `frames`. For example, a `tween` animation uses an image, such as a shape drawable, placed on stage as an `ImageView`. Its *x* and *y* position on the screen is altered in a looping structure. The result is that the object moves on the screen. Chapter 6 devotes a considerable amount of discussion to this topic.

Property animations are typically defined in XML files. Specific properties of the target object are modified over a set period of time. Examples of these properties are:

`rotation`

`rotationX`

`rotationY`

`scaleX`

`scaleY`

`pivotX`

`pivotY`

`x`

`y`

`alpha`

A common XML tag found in an animation XML file is `<set>`. This serves as a container that holds other animation elements (`<objectAnimator>`, `<valueAnimator>`, or other `<set>` elements).

`<set>` tags can be nested to further group animations together.

In the sample XML code shown below, an animated transition is implemented using an `objectAnimator`. The *x* and *y* properties are set to values 400 and 300, respectively. The animation will play over a duration of 500 milliseconds.

```
transition.xml
 1  <set>
 2  <objectAnimator
 3          android:propertyName="x"
 4          android:duration="500"
 5          android:valueTo="400"
 6          android:valueType="intType"/>
 7  <objectAnimator
 8          android:propertyName="y"
 9          android:duration="500"
10          android:valueTo="300"
11          android:valueType="intType"/>
12  </set>
```

■ Lab Example 3-4: Flip Cards with Animated Activity Transitions

The following lab example illustrates how an animated transition can be used when navigating between activities.

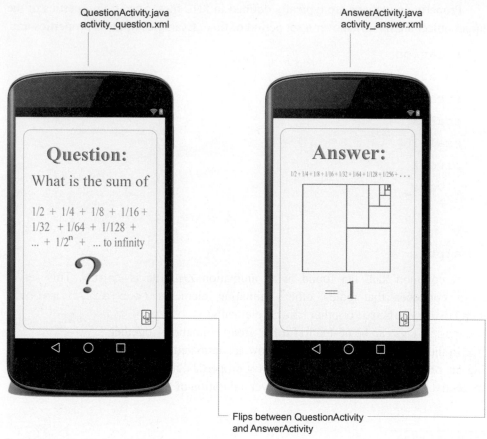

FIGURE 3-15 The front and back of a flip card.

Part 1: The Application Design

Students often prepare for tests and quizzes by scribbling notes on notecards. A flashcard is similar to this concept. It has two sides, such as a question on one side and the answer to the question on the other side.

The goal of this lab is not to create a complete stack of flashcards. That would be very useful to many people, but also time-consuming. Rather, the objective of this lab is to explore the use of animated transitions when navigating between activities. For example, consider a question card, such as the one shown in Figure 3-15, displayed on the screen in the form of a visual layout. When the user turns the card over, tapping the flip button located on the screen results in a customized animated transition that gives the user the sensory experience of the card being flipped.

To create a fully functioning Flashcard application, we would need to create many cards in a deck that could be shuffled. A deck would perhaps require a database of information. These topics will be discussed in the next chapters.

Part 2: Application Structure and Setup

The settings for the application are as follows:

- Application Name: Flip Card
- Project Name: FlipCard
- Package Name: `com.cornez.flipcard`
- Android Form: Phone and Tablet
- Minimum SDK: API 18: Android 4.3 (Jelly Bean)
- Target SDK: API 21: Android 5.0 (Lollipop)
- Compile with: API 21: Android 5.0 (Lollipop)
- Activity Name: `QuestionActivity`
- Layout Name: `activity_question`

The launcher icon for the application is set to the Android default `ic_launcher.pg` file. In addition to this graphic file, the drawable folder contains a background, a front card image, a back card image, and a flip button for the user to alternate between the two sides of the card. Figure 3-16 shows the complete project structure for this app.

The two activity files are representative of the two sides of the flashcard. The animation XML files are for transitioning cards in and out. This requires four animation files. Finally, the two layouts used in the application correspond with the two activities.

The orientation of the screen is locked into portrait mode, which is done in the `AndroidManifest.xml` file. In addition, a full screen is used and the titlebar is removed. Finally, since we have two activities, both are listed in the `AndroidManifest` file. The launch default activity is `QuestionActivity`, as shown in Lines 11–21 of the Android manifest file.

Lines 11–22:   The main activity of the application is defined as `QuestionActivity`. This activity is implemented as `QuestionActivity`.java.

Line 14:   `screenOrientation` is specified for individual activities.

Lines 23–29:   The secondary activity of the application is defined as `AnswerActivity` activity. This activity is implemented as `AnswerActivity`.java.

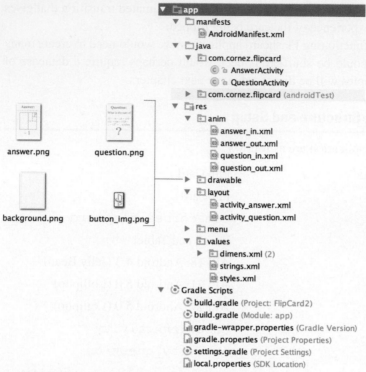

answer.png   question.png

background.png   button_img.png

FIGURE 3-16 Project structure of the Flip Card application.

```
AndroidManifest.xml
1  <?xml version="1.0" encoding="utf-8"?>
2  <manifest xmlns:android="http://schemas.android.com/apk/res/android"
3      package="com.cornez.flipcard" >
4
5  <application
6          android:allowBackup="true"
7          android:icon="@drawable/ic_launcher"
8          android:label="@string/app_name"
9          android:theme="@style/AppTheme" >
10
11 <!-- QUESTION ACTIVITY -->
12 <activity
13          android:name=".QuestionActivity"
14          android:screenOrientation="portrait"
15          android:label="@string/app_name" >
16 <intent-filter>
17 <action android:name="android.intent.action.MAIN" />
```

```
18   <category
19   android:name="android.intent.category.LAUNCHER" />
20   </intent-filter>
21   </activity>
22
23   <!-- ANSWER ACTIVITY -->
24   <activity
25               android:name=".AnswerActivity"
26               android:screenOrientation="portrait"
27               android:label="@string/app_name" >
28   </activity>
29   </application>
30
31   </manifest>
```

Part 3: External Value Resources

There are no external resources for the Flashcard app other than `strings.xml`, which contains text strings for the `ImageView` to be added to the layouts. As shown below, `strings.xml` has been edited to contain content descriptions.

```
strings.xml
1   <?xml version="1.0" encoding="utf-8"?>
2   <resources>
3
4   <string name="app_name">Flip Card</string>
5   <string name="hello_world">Hello world!</string>
6   <string name="action_settings">Settings</string>
7
8   <string name="question_card">Question</string>
9   <string name="answer_card">Answer</string>
10
11   </resources>
```

Part 4: The User Interface

This is a trivial app, because it contains exactly one card. The card question (card front) is visually implemented by `activity_question.xml`. The root element is a `RelativeLayout` containing a card background. These two elements, as seen in Figure 3-17, are the question image and the flip button.

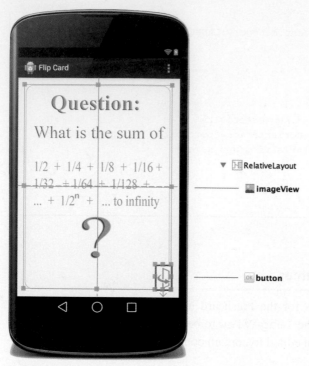

FIGURE 3-17 `activity_question.xml` represents the front side of the card.

```
activity_question.xml
1   <RelativeLayout
2   xmlns:android="http://schemas.android.com/apk/res/android"
3       xmlns:tools="http://schemas.android.com/tools"
4       android:layout_width="match_parent"
5       android:layout_height="match_parent"
6       android:paddingLeft="@dimen/activity_horizontal_margin"
7       android:paddingRight="@dimen/activity_horizontal_margin"
8       android:paddingTop="@dimen/activity_vertical_margin"
9       android:paddingBottom="@dimen/activity_vertical_margin"
10      tools:context=".QuestionActivity"
11      android:background="@drawable/background">
12
13
14  <ImageView
15          android:layout_width="wrap_content"
16          android:layout_height="wrap_content"
17          android:id="@+id/imageView"
18          android:layout_centerVertical="true"
19          android:layout_centerHorizontal="true"
20          android:src="@drawable/question"
```

```
21              android:contentDescription-"@string/answer_card" />
22
23
24   <Button
25          style="?android:attr/buttonStyleSmall"
26          android:layout_width="wrap_content"
27          android:layout_height="wrap_content"
28          android:id="@+id/button"
29          android:layout_alignParentBottom="true"
30          android:layout_alignParentStart="true"
31          android:layout_marginLeft="311dp"
32          android:background="@drawable/button_img" />
33   </RelativeLayout>
```

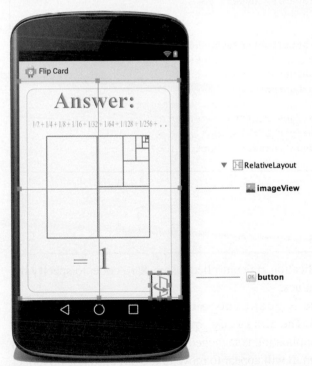

FIGURE 3-18 `activity_answer.xml` represents the back side of the flashcard.

The XML file `activity_answer.xml` is constructed similarly to the front side of the card. A consistent background is applied to the root element of each of the layouts. The XML file that implements `activity_answer` seen in Figure 3-18 is shown below.

```
activity_answer.xml
1   <?xml version="1.0" encoding="utf-8"?>
2   <RelativeLayout
3   xmlns:android="http://schemas.android.com/apk/res/android"
4       android:layout_width="match_parent"
5       android:layout_height="match_parent"
6       android:background="@drawable/background">
7
8   <ImageView
9           android:layout_width="wrap_content"
10          android:layout_height="wrap_content"
11          android:id="@+id/imageView"
12          android:layout_centerVertical="true"
13          android:layout_centerHorizontal="true"
14          android:contentDescription="@string/answer_card"
15          android:src="@drawable/answer" />
16
17  <Button
18          style="?android:attr/buttonStyleSmall"
19          android:layout_width="wrap_content"
20          android:layout_height="wrap_content"
21          android:id="@+id/button"
22          android:layout_alignParentBottom="true"
23          android:layout_alignParentStart="true"
24          android:layout_marginLeft="311dp"
25          android:background="@drawable/button_img" />
26  </RelativeLayout>
```

Part 5: Animated Transitions

The four transitions for this application are controlled, using XML code, to specify the animation properties and their values.

The first XML transition file is question_out.xml. This file describes the animation shown in Figure 3-19. The activity_question layout is initially displayed on the screen when the application is launched. The layout has a start position of 0. As it moves out of the screen, it will appear to move to the left until it is no longer visible on the screen. Its ending position is 100% of the screen.

Line 3:   Movement is constructed within a tag called <translate>. This tag, which represents a TranslateAnimation, is used to declare a starting x position, an ending x position, and a duration value.

The tag <translate> can be used for vertical and/or horizontal motion.

Line 4:   The attribute `android:fromXDelta` refers to the starting *x* offset position. The value can also be expressed in pixels relative to the normal position (such as "5"), in percentage relative to the element width (such as "5%"), or in percentage relative to the parent width (such as "5%p").

Line 5:   The attribute `android:toXDelta` refers to the ending *x* offset position. It supports attributes in any of the following three formats: (1) values from −100 to 100 ending with "%," indicating a percentage relative to itself; (2) values from −100 to 100 ending in "%p," indicating a percentage relative to its parent; or (3) a float value with no suffix, indicating an absolute value.

Line 6:   The attribute `android:duration` specifies how long the animation will last in milliseconds.

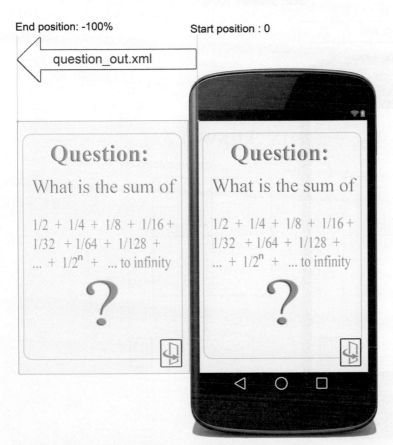

▌ FIGURE 3-19 A question exits the screen by moving to the right.

```
question_out.xml
1   <?xml version="1.0" encoding="utf-8"?>
2   <set xmlns:android="http://schemas.android.com/apk/res/android">
3   <translate
4           android:fromXDelta="0"
5           android:toXDelta="-100%"
6           android:duration="1250"/>
7   </set>
```

The second XML transition file describes the details, as depicted in Figure 3-20, for how the `answer_in.xml` layout will be moved from a position off the screen to its final location occupying the entire screen. The code is similar to the previous transition XML file, with only the values for the to/from properties altered. The XML code for `answer_in.xml` is shown below.

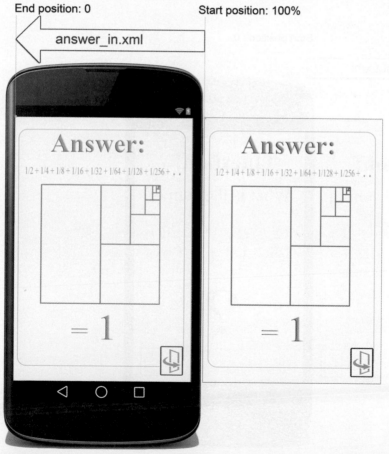

I FIGURE 3-20 An answer image enters the screen from the left.

```
answer_in.xml
1   <?xml version="1.0" encoding="utf-8"?>
2   <set xmlns:android="http://schemas.android.com/apk/res/android">
3   <translate
4       android:fromXDelta="100%"
5       android:toXDelta="0"
6       android:duration="1250" />
7   </set>
```

The animation XML file is used for the transitioning of the backside of the card; the answer, as it leaves the screen, is shown below in `answer_out.xml`.

```
answer_out.xml
1   <?xml version="1.0" encoding="utf-8"?>
2   <set xmlns:android="http://schemas.android.com/apk/res/android">
3   <translate
4       android:fromXDelta="0%"
5       android:toXDelta="100%"
6       android:duration="1250" />
7   </set>
```

The animation XML file is used for the transitioning of the frontside of the card; the question, as it moves back into the screen, is shown below in `question_in.xml`.

```
question_in.xml
1   <?xml version="1.0" encoding="utf-8"?>
2   <set xmlns:android="http://schemas.android.com/apk/res/android">
3   <translate
4           android:fromXDelta="-100%"
5           android:toXDelta="0%"
6           android:duration="1250"/>
7   </set>
```

Part 6: Source Code for Application

As a simple application, this lab example requires only two activities: the question side of the flashcard, and the answer side of the flashcard. `QuestionActivity` is the main activity of the application and will be launched when the application is launched for the first time. The Java code for `QuestionActivity` is shown below.

Line 17:   The visual content for the `Activity` is set to the layout named `activity_question.xml`.

Line 19:   `answerBtn` is used to reference the button `View` object from the active layout, `activity_question.xml`.

Lines 20–28: A listener event is registered to `answerBtn`, and the `onClick`
() handler is implemented as an anonymous inner class.

Lines 24–25: An `Intent` is instantiated to exit `QuestionActivity` and
launch `AnswerActivity`.

Lines 32–36: A transition animation will be initiated in the `onStart` ()
method of `QuestionActivity`. The animation will play out
as the activity becomes visible to the user.

QuestionActivity.java

```
1   package com.cornez.flipcard;
2
3   import android.app.Activity;
4   import android.content.Intent;
5   import android.os.Bundle;
6   import android.view.Menu;
7   import android.view.MenuItem;
8   import android.view.View;
9   import android.widget.Button;
10
11
12  public class QuestionActivity extends Activity {
13
14      @Override
15      protected void onCreate(Bundle savedInstanceState) {
16          super.onCreate(savedInstanceState);
17          setContentView(R.layout.activity_question);
18
19          Button answerBtn = (Button) findViewById(R.id.button);
20          answerBtn.setOnClickListener(new View.OnClickListener() {
21
22              @Override
23              public void onClick(View view) {
24                  Intent showAnswer = new Intent(QuestionActivity.this,
25                          AnswerActivity.class);
26                  startActivity(showAnswer);
27              }
28          });
29      }
30
31      @Override
32      protected void onStart() {
33          super.onStart();
34          overridePendingTransition(R.anim.question_out,
35          R.anim.answer_in);
36      }
37
38
```

```
39      @Override
40      public boolean onCreateOptionsMenu(Menu menu) {
41          // Inflate the menu
42          getMenuInflater().inflate(R.menu.question, menu);
43          return true;
44      }
45
46      @Override
47      public boolean onOptionsItemSelected(MenuItem item) {
48          // Handle action bar item clicks here. The action bar will
49          // automatically handle clicks on the Home/Up button, so long
50          // as you specify a parent activity in AndroidManifest.xml.
51          int id = item.getItemId();
52          if (id == R.id.action_settings) {
53              return true;
54          }
55          return super.onOptionsItemSelected(item);
56      }
57  }
```

AnswerActivity is the secondary activity of the application and will be launched when the user decides to flip the card to view the answer. The Java code for AnswerActivity is shown below:

Line 14:   The visual content for the activity is set to the layout named activity_answer.xml.

Line 16:   questionBtn is used to reference the button View object from the active layout, activity_answer.xml.

Lines 17–25:   A listener event is registered to answerBtn, and the onClick() handler is implemented as an anonymous inner class.

Lines 21–22:   An Intent is instantiated to exit the AnswerActivity and navigate back to the previously stopped QuestionActivity.

Lines 28–33:   A transition animation is initiated in the onStart() method of AnswerActivity. An animation will play out as the activity becomes visible to the user.

AnswerActivity.java
```
1  package com.cornez.flipcard;
2
3  import android.app.Activity;
4  import android.content.Intent;
5  import android.os.Bundle;
6  import android.view.View;
7  import android.widget.Button;
8
9
```

```
10  public class AnswerActivity  extends Activity {
11
12      protected void onCreate (Bundle savedInstance) {
13          super.onCreate(savedInstance);
14          setContentView(R.layout.activity_answer);
15
16          Button questionBtn = (Button) findViewById(R.id.button);
17          questionBtn.setOnClickListener(new View.OnClickListener() {
18
19              @Override
20              public void onClick(View view) {
21                  Intent showQuestion = new Intent(AnswerActivity.this,
22                          QuestionActivity.class);
23                  startActivity(showQuestion);
24              }
25          });
26
27      }
28      @Override
29      protected void onStart() {
30          super.onStart();
31          overridePendingTransition(R.anim.answer_out,
32              R.anim.question_in);
33      }
34
35  }
```

■ 3.7 Scene Transitions

With the release of KitKat, Android 4.4, a transitions framework was introduced that supports the definition of scene transitions.

Unlike frames, which will be discussed in Chapter 4, scenes are used specifically for transition animations. For example, scenes can be created as a View hierarchy, much like a layout. As a View hierarchy, scenes can be merged or transitioned into a defined View within an activity.

A scene contains values of various properties in the View hierarchy. As scenes enter or exit a View hierarchy, they will be animated based on these properties. In this manner, a scene defines a given state of the UI, whereas a transition defines the change from one scene to another.

Consider the following segment of code that illustrates how a scene is used in an activity:

Line 1:   The layout for the activity is established as
              activity_my.xml.

Line 2:   The root element of `activity_my.xml` is referenced by
                      `rootElement`, a `ViewGroup` for holding other `View`
                      elements.

Lines 5–9:   `scene1` and `scene2` are each assigned a `Scene`, which will
                      eventually be transitioned in and out of the `ViewGroup` root
                      element.

                      The method `getSceneForLayout()` requires three
                      arguments:

1. A `View` defined in the activity layout. Animated transitions take
   place in this `View`. In the code example below, `rootElement`
   is identified as the `View` object that displays the transition
   animation.

2. A scene layout resource file that contains the transition
   changes that occur. The two-scene layout resource files used
   in the code example are identified as `scene1_layout` and
   `scene2_layout`.

3. The context used in the process of inflating a scene layout resource. The context for this example is the current activity.

Line 11:   `scene1` is entered. The animation transition entails changing all
                      values that are specified by this scene.

```
1   setContentView(R.layout.activity_my);
2
3   ViewGroup rootElement = (ViewGroup) findViewById(R.id.rootContainer);
4
5   Scene scene1 = Scene.getSceneForLayout(rootElement,
6                   R.layout.scene1_layout, this);
7
8   Scene scene2 = Scene.getSceneForLayout(rootElement,
9                   R.layout.scene2_layout, this);
10
11  scene1.enter();
```

`Transitions` and `Scenes` produce animations based on specific properties,
such as visibility. A `Transition` holds information about animations that are run
on its targets during a `Scene` change. Every `Transition` object has two functions: (1) to capture property values and (2) to play animations based on changes to
the captured property values. For example, consider a `Transition` animation that
requires an object to fade into view. A `Transition` tracks changes using visibility
properties and then constructs and plays the animation based on the changes to those
properties.

Android developers can use the `TransitionManager` to coordinate `Scene` with `Transition` objects. More specifically, the `TransitionManager` manages the set of transitions that fire when there is a change of `Scene`. `TransitionManagers` can be declared in XML resource files inside the res/transition directory.

The following XML code example illustrates the delaration of scene transitions. Tag names are used to describe the relationship of a given transition to the from/to `Scene` information in that tag.

```
1    <transitionManager>
2    <transition
3                    android:fromScene="@layout/transition_scene1"
4                    android:toScene="@layout/transition_scene2"
5                    android:transition="@transition/changebounds"/>
6
7    <transition
8                    android:fromScene="@layout/transition_scene2"
9                    android:toScene="@layout/transition_scene1"
10                   android:transition="@transition/changebounds"/>
11
12   <transition
13                   android:toScene="@layout/transition_scene3"
14                   android:transition=
15                       "@transition/changebounds_fadein_together"/>
16
17   <transition
18                   android:fromScene="@layout/transition_scene3"
19                   android:toScene="@layout/transition_scene1"
20                   android:transition=
21                       "@transition/changebounds_fadeout_sequential"/>
22
23   <transition
24                   android:fromScene="@layout/transition_scene3"
25                   android:toScene="@layout/transition_scene2"
26                   android:transition=
27                       "@transition/changebounds_fadeout_sequential"/>
28   </transitionManager>
```

■ Lab Example 3-5: Pieces of a Painting–The Painting Scene App

The objective of the Painting Scene application is to explore the use of the `TransitionManager` and the construction of Scenes and Transitions.

Part 1: The Design

When the Painting Pieces application is launched for the first time, the user is presented with a famous Renaissance painting; however, the painting is not fully visible.

Much of the painting has been blocked out in small rectangular objects, as shown in Figure 3-21.

The idea of the app is similar to a flip card. The user can attempt to identify the famous painting and then tap the "show" button, located at the lower right corner of the screen, to reveal the complete painting and confirm the answer.

An animated transition is used to reveal the complete painting.

Show

FIGURE 3-21 Animation will occur with the gradual appearance of the painting.

Unlike the flashcard lab example, which performed a uniform `Transition` of a `ViewGroup`, the button in this lab triggers a complex animation. As shown in Figure 3-22, individual elements are animated to alter the scene in an interesting way.

 . . .  . . .

FIGURE 3-22 Animated Transition between Scenes.

Part 2: Application Structure and Setup

The settings for the application are as follows:

- Application Name: Paint Scene
- Project Name: PaintScene
- Package Name: `com.cornez.paintscene`
- Android Form: Phone and Tablet
- Minimum SDK: API 18: Android 4.3 (Jelly Bean)
- Target SDK: API 21: Android 5.0 (Lollipop)
- Compile with: API 21: Android 5.0 (Lollipop)
- Activity Name: `MainActivity`
- Layout Name: `activity_main`

The application launcher icon remains set to the Android default `ic_launcher.png` file. Figure 3-23 shows the final project structure for the completed application.

The painting is composed of multiple rectangular graphic objects. Similar to a jigsaw puzzle, these graphic elements are combined and arranged to build a complete painting. Each of these graphic elements must be added to the project. They are placed in the default drawable folder.

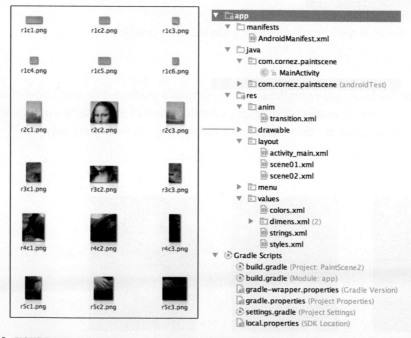

I FIGURE 3-23 Project structure for the Paint Scene application.

Three new XML code files have been added to the application. The Transition XML file, used to govern the animations, is placed in its own resource directory, anim. This directory must be created and placed within the res directory. Two scene resource files are placed in the layout directory, along with the activity layout.

Applications that require multiple activities must rely on the AndroidManifest file to declare them. When using scenes and a single activity, the manifest file needs only to declare the activity.

For the Paint Scene application, the orientation of the screen will be locked into portrait mode. The code for the manifest file is shown as follows:

AndroidManifest.xml

```
1   <?xml version="1.0" encoding="utf-8"?>
2   <manifest xmlns:android="http://schemas.android.com/apk/res/android"
3       package="com.cornez.paintscene" >
4
5   <application
6           android:allowBackup="true"
7           android:icon="@drawable/ic_launcher"
8           android:label="@string/app_name"
9           android:theme="@style/AppTheme" >
10  <activity
11              android:name=".MyActivity"
12              android:screenOrientation="portrait"
13              android:label="@string/app_name" >
14  <intent filter>
15  <action android:name="android.intent.action.MAIN" />
16
17  <category
18  android:name="android.intent.category.LAUNCHER" />
19  </intent-filter>
20  </activity>
21  </application>
22
23  </manifest>
```

Part 3: External Value Resources

The two value resource files used by the Paint Scene application are strings.xml and colors.xml. strings.xml will hold the labels for the two buttons. One button shows the complete painting, and one button returns it to its partially hidden View. A third string has been added to the content description for the pieces of the painting.

colors.xml stores one resource, the color black. This will provide a backdrop for the painting. When a piece of the painting has been removed or made invisible, the black backdrop appears.

The XML code for both these files is shown as follows:

strings.xml

```
1   <?xml version="1.0" encoding="utf-8"?>
2   <resources>
3
4   <string name="app_name">Paint Scene</string>
5   <string name="hello_world">Hello world!</string>
6   <string name="action_settings">Settings</string>
7
8   <string name="show">Show</string>
9   <string name="hide">Hide</string>
10  <string name="paint_square">Painting Piece</string>
11
12  </resources>
```

colors.xml

```
1   <?xml version="1.0" encoding="utf-8"?>
2   <resources>
3
4   <color name="black">#000000</color>
5
6   </resources>
```

Part 4: The User Interface and Scene Definitions

The user interface for the Paint Scene application consists of three files that will be grouped together.

`activity_my.xml` is the layout file that automatically launches the first time the application is launched. Its visual design is shown in Figure 3-24. The `activity_my.xml` layout contains a `ViewGroup` element for scenes to enter and exit.

Lines 14–20:   The `ViewGroup` object is defined as a `RelativeLayout`.

Line 15:   The id name of the `ViewGroup` is `painting_container`.

Line 20:   A black background is applied to the `ViewGroup`.

The XML code for the `activity_my.xml` file is listed as follows:

activity_my.xml

```
1   <RelativeLayout
2   xmlns:android="http://schemas.android.com/apk/res/android"
3   xmlns:tools="http://schemas.android.com/tools"
4       android:layout_width="match_parent"
5       android:layout_height="match_parent"
6       android:background="@color/black"
7       android:paddingBottom="@dimen/activity_vertical_margin"
8       android:paddingLeft="@dimen/activity_horizontal_margin"
```

```
9        android:paddingRight="@dimen/activity_horizontal_margin"
10       android:paddingTop="@dimen/activity_vertical_margin"
11       tools:context=".MyActivity">
12
13
14   <RelativeLayout
15          android:id="@+id/painting_container"
16          android:layout_width="fill_parent"
17          android:layout_height="fill_parent"
18          android:layout_centerHorizontal="true"
19          android:layout_centerVertical="true"
20          android:background="@color/black"></RelativeLayout>
21   </RelativeLayout>
```

▌ FIGURE 3-24 The graphic design of the layout `activity_my.xml`.

The scene layouts for the application hold the painting elements. There are 15 rectangular pieces that form a complete painting.

`scene01.xml` holds all of the painting elements, but it adjusts the visibility property for seven of them so they will not be visible to the user. The visual design for `scene01.xml` is shown in Figure 3-25. This layout contains `ImageViews` placed inside a `RelativeLayout` container.

The code listing for this layout appears as follows:

Line 11:	Each painting piece has a name that corresponds to its location on a grid. For example, the first painting piece is located on row 1, column 1; hence, its unique id is `r1c1`.
Line 16:	A generic content description is assigned to each painting piece.
Line 17:	Note that the name of the drawable matches the assigned id.

FIGURE 3-25 The visual design of the layout `scene01.xml`.

Line 18:   The `visibility` property is set to `invisible` for painting pieces that must be hidden.

Lines 152–159: A `Button` control is defined to allow the user to move to the next scene in the application. The handler for the `onClick` listener event is set to `changesScenes()`. This method is implemented in `MyActivity.java`. In addition, `changesScenes()` is generic in the sense that it will also be the handler for the `onClick` event for returning to the previously visited scene.

The XML code for `scene01.xml` is shown as follows:

```
scene01.sml
1   <?xml version="1.0" encoding="utf-8"?>
2   <merge xmlns:android="http://schemas.android.com/apk/res/android"
3       android:layout_width="match_parent"
4       android:layout_height="match_parent">
5
6   <RelativeLayout
7           android:layout_width="match_parent"
8           android:layout_height="match_parent" >
9
```

```
10   <ImageView
11               android:id="@+id/r1c1"
12               android:layout_width="wrap_content"
13               android:layout_height="wrap_content"
14               android:layout_alignParentLeft="true"
15               android:layout_alignParentTop="true"
16               android:contentDescription="@string/paint_square"
17               android:src="@drawable/r1c1"
18               android:visibility="invisible" />
19
20   <ImageView
21               android:id="@+id/r1c2"
22               android:layout_width="wrap_content"
23               android:layout_height="wrap_content"
24               android:layout_alignParentTop="true"
25               android:layout_toRightOf="@+id/r1c1"
26               android:contentDescription="@string/paint_square"
27               android:src="@drawable/r1c2" />
28
29   <ImageView
30               android:id="@+id/r1c3"
31               android:layout_width="wrap_content"
32               android:layout_height="wrap_content"
33               android:layout_alignParentTop="true"
34               android:layout_toRightOf="@+id/r1c2"
35               android:contentDescription="@string/paint_square"
36               android:src="@drawable/r1c3" />
37
38   <ImageView
39               android:id="@+id/r1c4"
40               android:layout_width="wrap_content"
41               android:layout_height="wrap_content"
42               android:layout_alignParentTop="true"
43               android:layout_toRightOf="@+id/r1c3"
44               android:contentDescription="@string/paint_square"
45               android:src="@drawable/r1c4"
46               android:visibility="invisible" />
47
48   <ImageView
49               android:id="@+id/r1c5"
50               android:layout_width="wrap_content"
51               android:layout_height="wrap_content"
52               android:layout_alignParentTop="true"
53               android:layout_toRightOf="@+id/r1c4"
54               android:contentDescription="@string/paint_square"
55               android:src="@drawable/r1c5" />
56
57   <ImageView
58               android:id="@+id/r1c6"
59               android:layout_width="wrap_content"
60               android:layout_height="wrap_content"
```

```
 61                android:layout_alignParentTop="true"
 62                android:layout_toRightOf="@+id/r1c5"
 63                android:contentDescription="@string/paint_square"
 64                android:src="@drawable/r1c6"
 65                android:visibility="invisible" />
 66
 67   <ImageView
 68                android:id="@+id/r2c1"
 69                android:layout_width="wrap_content"
 70                android:layout_height="wrap_content"
 71                android:layout_alignParentLeft="true"
 72                android:layout_below="@+id/r1c1"
 73                android:contentDescription="@string/paint_square"
 74                android:src="@drawable/r2c1" />
 75
 76   <ImageView
 77                android:id="@+id/r2c2"
 78                android:layout_width="wrap_content"
 79                android:layout_height="wrap_content"
 80                android:layout_alignTop="@+id/r2c1"
 81                android:layout_toRightOf="@+id/r2c1"
 82                android:contentDescription="@string/paint_square"
 83                android:src="@drawable/r2c2"
 84                android:visibility="invisible" />
 85
 86   <ImageView
 87                android:id="@+id/r2c3"
 88                android:layout_width="wrap_content"
 89                android:layout_height="wrap_content"
 90                android:layout_below="@+id/r1c3"
 91                android:layout_toRightOf="@+id/r2c2"
 92                android:contentDescription="@string/paint_square"
 93                android:src="@drawable/r2c3" />
 94
 95   <ImageView
 96                android:id="@+id/r3c1"
 97                android:layout_width="wrap_content"
 98                android:layout_height="wrap_content"
 99                android:layout_alignParentLeft="true"
100                android:layout_below="@+id/r2c1"
101                android:contentDescription="@string/paint_square"
102                android:src="@drawable/r3c1"
103                android:visibility="invisible" />
104
105   <ImageView
106                android:id="@+id/r3c2"
107                android:layout_width="wrap_content"
108                android:layout_height="wrap_content"
109                android:layout_alignTop="@+id/r3c1"
110                android:layout_toRightOf="@+id/r3c1"
111                android:contentDescription="@string/paint_square"
```

```
112                android:src="@drawable/r3c2" />
113
114  <ImageView
115                android:id="@+id/r3c3"
116                android:layout_width="wrap_content"
117                android:layout_height="wrap_content"
118                android:layout_alignTop="@+id/r3c1"
119                android:layout_toRightOf="@+id/r3c2"
120                android:contentDescription="@string/paint_square"
121                android:src="@drawable/r3c3"
122                android:visibility="invisible" />
123
124  <ImageView
125                android:id="@+id/r4c1"
126                android:layout_width="wrap_content"
127                android:layout_height="wrap_content"
128                android:layout_alignParentLeft="true"
129                android:layout_below="@+id/r3c1"
130                android:contentDescription="@string/paint_square"
131                android:src="@drawable/r4c1" />
132
133  <ImageView
134                android:id="@+id/r4c2"
135                android:layout_width="wrap_content"
136                android:layout_height="wrap_content"
137                android:layout_alignTop="@+id/r4c1"
138                android:layout_toRightOf="@+id/r4c1"
139                android:contentDescription="@string/paint_square"
140                android:src="@drawable/r4c2"
141                android:visibility="invisible" />
142
143  <ImageView
144                android:id="@+id/r4c3"
145                android:layout_width="wrap_content"
146                android:layout_height="wrap_content"
147                android:layout_alignTop="@+id/r4c1"
148                android:layout_toRightOf="@+id/r4c2"
149                android:contentDescription="@string/paint_square"
150                android:src="@drawable/r4c3" />
151
152  <Button
153                style="?android:attr/buttonStyleSmall"
154                android:layout_width="wrap_content"
155                android:layout_height="wrap_content"
156                android:layout_alignParentBottom="true"
157                android:layout_alignParentRight="true"
158                android:onClick="changeScenes"
159                android:text="@string/show" />
160      </RelativeLayout>
161
162  </merge>
```

FIGURE 3-26 The design for `scene02.xml`.

The `scene02.xml` layout, shown in Figure 3-26, is similar to `scene01.xml`, with two main differences between these files: (1) `scene02.xml` contains all "visible" `ImageViews`, and (2) `scene02.xml` contains a "Previous" button that triggers a return to the first scene. The XML code for `scene02.xml` is as follows:

```
scene02.xml
 1  <?xml version="1.0" encoding="utf-8"?>
 2  <merge xmlns:android="http://schemas.android.com/apk/res/android"
 3      android:layout_width="match_parent"
 4      android:layout_height="match_parent">
 5
 6  <RelativeLayout
 7          android:layout_width="match_parent"
 8          android:layout_height="match_parent" >
 9
10  <ImageView
11              android:id="@+id/r1c1"
12              android:layout_width="wrap_content"
13              android:layout_height="wrap_content"
14              android:layout_alignParentLeft="true"
15              android:layout_alignParentTop="true"
16              android:contentDescription="@string/paint_square"
```

```
17                 android:src="@drawable/r1c1" />
18
19     <ImageView
20                 android:id="@+id/r1c2"
21                 android:layout_width="wrap_content"
22                 android:layout_height="wrap_content"
23                 android:layout_alignParentTop="true"
24                 android:layout_toRightOf="@+id/r1c1"
25                 android:contentDescription="@string/paint_square"
26                 android:src="@drawable/r1c2" />
27
28     <ImageView
29                 android:id="@+id/r1c3"
30                 android:layout_width="wrap_content"
31                 android:layout_height="wrap_content"
32                 android:layout_alignParentTop="true"
33                 android:layout_toRightOf="@+id/r1c2"
34                 android:contentDescription="@string/paint_square"
35                 android:src="@drawable/r1c3" />
36
37     <ImageView
38                 android:id="@+id/r1c4"
39                 android:layout_width="wrap_content"
40                 android:layout_height="wrap_content"
41                 android:layout_alignParentTop="true"
42                 android:layout_toRightOf="@+id/r1c3"
43                 android:contentDescription="@string/paint_square"
44                 android:src="@drawable/r1c4" />
45
46     <ImageView
47                 android:id="@+id/r1c5"
48                 android:layout_width="wrap_content"
49                 android:layout_height="wrap_content"
50                 android:layout_alignParentTop="true"
51                 android:layout_toRightOf="@+id/r1c4"
52                 android:contentDescription="@string/paint_square"
53                 android:src="@drawable/r1c5" />
54
55     <ImageView
56                 android:id="@+id/r1c6"
57                 android:layout_width="wrap_content"
58                 android:layout_height="wrap_content"
59                 android:layout_alignParentTop="true"
60                 android:layout_toRightOf="@+id/r1c5"
61                 android:contentDescription="@string/paint_square"
62                 android:src="@drawable/r1c6" />
63
64     <ImageView
65                 android:id="@+id/r2c1"
66                 android:layout_width="wrap_content"
```

```
67                android:layout_height="wrap_content"
68                android:layout_alignParentLeft="true"
69                android:layout_below="@+id/r1c1"
70                android:contentDescription="@string/paint_square"
71                android:src="@drawable/r2c1" />
72
73   <ImageView
74                android:id="@+id/r2c2"
75                android:layout_width="wrap_content"
76                android:layout_height="wrap_content"
77                android:layout_alignTop="@+id/r2c1"
78                android:layout_toRightOf="@+id/r2c1"
79                android:contentDescription="@string/paint_square"
80                android:src="@drawable/r2c2" />
81
82   <ImageView
83                android:id="@+id/r2c3"
84                android:layout_width="wrap_content"
85                android:layout_height="wrap_content"
86                android:layout_below="@+id/r1c3"
87                android:layout_toRightOf="@+id/r2c2"
88                android:contentDescription="@string/paint_square"
89                android:src="@drawable/r2c3" />
90
91   <ImageView
92                android:id="@+id/r3c1"
93                android:layout_width="wrap_content"
94                android:layout_height="wrap_content"
95                android:layout_alignParentLeft="true"
96                android:layout_below="@+id/r2c1"
97                android:contentDescription="@string/paint_square"
98                android:src="@drawable/r3c1" />
99
100  <ImageView
101                android:id="@+id/r3c2"
102                android:layout_width="wrap_content"
103                android:layout_height="wrap_content"
104                android:layout_alignTop="@+id/r3c1"
105                android:layout_toRightOf="@+id/r3c1"
106                android:contentDescription="@string/paint_square"
107                android:src="@drawable/r3c2" />
108
109  <ImageView
110                android:id="@+id/r3c3"
111                android:layout_width="wrap_content"
112                android:layout_height="wrap_content"
113                android:layout_alignTop="@+id/r3c1"
114                android:layout_toRightOf="@+id/r3c2"
115                android:contentDescription="@string/paint_square"
116                android:src="@drawable/r3c3" />
```

```
117
118  <ImageView
119              android:id="@+id/r4c1"
120              android:layout_width="wrap_content"
121              android:layout_height="wrap_content"
122              android:layout_alignParentLeft="true"
123              android:layout_below="@+id/r3c1"
124              android:contentDescription="@string/paint_square"
125              android:src="@drawable/r4c1" />
126
127  <ImageView
128              android:id="@+id/r4c2"
129              android:layout_width="wrap_content"
130              android:layout_height="wrap_content"
131              android:layout_alignTop="@+id/r4c1"
132              android:layout_toRightOf="@+id/r4c1"
133              android:contentDescription="@string/paint_square"
134              android:src="@drawable/r4c2" />
135
136  <ImageView
137              android:id="@+id/r4c3"
138              android:layout_width="wrap_content"
139              android:layout_height="wrap_content"
140              android:layout_alignTop="@+id/r4c1"
141              android:layout_toRightOf="@+id/r4c2"
142              android:contentDescription="@string/paint_square"
143              android:src="@drawable/r4c3" />
144
145  <Button
146              style="?android:attr/buttonStyleSmall"
147              android:layout_width="wrap_content"
148              android:layout_height="wrap_content"
149              android:layout_alignParentBottom="true"
150              android:layout_alignParentLeft="true"
151              android:text="@string/hide"
152              android:onClick="changeScenes" />
153
154  </RelativeLayout>
155
156  </merge>
```

Part 5: Building the Animated Transitions between Scenes

The animated Transitions for this application is controlled using XML code to create animation specifications. The file that contains the animation properties is `transition.xml`. The XML code listing is as follows:

Line 3:   A `<transition Set>` is being used in this app because it enables more flexible choreography of transitions. If multiple elements need to be animated, as in this case, the order in which they are animated can be arranged.

Line 5:   The ordering sequence for the animation of painting elements is set to occur in sequence.

Lines 7–9:   A `<fade>` Transition animation is defined for a `fade_in` that lasts 1000 milliseconds (1 second).

Line 11–13:   The `fade_out` transition animation is defined.

The XML code listing for `transition.xml` appears as follows:

```
transition.xml
1   <?xml version="1.0" encoding="utf-8"?>
2
3   <transitionSet
4   xmlns:android="http://schemas.android.com/apk/res/android"
5       android:transitionOrdering="sequential">
6
7   <fade
8           android:duration="1000"
9           android:fadingMode="fade_in" />
10
11  <fade
12          android:duration="1000"
13          android:fadingMode="fade_out" />
14
15  </transitionSet>
```

Part 6: Source Code for Application

The application's activity is implemented in `MyActivity.java`. The code listing appears as follows:

Lines 20–21:   Two Scene objects are defined for the currently active Scene and the passive Scene. The active Scene, named `activeScene`, is the one currently visible to the user. The passive Scene, named `passiveScene`, is the one that is not visible. The values for these objects are dynamic.

Lines 28–29:   The ViewGroup object named `paintingContainer` is used to reference the layout items defined in `activity_my.xml`.

Lines 30–31:   A Transition object is assigned. `TransitionInflater` is used to inflate Scenes and Transitions from resource files. In this case, the `transition.xml` file is inflated.

Lines 33–34:   When the application is first launched, scene01.xml is displayed to the user. This scene is the active Scene. activeScene is assigned the layout scene01.xml.

Lines 35–36:   Because scene01.xml is the active Scene, scene02.xml is the passive Scene. scene02.xml is assigned to passiveScene.

Line 37:   The activeScene enters the stage.

Lines 40–48:   The onClick event handler is implemented. When the user navigates between the complete painting and the incomplete painting, this method is called by the button click. The values for activeScene and passiveScene are swapped. TransitionManager.go will change to the given Scene using the given Transition.

MyActivity.java

```
1   package com.cornez.paintscene;
2
3   import android.app.Activity;
4   import android.os.Bundle;
5   import android.transition.Scene;
6   import android.transition.Transition;
7   import android.transition.TransitionInflater;
8   import android.transition.TransitionManager;
9   import android.view.Menu;
10  import android.view.MenuItem;
11  import android.view.View;
12  import android.view.ViewGroup;
13
14
15  public class MyActivity extends Activity {
16
17      ViewGroup paintingContainer;
18      Transition transition;
19
20      Scene activeScene;
21      Scene passiveScene;
22
23      @Override
24      protected void onCreate(Bundle savedInstanceState) {
25          super.onCreate(savedInstanceState);
26          setContentView(R.layout.activity_my);
27
28          paintingContainer = (ViewGroup)
29              findViewById(R.id.painting_container);
30          transition = TransitionInflater.from(this).inflateTransition(
```

```
31                    R.anim.transition);
32
33          activeScene = Scene.getSceneForLayout(paintingContainer,
34                  R.layout.scene01, this);
35          passiveScene = Scene.getSceneForLayout(paintingContainer,
36                  R.layout.scene02, this);
37          activeScene.enter();
38      }
39
40      public void changeScenes(View view) {
41
42          Scene temp = passiveScene;
43          passiveScene = activeScene;
44          activeScene = temp;
45
46          TransitionManager.go(activeScene, transition);
47
48      }
49
50
51      @Override
52      public boolean onCreateOptionsMenu(Menu menu) {
53          // Inflate the menu;
54          getMenuInflater().inflate(R.menu.my, menu);
55          return true;
56      }
57
58      @Override
59      public boolean onOptionsItemSelected(MenuItem item) {
60          // Handle action bar item clicks here. The action bar will
61          // automatically handle clicks on the Home/Up button, so long
62          // as you specify a parent activity in AndroidManifest.xml.
63          int id = item.getItemId();
64          if (id == R.id.action_settings) {
65              return true;
66          }
67          return super.onOptionsItemSelected(item);
68      }
69 }
```

■ EXERCISES

3.1   Name the seven callback methods defined by the Activity class.

3.2   Explain the difference between onResume() and onStart().

3.3   Describe how an activity can be recreated after it has been destroyed.

3.4   Indicate the type of intent launched by the following segment of code. Explain.

```
1  public void launchActivity (View view) {
2  Intent intent = new Intent(getApplicationContext(),
3           XActivity.class);
4
5      startActivity(intent);
6  }
```

3.5 Write a short segment of Java code to launch a webpage.

3.6 Describe how data can be passed as a message object to an activity.

3.7 What is a common use of the ACTION_SEND action?

3.8 Given the following XML code, name the Activities within the application and the activity that launches when the application first launches.

```
1  <?xml version="1.0" encoding="utf-8"?>
2  <manifest xmlns:android="http://schemas.android.com/apk/res/android">
3
4  <application
5          android:allowBackup="true"
6          android:icon="@drawable/ic_launcher"
7          android:label="@string/app_name"
8          android:theme="@android:style >
9
10 <!-- MYACTIVITY CLASS: INPUT THE CAR PURCHASE INFORMATION -->
11 <activity
12             android:name=".BActivity"
13             android:label="@string/app_name" >
14 <intent-filter>
15 <action android:name="android.intent.action.MAIN" />
16 <category
17 android:name="android.intent.category.LAUNCHER" />
18 </intent-filter>
19 </activity>
20
21 <activity
22             android:name=".CActivity"
23             android:label="@string/app_name"
24 android:parentActivityName=".BActivity" >
25 <meta-data
26                 android:name="android.support.PARENT_ACTIVITY"
27                 android:value=".BActivity" />
28 </activity>
29 <activity
30             android:name=".DActivity"
31             android:label="@string/app_name"
32 android:parentActivityName=".BActivity" >
33 <meta-data
```

```
34                            android:name="android.support.PARENT_ACTIVITY"
35                            android:value=".BActivity" />
36   </activity>
37
38   </application>
39
40   </manifest>
```

3.9   Name five property animations that can be applied to activities.

3.10 What is the purpose of `<objectAnimator>`?

3.11 Briefly explain the concept of a scene transition.

3.12 Briefly describe the purpose of a `TransitionManager`.

4

Fragments, ActionBar, and Menus

Chapter Objectives

In this chapter you will:

- Explore how to build applications that use an ActionBar and Fragments.
- Understand the Fragment lifecycle.
- Learn to configure the ActionBar.
- Implement Fragments with Responsive Design Techniques.
- Explore animation in Fragment Transactions.
- Experiment with Fragments, ListViews, and ArrayAdapters.

■ 4.1 Fragmentation and Android Fragments

Android devices come in many shapes and screen sizes, and they have different performance characteristics. Multiple versions of Android are concurrently being used and supported at any given time. Often, companies produce their own variants on the system's user interface, which can change the look of default elements. It can be challenging, problematic, and time-consuming to develop an Android application that works optimally in this fragmented environment; however, fragmentation also has benefits for both users and developers. The availability of affordable Android devices makes them accessible to a large number of consumers. For developers, this translates into a wider audience and market for applications.

A well-designed app is partly characterized by its user interface, which must be as easy to navigate and use as possible. When designing and coding layouts, several factors should be considered, such as spacing, positioning, size, and the grouping of user interface controls. Layouts must be compatible to many physical screen sizes; as screen sizes vary, so do the positioning, spacing, and size of these control elements on the screen. The user interface layouts must resize correctly when run on different devices, and they must respond to changes, such as moving from portrait to landscape orientation.

The design concept behind Android's `Fragment` class was conceived with the goal of promoting reuse of, and interaction between, the different elements that make up an application. Rather than simply using an `Activity` and a Layout to define the complete user interface of an application screen, it is often more efficient to use fragments. The user interface can be divided into logical sections, with these sections represented by fragments. A fragment can then be reused in more than one screen within the application.

A `Fragment` is modeled as a subdivision of an `Activity`. In other words, a `Fragment` is integrated into an `Activity`; therefore, it needs an `Activity` to run. Using `Fragments` in building applications helps the developer easily present a consistently well-designed user interface. `Fragments` are particularly helpful in adapting a user experience across a wide range of devices.

■ 4.2 The Fragment Lifecycle

Fragments are associated with an activity and can be created, added, or removed while the activity is running. For example, an application can use one fragment for receiving its own input events, thus allowing the user to input information, and use another fragment for rendering output.

Like an Activity, a Fragment has its own lifecycle, as well as its own user interface. The Fragment's lifecycle is connected to the activity that owns it. Each fragment has its own callback methods in the standard Activity lifecycle.

The following code listing illustrates a Fragment class that overrides several of its callback methods that are joined with an activity.

Lines 3–9:   `onCreate()` is called to do initial creation of the fragment. Just as in an Activity, saved state changes can be restored in this method. `onCreate()` can be called while the fragment's activity is still in the process of being created.

Lines 11–17:   `onStart()` is called at the start of the fragment lifecycle. This method makes the fragment visible to the user, based on starting its containing activity. It is typical to apply user interface changes within this method.

Lines 19–27:   `onResume()` makes the fragment interact with the user, based on resuming its owner activity.

Lines 29–37:   `onPause()` is called when the fragment is no longer interacting with the user, either because its activity is being paused or because a fragment operation is modifying it within the activity.

Lines 39–46:   `onSaveInstanceState` is called to save the user interface state changes at the end of the activity lifecycle.

Lines 48–57:   onStop() is called when the fragment is no longer visible
                to the user, either because its activity is being stopped or be-
                cause a fragment operation is modifying it in the activity.
                onDestroyView() allows the fragment to clean up resources
                associated with its View.

Lines 60–66:   onDestroy() is called to do final cleanup of the fragment's
                state. onDetach() is called immediately before the fragment stops
                being associated with its activity.

```
1   public class MyFragmentA extends Fragment {
2
3       @Override
4       public void onCreate(Bundle savedInstanceState) {
5           super.onCreate(savedInstanceState);
6
7           Note:
8           Saved changes from savedInstanceState can be restored here.
9       }
10
11  @Override
12      public void onStart(){
13          super.onStart();
14
15          Note:
16          User interface changes can be applied to the visible fragment here.
17      }
18
19  @Override
20      public void onResume(){
21          super.onResume();
22
23          Note:
24          Paused user interface updates, threads, or processes
25          required by the fragment can be resumed here. These
26          elements were suspended when the fragment became inactive.
27  }
28
29  @Override
30      public void onPause(){
31
32          Note:
33          The suspension of user interface updates and threads, not needing the attention
34          of the paused Activity, can be placed here.
35          super.onPause();
36
37      }
```

```
38    @Override
39        public void onSaveInstanceState(Bundle savedInstanceState) {
40
41            Note:
42            The user interface state changes are saved to the savedInstanceState here.
43            This bundle will be passed to onCreate if the parent activity is killed or restarted.
44
45            super.onSaveInstanceState(savedInstanceState);
46        }
47
48    @Override
49        public void onStop(){
50
51            Note:
52            The suspension of any remaining user interface updates, or threads
53            that are not required when the Fragment is no longer visible, can
54            can be placed here.
55
56            super.onStop();
57        }
58
59    @Override
60        public void onDestroy(){
61
62            Note:
63                Fragment resources can be ended here.
64
65            super.onDestroy();
66        }
67    }
```

A fragment layout can be installed in an activity using setContentView(), as shown in the code segment that follows:

```
1
2    @Override
3    protected void onCreate(Bundle savedInstanceState) {
4        super.onCreate(savedInstanceState);
5
6        setContentView(R.layout.fragmentA_layout);
7    }
```

As previously illustrated, a Fragment has the same callback methods as an Activity; however, it also has its own set of callbacks. For example, when a fragment is no longer being used, it goes through a reverse series of callbacks, including onPause(), onStop(), and onDestroy(). Additionally, callbacks are made to onDestroyView() and onDetach() to carry out actions specific to Fragments.

The following list outlines the additional callbacks used in the lifecycle of a Fragment:

onCreateView()	This is a core lifecycle method that is called to bring a fragment up to a resumed state, interacting with the user. This callback method creates and returns the view hierarchy associated with the fragment.
onInflate()	Called every time the fragment is inflated.
onActivityCreated()	Called when the fragment's activity has been created and this fragment's view hierarchy is instantiated. Final initializations, such as restoring a state or retrieving a view, are often implemented here.
onAttach()	Called after the fragment has been attached (associated) to an activity.
onDestroyView()	Informs the fragment that its view is being destroyed so that it can clean up any associated resources. This is called after onStop() and before onDestroy().
onDetach()	Called when the fragment is no longer attached to its activity, after onDestroy(). This is the final call before the fragment object is released to the garbage collector.

The following code listing illustrates these callbacks in FragmentB:

```
1   public class MyFragmentB extends Fragment {
2
3       @Override
4       public void onInflate(Activity activity, AttributeSet attrs,
5                           Bundle savedInstanceState) {
6           super.onInflate(activity, attrs, savedInstanceState);
7       }
8
9       public View onCreateView(LayoutInflater inflater,
10                          ViewGroup container,
11                          Bundle savedInstanceState) {
12
13          // THE LAYOUT ASSOCIATED WITH MyFragmentB IS INFLATED.
14          return inflater.inflate(R.layout.fragment_b_my,
15              container, false);
16      }
17
18      @Override
19      public void onActivityCreated(Bundle savedInstanceState) {
20          super.onActivityCreated(savedInstanceState);
21      }
22
```

```
23      @Override
24      public void onAttach(Activity activity) {
25          super.onAttach(activity);
26      }
27
28      @Override
29      public void onDestroyView() {
30          super.onDestroyView();
31      }
32
33      @Override
34      public void onDetach() {
35          super.onDetach();
36      }
37  }
```

■ 4.3 Action Bar

The action bar is a vital and flexible design element for an application. A rectangular window feature that appears at the top of the screen, the action bar provides information and displays control elements to the user.

In a basic configuration, the action bar displays the application icon and a title. The title often identifies the running activity. In this simple format, users have an indication of where they are and a consistent identity from which to recognize the application.

In a more complex configuration, the action bar can feature user action control elements, navigation modes, and drop-down menus. The purpose of the action bar, as in the one shown in Figure 4-1, is to improve user interaction and provide a higher quality experience. It supports easy navigation through action controls, featured as tabs and drop-down lists.

The action bar was first introduced in Android 3.0. Support for older versions can also be achieved but requires the use of the Android Support Library. The action bar is included by default in all activities for applications with a minimum SdkVersion of 11.

An action bar can be constructed with the following features:

Application Icon:

The application icon can be used as a unique identification for an application. To the right of the icon is the View control, the title element that can specify the application name or the activity the user is currently using.

Action Items: Action items are buttons for the most used action of the application. To provide quick and easy access, it is also typical to include action buttons for the important actions that require accessibility and prominence. If all of the specified action buttons cannot be displayed on the screen, those that do not fit will automatically be moved to the action overflow menu.

Action Overflow:

The action overflow menu is a drop-down menu list that is often used for actions performed less frequently. This is also the location of actions that do not fit on the main action bar.

I FIGURE 4-1 The ActionBar of an application.

■ Lab Example 4-1: Fragments and the ActionBar: Menu Experiment

This lab features the Actionbar Experiment I application. It is a first look at the basics of fragments that also explores how an action bar is used so we can better understand its association with the user interface.

Part 1: The Design

Actionbar Experiment is an app that illustrates how fragments can use the `ActionBar` Android user interface component. This app combines four fragments into a single activity to build a multipane user interface. These fragments are basic, yet self-contained, components. Each fragment holds a photograph representing one meal in a given day: breakfast, snack, lunch, and dinner.

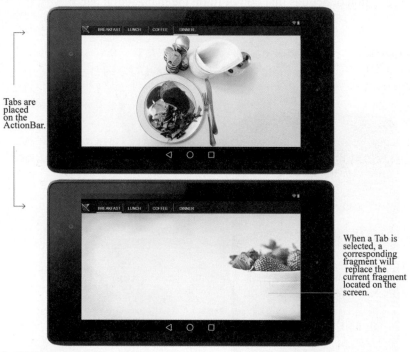

Tabs are placed on the ActionBar.

When a Tab is selected, a corresponding fragment will replace the current fragment located on the screen.

FIGURE 4-2 An Actionbar containing Tabs.

The action bar for this application displays a unique application icon. It also supports consistent navigation and view switching through the use of Tabs, as shown in Figure 4-2. The application is made up of four Tabs and four corresponding `Fragments`. When a Tab is selected, its corresponding `Fragment` replaces the fragment currently located on the screen.

Part 2: Application Structure and Setup

The settings for the application are as follows:

- Application Name: Actionbar Experiment
- Project Name: ActionbarExperiment

- Package Name: `com.cornez.actionbarexperiment`
- Android Form: Phone and Tablet
- Minimum SDK: API 18: Android 4.3 (Jelly Bean)
- Target SDK: API 21: Android 5.0 (Lollipop)
- Compile with: API 21: Android 5.0 (Lollipop)
- Activity Name: `MyActivity`
- Layout Name: `activity_my`

The application does not use the Android default `ic_launcher.pg` file. The launcher icon is the bitmap file provided in the textbook resources. This bitmap file stores the icon as a PNG and is added to the drawable folder, along with PNG files representing the meal photographs: breakfast, snack, lunch, and dinner.

The final project structure for the Actionbar Experiment application is shown in Figure 4-3. The project is driven by a single `Actvity`, `MyActivity.java`, and a set of `Fragment` subclass source files. The `Fragment` files are `Breakfast Fragment.java`, `SnackFragment.java`, `LunchFragment.java`, and `DinnerFragment.java`.

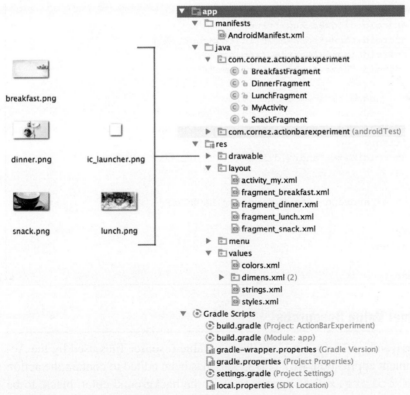

I FIGURE 4-3 Project structure for the ActionBar Experiment application.

In addition to the activity layout, `activity_my.xml`, each of the four Fragment classes have their own associated layout files. Finally, a `colors.xml` file is used to store a backdrop color.

The orientation of the screen will be locked into landscape mode. It should be noted that when an application is viewed in landscape mode, the action bar might be configured differently from the normal portrait view. Android automatically rearranges visible icons located on the action bar depending on several factors, such as the amount of space available to accommodate the icon, action control icons, and so forth. In landscape mode, for example, an "add" option is often shown as an icon on the action bar rather than in the drop-down menu.

Unlike an `Activity`, a `Fragment` is never declared in the `Android Manifest.xml` file. The following is the code listing for `AndroidManifest.xml` used by the Actionbar Experiment I application:

```
AndroidManifest.xml

 1  <?xml version="1.0" encoding="utf-8"?>
 2  <manifest xmlns:android="http://schemas.android.com/apk/res/android"
 3      package="com.cornez.actionbarexperiment">
 4
 5  <application
 6          android:allowBackup="true"
 7          android:icon="@drawable/ic_launcher"
 8          android:label="@string/app_name"
 9          android:theme="@style/AppTheme">
10  <activity
11              android:name=".MyActivity"
12              android:label="@string/app_name"
13              android:screenOrientation="landscape">
14  <intent-filter>
15  <action android:name="android.intent.action.MAIN" />
16
17  <category
18  android:name="android.intent.category.LAUNCHER" />
19  </intent-filter>
20  </activity>
21  </application>
22
23  </manifest>
```

Part 3: External Value Resources

`strings.xml` and `colors.xml` are the two value resource files used by the Actionbar Experiment application. `strings.xml` has been edited to contain the action bar Tab strings. `colors.xml` is created to store the background color, black, to be used as a backdrop for the fragments as they enter and exit the screen.

The XML code listings for `strings.xml` and `colors.xml` are as follows:

```
strings.xml
1  <?xml version="1.0" encoding="utf-8"?>
2  <resources>
3
4  <string name="app_name">Actionbar Experiment I</string>
5  <string name="hello_world">Hello world!</string>
6  <string name="action_settings">Settings</string>
7
8  <!-- ACTIONBAR TAB STRINGS -->
9  <string name="ui_tabname_breakfast">breakfast</string>
10 <string name="ui_tabname_lunch">lunch</string>
11 <string name="ui_tabname_snack">snack</string>
12 <string name="ui_tabname_dinner">dinner</string>
13
14 </resources>
```

```
colors.xml
1  <?xml version="1.0" encoding="utf-8"?>
2  <resources>
3
4      <color name="black">#000000</color>
5
6  </resources>
```

Part 4: Creating the User Interface and a Fragment

The user interface for the Actionbar Experiment application consists of five layouts. The layout associated with the running activity is always visible while the app is visible. This layout, `activity_my.xml`, uses a ViewGroup container, shown in Figure 4-4, to hold incoming and outgoing fragment layouts.

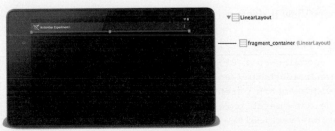

▌FIGURE 4-4 `activity_my.xml` contains a `LinearLayout` view for storing fragments.

The code listing for `activity_my.xml` is as follows:

Line 6:   A black backdrop is applied to the background of the root element, a `LinearLayout`.

Line 8:   The class `MyActivity` is the associated activity specified for this layout.

Lines 11–17:   A `LinearLayout` container `ViewGroup` is declared. The name assigned to this container is `fragment_container`.

`activity_my.xml`

```
1   <LinearLayout xmlns:android="http://schemas.android.com/apk/res/android"
2       xmlns:tools="http://schemas.android.com/tools"
3       android:layout_width="fill_parent"
4       android:layout_height="fill_parent"
5       android:layout_gravity="center"
6       android:background="@color/black"
7       android:orientation="vertical"
8       tools:context=".MyActivity">
9
10
11  <LinearLayout
12          android:id="@+id/fragment_container"
13          android:orientation="vertical"
14          android:layout_width="match_parent"
15          android:layout_height="wrap_content"
16          android:layout_gravity="center_horizontal">
17  </LinearLayout>
18
19  </LinearLayout>
```

Each of the four Fragments used by the app has an associated layout that stores the photograph of a meal. The code listing for these XML files is shown below. Figure 4-5 illustrates the graphic visual design of the layout for `fragment_snack.xml`. All four layouts will consistently feature the following properties:

Line 6:   A black backdrop is applied to the background of the root element, a `LinearLayout`.

Lines 8–14:   An ImageView is declared to store a drawable image.

`fragment_breakfast.xml`

```
1   <?xml version="1.0" encoding="utf-8"?>
2   <LinearLayout xmlns:android="http://schemas.android.com/apk/res/android"
3       android:layout_width="match_parent"
4       android:layout_height="match_parent"
5       android:orientation="vertical"
6       android:background="@color/black">
```

```
 7
 8  <ImageView
 9          android:id="@+id/imageView"
10          android:layout_width="fill_parent"
11          android:layout_height="fill_parent"
12          android:contentDescription="@string/ui_tabname_breakfast"
13          android:orientation="horizontal"
14          android:src="@drawable/breakfast" />
15
16  </LinearLayout>
```

FIGURE 4-5 The `fragment_snack.xml` layout shown in landscape orientation.

```
fragment_snack.xml
 1  <?xml version="1.0" encoding="utf-8"?>
 2  <LinearLayout xmlns:android="http://schemas.android.com/apk/res/android"
 3      android:layout_width="match_parent"
 4      android:layout_height="match_parent"
 5      android:orientation="vertical"
 6      android:background="@color/black">
 7
 8  <ImageView
 9          android:id="@+id/imageView"
10          android:layout_width="fill_parent"
11          android:layout_height="fill_parent"
12          android:contentDescription="@string/ui_tabname_snack"
13          android:orientation="horizontal"
14          android:src="@drawable/snack" />
15
16  </LinearLayout>
```

```
fragment_lunch.xml
 1  <?xml version="1.0" encoding="utf-8"?>
 2  <LinearLayout xmlns:android="http://schemas.android.com/apk/res/android"
 3      android:layout_width="match_parent"
 4      android:layout_height="match_parent"
 5      android:orientation="vertical"
 6      android:background="@color/black">
```

```
 7
 8   <ImageView
 9         android:id="@+id/imageView"
10         android:layout_width="fill_parent"
11         android:layout_height="fill_parent"
12         android:contentDescription="@string/ui_tabname_lunch"
13         android:orientation="horizontal"
14         android:src="@drawable/lunch" />
15
16   </LinearLayout>
```

fragment_dinner.xml

```
 1   <?xml version="1.0" encoding="utf-8"?>
 2   <LinearLayout xmlns:android="http://schemas.android.com/apk/res/android"
 3        android:layout_width="match_parent"
 4        android:layout_height="match_parent"
 5        android:orientation="vertical" >
 6
 7   <ImageView
 8         android:id="@+id/imageView"
 9         android:layout_width="fill_parent"
10         android:layout_height="fill_parent"
11         android:contentDescription="@string/ui_tabname_dinner"
12         android:orientation="horizontal"
13         android:src="@drawable/dinner"
14         android:background="@color/black" />
15
16   </LinearLayout>
```

Part 5: Defining the Fragment Subclasses

To create a fragment for use in an application, a subclass of Fragment must be created, if it does not already exist. A Fragment class uses code that looks very much like an Activity. It contains callback methods similar to an Activity, such as onCreate(). Oftentimes, you can convert an existing Android application to use Fragments by moving code from an activity's callback methods into the respective callback methods of the Fragment.

The BreakfastFragment class is an extension of the Fragment class. It has its own lifecycle, yet it is tied to MyActivity.

Lines 11–13:   The method onCreateView (LayoutInflater, ViewGroup, Bundle) is a core lifecycle method that is called to bring the fragment up to the resumed state (interacting with the user). This callback method creates and returns the view hierarchy associated with the fragment.

Line 16:   The inflate() method inflates a new view hierarchy from the specified XML resource; in this case, fragment_breakfast.xml. The container argument specifies the ViewGroup location where the fragment will be inflated.

The code listing for the implementation of the four Fragment subclasses is as follows. Each is responsible for inflating its associated user interface layout.

BreakfastFragment.java

```
1   package com.cornez.actionbarexperiment;
2
3   import android.app.Fragment;
4   import android.os.Bundle;
5   import android.view.LayoutInflater;
6   import android.view.View;
7   import android.view.ViewGroup;
8
9   public class BreakfastFragment extends Fragment {
10         @Override
11         public View onCreateView(LayoutInflater inflater,
12                              ViewGroup container,
13                              Bundle savedInstanceState) {
14
15             // Inflate the layout for this fragment
16             return inflater.inflate(R.layout.fragment_breakfast,
17                              container, false);
18      }
19  }
```

SnackFragment.java

```
1   package com.cornez. actionbarexperiment;
2
3   import android.app.Fragment;
4   import android.os.Bundle;
5   import android.view.LayoutInflater;
6   import android.view.View;
7   import android.view.ViewGroup;
8
9   public class CoffeeFragment extends Fragment {
10         @Override
11         public View onCreateView(LayoutInflater inflater,
12                              ViewGroup container,
13                              Bundle savedInstanceState) {
14
15             // Inflate the layout for this fragment
16             return inflater.inflate(R.layout.fragment_snack,
17                              container, false);
18      }
19  }
```

LunchFragment.java

```
1   package com.cornez.actionbarexperiment;
2
3   import android.app.Fragment;
4   import android.os.Bundle;
5   import android.view.LayoutInflater;
6   import android.view.View;
7   import android.view.ViewGroup;
8
9   public class LunchFragment extends Fragment {
10      @Override
11      public View onCreateView(LayoutInflater inflater,
12                              ViewGroup container,
13                              Bundle savedInstanceState) {
14
15          // Inflate the layout for this fragment
16          return inflater.inflate(R.layout.fragment_lunch,
17                                  container, false);
18      }
19  }
```

DinnerFragment.java

```
1   package com.cornez.actionbarexperiment;
2
3   import android.app.Fragment;
4   import android.os.Bundle;
5   import android.view.LayoutInflater;
6   import android.view.View;
7   import android.view.ViewGroup;
8
9   public class DinnerFragment extends Fragment {
10      @Override
11      public View onCreateView(LayoutInflater inflater,
12                              ViewGroup container,
13                              Bundle savedInstanceState) {
14
15          // Inflate the layout for this fragment
16          return inflater.inflate(R.layout.fragment_dinner,
17                                  container, false);
18      }
19  }
```

Part 6: Source Code for the App Activity

MyActivity is the sole Activity used by the Actionbar Experiment application. This Activity source file is responsible for displaying the app's user interface that will hold Fragments as they enter and exit the screen.

Lines 3, 5–6:   The imports for `ActionBar`, `Fragment`, and `FragmentTransaction` are required when configuring an `ActionBar` and binding its controls to an `Activity` or `Fragment`.

Lines 26–27:   The actionBar object is instantiated. Its navigation mode is set to `NAVIGATION_MODE_TABS`, which will allow the application to utilize Tabs for navigation.

Line 28:   The title element in the action bar can be disabled by setting the attribute `setDisplayShowTitleEnabled` to `false`.

Lines 31–38:   Four Tabs are constructed using `ActionBar.Tab`. Note that these tabs have not yet been added to the ActionBar.

Lines 41–44:   The Fragment objects used by the application (`breakfastFragment`, `snackFragment`, `lunchFragment`, and `dinnerFragment`) are instantiated.

MyActivity.java

```
1    package com.cornez.actionbarexperiment;
2
3    import android.app.ActionBar;
4    import android.app.Activity;
5    import android.app.Fragment;
6    import android.app.FragmentTransaction;
7    import android.content.Context;
8    import android.os.Bundle;
9    import android.view.Menu;
10   import android.view.MenuItem;
11
12   public class MyActivity extends Activity {
13
14       private static final String TAB_KEY_INDEX = "tab_key";
15       private Fragment breakfastFragment;
16       private Fragment lunchFragment;
17       private Fragment snackFragment;
18       private Fragment dinnerFragment;
19
20       @Override
21       protected void onCreate(Bundle savedInstanceState) {
22           super.onCreate(savedInstanceState);
23           setContentView(R.layout.activity_my);
24
25           // SET THE ACTIONBAR
26           ActionBar actionBar = getActionBar();
27           actionBar.setNavigationMode(ActionBar.NAVIGATION_MODE_TABS);
28           actionBar.setDisplayShowTitleEnabled(false);
29
```

```
30   // CREATE THE TABS AND BIND THEM TO THE ACTIONBAR
31         ActionBar.Tab breakfastTab = actionBar.newTab().setText(
32                 getString(R.string.ui_tabname_breakfast));
33         ActionBar.Tab lunchTab = actionBar.newTab().setText(
34                 getString(R.string.ui_tabname_lunch));
35         ActionBar.Tab snackTab = actionBar.newTab().setText(
36                 getString(R.string.ui_tabname_snack));
37         ActionBar.Tab dinnerTab = actionBar.newTab().setText(
38                 getString(R.string.ui_tabname_dinner));
39
40         // CREATE EACH FRAGMENT AND BIND THEM TO THE ACTIONBAR
41         breakfastFragment = new BreakfastFragment();
42   snackFragment = new SnackFragment();
43         lunchFragment = new LunchFragment();
44         dinnerFragment = new DinnerFragment();
```

Within the ActionBar, Tabs can trigger an event only if an event listener has been applied.

Lines 46–58:   A listener event is registered to each of the Tabs located on the ActionBar. Set the ActionBar.TabListener that will handle switching to and from a specific tab. The handler for the listener event is the anonymous class MyTabListener().

It should be noted that all tabs must have a TabListener set before being added to the ActionBar.

Lines 60–64:   Tabs are added to the ActionBar.

Lines 68–71:   If application has not been launched for the first time, the state of the navigation is restored using a constant, TAB_KEY_INDEX.

```
MyActivity.java    continued
45         // SET LISTENER EVENTS FOR EACH OF THE ACTIONBAR TABS
46         breakfastTab.setTabListener(new
47   MyTabsListener(breakfastFragment,
48                 getApplicationContext()));
49         snackTab.setTabListener(new
50   MyTabsListener(snackFragment,
51                 getApplicationContext()));
52
53         lunchTab.setTabListener(new
54   MyTabsListener(lunchFragment,
55                 getApplicationContext()));
56   dinnerTab.setTabListener(new
57   MyTabsListener(dinnerFragment,
58                 getApplicationContext()));
59
60         // ADD EACH OF THE TABS TO THE ACTIONBAR
```

```
61    actionBar.addTab(breakfastTab);
62    actionBar.addTab(lunchTab);
63    actionBar.addTab(snackTab);
64    actionBar.addTab(dinnerTab);
65
66
67    // RESTORE NAVIGATION
68    if (savedInstanceState != null) {
69        actionBar.setSelectedNavigationItem(
70            savedInstanceState.getInt(TAB_KEY_INDEX, 0));
71    }
72  }
```

The handler for the Tab listener events is the class `MyTabsListener`. This class implements the `ActionBar.TabListener` interface. Its callbacks will be invoked when a tab is focused, unfocused, added, or removed from the ActionBar.

Lines 76–78:   The constructor of this class assigns the Fragment whose layout will appear on the screen.

Lines 80–83:   Implementation for onTabReselected will not be used.

Lines 85–89:   When a Tab is selected from the ActionBar, its associated Fragment layout will replace the current layout located in the fragment_container within the activity layout.

When a Tab is unselected, the `remove()` method of `FragmentTransaction` will remove the existing fragment. If it was added to a container, its view will also be removed from that container.

MyActivity.java   *continued*

```
73  class MyTabsListener implements ActionBar.TabListener {
74      public Fragment fragment;
75
76      public MyTabsListener(Fragment f, Context context) {
77          fragment = f;
78      }
79
80      @Override
81      public void onTabReselected(ActionBar.Tab tab,
82  FragmentTransaction ft) {
83      }
84
85      @Override
86      public void onTabSelected(ActionBar.Tab tab,
87  FragmentTransaction ft) {
88          ft.replace(R.id.fragment_container, fragment);
```

```
89             }
90
91             @Override
92             public void onTabUnselected(ActionBar.Tab tab,
93   FragmentTransaction ft) {
94                 ft.remove(fragment);
95             }
96         }
97
98
99      @Override
100     public boolean onCreateOptionsMenu(Menu menu) {
101         // Inflate the menu;
102         getMenuInflater().inflate(R.menu.my, menu);
103         return true;
104     }
105
106     @Override
107     public boolean onOptionsItemSelected(MenuItem item) {
108         // Handle action bar item clicks here. The action bar will
109         // automatically handle clicks on the Home/Up button, so long
110         // as you specify a parent activity in AndroidManifest.xml.
111         int id = item.getItemId();
112         if (id == R.id.action_settings) {
113             return true;
114         }
115         return super.onOptionsItemSelected(item);
116     }
117 }
```

■ 4.4 ActionBar Configurations

Control elements that appear directly on the action bar as an icon and/or text are known as action buttons.

When an Activity starts, its associated layout is inflated on the screen and the action bar is populated with action buttons, such as the one shown in Figure 4-1. The activity's onCreateOptionsMenu() method is responsible for inflating a menu hierarchy from a specified XML resource file.

In the following sample code segment, onCreateOptionsMenu() calls getMenuInflater().inflate (R.menu.my, menu) to inflate the menu and add the defined items from the menu to the action bar. The name of the resource file in this example is my.xml. By default, every Activity supports an options menu of actions or options.

```
1   @Override
2       public boolean onCreateOptionsMenu(Menu menu) {
3           getMenuInflater().inflate(R.menu.my, menu);
4           return true;
5       }
```

The menu resource file, such as the example my.xml, is always located in the res/ menu directory of the project. The action button item definitions are specified using the <item> tag. The following XML file produced the action bar shown in Figure 4-1.

Lines 1–38:	Five button elements are defined using the <item> tag.
Lines 5–10:	The first action button is defined.
Line 6:	Each action button is given an identifier name, such as menuitem_search.
Line 7:	Many icon images are available through `android.R.drawable`. These are publicly accessible files and can be used in Android applications. Unique bitmaps for action button icons can also be constructed by the app developer and placed in the drawable folder. For the search action button, the icon value assigned `ic_menu_search`. A complete list of these R.drawable files can be found at `developer.android.com/reference/android/ R.drawable.html`.
Line 8:	`showAsAction` is an attribute that defines how the item will be displayed in the action bar. The possible values for this attribute are: `collapseActionView`, `ifRoom`, `never`, and `withText`.
	Action buttons that cannot fit (`ifRoom`) on the action bar, due to constraints in size, are placed in the action overflow menu. Action buttons that are less important to the activity or application can specifically designate the overflow menu as their required location.
Line 9:	`title` attribute represents the title associated with the item. The format required is a String value. The string `ui_menu_search` was defined in `strings.xml`.

res/menu/my.xml
```
1   <menu xmlns:android="http://schemas.android.com/apk/res/android"
2       xmlns:tools="http://schemas.android.com/tools"  >
3
4   <!-- ICONS ON THE ACTION BAR -->
5   <item
```

```
 6                android:id="@+id/menuitem_search"
 7                android:icon="@android:drawable/ic_menu_search"
 8                android:showAsAction="ifRoom"
 9                android:title="@string/ui_menu_search">
10  </item>
11  <item
12                android:id="@+id/menuitem_send"
13                android:icon="@android:drawable/ic_menu_send"
14                android:showAsAction="ifRoom"
15                android:title="@string/ui_menu_send">
16  </item>
17  <item
18                android:id="@+id/menuitem_share"
19                android:actionProviderClass=
20  "android.widget.ShareActionProvider"
21                android:icon="@android:drawable/ic_menu_share"
22                android:showAsAction="ifRoom"
23                android:title="@string/ui_menu_share">
24  </item>
25  <item
26                android:id="@+id/menuitem_about"
27                android:icon="@android:drawable/ic_menu_info_details"
28                android:showAsAction="ifRoom"
29                android:title="@string/ui_menu_about">
30  </item>
31  <item
32                android:id="@+id/menuitem_feedback"
33                android:icon="@android:drawable/ic_menu_help"
34                android:showAsAction="ifRoom"
35                android:title="@string/ui_menu_feedback">
36  </item>
37
38  </menu>
```

Several options are available when configuring the ActionBar. For example, if a menu item supplies both a title and an icon, as shown with the previous example, the action button always displays the icon by default. To display both the title and the icon, the withText value can be added to the showAsAction attribute.

The title of an action button should always be defined, even if it does not appear in the action bar. This provides flexibility in the application. For example, if the user performs a long-press on the button icon, a tool-tip containing the title will be revealed.

An action bar can be divided into two action bars: one on the top of the screen and the other on the bottom, as shown in Figure 4-6. This is helpful when more space is needed, such as when the action bar is found to be narrow. The top action bar contains

I FIGURE 4-6 Action bar with five action buttons and the overflow button.

the application icon and title. The bottom action bar has more room; thus, more of the action button will be visible to the user.

To split the action bar, the attribute `android:uiOptions` can be applied to the activity or the application in the AndroidManifest file. This option is supported in API level 14 and above. To add support for lower API levels, a metadata element must be applied. The following XML code segment is an example activity definition in an `AndroidManifest.xml` file:

Line 4:   A `splitActionBarWhenNarrow` value applied to the `android:uiOptions` attribute.

Lines 6–7:   UI options can be applied in a metadata element. Metadata is simply a name-value pair for an item of additional, arbitrary data that can be supplied to the parent component. A component element can contain any number of <metadata> subelements.

```
1   <activity
2   android:name="com.example.actionbar.MainActivity"
3   android:label="@string/app_name"
4   android:uiOptions="splitActionBarWhenNarrow" >
5
6   <meta-data android:name="android.support.UI_OPTIONS"
7   android:value="splitActionBarWhenNarrow" />
8   <intent-filter>
9   <action android:name="android.intent.action.MAIN" />
10  <category android:name="android.intent.category.LAUNCHER" />
11  </intent-filter>
12
13  </activity>
```

4.4.1 Overflow on the Action Bar

Narrow devices can often require the use of the overflow button. When creating layouts on devices with a narrow screen, it is best to use `ifRoom` to request that an item appear in the action bar. It is also a good design technique to allow the system to move elements into the overflow when there is not enough room. Figure 4-7 shows action buttons `Quit` and `Settings` placed in the overflow menu.

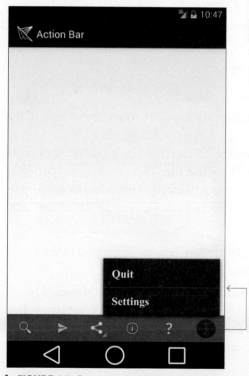

FIGURE 4-7 Buttons placed in the overflow menu display text titles.

The code for the XML menu resource file that produced the action bars displayed in Figure 4-7 is as follows:

```
res/menu/my.xml
1   <menu xmlns:android="http://schemas.android.com/apk/res/android"
2       xmlns:tools="http://schemas.android.com/tools"  >
3
4
5       <!-- ICONS ON THE ACTION BAR -->
6
7   <item
8           android:id="@+id/menuitem_search"
9           android:icon="@android:drawable/ic_menu_search"
10          android:showAsAction="ifRoom"
11          android:title="@string/ui_menu_search">
12  </item>
13  <item
14          android:id="@+id/menuitem_send"
15          android:icon="@android:drawable/ic_menu_send"
16          android:showAsAction="ifRoom"
17          android:title="@string/ui_menu_send">
18  </item>
19  <item
20          android:id="@+id/menuitem_share"
21          android:actionProviderClass=
22  "android.widget.ShareActionProvider"
23          android:icon="@android:drawable/ic_menu_share"
24          android:showAsAction="ifRoom"
25          android:title="@string/ui_menu_share">
26  </item>
27  <item
28          android:id="@+id/menuitem_about"
29          android:icon="@android:drawable/ic_menu_info_details"
30          android:showAsAction="ifRoom"
31          android:title="@string/ui_menu_about">
32  </item>
33  <item
34          android:id="@+id/menuitem_feedback"
35          android:icon="@android:drawable/ic_menu_help"
36          android:showAsAction="ifRoom"
37          android:title="@string/ui_menu_feedback">
38  </item>
39
40  <!-- ITEMS IN THE DROPDOWN MENU -->
41
42  <item
43          android:id="@+id/menuitem_quit"
44          android:icon=
```

```
45    "@android:drawable/ic_menu_close_clear_cancel"
46            android:showAsAction="never"
47            android:title="@string/ui_menu_quit">
48    </item>
49    <item
50            android:id="@+id/action_settings"
51            android:orderInCategory="100"
52            android:showAsAction="ifRoom"
53            android:title="@string/action_settings">
54    </item>
55
56
57    </menu>
```

4.4.2 Adding an Action View

An action view is simply a widget that appears in the action bar as a substitute for an action button. An action view provides quick access to heavily used actions. By placing these actions directly on the action bar, they appear as a consistent tool the user can easily utilize across multiple activities and fragments. From a developer's standpoint, the action bar can be designed once and used throughout the application screens.

Consider a collapsible search view widget. A search action view can be added as an embedded search view widget in the action bar.

To declare an action view, the `actionLayout` or `actionViewClass` attribute can be added to an item to specify either a layout resource or a widget class. The following segment of XML code adds a search view widget item to an action bar:

Line 3:   `actionViewClass` is an optional `View` class that uses an action view. `android.widget.SearchView` provides the user interface for entering a search query.

Line 5:   The `showAsAction` attribute is set to, or includes, the `collapseActionView` value. This is optional and declares that the action view should be collapsed into a button.

```
1    <item
2        android:id="@+id/menu_item_search"
3        android:actionViewClass="android.widget.SearchView"
4        android:icon="@drawable/icon_search"
5        android:showAsAction="collapseActionView"
6        android:title="@string/action_bar_button_search">
7    </item>
```

When a user executes a search request, the system starts your searchable activity and sends it to an activity action that performs the search.

■ Lab Example 4-2: Unit Conversion Calculator App

The objective of this lab example is to illustrate the use of the overflow menu as an option for presenting action tasks to the user. Using the overflow menu as a tool for application task navigation provides the user with action items that are available at all times, regardless of which activity or fragment is active. In addition, the overflow menu is often the first place users tend to look to understand what is included on the app.

Part 1: The Design

The Unit Conversion Calculator is a measurement converter, as illustrated in Figure 4-8. The user can use the conversion calculator to convert from one measure to another. To select the unit of measurement, the user chooses an option available from the overflow menu, as shown in Figure 4-9.

The application is designed to allow the user to input a unit value into a text field. The conversion to the target unit will automatically execute. Because the main purpose

I FIGURE 4-8 Unit Conversion Calculator.

of the app is to explore the overflow menu, the number of conversions available is kept to a minimum. Conversions include feet to meters, inches to centimeters, and pounds to grams. The user is also provided an action item for quitting the app. The `Quit` action item is placed last on the overflow menu.

As an added design feature, the user can show and hide the action bar by performing a single tap on unoccupied territory on the screen. This flexibility can be helpful when the user determines more screen space is needed.

It should be mentioned that long or poorly organized menus are difficult for users to scan. Long menus, in particular, can be overwhelming and confusing to the user. When given a large set of action items, it is better to reorganize them into other menus.

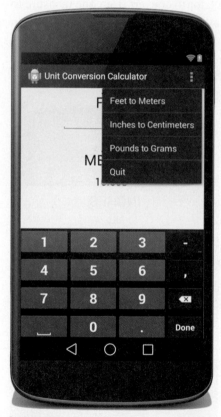

FIGURE 4-9 The Overflow menu contains Action Items.

Part 2: Application Structure and Setup

The settings for the Unit Conversion Calculator app are as follows:

- Application Name: Unit Conversion Calculator

- Project Name: UnitConversionCalculator
- Package Name: `com.cornez.unitconversioncalculator`
- Android Form: Phone and Tablet
- Minimum SDK: API 18: Android 4.3 (Jelly Bean)
- Target SDK: API 21: Android 5.0 (Lollipop)
- Compile with: API 21: Android 5.0 (Lollipop)
- Activity Name: `MyActivity`
- Layout Name: `activity_my`
- Menu name: `my`

The launcher is set to the Android default `ic_launcher.png` file. No additional drawable files are needed for this app. The final project structure is shown in Figure 4-10. The source file `conversion.java` is the only new file added to the project.

FIGURE 4-10 Project structure for the Unit Conversion Calculator app.

The application requires a single Activity class, `MyActivity.java`. Fragments are not used in this app. Changes are made to the auto-generated files `MyActivity.java`, `activity_my.xml`, `my.xml`, `strings.xml`, and `AndroidManifest.xml`.

The orientation of the screen for the application will be locked into portrait mode, which will be set within the activity. The complete attribute settings for the Android-Manifest are shown in the XML code listing as follows:

```
AndroidManifest.xml
1   <?xml version="1.0" encoding="utf-8"?>
2   <manifest xmlns:android="http://schemas.android.com/apk/res/android"
3       package="com.cornez.unitconversioncalculator" >
4
5   <application
6           android:allowBackup="true"
7           android:icon="@drawable/ic_launcher"
8           android:label="@string/app_name"
9           android:theme="@style/AppTheme" >
10  <activity
11              android:name=".MyActivity"
12              android:screenOrientation="portrait"
13              android:label="@string/app_name" >
14  <intent-filter>
15  <action android:name="android.intent.action.MAIN" />
16
17  <category
18  android:name="android.intent.category.LAUNCHER" />
19  </intent-filter>
20  </activity>
21  </application>
22
23  </manifest>
```

Part 3: Strings Value Resources

strings.xml is the only value resource, aside from the menu resource, required by the application. The new string elements are divided into two categories. The first category defines strings used by the application's layout file. The second category of strings represents the action bar overflow menu strings.

The complete strings.xml code is listed as follows:

```
strings.xml
1   <?xml version="1.0" encoding="utf-8"?>
2   <resources>
3
4   <string name="app_name">Unit Conversion Calculator</string>
5   <string name="hello_world">Hello world!</string>
6   <string name="action_settings">Settings</string>
7
8   <!-- LAYOUT ELEMENT STRINGS -->
9   <string name="feet">Feet</string>
10  <string name="meters">Meters</string>
11  <string name="inches">Inches</string>
12  <string name="centimeters">Centimeters</string>
13  <string name="pounds">Pounds</string>
```

```
14   <string name="grams">Grams</string>
15
16   <!-- ACTIONBAR ICON STRINGS -->
17   <string name="ui_menu_feet_meters">Feet to Meters</string>
18   <string name="ui_menu_inches_cent">Inches to Centimeters</string>
19   <string name="ui_menu_pounds_grams">Pounds to Grams</string>
20   <string name="ui_menu_quit">Quit</string>
21   <string name="zero">0.0</string>
22
23   </resources>
```

Part 4: The Action Bar and Menu Design

The action bar is configured to feature a limited number of elements: application icon, title, and the overflow menu. Action buttons are not used in this application. The overflow menu holds all the action elements (i.e., controls) for the application.

The code listing for the XML file, menu/my.xml, is shown below:

Line 3:   The context for the menu is an Activity. The activity for this application is implemented as MyActivity.class.

Lines 5–34:   Four action elements are defined as individual items using the <item> tag.

Line 9:   Each action item requires a resource ID.

Line 10:   To force an action item onto the overflow menu, the value is never applied to the showAsAction attribute.

Line 11:   The action title, as it appears on the overflow menu, is set using the appropriate strings.xml definition.

```
menu/my.xml
 1   <menu xmlns:android="http://schemas.android.com/apk/res/android"
 2       xmlns:tools="http://schemas.android.com/tools"
 3       tools:context=".MyActivity" >
 4
 5   <!-- ITEMS IN THE DROPDOWN OVERFLOW MENU -->
 6
 7   <!-- ACTION ITEM: FEET TO METERS -->
 8   <item
 9           android:id="@+id/menuitem_feet_meters"
10           android:showAsAction="never"
11           android:title="@string/ui_menu_feet_meters">
12   </item>
13
14   <!-- ACTION ITEM: INCHES TO CENTIMETERS -->
15   <item
16           android:id="@+id/menuitem_inches_cent"
```

```
17            android:showAsAction="never"
18            android:title="@string/ui_menu_inches_cent">
19  </item>
20
21  <!-- ACTION ITEM: POUNDS TO GRAMS -->
22  <item
23            android:id="@+id/menuitem_pounds_grams"
24            android:showAsAction="never"
25            android:title="@string/ui_menu_pounds_grams">
26  </item>
27
28  <!-- ACTION ITEM: QUIT -->
29  <item
30            android:id="@+id/menuitem_quit"
31            android:icon="@android:drawable/ic_menu_close_clear_cancel"
32            android:showAsAction="never"
33            android:title="@string/ui_menu_quit">
34  </item>
35
36  </menu>
```

Part 5: The Layout User Interface

A single layout, `activity_my.xml`, is used to support the entire user interface for the Unit Conversion Calculator application. This layout is bound to the activity `MyActivity.java`. Control elements for this layout are simple and arranged in a linear manner; however, the spacing between the elements requires a relative arrangement. As shown in the graphic layout design in Figure 4-11, the root element for the layout is a `RelativeLayout`, with an `EditText` providing the numeric input.

The XML code listing for `activity_my.xml` is shown below:

Lines 23–35:   The `EditText` input control is defined. It is given the identifier name `editText1`, which will be referenced in the `MyActivity`.

Line 31:   The alignment of the user's input into the text field will be centered along a horizontal axis.

Line 32:   A zero value hint text is displayed when the input text field is empty.

Line 33:   The type of data entered into the text field is restricted to a numeric value.

Lines 50–57:   The output text field, used to display the converted measurement, is given the identifier name `textView3`, which will be referenced in `MyActivity`.

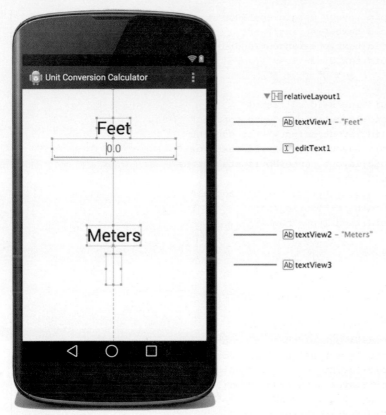

I FIGURE 4-11 The layout design for `activity_my.xml`.

```
activity_my.xml
1   <RelativeLayout
2   xmlns:android="http://schemas.android.com/apk/res/android"
3       xmlns:tools="http://schemas.android.com/tools"
4       android:layout_width="match_parent"
5       android:layout_height="match_parent"
6       android:paddingLeft="@dimen/activity_horizontal_margin"
7       android:paddingRight="@dimen/activity_horizontal_margin"
8       android:paddingTop="@dimen/activity_vertical_margin"
9       android:paddingBottom="@dimen/activity_vertical_margin"
10      tools:context=".MyActivity">
11
12  <!-- INPUT FIELDS: TEXTVIEW AND EDITTEXT -->
13  <TextView
14          android:id="@+id/textView1"
15          android:layout_width="wrap_content"
16          android:layout_height="wrap_content"
17          android:layout_alignParentTop="true"
18          android:layout_centerHorizontal="true"
```

```
19            android:layout_marginTop="30dp"
20            android:text="@string/feet"
21            android:textAppearance="?android:attr/textAppearanceLarge"
22            android:textSize="30sp" />
23
24    <EditText
25            android:id="@+id/editText1"
26            android:layout_width="wrap_content"
27            android:layout_height="wrap_content"
28            android:layout_below="@+id/textView1"
29            android:layout_centerHorizontal="true"
30            android:ems="10"
31            android:gravity="center_horizontal"
32            android:hint="@string/zero"
33            android:inputType="number" >
34
35    <requestFocus />
36    </EditText>
37
38    <!-- OUTPUT FIELDS: TEXTVIEW AND TEXTVIEW -->
39    <TextView
40            android:id="@+id/textView2"
41            android:layout_width="wrap_content"
42            android:layout_height="wrap_content"
43            android:layout_below="@+id/editText1"
44            android:layout_centerHorizontal="true"
45            android:layout_marginTop="40dp"
46            android:text="@string/meters"
47            android:textAppearance="?android:attr/textAppearanceLarge"
48            android:textSize="30sp" />
49
50    <TextView
51            android:id="@+id/textView3"
52            android:layout_width="wrap_content"
53            android:layout_height="wrap_content"
54            android:layout_below="@+id/textView2"
55            android:layout_centerHorizontal="true"
56            android:layout_marginTop="10dp"
57            android:textAppearance="?android:attr/textAppearanceLarge" />
58
59    </RelativeLayout>
```

Part 6: The Source Code

The two source files used by the application are MyActivity, which provides the
controller mechanism, and the Conversion class, which is used to implement the
data required by the conversions.

The Conversion class defines the data for a measurement object to be converted. This class also implements the logic for the computation of the conversion. The

data members of the class are used to describe the units of the conversion, the value to be converted, and result of the conversion. The code listing for Conversion is as follows:

```
Conversion.java
 1  package com.cornez.unitconversioncalculator;
 2
 3
 4  public class Conversion {
 5      static final int FEET = 1;
 6      static final int INCHES = 2;
 7      static final int POUNDS = 3;
 8      static final double METERS_PER_FEET = 0.3048;
 9      static final double CENTIMETERS_PER_INCH = 2.56;
10      static final double GRAMS_PER_LB = 453.592;
11
12      private int isA;
13      public String intputLabel;
14      public String outputLabel;
15
16      public Double inputValue;
17      public Double outputValue;
18
19      public Conversion() {
20          isA = FEET;
21
22          intputLabel = "FEET";
23          outputLabel = "METERS";
24          inputValue = 0.0;
25          outputValue = 0.0;
26      }
27
28      public void switch_toFeetMeters() {
29          isA = FEET;
30          intputLabel = "FEET";
31          outputLabel = "METERS";
32          compute();
33      }
34
35      public void switch_toInchesCentimeters() {
36          isA = INCHES;
37          intputLabel = "INCHES";
38          outputLabel = "CENTIMETERS";
39          compute();
40      }
41
42      public void switch_toPoundsGrams() {
43          isA = POUNDS;
44          intputLabel = "POUNDS";
45          outputLabel = "GRAMS";
```

```
46          compute();
47      }
48
49      public void compute() {
50
51          switch (isA) {
52              case FEET:
53                  outputValue = inputValue * METERS_PER_FEET;
54                  break;
55              case INCHES:
56                  outputValue = inputValue * CENTIMETERS_PER_INCH;
57                  break;
58
59              case POUNDS:
60                  outputValue = inputValue * GRAMS_PER_LB;
61                  break;
62          }
63      }
64
65  }
```

MyActivity will launch once the application has been activated. AndroidManifest specifies this activity as the main activity of the application. The Java code listing for MyActivity.java is shown below:

Lines 18–21:   All layout control elements need to be referenced because they are dynamic and will change, depending on the type of measurement conversion the user wants to apply to the input. The variables objects on Lines 18–21 include the unit measurement labels and the input and output measurement values.

Line 31:   A Conversion object is instantiated. The initial conversion type is set to "Feet to Meters" in the Conversion constructor.

Line 32:   The call to the method setUpReferenceDisplay() assigns references to the layout control elements. setUpReferenceDisplay appears on Lines 36–49.

Line 48:   addTextChangeListener() is applied to the input EditText control on the layout. This is a TextWatcher that is triggered when the user inputs a new number or edits the existing number.

Lines 51–71:   inputTextWatcher() is implemented as a TextWatcher. A try/catch is used to ensure the input is a valid number.

```
MyActivity.java
 1   package com.cornez.unitconversioncalculator;
 2
 3   import android.app.ActionBar;
 4   import android.app.Activity;
 5   import android.os.Bundle;
 6   import android.text.Editable;
 7   import android.text.TextWatcher;
 8   import android.view.Menu;
 9   import android.view.MenuItem;
10   import android.view.MotionEvent;
11   import android.widget.EditText;
12   import android.widget.TextView;
13
14
15   public class MyActivity extends Activity {
16
17   //REFERENCES TO THE USER INTERFACE ELEMENTS ON THE LAYOUT
18       private TextView inputLabel;
19       private TextView outputLabel;
20       private TextView outputMeasurement;
21       private EditText inputMeasurement;
22
23       Conversion conversion;
24
25
26       @Override
27       protected void onCreate(Bundle savedInstanceState) {
28           super.onCreate(savedInstanceState);
29           setContentView(R.layout.activity_my);
30
31           conversion = new Conversion();
32           setUpReferenceDisplay();
33
34       }
35
36       private void setUpReferenceDisplay () {
37           inputLabel = (TextView) findViewById(R.id.textView1);
38           inputLabel.setText(conversion.intputLabel);
39
40           outputLabel = (TextView) findViewById(R.id.textView2);
41           outputLabel.setText(conversion.outputLabel);
42
43           outputMeasurement = (TextView) findViewById(R.id.textView3);
44           outputMeasurement.setText(conversion.outputValue.toString());
45
46           inputMeasurement = (EditText) findViewById(R.id.editText1);
47           inputMeasurement.setText(conversion.inputValue.toString());
48           inputMeasurement.addTextChangedListener(inputTextWatcher);
49       }
```

```
50
51        private TextWatcher inputTextWatcher = new TextWatcher() {
52            //THE INPUT ELEMENT IS ATTACHED TO AN EDITABLE,
53            //THEREFORE THESE METHODS ARE CALLED WHEN THE TEXT IS CHANGED
54
55   public void onTextChanged(CharSequence s,
56                                        int start, int before, int count){
57            //CATCH AN EXCEPTION WHEN THE INPUT IS NOT A NUMBER
58            try {
59                conversion.inputValue =
60                                Double.parseDouble(s.toString());
61            }catch (NumberFormatException e){
62                conversion.inputValue = 0.0;
63            }
64            conversion.compute();
65            outputMeasurement.setText(
66                                conversion.outputValue.toString());
67        }
68        public void afterTextChanged(Editable s) {}
69        public void beforeTextChanged(CharSequence s,
70                                int start, int count, int after){}
71    };
```

Lines 72–78:   The onTouchEvent() is called when the user taps a single finger on a blank area of the screen. If the finger motion is registered as a simple "finger down" action, as opposed to gestures such as a swipe/fling, the event signals to the application that the user wants to hide or redisplay the action bar.

Lines 80–91:   The method toggleActionBar() is used to hide or show the action bar. Its current state is found using isShowing(). The visibility of the action bar is toggled accordingly.

Lines 95–99:   The menu hierarchy, specified by menu/my.xml, is inflated. The settings within my.xml will restrict the items to the overflow menu.

Lines 101–130: onOptionsItemSelected() is called when an action item located on the menu has been selected. This method identifies the item by its resource id. resetDisplay() processes the action and resets the display to the units of measurement specified by the menu item.

Lines 132–137: resetDisplay() resets the screen with new labels of conversion.

```
MyActivity.java     continued

72      @Override
73      public boolean onTouchEvent(MotionEvent event) {
74          if(event.getAction() == MotionEvent.ACTION_DOWN) {
75              toggleActionBar();
76          }
77          , true;
78      }
79
80      private void toggleActionBar() {
81          ActionBar actionBar = getActionBar();
82
83          if(actionBar != null) {
84              if(actionBar.isShowing()) {
85                  actionBar.hide();
86              }
87              else {
88                  actionBar.show();
89              }
90          }
91      }
92
93
94      @Override
95      public boolean onCreateOptionsMenu(Menu menu) {
96          // Inflate the menu
97          getMenuInflater().inflate(R.menu.my, menu);
98          return true;
99      }
100
101     @Override
102     public boolean onOptionsItemSelected(MenuItem item) {
103         // Handle action bar item clicks here. The action bar will
104         // automatically handle clicks on the Home/Up button, so long
105         // as you specify a parent activity in AndroidManifest.xml.
106         int id = item.getItemId();
107
108         if (id == R.id.menuitem_feet_meters){
109             conversion.switch_toFeetMeters();
110             resetDisplay();
111             return true;
112         }
113         else if (id == R.id.menuitem_inches_cent){
114             conversion.switch_toInchesCentimeters();
115             resetDisplay();
116             return true;
117         }
118         else if (id == R.id.menuitem_pounds_grams){
119             conversion.switch_toPoundsGrams();
120             resetDisplay();
```

```
121              return true;
122          }
123          else if (id == R.id.menuitem_quit){
124              //CLOSE ACTIVITY
125              finish();
126              return true;
127          }
128
129          return super.onOptionsItemSelected(item);
130      }
131
132      private void resetDisplay() {
133          inputLabel.setText(conversion.intputLabel);
134          outputLabel.setText(conversion.outputLabel);
135          outputMeasurement.setText(conversion.outputValue.toString());
136          inputMeasurement.setText(conversion.inputValue.toString());
137      }
138  }
```

■ 4.5 Responsive Design with Fragments

Responsive design techniques have been applied to web design to build websites that are able to work across different screen sizes. Responsive design techniques should also be applied to Android appplications for solving interactive design and layout problems within a responsive framework, such as the optimal arrangement of data elements in a fragmented environment.

In some ways, responsive design is similar to adaptive design, which was introduced in Chapter 2. At times, these two design techniques can overlap; however, responsive design and adaptive design have significant differences. To simplify, responsive design is used for heavy data-driven content. It uses screen grouping techniques and complex navigation to present data content in a more intuitive and device-sensitive way. Adaptive design is primarily used for the rearrangement of fixed user interface elements in an application. For example, adaptive design methods would not be ideal for solving problems related to the arrangement of data control elements for a database-driven application.

On an Android mobile device, responsive design revolves around a master/detail flow interface design pattern. In this design pattern, the user is provided with a list of items, which is referred to as the master list. Upon selecting one of the items, additional information relating to that item is then presented to the user within an area of the screen called a details panel. For example, consider an email application. One panel of the screen, the master list panel, displays a list of the inbox messages consisting of the address of the sender and the subject of the message. Upon selecting one of the email items from the list, the body of the email message appears in another panel of the screen, the detail panel.

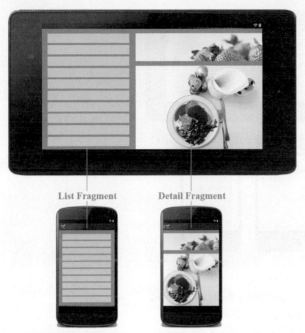

List Fragment   Detail Fragment

❘ FIGURE 4-12 Fragments can be combined or separated on a device.

This design concept is responsive in the sense that list and detail panels of the app can change based on the width of the device. On a large tablet-sized Android device, the screen is large enough to display both panels. The master list can appear as a narrow vertical panel along the left-hand edge of the screen, while the remainder of the screen can display the detail panel. This arrangement is referred to as a two-pane mode.

Small Android devices do not have a screen size large enough to combine lists and details together effectively on a screen. A solution for smaller Android devices is to display the master list within its own individual screen. The detail panel will also be displayed on a separate screen, which will appear when a selection is made from the master list. The detail screen must feature an action icon that allows the user to return to the master list.

In Android, responsive design makes use of Fragments. A user interface can be divided into multiple panes using Fragments and reused in more than one screen of an application, as shown in Figure 4-12. Fragments can be combined or separated on a device. Although a single screen is implemented as an `Activity` subclass, the individual content panes are implemented as `Fragment` subclasses.

When building an application that follows a similar master/detail design pattern, the application often needs a set of Java and XML layout resource files. As an example, consider a general application with a list of items and the details for a selected item to be displayed when the user selects the item from the list. Figure 4-13 shows the layout structure for such an application.

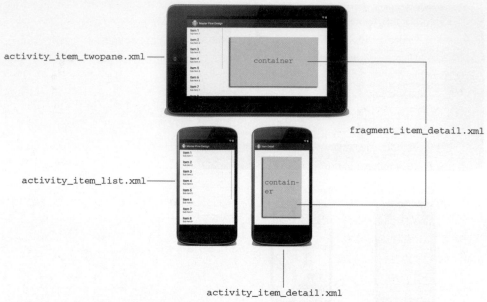

activity_item_twopane.xml

fragment_item_detail.xml

activity_item_list.xml

activity_item_detail.xml

▌ FIGURE 4-13 A layout design using fragments.

activity_item_twopane.xml is the layout that contains both the list of items and a container to display details. The container is used to hold a fragment. This layout is used when the application is running on a device large enough to support the two-pane mode.

The XML resource file named activity_item_list.xml is populated with the list of items, and is always used on devices that are too small to support the two-pane mode.

The activity_item_detail.xml layout resource file occupies its own screen, which means it is associated with another activity. This layout is inflated from the activity ItemActivityDetail.java, and it is used on small screens. The layout uses a container to place a fragment. The fragment_item_ detail.xml is the user interface for the detail pane.

Two separate activities are required to represent the item list activity (ItemListActivity.java) and the item detail activity (Item_Detail Activity.java).

ItemListActivity.java has a different presentation depending on the size of the device. On a large device, the activity presents the list of items and the item details side-by-side using two panes. The activity can do this by using a fragment. The ItemListFragment class can represent the list of items, and the Item DetailFragment class can represent the item details (if present). These classes must be created. On a small device, the activity can solely present the list of items. A selected item leads to an `ItemDetailActivity` representing item details.

`Item_DetailActivity.java` is a necessary activity that serves as a "shell" that is used to present an item detail fragment; it appears only when a small device is being used.

This sample application uses two Fragment source files: an item list fragment (`ItemListFragment.java`) and an item detail fragment (`ItemDetail-Fragment.java`).

`ItemListFragment.java` will be the list fragment class that represents a list of Items. `ItemDetailFragment.java` will be the fragment class representing a single-item detail on the screen.

If the display is large enough to support the two-pane mode, an instance of the `item_list` fragment from the `activity_item_twopane.xml` layout is created and displayed. If the display cannot accommodate both panes, the instance contained in the `activity_item_list.xml` file is used.

Lab Example 4-3: Shades App: A Fragment Experiment

This lab example explores using responsive design, with the use of Fragments, to create a responsive user interface that can be adapted from a two-pane to a single-pane configuration, based on a change in screen orientation.

Part 1: The Design

When launched, the Shades application provides the user with a fixed list of color shades: plum, blue, and gold. When a shade is selected, information about that shade is displayed. The user interface is designed to respond to changes in screen orientation. When the user is viewing the application in landscape mode, a two-pane configuration is used, displaying the list of shades in a left-hand pane and information about an individual shade in a right-hand pane. As the user rotates the device into portrait orientation, a single-pane configuration is used. One activity is used to display the list of shades. Once a shade is selected, a new activity appears on the screen with information about the shade. The two-pane and one-pane configurations for the Shades application are shown in Figure 4-14.

Fragments used with this master-detail pattern design provide the responsive framework for the application. In the default landscape mode, the main Activity contains two Fragments: a list Fragment and an information Fragment. When in portrait mode, the Activity contains only the list Fragment.

Selecting a shade from the master list either updates the information Fragment or launches a new activity, the information Fragment Activity.

Portrait orientation -
Selecting a list item
starts an activity containing a fragment.

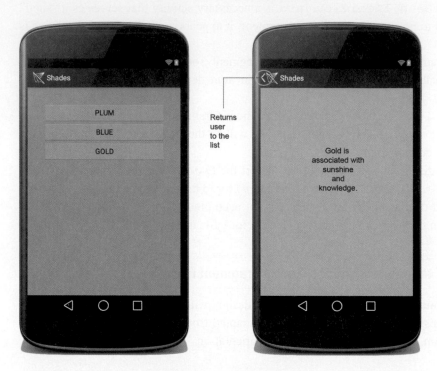

Returns
user
to the
list

Horizontal orientation-
Selecting a list item
updates the fragment on the right.

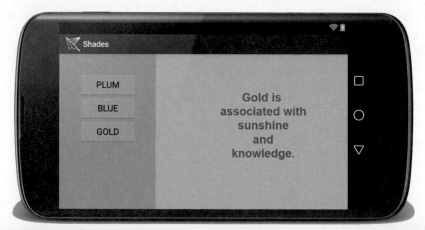

FIGURE 4-14 One- and two-pane configurations.

Part 2: Application Structure and Setup

The settings for the application are as follows:

- Application Name: Shades
- Project Name: Shades
- Package Name: `com.cornez.shades`
- Android Form: Phone and Tablet
- Minimum SDK: API 18: Android 4.3 (Jelly Bean)
- Target SDK: API 21: Android 5.0 (Lollipop)
- Compile with: API 21: Android 5.0 (Lollipop)
- Activity Name: `MyActivity`
- Layout Name: `activity_my`

The launch icon for the application is a PNG file added to the drawable folder. This bitmap file, also named `ic_launcher.png`, is provided in the textbook resource material. The application's final project structure is shown in Figure 4-1. The Java source files include two Activity classes and two Fragment classes. `MyActivity` is the main activity of the project. `MyActivity` uses `activity_my.xml` as its associated layout file.

`InformationActivity.java` is the `Activity` class that will be activated when the user is in portrait mode and has selected a shade. If the user remains in landscape mode during the entire application, `InformationActivity` will never launch.

As shown in the `res/layout` directory in Figure 4-15, the Shades app relies on three XML layout files: an activity layout and two fragment layouts. The activity layout, `activity_my.xml`, is the screen interface for the main activity of the application. Two versions of `activity_my.xml` are shown. The first version, designed for a landscape orientation, is located in the default `res/layout` folder and uses a two-pane layout. The second version of `activity_my.xml`, designed for a portrait screen orientation, is located in `res/layout-port` and uses a one-pane layout.

The two XML fragment layout files are `list_fragment_xml` and `information_fragment.xml`. Both files are used to structure the fragments of data, representing the shade list and the individual information, which will be inserted into the pane containers.

`AndroidManifest.xml` must declare both activities used by the Shades application, as shown below:

Lines 11–21:   `MyActivity.class` is specified as the main activity to be
                launched when the application is launched for the first time.

FIGURE 4-15 The final project structure for the Shades application.

Line 24–31:   The secondary activity, `InformationActivity.class`, is
set as the child activity of `MyActivity`.

```
AndroidManifest.xml
1   <?xml version="1.0" encoding="utf-8"?>
2   <manifest xmlns:android="http://schemas.android.com/apk/res/android"
3       package="com.cornez.shades" >
4
5   <application
6           android:allowBackup="true"
7           android:icon="@drawable/ic_launcher"
8           android:label="@string/app_name"
9           android:theme="@style/AppTheme" >
10
11  <!-- MAIN ACTIVITY -->
12  <activity
13              android:name=".MyActivity"
14              android:label="@string/app_name" >
15  <intent-filter>
16  <action android:name="android.intent.action.MAIN" />
17
```

```
18  <category
19  android:name="android.intent.category.LAUNCHER" />
20  </intent-filter>
21  </activity>
22
23  <!-- SECOND ACTIVITY TO DISPLAY DETAIL INFORMATION -->
24  <activity
25              android:name=".InformationActivity"
26              android:label="@string/app_name"
27              android:parentActivityName=".MyActivity" >
28  <meta-data
29              android:name="android.support.PARENT_ACTIVITY"
30              android:value=".MainActivity" />
31  </activity>
32  </application>
33
34  </manifest>
```

Part 3: External Value Resources

Color has been added to the Shades application to provide a visual demarcation for the two-pane configurations; this is primarily a visual cue. The pane used for the master list uses a caramel background color. The pane used for the information data uses a light-tan background color. The color definitions are placed in a newly added XML file colors.xml, which is located in res/values.

colors.xml
```
1  <?xml version="1.0" encoding="utf-8"?>
2  <resources>
3
4  <color name="caramel">#ac7d50</color>
5  <color name="light_tan">#c89b6d</color>
6
7  </resources>
```

The master list elements and the information about individual shades of color will be stored in strings.xml file. It should be noted that Shades is a simple application used to simplify and demonstrate how fragments can be used with a master/detail design pattern. Outside an example such as this, it is not practical to employ strings.xml as a data repository. More practical solutions will be explored later in the chapter, as well as in subsequent chapters.

The XML code listing for `strings.xml` is as follows:

```
strings.xml
1   <?xml version="1.0" encoding="utf-8"?>
2   <resources>
3
4   <string name="app_name">Shades</string>
5   <string name="hello_world">Hello world!</string>
6   <string name="action_settings">Settings</string>
7
8   <!-- SHADE LIST COLOR -->
9   <string name="gold">GOLD</string>
10  <string name="blue">BLUE</string>
11  <string name="plum">PLUM</string>
12
13  <!-- SHADE DETAIL INFORMATION -->
14  <string name="plum_is">Plum is a deep purple color.
15  It is used in weddings. </string>
16  <string name="blue_is">Blue is the color of peace
17  and trust.</string>
18  <string name="gold_is">Gold is associated with sunshine
19  and knowledge.</string>
20
21  </resources>
```

Part 4: Individual Fragment Layouts

As a component of an application's user interface, `Fragments` are designed with corresponding layouts. In this application, the master list fragment layout is defined by `list_fragment.xml`. The master list for this demonstration app is limited to three shades of color. Each shade is placed, as a button control, directly on the `list_fragment.xml` layout file, as shown in its visual representation in Figure 4-16. The layout's root container is set to a LinearLayout.

The code listing for `list_fragment.xml` appears below:

Line 5:   The background color, for this master list, is set to caramel.

Lines 11–12:   The width of each button will be uniform. The value `fill_parent`, assigned to the attribute `layout_width`, will stretch the width of the button to fill the layout.

Line 13:   The Activity uses the `contentDescription` attribute to update the information pane when the user selects a color shade.

FIGURE 4-16 `list_fragment.xml`.

```
list_fragment.xml
1   <?xml version="1.0" encoding="utf-8"?>
2   <LinearLayout xmlns:android="http://schemas.android.com/apk/res/android"
3       android:layout_width="match_parent"
4       android:layout_height="match_parent"
5       android:background="@color/caramel"
6       android:orientation="vertical"
7       android:padding="40dp"  >
8
9   <Button
10          android:id="@+id/button1"
11          android:layout_width="fill_parent"
12          android:layout_height="wrap_content"
13          android:contentDescription="@string/plum_is"
14          android:text="@string/plum" />
15
16  <Button
17          android:id="@+id/button2"
18          android:layout_width="fill_parent"
```

```
19            android:layout_height="wrap_content"
20            android:contentDescription="@string/blue_is"
21  android:text="@string/blue" />
22
23  <Button
24            android:id="@+id/button3"
25            android:layout_width="fill_parent"
26            android:layout_height="wrap_content"
27            android:contentDescription="@string/gold_is"
28            android:text="@string/gold" />
29
30
31  </LinearLayout>
```

The detail, or information, fragment layout is defined by the XML file
`information_fragment.xml`. Information about a selected shade is a text element. This text element is placed in a TextView, as shown in the visual representation
of the layout in Figure 4-17.

The XML code listing for information is shown below:

Line 2:   A RelativeLayout ViewGroup is used as the root element of the
                 layout file. This allows the text element to be placed freely on
                 the screen.

Lines 12–13:   The text element is set to appear in the center of the pane.

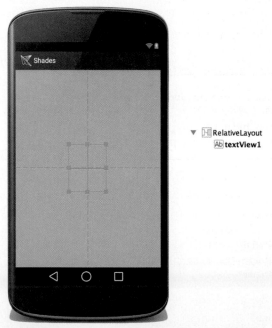

FIGURE 4-17 The layout, `information_fragment.xml`, used to hold color information.

```
information_fragment.xml
1   <?xml version="1.0" encoding="utf-8"?>
2   <RelativeLayout
3   xmlns:android="http://schemas.android.com/apk/res/android"
4       android:layout_width="match_parent"
5       android:layout_height="match_parent"
6       android:background="@color/light_tan" >
7
8   <TextView
9           android:id="@+id/textView1"
10          android:layout_width="wrap_content"
11          android:layout_height="wrap_content"
12          android:layout_centerHorizontal="true"
13          android:layout_centerVertical="true"
14          android:padding="50dp"
15          android:textAppearance="?android:attr/textAppearanceLarge" />
16
17  </RelativeLayout>
```

Part 5: The Main User Interface to Hold the Fragments

`activity_my.xml` provides two possible configurations. The Android operating system will choose the appropriate resources based on the current device characteristics. For this application experiment, the two layout configurations are placed in separate folders: `res/layout` and `res/layout-port`. The same name, `activity_my.xml`, is used in both locations.

It should be noted that using multiple layout folders works well for a simple application such as this one. For an application that is more complex, relying on a variety of folders to store versions of the same layout can be hard to maintain. For advanced applications, references can be used to refer to a specific item in Android from a particular resource folder. In addition, you can quickly calculate the suitability of a screen size, and you can apply pane configurations accordingly.

To keep the layout simple, the root element of the default main activity in a landscape orientation is a `LinearLayout`, as shown in Figure 4-18.

The XML code for `activity_my.xml` is listed below:

Line 4:   The orientation attribute of the LinearLayout is set to horizontal, which allows the Fragment elements to be placed side by side.

Lines 9–16:   The master list fragment is defined. The class associated with this `Fragment` is `ListFragment.class`.

Lines 18–26:   The information fragment is defined. The class associated with this `Fragment` is `InformationFragment`.

FIGURE 4-18 `activity_my.xml` uses a LinearLayout root element.

```
activity_my.xml    - located in layout
1  <LinearLayout xmlns:android="http://schemas.android.com/apk/res/
2  android"
3      xmlns:tools="http://schemas.android.com/tools"
4      android:baselineAligned="false"
5      android:layout_width="fill_parent"
6      android:layout_height="fill_parent"
7      android:orientation="horizontal" >
8
9  <!-- FRAGMENT: list_fragment.xml -->
10 <fragment
11        android:id="@+id/fragment1"
12        android:layout_width="0dp"
13        android:layout_weight="1"
14        android:layout_height="match_parent"
15        class="com.cornez.shades.ListFragment"
16        tools:layout="@layout/list_fragment">
17 </fragment>
18
19 <!-- FRAGMENT: information_fragment.xml -->
20 <fragment
21        android:id="@+id/fragment2"
22        android:layout_width="0dp"
23        android:layout_weight="2"
24        android:layout_height="match_parent"
```

```
24              class="com.cornez.shades.InformationFragment"
25              tools:layout="@layout/information_fragment">
26   </fragment>
27
28   </LinearLayout>
29
```

A second version of `activity_my.xml` will be created and placed in a new resource folder named `layout-port`. The Android system will select this second version of the layout when the current device is in a portrait orientation. The visual design for this version of the main activity layout is shown in Figure 4-19. It contains a LinearLayout with a single element, a `Fragment` container, and it is given the identifier name `fragment1`.

I FIGURE 4-19 The main layout designed for portrait orientation. Fragment1 is shown holding the color list.

This portrait version of `activity_my.xml` is used to define the single pane information Activity. This layout is a placeholder for the `ListFragment` class. The XML code for this file appears as follows:

```
activity_my.xml    - res/layout-port
1  <LinearLayout xmlns:android="http://schemas.android.com/apk/res/android"
2      xmlns:tools="http://schemas.android.com/tools"
3      android:baselineAligned="false"
4      android:layout_width="fill_parent"
5      android:layout_height="fill_parent"
6      android:orientation="vertical" >
7
8  <!-- FRAGMENT: list_fragment.xml -->
9  <fragment
10         android:id="@+id/fragment1"
11         android:layout_width="match_parent"
12         android:layout_height="match_parent"
13         class="com.cornez.shades.ListFragment"
14         tools:layout="@layout/list_fragment">
15  </fragment>
16
17
18  </LinearLayout>
```

Part 6: Coding the Application

Two Activities are used by this application: `MyActivity` and `Information Activity`. `MyActivity` is the main activity of the application and will always remain running while the application is in landscape mode. This activity displays fragments side by side with the master list on the left and the information detail on the right. When the system determines a single pane configuration, `MyActivity` is responsible for launching a second activity, `InformationActivity`, to display the information detail when required. The Java code for `MyActivity.java` is listed below:

Lines 18–26:   The information fragment is defined. The class associated with this `Fragment` is `InformationFragment`.

Lines 19–42:   The `onShadeItemSelected()` method is from the interface `OnItemSelectedListener`. This interface is declared in the ListFragment class and is discussed further in this lab example. The method `onShadeItemSelected()` is a handler for a listener event that is triggered when the user selects a shade from the master list.

Lines 23–30:   `findFragmentById()` is used to find a fragment identified by the given identifier. The InformationFragment is assigned, if it exists. If the fragment is present in the current configuration, the information about the selected shade is placed into the text element of this fragment.

Lines 33–41:   If a single-pane configuration is on display in the window, an
                 `Intent` is created to start another `Activity`, the Informatio-
                 nActivity, to display shade information. The information about
                 the shade is added onto the `Intent` and passed before the
                 `Activity` is started. The argument `link` is the specific infor-
                 mation about the shade choice selected.

```
MyActivity.java
1   package com.cornez.shades;
2
3   import android.app.Activity;
4   import android.content.Intent;
5   import android.os.Bundle;
6
7
8   public class MyActivity extends Activity implements
9           MyListFragment.OnItemSelectedListener {
10
11
12      @Override
13      protected void onCreate(Bundle savedInstanceState) {
14          super.onCreate(savedInstanceState);
15          setContentView(R.layout.activity_my);
16      }
17
18      @Override
19      public void onShadeItemSelected(String link) {
20
21          //TASK 1: CHECK IF THE INFORMATION FRAGMENT
22  EXISTS IN THIS LAYOUT
23          InformationFragment informationFragment = (InformationFragment)
24  getFragmentManager().findFragmentById(R.id.fragment2);
25
26          //TASK 2: CHECK IF A TWO PANE CONFIGURATION BEING DISPLAYED?
27          if (informationFragment != null &&
28  informationFragment.isInLayout()) {
29              informationFragment.setText(link);
30          }
31
32          //A SINGLE-PANE CONFIGURATION EXISTS
33          else {
34              // IF THE INFORMATION FRAGMENT DOES NOT EXIST IN THIS
35              // LAYOUT ACTIVATE THE INFORMATION ACTIVITY
36
37              Intent intent = new Intent (this,
38                          InformationActivity.class);
```

```
39            intent.putExtra("Information", link);
40            startActivity (intent);
41        }
42     }
43 }
```

The ListFragment is the Fragment class that provides the structure for the master list containing clickable buttons. ListFragment serves as a component to the MyActivity class.

The code listing for ListFragment.java appears as follows:

Line 12: A listener object, used for signaling and identifying which shade on the master list has been selected, is declared.

Line 13: When a shade from the master list is selected, the string information holds the detail information to be displayed.

Lines 21–24: ListFragment inflates its user interface view, list_fragment.xml, in the container set aside by activity_my.xml.

Lines 26–33: Each shade item on the master list is referenced by a button view. OnClicklistener events are registered to the buttons. The handler for this click event is ShadeChangeListener.

Lines 38–45: The onClick event handler ShadeChangeListener is implemented. view.getContentDescription() collects the View description stored in the XML definition for the button.

Lines 47–49: The public interface can support the passing of information to the controlling activity of a fragment. Often, communication between the fragment and its activity is managed through a public interface defined in the fragment. The public interface ListFragment.OnItemSelectedListener communicates which list item was selected.

Lines 52–61: onAttach() is called when a ListFragment is first attached to MyActivity.

Lines 62–64: updateDetail() communicates the shade information to MyActivity.

ListFragment.java

```
1  package com.cornez.shades;
2
3  import android.view.View;
4  import android.app.Activity;
5  import android.app.Fragment;
6  import android.os.Bundle;
```

```java
7   import android.view.LayoutInflater;
8   import android.view.View.OnClickListener;
9   import android.view.ViewGroup;
10  import android.widget.Button;
11
12  public class ListFragment extends Fragment {
13
14      private OnItemSelectedListener listener;
15      private String information;
16
17      @Override
18      public View onCreateView(LayoutInflater inflater,
19  ViewGroup container,
20                                  Bundle savedInstanceState) {
21          View view =
22  inflater.inflate(R.layout.list_fragment,
23  container,
24  false);
25
26          Button button1 = (Button) view.findViewById(R.id.button1);
27          button1.setOnClickListener(ShadeChangeListener);
28
29          Button button2 = (Button) view.findViewById(R.id.button2);
30          button2.setOnClickListener(ShadeChangeListener);
31
32          Button button3 = (Button) view.findViewById(R.id.button3);
33          button3.setOnClickListener(ShadeChangeListener);
34
35          return view;
36      }
37
38      private OnClickListener ShadeChangeListener =
39  new OnClickListener() {
40          public void onClick(View view) {
41              String description = (String) view.getContentDescription();
42              information = description;
43              updateDetail();
44          }
45      };
46
47      public interface OnItemSelectedListener {
48          public void onShadeItemSelected(String link);
49      }
50
51      @Override
52      public void onAttach(Activity activity) {
53          super.onAttach(activity);
54          if (activity instanceof OnItemSelectedListener) {
55              listener = (OnItemSelectedListener) activity;
56          } else {
```

```
57          throw new ClassCastException(activity.toString()
58                  + " must implement
59 MyListFragment.OnItemSelectedListener");
60          }
61      }
62
63      public void updateDetail() {
64          listener.onShadeItemSelected(information);
65      }
66 }
```

The `InformationFragment` class requires information about the selected shade item, which is then loaded into a TextView located on the associated layout. The Java code is listed below:

Lines 12–22:   `onCreateView ()` is called to instantiate the fragment's user interface view.

Lines 17–18:   The layout associated with the fragment, `information_fragment.xml`, is inflated and loaded into the container on `activity_my.xml`.

Line 19:   The view, specfically `R.layout.information_fragment`, is returned.

Lines 23–27:   The public method `setText()` sets the `TextView`, located on the layout `information_fragment.xml`, to the shade information.

```
InformationFragment.java
 1 package com.cornez.shades;
 2
 3 import android.app.Fragment;
 4 import android.os.Bundle;
 5 import android.view.LayoutInflater;
 6 import android.view.View;
 7 import android.view.ViewGroup;
 8 import android.widget.TextView;
 9
10 public class InformationFragment extends Fragment {
11
12     @Override
13     public View onCreateView(LayoutInflater inflater,
14 ViewGroup container,
15 Bundle savedInstanceState) {
16
17         View view = inflater.inflate(
18 R.layout.information_fragment, container, false);
19         return view;
```

```
20
21        }
22
23        public void setText (String shadeInfo) {
24            TextView view = (TextView)
25                         getView().findViewById(R.id.textView1);
26            view.setText(shadeInfo);
27        }
28 }
```

Part 7: Defining the Single-Pane Detail Activity

`InformationActivity.java` is the single-pane Activity that shows the detail information about a specific shade.

Lines 15–21:   If the orientation of the screen has returned to landscape mode, this single-pane Activity is no longer needed because the two-pane model does not fit comfortably on the screen. `getConfiguration ()` returns the current configuration, which can be matched with the constant `Configuration. ORIENTATION_LANDSCAPE`. `finish ()` and `return` finish the Activity and return to the starting Activity.

Line 27:   `setDisplayHomeAsUpEnabled()` enables the "up" control element located on the action bar.

Line 29:   The `Intent` that started this activity is returned by the call `getIntent ()`. The extended data (the passed shade information) is retrieved from this intent.

Lines 34–35:   A reference is made to the TextView located on the Fragment layout `information_fragment.xml`. The string value of the TextView is set to the information about the shade that was selected from the master list.

```
InformationActivity.java
1  package com.cornez.shades;
2
3  import android.app.Activity;
4  import android.content.Intent;
5  import android.content.res.Configuration;
6  import android.os.Bundle;
7  import android.widget.TextView;
8
9  public class InformationActivity extends Activity {
10
11       @Override
```

```
12        protected void onCreate(Bundle savedInstanceState) {
13            super.onCreate(savedInstanceState);
14
15            //TASK 1:  VERIFY THE ORIENTATION HAS BEEN SWITCHED
16            //         TO LANDSCAPE MODE.
17            if (getResources().getConfiguration().orientation ==
18    Configuration.ORIENTATION_LANDSCAPE) {
19                finish();
20                return;
21            }
22
23            //TASK 2: SET THE LAYOUT FOR THIS ACTIVITY
24            setContentView(R.layout.information_fragment);
25
26            //TASK 3: DISPLAY THE UP ICON IN THE ACTION BAR
27            getActionBar().setDisplayHomeAsUpEnabled(true);
28
29            //TASK 4: RETURN THE INTENT THAT STARTED THIS ACTIVITY
30            Intent intent = getIntent();
31            String shadeInformation = intent.getStringExtra("Information");
32
33            //TASK 5:
34            TextView information = (TextView) findViewById (R.id.textView1);
35            information.setText(shadeInformation);
36        }
37    }
```

■ 4.6 Animation in Fragment Transactions

Transition animations can be applied directly to fragments that are entering and exiting a transaction.

To manage fragments, the `FragmentManager` provides the structure that handles transactions between fragments. A transaction refers to the sequence of steps that add, replace, or remove fragments.

Operations performed by the `FragmentManager` occur inside a transaction. For example, the following code segment illustrates a Fragment transaction:

Line 1:   `getFragmentManager()` returns the `FragmentManager` for interacting with fragments associated with current activity.

Lines 3–4:   `FragmentTransaction` is the API for performing a set of `Fragment` –operations. A FragmentTransaction object is instantiated. `beginTransaction` initiates edit operations on the Fragments associated with this FragmentManager.

Lines 6–9:   A series of edit operations is performed on the fragment associated with the FragmentTransaction object instantiated on Lines 3–4. Common edit operations that can occur in a transaction are:

a. add()/remove(): to add and remove a Fragment from the FragmentManager.

b. attach()/detach(): to attach/detach a Fragment from the Activity (e.g., make it an active Fragment that can be seen by the user).

c. show()/hide(): to show or hide a Fragment by calling View.setVisibility() on the Fragment's root View.

Line 10:   commit() is called to mark the end of the transaction.

```
1   FragmentManager fragmentManager = getFragmentManager();
2
3   FragmentTransaction fragmentTransaction =
4   fragmentManager.beginTransaction();
5
6   fragmentTransaction.add(. . . );
7   fragmentTransaction.attach(. . . );
8   fragmentTransaction.hide(. . . );
9   fragmentTransaction.remove(. . . );
10
11  fragmentTransaction.commit();
```

Fragment transactions support transition animations. Two versions of the setCustomAnimations() method, from the FragmentTransaction class, are used to set the animation resources to be applied to fragments that are entering and exiting a given transaction.

The method setCustomAnimations(int enter, int exit) is used to play an animation for enter and exit operations. These animations, however, will not be played when popping the back stack.

popEnter and popExit animations can be played for enter and exit operations specifically when popping the back stack. The setCustom Animations (int enter, int exit, int popEnter, int popExit) method is used for this purpose.

■ Lab Example 4-4: Recipes–Fragments with Transition Animations

The objective of this lab example is to work with fragments in an application and to apply transition animations. This lab will explore the FragmentTransaction class, basic animation effects, and the Android interpolator.

Part 1: The App Design

The Recipes App was constructed for the purpose of demonstrating fragment transition animations; hence, it is very simple. The behavior of this application is similar to a flip card, with a swiveling rotation animation. The application is displayed in Figure 4-20. Upon first launching Recipe App, the user is presented with a photograph of a cooked dish. In the lower left corner is a button for flipping the photograph over to view the recipe directions. The photograph and the recipe directions are both Fragments that enter and exit within a transaction.

FIGURE 4-20 The Recipes app.

Part 2: Application Structure and Setup

The settings for the application are as follows:

- Application Name: Recipes
- Project Name: Recipes
- Android Form: Phone and Tablet
- Minimum SDK: API 18: Android 4.3 (Jelly Bean)

- Target SDK: API 21: Android 5.0 (Lollipop)
- Compile with: API 21: Android 5.0 (Lollipop)
- Activity Name: `MyActivity`
- Layout Name: `activity_my`

The application icon launcher is set to the Android default `ic_launcher.png` file, and a photograph of a cooked dish has been added to the drawable folder. The final application structure is shown in Figure 4-21. Two Java Fragment classes–one for the recipe photos and another for the recipe directions–,and a main Activity are the source files required by the application. The Activity and the Fragments each have an associated XML layout file.

An animation folder, `res/anim`, has been added to store the enter/exit animation definitions for "rotating" Fragments in and out of a transaction.

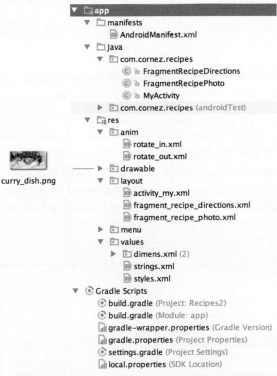

curry_dish.png

▌ FIGURE 4-21 Project structure for the Recipes application.

The AndroidManifest file for Recipes specifies a landscape orientation for the main activity and sets the main activity to the Java class `MyActivity`. The XML code for this file is listed as follows:

```
AndroidManifest.xml
1   <?xml version="1.0" encoding="utf-8"?>
2   <manifest xmlns:android="http://schemas.android.com/apk/res/android"
3       package="com.cornez.recipes" >
4
5   <application
6           android:allowBackup="true"
7           android:icon="@drawable/ic_launcher"
8           android:label="@string/app_name"
9           android:theme="@style/AppTheme" >
10  <activity
11              android:name=".MyActivity"
12              android:screenOrientation="landscape"
13              android:label="@string/app_name" >
14  <intent-filter>
15  <action android:name="android.intent.action.MAIN" />
16
17  <category
18  android:name="android.intent.category.LAUNCHER" />
19  </intent-filter>
20  </activity>
21  </application>
22
23  </manifest>
```

Part 3: Value Resources

`strings.xml` is the only required value resource file used by the Recipes app. As a demonstration application, this project stores its recipe data in the `strings.xml` file. To evolve this app into a more practical application, a database would be the optimal choice for the data source. The XML code for `strings.xml` is listed as follows:

```
strings.xml
1   <?xml version="1.0" encoding="utf-8"?>
2   <resources>
3
4   <string name="app_name">Recipes</string>
5   <string name="hello_world">Hello world!</string>
6   <string name="action_settings">Settings</string>
7
8   <!-- PHOTOGRAPH CONTENT DESCRIPTION -->
9   <string name="curry_dish">Curry Dish</string>
10
11  <!-- BUTTON LABEL TO FLIP BETWEEN THE PHOTO AND THE RECIPE -->
12  <string name="flip_btn">Flip Over</string>
13
14  <!-- RECIPE  TEXT -->
```

```
15  <string name="ingredients">2c. Vegetables sliced\n
16  1c. Curry powder\n
17  2c. Rice</string>
18  <string name="directions">Mix vegetables in a
19  bowl with curry powder.\n
20  Add rice.</string>
21
22  </resources>
```

Part 4: Designing Individual Fragments

The two `Fragments` for this application represent the front and back of a recipe flip card. The front of the card displays the photo of the cooked dish, and the back contains the directions of the recipe.

The layout for the photo fragment, `fragment_recipe_photo`, consists of an `ImageView` placed inside the root element, a `FrameLayout`. The visual layout structure is shown in Figure 4-22.

FIGURE 4-22 The visual layout design for `fragment_recipe_photo`.

The XML code for `fragment_recipe_photo.xml` is listed as follows:

Line 11:   The value `centerCrop` scales an image uniformly, which maintains the image's aspect ratio. This means the width and height of the image will be equal to or larger than the corresponding dimension of the view, minus padding.

```
fragment_recipe_photo.xml
1  <?xml version="1.0" encoding="utf-8"?>
2  <FrameLayout xmlns:android="http://schemas.android.com/apk/res/android"
3      android:layout_width="match_parent"
4      android:layout_height="match_parent">
5
6  <ImageView
```

```
 7              android:id="@+id/imageView1"
 8              android:layout_width="fill_parent"
 9              android:layout_height="fill_parent"
10              android:contentDescription="@string/curry_dish"
11              android:scaleType="centerCrop"
12              android:src="@drawable/curry_dish" />
13
14  </FrameLayout>
```

The visual design structure for `fragment_recipe_directions.xml` is shown in Figure 4-23.

FIGURE 4-23 The layout, `fragment_recipe.xml`, used to hold color information.

The XML code for `fragment_recipe_directions.xml` is listed as follows:

```
fragment_recipe_directions.xml
 1  <?xml version="1.0" encoding="utf-8"?>
 2  <RelativeLayout
 3  xmlns:android="http://schemas.android.com/apk/res/android"
 4      android:layout_width="match_parent"
 5      android:layout_height="match_parent">
 6
 7
```

```
8  <TextView
9          android:layout_width="wrap_content"
10         android:layout_height="wrap_content"
11         android:textAppearance="?android:attr/textAppearanceLarge"
12         android:text="@string/curry_dish"
13         android:id="@+id/textView1"
14         android:layout_alignParentTop="true"
15 android:layout_centerHorizontal="true"
16         android:layout_marginTop="5dp"
17         android:textSize="50sp" />
18
19 <TextView
20         android:layout_width="wrap_content"
21         android:layout_height="wrap_content"
22         android:textAppearance="?android:attr/textAppearanceMedium"
23         android:text="@string/ingredients"
24         android:id="@+id/textView2"
25         android:layout_below="@+id/textView1"
26         android:layout_alignEnd="@+id/textView1"
27         android:layout_marginTop="10dp"
28         android:textSize="30sp" />
29
30 <TextView
31         android:layout_width="wrap_content"
32         android:layout_height="wrap_content"
33         android:textAppearance="?android:attr/textAppearanceSmall"
34         android:text="@string/directions"
35         android:id="@+id/textView3"
36         android:layout_below="@+id/textView2"
37         android:layout_alignStart="@+id/textView2"
38         android:layout_marginTop="20dp"
39         android:textSize="25sp" />
40 </RelativeLayout>
```

Part 4: User Interface and Fragment Design

The application's user interface is designed to hold fragments. The main layout of the application, `activity_my.xml`, corresponds to the application's activity. The visual structure for this layout is shown in Figure 4-24. The layout consists of a `FrameLayout` placed inside the root element, a `RelativeLayout`. The Frame-Layout serves as a Fragment container, which allows a set of fragments to be moved in and out of the user's view on the screen. A Button control element is placed below the Fragment container and will be used to flip the recipe over.

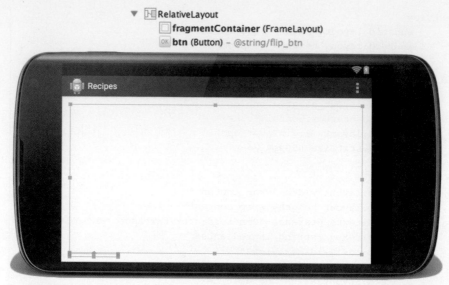

▼ ⊞ RelativeLayout
    ☐ **fragmentContainer** (FrameLayout)
    ᴼᴷ **btn** (Button) – @string/flip_btn

| FIGURE 4-24 The visual design for `activity_my.xml`.

The XML code for `activity_my.xml` is listed as follows:

activity_my.xml

```
1   <RelativeLayout
2   xmlns:android="http://schemas.android.com/apk/res/android"
3       xmlns:tools="http://schemas.android.com/tools"
4       android:layout_width="match_parent"
5       android:layout_height="match_parent"
6       android:paddingLeft="@dimen/activity_horizontal_margin"
7       android:paddingRight="@dimen/activity_horizontal_margin"
8       android:paddingTop="@dimen/activity_vertical_margin"
9       android:paddingBottom="@dimen/activity_vertical_margin"
10      tools:context=".MyActivity">
11
12  <FrameLayout
13          android:id="@+id/fragmentContainer"
14          android:layout_width="fill_parent"
15          android:layout_height="400dp"  >
16  </FrameLayout>
17
18  <Button
19          android:id="@+id/btn"
20          android:layout_width="wrap_content"
21          android:layout_height="wrap_content"
22          android:text="@string/flip_btn"
23          android:onClick="flipOver"
24          android:layout_below="@id/fragmentContainer"/>
25
26  </RelativeLayout>
```

Part 5: The Transition Animations

Fragments are transitioned into the container located on `activity_my.xml` with the help of the Android interpolator. An interpolator defines the rate of change of an animation. This allows the basic animation effects–such as alpha, scale, translate, and rotate–to be accelerated, decelerated, repeated, and so on.

Two XML files define the animation effects used to "flip" from the recipe photo to the recipe directions. Both animation XML files are placed in the anim folder, which was added to the project structure. `rotate_in.xml` characterizes how a fragment will enter the screen, and `rotate_out.xml` characterizes how a fragment will exit the screen.

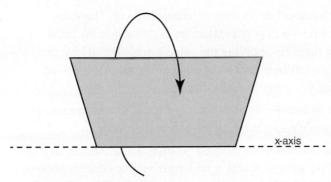

▌FIGURE 4-25 Animation effect rotationX rotates around the x-axis.

The XML code for `rotate_in.xml` is listed as follows:

Line 5:   The `<objectAnimator>` tag defines attributes of the target object that will be animated.

Line 6:   The animation effect `rotationX` performs a rotation around the x-axis, as shown in Figure 4-25.

Lines 8–9:   Values are set to define a rotation around the x-axis from 180 to 0 degrees.

Lines 11–13:   The interpolator moves the element after 1,500 milliseconds has passed.

```
rotate_in.xml
1   <?xml version="1.0" encoding="utf-8"?>
2   <set xmlns:android="http://schemas.android.com/apk/res/android">
3
4   <!—Rotate In -->
5   <objectAnimator
6           android:propertyName="rotationX"
```

```
 7
 8            android:valueFrom="180"
 9
10            android:valueTo="0"
11            android:interpolator="
12                @android:interpolator/accelerate_decelerate"
13                android:duration="1500"
14        />
    </set>
```

The XML code for `rotate_in.xml` and `rotate_out.xml` are listed as follows:

Lines 3–4:   A `<set>` can define its own ordering attribute. The value "`together`" will play animations as defined in the set at the same time. By applying the value `sequentially` to the `order` attribute, the set of animations would be played sequentially.

Lines 7–13:   The first animation set element is defined. ObjectAnimator is used to specify a rotation from −180 to 0 degrees.

Lines 16–23:   A second animation set element is defined to gradually fade the exiting Fragment so that it is no longer visible once the rotation ends. The interpolator alters the element after 500 milliseconds has passed.

```
rotate_out.xml
 1  <?xml version="1.0" encoding="utf-8"?>
 2
 3  <set xmlns:android="http://schemas.android.com/apk/res/android"
 4      android:ordering="together">
 5
 6  <!-- Rotate out -->
 7  <objectAnimator
 8          android:valueFrom="0"
 9          android:valueTo="180"
10          android:propertyName="rotationX"
11          android:interpolator=
12            "@android:interpolator/accelerate_decelerate"
13          android:duration="1500" />
14
15  <!-- Part-way through the rotation set the alpha to 0. -->
16  <objectAnimator
17          android:valueFrom="1.0"
18          android:valueTo="0.0"
19          android:propertyName="alpha"
```

```
20
21          android:interpolator=
22             "@android:interpolator/accelerate_decelerate"
23          android:duration="500" />
24
25  </set>
```

Part 6: Coding the Application

The primary activity of the application is `MyActivity`. This is the starting point for loading either one of the Fragments.

The Java code for `MyActivity.java` is listed as follows:

Lines 37–61:	`flipOver()` is the `onClick` event handler that is called when the user taps the "flip over" button located on the bottom of the screen.
Line 38:	`getFragmentManager()` returns the `FragmentManager` for interacting with fragments associated with the current activity. A transaction associated with the `FragmentManager` is initiated.
Lines 40–48:	Specific animation resources are set to run for the fragments that are entering and exiting in this transaction. In the second `setCustomAnimations()`, the `rotate_in` and `rotate_out` animations will be played for enter/exit operations specifically when popping the back stack.
Lines 54–55:	The `replace()` edit operations are specified for this transaction. For example, if the recipe photo is visible, recipe directions will replace it.
Line 58:	`commit()` is called to mark the end of the transaction.

```
MyActivity.java
1   package com.cornez.recipes;
2
3   import android.app.Activity;
4   import android.app.Fragment;
5   import android.app.FragmentManager;
6   import android.app.FragmentTransaction;
7   import android.os.Bundle;
8   import android.os.Handler;
9   import android.view.Menu;
10  import android.view.MenuItem;
11  import android.view.View;
12  import android.widget.Button;
13
```

```java
14
15  public class MyActivity extends Activity{
16
17      private Fragment mFragmentRecipeDirections;
18      private Fragment mFragmentRecipePhoto;
19      private FragmentTransaction mFragmentTransaction;
20
21      @Override
22      protected void onCreate(Bundle savedInstanceState) {
23          super.onCreate(savedInstanceState);
24          setContentView(R.layout.activity_my);
25
26          mFragmentRecipePhoto = new FragmentRecipePhoto();
27          mFragmentRecipeDirections = new FragmentRecipeDirections();
28
29          mFragmentTransaction = getFragmentManager().beginTransaction();
30          mFragmentTransaction.replace(R.id.fragmentContainer,
31                                      mFragmentRecipePhoto);
32          mFragmentTransaction.addToBackStack(null);
33          mFragmentTransaction.commit();
34
35      }
36
37      public void flipOver(View view) {
38          mFragmentTransaction = getFragmentManager().beginTransaction();
39
40          mFragmentTransaction.setCustomAnimations(
41                  R.anim.rotate_in,
42                  R.anim.rotate_out);
43
44          mFragmentTransaction.setCustomAnimations(
45                  R.anim.rotate_in,
46                  R.anim.rotate_out,
47                  R.anim.rotate_in,
48                  R.anim.rotate_out);
49
50          if(mFragmentRecipePhoto.isVisible()){
51              mFragmentTransaction.replace(R.id.fragmentContainer,
52                      mFragmentRecipeDirections);
53          }else{
54              mFragmentTransaction.replace(R.id.fragmentContainer,
55                      mFragmentRecipePhoto);
56          }
57
58          mFragmentTransaction.commit();
59      }
60
61      @Override
62      public boolean onCreateOptionsMenu(Menu menu) {
63          // Inflate the menu;
```

```
64          getMenuInflater().inflate(R.menu.my, menu);
65          return true;
66      }
67
68      @Override
69      public boolean onOptionsItemSelected(MenuItem item) {
70          // Handle action bar item clicks here. The action bar will
71          // automatically handle clicks on the Home/Up button, so long
72          // as you specify a parent activity in AndroidManifest.xml.
73          int id = item.getItemId();
74          if (id == R.id.action_settings) {
75              return true;
76          }
77          return super.onOptionsItemSelected(item);
78      }
79  }
```

The Recipes app has two fragments, each represented by an independent Fragment class. Both Fragment classes include a callback to onCreateView() to inflate its user interface view. The code listings for FragmentRecipePhoto.java and FragmentrecipeDirections.java appear as follows:

FragmentRecipePhoto.java

```
1  package com.cornez.recipes;
2
3  import android.app.Fragment;
4  import android.os.Bundle;
5  import android.view.LayoutInflater;
6  import android.view.View;
7  import android.view.ViewGroup;
8
9  public class FragmentRecipePhoto  extends Fragment {
10
11      @Override
12      public View onCreateView(LayoutInflater inflater,
13  ViewGroup container,
14                          Bundle savedInstanceState) {
15          return inflater.inflate(R.layout.fragment_recipe_photo, null);
16      }
17  }
```

FragmentRecipeDirections.java

```
1  package com.cornez.recipes;
2
3  import android.app.Fragment;
4  import android.os.Bundle;
5  import android.view.LayoutInflater;
```

```
 6  import android.view.View;
 7  import android.view.ViewGroup;
 8
 9  public class FragmentRecipeDirections extends Fragment {
10
11      @Override
12      public View onCreateView(LayoutInflater inflater,
13  ViewGroup container,
14      Bundle savedInstanceState) {
15
16      return inflater.inflate(R.layout.fragment_recipe_directions,
17      null);
18      }
19  }
```

■ 4.7 ListViews and Adapters

A `ListView` is similar to a `ScrollView`, which was introduced in Chapter 2. The `ScrollView` is an extension of the FrameLayout, and it is suitable for holding a single control element. As a scrollable control, it provides the user with the scroll mechanism to reveal more content than can be displayed on the screen at once. Scroll-Views are most often implemented with a LinearLayout. For example, a LinearLay-out, containing multiple View items, can be placed within a ScrollView. The items are made scrollable if the screen is not large enough to display them all. Placing many View items into a LinearLayout is not always practical. When dealing with a dynamic list of many `Views`, the `ScrollView` is not efficient.

A `ListView` is a specialized control that is optimized for displaying long lists of items. It is specifically designed to be efficient when creating, recycling, and displaying scrollable `Views`. The list items are inserted into the list using an `Adapter` that collects the data content from a source, such as an array or database query, and converts each item result into a view that is placed into the list.

When the data content for the layout is dynamic or not predetermined, it is possible to use a layout that subclasses an `AdapterView` to populate the layout with views at runtime. A subclass of the `AdapterView` class uses an `Adapter` to bind data to its associated layout. In this way, the `Adapter` serves as the controller between the data source and the `AdapterView` layout. The `Adapter` retrieves the data, then turns it into a layout `View`, and then adds to the `AdapterView` layout.

An AdapterView can be populated with data in two ways. An AdapterView, such as a ListView, can be filled with data by binding the AdapterView instance to an Adapter, which retrieves data from an external source and creates a View that represents each data entry.

Android provides several subclasses of Adapter that are useful for retrieving different kinds of data and building views for an AdapterView. A common adapter is an

ArrayAdapter. An ArrayAdapter is used when the data source is an array. By default, ArrayAdapter creates a view for each array item by calling toString() on each item and placing the contents in a TextView. For example, consider an array of strings that will be used to populate a ListView.

Lines 1–3:   An ArrayAdapter can be initialized, using a constructor, to specify the layout for each string and the string array.

The arguments for this constructor are:

a. The app Context

b. The layout that contains the TextView for each string in the array

c. The string array

Lines 7–8:   The setAdapter() is called to set the data behind the ListView.

To customize the appearance of items placed into a ListView, the toString() method can be overridden. To create a list item other than a TextView, such as an ImageView, the ArrayAdapter class can be extended and the getView() can be overridden to return the appropriate item type.

```
1   ArrayAdapter adapter = new ArrayAdapter<String>(
2          this,
3          android.R.layout.list_item,
4          myStringArray);
5
6   ListView listView = (ListView) findViewById(R.id.listview);
7   listView.setAdapter(adapter);
```

■ Lab Example 4-5: Redlands Music Events App–Adapters and ListViews

This lab explores the use of an Adapter and a ListView in a single Fragment context. A Fragment containing a ListView is arranged on the screen and filled with data from a Java data file. This is a first look at using an Adapter and a ListView; hence, the application will be kept very simple. A snapshot of the application is shown in Figure 4-26.

Part 1: Application Design

Every year, the City of Redlands puts on a music festival during the summer months. The scheduled events and the dates change from year to year, but the structure of the application itself remains much the same. An internal Java data file provides the data, containing a list of scheduled events and dates.

The layout holds a single Fragment.

The Fragment contains multiple Views, including a ListView populated with items.

The ListView is scrollable and uses dividers to visually separate its items.

Items in the ListView are retreived from a data file.

❙ FIGURE 4-26 A Fragment containing a ListView.

Part 2: Application Structure and Setup

The settings for the application are as follows:

- Application Name: Redlands Music Events
- Project Name: RedlandsMusicEvents
- Package Name: com.cornez.redlandsmusicevents
- Android Form: Phone and Tablet
- Minimum SDK: API 18: Android 4.3 (Jelly Bean)
- Target SDK: API 21: Android 5.0 (Lollipop)
- Compile with: API 21: Android 5.0 (Lollipop)

- Activity Name: MyActivity
- Layout Name: activity_my

The icon used to launch the application is the Android default icon stored in the ic_launcher.png file. To enhance the application's visual appeal, a background graphic, a Redlands music logo, and a unique graphic divider for separating the music event items have been added to the drawable default folder. The final application structure is shown in Figure 4-27.

The two Java classes represent the data source, MusicEvents.java, and the activity of the application, MyActivity.java. A Fragment class is not required for this simple application because the Fragment will be added to the main user interface and will not be removed at any time. The main activity and its fragment will each have an associated XML layout file, activity_my.xml and fragment_my.xml. A third layout file, list_item_event.xml, will provide the visual structure for items added to the music event list.

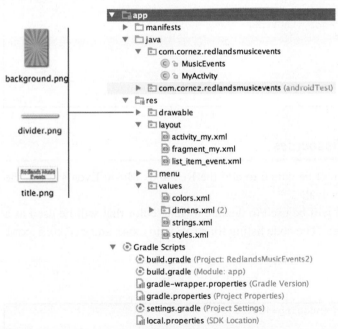

FIGURE 4-27 Project structure for the Redlands Music Events application.

The AndroidManifest file sets the main activity of the application to MyActivity. The action attribute of the intent-filter ensures that this activity will launch when the application launches for the first time. The orientation of the activity is restricted to landscape mode. The XML code for `AndroidManifest.xml` is listed as follows:

```
AndroidManifest.xml
1  <?xml version="1.0" encoding="utf-8"?>
2  <manifest xmlns:android="http://schemas.android.com/apk/res/android"
3      package="com.cornez.redlandsmusicevents" >
4
5  <application
6          android:allowBackup="true"
7          android:icon="@drawable/ic_launcher"
8          android:label="@string/app_name"
9          android:theme="@style/AppTheme" >
10 <activity
11          android:name=".MyActivity"
12          android:label="@string/app_name"
13          android:screenOrientation="portrait">
14 <intent-filter>
15 <action android:name="android.intent.action.MAIN" />
16 <category android:name=
17 "android.intent.category.LAUNCHER" />
18 </intent-filter>
19 </activity>
20 </application>
21
22 </manifest>
```

Part 3: External Value Resources

The `strings.xml` file will be edited to add the Redlands Music Events dates, the start and end data of the festival.

A `colors.xml` file will be used to declare a "tan" color that will be used as a backdrop by the `ListView`. The code listing for `strings.xml` and `colors.xml` are as follows:

```
strings.xml
1  <?xml version="1.0" encoding="utf-8"?>
2  <resources>
3
4  <string name="app_name">Redlands Music Events</string>
5  <string name="hello_world">Hello world!</string>
6  <string name="action_settings">Settings</string>
7  <string name="dates">July 24 - August 9</string>
8
9  </resources>
```

```
colors.xml
1  <?xml version="1.0" encoding="utf-8"?>
2  <resources>
3  <color name="tan">#EFC9A5</color>
4  </resources>
```

Part 4: The Event List Item

The event list item is an individual music event that will be added to the list of music events that make up the Redlands Music Festival. At its most basic, a music event item can be represented as a text element. The list_item_event.xml declares a TextView as its root element and sets the identifier to @+id/list_item_event_textView. The ArrayAdapter in the main activity references this identifier as it populates the ListView.

The XML code listing for list_item_event.xml appears as follows:

```
list_item_event.xml
1  <?xml version="1.0" encoding="utf-8"?>
2  <TextView xmlns:android="http://schemas.android.com/apk/res/android"
3      android:layout_width="match_parent"
4      android:layout_height="match_parent"
5      android:minHeight="?android:attr/listPreferredItemHeight"
6      android:gravity="center_vertical"
7      android:id="@+id/list_item_event_textView">
8  </TextView>
9
```

Part 5: The Activity XML File

The layout file that corresponds to the main activity of the application is represented by activity_my.xml. It uses a FrameLayout as the root element. No control elements have been added to this user interface.

```
activity__my.xml
1  <FrameLayout xmlns:android="http://schemas.android.com/apk/res/android"
2      xmlns:tools="http://schemas.android.com/tools"
3      android:id="@+id/container"
4      android:layout_width="match_parent"
5      android:layout_height="match_parent"
6      tools:context=".MyActivity"
7      tools:ignore="MergeRootFrame" >
8  </FrameLayout>
```

Part 6: The Fragment Layout File

The activitiy's fragment XML file holds all user interface elements used by the activity. The visual structure for `fragment_my.xml` is shown in Figure 4-28. The XML code for this fragment is listed as follows:

Line 11:   The background graphic, from the drawables folder, is applied to the background for the fragment.

Lines 13–23:   The Redlands Music logo is placed at the top of the screen.

Lines 25–35:   The dates for the music festival are placed in the Textview.

Lines 37–49:   The `ListView` that will hold all the music event items is defined. Its identifier is set for future referencing by the main activity. Visual attributes are set for color (tan) and alpha. Alpha will set the visibility of the View. The `divider` attribute is set to the bitmap file `divider.png`, stored in the drawable folder.

```
fragment_my.xml
1   <RelativeLayout
2   xmlns:android="http://schemas.android.com/apk/res/android"
3       xmlns:tools="http://schemas.android.com/tools"
4       android:layout_width="match_parent"
5       android:layout_height="match_parent"
6       android:paddingLeft="@dimen/activity_horizontal_margin"
7       android:paddingRight="@dimen/activity_horizontal_margin"
8       android:paddingTop="@dimen/activity_vertical_margin"
9       android:paddingBottom="@dimen/activity_vertical_margin"
10      tools:context=".MyActivity$PlaceholderFragment"
11      android:background="@drawable/background">
12
13  <ImageView
14          android:layout_width="wrap_content"
15          android:layout_height="wrap_content"
16
17          android:id="@+id/textView1"
18          android:layout_alignParentTop="true"
19          android:layout_centerHorizontal="true"
20
21          android:gravity="center_horizontal"
22          android:src="@drawable/title"
23          android:contentDescription="@string/app_name" />
24
25  <TextView
26          android:layout_width="wrap_content"
27          android:layout_height="wrap_content"
28          android:textAppearance="?android:attr/textAppearanceLarge"
```

```
29          android:text="@string/dates"
30          android:id="@+id/textView2"
31          android:layout_below="@+id/textView1"
32          android:layout_marginTop="42dp"
33          android:layout_centerHorizontal="true"
34          android:textSize="24sp"
35          android:gravity="center_horizontal" />
36
37  <ListView
38          android:layout_width="wrap_content"
39          android:layout_height="wrap_content"
40          android:id="@+id/listView_event"
41          android:layout_below="@+id/textView2"
42          android:layout_alignParentStart="true"
43          android:layout_marginTop="42dp"
44          android:background="@color/tan"
45          android:paddingLeft="25dp"
46          android:textFilterEnabled="false"
47          android:alpha=".7"
48          android:divider="@drawable/divider"
49          android:paddingRight="25dp" />
50  </RelativeLayout>
```

FIGURE 4-28 The layout design for the Music Festival application.

Part 7: Coding the Application

The purpose of `MusicEvents.java` is to provide a data source for the application. The `data[]` array contains a fixed set of music events. Each event includes the data of the event and the name. The code listing for `MusicEvents.java` is as follows:

```
MusicEvents.java
1  package com.cornez.redlandsmusicevents;
2
3  public class MusicEvents {
4
5      static public  String[] data = {
6              "6/24 - Object of Her Affection",
7              "6/25 - Electrogynous",
8              "6/26 - The Singing Head",
9              "6/27 - Saana the Foreigner",
10             "7/22 - Still",
11             "7/23 - Iceland",
12             "7/24 - Blacktop Highway",
13             "7/25 - For Now",
14             "8/04 - Beyond",
15             "8/07 - Destiny Six",
16             "8/08 - What and Why",
17             "8/09 - France is Gone!"
18     };
19 }
```

`MyActivity.java`, the main activity of the application, displays the fragment. Recall that a fragment requires an activity. The fragment XML file for this application holds all user interface elements used by the activity. The visual structure for `fragment_my.xml` is shown in Figure 4-1. The XML code for this fragment is listed as follows:

Line 25:   The activity user interface content is set to the layout file `activity_my.xml`.

Lines 27–31: When the activity is launched for the first time, a fragment transaction is processed to add `MusicEventFragment` to the activity layout container.

Lines 37–69: The `MusicEventFragment` class is implemented. All music event data are collected and processed within `onCreateView()`. `onCreateView()` will be called once, when the fragment instantiates its user interface view.

Lines 48–50:   The music event data are collected and first stored in eventData. This data will be assigned to seasonEvents, a Java List, as a collection of String items.

Lines 52–57:   Now that we have some music event data, an ArrayAdapter is created. The ArrayAdapter will take the music data and use it to populate the ListView to which it is attached.

Line 54:   The context of the activity is supplied to the ArrayAdapter.

Line 55:   The name of the layout ID is R.layout.list_item_event.

Line 56:   R.id.list_item_event_textView is the ID of the text-View to populate.

Lines 63–65:   The reference to the ListView is accessed and the adapter is attached to it.

```
MyActivity.java

 1   package com.cornez.redlandsmusicevents;
 2
 3   import android.app.Activity;
 4   import android.app.ActionBar;
 5   import android.app.Fragment;
 6   import android.os.Bundle;
 7   import android.view.LayoutInflater;
 8   import android.view.Menu;
 9   import android.view.MenuItem;
10   import android.view.View;
11   import android.view.ViewGroup;
12   import android.os.Build;
13   import android.widget.ArrayAdapter;
14   import android.widget.ListView;
15
16   import java.util.ArrayList;
17   import java.util.Arrays;
18   import java.util.List;
19
20   public class MyActivity extends Activity {
21
22       @Override
23       protected void onCreate(Bundle savedInstanceState) {
24           super.onCreate(savedInstanceState);
25           setContentView(R.layout.activity_my);
26
27           if (savedInstanceState == null) {
28               getFragmentManager().beginTransaction()
29                       .add(R.id.container, new MusicEventFragment())
30                       .commit();
31           }
32       }
```

```
33
34        /**
35         * The MusicEventFragment class
36         */
37        public static class MusicEventFragment extends Fragment {
38
39            public MusicEventFragment () {
40            }
41
42            @Override
43            public View onCreateView(LayoutInflater inflater,
44                                     ViewGroup container,
45                                     Bundle savedInstanceState) {
46
47                //COLLECT THE DATA FROM MUSIC EVENTS
48                String[] eventData = MusicEvents.data;
49                List<String> seasonEvents = new
50 ArrayList<String>(Arrays.asList(eventData));
51
52                ArrayAdapter<String> musicEventAdapter =
53                        new ArrayAdapter<String>(
54 getActivity(), // CURRENT CONTEXT - ACTIVITY
55 R.layout.list_item_event,
56 R.id.list_item_event_textView,
57 seasonEvents);
58
59                View rootView =
60 inflater.inflate(R.layout.fragment_my,
61 container, false);
62
63 ListView listView = (ListView)
64 rootView.findViewById(R.id.listView_event);
65                listView.setAdapter(musicEventAdapter);
66
67                return rootView;
68            }
69        }
70
71        @Override
72        public boolean onCreateOptionsMenu(Menu menu) {
73            // Inflate the menu;
74            getMenuInflater().inflate(R.menu.my, menu);
75            return true;
76        }
77
78        @Override
79        public boolean onOptionsItemSelected(MenuItem item) {
80            // Handle action bar item clicks here. The action bar will
81            // automatically handle clicks on the Home/Up button, so long
82            // as you specify a parent activity in AndroidManifest.xml.
```

```
83        int id = item.getItemId();
84        if (id == R.id.action_settings) {
85            return true;
86        }
87        return super.onOptionsItemSelected(item);
88    }
89 }
```

■ 4.8 Handling Click Events in a ListView

Often, a ListView is populated with items that need to respond to a click event. You can respond to click events on an item in an AdapterView by implementing the AdapterView.OnItemClickListener interface. The onItemClick () callback method will always be invoked when an item in the AdapterView has been clicked.

As shown in the following code segment, this onItemClick() callback uses four parameters:

1. parent: the AdapterView where the user has clicked.

2. view: the view within the AdapterView that was clicked. This is the view provided by the adapter.

3. position: the index position of the view in the adapter. To access the data associated with the selected item, the getItemAtPosition(position) method can be called.

4. id: the row id of the item that was clicked.

```
1  // AN ITEM CLICK HANDLER IMPLEMENTED AS AN ANONYMOUS CLASS
2  private OnItemClickListener mMessageClickedHandler = new
3  OnItemClickListener() {
4  public void onItemClick(AdapterView parent,
5  View view,
6  int position,
7  long id) {
8
9  // IDENTIFY THE ITEM THAT WAS CLICKED
10 // RESPOND TO THE CLICK
11 }
12 };
13
14 listView.setOnItemClickListener(mMessageClickedHandler);
```

■ **Lab Example 4-6: Shades (Part 2): Clickable Shades of Color in the ListView**

In Lab Example 4-3, a master list fragment was populated with buttons representing various shades of color. When the user clicked one of the buttons, detailed information about a specific shade of color appeared in a separate pane on the screen. This application was meant to be a simple introduction to fragments, but it is considered impractical because the buttons were placed individually within the layout design. With only three buttons, this example served as a good demonstration for a first look at the concepts of Fragments. In most cases, however, a more feasible approach to constructing a master list of items would be the utilization of a `ListView`. As a container, a `ListView` can be populated with a large and dynamic collection of clickable items. In addition, this master list can be built with items obtained from a dynamic source, such as an online database.

In this lab, we enhance the first version of the Shades application by employing a `ListView` for the display of items and an `Adapter` for populating the master list with items from a dummy source. Figure 4-29 shows Shades II, the new version of Shades. The master list of items will be more extensive and each item will be clickable. The fragment behavior of the application will remain the same.

Part 1: Application Structure and Setup

The final project structure for the Shades II application is shown in Figure 4-30. Two additional files from the original Shades have been added. A data source file, `DummyData`, will provide all the data elements. The second file added to the structure is `list-item-shade.xml`. This layout represents an individual list item to be added to the `ListView`.

It should be noted that the data file has been given the name DummyData because it is not an optimal design for a data source. Even though it is considerably more efficient than using a layout containing physical buttons, a better option is accessing data from a database file in the cloud. This topic will be discussed in Chapter 9.

Part 2: Defining the Layout Structure for an Individual Item to Be Added to the List

The human eye can distinguish nearly 2 million color shades, or perhaps even more. We will not be adding close to this number of color shades to the ListView, however. The goal is to add a more robust list than the set of three colors provided in the first version of Shades.

In the Shades II application, shades of color are added dynamically by creating a View object, populating it with a color, and adding it to the `Listview`. The blueprint

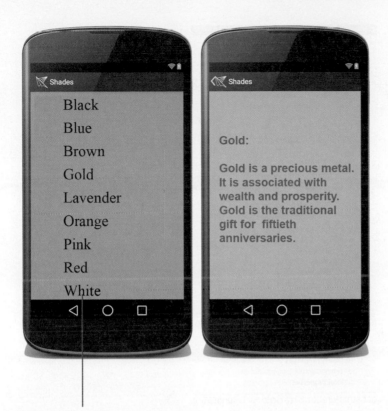

Scrollable, clickable, items in a `ListView`

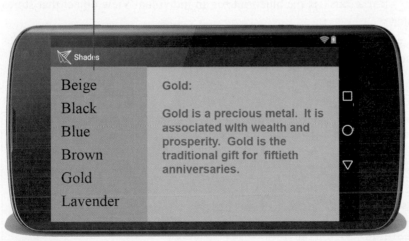

FIGURE 4-29 Shades II application features a scrollable list of clickable items.

A data file containing all shade information that will be added to a dynamic scrollable list.

A layout representing a single list item to be added to a scrollable ListView.

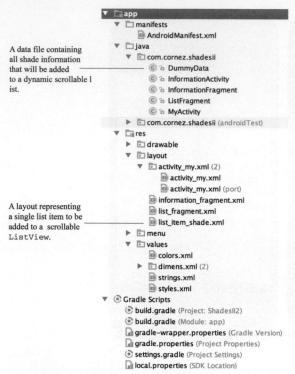

❙ FIGURE 4-30 Project structure for Shades II application.

of the View object can be defined as an XML file, specifically as a mini layout. The file list_item_shade.xml is the blueprint for an individual View object that stores a shade of color.

The root element of list_item_shade.xml is a TextView, which stores the text for the shade of color. The XML for this file is shown as follows:

list_item_shade.xml

```
1   <?xml version="1.0" encoding="utf-8"?>
2   <TextView xmlns:android="http://schemas.android.com/apk/res/android"
3
4
5       android:layout_width="match_parent"
6       android:layout_height="match_parent"
7       android:minHeight="?android:attr/listPreferredItemHeight"
8       android:gravity="center_vertical"
9       android:id="@+id/list_item_shade_textview"
10      android:textSize="40sp">
11
12
13  </TextView>
```

Part 3: Restructure `list_fragment.xml`

The layout for the master list, `list_fragment.xml`, will be restructured. Its container is a ListView named `listview_shades`, as shown in Figure 4-31.

FIGURE 4-31 The visual structure for the master list, `list_fragment.xml`.

The XML code list for `list_fragment.xml` is as follows:

```
list_fragment.xml
1   <?xml version="1.0" encoding="utf-8"?>
2   <LinearLayout xmlns:android="http://schemas.android.com/apk/res/android"
3       android:layout_width="match_parent"
4       android:layout_height="match_parent"
5       android:background="@color/caramel"
6       android:orientation="vertical"
7       android:padding="40dp"  >
8
9   <ListView
10          android:id="@+id/listview_shades"
11          android:layout_width="match_parent"
12          android:layout_height="match_parent" />
13
14
15  </LinearLayout>
```

Part 4: Defining the Data Source Application

Color data is provided by items stored in the Java file DummyData.java in two arrays of data. The first array contains the names of the colors, and the second array contains detailed information about each color.

This file represents pretend data for the ListView. For applications that require real data, the application code will still be used, but the data may be retrieved elsewhere, such as the cloud. To save space, the code below is incomplete. The finished code file can be found in the accompanying resources for this text.

DummyData.java

```
 1  package com.cornez.shadesii;
 2
 3
 4  public class DummyData {
 5      // Some dummy data for the ListView.
 6      // Here's a sample of shades and their meaning
 7      public static String[] shade_name = {
 8              "Tan", "Black", "Blue", "Brown", "Gold",
 9              "Lavender", "Orange", "Pink", "Red",
10              "White", "Yellow"};
11
12      public static String[] shade_detail = {
13              "Tan is a neutral color with a bit of warmth.",
14              "Black is the absence of color.",
15              "Blue is calming. It can be strong and steadfast.",
16              "Brown is a warm neutral color.",
17              "Gold is a precious metal.",
18              "Lavender is delicate and considered precious.",
19              "Orange is a stimulant.",
20              "Pink can create physical weakness in people.",
21              "Red is hot. It is a strong color.",
22              "White is often associated with hospitals,. ",
23              "Yellow is sunshine"
24      };
25  }
```

Part 5: Recoding MyListFragment

MyListFragment.java represents the master list in the master-detail flow pattern. Modifications, outlined in the Line commentary below, have been made to accommodate the ListView element in the Fragment.

Lines 28–31:   The shade dummy data is collected. The set of shade names, from the data source, is placed in the ordered list named shadeListing. The shade detail information is also placed in an ordered list, shadeNameDetail.

Lines 33–38: An `ArrayAdapter` is created to take `shadeListing` data and use it to populate the `ListView` it is attached to.

Lines 45–47: The object `listView` is assigned the reference to the `ListView` on the layout. The ArrayAdapter, `mShadeAdapter` is attached to the ListView, via the reference.

Lines 49–60: An `OnItemClickListener` listener event is registered for each new item added to the `ListView`. When the user clicks on a given item, the handler `onItemClick()` is called. Using the i parameter provided by `onItemClick()`, the position of the item clicked (the index) accessed. A string of information is constructed about the shade of color selected. The method `updateDetail ()` will be passed this information.

```
MyListFragment.java
1  package com.cornez.shadesii;
2
3  import android.view.View;
4  import android.app.Activity;
5  import android.app.Fragment;
6  import android.os.Bundle;
7  import android.view.LayoutInflater;
8  import android.view.ViewGroup;
9  import android.widget.AdapterView;
10 import android.widget.ArrayAdapter;
11 import android.widget.ListView;
12
13 import java.util.ArrayList;
14 import java.util.Arrays;
15 import java.util.List;
16
17 public class MyListFragment extends Fragment {
18
19     private OnItemSelectedListener listener;
20     List<String> shadelisting;         //MASTER LIST
21     List<String> shadeNameDetail;      //DETAIL
22
23     @Override
24     public View onCreateView(LayoutInflater inflater,
25 ViewGroup container,
26                             Bundle savedInstanceState) {
27
28         shadelisting = new
29 ArrayList<String>(Arrays.asList(DummyData.shade_name));
30         shadeNameDetail = new
31 ArrayList<String>(Arrays.asList(DummyData.shade_detail));
32
```

```
33  final ArrayAdapter<String> mShadeAdapter =
34              new ArrayAdapter<String>(
35                      getActivity(),
36                      R.layout.list_item_shade,
37                      R.id.list_item_shade_textview,
38                      shadelisting);
39
40      View rootView =
41              inflater.inflate(R.layout.color_list_fragment,
42                      container,
43                      false);
44
45  ListView listView = (ListView)
46  rootView.findViewById(R.id.listview_shades);
47      listView.setAdapter(mShadeAdapter);
48
49      listView.setOnItemClickListener(new
50  AdapterView.OnItemClickListener() {
51
52          @Override
53          public void onItemClick(AdapterView<?> adapterView,
54  View view, int i, long l) {
55              String shadeIndexString = mShadeAdapter.getItem(i);
56              String information = shadeIndexString + "\n\n\n"
57  + shadeNameDetail.get(i);
58              updateDetail(information);
59          }
60      });
61
62      return rootView;
63  }
64
65  public interface OnItemSelectedListener {
66      public void onShadeItemSelected (String link);
67  }
68
69  @Override
70  public void onAttach(Activity activity) {
71      super.onAttach(activity);
72      if (activity instanceof OnItemSelectedListener) {
73          listener = (OnItemSelectedListener) activity;
74      } else {
75          throw new ClassCastException(activity.toString()
76              + " must implement "
77              + " MyListFragment.OnItemSelectedListener");
78      }
79  }
80
81  public void updateDetail(String information) {
82      listener. onShadeItemSelected (information);
83  }
84 }
```

■ EXERCISES

4.1 Describe the Fragment lifecycle.

4.2 List the set of Fragment callback methods used by a Fragment.

4.3 Explain when `onInflate()` and `onActivityCreated()` are called.

4.4 Describe the features of a typical action bar.

4.5 Every `Activity` supports an options menu of actions. Describe what occurs in the code segment shown below:

```
1  @Override
2      public boolean onCreateOptionsMenu(Menu menu) {
3          getMenuInflater().inflate(R.menu.my, menu);
4          return true;
5      }
```

4.6 Explain the purpose of an action view.

4.7 How does adaptive design differ from responsive design?

4.8 Describe the master/detail design pattern.

4.9 How are `Adapters` used in a master/detail design?

5

Graphics, Drawing, and Audio

Chapter Objectives

In this chapter you will:

- Learn to draw to a canvas.
- Examine the process of adding drawn elements and user interface controls to a layout.
- Understand how to add and manipulate ImageViews programmatically.
- Build frame-by-frame animations.
- Explore a turn-based game containing animation.
- Understand the Android Animate library.
- Explore the MediaPlayer for audio.

■ 5.1 Graphics in Android

Graphics are an important part of any Android application. A graphic element can appear as a simple background image, an icon, a component in a sophisticated user interface, or as a moving object with interactive behavior in a game. Before developing an application, it is always a good idea to consider carefully what the graphical demands will be. Varying graphical tasks are often accomplished with varying techniques.

Two general techniques for adding graphics to an Android application are (1) placing an existing image into an ImageView, which can be inflated on the screen, or (2) drawing custom graphics in real time.

Often, ImageViews are populated with resources from drawables; images can also be read from a file on a device or downloaded from a URL. An ImageView graphic can be inflated at any time during the execution of an application. Once placed on the screen, these graphic elements can be manipulated in various ways. In the view hierarchy, parent views are responsible for editing the attributes of their child ImageViews, which can be done dynamically; this means that a graphic object can adjust to a changing environment, such as game play conditions or screen orientation. When the majority of an application's interface is fixed, it is practical to render the interface in advance, using `ImageViews`, and inflate those images at runtime. For example, a chess game requires multiple `ImageView` graphic elements representing the chessboard and chess pieces. The chessboard element is static and therefore can be added to the XML layout representing the game activity. Chess pieces are placed on the screen during runtime, with their initial positions set according to the player's color selection. As the chess game unfolds, chess pieces are repositioned or removed from the board when an opponent captures them.

Drawing custom graphic elements to be added to an activity is a technique that is generally suited for applications requiring more complex graphic needs. Drawing to a canvas or a `View` object makes use of Android native drawing tools. Custom drawing can be processor intensive and should be optimized.

■ 5.2 Adding and Manipulating ImageViews

Perhaps the easiest way to add graphics to an application is by referencing a bitmap file from the project's resources. In earlier chapters, graphics were added during the layout design. In this chapter, we explore the concept of inflating images and modifying them in real time.

Android supports three image file types: PNG, JPG, and GIF. PNG is established as the preferred format for an image file in Android. It is also acceptable to use a JPG. GIF bitmaps should always be avoided.

Bitmap files placed in `res/drawable/` may be automatically optimized with lossless image compression during the build process. For example, a true-color PNG image that does not require more than 256 colors may be converted to an 8-bit PNG with a color palette. This conversion will result in an image of equal quality but is optimized by requiring less memory.

Typically, an image resource is added to the `res/drawable/` folder before it can be referenced in an XML layout file and from an Activity.

The following code segment demonstrates how to build an ImageView that uses an image from the drawable directory and add it to the layout.

Line 6:   A `RelativeLayout` is constructed. The context of the layout is set to the Activity using the `this` argument.

Line 8:   An `ImageView` object named `imageView` is instantiated.

Line 10:   A photograph of Mt. Everest, defined by the drawable resource file `photo_of_everest.png`, is set as the content of this ImageView object. This segment of code assumes that `photo_of_everest.png` exists in the drawable directory.

Line 11:   The bounds are set to match the Drawable's dimensions. The argument true is used when the ImageView needs to adjust its bounds to preserve the aspect ratio of its drawable.

Line 13:   This sets the top position of this view relative to its parent. This method is meant to be called by the layout system and should not generally be called otherwise, because the property may be changed at any time by the layout.

Line 15:   The ImageView is added to the layout.

Line 16:   mRelativeLayout is set as the view content for the activity of the application. The layout is inflated, adding all top-level views to the activity.

```
1    RelativeLayout mRelativeLayout;
2
3    protected void onCreate(Bundle savedInstanceState) {
4        super.onCreate(savedInstanceState);
5
6        mRelativeLayout = new RelativeLayout (this);
7
8        ImageView imageView = new ImageView(this);
9
10       imageView. setImageDrawable (R.drawable.photo_of_everest);
11       imageView.setAdjustViewBounds(true);
12
13       imageView.setTop(10);
14
15       mRelativeLayout.addView(imageView);
16       setContentView(mRelativeLayout);
17    }
```

The Android resource system can be used to access an application's resources, such as the drawable bitmaps. For example, in some situations, it may be desirable to handle an image resource as a Drawable object. In the following segment of code, the object, everest, is assigned the drawable object associated with the resource ID, R.drawable.photo_of_everest.

Line 1:   The context of the application is the information about its environment. It allows access to application-specific resources. getBaseContext() returns the base context of the application.

Line 2:   getResources() returns a resources instance for the application's package.

Lines 3–4:   getDrawable() returns a drawable object associated with a resource ID, R.drawable.photo_of_everest.

```
1     Context mContext = getBaseContext();
2     Resources resource = mContext.getResources();
3     Drawable everest = resource.getDrawable
4                          (R.drawable.photo_of_everest);
```

A drawable resource is a general concept for a graphic that can be drawn to the screen. In addition to bitmaps, Android supports XML graphics, which are drawable resources defined in XML.

Consider the XML code segment in the example below. This code defines a graphical shape resource, as shown in Figure 5-1. As a drawable, it is placed in a drawable resource file, res/drawable/ directory.

Lines 3–4:   The root element of the drawable graphic is shape. Android provides four primitive shapes: line, oval, rectangle, and ring.

Lines 6–8:   The oval is outlined in dark red with a stroke width of 2dp.

Lines 10–11:   The interior of the oval is filled with a solid color, grey. Additional shape attributes can be applied using the tags <gradient>, <padding>, <stroke>, and <corners>.

Lines 12–14:   The height and width are both set to 50dp, a perfect circle. Figure 5-1 shows the graphic produced by the XML drawable.

res/drawable/circle.xml

```
1    <?xml version="1.0" encoding="utf-8"?>
2
3    <shape xmlns:android="http://schemas.android.com/apk/res/android"
4        android:shape="oval">
5
6        <stroke
7            android:width="2dp"
8            android:color="#660000" />
9
10       <solid
11           android:color="#999999" />
12       <size
13           android:height="50dp"
14           android:width="50dp" />
15
16   </shape>
```

FIGURE 5-1 Graphic created as an XML Drawable.

Lab Example 5-1: Fibonacci Flower Application

Bitmap graphics play a significant role in much of what we see on smart devices. Creating artwork algorithmically is an interesting endeavor, as well as an efficient method for producing remarkably detailed designs. This lab example explores the dynamic ability of manipulating `ImageView` objects and adding them to a layout.

Part 1: The Design

The Fibonacci Flower application allows the user to build an artwork with constraints built in. This is an ideal application for illustrating how bitmaps can be placed on the screen and altered programmatically.

The constraint for the artwork is the Golden Ratio; mathematicians, computer scientists, and graphic designers make frequent use of this ratio, which is derived from the Fibonacci series. Leonardi Fibonacci was an Italian mathematician who created the sequence of numbers in which each term is the sum of the two preceding terms. The value of the first term is 1, as is the second term. The third term in the series is computed as $1 + 1$ (term 1 + term 2). The first 14 terms in the sequence are as follows:

Term 1:	1 First Term
Term 2:	1 Second Term
Term 3:	$2 = 1 + 1$
Term 4:	$3 = 1 + 2$
Term 5:	$5 = 2 + 3$
Term 6:	$8 = 3 + 5$

Term 7: $13 = 5 + 8$

Term 8: $21 = 8 + 13$

Term 9: $34 = 13 + 21$

Term 10: $55 = 21 + 34$

Term 11: $89 = 34 + 55$

Term 12: $144 = 55 + 89$

Term 13: $233 = 89 + 144$

Term 14: $377 = 144 + 233$

An important aspect of this sequence is the ratio produced when dividing successive terms. For example, when the 9th term is divided by the 10th term, the ratio of 0.61818182 is produced. When the 13th term is divided by the 14th term, the result is 0.61803279 is produced. As the terms become larger and larger, the ratio between two successive terms converges to approximately 0.6180339. This so-called Golden Ratio is considered to be extraordinary because of its common occurrence in nature.

For this application, the user is provided with two types of flower petals, Pink and Gold, in which to build a Fibonacci flower. The flower can be built one petal at a time by tapping one of the petal buttons, located at the top of the screen. As petals are placed on the screen, they are manipulated, using a Lorenz attractor, to produce a flower that resembles a butterfly. Figure 5-2 shows four screenshots of the application. The first screenshot shows the initial application screen as it appears when it is launched for the first time. The remaining three screenshots show petals added to the screen in a particular formation. The user can use the buttons to choose the petal to add to the flower, while the algorithm will manipulate it and arrange it on the screen.

In addition to the petal selection buttons, a "clear" button is placed on the bottom of the screen to allow users to clear away the petals to begin creating a new flower.

Part 2: Application Structure and Setup

The settings for the application are as follows:

- Application Name: Fibonacci Flower
- Project Name: FibonacciFlower
- Package Name: `com.cornez.fibonacciflower`
- Android Form: Phone and Tablet
- Minimum SDK: API 18: Android 4.3 (Jelly Bean)
- Target SDK: API 21: Android 5.0 (Lollipop)
- Compile with: API 21: Android 5.0 (Lollipop)
- Activity Name: `MyActivity`
- Layout Name: `activity_my`

FIGURE 5-2 The Fibonacci Flower app allows the user to build a flower artwork.

The icon that launches the Fibonacci Flower application is set to the Android default `ic_launcher.png` file. The two drawable bitmap files required by the application are `petal_a.png` and `petal_b.png`. These files can be found in the textbook resources and should be placed in `res/drawable`.

The final project structure is shown in Figure 5-3. The Java source file, `MyActivity`, is the only activity of the application. `Flower.java` is a blueprint for a Fibonacci flower artwork.

Three XML files will be used by the application: (1) `activity_my.xml`, (2) `petal_gold.xml`, and (3) `petal_pink.xml`. `activity_my.xml` is the user interface for `MyActivity`. `petal_gold.xml` and `petal_pink.xml` are also technically layout files; however, their primary function is not as a user interface, but instead as a graphic bitmap container. Each is used to represent a class of petals visually. For example, when a petal graphic is created and added to the screen, it is generated from one of the petal XML files.

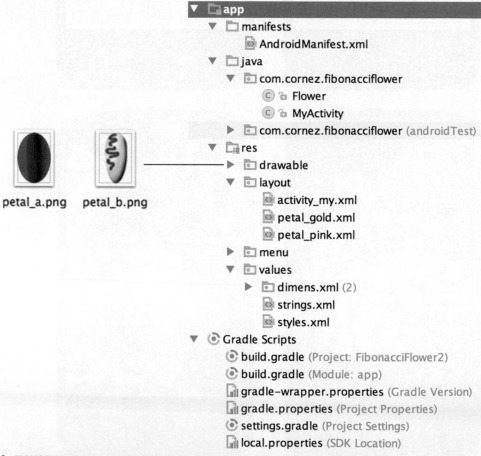

FIGURE 5-3 Project structure for the Fibonnaci Flower application.

The orientation of the screen is locked into portrait mode. The screen is presented in a fullscreen configuration with the title bar eliminated. These attributes are set in the `AndroidManifest.xml` file, as shown below:

```
AndroidManifest.xml
1  <?xml version="1.0" encoding="utf-8"?>
2  <manifest xmlns:android="http://schemas.android.com/apk/res/android"
3      package="com.cornez.fibonacciflower" >
4
5      <application
6          android:allowBackup="true"
7          android:icon="@drawable/ic_launcher"
8          android:label="@string/app_name"
9          android:theme="@android:style/
10                         Theme.Light.NoTitleBar.Fullscreen">
11
12      <activity
13          android:name=".MyActivity"
14          android:screenOrientation="portrait"
15          android:label="@string/app_name" >
16          <intent-filter>
17              <action android:name="android.intent.action.MAIN" />
18
19              <category android:name=
20                         "android.intent.category.LAUNCHER" />
21          </intent-filter>
22      </activity>
23
24      </application>
25
26  </manifest>
```

Part 3: The User Interface

The user interface uses strings for three of the interactive buttons. The `strings.xml` file is shown below with the button labels added:

```
strings.xml
1  <?xml version="1.0" encoding="utf-8"?>
2  <resources>
3
4      <string name="app_name">Fibonacci Flower</string>
5      <string name="hello_world">Hello world!</string>
6      <string name="action_settings">Settings</string>
7
8      <!-- BUTTON LABELS -->
9      <string name="pink_btn">Add Pink</string>
```

```
10      <string name="gold_btn">Add Gold</string>
11      <string name="clear_btn">CLEAR</string>
12
13  </resources>
```

The application is controlled by a single activity, MyActivity. My Activity will launch with activity_my.xml. The root layout element for activity_my.xml is a RelativeLayout, which supports a flexible arrangement for the buttons. The coordinate system for a RelativeLayout is shown in

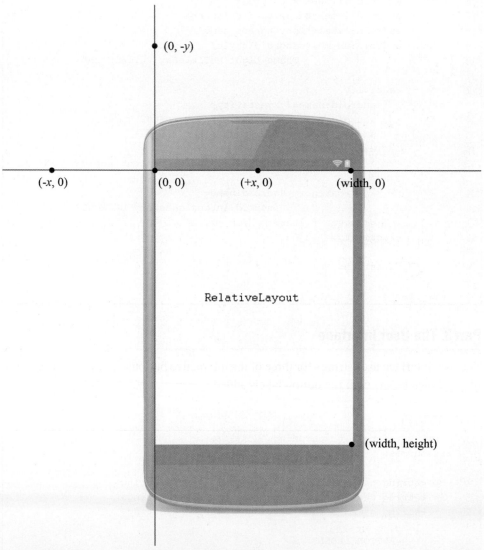

| FIGURE 5-4 The coordinate system for a RelativeLayout.

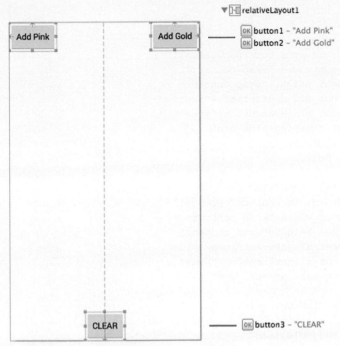

	▼ relativeLayout1
	OK button1 – "Add Pink"
	OK button2 – "Add Gold"
	OK button3 – "CLEAR"

❙ FIGURE 5-5 The layout structure and design of `activity_my.xml`.

Figure 5-4. It is important to understand the coordinate system that is supported by the layout used, because they do not all use the same system.

The layout graphic design for the `activity_my.xml` is shown in Figure 5-5. The XML code for `activity_my.xml` is listed as follows:

Line 10:   The `RelativeLayout` root view must be given an id name. This name will be referenced in `MyActivity` as petals are inflated and positioned within the layout.

```
activity_my.xml
 1   <RelativeLayout
 2       xmlns:android="http://schemas.android.com/apk/res/android"
 3       xmlns:tools="http://schemas.android.com/tools"
 4       android:layout_width="match_parent"
 5       android:layout_height="match_parent"
 6       android:paddingLeft="@dimen/activity_horizontal_margin"
 7       android:paddingRight="@dimen/activity_horizontal_margin"
 8       android:paddingTop="@dimen/activity_vertical_margin"
 9       android:paddingBottom="@dimen/activity_vertical_margin"
10       android:id= "@+id/relativeLayout1"
11       tools:context=".MyActivity">
12
```

```
13        <!-- PINK PETAL BUTTON -->
14        <Button
15            android:id="@+id/button1"
16            style="?android:attr/buttonStyleSmall"
17            android:layout_width="wrap_content"
18            android:layout_height="wrap_content"
19            android:layout_alignParentLeft="true"
20            android:layout_alignParentTop="true"
21            android:text="@string/pink_btn" />
22
23        <!-- GOLD PETAL BUTTON -->
24        <Button
25            android:id="@+id/button2"
26            style="?android:attr/buttonStyleSmall"
27            android:layout_width="wrap_content"
28            android:layout_height="wrap_content"
29            android:layout_alignParentRight="true"
30            android:layout_alignParentTop="true"
31            android:text="@string/gold_btn" />
32
33        <!-- CLEAR ALL PETALS BUTTON -->
34        <Button
35            android:id="@+id/button3"
36            style="?android:attr/buttonStyleSmall"
37            android:layout_width="wrap_content"
38            android:layout_height="wrap_content"
39            android:layout_alignParentBottom="true"
40            android:layout_centerHorizontal="true"
41            android:text="@string/clear_btn" />
42
43    </RelativeLayout>
```

ImageView – petal_a

FIGURE 5-6 The layout structure for `petal_pink.xml` contains a drawable.

ImageView – petal_b

FIGURE 5-7 The layout structure for `petal_gold.xml`.

The two petal layout files use an `ImageView` as their root element. There are no other views contained within these layouts. Their view structures are shown in Figures 5-6 and 5-7. The XML code for the petal files are listed as follows:

Line 5:   The `contentDescription` attribute is not used by Java source code; however, it is customary to add a description for all image elements.

```
petal_pink.xml
1  <?xml version="1.0" encoding="utf-8"?>
2  <ImageView xmlns:android="http://schemas.android.com/apk/res/android"
3      android:layout_width="match_parent"
4      android:layout_height="match_parent"
5      android:contentDescription="@string/pink_btn"
6      android:src="@drawable/petal_a" >
7
8  </ImageView>
```

```
petal_gold.xml
1  <?xml version="1.0" encoding="utf-8"?>
2  <ImageView xmlns:android="http://schemas.android.com/apk/res/android"
3      android:layout_width="match_parent"
4      android:layout_height="match_parent"
5      android:contentDescription="@string/gold_btn"
6      android:src="@drawable/petal_b"  >
7
8  </ImageView>
```

Part 4: Source Code for Application

Flower.java is the blueprint for a given flower that is seen on the screen. Flower.java relies on the Golden Ratio, which is common for giving computer-generated images the appearance of natural harmony. To create a Fibonacci flower for this application, the Golden Ratio is used repeatedly to offset the angle of each petal before it is placed on the screen.

In addition, each petal added to the screen is generated 3% wider and 3% longer than the previous one. The petal's angle of rotation is increased by 360 degrees multiplied by the Golden Ratio. This result for the first two petals placed on the screen is illustrated in Figure 5-8. The second petal is slightly wider and longer and offset at an angle of 233 degrees (360 * 0.6180339).

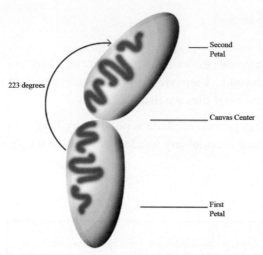

FIGURE 5-8 A flower petal will rotate at the center of the canvas.

The Java code listing for Flower.java appears as follows:

Lines 5–7:	The Golden Ratio and the growth factors are stored as constants.
Lines 10–16:	Each petal within the flower has a set of attributes that will be edited to manipulate the appearance of a petal graphic before it appears on the screen.
Lines 18–24:	The class constructor initializes the first petal of the flower. The data member degenerate is set to 1.001. This value will remain constant and will be applied to the angle of each flower petal.
Lines 76–81:	Once a flower petal has been added to the screen, petal values will be updated, which will then be applied to the next petal in the sequence.

```
Flower.java
1   package com.cornez.fibonacciflower;
2
3   public class Flower {
4
5       public final double GOLDEN_RATIO = .618033989;
6       public final double GROW_WIDTH = .03 * GOLDEN_RATIO;
7       public final double GROW_HEIGHT = .03 * GOLDEN_RATIO;
8
9       //PETAL ATTRIBUTES
10      private double angle;
11      private int rotate;
12      private float scaleX;
13      private float scaleY;
14      private int xCenter;
15      private int yCenter;
16      private float degenerate;
17
18      public Flower() {
19          rotate - 0;
20          scaleX = (float) .3;
21          scaleY = (float) .3;
22          degenerate = (float) 1.001;
23          angle = 360 * GOLDEN_RATIO;
24      }
25
26      public void initialize() {
27          //TASK 1: INITIALIZE THE SETTINGS
28          //        FOR THE FIRST FLOWER PETAL
29          rotate = 0;
30          scaleX = (float) .3;
31          scaleY = (float) .3;
32          degenerate = (float) 1.001;
33          angle = 360 * GOLDEN_RATIO;
34
35      }
36
37      public float getScaleX(){
38          return scaleX;
39      }
40      public void setScaleX(float scale){
41          scaleX = scale;
42      }
43      public float getScaleY(){
44          return scaleY;
45      }
46      public void setScaleY(float scale){
47          scaleX = scale;
48      }
49      public void setRotate(int rot) {
```

```
50        rotate =rot;
51    }
52    public int getRotate() {
53        return rotate;
54    }
55    public void set_xCenter(int x){
56        xCenter = x;
57    }
58    public int get_xCenter(){
59        return xCenter;
60    }
61
62    public void set_yCenter(int y){
63        yCenter = y;
64    }
65    public int get_yCenter(){
66        return yCenter;
67    }
68
69    public void setDegenerate(float deg){
70        degenerate = deg;
71    }
72    public void initializeAngle (){
73        angle = 360 * GOLDEN_RATIO;
74    }
75
76    public void updatePetalValues() {
77        rotate += angle;
78        scaleX += scaleX * GROW_WIDTH;
79        scaleY += scaleY * GROW_HEIGHT;
80        angle *= degenerate;
81    }
82 }
```

The Java code listing for MyActivity.java appears as follows:

Line 6:   DisplayMetrics is a utility public class that is used to access general information describing the display screen. This includes its size, density, and font scaling.

Line 7:   The LayoutInflater class is used in MyActivity to instantiate a petal layout XML file, which will allow a petal graphic bitmap to appear on the screen.

Line 15:   An ArrayList is used to store all petal graphic elements placed on the screen.

Lines 42–43:   getSystemService() returns a system-level service for a LayoutInflater, which is used to inflate layout resources in this context.

Lines 55–59:   The RelativeLayout will hold all flower petals. The petals will be positioned in the center of the layout, which is specified as width/2, height/2. `getWindowManager()` retrieves the window manager for showing custom windows. `getDefaultDisplay()` returns a default display.

Lines 82–97:   A petal ImageView object is created based on the text value of the button that was clicked. The new view hierarchy is inflated from the specified petal XML resource.

The visual properties for the ImageView are set. `setPivotY()` sets the *y* location of the point around which the petal is rotated and scaled. By default, the pivot point is centered on the object. `setPivotX()` is the same, except the *x* pivot location is set. `setScaleX ()` sets the amount that the petal is scaled in *x* around the pivot point, as a proportion of the view's unscaled width. For `setScaleX` and `setScaleY`, a value of 1 means that no scaling is applied.

`setRotation()` sets the degrees that the petal is rotated around the pivot point. Increasing values result in a clockwise rotation.

Line 100:   The petal `ImageView` object is added to `relativeLayout`. Properties are applied before the object is added to the layout. The number zero refers to the layer index of the petal being added. By specifying zero, petals will be placed underneath the existing flower petals.

Lines 112–126: Petals are cleared when the user clicks the "clear" button. The `onClick()` handler uses `removeView()` to eliminate the View from the `RelativeLayout`. In addition, all petals are cleared from the `ArrayList`.

```
MyActivity.java
 1  package com.cornez.fibonacciflower;
 2
 3  import android.app.Activity;
 4  import android.content.Context;
 5  import android.os.Bundle;
 6  import android.util.DisplayMetrics;
 7  import android.view.LayoutInflater;
 8  import android.view.Menu;
 9  import android.view.MenuItem;
10  import android.view.View;
11  import android.widget.Button;
12  import android.widget.ImageView;
```

```java
13    import android.widget.RelativeLayout;
14
15    import java.util.ArrayList;
16
17
18    public class MyActivity extends Activity {
19
20        private ArrayList<ImageView> allPetals;
21        private LayoutInflater layoutInflater;
22
23        private Button pinkBtn;
24        private Button goldBtn;
25        private Button clearBtn;
26        private RelativeLayout relativeLayout;
27
28        Flower myFlower;
29
30        @Override
31        protected void onCreate(Bundle savedInstanceState) {
32            super.onCreate(savedInstanceState);
33            setContentView(R.layout.activity_my);
34
35            myFlower = new Flower();
36            allPetals = new ArrayList <ImageView>();
37
38            //INITIALIZE THE GENERATION OF THE FIBONACCI ARTWORK
39            initialize();
40
41            //CREATE A LAYOUT INFLATER TO ADD PETALS TO RELATIVE LAYOUT
42            layoutInflater = (LayoutInflater)
43                getSystemService(Context.LAYOUT_INFLATER_SERVICE);
44
45            relativeLayout = (RelativeLayout)
46                findViewById(R.id.relativeLayout1);
47            pinkBtn = (Button) findViewById(R.id.button1);
48            goldBtn = (Button) findViewById(R.id.button2);
49            clearBtn = (Button) findViewById(R.id.button3);
50            pinkBtn.setOnClickListener(addPetal);
51            goldBtn.setOnClickListener(addPetal);
52            clearBtn.setOnClickListener(clearPetals);
53
54            //SET THE CENTER COORDINATE
55            DisplayMetrics metrics = new DisplayMetrics();
56            getWindowManager().getDefaultDisplay().getMetrics(metrics);
57            myFlower.set_xCenter(metrics.widthPixels / 2);
58            myFlower.set_yCenter(metrics.heightPixels / 2);
59
60        }
61
```

```
62    private void initialize(){
63        //TASK 1: INITIALIZE THE SETTINGS FOR THE FIRST PETAL
64
65        myFlower.setRotate(0);
66        myFlower.setScaleX((float) .3);
67        myFlower.setScaleY((float) .3);
68        myFlower.setDegenerate((float) 1.001);
69        myFlower.initializeAngle();
70
71    }
72
73    //ON CLICK BUTTON HANDLER FOR ADDING A FLOWER PETAL TO THE SCREEN
74    private View.OnClickListener addPetal = new View.OnClickListener() {
75        public void onClick (View view) {
76
77
78            //TASK 1:  INSTANTIATE A VIEW TO STORE A PETAL GRAPHIC
79            ImageView petal;
80
81            // INFLATE THE CORRECT PETAL
82            String buttonText = ((Button) view).getText().toString();
83            if (buttonText.equals("Add Pink"))
84                petal = (ImageView)
85                    layoutInflater.inflate(R.layout.petal_pink, null);
86            else
87                petal = (ImageView)
88                    layoutInflater.inflate(R.layout.petal_gold, null);
89
90            //TASK 2: SET THE VISUAL PROPERTIES OF THE PETAL
91            petal.setX(myFlower.get_xCenter());
92            petal.setY(myFlower.get_yCenter());
93            petal.setPivotY(0);
94            petal.setPivotX(100);
95            petal.setScaleX(myFlower.getScaleX());
96            petal.setScaleY(myFlower.getScaleY());
97            petal.setRotation(myFlower.getRotate());
98
99            //TASK 3: PLACE THE INFLATED IMAGEVIEW IN THE MAIN LAYOUT
100           relativeLayout.addView(petal, 0);
101
102           //TASK 4: ADD THE IMAGEVIEW OF THE PETAL TO THE ARRAYLIST
103           allPetals.add(petal);
104
105           //TASK 5: UPDATE THE ANGLE AND SCALE
106           //        FOR THE NEXT PETAL TO BE ADDED
107           myFlower.updatePetalValues();
108        }
109    };
110
```

```
111    //ON CLICK BUTTON HANDLER TO CLEAR ALL PETALS ON THE SCREEN
112    private View.OnClickListener clearPetals  =
113        new View.OnClickListener() {
114
115        public void onClick (View view) {
116            //TASK 1: REMOVE ALL PETAL IMAGE VIEW FROM THE LAYOUT
117            for (int i = 0; i < allPetals.size(); i++) {
118                ImageView petal = allPetals.get(i);
119                relativeLayout.removeView(petal);
120            }
121
122            //TASK 2:CLEAR THE ARRAYLIST AND RESET ALL VARIABLES
123            allPetals.clear();
124            initialize();
125        }
126    };
127
128    @Override
129    public boolean onCreateOptionsMenu(Menu menu) {
130        // Inflate the menu.
131        getMenuInflater().inflate(R.menu.my, menu);
132        return true;
133    }
134
135    @Override
136    public boolean onOptionsItemSelected(MenuItem item) {
137        // Handle action bar item clicks here. The action bar will
138        // automatically handle clicks on the Home/Up button, so long
139        // as you specify a parent activity in AndroidManifest.xml.
140        int id = item.getItemId();
141        if (id == R.id.action_settings) {
142            return true;
143        }
144        return super.onOptionsItemSelected(item);
145    }
146 }
```

■ 5.3 Drawing and the Canvas Class

When an application requires specialized drawing, or the control of animated graphics, a Canvas can be used. A Canvas provides an interface to the actual surface upon which graphics will be drawn. The purpose of the canvas is to hold the results of the "draw" calls. By using the Canvas, a drawing is actually performed on an underlying Bitmap, which is placed into the window.

Optimizing an application that requires extensive custom drawing can sometimes be difficult. The use of custom drawing code should be limited to situations where the content display needs to change dynamically. Consider the game of Pong, as shown in Figure 5-9. Pong can be created as a drawing application, which means it requires custom drawing code to track the movement of the paddle and update the screen as the user drags the paddle back and forth. The application also needs to update the drawing of the two-dimensional ball to reflect its changing position as it bounces off the walls and the paddle.

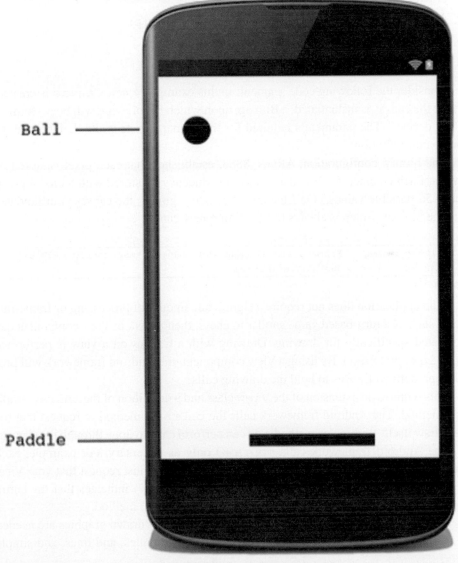

Ball

Paddle

I FIGURE 5-9 The game of Pong can be created using a custom drawing code.

Drawing custom graphics can be performed in two ways: (1) graphics can be drawn into a View object, or (2) they can be drawn directly to a `Canvas`. Drawing to a `View` is a good choice when simple static graphics are needed. Game applications, such as Pong, need dynamic visuals that require the application to regularly redraw itself to a canvas.

The android.graphics package provides canvas tools, color filters, points, and rectangles. The Android `Canvas` class has a set of drawing methods, such as `drawBitmap()`, `drawRect()`, and `drawText()`. To draw something, four basic components are needed:

1. A Bitmap to hold the pixels.
2. A Canvas to host the draw calls (writing into the bitmap).
3. A drawing primitive (e.g., Rect, Path, text, Bitmap).
4. Paint (to describe the colors and styles for the drawing).

Consider the following code segment; in this example, a new `Canvas` is created. Before the canvas is instantiated, a Bitmap, upon which the drawing will be performed, is first defined. The parameters required for the bitmap are its width, height, and the bitmap configuration.

The bitmap configuration, ARGN_8888, establishes that each pixel is stored on 4 bytes. Each channel (RGB and alpha for translucency) is stored with 8 bits of precision (256 possible values.) On Line 2 of the code segment, the canvas is instantiated with the bitmap, which is always required for a new canvas.

```
1   Bitmap bitmap = Bitmap.createBitmap(100, 100, Bitmap.Config.ARGB_8888);
2   Canvas canvas = new Canvas(bitmap);
```

If an application does not require a significant amount of processing or frame-rate speed, such as a turn-based game similar to chess, then a custom View component can be created specifically for drawing. Drawing with a Canvas on a view is performed with `View.onDraw()`. By using a View component, the Android framework will provide a predefined Canvas to hold the drawing calls.

This requires an extension of the `View` class and a definition of the `onDraw()` callback method. The Android framework calls the `onDraw()` method to request that the View draw itself. Within this method, you can perform calls to draw through the Canvas.

The Android framework calls `onDraw()` only as necessary. For example, each time your application is prepared to redraw a canvas, you must request that your View be invalidated by calling `invalidate()`. `invalidate()` indicates that the entire view will be drawn again. Android then calls the `onDraw()` method.

A ShapeDrawable is a good option when dynamically drawn graphics are needed for an application. Primitive shapes, such as ovals, rectangles, and lines, and simple styles can be programmatically built easily. Consider the class CustomView, implemented in the following code segment. CustomView is an extension of the View class that draws a primitive oval shape.

Line 2:   A ShapeDrawable is a drawable object that draws only primitive shapes. A ShapeDrawable uses a Shape object and manages its appearance on the screen. If no Shape is specified, the ShapeDrawable will default to a rectangle. As we saw previously in Section 5.2 of this chapter, an object can also be defined in an XML file using the <shape> tag.

Line 13:   The paint color for the oval shape is set. The color value 0xff74AC23 is an integer containing alpha, as well as red, green, and blue values.

Line 14:   setBounds() specifies a bounding rectangle for the Drawable. This is where the oval shape appears when its draw() method is called.

```
1    public class CustomView extends View {
2        private ShapeDrawable mDrawable;
3
4        public CustomView(Context context) {
5            super(context);
6
7            int x = 10;
8            int y = 10;
9            int width = 50;
10           int height = 50;
11
12           mDrawable = new ShapeDrawable(new OvalShape());
13           mDrawable.getPaint().setColor(0xff74AC23);
14           mDrawable.setBounds(x, y, x + width, y + height);
15       }
16
17       protected void onDraw(Canvas canvas) {
18           mDrawable.draw(canvas);
19       }
20   }
```

A ShapeDrawable is an extension of Drawable. This is convenient because it can be used anywhere a Drawable is expected, such as the background of a View.

A drawable can also be built as its own custom View and then added to a layout. In the code segment below, the CustomView object is set as the layout content in onCreate().

```
1        CustomView mCustomView;
2
3        protected void onCreate(Bundle savedInstanceState) {
4            super.onCreate(savedInstanceState);
5            mCustomDrawableView = new
6                    CustomView(this);
7
8            setContentView(mCustomView);
9        }
```

■ Lab Example 5-2: Drawing Experiment 1: Bull's-Eye Drawing

This lab example explores the concept of building a custom `View`, drawing a Bull's Eye within the `View`, and displaying it on the screen as the layout associated with `MyActivity`. The Bull's-Eye View is dynamic in the sense that it redraws itself when the user changes orientation on the device. Figure 5-10 shows the Bull's Eye configured for portrait and landscape orientations.

Part 1: The Design

The width of the Bull's Eye is set to span the width of the device, regardless of the device's orientation. The drawing is created using five circles, with different sizes, sharing the same center.

The window containing the layout does not feature a title, and it occupies the full screen.

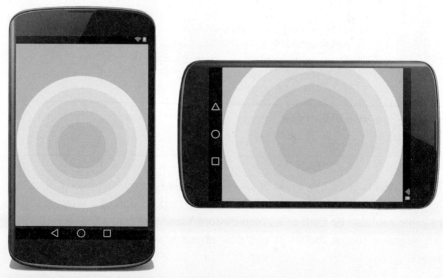

❙ FIGURE 5-10 The Bull's-Eye App running in portrait and landscape orientation.

Part 2: Application Structure and Setup

The application structure is very simple, as this project is intended to be an experiment in drawing rather than an interactive app.

The settings for the application are as follows:

- Application Name: Bulls Eye
- Project Name: BullsEye
- Package Name: `com.cornez.bullseye`
- Android Form: Phone and Tablet
- Minimum SDK: API 18: Android 4.3 (Jelly Bean)
- Target SDK: API 21: Android 5.0 (Lollipop)
- Compile with: API 21: Android 5.0 (Lollipop)
- Activity Name: `MyActivity`

The icon launcher will remain set to the Android default `ic_launcher.png` file. No changes are required. The final project structure resembles the structure shown in Figure 5-11.

▼ app
- **▼ manifests**
  - AndroidManifest.xml
- **▼ java**
  - **▼ com.cornez.bullseye**
    - C BullsEyeView
    - C MyActivity
  - ▶ com.cornez.bullseye (androidTest)
- **▼ res**
  - ▶ drawable
  - ▶ layout
  - ▶ menu
  - ▶ values
- **▼ Gradle Scripts**
  - build.gradle (Project: BullsEye2)
  - build.gradle (Module: app)
  - gradle-wrapper.properties (Gradle Version)
  - gradle.properties (Project Properties)
  - settings.gradle (Project Settings)
  - local.properties (SDK Location)

FIGURE 5-11 The Project Structure of the Bull's-Eye application.

MyActivity is the main Activity for the application. BullsEyeView is an extended View class with an implemented onDraw() method. The Bull's-Eye graphic will be drawn into this View.

The AndroidManifest.xml file contains the settings for the main Activity. The android:theme setting is overridden in MyActivity. The XML code for AndroidManifest.xml appears as follows. No layout XML file is used in the Bull's-Eye application. Instead, a layout will be constructed programmatically in Java.

```
AndroidManifest.xml
1   <?xml version="1.0" encoding="utf-8"?>
2   <manifest xmlns:android="http://schemas.android.com/apk/res/android"
3       package="com.cornez.bullseye" >
4
5       <application
6           android:allowBackup="true"
7           android:icon="@drawable/ic_launcher"
8           android:label="@string/app_name"
9           android:theme="@style/AppTheme" >
10          <activity
11              android:name=".MyActivity"
12              android:label="@string/app_name" >
13              <intent-filter>
14                  <action android:name="android.intent.action.MAIN" />
15
16                  <category
17                      android:name="android.intent.category.LAUNCHER" />
18              </intent-filter>
19          </activity>
20      </application>
21
22  </manifest>
```

Part 3: Source Code for Application

The Activity for the application is MyActivity. As a drawing app experiment, it performs two simple functions: (1) it configures the screen window, and (2) it sets the layout to a drawable. The drawable will be constructed programmatically.

Line 21:   requestWindowFeature () enables specific window features, specifically a "no title" feature. This turns off the title at the top of the screen.

Lines 22–24:   getWindow() retrieves the current window for the running activity. This call is used to access parts of the Window API directly.

A call to setFlags(int flags, int mask) sets the behaviorial options of a window. The window flag FLAG_FULLSCREEN is used to display the Activity in fullscreen. The flags parameter specifies the window flags, and the mask parameter identifies which of the window flag bits to modify. To hide the Status Bar on the device when the application is started, the window flag FLAG_FULLSCREEN is passed to both parameters.

The following is a brief list of useful window flags:

a. FLAG_FULLSCREEN hides all screen decorations (such as the status bar) while this window is displayed.

b. FLAG_KEEP_SCREEN_ON keeps the device's screen turned on as long as the window is visible to the user.

c. FLAG_SHOW_WALLPAPER allows the system wallpaper to be shown behind the activity window.

d. FLAG_TRANSLUCENT_NAVIGATION sets the navigation bar to translucent, with minimal system-provided background protection.

Window flags are often required to be set before the first call to setContentView(View).

Line 26:   A BullsEyeView View is instantiated. This View, containing the bull's-eye graphic, will be bound to MyActivity in the next instruction.

Line 27:   The activity content is set to the explicit view, bullsEyeView. This view is placed directly into the activity's view hierarchy. When the user alters the orientation of the device, the activity is restarted. The restart in the activity will force a call to the onDraw() method in the BullsEyeView class.

MyActivity.java

```
1   package com.cornez.bullseye;
2
3   import android.app.Activity;
4   import android.os.Bundle;
5   import android.view.Menu;
6   import android.view.MenuItem;
7   import android.view.Window;
8   import android.view.WindowManager;
9
10
```

```
11  public class MyActivity extends Activity {
12
13      BullsEyeView bullsEyeView;
14
15      @Override
16      protected void onCreate(Bundle savedInstanceState) {
17          super.onCreate(savedInstanceState);
18
19          //WINDOW PROPERTIES ARE SET
20          //THIS ANDROID WINDOW WILL NOT FEATURE A TITLE
21          requestWindowFeature(Window.FEATURE_NO_TITLE);
22          getWindow().setFlags(
23                  WindowManager.LayoutParams.FLAG_FULLSCREEN,
24                  WindowManager.LayoutParams.FLAG_FULLSCREEN);
25
26          bullsEyeView = new BullsEyeView(this);
27          setContentView(bullsEyeView);
28      }
29
30
31
32      @Override
33      public boolean onCreateOptionsMenu(Menu menu) {
34          // Inflate the menu.
35          getMenuInflater().inflate(R.menu.my, menu);
36          return true;
37      }
38
39      @Override
40      public boolean onOptionsItemSelected(MenuItem item) {
41          // Handle action bar item clicks here. The action bar will
42          // automatically handle clicks on the Home/Up button, so long
43          // as you specify a parent activity in AndroidManifest.xml.
44          int id = item.getItemId();
45          if (id == R.id.action_settings) {
46              return true;
47          }
48          return super.onOptionsItemSelected(item);
49      }
50  }
```

The BullsEyeView.java class is the data model for the graphic element. A mix of colors is applied to a Paint object, which is used to fill a single circle. After each circle is drawn, paint is mixed again and the process repeats itself.

Line 5:   The Color class defines methods for creating and converting color integers. Colors are made up of 4 bytes: alpha, red, green, and blue. Transparency is stored solely in the alpha component, not in the color components. Color values range between 0 and

255: 0 means no contribution for that color, and 255 means 100% contribution. For example, opaque-black would be 0xFF000000 (100% opaque, but no contributions from red, green, or blue).

Line 6:   The `Paint` class holds the style and color information about how to draw geometries, text, and bitmaps.

Line 7:   The Style class provides the specifics for how a primitive shape is drawn. For example, it can be filled with color, have a stroke applied, or both. The default is a filled shape.

Line 10:   `BullsEyeView` is extended as a `View`. This allows `BullsEyeView` to support drawing and event handling.

Lines 22–27:   The color values for red, green, and blue are mixed to fill the first circle of the bull's eye. An instance of `Paint` is created so new paint can be applied to newly drawn circles.

Line 30:   `onDraw()` is implemented to perform the drawing needs for this View. The canvas represents the background for the drawing.

Lines 31–32:   `getWidth()` returns the width of the current drawing layer, the canvas. The center of the canvas is the width divided by 2 and the height divided by 2.

Lines 41–59:   Five circles will be drawn, each one smaller than the previous one. Each circle is colored with a new mix of red, green, and blue and is drawn on top of the previous circle.

```
BullsEyeView.java
1   package com.cornez.bullseye;
2
3   import android.content.Context;
4   import android.graphics.Canvas;
5   import android.graphics.Color;
6   import android.graphics.Paint;
7   import android.graphics.Paint.Style;
8   import android.view.View;
9
10  public class BullsEyeView  extends View {
11
12      private Paint paint;
13
14      //VALUES FOR THE RED, GREEN, AND BLUE VALUES
15      private int redVal;
16      private int greenVal;
17      private int blueVal;
18
19      public BullsEyeView (Context context) {
20          super(context);
21
```

```
22          //INITIAL VALUES FOR RED, GREEN, AND BLUE
23          redVal = 248;
24          greenVal = 232;
25          blueVal = 198;
26
27          paint = new Paint();
28      }
29
30      public void onDraw (Canvas canvas) {
31          //INITIALIZE THE CENTER OF THE CANVAS
32          float centerX = canvas. getWidth() / 2;
33          float centerY = canvas.getHeight() / 2;
34
35          //INITIALIZE THE RADIUS FOR THE FIRST RING
36          float radius = canvas.getHeight() / 2;
37
38          //TASK 1: FILL THE ENTIRE CANVAS WITH A BEIGE COLOR
39          canvas.drawRGB(194,  183,  158);
40
41          //TASK 2: DRAW A SET OF FIVE RINGS
42          int ringRed = redVal;
43          int ringGreen = greenVal;
44          int ringBlue = blueVal;
45
46          for (int i = 1; i <= 5; i++) {
47              //DRAW A SINGLE RING
48              paint.setStyle(Style.FILL);
49              paint.setColor(Color.rgb(ringRed, ringGreen, ringBlue));
50              canvas.drawCircle(centerX, centerY, radius,  paint);
51
52              //RESET THE COLOR AND SIZE FOR THE NEXT RING
53              ringRed -= 13;
54              ringGreen -= 13;
55              ringBlue -= 13;
56              radius -= 120;
57          }
58      }
59 }
```

5.4 Recursive Drawing

Drawing can be applied to an application in varied ways. One area that relies heavily on drawing is the generation of fractal terrain. The terrain in an environment can be a crucial user interface element, particularly in a game application. Fractals are inherent to the development of terrain drawings, mainly because fractal-based terrain is simple to implement and scales well, as fractals are self-similar. Recursive drawing algorithms are often used to produce landscape fractal images.

The math behind recursive drawing algorithms (fractals) can be simple or complex, depending on the requirements of the application. The key concept behind any fractal is self-similarity. An object is said to be self-similar when magnified subsets of the object are identical to the whole and to each other. Landscape terrain falls into the "self-similar" category. For example, a single branch of a tree has the same structure as the tree itself. A recursively generated tree, such as in Figure 5-12, still looks like a tree, regardless of the scale in which it is displayed.

❚ FIGURE 5-12 Recursive drawing.

The textures of natural objects, such as trees, mountains, and stones, have fractal properties. Almost any item that does not have an absolutely smooth, glassy surface contains bumps, pits, and grooves. The sizes of these features vary by fractal laws; many will be very small, some will be bigger, and a few are relatively large. The distribution of these bumps, pits, and grooves across an object's surface is not entirely random, but it has a fractal nature.

When drawing fractal elements in an application, realistic-looking texture can be rendered quickly. This has advantages to the alternative, which would create hundreds of still images that would occupy memory on a device.

To be effective on a mobile device, the terrain needs to meet a number of requirements, many of which can be mutually opposing. A terrain should appear to be continuous to the user and must render quickly, yet it must be simplified, where possible, to reduce the load on a low-processing device.

■ Lab Example 5-3: C-Curve Recursive Drawing

This lab experiments with the concept of layering—including drawn elements—onto an existing layout. This is done programmatically, as well as with an XML layout. We will use recursive drawing to construct a well-recognized fractal pattern, known as the C-curve.

Part 1: The Design

The C-curve fractal is a geometric pattern that can be subdivided into many smaller imitations, that is, self-similar copies of the larger pattern. If you enlarge any small portion of the complete fractal, it will have the same structure as the larger complete work. Figure 5-13 shows several screenshots of the C-curve application.

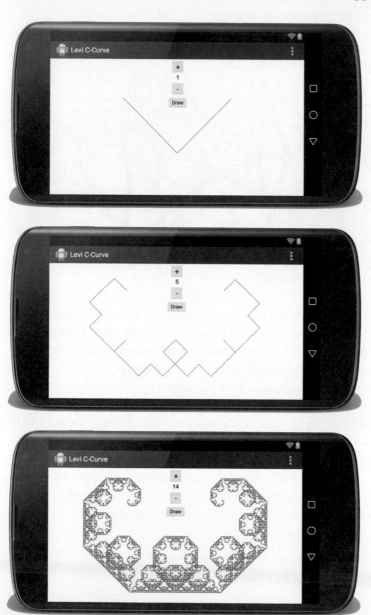

FIGURE 5-13 Screenshots of the C-curve application.

When the application launches, the user will see a "number stepper." This user interface control allows the user to select a C-curve level, which determines the complexity of the final design.

Part 2: Application Structure and Setup

The settings for the application are as follows:

- Application Name: Levi C-Curve
- Project Name: LeviC_Curve
- Package Name: `com.cornez.leviccurve`
- Android Form: Phone and Tablet
- Minimum SDK: API 18: Android 4.3 (Jelly Bean)
- Target SDK: API 21: Android 5.0 (Lollipop)
- Compile with: API 21: Android 5.0 (Lollipop)
- Activity Name: `MyActivity`
- Layout Name: `activity_my`

The launcher is set to Android's default `ic_launcher.png` file. No bitmap files are used in this application.

The final project structure, shown in Figure 5-14, contains three source files and one layout file. The C-curve application uses a single activity, `MyActivity.java`, which sets the screen user interface to `activity_my.xml`.

FIGURE 5-14 Project structure for the Levi C-Curve application.

The theme for the application has been set in the AndroidManifest file, along with a landscape screen orientation. The XML code listing for `AndroidManifest.xml` appears as follows:

```
AndroidManifest.xml
1   <?xml version="1.0" encoding="utf-8"?>
2   <manifest xmlns:android="http://schemas.android.com/apk/res/android"
3       package="com.cornez.levic_curve" >
4
5       <application
6           android:allowBackup="true"
7           android:icon="@drawable/ic_launcher"
8           android:label="@string/app_name"
9           android:theme="@style/AppTheme" >
10          <activity
11              android:screenOrientation="landscape"
12              android:name=".MyActivity"
13              android:label="@string/app_name" >
14              <intent-filter>
15                  <action android:name="android.intent.action.MAIN" />
16
17                  <category
18                      android:name="android.intent.category.LAUNCHER" />
19              </intent-filter>
20          </activity>
21      </application>
22
23  </manifest>
```

Part 3: The User Interface Design

A NumberPicker widget enables the user to select a number from a predefined range. This lab features a custom-built NumberPicker, or rather, a number stepper, which is a control that is used to limit the range of values that a user can input. The number stepper constrains input within the onClick handler. By using an increase button or decrease button, the user can choose a level from 0 through 14. As shown in Figure 5-15,

❙ FIGURE 5-15 A "number stepper" is built, using `Buttons` and a `TextView`.

the decrease button contains a minus sign, and the increase button contains a plus sign. The user does not have direct access to the numeric value that appears between these two buttons.

The `strings.xml` file defines the button labels used by the number stepper. In addition to the number stepper's increment and decrement buttons, a draw button activates the C-curve recursive drawing. The label is defined on Line 9. The XML code for `strings.xml` is listed as follows:

```
strings.xml
1   <?xml version="1.0" encoding="utf-8"?>
2   <resources>
3
4       <string name="app_name">Levi C-Curve</string>
5       <string name="hello_world">Hello world!</string>
6       <string name="action_settings">Settings</string>
7
8       <!--BUTTON LABELS -->
9       <string name="draw_btn">Draw</string>
10      <string name="up_btn">+</string>
11      <string name="down_btn">-</string>
12      <string name="start_level">1</string>
13
14  </resources>
```

FIGURE 5-16 The layout structure for `activity_my.xml`.

The `View` hierarchical structure for the layout file `activity_my.xml` is shown in Figure 5-16. The number stepper contains `button1`, `textView1`, and `button2`. The root element in `activity_my.xml` is set to a `RelativeLayout`. The XML code listing for `activity_my.xml` is shown below.

Line 6:   It is important that the `RelativeLayout` root is given an identifier name, as this view will be referenced in the main activity of the application.

Line 15:   The method stepUp() is the onClick event handler for the
                increment button.

Line 33:   The method stepDown() is the onClick event handler for the
                decrement button.

Line 45:   The method drawFractal() handles the onClick event for
                the Draw button.

```
activity_my.xml
1   <RelativeLayout
2   xmlns:android="http://schemas.android.com/apk/res/android"
3       xmlns:tools="http://schemas.android.com/tools"
4       android:layout_width="match_parent"
5       android:layout_height="match_parent"
6       android:id="@+id/relativeLayout"
7       tools:context=".MyActivity">
8
9       <Button
10          android:id="@+id/button1"
11          android:layout_width="35dp"
12          android:layout_height="35dp"
13          android:layout_alignParentTop="true"
14          android:layout_centerHorizontal="true"
15          android:onClick="stepUp"
16          android:text="@string/up_btn"
17          android:gravity="center" />
18
19      <TextView
20          android:id="@+id/textView1"
21          android:layout_width="wrap_content"
22          android:layout_height="wrap_content"
23          android:layout_below="@+id/button1"
24          android:layout_centerHorizontal="true"
25          android:text="@string/start_level" />
26
27      <Button
28          android:id="@+id/button2"
29          android:layout_width="35dp"
30          android:layout_height="35dp"
31          android:layout_below="@+id/textView1"
32          android:layout_centerHorizontal="true"
33          android:onClick="stepDown"
34          android:text="@string/down_btn"
35          android:gravity="center" />
36
37      <Button
38          android:id="@+id/button3"
39          style="?android:attr/buttonStyleSmall"
```

```
40          android:layout_width="wrap_content"
41          android:layout_height="30dp"
42          android:layout_below="@+id/button2"
43          android:layout_centerHorizontal="true"
44          android:text="@string/draw_btn"
45          android:onClick="drawFractal"
46          android:textSize="12sp" />
47
48    </RelativeLayout>
```

Part 4: Source Code for Application

`MyActivity`, launched when the application is loaded, collects the user's input and initiates the recursive drawing based on the input. MyActivity is primarily responsible for arranging the relevant views of the user interface and presenting them in appropriate places on the screen.

Lines 14–15: `levelsTV` is the `TextView` that is used to display the numeric level as a string to the user. The integer variable `level` is the numeric value. This variable is initialized to one on Line 29.

Lines 16–17: The user interface is arranged in layers. The main layout is the `RelativeLayout` layer, the root element of `activity_my.xml`. A `FractalView` layer is added to this root element, as shown in Figure 5-17. The `FractalView` object will hold a `Canvas`, the final layer.

Line 27: The FractalView object is added as a child view to the Relative-Layout. The zero position is the index position at which the child object has been added.

Line 30: A reference to the levels `TextView` is assigned to `levelsTV`, which is the numeric text element of the number stepper.

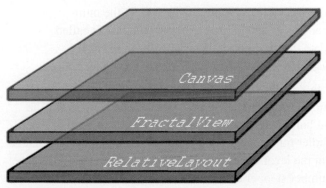

FIGURE 5-17 Layers applied to the C-curve user interface.

```
MyActivity.java
 1   package com.cornez.levic_curve;
 2
 3   import android.app.Activity;
 4   import android.os.Bundle;
 5   import android.view.Menu;
 6   import android.view.MenuItem;
 7   import android.view.View;
 8   import android.widget.RelativeLayout;
 9   import android.widget.TextView;
10
11
12   public class MyActivity extends Activity {
13
14       private TextView levelsTV;
15       private Integer level;
16       private RelativeLayout relativeLayout;
17       private FractalView fractalView;
18
19       @Override
20       protected void onCreate(Bundle savedInstanceState) {
21           super.onCreate(savedInstanceState);
22           setContentView(R.layout.activity_my);
23
24           relativeLayout = (RelativeLayout)
25                   findViewById(R.id.relativeLayout);
26           fractalView = new FractalView(this);
27           relativeLayout.addView(fractalView, 0);
28
29           level = 1;
30           levelsTV = (TextView) findViewById(R.id.textView1);
31       }
32
```

Lines 33–36:   drawFractal() is the event handler for the "draw" button. The fractal level, input by the user in the number stepper, is set. The invalidate() method is called to invalidate the entire fractalView. This will result in onDraw(android.graphics.Canvas) being called, which will draw the lines that make up the C-curve fractal.

Lines 38–51:   The method stepUp() is the onClick event handler for the increment button. The method stepDown() is the onClick event handler for the decrement button. Both handlers increment/decrement the level variable and update the TextView display for the number stepper control.

```
MyActivity.java (continued)
33       public void drawFractal(View view) {
34           fractalView.level = level;
35           fractalView.invalidate();
36       }
37
38       // NUMBERS FOR STEP UP AND STEP DOWN CAN RANGE FROM 1 THROUGH 14
39       public void stepUp(View view) {
40           if (level < 14) {
41               level++;
42               levelsTV.setText(level.toString());
43           }
44       }
45
46       public void stepDown(View view) {
47           if (level > 1) {
48               level--;
49               levelsTV.setText(level.toString());
50           }
51       }
52
53       @Override
54       public boolean onCreateOptionsMenu(Menu menu) {
55           // Inflate the menu.
56           getMenuInflater().inflate(R.menu.my, menu);
57           return true;
58       }
59
60       @Override
61       public boolean onOptionsItemSelected(MenuItem item) {
62           // Handle action bar item clicks here. The action bar will
63           // automatically handle clicks on the Home/Up button, so long
64           // as you specify a parent activity in AndroidManifest.xml.
65           int id = item.getItemId();
66           if (id == R.id.action_settings) {
67               return true;
68           }
69           return super.onOptionsItemSelected(item);
70       }
71   }
```

The FractalView class is a View that occupies a rectangular area on the RelativeLayout in activity_my.xml. FractalView is responsible for drawing the C-curve fractal.

Lines 8–12:   The C-curve fractal is constructed with many line drawings
                 that recursively begin at point ($x1$, $y1$) and end at point ($x2$, $y2$).

These line drawings will occur on the canvas provided by this `FractalView` class.

Line 14:   The `Fractal` class is the fractal generator.

Lines 24–36:   The method onDraw() initializes the fractal (*x1*, *y1*) and (*x2*, *y2*) settings and then calls `fractal.drawCurve()` to draw the fractal lines to the canvas. onDraw() is called by `fractalView.invalidate()` in `MyActivity`.

Lines 25–29:   The initial points for the first line in the fractal are set so that the C-curve appears in the center of the screen, no matter the screen size.

Line 32:   If a previous recursive drawing appears on the canvas, it is wiped clean by covering the canvas in white paint.

Line 35:   When calling drawCCurve() to generate the recursive drawing, it must be past the `Canvas` object provided by `FractalView`.

```
FractalView.java
1   package com.cornez.levic_curve;
2   import android.content.Context;
3   import android.graphics.Canvas;
4   import android.view.View;
5
6   public class FractalView extends View {
7
8       private float x1;
9       private float y1;
10      private float x2;
11      private float y2;
12      public int level;
13
14      private Fractal fractal;
15
16      public FractalView (Context context) {
17          super (context);
18
19          //CREATE A FRACTAL OBJECT
20          level = 2;
21          fractal = new Fractal();
22      }
23
24      protected void onDraw (Canvas canvas){
25          //TASK 1: GET THE DIMENSIONS OF THE CANVAS
26          x1 = canvas.getWidth() / 3;
27          y1 = canvas.getHeight() / 4;
28          x2 = canvas.getWidth() - x1;
29          y2 = y1;
30
```

```
31        //TASK 2:  FILL THE CANVAS WITH WHITE PAINT
32        canvas.drawRGB(255, 255, 255);
33
34        //TASK 3: DRAW THE CCURVE
35        fractal.drawCCurve(canvas, x1, y1, x2, y2, level);
36     }
37
38   }
```

In this application, the C-curve is generated recursively. To better understand its construction, the first four levels are illustrated in Figure 5-18. Consider the most primitive level, Level 0. At this level, the fractal starts with a straight line drawn from point $(x1, y1)$ to the point $(x2, y2)$. This basic line always occurs at the primitive state in the recursion.

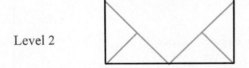

Level 0

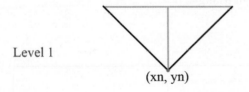

Level 1

Level 2

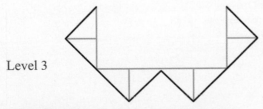

Level 3

FIGURE 5-18 The C-curve from Level 0 to Level 3.

At Level 1 of the fractal, an isosceles right triangle is built using the line at Level 0 as its hypotenuse. The first line is drawn from the point $(x1, y1)$ to the point (xn, yn). The second line is drawn between points (xn, yn) and $(x2, y2)$.

The point at (xn, yn) is computed as follows:

$$xn = (x1 + x2)/2 + (y1 - y2)/2$$

$$yn = (x2 - x1)/2 + (y1 + y2)/2$$

At Level 2, two new lines are used to form the foundation for another right-angled isosceles triangle. At every new level, two new lines from two sides of a respective triangle are constructed to replace an existing line. At Level 0, there are 2^0 lines. Level 1 draws 2^1 lines, and Level 3 generates 2^3 lines. Level n would be constructed with 2^n lines.

The Fractal class is simply the engine that constructs a C-curve. The class contains a recursive method, but it contains no data.

Lines 8–9:   The Canvas parameter is required in order to draw to the FractalView.

Lines 17–18:   The primitive state for the recursion is Level 0. This results in a single line drawn to the canvas.

Lines 19–24:   The method drawCCurve() is called recursively to replace one line with two new lines, based on the computation of an x, y point in an isosceles right triangle.

```
Fractal.java
1   package com.cornez.levic_curve;
2
3          import android.graphics.Canvas;
4          import android.graphics.Color;
5          import android.graphics.Paint;
6
7   public class Fractal {
8
9       public void drawCCurve (Canvas canvas, float x1,
10          float y1, float x2, float y2, int level){
11
12          //PAINT COLOR IS SET TO RED
13          //LINE STROKE IS SET TO 1
14          Paint paint = new Paint();
15          paint.setColor(Color.rgb(255, 0, 0));
16          paint.setStrokeWidth(1);
17
18          if (level == 0)
19              canvas.drawLine(x1,  y1,  x2,  y2,  paint);
20          else {
```

```
21      float xn = (x1 + x2) / 2 + (y1 - y2) / 2;
22      float yn = (x2 - x1) / 2 + (y1 + y2) / 2;
23      drawCCurve(canvas, x1, y1, xn, yn, level -1);
24      drawCCurve(canvas, xn, yn, x2, y2, level -1);
25          }
26      }
27
28  }
```

■ 5.5 Frame-by-Frame and Film Loop Animations

Frame-by-frame animation is a sequence of images that are displayed in rapid succession, one after the other. A film loop is an animated sequence that you can use like a single View object. For example, to create an animation of a character dancing on the stage, a set of bitmaps is placed in the Drawable directory and the images are displayed on the screen within a View. To create a film loop, the sequence of bitmaps that shows the character dancing is created as a View object that can be animated across the screen. When the animation is run, the character dances and moves across the screen at the same time.

Any Drawable subclass that supports the inflate() method can be used to create an animation. An animated element can be defined in XML and instantiated in an application's source code. If a Drawable animation uses properties that will change during the runtime of the application, these values can be initialized once the object is instantiated.

Transition animations are introduced in Chapter 3. Consider the following XML definition for a transition. The XML file, saved as res/drawable /open_close.xml, contains two Drawables defined in the <item> tag, image_open, and image_close. Once instantiated, this container of nested Drawables can be set as the content of an ImageView. Frame-by-frame animations and film loops can be built in a similar fashion.

```
1  <?xml version="1.0" encoding="utf-8"?>
2
3  <transition xmlns:android="http://schemas.android.com/apk/res/android">
4      <item android:drawable="@drawable/image_open"></item>
5      <item android:drawable="@drawable/image_close"></item>
6  </transition>
```

Animations in Android are Drawable animations. They require a set of drawable items, such as the items used in the above transition example, res/drawable/ open_close.xml.

A frame-by-frame animation is prepared as a series of timeline frames to be displayed in an ordered sequence with a time delay. Frame and film loop animations fall under the category of `View` animations because the ordered sequence of images appears within an `ImageView`.

To understand Drawable animation, consider the simple Dance application shown in Figure 5-19. When the application is launched for the first time, a still image of a cartoon character appears on the screen. Below the character is a button that can activate the frame-by-frame animation. The animation relies on a sequence of dance moves that form a complete dance when it is displayed as a running loop.

▌ FIGURE 5-19 Animation that begins with an `onClick` event.

The sequence of images comprising the dance moves are placed into the application's drawables folders. The bitmap images shown in Figure 5-20 were used to create the Dance animation. When giving images file names, consider using a numeric indicator for the order in which they will appear.

A Drawable animation relies on an ordered list specifying how the images will appear; this ordered list is defined as an XML file. The duration of an individual image on the screen is also specified in this animation resource file. For example, in the animation resource XML code below, the root element is `<animation-list>`. This root element is a container for a set of eight images that constitutes a dancing film loop. Each prebuilt image is located in the drawable directory, such as `drawable/dancer1`. The duration value for a frame image is an integer value (100 milliseconds) that indicates how long the item appears on the screen before it is replaced by the next image in the sequence.

The XML code for a Drawable dancing animation, `res/anim/dance_animation.xml`, appears as follows. The `res/anim` directory is created specifically for Drawable animations.

```
1   <animation-list
2   xmlns:android="http://schemas.android.com/apk/res/android"
3       android:oneshot="false" >
4
5       <item
6           android:drawable="@drawable/dancer1"
7           android:duration="100"/>
8       <item
9           android:drawable="@drawable/dancer2"
10          android:duration="100"/>
11      <item
12          android:drawable="@drawable/dancer3"
13          android:duration="100"/>
14      <item
15          android:drawable="@drawable/dancer4"
16          android:duration="100"/>
17      <item
18          android:drawable="@drawable/dancer5"
19          android:duration="100"/>
20      <item
21          android:drawable="@drawable/dancer6"
22          android:duration="100"/>
23      <item
24          android:drawable="@drawable/dancer7"
25          android:duration="100"/>
26      <item
27          android:drawable="@drawable/dancer8"
28          android:duration="100"/>
29
30  </animation-list>
```

An `ImageView` is the container used for holding the animation element. In the following code segment, an ImageView, `dancerView`, is referenced from the main activity layout.

Lines 4–5:   The Drawable animation `res/anim/dance_animation` `.xml` is set as the background resource for the `dancerView`. A Drawable object is then created, based on this background.

Line 7:   The animation is started.

```
1   ImageView dancerView = (ImageView) findViewById(R.id.imageView1);
2
3   dancerView.setBackgroundResource(R.drawable.dance_animation);
4   AnimationDrawable danceAnimation = (AnimationDrawable)
5       dancerView.getBackground();
6
7   danceAnimation.start();
```

dancer1.png   dancer2 .png   dancer3.png   dancer4 png

dancer5.png   dancer6.png   dancer7.png   dancer8.png

❘ FIGURE 5-20 Bitmap images, numbered sequentially, create the Dance animation.

Film loops and frame-by-frame animations are suited only to cases where you have either already created the frame images or you plan to implement them as drawables. For more detailed control over animations, property or tween animations are best. These types of animations, both of which are more complex, are discussed in Chapter 6.

In many cases, an animation is intended to enhance interaction with UI items such as buttons, rather than to be a standalone component. Animations can provide the user with helpful visual cues. These animations should not intrude on a given operation or distract from it.

■ Lab Example 5-4: Animated Maze Chase

In this lab, we explore the use of a frame-by-frame animation that is programmatically added to the main activity layout. In addition, the main activity layout includes a drawn canvas. Interactions for this application feature both of these elements. Maze Chase is not a complete game in which a user competes against an opponent; instead, this is a lab exercise that examines how to combine a drawing algorithm with animation and interactivity.

Part 1: The Design

The user who launches the application is presented with a graphic image of a "perfect" maze. A different maze is generated each time the application launches. A perfect maze is one in which exactly one path exists between any two given cells, such as the one shown in the application screenshot in Figure 5-21.

A film loop animation of a pig is positioned in a maze cell. The pig is animated with nuanced facial movements. The control buttons are provided to move the pig up, down, left, or right into an open cell. If a cell is walled off, the pig will remain in its cell.

Part 2: Application Structure and Setup

The settings for the Maze Chase application are as follows:

- Application Name: Maze Chase
- Project Name: MazeChase
- Package Name: `com.cornez.mazechase`
- Android Form: Phone and Tablet
- Minimum SDK: API 18: Android 4.3 (Jelly Bean)
- Target SDK: API 21: Android 5.0 (Lollipop)
- Compile with: API 21: Android 5.0 (Lollipop)
- Activity Name: `MyActivity`
- Layout Name: `activity_my`

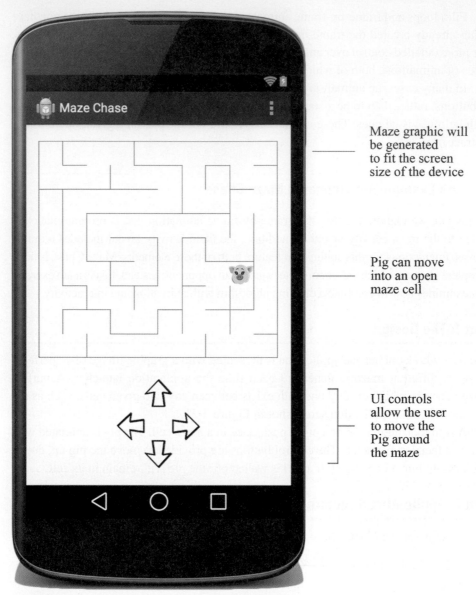

FIGURE 5-21 An animated pig moves in a "perfect" maze.

The icon launcher for the application is set to Android's default ic_ launcher.png file. Seven additional bitmap files, used for the pig animation and the control buttons, are added to the drawable folders. Figure 5-22 shows the final project structure for the Maze Chase application. This application is driven by a single activity, MyActivity. The layout associated with MyActivity is activity_my.xml. Additional files are used for a drawing canvas, animation, and the data model for a maze cell.

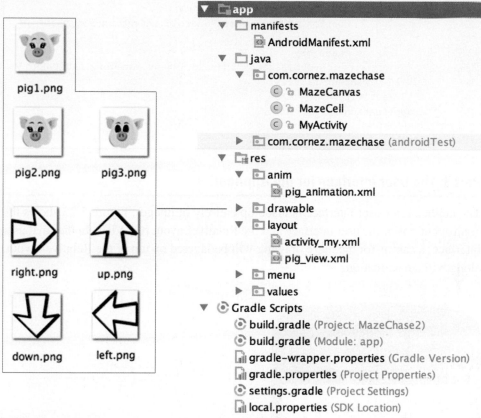

▌ FIGURE 5-22 Project structure for the Maze Chase application.

The orientation of the screen is locked into portrait mode and the main activity is set to `MyActivity`. The XML code listing for `AndroidManifest.xml` appears as follows:

```
AndroidManifest.xml
1   <?xml version="1.0" encoding="utf-8"?>
2   <manifest xmlns:android="http://schemas.android.com/apk/res/android"
3       package="com.cornez.mazechase" >
4
5       <application
6           android:allowBackup="true"
7           android:icon="@drawable/ic_launcher"
8           android:label="@string/app_name"
9           android:theme="@style/AppTheme" >
10          <activity
11              android:name=".MyActivity"
12              android:screenOrientation="portrait"
13              android:label="@string/app_name" >
```

```
14                <intent-filter>
15                    <action android:name="android.intent.action.MAIN" />
16
17                    <category
18                        android:name="android.intent.category.LAUNCHER" />
19                </intent-filter>
20            </activity>
21        </application>
22
23    </manifest>
```

Part 3: The User Interface for the Application

The application's user interface is made up entirely of images. Figure 5-23 shows the control buttons of the user interface and the RelativeLayout root View. In the final user interface, a canvas for the maze drawing will be layered on top of the RelativeLayout, along with an animation.

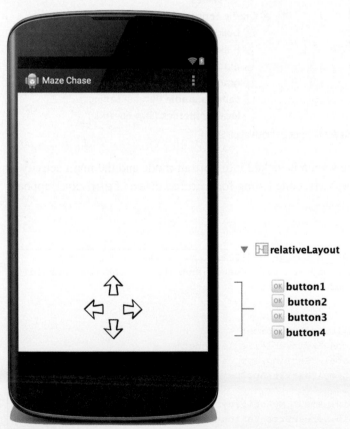

FIGURE 5-23 The activity_my.xml layout structure.

Given that the user interface consists of graphics and an animation, it appears that text strings will not be needed. Nevertheless, a well-constructed graphical application requires content descriptions for the image elements, such as the control buttons and the animated pig that moves around the maze. The XML code for `strings.xml` includes the descriptions for the graphic component.

```
strings.xml
1   <?xml version="1.0" encoding="utf-8"?>
2   <resources>
3
4       <string name="app_name">Maze Chase</string>
5       <string name="hello_world">Hello world!</string>
6       <string name="action_settings">Settings</string>
7
8       <string name="up_button">Up button</string>
9       <string name="down_button">Down button</string>
10      <string name="left_button">Left button</string>
11      <string name="right_button">Right button</string>
12      <string name="pig">Pig</string>
13
14  </resources>
```

The file that provides the layout elements for `MyActivity` is `activity _my.xml`. It contains a `RelativeLayout` root element. Its view hierarchical structure is shown in Figure 5-23. The XML code for this layout is shown below. `onClick` event handlers have been identified for each of the control buttons. An id has been applied to the root element, `@+id/relativeLayout`, which will be used by `MyActivity.java` to add a canvas layer for drawing a perfect maze.

```
activity_my.xml
1   <RelativeLayout
2   xmlns:android="http://schemas.android.com/apk/res/android"
3       xmlns:tools="http://schemas.android.com/tools"
4       android:layout_width="match_parent"
5       android:layout_height="match_parent"
6
7       android:id="@+id/relativeLayout"
8       tools:context=".MyActivity">
9
10      <Button
11          android:id="@+id/button1"
12          style="?android:attr/buttonStyleSmall"
13          android:layout_width="40dp"
14          android:layout_height="40dp"
15          android:layout_alignParentBottom="true"
16          android:layout_centerHorizontal="true"
```

```
17          android:layout_marginBottom="113dp"
18          android:background="@drawable/up"
19          android:onClick="goUp" />
20
21      <Button
22          android:id="@+id/button2"
23          style="?android:attr/buttonStyleSmall"
24          android:layout_width="40dp"
25          android:layout_height="40dp"
26          android:layout_alignTop="@+id/button1"
27          android:layout_marginTop="48dp"
28          android:layout_toLeftOf="@+id/button1"
29          android:background="@drawable/left"
30          android:onClick="goLeft" />
31
32      <Button
33          android:id="@+id/button3"
34          style="?android:attr/buttonStyleSmall"
35          android:layout_width="40dp"
36          android:layout_height="40dp"
37          android:layout_alignTop="@+id/button2"
38          android:layout_toRightOf="@+id/button1"
39          android:background="@drawable/right"
40          android:onClick="goRight" />
41
42      <Button
43          android:id="@+id/button4"
44          style="?android:attr/buttonStyleSmall"
45          android:layout_width="40dp"
46          android:layout_height="40dp"
47          android:layout_below="@+id/button2"
48          android:layout_centerHorizontal="true"
49          android:background="@drawable/down"
50          android:onClick="goDown" />
51
52
53  </RelativeLayout>
```

Part 4: Animation Resources

The animated component, the pig, takes the form of a film loop. The pig appears as an idle animation; it does not perform an action. The idle animation, featuring wiggling ears and blinking eyes, is constructed using three bitmap images. The bitmap images shown in Figure 5-24 contain very nuanced changes, but when they are placed as frames in a film loop, the character becomes vibrant. Small changes such as these can have an enormous impact in a game application.

The bitmap images shown in Figure 5-24 are all PNG files. A small border around each image has been left bare, making that portion of the image transparent. This allows the lines in the maze to show through when the pig is placed in a cell that is the same size as the pig.

Ear wiggles   **Eyes blink**

❚ FIGURE 5-24 Bitmaps representing frames in the pig animation.

The frame-by-frame animation is defined in XML. Each bitmap image is placed in a particular order in an animation list container, specifically the `<animation-list>`. The `duration` attribute is used to set the frame rate. For example, each pig image is displayed on the screen for the duration of 200 milliseconds. The XML code for `pig_animation.xml` is shown as follows. This file will be placed in `res/anim`.

pig_animation.xml

```
1   <?xml version="1.0" encoding="utf-8"?>
2
3   <animation-list
4   xmlns:android="http://schemas.android.com/apk/res/android"
5       android:oneshot="false">
6
7       <item
8           android:drawable="@drawable/pig1"
9           android:duration="200" />
10      <item
11          android:drawable="@drawable/pig2"
12          android:duration="200" />
13      <item
14          android:drawable="@drawable/pig3"
15          android:duration="200" />
16
17  </animation-list>
```

Part 5: The Animated Film Loop

The <animation-list> in pig_animation.xml is used to define the frame structure of the animation. To create the actual film loop, an ImageView is used to hold the frame-by-frame structure. The film loop for the pig animation is stored as an independent XML file within res/layout. This file, named pig_view.xml, is structured as shown in Figure 5-25.

I FIGURE 5-25 The pig_view.xml layout file contains an ImageView.

As a container for the pig animation, pig_view.xml requires an ImageView as its root element. For this lab exercise, the XML code does not assign an image source, leaving the View empty, as shown in Figure 5-25. An identifier value, @id/pig, will be used to access this View from the Java source code, which will assign it the animation. The XML code for pig_view.xml is listed as follows:

```
pig_view.xml
1  <?xml version="1.0" encoding="utf-8"?>
2  <ImageView xmlns:android="http://schemas.android.com/apk/res/android"
3      android:layout_width="match_parent"
4      android:layout_height="match_parent"
5      android:id="@+id/pig" >
6
7  </ImageView>
```

Part 6: Source Code for Application

`MyActivity.java` drives the application.

Line 5:	`AnimationDrawable` is a `Drawable` container. This class allows the code to instantiate a frame-by-frame animation.
Line 17:	`pig` is the `ImageView` that stores the animated film loop of the pig.
Lines 19–20:	The (x, y) location of the pig element on the screen is stored in `xPos` and `yPos`. For simplicity, the location is defined in `MyActivity`, rather than in a separate class.
Line 21:	`maze` is a canvas for drawing, as well as the data that are used to render the drawing. The data are used to determine whethr or not the pig is allowed to move into an adjacent cell.
Lines 23, 31:	Each cell in the maze can be uniquely identified by a number. The pig can be tracked by its `cellId`, which is initialized to 22: the 11th column in the 11th row.
Lines 34–38:	A perfect maze is drawn on a canvas, which is then added to the `RelativeLayout`.
Lines 40–42:	Prior to placing an existing ImageView onto the RelativeLayout, a `LayoutInflater` must be instantiated to perform the work.
Lines 44–47:	An instance of the pig film loop animation is inflated. This object's background is set to the pig frame-by-frame animation.
Lines 50–52:	An `AnimationDrawable` object is used to create the frame-by-frame animations that have been defined by the series of pig Drawable objects, which was set as the View object's background. The film loop animation is started.
Lines 54–58:	The film loop is running, but the user cannot see it because it has not yet been added to the screen. The position and scale of the pig ImageView are set, and the view is added to the RelativeLayout at index 1. By adding the ImageView at index 1, it will be layered above the drawing canvas containing the maze and the controls.

```
MyActivity.java
1   package com.cornez.mazechase;
2
3   import android.app.Activity;
4   import android.content.Context;
5   import android.graphics.drawable.AnimationDrawable;
6   import android.os.Bundle;
7   import android.view.LayoutInflater;
8   import android.view.Menu;
9   import android.view.MenuItem;
```

```
10   import android.view.View;
11   import android.widget.ImageView;
12   import android.widget.RelativeLayout;
13
14
15   public class MyActivity extends Activity {
16       private RelativeLayout relativeLayout;
17       private ImageView pig;
18       private LayoutInflater layoutInflater;
19       private float xPos;
20       private float yPos;
21       private MazeCanvas maze;
22
23       private int cellId;
24
25       @Override
26       protected void onCreate(Bundle savedInstanceState) {
27           super.onCreate(savedInstanceState);
28           setContentView(R.layout.activity_my);
29           xPos = 10;
30           yPos = 10;
31           cellId = 22;
32
33
34           // CONSTRUCT THE MAZE AND ADD IT TO THE RELATIVE LAYOUT
35           maze = new MazeCanvas(this);
36           relativeLayout = (RelativeLayout)
37                   findViewById(R.id.relativeLayout);
38           relativeLayout.addView(maze, 0);
39
40           // CREATE A LAYOUT INFLATER
41           layoutInflater = (LayoutInflater)
42                   getSystemService(Context.LAYOUT_INFLATER_SERVICE);
43
44           // SET THE BACKGROUND OF THE IMAGEVIEW TO THE PIG ANIMATION
45           pig = (ImageView) layoutInflater.inflate(
46                   R.layout.pig_view, null);
47           pig.setBackgroundResource(R.anim.pig_animation);
48
49           // CREATE AN ANIMATION DRAWABLE OBJECT BASED ON THIS BACKGROUND
50           AnimationDrawable pigAnimate = (AnimationDrawable)
51                   pig.getBackground();
52           pigAnimate.start();
53
54           pig.setX(xPos);
55           pig.setY(yPos);
56           pig.setScaleX(.15f);
57           pig.setScaleY(.15f);
58           relativeLayout.addView(pig, 1);
59
60       }
```

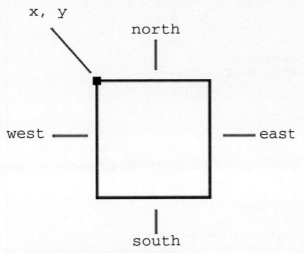

I FIGURE 5-26 The model for a `MazeCell` object.

The user moves the pig, using the arrow buttons provided by the user interface. The maze structure controls the pig's movement within the maze; in particular; the attributes of the maze cells control the movement. Four walls, as shown in Figure 5-26, characterize a maze cell: north, south, east, and west. If an adjacent wall to the pig is open, the pig may enter the cell. Lines 61–91 of `MyActivity.java` are the implementation of the `onClick` handlers that control the pig's movement into a given cell.

```
MyActivity.java (continued)
61   public void goUp(View view) {
62           if (maze.board[cellId].north == false){
63               yPos -= 100;
64               pig.setY(yPos);
65               cellId -= maze.COLS;
66           }
67       }
68
69       public void goLeft(View view) {
70           if (maze.board[cellId].west == false){
71               xPos -= 100;
72               pig.setX(xPos);
73               cellId--;
74           }
75       }
76
77       public void goRight(View view) {
78           if (maze.board[cellId].east == false){
79               xPos += 100;
80               pig.setX(xPos);
81               cellId++;
```

```
82                    }
83              }
84
85          public void goDown(View view) {
86              if (maze.board[cellId].south == false){
87                  yPos += 100;
88                  pig.setY(yPos);
89                  cellId += maze.COLS;
90              }
91          }
92
93
94          @Override
95          public boolean onCreateOptionsMenu(Menu menu) {
96              // Inflate the menu.
97              getMenuInflater().inflate(R.menu.my, menu);
98              return true;
99          }
100
101         @Override
102         public boolean onOptionsItemSelected(MenuItem item) {
103             // Handle action bar item clicks here. The action bar will
104             // automatically handle clicks on the Home/Up button, so long
105             // as you specify a parent activity in AndroidManifest.xml.
106             int id = item.getItemId();
107             if (id == R.id.action_settings) {
108                 return true;
109             }
110             return super.onOptionsItemSelected(item);
111         }
112 }
```

The definition of the maze cell is represented by the `MazeCell.java` class. The Java code for this class is as follows. All the cell data members have been made public for quick and simple access.

MazeCell.java

```
1    package com.cornez.mazechase;
2    public class MazeCell {
3        public int x;
4        public int y;
5        public int id;
6        public boolean visited;
7        public boolean north;
8        public boolean south;
9        public boolean east;
10       public boolean west;
11
```

```
12      //NEW CELLS ARE INSTANTIATED WITH ALL WALLS INTACT
13      public MazeCell (int xPos, int yPos, int cellId){
14          x = xPos;
15          y = yPos;
16          visited = false;
17          north = true;
18          south = true;
19          east = true;
20          west = true;
21      }
22  }
```

Part 7: Constructing a Perfect Maze

In computer science terms, a perfect maze is characterized as a minimal spanning tree over a set of cells. The task of carving out a path from one cell to the next is based on the concept of a depth-first-search, which uses a stack data structure.

Creating a perfect maze involves building the maze cell by cell while making sure that no loops exist and that no cell ends up isolated.

Lines 27–79:   The maze for this application will be instantiated from the MazeCanvas class. Each maze cell will be drawn row by row.

Lines 81–161:   The backtracker() method belongs to a class of algorithms that share a common operational goal:

1. Begin with an array of maze cells with all of the walls intact.

2. Choose a starting cell.

3. Repeatedly select a random adjacent cell in the maze—one that has been unvisited—and open the wall between the two. Continue to do this until every cell has been visited and a wall has been eliminated during the visit.

The resulting maze contains no circular paths; every cell is connected to every other cell by exactly one path. The backtracker() method uses an iterative loop and a stack to carve out its paths.

The process of creating a perfect maze, such as the one shown in Figure 5-21, is done in stages. In Stage 1, the maze is built containing a two-dimensional array representing the maze cells. As shown in the first image of Figure 5-27, all the walls are initially intact. An empty stack is also constructed. The stack will be used to ensure that no loops exist in the path and that no cells end up isolated.

Stage 1 is the beginning of the backtracker procedure. The starting cell, 0, is selected and placed on the stack. Cell 0 cannot be visited again. At each stage in the process, a random, unvisited cell is chosen from the possible adjacent cells. Once the cell has been selected, it is tagged as visited, pushed onto the stack, and its adjacent wall is eliminated.

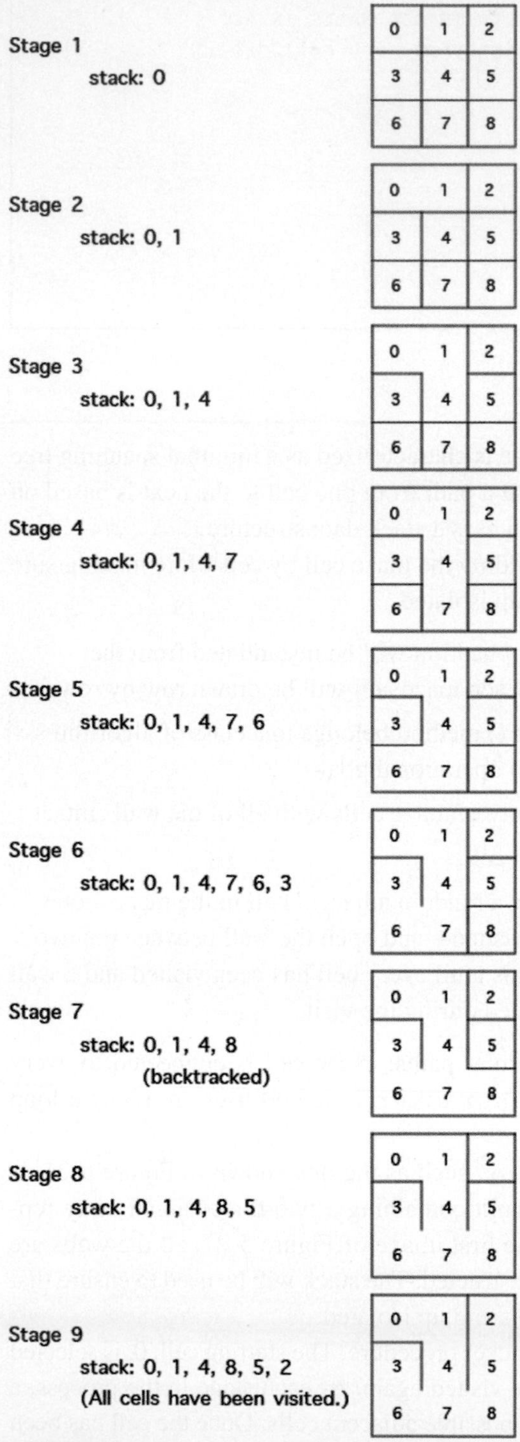

Stage 1
    stack: 0

Stage 2
    stack: 0, 1

Stage 3
    stack: 0, 1, 4

Stage 4
    stack: 0, 1, 4, 7

Stage 5
    stack: 0, 1, 4, 7, 6

Stage 6
    stack: 0, 1, 4, 7, 6, 3

Stage 7
    stack: 0, 1, 4, 8
       (backtracked)

Stage 8
    stack: 0, 1, 4, 8, 5

Stage 9
    stack: 0, 1, 4, 8, 5, 2
   (All cells have been visited.)

❘ FIGURE 5-27

In Stage 7, no unvisited cells are adjacent to cell 3. At this point, the stack is used for backtracking to a cell that has unvisited neighbors. Finally, at Stage 9, the process is complete once all the cells have been visited.

MazeCanvas.java

```java
1   package com.cornez.mazechase;
2
3   import android.content.Context;
4   import android.graphics.Canvas;
5   import android.graphics.Color;
6   import android.graphics.Paint;
7   import android.view.View;
8
9   import java.util.Stack;
10
11  public class MazeCanvas extends View {
12
13      //MAZE DIMENSIONS
14      public final int COLS = 10;
15      public final int ROWS = 9;
16      final int N_CELLS = COLS * ROWS;
17      final int SIZE = 100;
18      final int OFFSET = 100;
19
20
21      //ARRAY OF MAZE CELLS
22      public MazeCell [] board;
23
24      private Paint paint;
25
26
27      public MazeCanvas (Context context){
28
29          super(context);
30
31          //TASK 1: DECLARE A MAZE ARRAY OF SIZE N_CELLS TO HOLD THE CELLS
32          board = new MazeCell[N_CELLS];
33
34          //TASK 2: INSTANTIATE CELL OBJECTS FOR EACH CELL IN THE MAZE
35          int cellId = 0;
36          for (int r = 0; r < ROWS; r++){
37              for (int c = 0; c < COLS; c++){
38                  //STEP 1: GENERATE A MAZE CELL WITH THE X, Y AND CELL ID
39                  int x = c * SIZE + OFFSET;
40                  int y = r * SIZE + OFFSET;
41                  MazeCell cell = new MazeCell(x, y, cellId);
42
43                  //STEP 2: PLACE THE CELL IN THE MAZE
44                  board[cellId] = cell;
```

```
45                        cellId++;
46                  }
47            }
48
49            //TASK 3: SET THE PAINT FOR THE MAZE
50            paint = new Paint();
51            paint.setColor(Color.BLACK);
52            paint.setStrokeWidth(2.0f);
53
54            //TASK 4: USE A BACKTRACKER METHOD TO BREAK DOWN THE WALLS
55            backtrackMaze();
56      }
57
58
59
60      public void onDraw(Canvas canvas){
61            //TASK 1: FILL THE CANVAS WITH WHITE PAINT
62            canvas.drawRGB(255,  255,  255);
63
64            //TASK 2: DRAW THE LINES FOR EVERY CELL
65            for (int i = 0; i < N_CELLS; i++){
66                  int x = board[i].x;
67                  int y = board[i].y;
68
69                  if (board[i].north)
70                        canvas.drawLine(x,  y, x+SIZE, y, paint);
71                  if (board[i].south)
72                        canvas.drawLine(x,  y+SIZE, x+SIZE, y+SIZE, paint);
73                  if (board[i].east)
74                        canvas.drawLine(x+SIZE,  y, x+SIZE, y+SIZE, paint);
75                  if (board[i].west)
76                        canvas.drawLine(x,  y, x, y+SIZE, paint);
77            }
78
79      }
80
81      public void backtrackMaze() {
82            // TASK 1: CREATE THE BACKTRACKER VARIABLES AND INITIALIZE THEM
83            Stack<Integer> stack = new Stack<Integer>();
84            int top;
85
86            // TASK 2: VISIT THE FIRST CELL AND PUSH IT ONTO THE STACK
87            int visitedCells = 1; // COUNTS HOW MANY CELLS HAVE BEEN VISITED
88            int cellID = 0; // THE FIRST CELL IN THE MAZE
89            board[cellID].visited = true;
90            stack.push(cellID);
91
92            // TASK 3: BACKTRACK UNTIL ALL THE CELLS HAVE BEEN VISITED
93            while (visitedCells < N_CELLS) {
94                  //STEP 1: WHICH WALLS CAN BE TAKEN DOWN FOR A GIVEN CELL?
```

```
95              String possibleWalls = "";
96              if (board[cellID].north == true && cellID >= COLS) {
97                  if (!board[cellID - COLS].visited) {
98                      possibleWalls += "N";
99                  }
100             }
101             if (board[cellID].west == true && cellID % COLS != 0) {
102                 if (!board[cellID - 1].visited) {
103                     possibleWalls += "W";
104                 }
105             }
106             if (board[cellID].east == true &&
107                 cellID % COLS != COLS - 1) {
108                 if (!board[cellID + 1].visited) {
109                     possibleWalls += "E";
110                 }
111             }
112             if (board[cellID].south == true &&
113                 cellID < COLS * ROWS - COLS) {
114                 if (!board[cellID + COLS].visited) {
115                     possibleWalls += "S";
116                 }
117             }
118
119             //STEP 2: RANDOMLY SELECT A RANDOM WALL
120             //        FROM AVAILABLE WALLS
121             if (possibleWalls.length() > 0) {
122                 int index = Math.round((int)(Math.random()
123                     *possibleWalls.length()));
124                 char randomWall = possibleWalls.charAt(index);
125
126                 switch (randomWall) {
127                     case 'N':
128                         board[cellID].north = false;
129                         board[cellID - COLS].south = false;
130                         cellID -= COLS;
131                         break;
132                     case 'S':
133                         board[cellID].south = false;
134                         board[cellID + COLS].north = false;
135                         cellID += COLS;
136                         break;
137                     case 'E':
138                         board[cellID].east = false;
139                         board[cellID + 1].west = false;
140                         cellID++;
141                         break;
142                     case 'W':
143                         board[cellID].west = false;
144                         board[cellID - 1].east = false;
```

```
145                    cellID--;
146                }
147                board[cellID].visited = true;
148                stack.push(cellID);
149                visitedCells++;
150
151            }
152            //IF THERE ARE NO WALLS TO BUST DOWN,
153            //BACKTRACK BY GRABBING THE TOP OF THE STACK
154            else {
155                top = stack.pop();
156                if (top == cellID){
157                    cellID = stack.pop();
158                    stack.push(cellID);
159                }
160            }
161        }
162
163    }
164 }
```

■ 5.6 Animate Library

Beginning with KitKat, Android 4.4, the transitions framework allows the definition of scene animations. These are typically view hierarchies that describe how to animate or custom transform a scene based on specific properties, such as layout bounds, or visibility. There is also an abstraction for an animation that can be applied to Views, Surfaces, or other objects.

To generate simple tweened animations, Android provides a packaged called android.view.animation. The following are a collection of classes that support basic animations:

AlphaAnimation:	Animates the changing transparency of an object
RotateAnimation:	Rotates animation of an object
ScaleAnimation:	Animates the scaling of an object
TranslateAnimation:	Moves an object

Unlike frame-by-frame animations, these classes control the specific `View` property of an object on display on the screen. The four standard animation attributes used when generating tweens are as follows:

1. `android:startOffset`: The start time (in milliseconds) of a transformation, where 0 is the start time of the root animation set.

2. `android:duration`:   The duration (in milliseconds) of a transformation.

3. `android:fillafter:`   Whether you want the transformation you apply to continue after the duration of the transformation has expired. If false, the original value will immediately be applied when the transformation is done. Suppose, for example, you want to make a dot move down and then right in an "L" shape. If this value is not true, at the end of the down motion, the text box will immediately jump back to the top before moving right.

4. `android:fillBefore:`   True if you want this transformation to be applied at time zero, regardless of your start time value (you will probably never need this).

Consider the following segment of code. This code assumes that an `ImageView` named `imageView` has been inflated and placed within the layout for the running activity. The animation, `alpha`, controls the transparency of `imageView` so that it animates from full view to complete transparency. `setFillAfter()` is used to apply the transformation after the animation ends. If `setfillAfter()` is passed a true argument, the final transformation will persist once the animation is completed.

```
1   AlphaAnimation alpha = new AlphaAnimation(1.0f, 0.0f);
2   alpha.setDuration(3000);
3   alpha.setFillAfter(true);
4   imageView.startAnimation(alpha);
```

In the case of rotation, movement will take place in the *X-Y* plane. The center point of rotation can be specified as an *x*, *y* coordinate, where (0, 0) is the top left point. When not specified, the default point of rotation is set as (0, 0). The following segment of code rotates the `imageView` from a starting point of 0 degrees and an ending point of 90 degrees. Line 11 sets the acceleration curve for the animation, which defaults to a linear interpolation.

```
1    RotateAnimation mRotate = new RotateAnimation(
2        0,
3        90,
4        Animation.RELATIVE_TO_SELF,
5        0.5f,
6        Animation.RELATIVE_TO_SELF,
7        0.5f);
8    mRotate.setDuration(200);
9    mRotate.setFillAfter(true);
10
11   mRotate.setInterpolator(new AccelerateInterpolator());
12
13   imageView.startAnimation(mRotate);
```

■ Lab Example 5-5: Gears Churning Basic Rotating Animation

The Android `android.view.animation` package provides classes that handle tween animations. This lab example explores the creation of a simple animation that involves a tweened element, such as rotation. A tween animation can perform a series of simple transformations in regard to position, size, rotation, and so on.

Part 1: The Design

The Gear Churn application contains graphics, specifically two gears, that are animated. When the user taps the button labeled "Rotate Gears," the wheels of the gears slowly churn, as shown in Figure 5-28. Tween settings are applied so that the gears move in sync: The smallest gear rotates clockwise while the larger gear rotates counterclockwise. The tween performs the animation with a starting point and an ending point, so that the rotations are not performed continuously and eventually come to an end.

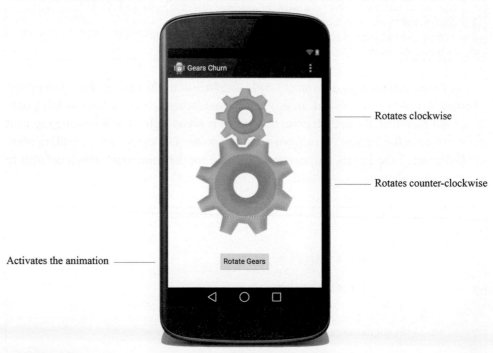

Rotates clockwise

Rotates counter-clockwise

Activates the animation

▌ FIGURE 5-28

Part 2: Application Structure and Setup

The settings for the application are as follows:

- Application Name: Gears Churn
- Project Name: GearsChurn
- Package Name: `com.cornez.gearschurn`
- Android Form: Phone and Tablet
- Minimum SDK: API 18: Android 4.3 (Jelly Bean)
- Target SDK: API 21: Android 5.0 (Lollipop)
- Compile with: API 21: Android 5.0 (Lollipop)
- Activity Name: `MyActivity`
- Layout Name: `activity_my`

The `AndroidManifest.xml` file sets the launch icon to the Android default `ic-launcher.png` file. The main activity of the application is `MyActivity` and its associated user interface is `activity_my.xml`.

AndroidManifest.xml

```
1   <?xml version="1.0" encoding="utf-8"?>
2   <manifest xmlns:android="http://schemas.android.com/apk/res/android"
3       package="com.cornez.gearschurn" >
4
5       <application
6           android:allowBackup="true"
7           android:icon="@drawable/ic_launcher"
8           android:label="@string/app_name"
9           android:theme="@style/AppTheme" >
10          <activity
11              android:name=".MyActivity"
12              android:screenOrientation="portrait"
13              android:label="@string/app_name" >
14              <intent-filter>
15                  <action android:name="android.intent.action.MAIN" />
16
17                  <category
18                      android:name="android.intent.category.LAUNCHER" />
19              </intent-filter>
20          </activity>
21      </application>
22
23  </manifest>
24
```

Two bitmap images, `gear1.png` and `gear2.png`, are added to the `Drawables` directory. The final project structure for this application appears in Figure 5-29. `Gear` class will be used as the data model for each gear.

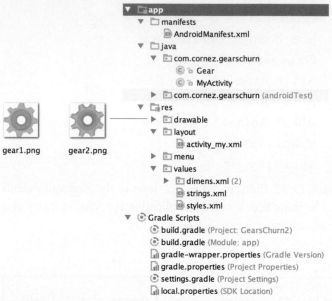

FIGURE 5-29 The Project Structure of the Gears Churn application.

Part 3: The User Interface

The user interface relies on strings.xml and the two drawable images: gear1 and gear2. Figure 5-30 shows the hierarchical `View` structure of the graphic elements and the button, which constitute the application's layout design. The added string values are used for image descriptions and the button label that appears on the screen. The XML code for `strings.xml` appears as follows:

```
strings.xml
1   <?xml version="1.0" encoding="utf-8"?>
2   <resources>
3
4       <string name="app_name">Gears Churn</string>
5       <string name="hello_world">Hello world!</string>
6       <string name="action_settings">Settings</string>
7
8       <string name="gear_large">Large gear</string>
9       <string name="gear_small">Small gear</string>
10      <string name="rotate_btn">Rotate Gears</string>
11
12  </resources>
```

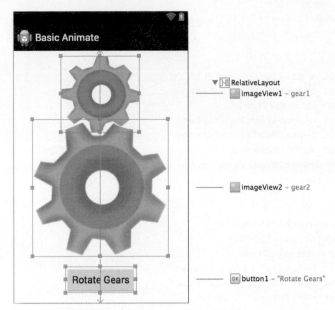

FIGURE 5-30 The layout design for `activity_my.xml`.

The layout design for `activity_my.xml` requires strict adherence to the placement of the gears. The teeth of the gears must fit together to provide an animation that appears to churn at the correct angles. The first gear is placed 10dps from the top of the screen. The larger gear has a width and height of 250dps and is positioned at −25dps below the smaller gear. This overlap allows the teeth of the smaller gear to fit correctly into the gap provided by the larger gear.

The button View is assigned an event handler named `animateGears()`. The button has been given a unique identifier name; however, this is a convention of RelativeLayouts, rather than a requirement. Nevertheless, the `ImageViews` that hold the gear bitmaps both require identifier names. This will allow `MyActivity.java` to be accessed and for the gears to be customized with an animation. The names that have been generically assigned to the gears are `imageView1` and `imageView2`.

The XML code for `activity_my.xml` appears as follows:

```
activity_my.xml
1   <RelativeLayout
2   xmlns:android="http://schemas.android.com/apk/res/android"
3       xmlns:tools="http://schemas.android.com/tools"
4       android:layout_width="match_parent"
5       android:layout_height="match_parent"
6       android:paddingLeft="@dimen/activity_horizontal_margin"
7       android:paddingRight="@dimen/activity_horizontal_margin"
8       android:paddingTop="@dimen/activity_vertical_margin"
9       android:paddingBottom="@dimen/activity_vertical_margin"
```

```
10        tools:context=".MyActivity">
11
12
13    <ImageView
14        android:layout_width="wrap_content"
15        android:layout_height="wrap_content"
16        android:id="@+id/imageView1"
17        android:layout_alignParentTop="true"
18        android:layout_centerHorizontal="true"
19        android:layout_marginTop="10dp"
20        android:src="@drawable/gear1"
21        android:contentDescription="@string/gear_small" />
22
23    <ImageView
24        android:layout_width="250dp"
25        android:layout_height="250dp"
26        android:id="@+id/imageView2"
27        android:layout_below="@+id/imageView1"
28        android:layout_centerHorizontal="true"
29        android:layout_marginTop="-25dp"
30        android:src="@drawable/gear2"
31        android:contentDescription="@string/gear_large" />
32
33    <Button
34        android:layout_width="wrap_content"
35        android:layout_height="wrap_content"
36        android:text="@string/rotate_btn"
37        android:id="@+id/button"
38        android:layout_below="@+id/imageView2"
39        android:layout_centerHorizontal="true"
40        android:layout_marginTop="38dp"
41        android:onClick="animateGears"/>
42
43
44  </RelativeLayout>
```

Part 4: Source Code for Application

As the class that represents a gear's data, the Gear class has two data members: mStartDegree and mEndDegree. These data members are used to customize the tween animation. For example, an idle gear has an initial starting degree before it begins to rotate. Once the animation begins, the gear rotates until it reaches an end degree, at which point it stops and becomes idle again. The Java code listing for Gear.java appears as follows:

```
Gear.java
1   package com.cornez.gearschurn;
2
3   public class Gear {
4
5       private int mStartDegree;
6       private int mEndDegree;
7
8       public Gear(){
9           mStartDegree = 0;
10          mEndDegree = 0;
11      }
12
13      public void setStartDegree(int startDegree){
14          mStartDegree = startDegree;
15      }
16      public int getStartDegree(){
17          return mStartDegree;
18      }
19      public void setEndDegree(int endDegree){
20          mEndDegree = endDegree;
21      }
22      public int getEndDegree(){
23          return mEndDegree;
24      }
25  }
```

MyActivity.java is the controller of the application, and it is the sole activity. The Java code listing for this source file appears as follows:

Lines 8–9:   The imported Animation class provides the animation behavior that can be applied to the gears. The RotationAnimation class is an extension of Animation. Both classes are required for the rotation tween used in this application.

Lines 15–16:   The two ImageView objects holding the gear bitmaps need to be referenced in order to be animated. The small gear is referenced by gear1Img and the large gear is referenced by gear2Img. The references are assigned on Lines 30 and 31.

Lines 18–19:   Two Gear objects are declared. gear1 and gear2 hold the tween information for the ImageViews named gear1Img and gear2Img, respectively. gear1 and gear2 are instantiated on Lines 38 and 43.

Lines 36–46:   The idle positions for the gears are set. The starting angle is zero for both gears. Because gear1 will move in a clockwise rotation, its ending angle will be 360 degrees. The second gear, gear2, will move counterclockwise, and therefore, its ending angle will be −360 degrees.

```
MyActivity.java
1    package com.cornez.gearschurn;
2
3    import android.app.Activity;
4    import android.os.Bundle;
5    import android.view.Menu;
6    import android.view.MenuItem;
7    import android.view.View;
8    import android.view.animation.Animation;
9    import android.view.animation.RotateAnimation;
10   import android.widget.ImageView;
11
12
13   public class MyActivity extends Activity {
14
15       private ImageView gear1Img;
16       private ImageView gear2Img;
17
18       private Gear gear1;
19       private Gear gear2;
20
21       private float currentDegree;
22       private float degree;
23
24
25       @Override
26       protected void onCreate(Bundle savedInstanceState) {
27           super.onCreate(savedInstanceState);
28           setContentView(R.layout.activity_my);
29
30           gear1Img = (ImageView) findViewById(R.id.imageView1);
31           gear2Img = (ImageView) findViewById(R.id.imageView2);
32
33           initializeGears();
34       }
35
36       private void initializeGears(){
37           //GEAR 1 WILL MOVE IN A CLOCKWISE DIRECTION
38           gear1 = new Gear();
39           gear1.setStartDegree(0);
40           gear1.setEndDegree(360);
41
```

```
42              //GEAR 1 WILL MOVE IN A COUNTER-CLOCKWISE DIRECTION
43              gear2 = new Gear();
44              gear2.setStartDegree(0);
45              gear2.setEndDegree(-360);
46          }
```

Lines 50–56:   RotateAnimation is a tween animation that controls the rotation of an object. This rotation takes place in the *x, y* plane. The parameters for this animation are:

fromDegrees: Rotation offset to apply at the start of the animation.

toDegrees: Rotation offset to apply at the end of the animation.

pivotXType: Specifies how pivotXValue should be interpreted. There are three possible options: (1) Animation.ABSOLUTE, (2) Animation.RELATIVE_TO_SELF, or (3) Animation.RELATIVE_TO_ PARENT.

pivotXValue: The *x* coordinate of the point about which the object is being rotated, specified as an absolute number where 0 is the left edge.

pivotYType: Specifies how pivotYValue should be interpreted.

pivotYValue: The *y* coordinate of the point about which the object is being rotated, specified as an absolute number where 0 is the top edge.

Line 57:   setDuration() sets how long the animation should last. It should be noted that duration cannot be negative.

Line 59:   setFillAfter () set to true. This means the transformation that this animation performs will persist when it is finished.

MyActivity.java (*continued*)

```
47          public void animateGears(View view){
48              final int DELAY = 1000;
49
50              RotateAnimation ra1 = new RotateAnimation(
51                                  gear1.getStartDegree(),
52                                  gear1.getEndDegree(),
53                                  Animation.RELATIVE_TO_SELF,
54                                  0.5f,
```

```
55                              Animation.RELATIVE_TO_SELF,
56                              0.5f);
57          ra1.setDuration(DELAY);
58          ra1.setFillAfter(true);
59          gear1Img.startAnimation(ra1);
60
61          RotateAnimation ra2 = new RotateAnimation(
62                              gear2.getStartDegree(),
63                              gear2.getEndDegree(),
64                              Animation.RELATIVE_TO_SELF,
65                              0.5f,
66                              Animation.RELATIVE_TO_SELF,
67                              0.5f);
68          ra2.setDuration(DELAY);
69          ra2.setFillAfter(true);
70          gear2Img.startAnimation(ra2);
71      }
72
73      @Override
74      public boolean onCreateOptionsMenu(Menu menu) {
75          // Inflate the menu.
76          getMenuInflater().inflate(R.menu.my, menu);
77          return true;
78      }
79
80      @Override
81      public boolean onOptionsItemSelected(MenuItem item) {
82          // Handle action bar item clicks here. The action bar will
83          // automatically handle clicks on the Home/Up button, so long
84          // as you specify a parent activity in AndroidManifest.xml.
85          int id = item.getItemId();
86          if (id == R.id.action_settings) {
87              return true;
88          }
89          return super.onOptionsItemSelected(item);
90      }
91  }
```

■ 5.7 Audio

A basic understanding of audio file formats and conversions is required when developing applications that use audio media. An audio file is characterized by its file format (audio container) and its data format (audio encoding). The data format of an audio file refers to the content and how it has been encoded. For example, WAV is a file format that can contain audio that is encoded in PCM. PCM describes the technique used to

TABLE 5-1 Android supports these common data formats.

AAC	AAC stands for "Advanced Audio Coding," and it was designed to be the successor of MP3. As you would guess, it compresses the original sound, resulting in disk savings but lower quality. The loss of quality is not always noticeable, however, depending on how low you set the bit rate. In practice, AAC usually does better compression than MP3, especially at bit rates below 128kbit/s. The supported file formats for AAC are: 3GPP (.3gp) MPEG-4 (.mp4, .m4a) ADTS MPEG-TS
HE-AAC	HE-AAC is a superset of AAC, where the HE stands for "high efficiency." HE-AAC is optimized for low-bit-rate audio, such as streaming audio. The supported file formats for HE-AAC are the same as AAC.
AMR	AMR stands for "Adaptive Multi-Rate" and is another encoding optimized for speech, featuring very low bit rates. The supported file format for AMR is 3GPP (.3gp).
MP3	The format we all know and love: MP3. MP3 is still a very popular format after all of these years, and it is supported by the iPhone. MP3 supports its own file format.
PCM	This stands for linear "Pulse Code Modulation," and it describes the technique used to convert analog sound data into a digital format, or in simple terms, into uncompressed data. Because the data are uncompressed, PCM is the fastest to play and is the preferred encoding for audio on an Android device when space is not an issue. The supported file format for PCM is WAV.
FLAC	FLAC stands for "Free Lossless Audio Codec." This audio format is similar to MP3, but it is lossless, meaning that audio is compressed in FLAC without any loss in quality. FLAC is nonproprietary and has an open-source reference implementation. FLAC supports its own file format.

convert analog sound data into a digital format. Table 5-1 lists common data formats, or audio encoding, supported by Android.

You can play audio in an Android application in several ways. Android uses two APIs for this purpose: `SoundPool` and `MediaPlayer`.

5.7.1 `SoundPool`

`SoundPool` provides an easy way to play short audio files, which is particularly useful for audio alerts and simple game sounds (such as making a "click" when moving a game piece).

It can repeat sounds and play several sounds simultaneously. Typically, sound files played with SoundPool should not exceed 1 MB.

Examine the following code segment:

Lines 1–4:   A SoundPool object is instantiated using three arguments: (1) maxStreams, the maximum number of simultaneous streams allowed for this SoundPool object; (2) the streamType, specified as AudioManager.STREAM_MUSIC. This is the audio stream type as described in AudioManager. Android supports different audio streams for different purposes. Game applications normally use STREAM_MUSIC; and (3) srcQuality, which specifies the sample-rate converter quality. Currently this has no effect. Zero is used for the default.

Line 6:   The sound R.raw.explosion is loaded. The directory for sound files is res/raw. Note that the extension is dropped. For example, if you want to load a sound from the raw resource file "explosion.mp3," you would specify R.raw.explosion as the resource ID. You cannot have both an explosion.wav and an explosion.mp3 in the res/raw directory. load() returns a nonzero streamID if successful, zero if it fails. The streamID can be used to further control playback.

Lines 8–12:   Attributes for the explosion sound are set. The values for left volume and right volume can range from 0.0 to 1.0, with 1.0 representing the maximum volume. Priority refers to the stream priority. Zero is the lowest priority. The loop attribute refers to how many times the sound will loop. For example, zero means no loop; it will play once and end. A value of −1 forces a forever loop. The last attribute is rate, the playback rate (pitch). By specifying a 1.0, the playback will occur at a normal rate. This value for rate can range from .5 to 2.0. A value of 2.0 means playback twice as fast, and a value of 0.5 means playback at half speed.

Lines 14–19:   The explosion sound, specified by its soundID, is played. Calling play() may cause another sound to stop playing if the maximum number of active streams is exceeded. Otherwise, the sound will be layered over the sound currently playing.

```
1    SoundPool soundPool = new SoundPool(
2            maxStreams,
3            AudioManager.STREAM_MUSIC,
4            0);
5
6    int soundId = soundPool.load(this, R.raw.explosion, 1));
7
```

```
8      float leftVolume = 1;
9      float rightVolume = 1
10     int priority = 1;
11     int loop = 0;
12     float rate = 1.0f;
13
14     soundPool.play(soundId,
15               leftVolume,
16               rightVolume,
17               priority,
18               loop,
19               rate);
```

SoundPool has many advantages. You can play several sounds at once (using a different SoundPool for each sound), and you can play sounds even when your app is in the background. However, SoundPool can be extremely slow for large raw files. If a large sound has not fully loaded, there may be a noticeable delay when it is triggered.

5.7.2 `MediaPlayer`

`MediaPlayer` provides the resources for handling media playback. For example, an application can use `MediaPlayer` to create an interface between the user and a music file. The interface may include playback controls for interacting with playback components and for sending notification as the playback elapses.

For applications that require the retrieval of audio files located on the device, the `ContentResolver` class is used to access these files, the `MediaPlayer` class is used to play audio, and the `MediaController` class is used to control playback. The `MediaPlayer` class can be used to control playback of both audio and video files and streams.

Android supports a variety of common media types, allowing the integration of audio, video, and images into an application. Audio files used with `MediaPlayer` are often stand-alone files in the filesystem, or they arrive from a data stream over a network connection. As in `SoundPool`, audio files can also be stored in the application's resources (raw resources).

The code segment below illustrates how a raw audio resource of an explosion is played using `MediaPlayer`. `mediaController` is a view containing controls for a `MediaPlayer`. Typically this view contains buttons such as "Play/Pause," "Rewind," "Fast Forward," and a progress slider.

MediaController takes care of synchronizing the controls with the state of the `MediaPlayer`. The way to use this class is to instantiate it programatically. The `MediaController` creates a default set of controls and puts them in a floating window. For the control window to appear, a `setAnchorView()` must be specified.

```
1   MediaPlayer mediaPlayer = new MediaPlayer();
2   MediaController mediaController = new MediaController(this);
3
4   mediaController.setMediaPlayer(this);
5   mediaController.setAnchorView(findViewById(R.id.playback_view));
6
7   try {
8     mediaPlayer.setDataSource(R.raw.explosion);
9     mediaPlayer.prepare();
10    mediaPlayer.start();
11  } catch (IOException e) {
12    Log.e(TAG, "Could not open the audio file for playback.", e);
13  }
```

The view that acts as the anchor for the playback control window will disappear if it has been left idle for three seconds. By using an `onTouchEvent()` shown in the following code segment, the playback controls will reappear when the user touches the anchor view.

```
1
2     @Override
3     public boolean onTouchEvent(MotionEvent event) {
4         mediaController.show();
5         return false;
6     }
```

Lab Example 5-6: Simple Jukebox Sound Effects

This lab explores a simple implementation of sound effects, played with the `SoundPool` and `MediaPlayer`. As Figure 5-31 illustrates, `SoundPool` is used to play short sound bursts, such as a brief bell clang or a quick clang on a gong. `MediaPlayer` is used for longer sounds, such as a drum solo.

Part 1: The Design

The Sound Jukebox application contains a collection of sound effects. The users of this application can create sound punctuations to enhance speech. For example, a scary description of an event might be followed by a "spooky cry" sound effect.

Sounds will be preloaded or configured when the application launches for the first time. Sounds using SoundPool can result in very slow loads. Often. a preloaded SoundPool audio will continue to load for a delayed period.

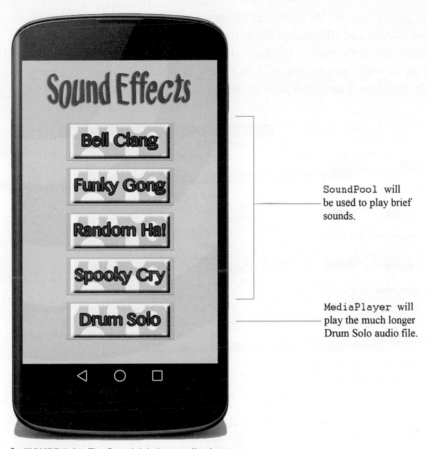

SoundPool will
be used to play brief
sounds.

MediaPlayer will
play the much longer
Drum Solo audio file.

FIGURE 5-31 The Sound Jukebox application.

Part 2: Application Structure and Setup

The settings for the application are as follows:

- Application Name: Sound Jukebox
- Project Name: SoundJukebox
- Package Name: com.cornez.soundjukebox
- Android Form: Phone and Tablet
- Minimum SDK: API 18: Android 4.3 (Jelly Bean)
- Target SDK: API 21: Android 5.0 (Lollipop)
- Compile with: API 21: Android 5.0 (Lollipop)
- Activity Name: MyActivity
- Layout Name: activity_my

The final project structure for the Sound Jukebox application is shown in Figure 5-32. The audio files, WAVs, and MP3 are not Drawables and should not be placed in a drawable folder. A separate directory, res/raw, is used to store all audio files. This directory must be created. During the build process, the `R.java` class automatically stores the generated identifiers for these files. The launch icon for the application is the default Android icon.

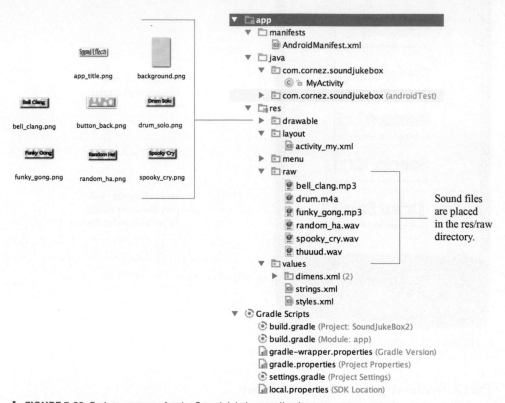

FIGURE 5-32 Project structure for the Sound Jukebox application.

The orientation of the screen is locked into portrait mode, and a fullscreen is used. The code listing for `AndroidManifest.xml` is shown as follows. The main activity of the application is `MyActivity.java`.

```
AndroidManifest.xml
1   <?xml version="1.0" encoding="utf-8"?>
2   <manifest xmlns:android="http://schemas.android.com/apk/res/android"
3       package="com.cornez.soundjukebox" >
4
5       <application
6           android:allowBackup="true"
7           android:icon="@drawable/ic_launcher"
```

```
8             android:label="@string/app_name"
9             android:theme="@android:style/
10                    Theme.Holo.NoActionBar.Fullscreen" >
11        <activity
12            android:name=".MyActivity"
13            android:screenOrientation="portrait"
14            android:label="@string/app_name" >
15            <intent-filter>
16                <action android:name="android.intent.action.MAIN" />
17
18                <category
19                    android:name="android.intent.category.LAUNCHER" />
20            </intent-filter>
21        </activity>
22    </application>
23
24 </manifest>
```

Part 3: Value Resources and the User Interface

The user interface consists of buttons that allow the user to activate a sound effect. For visual interest, `ImageButton` widgets are used for this purpose. `ImageButton` widgets are treated as `ImageViews` in the sense that they should be assigned a content description. `strings.xml`, listed below, stores the content descriptions.

FIGURE 5-33 The user interface for the Sound Jukebox Application.

```
strings.xml
1  <?xml version="1.0" encoding="utf-8"?>
2  <resources>
3
4      <string name="app_name">Sound Jukebox</string>
5      <string name="hello_world">Hello world!</string>
6      <string name="action_settings">Settings</string>
7
8      <!--  SOUND EFFECTS -->
9      <string name="bell_clang">Bell Clang</string>
10     <string name="funky_gong">Funky Gong</string>
11     <string name="random_ha">Random Ha</string>
12     <string name="spooky_cry">Spooky Cry</string>
13     <string name="drum_solo">Drum Solo</string>
14
15 </resources>
```

The layout associated with the application activity is `activity_my.xml`, shown in Figure 5-33. The code listing for this layout is displayed as follows:

```
activity_my.xml
1  <RelativeLayout
2  xmlns:android="http://schemas.android.com/apk/res/android"
3      xmlns:tools="http://schemas.android.com/tools"
4      android:layout_width="match_parent"
5      android:layout_height="match_parent"
6      android:id="@+id/relativeLayout"
7      tools:context=".MyActivity"
8      android:background="@drawable/background">
9
10
11     <ImageView
12         android:layout_width="wrap_content"
13         android:layout_height="wrap_content"
14         android:id="@+id/imageView"
15         android:layout_alignParentTop="true"
16         android:layout_marginTop="20dp"
17         android:layout_centerHorizontal="true"
18         android:src="@drawable/app_title"
19         android:contentDescription="@string/app_name" />
20
21     <ImageButton
22         android:layout_width="wrap_content"
23         android:layout_height="wrap_content"
24         android:id="@+id/imageButton1"
25         android:layout_below="@+id/imageView"
26         android:layout_centerHorizontal="true"
27         android:layout_marginTop="20dp"
28         android:src="@drawable/bell_clang"
```

```
29          android:contentDescription="@string/bell_clang" />
30
31      <ImageButton
32          android:layout_width="wrap_content"
33          android:layout_height="wrap_content"
34          android:id="@+id/imageButton2"
35          android:layout_below="@+id/imageButton1"
36          android:layout_centerHorizontal="true"
37          android:layout_marginTop="5dp"
38          android:src="@drawable/funky_gong"
39          android:contentDescription="@string/funky_gong" />
40
41      <ImageButton
42          android:layout_width="wrap_content"
43          android:layout_height="wrap_content"
44          android:id="@+id/imageButton3"
45          android:layout_below="@+id/imageButton2"
46          android:layout_centerHorizontal="true"
47          android:layout_marginTop="5dp"
48          android:src="@drawable/random_ha"
49          android:contentDescription="@string/random_ha" />
50
51      <ImageButton
52          android:layout_width="wrap_content"
53          android:layout_height="wrap_content"
54          android:id="@+id/imageButton4"
55          android:layout_below="@+id/imageButton3"
56          android:layout_centerHorizontal="true"
57          android:layout_marginTop="5dp"
58          android:src="@drawable/spooky_cry"
59          android:contentDescription="@string/spooky_cry" />
60
61      <ImageButton
62          android:layout_width="wrap_content"
63          android:layout_height="wrap_content"
64          android:id="@+id/imageButton5"
65          android:layout_below="@+id/imageButton4"
66          android:layout_centerHorizontal="true"
67          android:layout_marginTop="5dp"
68          android:src="@drawable/drum_solo"
69          android:contentDescription="@string/drum_solo" />
70  </RelativeLayout>
```

Part 4: Source Code for Application

To simplify the implementation of audio playback, this application uses no data models. An adapter for a scrolling list of data would be implemented to construct Sound Jukebox into a sophisticated application. The code listing for the application's activity, MyActivity.java, is listed as follows. A unique object references each

ImageButton element. An onClick listener event is applied to each button, which triggers the handler `playsoundEffect()`.

Unlike a normal array of integers, there can be gaps in the indices. Therefore, we use `SparseIntArrays` to map integers to integers. `SparseIntArray` is memory efficient because it avoids auto-boxing keys and values, and its data structure does not rely on an extra entry object for each mapping, as compared to HashMap.

The `SparseIntArray` container keeps its mappings in an array data structure, using a binary search to find keys. The implementation is not intended to be appropriate for data structures that may contain large numbers of items. It is generally slower than a traditional `HashMap`, since lookups require a binary search, and adds and removes require inserting and deleting entries in the array. For containers holding up to hundreds of items, the performance difference—less than 50%—is not significant. It is possible to iterate over the items in this container using `keyAt()` and `valueAt()`. Iterating over the keys using `keyAt()` with ascending values of the index returns the keys in ascending order, or the values corresponding to the keys in ascending order in the case of `valueAt()`. On Lines 46–49, `put(int key, int value)` is used to add a mapping from the specified key to the specified sound file.

MyActivity.java

```
1    package com.cornez.soundjukebox;
2
3    import android.app.Activity;
4    import android.media.AudioManager;
5    import android.media.MediaPlayer;
6    import android.media.SoundPool;
7    import android.os.Bundle;
8    import android.util.SparseIntArray;
9    import android.view.Menu;
10   import android.view.MenuItem;
11   import android.view.View;
12   import android.widget.ImageButton;
13   import android.widget.MediaController;
14   import android.widget.RelativeLayout;
15   import android.widget.Toast;
16
17   public class MyActivity extends Activity {
18
19       private ImageButton bellClangBtn;
20       private ImageButton funkyGongBtn;
21       private ImageButton spookyCryBtn;
22       private ImageButton randomHaBtn;
23       private ImageButton drumSoloBtn;
24
25       private SoundPool soundPool;
26       private SparseIntArray soundMap;
27
```

```
28    private MediaPlayer mMediaPlayer;
29    private MediaController mMediaController;
30
31    @Override
32    protected void onCreate(Bundle savedInstanceState) {
33        super.onCreate(savedInstanceState);
34        setContentView(R.layout.activity_my);
35
36        configureSounds();
37        initializeJukeBoxBtns();
38    }
39
40    private void configureSounds() {
41
42        // CONFIGURE THE SOUNDS USE IN THE JUKEBOX
43        // PRE-LOAD THE FIRST FOUR SOUNDS
44        soundPool = new SoundPool(1, AudioManager.STREAM_MUSIC, 0);
45        soundMap - new SparseIntArray(4);
46        soundMap.put(1, soundPool.load(this, R.raw.bell_clang, 1));
47        soundMap.put(2, soundPool.load(this, R.raw.funky_gong, 1));
48        soundMap.put(3, soundPool.load(this, R.raw.spooky_cry, 1));
49        soundMap.put(4, soundPool.load(this, R.raw.random_ha, 1));
50
51        // FIFTH SOUND WILL BE PLAYED IN MEDIA PLAYER
52        mMediaPlayer = MediaPlayer.create(this, R.raw.drum);
53        mMediaController = new MediaController(this);
54        mMediaController.setEnabled(true);
55    }
56
57    private void initializeJukeBoxBtns() {
58        // SET REFERENCES TO THE SOUND EFFECT BUTTONS ON THE LAYOUT
59
60        bellClangBtn = (ImageButton) findViewById(R.id.imageButton1);
61        funkyGongBtn = (ImageButton) findViewById(R.id.imageButton2);
62        spookyCryBtn = (ImageButton) findViewById(R.id.imageButton3);
63        randomHaBtn = (ImageButton) findViewById(R.id.imageButton4);
64        drumSoloBtn = (ImageButton) findViewById(R.id.imageButton5);
65
66        // REGISTER LISTENER EVENTS FOR THE BUTTONS ON THE LAYOUT
67        bellClangBtn.setOnClickListener(playSoundEffect);
68        funkyGongBtn.setOnClickListener(playSoundEffect);
69        spookyCryBtn.setOnClickListener(playSoundEffect);
70        randomHaBtn.setOnClickListener(playSoundEffect);
71        drumSoloBtn.setOnClickListener(playSoundEffect);
72    }
73
74    private View.OnClickListener playSoundEffect = new
75            View.OnClickListener() {
76        public void onClick(View btn) {
77
```

```
78            // IDENTIFY THE SOUND TO BE PLAYED
79            String soundName = (String) btn.getContentDescription();
80
81            // PLAY THE SOUND
82            if (soundName.contentEquals("Bell Clang")) {
83                soundPool.play(1, 1, 1, 1, 0, 1.0f);
84            }
85            else if (soundName.contentEquals("Funky Gong")) {
86                soundPool.play(2, 1, 1, 1, 0, 1.0f);
87            }
88            else if (soundName.contentEquals("Random Ha"))
89                soundPool.play(3, 1, 1, 1, 0, 1.0f);
90            else if (soundName.contentEquals("Spooky Cry"))
91                soundPool.play(4, 1, 1, 1, 0, 1.0f);
92            else if (soundName.contentEquals("Drum Solo")) {
93                mMediaController.show();
94                mMediaPlayer.start();
95            }
96        }
97    };
98
99    @Override
100   public boolean onCreateOptionsMenu(Menu menu) {
101       // Inflate the menu.
102       getMenuInflater().inflate(R.menu.my, menu);
103       return true;
104   }
105
106   @Override
107   public boolean onOptionsItemSelected(MenuItem item) {
108       // Handle action bar item clicks here. The action bar will
109       // automatically handle clicks on the Home/Up button, so long
110       // as you specify a parent activity in AndroidManifest.xml.
111       int id = item.getItemId();
112       if (id == R.id.action_settings) {
113           return true;
114       }
115       return super.onOptionsItemSelected(item);
116   }
117 }
```

■ Exercises

5.1 Describe the steps for creating an XML graphic element to be stored as a drawable resource file.

5.2 Explain when `onInflate()` and `onActivityCreated()` are called.

5.3 Describe the coordinate system used by a `RelativeLayout`. How does this compare with the coordinate system used in a `FrameView`?

5.4 List the properties that must be set for an `ImageView` that will result in the rotation around a pivot point.

5.5 Write a segment of code to remove an `ImageView` object from the screen during runtime.

5.6 What is the relationship between a `Bitmap` and a `Canvas`?

5.7 Briefly explain the purpose of `requestWindowFeature()`?

5.8 Create a frame-by-frame animation. Describe the steps that are required.

5.9 What parameters are required for `RotateAnimation()`?

5.10 Briefly describe the purpose of `SoundPool` and `MediaPlayer`.

6 Threads, Handlers, and Programmatic Movement

Chapter Objectives

In this chapter you will:

- Understand the benefits of multithreading on Android.
- Understand multithreading fundamentals.
- Know the `Thread` class and the `Runnable` interface.
- Understand an `AsyncTask`.
- Learn to implement canvas movement using surface views.
- Learn to communicate between threads.

■ 6.1 Multithreading and Multicore Processing

Since the early days of Cupcake, Android-powered devices have grown enormously in multitasking capability. Even fairly recent mobile devices have more resource constraints (such as CPU, memory, and battery power) than a desktop computer; this makes multitasking more difficult on a mobile device. Nevertheless, Android users have always expected their devices—even those running on a single-core processor— to be able to perform or appear to perform multiple tasks at the same time. A simple example is that Android users have never had to actively manage whether an application is open or closed, as a result of its multitasking capability.

One of the biggest challenges chip designers face is a CPU's heat emission. CPUs with a single core produce excess heat, which makes them inefficient in terms of power consumption. To solve this problem, chip designers created a multicore processor. Today, the processing on a mobile device is divided between multiple cores, which reduces heat emissions and consequently reduces power consumption.

Most of the mobile devices available today use multicore application processors with dual-core and quad-core power. This feature is essential to run the large collection of sensor components embedded on the mobile device. At a minimum, a typical smartphone comes equipped with an accelerometer, magnetic sensor, and GPS. These sensors make devices intuitive and are often required for use with applications. For example, a proximity sensor is helpful during phone calls, as it turns off the screen when a user's face remains out of range for a given period of time. The accelerometer senses movement and orientation, which is useful for interesting game play and for intuitively flipping the screen into landscape mode and back again. These sensors constantly gather large amounts of data and need continuous processing. As an application developer, it is advisable to understand how to achieve performance gains and to write code specifically to take advantage of multiple cores for additional optimization.

Android is a Linux-based operating system; therefore, it uses processes and thread management models to manage running applications, services, and the other elements of the system. In fact, the most rudimentary of all applications is one that runs on a single processor with a single thread of execution.

One of Android Java's most impressive features is its built-in support for multithread programming. When an application does several things at once, it is called *multithreading*. Other terms are used for multithreading, such as *parallelism* and *concurrency*. Such an application can do several things seemingly at once: perform computations, display an animation, play sounds, and allow the user to interact. Each of these tasks can be performed on a separate thread of execution. A multithreaded Android application contains two or more threads. A principal advantage of multithreading is that it enables programmers to write very efficient applications because it allows the use of any idle time that may accrue while other segments of code are being processed. Each thread runs as a separate path of execution that is managed by its own stack, the *call stack*. The *call stack* is used to manage method calling, parameter passing, and storage for a called method's local variables.

Multitasking can be subdivided into two categories: process-based multitasking and thread-based multitasking. Process-based multitasking is the feature that allows a device to execute two or more programs concurrently. For example, it is process-based multitasking that allows users to run the device calculator and browse the Internet at the same time. In process-based multitasking, an app is the smallest unit of code that can be dispatched by the scheduler.

In a thread-based multitasking environment, the thread is the smallest unit of dispatchable code. This means that a single program can perform two or more tasks at once. Although Android Apps make use of process-based multitasking environments, process-based multitasking is not under the control of Java. Each virtual machine instance has at least one main thread. In Android, the main thread is the UI thread. This single thread is responsible for handling all the UI events. Even a simple single-threaded application can benefit from parallel processing on different cores. For example, if an application uses a media server, then the media processing and the UI rendering logic can run on different cores at the same time.

In Android, the system guards against applications that are insufficiently responsive for a period of time by displaying a dialogue that says an app has stopped responding. If an application has been unresponsive for a considerable period of time, the system will offer the user an option to quit the application, as shown in Figure 6-1. This is called "Application Not Responding," or ANR. An ANR dialog, which appears only when an application is unresponsive, should always be avoided.

The use of multiple threads is the best solution to a poorly performing application, or even worse, an unresponsive application. Threads have been an essential part of computer science and a versatile tool for programmers for decades. Most modern operating systems support threads, and Android is no exception. Android support for threads enables programmers to split their programs into multiple units that execute commands and instructions in parallel.

A thread is the smallest unit of processing that can be scheduled by an operating system. An app's processing tasks can be broken into threads, which can then be scheduled simultaneously by the operating system. This method helps the programmer take care of longer processes in a separate thread, so that the main thread (in which the UI is running) remains quick and responsive to the user.

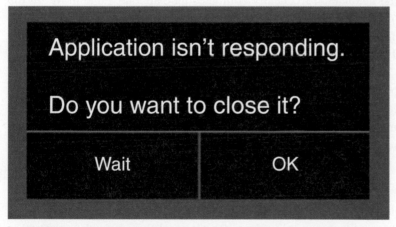

| FIGURE 6-1 An ANR (Application Not Responding) dialogue displayed to the user.

Programmers often perform complex and time-consuming tasks within Android apps. If these tasks are not segmented in separate threads, they might cause applications to crash or just be slow and inefficient. The benefits of using separate threads outweigh the drawbacks, so you should use them often to make snappy, responsive, crash-proof Android apps.

To utilize the maximum potential of the available processing power on multicore devices, applications should be written with concurrency in mind. Android applications should be designed to allow separate threads to process tasks that can be executed in parallel. Categories of operations that can be carried out on separate background threads are as follows:

- Heavy calculations
- An Object's long initialization
- Networking
- Database operations

◼ 6.2 Main Thread and Background Thread

Android UI threads are distinct from background threads. When an activity is created, it runs by default in the UI thread of the application. All of the commands issued by the Android operating system, such as `onClick and onCreate`, are sent to and processed by this UI thread.

When a substantial amount of processing is performed on the UI thread, the application may be too busy to respond to messages sent by the Android operating system. For example, if an application frequently computes an elaborate game move on the UI thread, the I/O operations of the system, such as processing incoming user input events, may perform sluggishly or can be blocked. Computations should always be written efficiently, but even the most efficient code requires time to run. To improve performance, it is good practice to execute tasks that might take a long time in a separate background thread rather than in the UI thread. The UI thread, which drives the user interface, must remain unblocked and responsive to user input sent by the Android operating system.

When writing multithreaded applications in Android, it is a good idea to keep several things in mind about the UI thread:

- The UI thread should not perform tasks that take longer than a few seconds.
- The user interface cannot be updated from a background thread. Only the UI thread should update the user interface. Background threads in the application should return data back to the UI thread for changes to UI elements.
- An Android application has no single point of entry; it can be entered from an Activity, Service, or a Broadcast Receiver, all of which run on the UI thread.

Java's multithreading system is built on the `Thread` class and its companion interface, `Runnable`. Both are packaged in `java.lang`. The `java.lang.Thread` class, available in the Java JDK, provides methods to start and manage multiple threads running concurrently.

■ 6.3 Thread Approaches

From the main UI thread, programmers can create other threads by instantiating an object of type `Thread`. The `Thread` class encapsulates an object that is runnable. Two ways in which a runnable object can be created are:

1. Implement the `Runnable` interface.
2. Extend the `Thread` class.

Both implementation approaches use the `Thread` class to instantiate, access, and control the thread. The only difference between these two approaches is how a thread-enabled class is created. The `start()` method must be called to execute a new Thread, regardless of the approach.

6.3.1 Implementing a Runnable Interface

The `Runnable` interface abstracts a unit of executable code. For example, you can construct a thread on any object that implements the `Runnable` interface. `Runnable` defines only one method called `run()`. This approach is illustrated in the code segment shown below. It is assumed a class exists that implements `Runnable`.

On Line 8, an object of type `Thread` is instantiated on an object of the `Runnable` class. On Line 9, the new thread, `t1`, will not begin execution until the `start()` method is called.

```
1   public class MyActivity extends Activity {
2   @Override
3       public void onCreate(Bundle savedInstanceState) {
4           super.onCreate(savedInstanceState);
5           setContentView (R.layout.activity_main);
6
7           Runnable myRunnable1 = new MyRunnableClass();
8           Thread t1 = new Thread(myRunnable);
9           t1.start();
10  }
```

An application that creates an instance of `Thread` must provide the code that will run in that thread. The `Runnable` interface defines a single method, `run ()`, as shown on Lines 14 and 15, which contains the code to be executed in the thread. This `Runnable` object is instantiated on Line 7. The `Runnable` object is passed to the Thread constructor when the Thread object is instantiated on Line 8. When `start()` is called by the `Thread` object (Line 9), the `run()` method will be executed in that thread.

The code below shows the `MyRunnableClass` that implements the `Runnable` interface:

```
11  public class MyRunnableClass implements Runnable {
12
13    @Override
14    public void run() {
15      // operations to be performed on a background thread
16    }
17  }
```

6.3.2 Extend the Thread Class

A `Thread` class can also be constructed that implements the `Runnable` interface. This approach is illustrated in the two code segments shown below. On Line 7 an object of a `Thread` subclass is instantiated. This thread will not begin its execution until the `start()` method is called.

The `Thread` class itself implements `Runnable` through its `run()` method. An application can subclass `Thread`, providing its own implementation of a run, as shown on Lines 13–15.

```
1  public class MyActivity extends Activity {
2  @Override
3     public void onCreate(Bundle savedInstanceState) {
4         super.onCreate(savedInstanceState);
5         setContentView (R.layout.activity_my);
6
7         MyThreadClass thread2 = new MyThreadClass ();
8         thread2.start();
9  }
```

```
10  public class MyThreadClassextendsThread {
11
12    @Override
13    public void run() {
14      // operations to be performed on a background thread
15    }
16  }
```

■ 6.4 UI Modification and the Handler Class

The UI thread is the main thread of execution for a given Android application. Every application has its own UI thread that runs UI objects. All of the application components, including activities, services, and intent receivers, are created in this thread. In addition, system calls to these components are performed on this thread.

Only the UI thread can modify the user interface. Modification to the UI cannot be directly performed from a background thread. Consider the following code for MyActivity. The layout associated with this activity contains a TextView and a Button. The TextView, referenced by mTextview, requires an update to its content when the user clicks the button. The button onClick() event is handled by the method updateText(), as shown on Lines 18–25. A background thread is created to handle the update operation.

The instruction on Line 22 is designed to set the text content within the TextView component to a new value. However, since the TextView is updated by a call from a background thread, it will end in an application crash.

```
1   import android.app.Activity;
2   import android.os.Bundle;
3   import android.view.View;
4   import android.widget.TextView;
5
6   public class MyActivity extends Activity {
7
8       private TextView mTextview;
9
10      @Override
11      public final void onCreate(Bundle savedInstanceState) {
12          super.onCreate(savedInstanceState);
13          setContentView(R.layout.activity_my);
14
15          mTextview = (TextView) findViewById(R.id.textView1);
16      }
17
18      public void updateText(View view) {
19          new Thread(new Runnable() {
20              @Override
21              public void run() {
22                  mTextview.setText("Just clicked");
23              }
24          }).start();
25      }
26  }
```

A stack trace, such as the one shown below, will appear in the Logcat console when an uncaught thread exception has been attempted. The exception that caused the crash has occurred because the specified TextView can be modified only from the UI thread. A solution to this problem is to communicate to the UI thread that an update to the TextView needs to be performed. The UI thread can then act on that request.

```
1    10-10 05:08:35.251      9564-9584/com.cornez.junk3 W/dalvikvm:
2                            threadid=11: thread exiting with uncaught
3                            exception (group=0x415e0ba8)
4    10-10 05:08:35.251      9564-9584/com.cornez.junk3 E/AndroidRuntime:
5                            FATAL EXCEPTION: Thread-5841
6         Process: com.cornez.junk3, PID: 9564
7         android.view.ViewRootImpl$CalledFromWrongThreadException:
8                            Only the original thread that created a
9                            view hierarchy can touch its views.
10              at android.view.ViewRootImpl.checkThread
11                  (ViewRootImpl.java:6024)
12              at android.view.ViewRootImpl.requestLayout
13                  (ViewRootImpl.java:820)
14              at android.view.View.requestLayout(View.java:16431)
15              at android.widget.RelativeLayout.requestLayout
16                  (RelativeLayout.java:352)
17              at android.view.View.requestLayout(View.java:16431)
18              at android.widget.TextView.checkForRelayout
19                  (TextView.java:6600)
20              at android.widget.TextView.setText(TextView.java:3813)
21              at com.cornez.junk3.MyActivity$1.run(MainActivity.java:38)
22              at java.lang.Thread.run(Thread.java:841)
```

A Handler is part of the Android system's framework for managing threads and is designed for interthread communication. It combines features from a BlockingQueue and a message listener.

Interaction between an Android thread and the UI thread is accomplished using a UI thread Handler object and posting Messages and Runnable objects to a message queue.

A Handler object created on the UI thread exposes a thread-safe message queue on which background threads can asynchronously add either messages or requests for foreground runnables to act on their behalf.

When a Handler is created for a new thread, it is bound to the message queue of the thread in which it is created. The Handler delivers messages and runnables to this message queue and executes them as they are retrieved off the queue.

In the following example, the main UI thread establishes a Handler to get messages from the background threads. On Lines 19–22, a background thread is implemented when the user clicks a button. The Handler, named mHandler, will provide communication between the UI thread and the background thread.

The method call sendEmptyMessage(), on Line 25, is used to add a message to the UI MessageQueue. This particular message is categorized as an empty message containing an integer value of zero. This integer value is referred to as a "what" value and is used to attach a code to the empty message, which will be added to the MessageQueue. A "true" is returned by the method call if the message was successfully placed into the message queue. If the message failed to be added to the queue, a "false" is returned.

Each background thread can also define its own `Handler`. A `Handler` processes messages and `Runnable` objects associated with the current thread message queue. A `Handler` defined by a background thread creates a local message queue, which can be used to receive messages from other threads, including the UI thread.

```
1   public class MyActivity extends Activity {
2
3       private ImageView imageView;
4       private TextView textView;
5
6       @Override
7       protected void onCreate(Bundle savedInstanceState) {
8           super.onCreate(savedInstanceState);
9           setContentView(R.layout.activity_my);
10
11          textView = (TextView) findViewById(R.id.textView);
12          imageView = (ImageView) findViewById(R.id.imageView);
13
14
15          Button mButton = (Button) findViewById(R.id.button);
16          mButton.setOnClickListener(new View.OnClickListener() {
17              @Override
18              public void onClick(View view) {
19                  new Thread() {
20                      public void run() {
21                          Thread work occurs here
22                          .
23                          .
24                          .
25                          mHandler.sendEmptyMessage(0);
26                      }
27                  }.start();
28              }
29          });
30      }
31
32      public Handler mHandler = new Handler() {
33
34          public void handleMessage(android.os.Message message){
35              super.handleMessage(message);
36
37              //UPDATE UI COMPONENTS
38              textView.setText(textString);
39              imageView.setImageBitmap(bitmap);
40          }
41      };
```

A `Handler` can send and process messages and `Runnable` objects associated with a thread's `MessageQueue`. Each `Handler` instance is associated with a single thread. When a new `Handler` is created, it is bound to the thread and the message queue of the thread that is creating it.

A handler's message queue uses the `obtainMessage()` method to control communication. Consider the following example. A background thread that wants to communicate with the main UI thread must request a message token using the `obtainMessage()` method, as shown on Line 9. Once obtained, the background thread can fill data into the message token and attach it to the handler's message queue using the `sendMessage()` method, as shown on Line 11.

The `Handler` for this thread, named `threadHandler`, will need to use the `handleMessage()` method to attend continuously to new messages delivered from the main thread.

```
1    Thread backgroundThread = new Thread (new Runnable() {
2        @Override
3        public void run () {
4            // do background work
5            .
6            .
7            .
8
9            Message msg = threadHandler.obtainMessage();
10           // Deliver message to main's message queue.
11           threadHandler.sendMessage(msg);
12       }
13   });
14
15   //Start the execution of the parallel thread
16   backgroundThread.start();
```

The segment of code shown below is the `Handler` definition that is bound to the background thread in the above example. Lines 3–9 show the `handleMessage()` method. The UI components named `textView` and `imageView` are updated within this method.

```
1
2        public Handler threadHandler = new Handler() {
3            public void handleMessage (android.os.Message message) {
4                super.handleMessage(msg);
5
6                //UPDATE UI COMPONENTS
7                textView.setText(textString);
8                imageView.setImageBitmap(bitmap);
9            }
10       };
```

▪ Lab Example 6-1: Background Thread and Handler—Counting

This lab provides a first look at creating a background thread and handler for updating a UI element. The background thread for this simple example does not require a message; rather, it uses an empty message.

Part 1: The Design

The application, Counting Thread Example, features a `TextView` element that is updated every second. Figure 6-2 shows the application 34 seconds after the application has launched. The number zero appears in the `TextView` when the application first launches. After every second, the number is incremented.

▌ FIGURE 6-2 Thread Basics application shows a simple counter running in a separate thread.

Part 2: Application Structure and Setup

The settings for the application are as follows:

- Application Name: Counting Thread Example
- Project Name: CountingThreadExample

- Package Name: `com.cornez.countingthreadexample`
- Android Form: Phone and Tablet
- Minimum SDK: API 18: Android 4.3 (Jelly Bean)
- Target SDK: API 21: Android 5.0 (Lollipop)
- Compile with: API 21: Android 5.0 (Lollipop)
- Activity Name: `MyActivity`
- Layout Name: `activity_my`

The structure for the final application is shown in Figure 6-3. The Java source file, `MyActivity`, will define the single activity of the application, along with the background thread and its associated handler. The layout for `MyActivity` is `activity_my.xml`.

| FIGURE 6-3 Final Project structure for the application.

A portrait orientation of the screen is specified in `AndroidManifest.xml`. The single activity of the application is specified on Lines 10–20. The complete XML for `AndroidManifest.xml` is shown as follows:

```
AndroidManifest.xml
1   <?xml version="1.0" encoding="utf-8"?>
2   <manifest xmlns:android="http://schemas.android.com/apk/res/android"
3       package="com.cornez.countingthreadexample" >
4
5       <application
6           android:allowBackup="true"
7           android:icon="@drawable/ic_launcher"
```

```
 8          android:label="@string/app_name"
 9          android:theme="@style/AppTheme" >
10          <activity
11              android:name=".MyActivity"
12              android:screenOrientation="portrait"
13              android:label="@string/app_name" >
14              <intent-filter>
15                  <action android:name="android.intent.action.MAIN" />
16
17                  <category
18                      android:name="android.intent.category.LAUNCHER" />
19              </intent-filter>
20          </activity>
21      </application>
22
23  </manifest>
```

Part 3: The User Interface

As an exploration of a simple background thread with a handler, the layout design for this application is minimized to include a single UI element: a TextView. The complete XML code for the layout, activity_my.xml, is shown below. The TextView, defined on Lines 12–20, is used to display a counting integer that begins with zero when the application launches and is incremented at every second. The layout design is illustrated in Figure 6-4.

```
activity_my.xml
 1  <RelativeLayout
 2  xmlns:android="http://schemas.android.com/apk/res/android"
 3      xmlns:tools="http://schemas.android.com/tools"
 4      android:layout_width="match_parent"
 5      android:layout_height="match_parent"
 6      android:paddingLeft="@dimen/activity_horizontal_margin"
 7      android:paddingRight="@dimen/activity_horizontal_margin"
 8      android:paddingTop="@dimen/activity_vertical_margin"
 9      android:paddingBottom="@dimen/activity_vertical_margin"
10      tools:context=".MyActivity">
11
12      <TextView
13          android:layout_width="wrap_content"
14          android:layout_height="wrap_content"
15          android:textAppearance="?android:attr/textAppearanceLarge"
16          android:text="0"
17          android:id="@+id/textView"
18          android:layout_centerVertical="true"
19          android:layout_centerHorizontal="true"
20          android:textSize="100sp" />
21  </RelativeLayout>
22
```

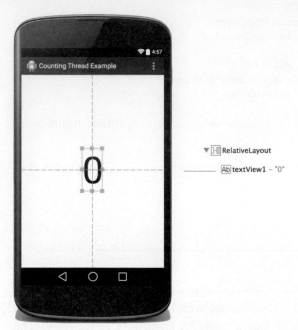

▼ ⊟ RelativeLayout
——————— Ab textView1 – "0"

FIGURE 6-4 The layout design shown in the Graphical Layout Editor.

Part 4: Source Code for Application

A single Activity for the application, `MyActivity`, is used to host the `Runnable` object that will be used to run code in the background thread. The Java code for `MyActivity` is as follows:

Line 15: An `Integer` object, `count`, will hold the counting data value, which is initialized to zero on Line 27.

Line 30: A new `Thread` is constructed, `thread`. A `Runnable` named `countNumbers` is passed to the `Thread` constructor.

Line 31: The `start()` method must be called to execute the `Thread`. The method call `thread.start()` automatically initiates a call to the `run()` method of the `Runnable` task, which was passed to the `Thread` during its instantiation.

Lines 38–41: The `onStart()` callback for the Activity is used to reinitialize count to zero. This means that the counter will set to zero each time the application is launched.

Lines 44–57: The `Runnable` named `countNumbers` is defined as an inner class. This object is bound to the background thread on Line 30. The `Runnable` interface defines a single method, `run()`, which contains the code executed in the thread.

There are two advantages to making a runnable class into an inner class. (1) If the run() is short, it can be placed where it is needed, without cluttering up the remainder of the source code. (2) The run() method can access instance variables and methods of the surrounding activity.

Lines 49:	The count value is incremented.
Line 50:	Thread.sleep() causes the background thread to suspend execution for 1000 milliseconds, one second. This is an efficient means of making processor time available to the other threads in an application or other applications that might be running. Sleep times are not guaranteed to be precise, because they are limited by the facilities provided by the underlying Android system. Also, the sleep period can be terminated by a system interrupt. Do not assume that invoking sleep() will suspend the thread for precisely the time period specified.
Line 51:	A message, containing a zero value, is sent to the Handler object named threadHandler.
	The sendEmptyMessage(0) is the callback on the UI thread's threadHandler to signal that the background thread has finished its work. In this example, we are sending an empty message. As shown earlier, this is a means of communication and exchange of data from a child thread (the background thread) to a parent thread (the UI thread).
Lines 60–64:	The count data from the task object running on the background thread is passed to an object on the UI thread. Because the Handler is running on the UI thread, it can place the count data in the UI object named countTextView. The handleMessage() method is implemented to receive messages. In this example, the message is not used. Typically a message contains a description and arbitrary data object.

```
MyActivity.java
 1   package com.cornez.countingthreadexample;
 2
 3   import android.app.Activity;
 4   import android.os.Bundle;
 5   import android.os.Handler;
 6   import android.view.Menu;
 7   import android.view.MenuItem;
 8   import android.widget.TextView;
 9
10
```

```
11   public class MyActivity extends Activity {
12
13       //DECLARE UI TEXTVIEW AND COUNT OBJECT
14       private TextView countTextView;
15       private Integer count;
16
17
18       @Override
19       protected void onCreate(Bundle savedInstanceState) {
20           super.onCreate(savedInstanceState);
21           setContentView(R.layout.activity_my);
22
23           //REFERENCE THE TEXTVIEW UI ELEMENT ON THE LAYOUT
24           countTextView = (TextView) findViewById(R.id.textView);
25
26           //INITIALIZE THE COUNTER
27           count = 0;
28
29           //CREATE A THREAD AND START IT
30           Thread thread = new Thread (countNumbers);
31           thread.start();
32
33       }
34
35       //INITIALIZE THE COUNTER TO ZERO EACH TIME THE
36       //APPLICATION LAUNCHES
37       @Override
38       protected void onStart() {
39           super.onStart();
40           count = 0;
41       }
42
43       //*************RUNNABLE **************/
44       private Runnable countNumbers = new Runnable () {
45           private static final int DELAY = 1000;
46           public void run() {
47               try {
48                   while (true) {
49                       count ++;
50                       Thread.sleep (DELAY);
51                       threadHandler.sendEmptyMessage(0);
52                   }
53               } catch (InterruptedException e){
54           e.printStackTrace();
55               }
56           }
57       };
58
```

```
59    //*************HANDLER****************/
60    public Handler threadHandler = new Handler() {
61        public void handleMessage (android.os.Message message){
62            countTextView.setText(count.toString());
63        }
64    };
65
66    @Override
67    public boolean onCreateOptionsMenu(Menu menu) {
68        // Inflate the menu;
69        getMenuInflater().inflate(R.menu.my, menu);
70        return true;
71    }
72
73    @Override
74    public boolean onOptionsItemSelected(MenuItem item) {
75        // Handle action bar item clicks here. The action bar will
76        // automatically handle clicks on the Home/Up button, so long
77        // as you specify a parent activity in AndroidManifest.xml.
78        int id = item.getItemId();
79        if (id == R.id.action_settings) {
80            return true;
81        }
82        return super.onOptionsItemSelected(item);
83    }
84 }
```

■ 6.5 Loopers

Looper is a class within the Android user interface that can be used in tandem with the Handler class to provide a framework for implementing a concurrency pattern.

The following is an example of a basic concurrency pattern in which the UI thread accesses the MessageQueue, which holds units of work that can be executed or processed. Units of work are Messages or Runnables.

- Background threads can push new units of work onto the MessageQueue at any time.
- The UI thread processes the queued units of work one after another.
- If there are no work units on the MessageQueue, it waits until one appears in the queue.
- Processing the MessageQueue can be quit at any time, and units of work can be removed from the queue.

A `Looper` is the mechanism that allows these units of work to be executed or processed sequentially on a single thread. A `Handler` is used to schedule those units of work for execution by pushing them onto a `MessageQueue`.

By default, an application has at least one Looper. This `Looper` is implicitly attached to the UI Thread.

A default Looper exists as a message-handling loop that reads and processes items from the UI `MessageQueue`. A Handler can be created and associated with the UI thread. Once a `Runnable` is attached to it, its UI updates can be implemented via the default Looper. It is also possible to implement Loopers and perform message processing on a background thread.

The `Looper` class provides a `MessageQueue` when a Looper object is instantiated. This `MessageQueue` will automatically be associated with the thread from which it is created. This association cannot be altered. In addition, the `Looper` cannot be reattached to another thread. `Handlers` are attached to `Loopers` and their associated threads. A `Handler` sends `Messages` and `Runnables` to the `MessageQueue` associated with a thread. When a `Looper` processes a message, it routes the message back to the `Handler`, thus allowing the event to be processed on the appropriate thread.

When you instantiate a Handler based on a particular `Looper` instance, the `Handler` runs on the same thread as the `Looper`.

Consider the following segment of code that implements a background thread.

Line 5:   `Looper.prepare()` will create a `MessageQueue` and bind it to the current thread, which is detected implicitly.

Line 7:   When a `Handler` is created, it is associated by default with the current thread. In addition, the `Handler` will automatically be bound to the Looper that is attached to the current thread. It is not necessary to specify the Looper explicitly. In this example, `mHandler` is specifically used to communicate with the Looper.

                 When creating a `Handler` within the UI thread, the background threads and the UI thread can communicate with each other using the `Handler`. Each `Handler` instance is associated with a single thread and that thread's `MessageQueue`.

Line 13:   By calling `Looper.loop`, the thread will begin looping through the message queue. The processing of messages and runnables in the message queue will be continual until a `quit()` call is executed. `Looper.quit()` will complete the processing of the current message, but it will end processing for other messages left in its queue.

```
1   class BackgroundThread extends Thread {
2       public Handler mHandler;
3
4       public void run() {
5           Looper.prepare();
6
7           mHandler = new Handler() {
8               public void handleMessage(Message msg) {
9                   // process incoming messages here
10              }
11          };
12
13          Looper.loop();
14      }
15  }
```

Messages and Runnables are added to a MessageQueue through the `Handler` object associated with the Looper. Access to the `MessageQueue` is provided by a set of Post- and Send-type methods in the Handler class.

Post-type methods are used to add `Runnable` objects to the `MessageQueue`. For example, at its most basic, the method `post()` will simply add a `Runnable` object to the `MessageQueue`. To schedule a time of execution for a `Runnable` object, the method `postAtTime()` can be used to supply a specific time. When a runnable object requires a delay in execution, the method `postdelayed()` will add the `Runnable` object, along with a delay time in milliseconds.

The `Handler` class provides Send-type methods for adding Message objects to the MessageQueue. As illustrated in Lab Example 6-1, the simplest of these methods is `sendEmptyMessage()`, which passes an integer value that can be used to specify a message operation. To add a specific Message object to the MessageQueue, the method `sendMessage()` can be used. Similar to Runnable objects that require execution at specific times or delay times, Message objects can be time-stamped for delivery at a specific time. These methods are `sendMessageAtTime()` and `sendMessageDelayed()`. An empty message delivery can also be time-stamped using `sendEmptyMessageAtTime()` and `sendEmptyMessageDelayed()`.

In the following segment of code, three Runnable objects and three Message objects are pushed onto a single `MessageQueue`. In the final statement, the `Handler` clears the `mRunnable` objects from the `MessageQueue`.

```
1   mHandler.post(mRunnable);
2   mHandler.postAtTime(mRunnable, aTime);
3   mHandler.postDelayed(mRunnable, 1000);
4
```

```
5   mHandler.sendMessage(mMessage);
6   mHandler.sendMessageAtTime(mMessage, aTime);
7   mHandler.sendMessageDelayed(mMessage, 1000);
8
9   mHandler.removeCallbacks(mRunnable);
```

Lab Example 6-2: Digital StopWatch

This lab example explores the creation of a digital stopwatch. The stopwatch application, shown in Figure 6-5, requires continual updates to the UI timer display once the stopwatch is started. Updates at regular intervals allow us to explore the implementation of a concurrency pattern.

Part 1: The Design

This lab illustrates the coordination between the UI thread, a handler, and the default UI Looper. More specifically, the Stopwatch application demonstrates the versatility of Handlers and Loopers for creating repetition that continually updates UI elements in the UI Thread.

FIGURE 6-5 An application for a digital stopwatch.

Part 2: Application Structure and Setup

The settings for the application are as follows:

- Application Name: Stop Watch
- Project Name: StopWatch
- Package Name: `com.cornez.stopwatch`
- Android Form: Phone and Tablet
- Minimum SDK: API 18: Android 4.3 (Jelly Bean)
- Target SDK: API 21: Android 5.0 (Lollipop)
- Compile with: API 21: Android 5.0 (Lollipop)
- Activity Name: `MyActivity`
- Layout Name: `activity_my`

The launcher is set to the Android default `ic_launcher.png` file.

The project structure, shown in Figure 6-6, contains two Java source files and a single layout file. The `MyActivity` will set the screen content to `activity_my.xml`, and `WatchTime` is the class that will model the digital stopwatch time displayed on the screen. The drawable resource, `background.png`, adds visual context to the application. This file can be found in the textbook resources.

background.png

▼ 🗁 app
  ▼ 🗁 manifests
      📄 AndroidManifest.xml
  ▼ 🗁 java
    ▼ 🗁 com.cornez.stopwatch
      ⓒ 🗋 MyActivity
      ⓒ 🗋 WatchTime
    ▶ 🗁 com.cornez.stopwatch (androidTest)
  ▼ 🗁 res
    ▶ 🗁 drawable
    ▼ 🗁 layout
      📄 activity_my.xml
    ▶ 🗁 menu
    ▼ 🗁 values
      ▶ 🗁 dimens.xml (2)
      📄 strings.xml
      📄 styles.xml
  ▼ ⓒ Gradle Scripts
    ⓒ build.gradle (Project: StopWatch2)
    ⓒ build.gradle (Module: app)
    📄 gradle-wrapper.properties (Gradle Version)
    📄 gradle.properties (Project Properties)
    ⓒ settings.gradle (Project Settings)
    📄 local.properties (SDK Location)

❚ FIGURE 6-6 Project structure for the Stop Watch application.

The single critical component in the manifest file is the specification of `MyActivity` as the main activity. No other activities are started by this activity or will be used by the application. The orientation for the main activity is set to portrait. The complete XML code for `AndroidManifest.xml` is shown as follows:

```
AndroidManifest.xml
1   <?xml version="1.0" encoding="utf-8"?>
2   <manifest xmlns:android="http://schemas.android.com/apk/res/android"
3       package="com.cornez.stopwatch" >
4
5       <application
6           android:allowBackup="true"
7           android:icon="@drawable/ic_launcher"
8           android:label="@string/app_name"
9           android:theme="@style/AppTheme" >
10          <activity
11              android:name=".MyActivity"
12              android:screenOrientation="portrait"
13              android:label="@string/app_name" >
14              <intent-filter>
15                  <action android:name="android.intent.action.MAIN" />
16
17                  <category
18                      android:name="android.intent.category.LAUNCHER" />
19              </intent-filter>
20          </activity>
21      </application>
22
23  </manifest>
```

Part 3: The User Interface

The StopWatch application uses values from the `strings.xml` file to store static button labels used in the layout associated with `MyActivity`. The XML code for this file is as follows:

```
strings.xml
1   <?xml version="1.0" encoding="utf-8"?>
2   <resources>
3
4       <string name="app_name">Stop Watch</string>
5       <string name="hello_world">Hello world!</string>
6
7       <string name="timer">00:00:00</string>
8       <string name="start_btn">Start</string>
9       <string name="stop_btn">Stop</string>
10      <string name="reset_btn">Reset</string>
11  </resources>
```

The user interface for the application is `activity_my.xml`. This layout file places UI objects relative to each other on the screen within a `RelativeLayout` root element. To provide appeal, this root element contains a background set to a drawable-`background.png`.

The digits on display is updated as the stopwatch counts down. A `TextView` is used for the dynamic display of the stopwatch timer digits, `00:00:00`, as shown in the completed layout in Figure 6-7. The `textSize` for this `TextView` is increased to 50dp so that the digits are easily visible to the user.

‖ FIGURE 6-7 The layout structure for `activity_my.xml`.

The complete XML code for `activity_my.xml` is shown as follows. The three buttons—Start, Stop, and Reset—are registered to `onClick()` events.

activity_my.xml

```
1   <RelativeLayout
2   xmlns:android="http://schemas.android.com/apk/res/android"
3       xmlns:tools="http://schemas.android.com/tools"
4       android:layout_width="match_parent"
5       android:layout_height="match_parent"
6       android:paddingLeft="@dimen/activity_horizontal_margin"
7       android:paddingRight="@dimen/activity_horizontal_margin"
8       android:paddingTop="@dimen/activity_vertical_margin"
9       android:paddingBottom="@dimen/activity_vertical_margin"
10      tools:context=".MyActivity"
11      android:background="@drawable/background">
12
```

```
13        <TextView
14            android:layout_width="wrap_content"
15            android:layout_height="wrap_content"
16            android:text="@string/timer"
17            android:id="@+id/textView1"
18            android:layout_centerVertical="true"
19            android:layout_centerHorizontal="true"
20            android:textSize="75sp"/>
21
22        <Button
23            android:layout_width="wrap_content"
24            android:layout_height="wrap_content"
25            android:text="@string/start_btn"
26            android:id="@+id/button1"
27            android:onClick="startTimer"
28            android:layout_alignParentBottom="true"
29            android:layout_alignStart="@id/textView1"
30            android:layout_marginBottom="57dp" />
31
32        <Button
33            android:layout_width="wrap_content"
34            android:layout_height="wrap_content"
35            android:text="@string/stop_btn"
36            android:id="@+id/button2"
37            android:onClick="stopTimer"
38            android:layout_alignBottom="@+id/button1"
39            android:layout_centerHorizontal="true" />
40
41        <Button
42            android:layout_width="wrap_content"
43            android:layout_height="wrap_content"
44            android:text="@string/reset_btn"
45            android:id="@+id/button3"
46            android:onClick="resetTimer"
47            android:layout_alignTop="@+id/button2"
48            android:layout_alignEnd="@id/textView1" />
49    </RelativeLayout>
```

Part 4: The Time Data Model for StopWatch

The WatchTime class is used to model the watch time data for the stopwatch. This class requires three data elements for time: start time, update time, and a stored time for when the stopwatch has been stopped but not reset. The complete Java code for the WatchTime class appears as follows:

Line 6:   mStartTime will hold the system clock time when the stopwatch is first started.

Line 7:   mTimeUpdate is the time that will appear in the stopwatch display. This value will be continually updated at intervals.

Line 8:   mStoredTime is used to hold the current stop time when the user has clicked the Stop button. Once the user clicks on the Start button, the stopwatch can resume the clock at the stored time rather than restarting at zero time.

Lines 16–20:   All time components are reset to their initial value of zero.

```
WatchTime.java
1   package com.cornez.stopwatch;
2
3   public class WatchTime {
4
5       // TIME ELEMENTS
6       private long mStartTime;
7       private long mTimeUpdate;
8       private long mStoredTime;
9
10      public WatchTime() {
11          mStartTime = 0L;
12          mTimeUpdate = 0L;
13          mStoredTime = 0L;
14      }
15
16      public void resetWatchTime() {
17          mStartTime = 0L;
18          mStoredTime = 0L;
19          mTimeUpdate = 0L;
20      }
21
22      public void setStartTime(long startTime){
23          mStartTime = startTime;
24      }
25      public long getStartTime(){
26          return mStartTime;
27      }
28      public void setTimeUpdate(long timeUpdate){
29          mTimeUpdate = timeUpdate;
30      }
31      public long getTimeUpdate(){
32          return mTimeUpdate;
33      }
34      public void addStoredTime(long timeInMilliseconds){
35          mStoredTime += timeInMilliseconds;
36      }
37      public long getStoredTime(){
38          return mStoredTime;
39      }
40  }
```

Part 5: The Controller for the Application

As the single activity for the application, `MyActivity` is the controller element of the application. It enables and disables the buttons on the stopwatch, displays the stopwatch time, and responds to starts, stops, and resets.

The activity relies on the default UI `Looper`, which manages the Message-Queue processing. More specifically, this activity uses the Looper to perform updates on the UI thread.

The Java code for `MyActivity` is shown below:

Lines 23–24:	The `watchTime` and `timeInMilliseconds` are used to calculate the digital time that will be displayed to the user. `timeInMilliseconds` will hold the current time difference value in milliseconds. This is the system clock time minus the stopwatch start time.
Line 27:	The `Handler` is the interface to the `MessageQueue` that the default `Looper` is continually processing. When code is executing in a thread and needs to interact with the user interface, it must do so by synchronizing with the main UI thread. `mHandler` is implemented to update the user interface, specifically the digits on the stopwatch display.
	Note that the default `Looper` does not need to be instantiated. It is an automatic component in an Android application. In addition, the default `Looper` is directly attached to the UI Thread.
Lines 30–51:	The `onCreate()` method disables the Stop and Reset buttons. These buttons are logically unusable until the user starts timing on the stopwatch. `onCreate()` instantiates the `watchTime` object.
Line 50:	By instantiating the `Handler` within `onCreate()`, `mHandler` is bound to the UI thread and its default `Looper`.

```
MyActivity.java
 1   package com.cornez.stopwatch;
 2
 3   import android.app.Activity;
 4   import android.os.Bundle;
 5   import android.os.Handler;
 6   import android.os.SystemClock;
 7   import android.view.Menu;
 8   import android.view.MenuItem;
 9   import android.view.View;
10   import android.widget.Button;
11   import android.widget.TextView;
12
13
```

```
14   public class MyActivity extends Activity {
15
16       // UI ELEMENTS: BUTTONS WILL TOGGLE IN VISIBILITY
17       private TextView timeDisplay;
18       private Button startBtn;
19       private Button stopBtn;
20       private Button resetBtn;
21
22       // TIME ELEMENTS
23       private WatchTime watchTime;
24       private long timeInMilliseconds = 0L;
25
26       // THE HANDLER FOR THE THREAD ELEMENT
27       private Handler mHandler;
28
29       @Override
30       protected void onCreate(Bundle savedInstanceState) {
31           // TASK 1: ACTIVATE THE ACTIVITY AND THE LAYOUT
32           super.onCreate(savedInstanceState);
33           setContentView(R.layout.activity_my);
34
35           // TASK 2: CREATE REFERENCES TO UI COMPONENTS
36           timeDisplay = (TextView) findViewById(R.id.textView1);
37           startBtn = (Button) findViewById(R.id.button1);
38           stopBtn = (Button) findViewById(R.id.button2);
39           resetBtn = (Button) findViewById(R.id.button3);
40
41           // TASK 3: HIDE THE STOP BUTTON
42           stopBtn.setEnabled(false);
43           resetBtn.setEnabled(false);
44
45
46           // TASK 4: INSTANTIATE THE OBJECT THAT MODELS THE STOPWATCH TIME
47           watchTime = new WatchTime();
48
49           //TASK 5: INSTANTIATE A HANDLER TO RUN ON THE UI THREAD
50           mHandler = new Handler();
51       }
```

When the user clicks the Start button, the method `startTimer()` is executed.

Lines 55–57:   When the application is launched for the first time, the Stop button is made available to user, while the Start and Reset buttons are disabled.

Line 60:   The start time of the stopwatch is set to the system clock.

Line 61:   The `postDelay()` method call will cause `updateTimerRunnable` to be added to the `MessageQueue` and specifies that it will be run after a delay of 20 milliseconds. The default Looper is used to process this unit of work and remove it from the MessageQueue.

Lines 65–88:   A Runnable, representing the collection of tasks responsible for updating the stopwatch time, is implemented.

Line 86:   mHandler pushes a Runnable object to the MessageQueue, this time with no delay time. By performing this task within run(), continual updates will be made to the stopwatch time display. Updates to the time display will stop once the callbacks from the MessageQueue are removed.

MyActivity.java *(continued)*

```
52      public void startTimer(View view) {
53          // TASK 1: SET THE START BUTTON TO INVISIBLE
54          //         AND THE STOP BUTTON TO VISIBLE
55          stopBtn.setEnabled(true);
56          startBtn.setEnabled(false);
57          resetBtn.setEnabled(false);
58
59          // TASK 2: SET THE START TIME AND CALL THE CUSTOM HANDLER
60          watchTime.setStartTime(SystemClock.uptimeMillis());
61          mHandler.postDelayed(updateTimerRunnable, 20);
62      }
63
64      //RUNNABLE OBJECT
65      private Runnable updateTimerRunnable= new Runnable() {
66          public void run() {
67
68              // TASK 1: COMPUTE THE TIME DIFFERENCE
69              timeInMilliseconds = SystemClock.uptimeMillis() -
70                                  watchTime.getStartTime();
71              watchTime.setTimeUpdate(watchTime.getStoredTime() +
72                                  timeInMilliseconds);
73              int time = (int) (watchTime.getTimeUpdate() / 1000);
74
75              // TASK 2: COMPUTE MINUTES, SECONDS, AND MILLISECONDS
76              int minutes = time / 60;
77              int seconds = time % 60;
78              int milliseconds = (int) (watchTime.getTimeUpdate() % 1000);
79
80              // TASK 3: DISPLAY THE TIME IN THE TEXTVIEW
81              timeDisplay.setText(String.format("%02d", minutes) + ":"
82                      + String.format("%02d", seconds) + ":"
83                      + String.format("%02d", milliseconds));
84
85              // TASK 4: SPECIFY NO TIME LAPSE BETWEEN POSTING
86              mHandler.postDelayed(this, 0);
87          }
88      };
```

Once the user clicks the Stop button, the method `stopTimer()` is executed.

Lines 92–94:   The Stop button is appropriately disabled and the Start and Reset buttons are reenabled.

Line 98:   The method call `mHandler.removeCallbacks` `(updateTimerRunnable)` is used to remove any pending `Runnable` objects that were previously placed onto the `MessageQueue`. This will effectively stop updates made to the stopwatch time display.

Lines 103–109:   Once the user clicks the Reset button, the method `resetTimer()` is executed. Data in the `watchTime` object is set to zero and the time display will now read 00:00:00.

```
MyActivity.java  (continued)
89      public void stopTimer(View view) {
90          // TASK 1: DISABLE THE START BUTTON
91          //         AND ENABLE THE STOP BUTTON
92          stopBtn.setEnabled(false);
93          startBtn.setEnabled(true);
94          resetBtn.setEnabled(true);
95
96          // TASK 2: UPDATE THE STORED TIME VALUE
97          watchTime.addStoredTime(timeInMilliseconds);
98
99          // TASK 3: HANDLER CLEARS THE MESSAGE QUEUE
100         mHandler.removeCallbacks(updateTimerRunnable);
101     }
102
103     public void resetTimer(View view) {
104         watchTime.resetWatchTime();
105         timeInMilliseconds = 0L;
106
107         int minutes = 0;
108         int seconds = 0;
109         int milliseconds = 0;
110
111         // TASK 3: DISPLAY THE TIME IN THE TEXTVIEW
112         timeDisplay.setText(String.format("%02d", minutes) + ":"
113             + String.format("%02d", seconds) + ":"
114             + String.format("%02d", milliseconds));
115     }
116
117     @Override
118     public boolean onCreateOptionsMenu(Menu menu) {
119         // Inflate the menu.
120         getMenuInflater().inflate(R.menu.my, menu);
121         return true;
122     }
```

```
123
124        @Override
125        public boolean onOptionsItemSelected(MenuItem item) {
126            // Handle action bar item clicks here. The action bar will
127            // automatically handle clicks on the Home/Up button, so long
128            // as you specify a parent activity in AndroidManifest.xml.
129            int id = item.getItemId();
130            if (id == R.id.action_settings) {
131                return true;
132            }
133            return super.onOptionsItemSelected(item);
134        }
135    }
```

■ 6.6 Canvas Movement and Views

Animation means change, such as motion. Chapter 5 explored animation in the form of frames: a series of still images shown very rapidly to simulate motion or change. Frame-by-frame animation goes back to the earliest days of cartoon animation, where the individual pictures were drawn on sheets of cellophane and became known as cels. This type of animation is static, in the sense that it is predictable. In this chapter, we explore programmatic animation, or dynamic animation, which can be generated by user or program influence. It should be noted that programmatic animation is often combined with frame-by-frame animation.

The connection of programmatic animation to time is an important one. When using a canvas, programmatic animation can be achieved by continually redrawing graphic elements to a canvas at specified time intervals. For example, a ball moving across the screen doesn't move from spot to spot. It disappears and reappears in another location in the next time interval.

Programatic animation can be achieved through the use of a Canvas. As demonstrated in Chapter 5, a canvas is provided by View.onDraw(). This means that to build movement, a custom View can be constructed that contains an implementation of the onDraw() callback method. The most convenient aspect of this feature is the provision of the predefined Canvas, which is automatically supplied by the Android framework. This means that onDraw() callbacks can be performed again and again at scheduled time intervals.

Consider the code segment below. MyView is implemented as a View class with an onDraw() and a reDraw() method. Typically, onDraw() is called by the Android framework to request that MyView draw itself. In this example, if onDraw() is called at regular intervals, the canvas will fill with red circles at various locations. Animation can be achieved when the canvas is wiped with white paint (Line 10) before redrawing the circles (Line 11).

```
1   public class MyView  extends View{
2
3       public MyView (Context context) {
4           super(context);
5       }
6
7       @Override
8       protected void onDraw(Canvas canvas) {
9           canvas.drawRGB(255,   255,   255);
10          paint.setColor(Color.rgb(255, 0, 0));
11          canvas.drawCircle(x, y, radius, paint);
12      }
13
14      public void reDraw () {
15          invalidate();
16      }
17  }
```

Keep in mind that the onDraw() method is called only when necessary by the Android framework. When a drawing component needs to be rendered, a request must be submitted to the View to be invalidated. This was performed by the method reDraw() in the code segment above. The method call invalidate() simply indicates that the View needs to be redrawn.

When an invalidate() request is submitted, precision is not guaranteed when time delays are specified in a thread Runnable. It is possible that a resulting animation may not be entirely smooth because callbacks are not always instantaneous.

Lab Example 6-3: Animated Dial Using a Simple View

This lab example demonstrates animation using a custom View. As shown in Figure 6-8, a rotating dial will be animated, with the dial moving rapidly in a clockwise direction.

Part 1: The Design

The image of the dial can be drawn at any given time by simply specifying its computed angle. It moves in increments of that angle at each time interval. The invalidate() method will request a redraw when the system finds time to perform the task. This will create a continuous rendering.

FIGURE 6-8 Linear animation using `onDraw()`.

Part 2: Application Structure and Setup

The settings for the application are as follows:

- Application Name: Animated Dial
- Project Name: AnimatedDial
- Package Name: `com.cornez.animateddial`
- Android Form: Phone and Tablet

- Minimum SDK: API 18: Android 4.3 (Jelly Bean)
- Target SDK: API 21: Android 5.0 (Lollipop)
- Compile with: API 21: Android 5.0 (Lollipop)
- Activity Name: `MyActivity`

The project structure, shown in Figure 6-9, contains two source files and the manifest file. DialView is the custom View containing a Canvas. The `MyActivity.java` is the controller of the application and will set the screen content to the custom View. No other files will be edited for the application.

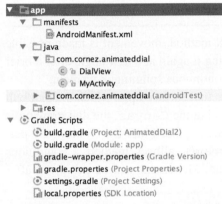

▮ **FIGURE 6-9** Project structure for the Animated Dial application.

The theme for this application has been set. The action bar has been eliminated from the screen, and fullscreen usage has been specified. The XML code for `AndroidManifest.xml` is shown as follows:

```
AndroidManifest.xml
1   <?xml version="1.0" encoding="utf-8"?>
2   <manifest xmlns:android="http://schemas.android.com/apk/res/android"
3       package="com.cornez.animateddial" >
4
5       <application
6           android:allowBackup="true"
7           android:icon="@drawable/ic_launcher"
8           android:label="@string/app_name"
9           android:theme="@android:style/
10                      Theme.Holo.Light.NoActionBar.Fullscreen">
11      <activity
12          android:name=".MyActivity"
13          android:label="@string/app_name" >
14          <intent-filter>
```

```
15                    <action android:name="android.intent.action.MAIN" />
16
17            <category
18                android:name="android.intent.category.LAUNCHER" />
19          </intent-filter>
20        </activity>
21    </application>
22
23 </manifest>
```

Part 3: A Custom View Containing a Canvas

By using the canvas and an onDraw() callback method, movement is made possible by first deleting the dial graphic and then drawing it again at a new angle after a brief pause. In this manner, the human eye will see continuous spinning movement.

The Canvas works as an interface to the actual surface upon which the dial will be drawn; it will hold all of the "draw" calls. Using the Canvas, the dial drawing is actually created on an underlying Bitmap, which is placed into the window. By performing frequent and regular calls to the onDraw() callback method, a continuous rendering will be produced within the UI thread. Movement will be perceived after each rendering.

The Java source code for DialView is shown below:

Line 10:   DialView is a customized View, which occupies a rectangular canvas area on the screen. It extends from the View class and will be responsible for drawing the graphic dial image.

Lines 12–13:   Changes in the graphic image of the dial will be based on the angle of the dial line. This line angle will be incremented by one at each time interval, creating the appearance of clockwise movement. The Paint object will dictate the color and size attributes of the dial, as well as the auxiliary dial elements.

Lines 23–24:   The style and stroke width are set for the dial graphic. In addition, all draw operations will use antialiasing, ensuring smooth graphics when possible.

Lines 28–65:   The onDraw() is called when the custom view, DialView, needs to render its graphic content to the canvas. The changes in the dial image are computed based on an angle value, as shown in Figure 6-10.

Line 68:   The call to invalidate() will tell the system to redraw the DialView as soon as it finds time to perform this task. This is a continuous rendering, albeit relatively slow. This method must

Initial angle is zero.

Angle is
incremented.

The dial is drawn as a line.
After short delays, the line is redrawn.

FIGURE 6-10 The angle of the rotating dial will be incremented after each delay.

be called from a UI thread. It should be noted that to perform a canvas drawing from a non-UI thread, a postInvalidate() call can be used.

```
DialView.java
1   package com.cornez.animateddial;
2
3   import android.content.Context;
4   import android.graphics.Canvas;
5   import android.graphics.Color;
6   import android.graphics.Paint;
7   import android.view.View;
8
9
10  public class DialView  extends View{
11
12      private float angle;
13      private Paint paint;
14
15      public DialView (Context context) {
16          super(context);
17
18          //SET THE ANGLE
19          angle = 0;
20
```

```
21          //INITIALIZE THE PAINT
22          paint = new Paint(Paint.ANTI_ALIAS_FLAG);
23          paint.setStyle(Paint.Style.STROKE);
24          paint.setStrokeWidth(150);
25
26      }
27      @Override
28      protected void onDraw(Canvas canvas) {
29
30          //TASK 1: FILL THE BACKGROUND OF THE CANVAS
31          canvas.drawRGB(248,  232,  198);
32
33          //TASK 2: COMPUTE THE WIDTH AND HEIGHT OF THE CANVAS
34          //         THIS WILL CHANGE DEPENDING ON ORIENTATION
35          int w = getMeasuredWidth();
36          int h = getMeasuredHeight();
37          int radius;
38          if (w > h) {
39              radius = h/2;
40          }else {
41              radius = w/2;
42          }
43
44          //TASK 3: DRAW THE CIRCLES
45          paint.setColor(Color.rgb(126, 79, 43));
46          canvas.drawCircle(w/2, h/2, radius, paint);
47
48          paint.setColor(Color.rgb(224, 153, 78));
49          canvas.drawCircle(w/2, h/2, radius/2, paint);
50
51          paint.setColor(Color.rgb(207, 69, 56));
52          canvas.drawCircle(w/2, h/2, radius/4, paint);
53
54          //TASK 4: COMPUTE THE NEW ANGLE
55          angle += 1;
56          if (angle > 360)
57              angle = 0;
58
59          //TASK 5: DRAW THE LINE FROM THE CENTER TO THE RIM
60          float radians = (float) (angle * (180/Math.PI));
61          float stopX = (float) (w/2 + radius * Math.sin(radians));
62          float stopY = (float) (h/2 - radius * Math.cos(radians));
63          paint.setColor(Color.rgb(132, 175, 166));
64          canvas.drawLine(w/2, h/2, stopX, stopY, paint);
65      }
66
67      public void update () {
68          invalidate();
69      }
70  }
```

Part 4: The Application Activity

MyActivity is the controller for the application. It instantiates the background thread and uses the Handler to control the UI updates. The complete code for MyActivity is shown as follows:

Line 12:	The animationThread will be the background thread that updates the MessageQueue with Runnable tasks for performing canvas redraws at regular intervals. Performing this task on a background thread will ensure the UI thread is not blocked.
Line 13:	dialView is declared.
Line 20:	The DialView object, containing the canvas, is set as the content screen for the activity.
Lines 26–27:	The background thread, animationThread, is instantiated and started. Its Runnable object is set to runningAnimation, whose run() method will be executed by the thread.
Lines 30–43:	An inner Runnable class is defined and instantiated. The run() method will produce a delay between messages sent to the MessageQueue.
Lines 45–49:	An inner Handler class is defined and instantiated. The threadHandler object will rely on handleMessage() to update the canvas. This is performed by the call dialView.update().
Lines 52–55:	All posts sent to the MessageQueue are removed.

```
MyActivity.java
 1   package com.cornez.animateddial;
 2
 3   import android.app.Activity;
 4   import android.os.Bundle;
 5   import android.os.Handler;
 6   import android.view.Menu;
 7   import android.view.MenuItem;
 8
 9
10   public class MyActivity extends Activity {
11
12       private Thread animationThread;
13       private DialView dialView;
14
```

```
15      @Override
16      protected void onCreate(Bundle savedInstanceState) {
17          super.onCreate(savedInstanceState);
18
19          //INSTANTIATE A DIAL VIEW OBJECT
20          dialView = new DialView(this);
21
22          //SET THE CONTENT OF THIS ACTIVITY TO THE DIAL VIEW
23          setContentView(dialView);
24
25          //CONSTRUCT A THREAD TO ANIMATE THE DIAL
26          animationThread = new Thread(runningAnimation);
27          animationThread.start();
28      }
29
30      private Runnable runningAnimation = new Runnable() {
31          private static final int DELAY = 200;
32
33          public void run() {
34              try {
35                  while (true) {
36                      Thread.sleep(DELAY);
37                      threadHandler.sendEmptyMessage(0);
38                  }
39              } catch (InterruptedException e) {
40                  e.printStackTrace();
41              }
42          }
43      };
44
45      public Handler threadHandler = new Handler() {
46          public void handleMessage(android.os.Message msg) {
47              dialView.update();
48          }
49      };
50
51      @Override
52      protected void onPause() {
53          super.onPause();
54          threadHandler.removeCallbacks(runningAnimation);
55      }
56
57
58      @Override
59      public boolean onCreateOptionsMenu(Menu menu) {
60          // Inflate the menu.
61          getMenuInflater().inflate(R.menu.my, menu);
62          return true;
63      }
64
```

```
65      @Override
66      public boolean onOptionsItemSelected(MenuItem item) {
67          // Handle action bar item clicks here. The action bar will
68          // automatically handle clicks on the Home/Up button, so long
69          // as you specify a parent activity in AndroidManifest.xml.
70          int id = item.getItemId();
71          if (id == R.id.action_settings) {
72              return true;
73          }
74          return super.onOptionsItemSelected(item);
75      }
76  }
```

■ 6.7 SurfaceViews

A View object cannot be updated on a background thread; however, Android provides a SurfaceView class to construct objects with a dedicated drawing surface that can be updated on a background thread. SurfaceViews contain a rendering mechanism that allows threads to update the surface's content without the use of a Handler. This means that drawing to a SurfaceView object can be rendered quickly, without having to wait until the System's View hierarchy is ready to draw.

A SurfaceView is derived from the View class. It provides more resources than Views and was created with the objective of delivering a drawing surface for a background thread. This drawing surface can be rendered at anytime, which makes it ideal for use in video playback, camera previews, and two-dimensional games.

The dedicated drawing surface provided by a SurfaceView is a collection of pixels. These pixels are composited onto the display. Every window on the display, such as a fullscreen activity and the status bar, has its own surface that it draws to. No matter what type of rendering API developers use, everything is rendered onto a surface. Every window that is created on the Android platform is backed by a surface. All of the visible surfaces rendered are composited onto the display.

When a SurfaceView object is instantiated in an Activity, its dedicated drawing surface can be formatted for size. As shown in Figure 6-11, the SurfaceView object sits behind the window of the application. Its drawing surface can be viewed through a hole punched into the window. The view hierarchy will take care of correctly compositing with the Surface any siblings of the SurfaceView that would normally appear on top of it. This allows UI components, such as interactive buttons and text fields, to be placed on top of the SurfaceView.

Access to the dedicated drawing surface is provided by a SurfaceHolder. A SurfaceHolder is an interface that can be retrieved by calling getHolder(). The drawing surface will be created and rendered while the SurfaceView window is visible. The SurfaceHolder interface requires the implementation of surface

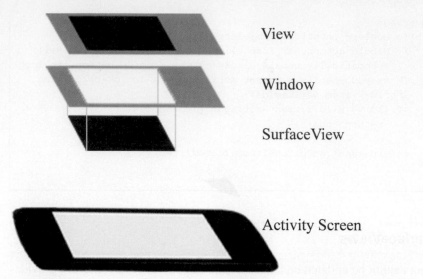

View

Window

SurfaceView

Activity Screen

I FIGURE 6-11 The SurfaceView object is positioned behind the window of the application.

Created(SurfaceHolder) and surface Destroyed (SurfaceHolder).
These two callback methods signal when the surface is created and destroyed, which
corresponds with the window being shown and hidden.

■ Lab Example 6-4: Ball Animation Using a SurfaceHolder

This lab example explores the use of a SurfaceView to implement movement. As
shown in Figure 6-12, a ball is made to bounce around the screen at a constant velocity.
The application will rely on a SurfaceView object, which will be added to the root
element of the layout XML file associated with the activity of the application. The ball
graphic element, drawn directly onto the SurfaceView object, will be continuously
relocated and rendered in a dedicated thread.

Part 1: The Design

When an application requires the use of a SurfaceView, the architecture of the application is typically more complex than when a simple canvas is used. In this application,
we will keep the structure as simple as possible by using a single Activity. The goal of
this application is to create a ball that moves in two dimensions, bouncing off the ceiling, floor, left wall, and right wall of the window. To ensure that the process required
for the bouncing ball does not monopolize the resources for the device, the application
will be structured with two threads running at once: the UI thread and a background
thread. The background thread will be bound to a SurfaceView that is continually rendered. This background thread will control the ball movement.

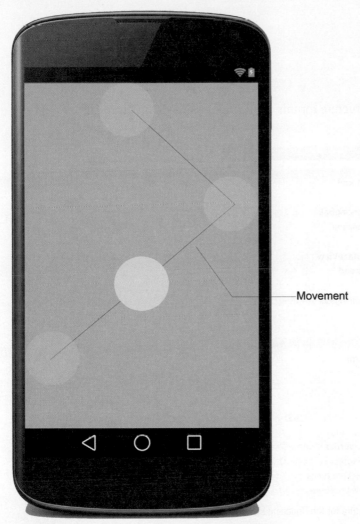

Movement

┃ FIGURE 6-12 Bouncing Ball animation uses a SurfaceView.

Part 2: Application Structure and Setup

The settings for the application are as follows:

- Application Name: Bouncing Ball
- Project Name: BouncingBall
- Package Name: `com.cornez.bouncingball`
- Android Form: Phone and Tablet
- Minimum SDK: API 18: Android 4.3 (Jelly Bean)

- Target SDK: API 21: Android 5.0 (Lollipop)
- Compile with: API 21: Android 5.0 (Lollipop)
- Activity Name: `MyActivity`
- Layout Name: `activity_my`

The final project structure for this application is shown in Figure 6-13.

❙ FIGURE 6-13 Project Structure for the Bouncing Ball application.

The relationship between the Java source code components is illustrated in Figure 6-14.

In addition to the SurfaceView, BounceSurfaceView, and the background thread-BounceThread, the application uses two models: Ball and AnimationArena.

The Ball class models a spherical graphic in motion. The AnimationArena class is used to model the game world where the ball can move. In a more complicated game application, AnimationArena would be used to group together all of the game objects, such as game obstacles and enemies, into a single world. In this application, the game world is very basic: a single Ball object. Updates and rendering of the game world will be delegated to AnimationArena.

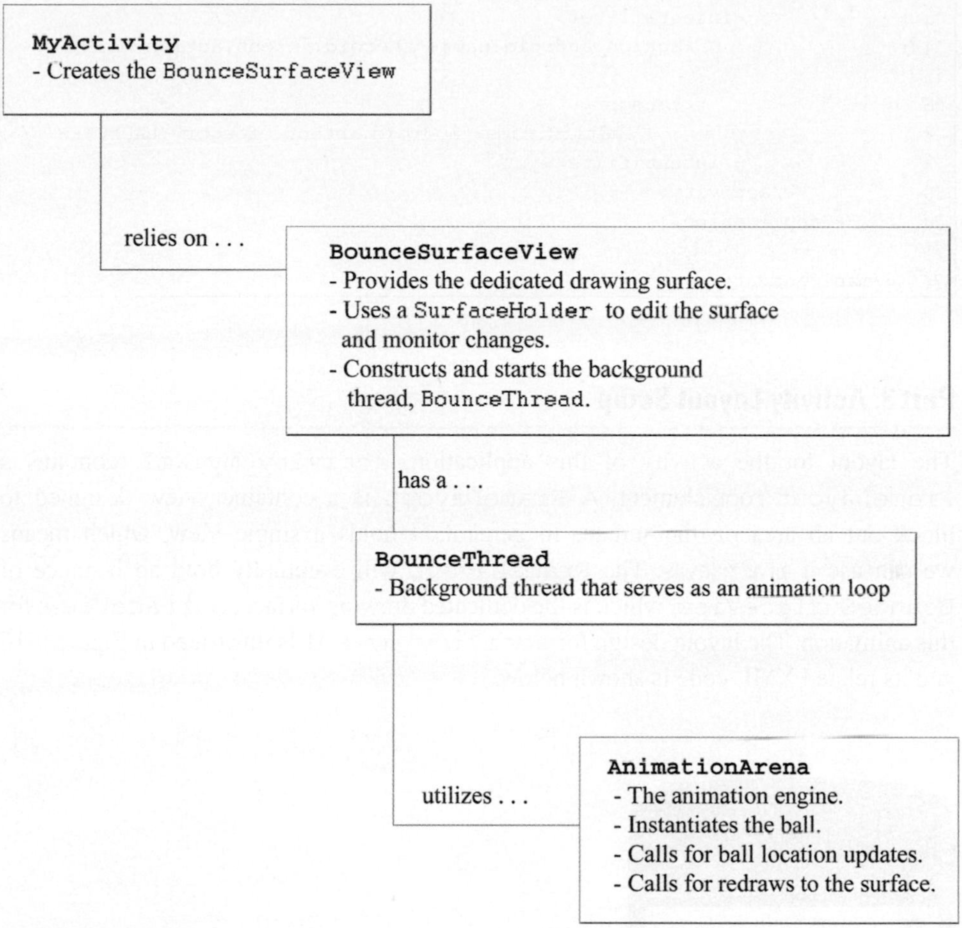

```
MyActivity
- Creates the BounceSurfaceView
```

relies on . . .

```
BounceSurfaceView
- Provides the dedicated drawing surface.
- Uses a SurfaceHolder to edit the surface
  and monitor changes.
- Constructs and starts the background
  thread, BounceThread.
```

has a . . .

```
BounceThread
- Background thread that serves as an animation loop
```

utilizes . . .

```
AnimationArena
- The animation engine.
- Instantiates the ball.
- Calls for ball location updates.
- Calls for redraws to the surface.
```

| FIGURE 6-14 Animation elements.

The XML code for `AndroidManifest.xml` is shown as follows:

AndroidManifest.xml

```
1   <?xml version="1.0" encoding="utf-8"?>
2   <manifest xmlns:android="http://schemas.android.com/apk/res/android"
3       package="com.cornez.bouncingball" >
4
5       <application
6           android:allowBackup="true"
7           android:icon="@drawable/ic_launcher"
8           android:label="@string/app_name"
9           android:theme="@style/AppTheme" >
10          <activity
11              android:name=".MyActivity"
12              android:label="@string/app_name" >
```

```
13              <intent-filter>
14                  <action android:name="android.intent.action.MAIN" />
15
16                  <category
17                      android:name="android.intent.category.LAUNCHER" />
18              </intent-filter>
19          </activity>
20      </application>
21
22  </manifest>
```

Part 3: Activity Layout Setup

The layout for the activity of this application, `activity_my.xml`, contains a `FrameLayout` root element. A `FrameLayout` is a container view designed to block out an area on the screen. In general, it holds a single view, which means we can use it as a canvas. The `FrameLayout` will eventually hold an instance of `BounceSurfaceView`, which is the dedicated drawing surface, `SurfaceView`, for this animation. The layout design for `activity_my.xml` is illustrated in Figure 6-15 and its related XML code is shown below.

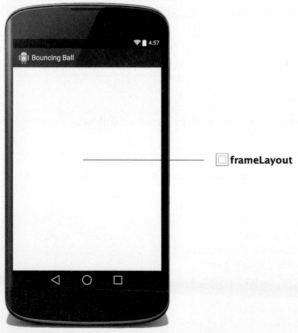

FIGURE 6-15 `activity_my.xml` contains a `FrameLayout` named `frameLayout`.

```
activity_my.xml
1
2   <?xml version="1.0" encoding="utf-8"?>
3   <FrameLayout xmlns:android="http://schemas.android.com/apk/res/android"
4       android:layout_width="match_parent"
5       android:layout_height="match_parent"
6       android:id="@+id/frameLayout">
7   </FrameLayout>
```

Part 4: `Ball` Class

`Ball` class provides the blueprint for the ball in motion. It is characterized by location, size, velocity, and collision detection. The details of the collisions have been established directly in the `Ball` class. As shown in Figure 6-16, this application will require four boundary limits of the viewable drawing surface. These limits represent the topmost, bottommost, leftmost, and rightmost boundaries of where the ball can move in the game area.

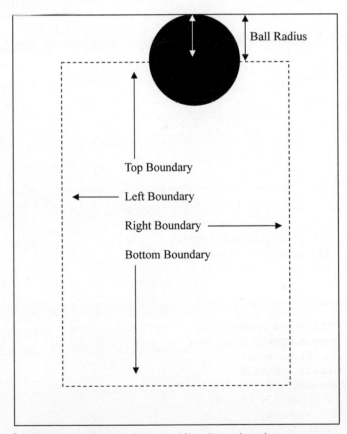

I FIGURE 6-16 Ball boundaries used for collision detection.

It is necessary to detect collisions because the ball's velocity will be reversed once it collides with wall boundaries. To establish boundaries and collisions, we consider that a ball's origin is located at its center. The ball collides with the top boundary when its *y* position is less than or equal to zero (the topmost edge of the drawing surface) plus the ball's radius.

The Java code for the Ball class is shown as follows:

Lines 22–46:   move() will be called repeatedly to move the ball and check for and respond to collisions.

Lines 48–53:   The draw() method will be called to render the ball on the background thread.

Ball.java

```java
1   package com.cornez.bouncingball;
2
3   import android.graphics.Canvas;
4   import android.graphics.Color;
5   import android.graphics.Paint;
6
7   public class Ball {
8       private final int RADIUS = 100;
9       private final int REVERSE = -1;
10      private int x;
11      private int y;
12      private int velX;
13      private int velY;
14
15      public Ball() {
16          x = 100;
17          y = 100;
18          velX = 10;
19          velY = 10;
20      }
21
22      public void move(int leftWall, int topWall,
23                       int rightWall, int bottomWall) {
24          //MOVE BALL
25          x += velX;
26          y += velY;
27
28          //CHECK FOR COLLISIONS ALONG WALLS
29          //TOP AND BOTTOM BOUNDARY COLLISION
30          if (y > bottomWall - RADIUS) {
31              y = bottomWall - RADIUS;
32              velY *= REVERSE;
33          } else if (y < topWall + RADIUS) {
34              y = topWall + RADIUS;
35              velY *= REVERSE;
36          }
```

```
37
38            //LEFT AND RIGHT BOUNDARY COLLISION
39            if (x > rightWall - RADIUS) {
40                x = rightWall - RADIUS;
41                velX *= REVERSE;
42            } else if (x < leftWall + RADIUS) {
43                x = leftWall + RADIUS;
44                velX *= REVERSE;
45            }
46        }
47
48        public void draw(Canvas canvas) {
49
50            Paint paint = new Paint();
51            paint.setColor(Color.rgb(211, 216, 156));
52            canvas.drawCircle(x, y, RADIUS, paint);
53        }
54    }
```

Part 5: The Drawing Surface

The BounceSurfaceView class is created by extending the SurfaceView class. This class will allow us to create a View that can be rendered within a background thread. The surface content for this View will be updated quickly and without the use of a Handler. An instance of BounceSurfaceView will eventually be added to the layout associated with the application's activity.

Lines 8–9:   The SurfaceView class will implement a SurfaceHolder interface. This interface will provide the controls that will be used to edit, or re-render, the drawing surface.

Line 11:   The background thread for this application will be associated with the drawing surface. All rendering tasks will occur on this thread.

Lines 16–17:   holder is the SurfaceHolder interface object that will be used to provide the access and control over the underlying drawing surface. addCallback() will add a callback interface for this holder.

Line 20:   A background thread is created, bounceThread. This thread will be linked to holder to facilitate updates to the drawing surface of the SurfaceView.

Lines 24–36:   The SurfaceHolder interface requires the implementation of three callback methods. These methods will supply notification when the drawing surface is created, changed, and destroyed. When the drawing surface is created, the background thread, bounceThread will be started. When the drawing surface is destroyed, the bounceThread is nullified.

BounceSurfaceView.java

```
1   package com.cornez.bouncingball;
2
3   import android.content.Context;
4   import android.util.AttributeSet;
5   import android.view.SurfaceHolder;
6   import android.view.SurfaceView;
7
8   public class BounceSurfaceView extends SurfaceView implements
9           SurfaceHolder.Callback {
10
11      private BounceThread bounceThread;
12
13      public BounceSurfaceView (Context context, AttributeSet attrs){
14          super (context, attrs);
15
16          SurfaceHolder holder = getHolder();
17          holder.addCallback(this);
18
19          //CREATE A NEW THREAD
20          bounceThread = new BounceThread (holder);
21      }
22
23      //IMPLEMENT THE INHERITED ABSTRACT METHODS
24      public void surfaceCreated (SurfaceHolder holder) {
25          bounceThread.start();
26      }
27      public void surfaceChanged (SurfaceHolder holder, int format,
28                                      int width, int height) {
29      }
30
31      public void surfaceDestroyed (SurfaceHolder holder) {
32          bounceThread.endBounce();
33          Thread dummyThread = bounceThread;
34          bounceThread = null;
35          dummyThread.interrupt();
36      }
37  }
```

Part 6: The Activity of the Application

MyActivity is the single Activity used by the application. Its controller role, which is to inflate the layout associated with the application and to add a SurfaceView to the inflated layout, is kept to a minimum.

Lines 24–26:   A BounceSurfaceView object is instantiated and added to the FrameLayout root element of the activity_my.xml layout. The surface content for this View will be updated in a background thread.

```
MyActivity.java
1   package com.cornez.bouncingball;
2
3   import android.app.Activity;
4   import android.os.Bundle;
5   import android.view.Menu;
6   import android.view.MenuItem;
7   import android.widget.FrameLayout;
8
9   public class MyActivity extends Activity {
10
11      @Override
12      protected void onCreate(Bundle savedInstanceState) {
13          super.onCreate(savedInstanceState);
14
15          // INFLATE THE LAYOUT CONTAINING THE FRAMELAYOUT ELEMENT
16          setContentView(R.layout.activity_my);
17
18          // REFERENCE THE FRAMELAYOUT ELEMENT
19          FrameLayout frameLayout = (FrameLayout)
20                          findViewById(R.id.frameLayout);
21
22          // INSTANTIATE A CUSTOM SURFACE VIEW
23          // ADD IT TO THE FRAMELAYOUT
24          BounceSurfaceView bounceSurfaceView = new
25                          BounceSurfaceView(this, null);
26          frameLayout.addView(bounceSurfaceView);
27      }
28
29      @Override
30      public boolean onCreateOptionsMenu(Menu menu) {
31          // Inflate the menu.
32          getMenuInflater().inflate(R.menu.my, menu);
33          return true;
34      }
35
36      @Override
37      public boolean onOptionsItemSelected(MenuItem item) {
38          // Handle action bar item clicks here. The action bar will
39          // automatically handle clicks on the Home/Up button, so long
40          // as you specify a parent activity in AndroidManifest.xml.
41          int id = item.getItemId();
42          if (id == R.id.action_settings) {
43              return true;
44          }
45          return super.onOptionsItemSelected(item);
46      }
47   }
```

Part 7: Background Thread

BounceThread is the class that models the background thread for the application. It is implemented as a separate class that extends the Thread class. As an extension of Thread, it will provide the essential run() method, which will serve as the animation loop.

Lines 8–16:   This background thread will be responsible for executing updates to an AnimationArena object. This object is instantiated in the thread and is the arena that holds the ball object that will be set in motion. This thread will be used to execute the updates to the AnimationArena object and control access to the drawing surface. The SurfaceHolder will control access to the surface.

Lines 21:   When making changes to the underlying drawing surface of a SurfaceView, the surface should be locked prior to rendering. This makes the surface unavailable to anyone else. After performing a lock, editing pixels in the surface can take place. A clean Canvas object will be returned for use when drawing onto the surface's bitmap.

Lines 22–23:   animationArena.update() is called to update the location of the ball.

Line 24:   animationArena.draw() will pass the Canvas object for re-rendering the ball in its new location.

Line 25:   unlockCanvasAndPost(canvas) signals that editing pixels in the surface is now complete. The surface's current pixels, drawn onto the canvas, will be displayed on the screen.

Lines 32–34:   A method for ending the animation is implemented.

BounceThread.java

```
1    package com.cornez.bouncingball;
2
3    import android.graphics.Canvas;
4    import android.view.SurfaceHolder;
5
6    public class BounceThread extends Thread {
7
8        private SurfaceHolder surfaceHolder;
9        private AnimationArena animationArena;
10       private boolean isRunning;
11
12       public BounceThread (SurfaceHolder sh){
13           isRunning = true;
14           surfaceHolder = sh;
15           animationArena = new AnimationArena();
16       }
```

```
17
18      public void run() {
19          try {
20              while (isRunning) {
21                  Canvas canvas = surfaceHolder.lockCanvas();
22                  animationArena.update(canvas.getWidth(),
23                          canvas.getHeight());
24                  animationArena.draw(canvas);
25                  surfaceHolder.unlockCanvasAndPost(canvas);
26              }
27          }catch (NullPointerException e){
28              e.printStackTrace();
29          }
30      }
31
32      public void endBounce() {
33          isRunning = false;
34      }
35  }
```

Part 8: AnimationArena for the Game World Model

The AnimationArena class is essentially the model for the game world. This class holds the ball and implements a set of methods that controls when the ball moves and is drawn to the canvas.

The background thread of the application will call the update() and draw() methods over and over again to create animation. The Java code for AnimationArena is shown as follows:

AnimationArena.java

```
1   package com.cornez.bouncingball;
2
3   import android.graphics.Canvas;
4
5   public class AnimationArena {
6       private Ball mBall;
7
8       public AnimationArena () {
9           //INSTANTIATE THE BALL
10          mBall = new Ball();
11      }
12
13      public void update (int width, int height) {
14          mBall.move(0, 0, width, height);
15      }
16
```

```
17      public void draw (Canvas canvas) {
18          //WIPE THE CANVAS CLEAN
19          canvas.drawRGB(156, 174, 216);
20
21          //DRAW THE BALL
22          mBall.draw(canvas);
23      }
24  }
```

■ 6.8 Efficient Threading

Developing applications with multiple threads requires careful programming. Concurrency is not a trivial subject and can be very challenging. Despite the complexities, there are obvious advantages of multithreading, such as the provision of greater responsiveness by using idle time to perform background tasks. It might seem that if a little threading improves efficiency, the employment of many threads must be better. In fact, having too many threads can lead to a sluggish application.

The impact of having too many threads in an application can result in the following two conditions. First, partitioning a fixed amount of work among too many threads gives each thread too little work. In this case, the overhead of starting and terminating threads swamps the useful work. Second, having too many threads running incurs overhead in the way they share finite processing resources. On a given device, the number of threads that can execute concurrently is limited by the number of processors. When the start() method is called on a thread, that thread may or may not start executing immediately, depending on the number of processors built into the device, as well as the number of threads currently waiting to execute.

Multithreaded code should be tested for efficiency and should provide a useful abstraction of concurrent execution. Applications should be designed so that few background threads are responsible for waiting until a task is available, executing it, and notifying other components of the program when it is complete. Because threads are able to share execution resources, thread-safe mechanisms, such as locks and queues, can be used to control access.

Sophisticated locking idioms are supported by the java.util package. When designing applications that require multiple threads, it is advisable to strategize the detection of possible deadlocks. Deadlocks occur when a given thread is waiting for a previous thread to finish; likewise, that thread is waiting for the previous one to complete. These deadlocks must be avoided, or they must be resolved when they occur. While threads are communicating through state variables on shared memory, they can use the Java library's built-in signaling mechanism that lets a thread notify other threads of changes in the state. Lock is a Java utility

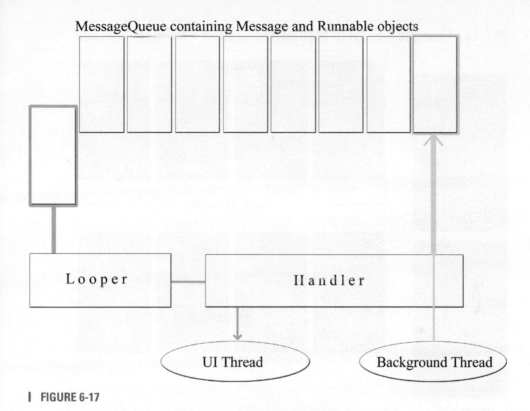

MessageQueue containing Message and Runnable objects

Looper

Handler

UI Thread

Background Thread

| FIGURE 6-17

that provides locking operations that control access to a shared resource by multiple threads. A lock provides exclusive access to a shared resource: only one thread at a time can acquire the lock, and all access to the shared resource requires that the lock be acquired first.

The most common thread communication between threads occurs between the UI thread and background threads. As illustrated in previous lab examples, the UI thread offloads long tasks by sending data messages to be processed on background threads. Multithreaded applications should follow an efficient message passing mechanism, such as the one illustrated in Figure 6-17. This diagram shows messages passed between a background thread and the UI thread.

The background thread adds messages to the queue, using the Handler connected to the UI thread. The Looper runs in the UI thread and retrieves messages from the queue in a First-In, First-Out order. The Handler is then responsible for processing the messages on the UI thread. In applications that create multiple Handler instances for processing messages on a thread, the Looper must be used to ensure that messages are dispatched to the correct Handler.

■ **Lab Example 6-5: Art in Motion Application—Multiple Threads**

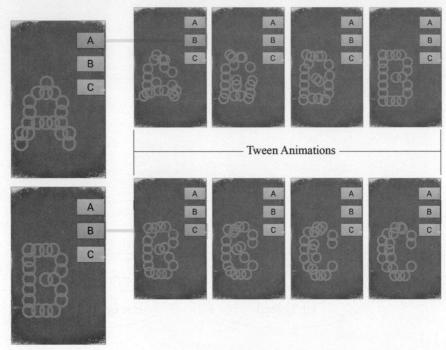

FIGURE 6-18 An Art "Letter" is created as spherical objects are "eased" into a target position.

This application explores proportional motion animation using a canvas and two background threads. A single Handler will be implemented to update drawings in the canvas. As shown in Figure 6-18, the letters A, B, and C are formed with 19 spherical objects. When the user launches the Art In Motion application for the first time, all 19 spheres are positioned in the exact same location on the canvas. When the user clicks on one of the letter buttons, the spheres "ease" into position until they have formed the letter clicked by the user.

Part 1: Animation Movement Design

Velocity, the fundamental property of an object that is moving, is characterized by direction and speed. The concept of proportional motion is an easing motion that involves moving an object from an existing position to a target position. The easing motion is evident as the object appears to slide into the target and then eventually stops.

Creating an easing motion requires that velocity is computed proportional to distance. For example, the further away from the target, the faster the object moves. As an object gets very close to the target, it moves an imperceptible amount. As Figure 6-19 shows, the illusion of an easing motion is achieved by repositioning the spherical object half the distance to the target position at each interval. The new velocity of the moving object is recomputed at each interval.

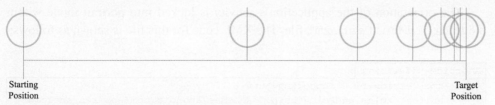

▌ FIGURE 6-19 A spherical object is eased into a target position.

Part 2: Application Structure and Setup

The settings for the application are as follows:

- Application Name: Art In Motion
- Project Name: ArtInMotion
- Package Name: `com.cornez.artinmotion`
- Android Form: Phone and Tablet
- Minimum SDK: API 18: Android 4.3 (Jelly Bean)
- Target SDK: API 21: Android 5.0 (Lollipop)
- Compile with: API 21: Android 5.0 (Lollipop)
- Activity Name: `MyActivity`
- Layout Name: `activity_my`

The final project structure for the application is shown in Figure 6-20.

▌ FIGURE 6-20 Project structure for Art in Motion animation.

The orientation of the application's activity is locked into portrait mode within the `AndroidManifest.xml` file. The XML code for this file is shown as follows:

```
AndroidManifest.xml
1   <?xml version="1.0" encoding="utf-8"?>
2   <manifest xmlns:android="http://schemas.android.com/apk/res/android"
3       package="com.cornez.artinmotion" >
4
5       <application
6           android:allowBackup="true"
7           android:icon="@drawable/ic_launcher"
8           android:label="@string/app_name"
9           android:theme="@style/AppTheme" >
10          <activity
11              android:name=".MyActivity"
12              android:screenOrientation="portrait"
13              android:label="@string/app_name" >
14              <intent-filter>
15                  <action
16                      android:name="android.intent.action.MAIN" />
17                  <category
18                      android:name="android.intent.category.LAUNCHER" />
19              </intent-filter>
20          </activity>
21      </application>
22
23  </manifest>
```

Part 3: The User Interface External Value Resources

The external string values for the button labels, A, B, and C, are set in `strings.xml`. This file is shown as follows:

```
strings.xml
1   <?xml version="1.0" encoding="utf-8"?>
2   <resources>
3
4       <string name="app_name">Art in Motion</string>
5       <string name="hello_world">Hello world!</string>
6       <string name="action_settings">Settings</string>
7
8       <string name="a_btn">A</string>
9       <string name="b_btn">B</string>
10      <string name="c_btn">C</string>
11
12  </resources>
```

The layout associated with the main activity is `activity_my.xml`, shown in Figure 6-21.

❙ FIGURE 6-21 The layout structure for `activity_my.xml`.

`activity_my.xml` requires a reference to the root element, `relativeLayout1`. This reference will be used programmatically to add a customized `View` to the layout. This customized View is designed to contain a drawing canvas that will hold animated spheres. The XML code for `activity_my.xml` is shown as follows:

```
activity_my.xml
1   <RelativeLayout
2   xmlns:android="http://schemas.android.com/apk/res/android"
3       xmlns:tools="http://schemas.android.com/tools"
4       android:layout_width="match_parent"
5       android:layout_height="match_parent"
6       android:paddingLeft="@dimen/activity_horizontal_margin"
7       android:paddingRight="@dimen/activity_horizontal_margin"
```

```
 8        android:paddingTop="@dimen/activity_vertical_margin"
 9        android:paddingBottom="@dimen/activity_vertical_margin"
10        android:id="@+id/relativeLayout1"
11        tools:context=".MyActivity"
12        android:background="@drawable/artback">
13
14        <Button
15            android:id="@+id/button1"
16            android:layout_width="100dp"
17            android:layout_height="wrap_content"
18            android:layout_alignParentRight="true"
19            android:layout_alignParentTop="true"
20            android:layout_marginTop="40dp"
21            android:alpha=".7"
22            android:onClick="createA"
23            android:text="@string/a_btn"
24            android:textSize="35sp" />
25
26        <Button
27            android:id="@+id/button2"
28            android:layout_width="100dp"
29            android:layout_height="wrap_content"
30            android:layout_alignParentRight="true"
31            android:layout_below="@+id/button1"
32            android:layout_marginTop="20dp"
33            android:alpha=".7"
34            android:onClick="createB"
35            android:text="@string/b_btn"
36            android:textSize="35sp" />
37
38        <Button
39            android:id="@+id/button3"
40            android:layout_width="100dp"
41            android:layout_height="wrap_content"
42            android:layout_alignParentRight="true"
43            android:layout_below="@+id/button2"
44            android:layout_marginTop="20dp"
45            android:alpha=".7"
46            android:onClick="createC"
47            android:text="@string/c_btn"
48            android:textSize="35sp" />
49
50    </RelativeLayout>
```

Part 4: Designing the Art Letters

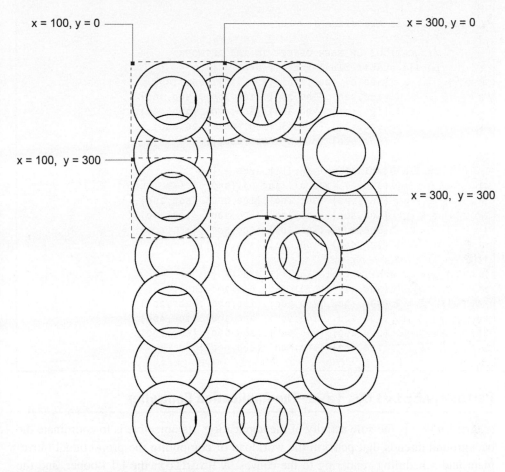

FIGURE 6-22 The *x, y* position of spheres on a grid are used to form the letter B.

Each of the "art" letters for A, B, and C is composed of an arrangement of spheres. For example, the arrangement of spheres that form the letter B is shown in Figure 6-22. The location of these spheres is specified in the file `ArtDesign.java` as two-dimensional arrays. These *x, y* locations are used to establish final target positions when computing proportional movement. The Java code for `ArtDesign.java` is shown as follows:

```
ArtDesign.java
1   package com.cornez.artinmotion;
2
3   public class ArtDesign {
4
5       //LOCATIONS OF EACH OBJECT IN THE ARTWORK
6       public static final int[][] artA = {
7               {300,0},{200,100},{300,100},{400,100},
8               {100,200},{500,200},{100,300},{500,300},
9               {100,400},{200,400},{300,400},{400,400},
10              {500,400},{0,500},{100,500},{500,500},
11              {600,500},{0,600},{600,600}};
12
13      public static final int[][] artB = {
14              {100,0},{200,0},{300,0},{400,0},
15              {100,100},{500,100},{100,200},{500,200},
16              {100,300},{300,300},{400,300},{100,400},
17              {500,400},{100,500},{500,500},{100,600},
18              {200,600},{300,600},{400,600}};
19
20      public static final int[][] artC = {
21              {300,0},{400,0},{500,0},{200,100},
22              {300,100},{600,100},{100,200},{200,200},
23              {600,200},{100,300},{200,300},{100,400},
24              {200,400},{200,500},{300,500},{600,500},
25              {300,600},{400,600},{500,600}};
26  }
```

Part 5: `MyActivity.java`–The Application Controller

`MyActivity` is the sole activity of the application. Its objective is to coordinate the background threads that perform the workload of computing the proportional movement and scheduling rendering to the canvas. A `Handler`, the UI Looper, and the `MessageQueue` are used to synchronize the animation process. The Java code for `MyActivity` is shown as follows:

```
MyActivity.java
1   package com.cornez.artinmotion;
2
3   import android.app.Activity;
4   import android.os.Bundle;
5   import android.os.Handler;
6   import android.view.Menu;
7   import android.view.MenuItem;
8   import android.view.View;
```

```
9   import android.widget.RelativeLayout;
10
11  public class MyActivity extends Activity {
12
13      //ANIMATION IS SPLIT INTO TWO THREADS:
14      //          CALCULATING MOVEMENT
15      //          DRAWING MOVEMENT
16      private Thread calculateMovementThread;
17      private Thread drawMovementThread;
18
19      //HOW MANY MOVING OBJECTS IN THE ARTWORK
20      private final int OBJECTS_N = 19;
21
22      //ARTWORK OBJECTS MOVE FROM A CURRENT POSITION TO
23      //A FINAL DESTINATION FORMING THE FINAL ARTWORK.
24      private int[][] currentPosition = new int[19][2];
25      private int[][] finalDestination = new int[19][2];
26
27      private ArtWorkView artworkView;
28      private RelativeLayout mainLayout;
29
30      @Override
31      protected void onCreate(Bundle savedInstanceState) {
32          super.onCreate(savedInstanceState);
33
34          //TASK 1: SET THE LAYOUT
35          setContentView(R.layout.activity_my);
36
37          //TASK 2: INITIALIZE THE STARTING
38          //        AND ENDING ART LOCATIONS
39          initialize();
40
41          //TASK 3: CREATE REFERENCES TO THE RELATIVELAYOUT CONTAINER
42          //        AND ADD THE ARTWORK VIEW TO THE LAYOUT
43          mainLayout = (RelativeLayout)
44                      findViewById(R.id.relativeLayout1);
45          artworkView = new ArtWorkView(this);
46          mainLayout.addView(artworkView, 0);
47
48          //TASK 4: CONSTRUCT THE THREADS TO CALCULATE MOVEMENT
49          //        AND ANIMATE (DRAW) THE MOVEMENT
50          calculateMovementThread = new Thread(calculateMovement);
51          drawMovementThread = new Thread(drawMovement);
52
53          //TASK 5: START THE THREADS
54          calculateMovementThread.start();
55          drawMovementThread.start();
56      }
```

Lines 58–66:   The current position of each moving sphere is updated at regular intervals. The target position is used to compute the next current position of a given sphere. This data is stored in the array's finalDestination and currentPosition.

Lines 69–88:   The onClick() event handlers are implemented for A, B, and C buttons.

MyActivity.java (*continued*)

```
57      //****** CURRENT AND TARGET ARTWORK LOCATIONS ******
58      private void initialize() {
59          for (int i = 0; i < OBJECTS_N; i++){
60              finalDestination[i][0] = 200;  //X POSITION
61              finalDestination[i][1] = 200;  //Y POSITION
62
63              currentPosition[i][0] = 20;
64              currentPosition[i][1] = 20;
65          }
66      }
67
68      //****** BUTTONS EVENT HANDLERS ******
69      public void createA (View view){
70          for (int i = 0; i < OBJECTS_N; i++){
71              finalDestination[i][0] = ArtDesign.artA[i][0];
72              finalDestination[i][1] = ArtDesign.artA[i][1];
73          }
74      }
75
76      public void createB (View view){
77          for (int i = 0; i < OBJECTS_N; i++){
78              finalDestination[i][0] = ArtDesign.artB[i][0];
79              finalDestination[i][1] = ArtDesign.artB[i][1];
80          }
81      }
82
83      public void createC (View view){
84          for (int i = 0; i < OBJECTS_N; i++){
85              finalDestination[i][0] = ArtDesign.artC[i][0];
86              finalDestination[i][1] = ArtDesign.artC[i][1];
87          }
88      }
```

The unit of work on background threads is divided into movement calculations and drawing.

Lines 91–108:   The calculateMovement is a Runnable, bound to the calculateMovementThread, that computes positions of spheres on the canvas. These positions will be calculated at intervals spaced at approximately 200 milliseconds apart. Current positions are based on the distance to the target position divided by 5. This means that a sphere will travel 1/5th of the distance to its target destination at each time interval. `finalDestination[i][0]` refers to the *x* position and `finalDestination[i][1]` refers to the *y* position.

Lines 110–120: The drawMovement Runnable is associated with the drawmovementThread. The threadHandler is used to send empty messages to the MessageQueue at intervals of approximately 200 milliseconds.

`MyActivity.java` (*continued*)

```
89
90      //***** RUNNABLES *****
91      private Runnable calculateMovement = new Runnable() {
92          private static final int DELAY = 200;
93          public void run() {
94              try {
95                  while (true){
96                      for (int i = 0; i < OBJECTS_N; i++){
97                          currentPosition[i][0] +=
98                                      (finalDestination[i][0] -
99                                      currentPosition[i][0])/ 5;
100                         currentPosition[i][1] +=
101                                     (finalDestination[i][1] -
102                                     currentPosition[i][1])/ 5;
103                     }
104                     Thread.sleep(DELAY);
105                 }
106             } catch (InterruptedException e) {}
107         }
108     };
109
110     private Runnable drawMovement = new Runnable() {
111         private static final int DELAY = 200;
112         public void run() {
113             try {
114                 while (true){
115                     Thread.sleep(DELAY);
116                     threadHandler.sendEmptyMessage(0);
117                 }
118             } catch (InterruptedException e) {}
119         }
120     };
```

Lines 123–125:   handleMessage() is used to process messages from the MessageQueue. Each message it processes results in a call to artworkView.update(currentPosition), which will redraw the spheres on the canvas in their recomputed current positions.

```
MyActivity.java (continued)
121    //****** HANDLER FOR UPDATING ARTWORK BETWEEN DELAYS ******
122    public Handler threadHandler = new Handler() {
123        public void handleMessage(android.os.Message msg){
124            artworkView.update(currentPosition);
125        }
126    };
127
128    @Override
129    public boolean onCreateOptionsMenu(Menu menu) {
130        // Inflate the menu.
131        getMenuInflater().inflate(R.menu.my, menu);
132        return true;
133    }
134
135    @Override
136    public boolean onOptionsItemSelected(MenuItem item) {
137        // Handle action bar item clicks here. The action bar will
138        // automatically handle clicks on the Home/Up button, so long
139        // as you specify a parent activity in AndroidManifest.xml.
140        int id = item.getItemId();
141        if (id == R.id.action_settings) {
142            return true;
143        }
144        return super.onOptionsItemSelected(item);
145    }
146 }
```

Part 6: `ArtWorkView.java`—The Custom View Containing a Canvas

ArtWorkView is the class that models the custom View. onDraw() is implemented to perform drawing. The Java code for ArtWorkView is shown as follows.

```
ArtWorkView.java
1    package com.cornez.artinmotion;
2
3    import android.content.Context;
4    import android.graphics.Canvas;
5    import android.graphics.Color;
6    import android.graphics.Paint;
7    import android.view.View;
8
```

```
9   import java.util.Arrays;
10
11  public class ArtWorkView extends View {
12
13      private Paint paint;
14      private int[][] artPositions;
15
16      public ArtWorkView(Context context) {
17          super(context);
18
19          //HOLDS THE POSITIONS FOR EACH SPHERE IN THE ARTWORK
20          artPositions = new int[19][2];
21
22          //SPECIFY THE PAINT COLOR AND STYLE
23          int aquaBlue = Color.argb(255, 148, 205, 204);
24          paint = new Paint();
25          paint.setStyle(Paint.Style.STROKE);
26          paint.setStrokeWidth(15.0f);
27          paint.setColor(aquaBlue);
28      }
29
30      @Override
31      protected void onDraw(Canvas canvas) {
32          //DRAW EACH OF THE SPHERES ON THE CANVAS
33          for (int i = 0; i < 19; i++) {
34              canvas.drawCircle(artPositions[i][0] + 300,
35                      artPositions[i][1] + 400, 80, paint);
36          }
37      }
38
39      public void update(int[][] values) {
40          artPositions = Arrays.copyOf(values, values.length);
41          invalidate();
42      }
43  }
```

■ 6.9 Materials and Functionality

With the release of Lollipop in October 2014, new visual enhancement features were added to the platform and given the name Material Design. One specific feature that stood out was fluid animations. Material is partly a metaphor for a system of motion; surfaces and edges of material provide visual cues. The use of familiar tactile attributes helps users quickly comprehend how to maneuver. Movement is important for providing understanding that leads to instinctive interactions.

Applying material design to an application requires the android: Theme attribute in AndroidManifest.xml to be set to Material. This specification provides a collection of default animations for touch feedback and activity transitions.

Beginning with Android 5.0 (ApI level 21), animations can be customized as transitions. Two interesting animations provided by Material Design are "circular reveal" and "curved motion." These transitions do not require the use of a background thread to execute.

Consider the following onCreate() callback method for MyActivity. The single objective of this code is to reveal a previously invisible ImageView using an Animator object, anim. anim is created and configured within the activity and will therefore execute on the UI thread.

The method calls getLeft(), getRight(), getTop(), and getBottom() are used to get the pixel positions of the ImageView relative to the parent.

The createCircularReveal() method call returns an animation object that transitions the ImageView into full view in a clipping circle motion. View AnimationUtils defines a collection of common animation utilities to apply to View objects. The call to start() is required to set the animation in motion.

```
1   public class MyActivity extends Activity {
2
3       @Override
4       protected void onCreate(Bundle savedInstanceState) {
5           super.onCreate(savedInstanceState);
6           setContentView(R.layout.activity_my);
7
8           //TASK 1: REFERENCE THE TEXTVIEW IN THE LAYOUT
9           ImageView imageView = findViewById(R.id. imageView);
10
11          //TASK 2: COMPUTE THE CENTER OF THE CLIPPING
12          int centerX = (imageView.getLeft() + imageView.getRight()) / 2;
13          int centerY = (imageView.getTop() + imageView.getBottom()) / 2;
14
15          //TASK 3: COMPUTE THE STARTING AND ENDING RADIUS OF THE CIRCLE
16          int startRadius = 0;
17          int endRadius = imageView.getWidth();
18
19          //TASK 4: CREATE THE ANIMATOR TO RUN IN THE UI THREAD
20          Animator anim =
21                  ViewAnimationUtils.createCircularReveal(
22                          imageView, centerX, centerY, 0, endRadius);
23          //TASK 5: START THE ANIMATION
24          anim.start();
25      }
```

When start() is called within a background thread, a Looper should be used to avoid a runtime exception. When the animation is used to update properties of objects in the view hierarchy, a UI thread is required to perform View updates.

Activity transitions in material design support the visual connections between different states, using motion and transformations between common elements. For example, it is possible to specify custom animations for entering and exiting transitions, as well as for transitions of shared elements between activities; these transitions include explode, slide, and fade. A system-managed processing thread called RenderThread keeps animations smooth, even when there are delays in the main UI thread.

`ValueAnimator`, an extension of `Animator`, can be used to provide a timing engine for running animations that calculate animated values and set them on target objects. These animations use a single timing pulse that runs in a custom handler to ensure that property changes happen on the UI thread.

The code segment below illustrates a circular reveal animation that changes the visibility of an ImageView at a specified time using an animation listener. The `showImageView`() method uses a DELAY value that will cause the animation to be spread over a period of two seconds. The `hideImageView`() method will produce a rapid circular reveal.

```
1    private void hideImageView() {
2        int centerX = (imageView.getLeft() + imageView.getRight()) / 2;
3        int centerY = (imageView.getTop() + imageView.getBottom()) / 2;
4        int startRadius = 0;
5        int endRadius = imageView.getWidth();
6
7        ValueAnimator animUtil =
8                ViewAnimationUtils.createCircularReveal(imageView,
9                        centerX, centerY, endRadius, startRadius);
10
11        animUtil.addListener(new AnimatorListenerAdapter() {
12
13            @Override
14            public void onAnimationEnd(Animator animation) {
15                super.onAnimationEnd(animation);
16                imageView.setVisibility(View.INVISIBLE);
17            }
18        });
19        animUtil.start();
20    }
21
22    private void showImageView() {
23        final int DELAY = 2000;
24        int centerX = (imageView.getLeft() + imageView.getRight()) / 2;
25        int centerY = (imageView.getTop() + imageView.getBottom()) / 2;
26        int startRadius = 0;
27        int endRadius = imageView.getWidth();
28
29        ValueAnimator animUtil =
30                ViewAnimationUtils.createCircularReveal(imageView,
```

```
31                          centerX, centerY, startRadius, endRadius);
32
33          animUtil.setDuration(DELAY);
34          animUtil.addListener( new AnimatorListenerAdapter() {
35              @Override
36              public void onAnimationStart(Animator animation) {
37                  super.onAnimationStart(animation);
38                  imageView.setVisibility(View.VISIBLE);
39              }
40          });
41          animUtil.start();
42      }
```

■ Lab Example 6-6: Virtual Pet Fish—Animated ImageViews

Android users often have high expectations for the production values of the apps they use on their devices. Applications providing the same basic functionality often compete with each other on Google Play. The most outstanding products are delivered with high-end production values that can include graphics, sound and music, and a narrative.

Sophisticated visual graphics may not make an application any better, but they will contribute to a more satisfying experience for the user. Visuals furnish a well-developed representation of a brand and provide an interesting context for an application.

Part 1: The Design

This lab explores animated movement, using imported higher-quality graphics. The completed application, a dynamic aquarium containing a fish, is shown in Figure 6-23. The fish is a virtual pet. As the fish swims within the aquarium, it will burn calories and will eventually become hungry. Once hungry, the fish will feed at the bottom of the aquarium. When the fish is not searching for a meal to supply calories, it will explore the top part of the aquarium.

Part 2: Application Structure and Setup

The settings for the application are as follows:

- Application Name: Virtual Fish
- Project Name: VirtualFish
- Package Name: `com.cornez.virtualfish`
- Android Form: Phone and Tablet
- Minimum SDK: API 18: Android 4.3 (Jelly Bean)

| FIGURE 6-23 The Virtual Pet Fish application.

- Target SDK: API 21: Android 5.0 (Lollipop)
- Compile with: API 21: Android 5.0 (Lollipop)
- Activity Name: `MyActivity`
- Layout Name: `activity_my`

The application is to be divided into three parts:

1. `Fish.java` (Model): The behavior of the virtual fish is driven by logic rules that primarily deal with the current state of hunger.

2. Visuals (`Views`): A small set of `ImageViews` is used to depict the elements in the fishtank, including the fish, foliage, and water.

3. `MyActivity.java` (Controller): The main activity of the application requires two threads: the UI thread and a background thread. The UI thread is responsible for updating the visuals, while the background thread provides the logic and calculations determining how the fish will behave.

The project structure for the application is shown in Figure 6-24. Three graphic PNG files are stored in the `res/drawable` folders. `background.png` provides the water context for the aquarium. The other two visuals, `fish.png` and `foliage.png`, will be layered over the background in the final application. This will provide an interesting visual effect.

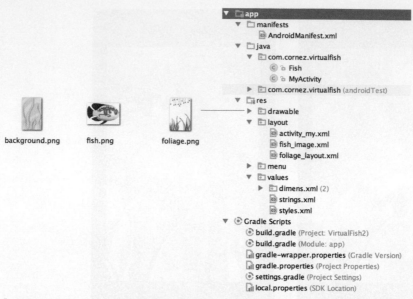

FIGURE 6-24 Final Project structure for the Virtual Fish application.

The orientation of the screen is locked into portrait mode. In addition, a fullscreen will be used with the titlebar removed. The XML code for `AndroidManifest.xml` is shown as follows:

```
AndroidManifest.xml
1  <?xml version="1.0" encoding="utf-8"?>
2  <manifest xmlns:android="http://schemas.android.com/apk/res/android"
3      package="com.cornez.virtualfish" >
4
5      <application
6          android:allowBackup="true"
7          android:icon="@drawable/ic_launcher"
8          android:label="@string/app_name"
9          android:theme="@android:style/Theme.Holo.
10                    Light.NoActionBar.Fullscreen">
11          <activity
12              android:name=".MyActivity"
13              android:screenOrientation="portrait"
14              android:label="@string/app_name" >
15              <intent-filter>
16                  <action android:name="android.intent.action.MAIN" />
17                  <category
18                      android:name="android.intent.category.LAUNCHER" />
19              </intent-filter>
20          </activity>
21      </application>
22
23  </manifest>
```

Part 3: The User Interface and Graphic Elements

☐ **container** (FrameLayout)

❙ **FIGURE 6-25** The layout design shown in the Graphical Layout Editor.

A `FrameLayout` is primarily used to hold a single child view. It can be difficult to organize child views in a way that is scalable to different screen sizes, and child views can overlap each other. However, when a `View` is added programmatically to a `FrameLayout`, its position can be controlled very easily. In addition, multiple `View` elements can be layered in a useful way. This is advantageous when creating games and applying movement to View elements.

The user interface screen for the Virtual Fish application is the layout file `activity_my.xml`. This UI screen will be bound to the `Activity` of the application and will use a `FrameLayout` as the root element. No other `View` elements will be specified in the XML file. As shown in Figure 6-25, the background for the `FrameLayout` is set to the drawable representing the water in the aquarium-`background.png`.

The `FrameLayout` will serve as a container for the aquarium, with additional visual elements being added programmatically when the `Activity` of the application is launched for the first time. The XML code for `activity_my.xml` is shown as follows:

Line 5:   The id for the `FrameLayout` is specified as `container`. This will allow additional elements to be added to the aquarium.

Line 7:   The image of water is applied to the background.

```
activity_my.xml
1  <FrameLayout xmlns:android="http://schemas.android.com/apk/res/android"
2      xmlns:tools="http://schemas.android.com/tools"
3      android:layout_width="match_parent"
4      android:layout_height="match_parent"
5      android:id="@+id/container"
6      tools:context=".MyActivity"
7      android:background="@drawable/background">
8  </FrameLayout>
```

The fish graphic will be added to the `FrameLayout` by inflating an `ImageView` XML file, depicted in Figure 6-26. The XML layout file is `fish_image.xml` and is located in `app/src/main/res/layout`.

ImageView – @drawable/fish

❚ FIGURE 6-26 The image of a fish is stored as an XML layout.

The XML code for `fish_image.xml` is shown as follows:

Line 2:   An ImageView is specified as the root element of the layout.

Line 5:   The image of a fish is identified as the source for the layout.

```
fish_image.xml
1  <?xml version="1.0" encoding="utf-8"?>
2  <ImageView xmlns:android="http://schemas.android.com/apk/res/android"
3      android:layout_width="match_parent"
4      android:layout_height="match_parent"
5      android:src="@drawable/fish"
6      android:contentDescription="@string/app_name">
7
8  </ImageView>
```

Similar to the fish graphic, the image of foliage will also be added to the aquarium during runtime. By doing this programmatically, this allows us to position the fish between the water and the foliage. This provides an attractive visual effect, with the fish being able to swim behind the foliage as it searches for food.

ImageView – @drawable/foliage

▌ FIGURE 6-27 The graphic of foliage is represented as an XML file.

The XML code for `foliage_layout.xml` is shown as follows. As illustrated in Figure 6-27, the root element of the layout is an `ImageView`. `foliage.png` is specified as the image source, as shown on Line 5.

```
foliage_layout.xml
1   <?xml version="1.0" encoding="utf-8"?>
2   <ImageView xmlns:android="http://schemas.android.com/apk/res/android"
3       android:layout_width="match_parent"
4       android:layout_height="match_parent"
5       android:src="@drawable/foliage"
6       android:contentDescription="@string/foliage">
7
8   </ImageView>
```

Part 4: Modeling the Behavior of the Fish

The `Fish` class is used to model a virtual fish living in the aquarium. The behavior of a fish will be governed by rules related to hunger or, more specifically, the amount of food in its stomach. For example, when the fish is hungry, it will actively search for food. If the fish has food in its stomach, it will swim around the tank while burning calories and depleting the food in its stomach. Once the fuel in the stomach has been used up, the fish will again seek out food. As the fish eats, food is added to his stomach. When the amount of food in the stomach has reached full capacity, the fish will leave its food and begin swimming around the tank. The state of the fish at any given moment is described by one of three conditions:

IsHungry: The fish is hungry and actively searching for food.

IsSwimming: The fish has food in its stomach and is looking for specific spots in the aquarium to play. As the pet swims, calories are burned until it becomes hungry again.

IsEating: A fish is eating when its state was previously changed from isHungry and is in close proximity to food. The fish remains stationary as it refuels. Once the stomach has reached its full capacity, the state of the fish is set to IsSwimming.

In addition to the x and y position of the fish, further attributes are defined as follows:

mCondition: This attribute specifies the current state of the fish: IsHungry, IsSwimming, or IsEating.

mVelocity: This attribute refers to the easing velocity, or proportional movement of the fish.

mStomachCapacity and mFoodInStomach: In this lab example, the maximum capacity of a fish's stomach is set to 80. When multiple fish are added to the aquarium, this value can be randomized. When a Fish object is instantiated, its stomach will be set to full, as shown on Line 30.

mTankWidth and mTankHeight: Food is located at the bottom area of the tank. Play locations will be computed within the top area of the tank. Both computations will rely on the height and width of the Android device.

mDirection: As the fish moves around the aquarium, the direction it faces will change, as shown in Figure 6-28.

1   -1

FIGURE 6-28 mDirection refers to the direction a Fish object faces.

```
Fish.java
1   package com.cornez.virtualfish;
2
3   public class Fish {
4       // FISH ARTWORK OBJECT HAS A CURRENT
5       // POSITION TO THAT CAN BE ACCESSED PUBLICLY
6       public int x;
7       public int y;
8
9
10      public static final int IsHungry = 1;
11      public static final int IsSwimming = 2;
12      public static final int IsEating = 3;
13
14      private int mCondition;
15      private int mVelocity;
16      private int mStomachCapacity;
17      private int mFoodInStomach;
18      private int mTankWidth;
19      private int mTankHeight;
20      private int mDirection;
21
22      private int playX, playY;
23      private int foodX, foodY;
24
25      public Fish(int xPos, int yPos, int condition,
26                      int tankWidth, int tankHeight) {
27          mCondition = condition;
28          mVelocity = 3;
29          mStomachCapacity = 80;
30          mFoodInStomach = mStomachCapacity;
31          mTankWidth = tankWidth;
32          mTankHeight = tankHeight;
33          x = xPos;
34          y = yPos;
35          mDirection = 1;
36
37          // FOOD AND EXPLORE LOCATIONS ARE FIXED
38          // IN THE TOP AND BOTTOM OF THE TANK
39          foodY = (int) tankHeight / 2 - 100;
40          foodX = (int) (Math.ceil(Math.random() * mTankWidth) -
41                          mTankWidth / 2);
42          playY = (int) -(Math.random() * mTankHeight / 2) + 100;
43          playX = (int) (Math.ceil(Math.random() * mTankWidth) -
44                          mTankWidth / 2);
45      }
46
47      public void move() {
48          //EXAMINE POSSIBLE CONDITIONS
```

```
49          switch (mCondition) {
50              case IsSwimming:
51                  swim();
52                  break;
53              case IsHungry:
54                  findFood();
55                  break;
56              case IsEating:
57                  eatFood();
58          }
59      }
60
61      private void swim() {
62          //TASK 1: BURN A CALORIE OF FOOD;
63          mFoodInStomach--;
64
65          //TASK 2: SWIM TOWARD A POINT OF INTEREST: playX, playY
66          int xDistance = playX - x;
67          int yDistance = playY - y;
68          x += xDistance / mVelocity;
69          y += yDistance / mVelocity;
70          if (playX < x) {
71              mDirection = -1;
72          } else {
73              mDirection = 1;
74          }
75
76          //TASK 3: FIND ANOTHER PLACE TO EXPLORE
77          //          IN THE TOP HALF OF THE TANK
78          if (Math.abs(xDistance) < 5 && Math.abs(yDistance) < 5) {
79              playX = (int) (Math.ceil(Math.random() * mTankWidth) -
80                          mTankWidth / 2);
81              playY = (int) -(Math.random() * mTankHeight / 2) + 100;
82          }
83
84          //TASK 4: DETERMINE IF STOMACH IS EMPTY
85          if (mFoodInStomach <= 0) {
86              mCondition = IsHungry;
87              //FIND A PLACE TO EAT IN THE BOTTOM OF THE TANK
88              foodX = (int) (Math.ceil(Math.random() * mTankWidth) -
89                          mTankWidth / 2) - 100;
90          }
91      }
92
93      private void findFood() {
94
95          //TASK : SWIM TOWARD FOOD: foodX, foodY
96          int xDistance = foodX - x;
```

```
97      int yDistance = foodY - y;
98
99      x += xDistance / mVelocity;
100     y += yDistance / mVelocity;
101
102     //TURN FISH IN DIRECTION OF FOOD
103     if (foodX < x) {
104         mDirection = -1;
105     } else {
106         mDirection = 1;
107     }
108
109     //TASK 3: DETERMINE IF FOOD IS FOUND
110     if (Math.abs((x - foodX)) <= 10 && Math.abs(y - foodY) <= 10) {
111         mCondition = IsEating;
112     }
113 }
114
115 private void eatFood() {
116
117     //TASK 1: ADD A CALORIE OF FOOD TO THE STOMACH;
118     mFoodInStomach += 4;
119
120     //TASK 3: DETERMINE IF STOMACH IS FULL
121     if (mFoodInStomach >= mStomachCapacity) {
122         mCondition = IsSwimming;
123
124         //FIND A NEW PLACE TO PLAY
125         playX = (int) (Math.ceil(Math.random() * mTankWidth) -
126                         mTankWidth / 2);
127         playY = (int) -(Math.random() * mTankHeight / 2) + 100;
128     }
129 }
130
131 public int getFacingDirection() {
132     return mDirection;
133 }
134 }
```

Part 5: The Application Activity

As the sole activity of the application, MyActivity is the controller that initializes the application threads and controls communication between elements. Two threads will be used to perform the application workloads. The UI thread will update the image elements, specifically repositioning and scaling the fish: ImageView. A background thread, `calculateMovementThread`, will perform the calculations that determine the *x, y* location and facing direction of the fish.

The Java code for `MyActivity` is shown as follows:

MyActivity.java

```
1    package com.cornez.virtualfish;
2
3    import android.app.Activity;
4    import android.content.Context;
5    import android.graphics.Point;
6    import android.os.Bundle;
7    import android.os.Handler;
8    import android.view.Display;
9    import android.view.LayoutInflater;
10   import android.view.Menu;
11   import android.view.MenuItem;
12   import android.widget.FrameLayout;
13   import android.widget.ImageView;
14
15   public class MyActivity extends Activity {
16
17       //ANIMATION IS SPLIT INTO TWO THREADS:
18       //          CALCULATING MOVEMENT
19       //           FISH TANK UPDATES: UI THREAD
20       private Thread calculateMovementThread;
21
22       // FISH TANK ELEMENTS AND PROPERTIES
23       private ImageView fishImageView;
24       private Fish mFish;
25       private int tankWidth;
26       private int tankHeight;
27       private FrameLayout fishTankLayout;
28
29       @Override
30       protected void onCreate(Bundle savedInstanceState) {
31           super.onCreate(savedInstanceState);
32
33           //TASK 1: SET THE LAYOUT
34           setContentView(R.layout.activity_my);
35
36           //TASK 2: CREATE REFERENCES TO THE FRAME LAYOUT CONTAINER
37           fishTankLayout = (FrameLayout) findViewById(R.id.container);
38
39           //TASK 4: GET THE DIMENSIONS OF THE SCREEN
40           //          TO USE FOR THE TANK SIZE
41           Display display = getWindowManager().getDefaultDisplay();
42           Point size = new Point();
43           display.getSize(size);
44           tankWidth = size.x;
45           tankHeight = size.y;
```

```
46
47          //TASK 2: INSTANTIATE A FISH
48          int initialXPosition = 0;
49          int initialYPosition = 0;
50          mFish = new Fish(initialXPosition, initialYPosition,
51                           Fish.IsSwimming, tankWidth, tankHeight);
52
53          //TASK 3: BUILD THE TANK ELEMENTS
54          buildTank();
55
56          //TASK 4: CONSTRUCT THE THREAD TO CALCULATE MOVEMENT
57          //          AND ANIMATE THE MOVEMENT
58          calculateMovementThread = new Thread(calculateMovement);
59
60          //TASK 5: START THE THREAD
61          calculateMovementThread.start();
62      }
63
64      private void buildTank() {
65          //TASK 1: CREATE A LAYOUT INFLATER TO
66          //          ADD VISUAL VIEWS TO THE LAYOUT
67          LayoutInflater layoutInflater;
68          layoutInflater = (LayoutInflater)
69                  getSystemService(Context.LAYOUT_INFLATER_SERVICE);
70
71          //TASK 2: ADD THE FOLIAGE
72          ImageView foliageImageView = (ImageView)
73              layoutInflater.inflate(R.layout.foliage_layout, null);
74          foliageImageView.setX((float) 0);
75          foliageImageView.setY((float) 0);
76          foliageImageView.setAlpha((float) .97);
77          fishTankLayout.addView(foliageImageView, 0);
78
79          //TASK 3: ADD THE VIRTUAL FISH
80          fishImageView = (ImageView)
81              layoutInflater.inflate(R.layout.fish_image, null);
82          fishImageView.setScaleX((float) .3);
83          fishImageView.setScaleY((float) .3);
84          fishImageView.setX(mFish.x);
85          fishImageView.setY(mFish.y);
86          fishTankLayout.addView(fishImageView, 0);
87      }
```

Lines 89–103: An inner class implementation is used to define the Runnable
work unit that executes on the background thread. Anima-
tion is achieved by performing fish movement computations
and then pausing 200 milliseconds before adding a message to
the MessageQueue. The MessageQueue is regulated by the
Handler named updateTankHandler.

Lines 106–117: The instructions in the `Handler` are performed on the UI thread, which allows updates to `View` elements such as `fishImageView`.

MyActivity.java (*continued*)

```
88      //******************* RUNNABLE *********************
89      private Runnable calculateMovement = new Runnable() {
90          private static final int DELAY = 200;
91
92          public void run() {
93              try {
94                  while (true) {
95                      mFish.move();
96                      Thread.sleep(DELAY);
97                      updateTankHandler.sendEmptyMessage(0);
98                  }
99              } catch (InterruptedException e) {
100                     e.printStackTrace();
101             }
102         }
103     };
104
105     //***** HANDLER FOR UPDATING THE FISH BETWEEN SLEEP DELAYS ******
106     public Handler updateTankHandler = new Handler() {
107         public void handleMessage(android.os.Message msg) {
108
109             //TASK 1: FACE THE FISH IN THE CORRECT DIRECTION
110             fishImageView.setScaleX((float) (.3 *
111                                     mFish.getFacingDirection()));
112
113             //TASK 2: SET THE FISH AT THE CORRECT XY LOCATION
114             fishImageView.setX((float) mFish.x);
115             fishImageView.setY((float) mFish.y);
116         }
117     };
118
119     @Override
120     public boolean onCreateOptionsMenu(Menu menu) {
121         // Inflate the menu.
122         getMenuInflater().inflate(R.menu.my, menu);
123         return true;
124     }
125
126     @Override
127     public boolean onOptionsItemSelected(MenuItem item) {
128         // Handle action bar item clicks here. The action bar will
129         // automatically handle clicks on the Home/Up button, so long
130         // as you specify a parent activity in AndroidManifest.xml.
```

```
131        int id = item.getItemId();
132        if (id == R.id.action_settings) {
133            return true;
134        }
135        return super.onOptionsItemSelected(item);
136    }
137 }
```

■ 6.10 AsyncTasks

In general, when performing parallel tasks running longer than a few seconds, it is best to use Java threads rather than the UI thread. As an alternate solution, Android provides an AsyncTask class as a convenient way to execute work units in parallel.

The AsyncTask class is similar to a thread in that it allows background work to execute outside the UI thread; however, it enables easy use of the UI thread by publishing background operation results on the UI thread. In addition, AsyncTask does not require the creation of a thread or handler. AsyncTask is an easy option for developers because it offers an uncomplicated framework for performing short-term background work.

AsyncTask is designed to be a helper class for Thread and Handler, and it does not constitute a generic threading mechanism. AsyncTask operations should not be used for long-running work. For example, in many cases, a networking operation requires a long process that is better performed using the Thread/Handler method. Ideally, AsyncTask should be used for tasks that take a few seconds at most.

AsyncTask is an abstract class that is designed to work with the UI thread in a seamless and convenient way. Within the asynchronous framework, a task is defined by a series of instructions that run on a background thread and whose results are published on the UI thread. The following four steps, each implemented as a callback method, define an asynchronous process:

onPreExecute():	This method is the first step in the asynchronous process and is called before the background tasks are performed. The objective of this step is to set up any required preliminary tasks before background work begins executing. onPreExecute() is invoked on the UI thread.
doInBackground():	Once onPreExecute() has finished executing, the second step, doInBackground(), is invoked on a background thread. All code performing the background work is placed in this method. Parameters used by the asynchronous task must be passed to this method, and the final results of the

completed background work are returned. During the execution of doInBackground(), calls can be made to publishProgress() to publish update values on the UI thread.

The AsyncTask class will automatically create a background thread for the doInBackground() step. Once the thread is no longer needed, it will release and destroy the thread. In addition, an AsyncTask can be canceled by invoking the cancel() method.

onProgressUpdate():   While the background tasks are being processed by doInBackground(), updates to the display are made by calling publishProgress(), which invokes onProgressUpdate() on the UI thread.

onPostExecute():   This method is the final step in the asynchronous process and is called once the doInBackground() method completes processing. As with onPreExecute(), this method is invoked on the UI thread. The final result from doInBackground() is passed to this method.

To create an AsyncTask, a subclass is constructed that inherits from AsyncTask. In addition, the defining callback methods are overridden. At a minimum, doInBackground() must be implemented.

Consider the following code segment that creates a photographic filter for a camera photograph. Computing a filter for a photograph is a relatively long operation that needs to be performed in the background. While the filter operation is processing, the user will observe a spinning ProgressBar, providing a visual indication that the process is on course. Once the filter has completed, the ProgressBar will be removed from the screen and the resulting filtered photograph will appear in an ImageView.

Lines 1–2:   An AsyncTask is defined by three generic types: Params, Progress, and Result. The first type, Params, describes the type of parameters sent to the task upon execution. In this code example, no parameters are used; hence, Params is specified as Void. The second type, Progress, defines the type of value published during the background computation. In this example, a dialog is used to provide the user with feedback indicating how far along the filter process is from completion. The third type, Result, is the end result of the background computation. In this example, a Bitmap containing the filtered photograph is the AsyncTask result.

Lines 4–10:   The first step in the asynchronous process is defined. `onPreExecute()` is overridden to display a progress bar.

Lines 12–23:   `doInBackground ()` defines the tasks that will be performed in the background. `publishProgress()` will post progress changes to the user. A `Bitmap`, the final filtered photograph, will be returned once this step has been completed.

Lines 25–27:   Updates to UI elements are published by `onProgressUpdate()` while the background operations are performed in `doInBackground()`. This step allows you to notify the user of progress.

Lines 29–39:   `onPostExecute()` is called to complete the asynchronous process. The final result is passed to this last step.

```
1    private class PhotoFilterAsyncTask extends AsyncTask
2                        <Void, Integer, Bitmap> {
3
4        @Override
5        protected void onPreExecute() {
6            super.onPreExecute();
7
8            //DISPLAY THE PROGRESS BAR
9            mProgressBar.setAlpha(1);
10       }
11
12       @Override
13       protected Bitmap doInBackground(Void... params) {
14           //TASK 1: ACCESS THE PHOTOGRAPH CAPTURED BY THE CAMERA
15           Bitmap photo = photoCaptured;
16           Bitmap filter = new Bitmap();
17           for (int y = 0; y < photo.getHeight(); y++){
18               for (int x = 0; x < photo.getWidth(); x++)
19                   BuildFilter(photo, x, y, filter);
20           publishProgress((int) ((y*x + x /
21                   (float) photo.getWidth * photo.getHeight) * 100));
22           return filter;
23       }
24
25       protected void onProgressUpdate(Integer... progress) {
26           setProgressPercent(progress[0]);
27       }
28
29       @Override
30       protected void onPostExecute(Bitmap result) {
31           super.onPostExecute(result);
32
```

```
33            //TURN THE PROGRESS BAR OFF - MAKE IT INVISIBLE
34            mProgressBar.setAlpha(0);
35
36            //DISPLAY THE FILTERED PHOTO
37            filterImage.setImageBitmap(result);
38        }
39    }
```

■ Lab Example 6-7: AsyncTask to Read a File in the Background

This lab illustrates the creation of an asynchronous process. Specifically, the example application built in this lab will be used to explore the four steps of AsyncTask: onPreExecute(),doInBackground(Params...),onProgressUpdate (Progress...), and onPostExecute(Result).

Part 1: The Design

This lab application is designed to simulate the downloading of a document. The download will occur in an AsyncTask background thread. The progress of the download will be updated and displayed in a ProgressBar. In addition, a textfield is used to provide specific asyncronous callback information, as shown in Figure 6-29.

FIGURE 6-29 An AsyncTask experiment application.

Part 2: Application Structure and Setup

The settings for the application are as follows:

- Application Name: AsyncTask Explore
- Project Name: AsyncTaskExplore
- Package Name: `com.cornez.asynctaskexplore`
- Android Form: Phone and Tablet
- Minimum SDK: API 18: Android 4.3 (Jelly Bean)
- Target SDK: API 21: Android 5.0 (Lollipop)
- Compile with: API 21: Android 5.0 (Lollipop)
- Activity Name: `MyActivity`
- Layout Name: `activity_my`

The project structure, shown in Figure 6-30, contains a single `Activity` and an associated layout file. The `strings.xml` file is the only required value resource for the application.

▌ FIGURE 6-30 Project structure for the `AsyncTask` Exploration application.

The orientation of the application will be specified as portrait within the Android-Manifest file. Depending on the Android platform, an error can occur when a user rotates the device while an asynchronous background thread is in progress. This is caused when an Activity lifecycle is required to restart. The AsyncTask reference to the Activity may become invalid.

A simple solution is to permanently lock the screen orientation of the activity, as shown on Line 11 of the AndroidManifest file. A second solution will be discussed in the implementation of the AsyncTask subclass.

AndroidManifest.xml

```
1   <?xml version="1.0" encoding="utf-8"?>
2   <manifest xmlns:android="http://schemas.android.com/apk/res/android"
3       package="com.cornez.asynctaskexplore" >
4
5       <application
6           android:allowBackup="true"
7           android:icon="@drawable/ic_launcher"
8           android:label="@string/app_name"
9           android:theme="@style/AppTheme" >
10          <activity
11              android:screenOrientation="portrait"
12              android:name=".MyActivity"
13              android:label="@string/app_name" >
14              <intent-filter>
15                  <action android:name="android.intent.action.MAIN" />
16
17                  <category
18                      android:name="android.intent.category.LAUNCHER" />
19              </intent-filter>
20          </activity>
21      </application>
22
23  </manifest>
```

Part 3: The Application User Interface

The application uses text strings for labeling buttons and providing a title to the asynchronous feedback. The XML code for the strings file is shown as follows:

strings.xml

```
1   <?xml version="1.0" encoding="utf-8"?>
2   <resources>
3
4       <string name="app_name">AsyncTask Explore</string>
5       <string name="hello_world">Hello world!</string>
6       <string name="action_settings">Settings</string>
7
8       <string name="download_btn">Download</string>
9       <string name="progress">downloading 0%</string>
10      <string name="async_callbacks">call backs</string>
11      <string name="clear_btn">Clear Display</string>
12
13  </resources>
```

The layout design for the `activity_my`, the activity user interface, is shown in Figure 6-31. A `RelativeLayout` is used, along with a scrollable text element for detailed feedback. Both layout buttons contain `onClick` event handlers specified in the XML document.

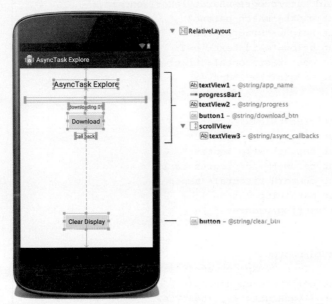

▮ FIGURE 6-31 The layout structure for `activity_my.xml`.

The XML code for `activity_my.xml` is shown as follows:

```
activity_my.xml
1   <RelativeLayout
2   xmlns:android="http://schemas.android.com/apk/res/android"
3       xmlns:tools="http://schemas.android.com/tools"
4       android:layout_width="match_parent"
5       android:layout_height="match_parent"
6       android:paddingLeft="@dimen/activity_horizontal_margin"
7       android:paddingRight="@dimen/activity_horizontal_margin"
8       android:paddingTop="@dimen/activity_vertical_margin"
9       android:paddingBottom="@dimen/activity_vertical_margin"
10      tools:context=".MyActivity">
11
12      <TextView
13          android:id="@+id/textView1"
14          android:layout_width="wrap_content"
15          android:layout_height="wrap_content"
16          android:layout_alignParentTop="true"
17          android:layout_centerHorizontal="true"
18          android:layout_marginTop="18dp"
```

```
19              android:text="@string/app_name"
20              android:textAppearance="?android:attr/textAppearanceLarge" />
21
22          <ProgressBar
23              android:id="@+id/progressBar1"
24              style="?android:attr/progressBarStyleHorizontal"
25              android:layout_width="match_parent"
26              android:layout_height="wrap_content"
27              android:layout_below="@+id/textView1"
28              android:layout_centerHorizontal="true"
29              android:layout_marginTop="25dp" />
30
31          <TextView
32              android:id="@+id/textView2"
33              android:layout_width="wrap_content"
34              android:layout_height="wrap_content"
35              android:layout_below="@+id/progressBar1"
36              android:layout_centerHorizontal="true"
37              android:layout_marginTop="3dp"
38              android:text="@string/progress" />
39
40          <Button
41              android:id="@+id/button1"
42              android:layout_width="wrap_content"
43              android:layout_height="wrap_content"
44              android:layout_alignRight="@+id/textView2"
45              android:layout_below="@+id/textView2"
46              android:layout_marginTop="10dp"
47              android:onClick="startDownload"
48              android:text="@string/download_btn" />
49
50          <ScrollView
51              android:layout_width="wrap_content"
52              android:layout_height="wrap_content"
53              android:id="@+id/scrollView"
54              android:layout_below="@+id/button1"
55              android:layout_centerHorizontal="true"
56              android:layout_marginTop="10dp" >
57
58              <TextView
59                  android:layout_width="wrap_content"
60                  android:layout_height="wrap_content"
61                  android:text="@string/async_callbacks"
62                  android:id="@+id/textView3" />
63          </ScrollView>
64
65          <Button
66              android:layout_width="wrap_content"
67              android:layout_height="wrap_content"
68              android:text="@string/clear_btn"
```

```
69              android:id="@+id/button"
70              android:layout_alignParentBottom="true"
71              android:layout_centerHorizontal="true"
72              android:layout_marginBottom="35dp"
73              android:onClick="clearDisplay"/>
74
75   </RelativeLayout>
```

Part 5: `Activity` Code for Application

The application requires the use of a single Activity. All operations are defined within this element file. The onCreate() method declares the ProgressBar, referenced by downloadProgressBar, which will be updated while the AsyncTask is running in the background. The Java code for MyActivity is shown as follows:

Line 27:	downloadBtn is the button that triggers the download AsyncTask operation.
Lines 29–30:	A TextView, named downloadProgressTextView, is used to provide a percentage amount of the current download. The ProgressBar element will be updated while AsyncTask is running in the background.
Lines 31–32:	A TextView, named callBackDisplayTextView, is used to provide constant feedback of the download AsyncTask process. This text field will show the sequence of callbacks that occur.
Lines 35–43:	The methods clearDisplay() and startDownload() are both button event handlers. clearDisplay() will clear the display listing the feedback of events. startDownload() will execute an AsyncTask.

MyActivity.java

```
1   package com.cornez.asynctaskexplore;
2
3   import android.app.Activity;
4   import android.os.AsyncTask;
5   import android.os.Bundle;
6   import android.os.SystemClock;
7   import android.view.Menu;
8   import android.view.MenuItem;
9   import android.view.View;
10  import android.widget.Button;
11  import android.widget.ProgressBar;
12  import android.widget.TextView;
13
```

```
14   public class MyActivity extends Activity {
15       private Button downloadBtn;
16       private ProgressBar downloadProgressBar;
17       private TextView downloadProgressTextView;
18       private TextView callBackDisplayTextView;
19
20       @Override
21       protected void onCreate(Bundle savedInstanceState) {
22           super.onCreate(savedInstanceState);
23           setContentView(R.layout.activity_my);
24
25           downloadProgressBar = (ProgressBar)
26                               findViewById(R.id.progressBar1);
27           downloadBtn = (Button) findViewById(R.id.button1);
28
29           downloadProgressTextView = (TextView)
30                               findViewById(R.id.textView2);
31           callBackDisplayTextView = (TextView)
32                               findViewById(R.id.textView3);
33       }
34
35       public void clearDisplay(View view) {
36           callBackDisplayTextView.setText(" ");
37       }
38
39       public void startDownload(View view) {
40           // DOWNLOAD IS PERFORMED.
41           downloadBtn.setEnabled(false);
42           new PerformAsyncTask().execute();
43       }
```

Lines 44–123:   An `AsyncTask` inner class is implemented to simulate the downloading of a file in the background. The `PerformAsyncTask` extends `AsyncTask`. `onPreExecute()` and `onPostExecute()` offer access to the UI before and after the heavy workload occurs in `doInBackground()`.

Lines 54–66:   A temporary locking of the screen is performed in OnPreExecute(). This will prevent an orientation change to the device while the AsyncTask is processing work in the background.

Line 91:   The `publishProgress()` method is invoked from `doInBackground()`. This method call will publish updates on the UI thread while the background tasks are still running. A call to this method will trigger the execution of `onProgressUpdate()` on the UI thread.

```
MyActivity.java  (continued)
44      private class PerformAsyncTask extends AsyncTask
45                          <Void, Integer, Void> {
46          int progress_status;
47
48          @Override
49          protected void onPreExecute() {
50              // UPDATE THE UI IMMEDIATELY BEFORE
51              // BACKGROUND WORK IS PERFORMED
52              super.onPreExecute();
53
54              callBackDisplayTextView.setText(
55                      callBackDisplayTextView.getText()
56                      + "\n\nLock the screen orientation()");
57              int currentOrientation =
58                      getResources().getConfiguration().orientation;
59              if (currentOrientation ==
60                      Configuration.ORIENTATION_PORTRAIT) {
61                  setRequestedOrientation(
62                      ActivityInfo.SCREEN_ORIENTATION_PORTRAIT);
63              } else {
64                  setRequestedOrientation(
65                      ActivityInfo.SCREEN_ORIENTATION_LANDSCAPE);
66              }
67
68              callBackDisplayTextView.setText(
69                      callBackDisplayTextView.getText()
70                      + "\nInvoke onPreExecute()");
71              progress_status = 0;
72              downloadProgressTextView.setText("downloading 0%");
73
74              callBackDisplayTextView.setText(
75                      callBackDisplayTextView.getText()
76                      + "\nCompleted onPreExecute()");
77              callBackDisplayTextView.setText(
78                      callBackDisplayTextView.getText()
79                      + "\nInvoke doInBackground()");
80              callBackDisplayTextView.setText(
81                      callBackDisplayTextView.getText()
82                      + "\nPerforming background work...");
83          }
84
85          @Override
86          protected Void doInBackground(Void... params) {
87
88              while (progress_status < 100) {
89                  progress_status += 2;
90
91                  publishProgress(progress_status);
92                  SystemClock.sleep(300);
93              }
```

```
 94                        return null;
 95              }
 96
 97          @Override
 98          protected void onProgressUpdate(Integer... values) {
 99              super.onProgressUpdate(values);
100
101              // UPDATE THE UI AS BACKGROUND TASKS ARE BEING PERFORMED
102              downloadProgressBar.setProgress(values[0]);
103              downloadProgressTextView.setText("downloading "
104                      + values[0] + "%");
105          }
106
107          @Override
108          protected void onPostExecute(Void result) {
109              super.onPostExecute(result);
110
111              // UPDATE THE FINAL UI IMMEDIATELY
112              // AFTER THE TASK IS EXECUTED
113              callBackDisplayTextView.setText(
114                      callBackDisplayTextView.getText()
115                      + "\nCompleted backgound work");
116              callBackDisplayTextView.setText(
117                      callBackDisplayTextView.getText()
118                      + "\nInvoke onPostExecute()");
119
120              downloadProgressTextView.setText("download complete");
121              downloadBtn.setEnabled(true);
122          }
123      };
124
125
126      @Override
127      public boolean onCreateOptionsMenu(Menu menu) {
128          // Inflate the menu.
129          getMenuInflater().inflate(R.menu.my, menu);
130          return true;
131      }
132
133      @Override
134      public boolean onOptionsItemSelected(MenuItem item) {
135          // Handle action bar item clicks here. The action bar will
136          // automatically handle clicks on the Home/Up button, so long
137          // as you specify a parent activity in AndroidManifest.xml.
138          int id = item.getItemId();
139          if (id == R.id.action_settings) {
140              return true;
141          }
142          return super.onOptionsItemSelected(item);
143      }
144
145 }
```

■ Exercises

6.1 What is multithreading?

6.2 What does the acrynom ANR stand for? Provide several reasons why an ANR will occur.

6.3 What tasks should be performed only on the UI thread?

6.4 Briefly describe two approaches to creating threads in an Android application.

6.5 List three application components that are created on the UI thread.

6.6 Explain the purpose of the `MessageQueue`.

6.7 What is the purpose of a call to `Looper.loop()`?

6.8 How is an AsyncTask similar to a Thread? How is it different?

6.9 Briefly describe the four callback methods implemented in an asynchronous process.

7 Touch Gestures

Chapter Objectives

In this chapter you will:

- Learn to code the detection of and response to touch gestures.
- Find patterns of common touches to create touch gestures that can be interpreted by an Android device.
- Learn about MotionEvents.
- Understand the differences between touch events and motion events.
- Learn how to build applications using multitouch gestures.

■ 7.1 Touchscreens

As users of Android devices, we often take touch input for granted. We double tap, fling our fingers across screens, pinch images, and perform other touch gestures that were not widely available as characteristics of screen interfaces prior to January 2007. The naturalness and variety of touch-based hand gestures play an integral role in application interfaces.

Touchscreens are an essential feature of Android devices. On a typical Android device, the high-resolution touchscreen is often the most expensive element on the device. Even though touchscreen technology has been around since the 1960s, it was not an assumed interface component until the mobile device market triggered its explosive growth. Today, Android application interfaces depend on interactions with touchscreens. Understanding touchscreen implementation is crucial to Android application development.

Not all touchscreens are created equal. Many different touch technologies are available to design engineers. Some touchscreens rely on infrared light, some use sound waves, and some use force sensors. All of these technologies have their advantages and disadvantages, ranging from size, accuracy, reliability, durability, number of touches sensed, and cost. Only two of these technologies, however, dominate the market in mobile devices: capacitive touchscreens and resistive touchscreens.

Most Android devices are equipped with a capacitive touchscreen, which relies on the electrical properties of the human body to detect when and where the user is touching the display. Capacitive technology provides numerous design opportunities for Android developers because interactivity can be detected with the slightest touch of a finger. An Android touchscreen is usually made of one insulating layer, such as glass, which is coated by a transparent conductive material on the inside. Since the human body is conductive, electricity can pass through it, and the Android touchscreen can use this conductivity as input. When a user touches a capacitive touchscreen, a change in the screen's electrical field occurs on the screen surrounding the fingertip. This change is registered, and the location of the touch can be computed. Because capacitive touchscreens rely on the electrical change caused by a light touch of a finger, users cannot wear gloves or tap with their fingernails. Fingernails and gloves are not conductive, and the touch does not cause any change in the electrostatic field.

This chapter describes how to write applications that allow users to interact via touch gestures. Unlike traditional desktop applications, mobile devices tend to be small, which is an essential reason for their ubiquity. People use them anywhere and everywhere, which means that application developers must pay sufficient attention to the user experience to ensure that interactivity is easy and intuitive. In an exploration of basic interactivity in Chapter 2, we examined the use of buttons and other user interface components, such as radio buttons, checkboxes, and text input. Interaction with all of these components involved the use of a touchscreen and listener events.

7.2 Touch Gestures

The Android API has large support for gestures, as they are the primary way in which users interact with most Android devices. Touch gestures represent a fundamental form of communication with an Android device. A touch gesture is an action, typically a movement of a user's finger on a touchscreen, recognized by the device to perform a specified function. For example, to interact with items on the touchscreen, users use touch gestures, such as tapping a button. The functions associated with a touch gesture are customizable and can be tailored to meet the specific needs of an application.

As human interfaces become more intelligent and intuitive, more and more gestures are used to control device applications. A touch gesture in Android can involve one or more fingers on the touchscreen. A multitouch gesture refers to a touchscreen's ability to recognize the presence of two-finger contact points. This plural-point awareness is often used to implement more advanced functionality, such as a pinch open for zooming in on a display object on the screen.

Gestures for touchscreen interactivity are inherently intuitive because they mirror known user actions. Using a touchscreen, the user can interact directly with an application through simple gestures that involve one or more fingers. A touch gesture involves input through the placement and motions of fingers on the touch-sensitive screen. By echoing a natural action, touch gestures provide for a richer user experience; ultimately, gestures or touch interactions translate into easier-to use-applications.

Gesture listeners, which cater to the most generic gesture inputs, have been part of the Android API since its creation. The common touch gestures for Android devices, shown in Figure 7-1, are single tap, double tap, long press, scroll, drag, fling, pinch open, and pinch close. The first six are single-touch gestures and the last two are multitouch.

A single tapping gesture is similar to the clicking of a mouse; we think of it as the activity that activates the given functionality of an icon or menu selection. This gesture is often referred to simply as "touch." The double-tap gesture is commonly known as a secondary gesture for text selection. It is also used to provide a zooming action that is typically associated with magnifying content on the screen.

For applications that require editing and data entry, a long press is useful for indicating data selection. For example, when the user places a finger on a word and performs a long press, the word is highlighted. In this way, a long press gesture allows users to select one or more items on the screen.

A dragging touch gesture is typically associated with the act of dropping. A drag-and-drop is a combined gesture that allows users to rearrange data within a view. Users can drag data from one container and release, or drop, the item into another container.

A quick fling of a finger across the surface of a touchscreen is called flinging; on iPhone devices, this is referred to as swiping. Flinging is often used for scrolling overflowing content or navigating between views in the same hierarchy. This gesture is also used in games where direction and velocity can be applied to an object that is set in motion.

The difference between a scroll and a fling gesture is that the user lifts a finger at the end of the gesture in order to make it a fling. In addition, a fling movement tends to be more rapid. For Android developers, these two events are similar and difficult to tell apart. From the user's perspective, using both gestures in a single user interface can be confusing because they are so similar. For example, it is very difficult to keep the ordinary scroll behavior and still detect the fling.

Pinch open is the gesture most commonly known for zooming into the content displayed on the screen. Hence, its counterpart, pinch close, is frequently associated with zooming out of the content.

■ 7.3 The Basics of Touch Events

Android provides a variety of classes and APIs to help create and recognize simple and complex patterns of single and multiple touches. These touch patterns can be turned into input for applications. Although application developers may not always depend on touch gestures for basic behaviors (because the gestures may not be available to users in all contexts), adding touch-based interaction to an application can unlock extra functionality and interaction possibilities.

All Android touch gestures begin when the user first places a finger on the touchscreen. Every touch gesture that occurs on a touchscreen triggers an `onTouch-Event()`. The specific details of each touch event, such as the location of the finger or fingers, the amount of pressure applied by the touch, and the size of the finger, are provided as identification of the gesture. The position of the finger, or multiple fingers if it is a multitouch gesture, is tracked until the finger is removed from the screen. Each individual finger in a gesture is referred to as a pointer.

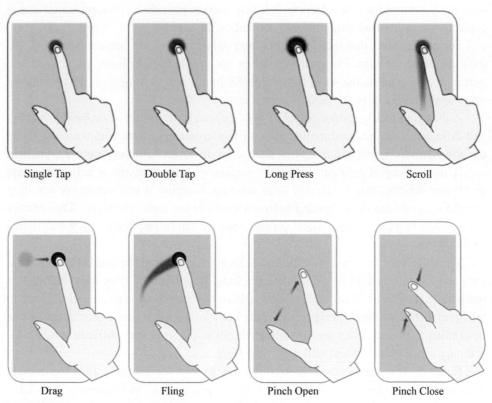

| Single Tap | Double Tap | Long Press | Scroll |

| Drag | Fling | Pinch Open | Pinch Close |

FIGURE 7-1 Common touch gestures for Android devices.

The `MotionEvent` class, discussed more thoroughly in Section 7-5, provides a collection of methods to report on the properties of a given touch gesture. Motion events describe movements in terms of an action code and a set of axis values. Each action code specifies a state change produced by a touch occurrence, such as a pointer going up or down. The axis values describe the position and movement properties.

For example, when the user taps the screen, the system delivers a touch event to the appropriate view with the action code `ACTION_DOWN` and a set of axis values that include the *x* and *y* coordinates of the touch and information about the pressure, size, and orientation of the contact area.

To understand gestures and how they work, we must be familiar with three basic `MotionEvents`, which can be combined to create touch gestures. These basic motion events are identified by the following action codes:

```
ACTION_DOWN

ACTION_MOVE

ACTION_UP
```

A `MotionEvent` object can be used to provide the details of all events involving finger movement. For example, when the first touch on a View occurs, the `MotionEvent` object contains an action type of `ACTION_DOWN` and the *x*, *y* coordinates of the touch. When the finger is lifted from the screen, an `ACTION_UP` event is generated. `ACTION_MOVE` events represent any motion of the touch between the `ACTION_DOWN` and `ACTION_UP` events. A specific View object located on the screen can also intercept these actions. A touch gesture can be associated with a View object through the registration of an `onTouchListener` event and the implementation of a corresponding `onTouch()` callback method. The callback method receives both a reference to the `View` object on which the touch gesture was triggered and an object of type `MotionEvent`.

■ 7.4 Gesture Detector

Android provides several approaches to touchscreen event handling. The easiest approach is to use the `GestureDetector` class for detecting specific touch gestures. This approach uses the `OnGestureListener` to signal when a gesture occurs and then pass the triggered motion event to the `GestureDetector`'s `onTouchEvent()` method. The `onTouchEvent()` method then analyzes this new event, along with previous events, to determine exactly which action patterns are occurring on the screen. The ease with which a gesture pattern can be accurately classified makes this method very practical. For example, when detecting a fling gesture, a specific pattern of touch events is signaled: a down touch, followed by one or more scroll touches, before ending with a fling. The scroll events produced by a fling gesture can provide information about the velocity of a moving finger and the distance it has traveled on the screen. The execution of the `on-Down()`, `onScroll()`, and `onFling()` callback methods completes the fling gesture. The `GestureDetector` simplifies motion events by identifying the triggered event and delegating calls to a `GestureListener` object. In this manner, a Gesture object can receive callbacks for specific gestures that the `GestureDetector` recognizes.

GestureDetector has limited usage for Android application because it is not able to handle all types of gestures. For example, modifications are needed to recreate more complex gestures, such as fling left and fling right. At its simplest, Gesture-Detector is ideal for interfaces that involve simple and generic touch gestures. More specifically, the GestureDetector.OnGestureListener callback is used for signaling when a particular motion event has occurred. The callback methods contained in the GestureDetector class are onDown(), onLongPress(), onShowPress(), onSingleTapUp(), and onDoubleTap(). Table 7-1 shows a sequence of callback methods for several basic gestures.

The onDown() method is automatically called when a tap occurs with the down MotionEvent that triggered it. This callback is triggered every time a finger touches the screen. This is an important event because most other events will be preceeded with a finger touching the screen. For every ACTION_DOWN motion event, an onDown() is called.

The onLongPress() is called when a long press occurs with the initial onDown MotionEvent that triggered it. The event parameter for a long press is the initial onDown motion event that preceded the longPress motion. The onShowPress() callback occurs whenever the user has performed an onDown motion but has not yet completed any other movement. This event commonly provides visual feedback to let the user know that the action has been recognized (i.e., highlighting an element). The parameter for an onShowPress motion event is the initial onDown motion event that preceded the onShowPress. In some instances, this motion event might not get called at all. For example, when a user taps a finger on the screen very quickly, it is possible it will be considered an unintentional touch.

The onSingleTapUp() callback occurs when a tap gesture takes place with an up motion that triggered it. For example, a tap gesture happens when an ACTION_DOWN event is followed by an ACTION_UP event. A common pattern for this gesture is a single tap, where the user quickly touches the screen and then, just as quickly, removes the finger from the touchscreen. The required parameter for onSingleTapUp is an up motion that completes the first tap.

Similar to the onSingleTapUp() callback, onSingleTapConfirmed() occurs when a detected tap gesture is confirmed by the system as a single tap and not as part of a double-tap gesture. A double-tap event is recognized as two consecutive tap gestures. The onDoubleTap() callback occurs when a two-tap event is detected.

As shown in Table 7-1, when a fling gesture is detected, callbacks occur on four methods: onDown, onShowPress(), onScroll(), and onFling(). A fling gesture is recognized when there is an ACTION_DOWN followed by one or more ACTION_MOVE events and finally terminated by an ACTION_UP event. A fling is a constrained type of action. To be recognized as a fling, the ACTION_DOWN, ACTION_MOVE, and

TABLE 7-1 Sequences of callback methods for basic gestures

Gesture	Sequence of Callback Methods
Single Tap	onDown onShowPress() onSingleTapUp() onSingleTapConfirmed()
Double Tap	onDown onShowPress() onSingleTapUp() onDoubleTap() onDoubleTapEvent() onDown() onShowPress() onDoubleTapEvent()
Fling	onDown onShowPress() onScroll() onScroll() … onScroll() onFling()
Scroll	onDown onShowPress() onScroll() onScroll() … onScroll()

ACTION_UP events must take place with a specific velocity pattern. For example, when the user places a finger on the touchscreen and moves it slowly before removing it, this unrestrained sequence is not recognized as a fling gesture.

The last gesture sequence in Table 7-1 represents a scrolling gesture, which is very similar to a fling gesture. Scrolling the content on display on a touchscreen is a common task and is detected and processed on an Android device with callbacks to onDown(), onShowPress(), and a series of onScroll(). The onScroll() callback is typically called when there is an ACTION_MOVE event. This involves the user placing a finger on the screen and moving it for a period of time before removing it from the screen. During this period, there will be a chain of repeated method calls to onScroll().

■ Lab Example 7-1: Touch Experiment 1: Touch Events Using GestureDetector

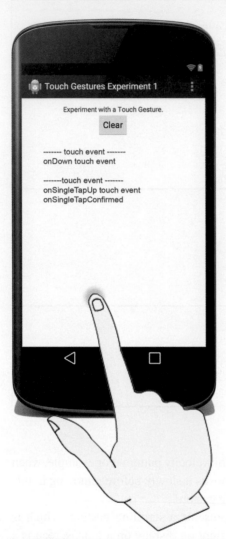

■ **FIGURE 7-2** A Touch Gesture application for exploring basic touch events.

This lab example provides an opportunity to explore all simple touch gestures that involve the detection of a single-finger touch event. A collection of gestures can be tested, ranging from a single tap to a fling event. As each gesture is produced, a scrollable text field will provide a list of the touch events and triggered callbacks that occur. Figure 7-2 illustrates the touch events that are triggered when the user performs a single tap on the touchscreen.

Part 1: Application Structure and Setup

The goal of this lab is to recognize simple touch patterns and to develop an application that utilizes `GestureDetector` and `MotionEvent`. The application in this example is simple and involves the implementation of the `onGestureListener`, the creation of a `GestureDetector` object and the construction of the `onTouch-Event()` method.

The settings for the application are as follows:

- Application Name: Touch Gestures Experiment 1
- Project Name: TouchGesturesExperiment1
- Package Name: `com.cornez.touchgesturesexperiment1`
- Android Form: Phone and Tablet
- Minimum SDK: API 18: Android 4.3 (Jelly Bean)
- Target SDK: API 21: Android 5.0 (Lollipop)
- Compile with: API 21: Android 5.0 (Lollipop)
- Activity Name: `MyActivity`
- Layout Name: `activity_my`

The project structure for the application is shown in Figure 7-3.

FIGURE 7-3 Final project structure for the Touch Experiment application.

The application will use a single layout associated with one main activity.

The activity is specified as `MyActivity` in the Android Manifest file. The XML code for the manifest file is shown as follows:

```
AndroidManifest.xml
1   <?xml version="1.0" encoding="utf-8"?>
2   <manifest xmlns:android="http://schemas.android.com/apk/res/android"
3       package="com.cornez.touchgesturesexperiment1" >
4
5       <application
6           android:allowBackup="true"
7           android:icon="@drawable/ic_launcher"
8           android:label="@string/app_name"
9           android:theme="@style/AppTheme" >
10          <activity
11              android:name=".MyActivity"
12              android:label="@string/app_name" >
13              <intent-filter>
14                  <action android:name="android.intent.action.MAIN" />
15
16                  <category
17                      android:name="android.intent.category.LAUNCHER" />
18              </intent-filter>
19          </activity>
20      </application>
21
22  </manifest>
```

Part 2: The User Interface

After performing each touch gesture experiment, a button labeled "Clear" can be used to empty the scrolling text field. This will create a clean slate for reporting the results of the Touch Gestures experiment. The application string requirements for labeling the button, emptying the text field, and providing a title for the application are shown as follows in `strings.xml`:

```
strings.xml
1   <?xml version="1.0" encoding="utf-8"?>
2   <resources>
3
4       <string name="app_name">Touch Gestures Experiment 1</string>
5       <string name="hello_world">Hello world!</string>
6       <string name="action_settings">Settings</string>
7
8       <string name="clear_btn">Clear</string>
9       <string name="empty">\n</string>
10      <string name="experiment">Experiment with a Touch Gesture.</string>
11
12  </resources>
```

The layout file associated with the application's activity is shown in Figure 7-4. This file, `activity_my.xml`, uses a `RelativeLayout` as its root element. Several touch experiments produce extensive method callbacks to touch events, such as fling gestures. Depending on the size of the touchscreen, this information may require a scrollable TextView to accommodate the full text. To provide a scrolling feature for the text field, a `TextView` is placed within a `ScrollView`.

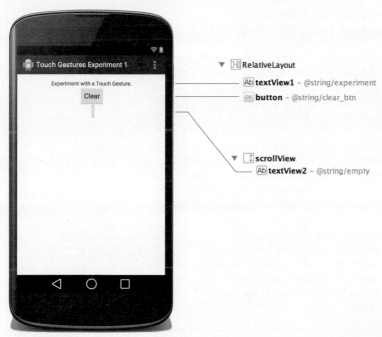

▼ ▣ RelativeLayout
     [Ab] textView1 – @string/experiment
     [OK] button – @string/clear_btn

▼ ⬍ scrollView
     [Ab] textView2 – @string/empty

❚ FIGURE 7-4 The hierarchical structure for the user interface screen, `activity_my.xml`.

The XML for `activity_my.xml` is shown as follows. The `onClick` event handler for the button defined in Lines 20–27 is specified as `clearLog`.

```
activity_my.xml
1    <RelativeLayout
2    xmlns:android="http://schemas.android.com/apk/res/android"
3        xmlns:tools="http://schemas.android.com/tools"
4        android:layout_width="match_parent"
5        android:layout_height="match_parent"
6        android:paddingBottom="@dimen/activity_vertical_margin"
7        android:paddingLeft="@dimen/activity_horizontal_margin"
8        android:paddingRight="@dimen/activity_horizontal_margin"
9        android:paddingTop="@dimen/activity_vertical_margin"
10       tools:context=".MyActivity">
11
```

```
12          <TextView
13              android:id="@+id/textView1"
14              android:layout_width="wrap_content"
15              android:layout_height="wrap_content"
16              android:layout_alignParentTop="true"
17              android:layout_centerHorizontal="true"
18              android:text="@string/experiment" />
19
20          <Button
21              android:id="@+id/button"
22              android:layout_width="wrap_content"
23              android:layout_height="wrap_content"
24              android:layout_below="@+id/textView1"
25              android:layout_centerHorizontal="true"
26              android:onClick="clearLog"
27              android:text="@string/clear_btn" />
28
29          <ScrollView
30              android:id="@+id/scrollView"
31              android:layout_width="wrap_content"
32              android:layout_height="wrap_content"
33              android:layout_below="@+id/button"
34              android:layout_centerHorizontal="true">
35
36              <TextView
37                  android:id="@+id/textView2"
38                  android:layout_width="wrap_content"
39                  android:layout_height="wrap_content"
40                  android:text="@string/empty" />
41          </ScrollView>
42      </RelativeLayout>
```

Part 3: Source Code for Application

A single source file is used by the application, the main activity. The first lines of code in this file are used to import the required libraries. Lines 5 and 8 import the required libraries for listening for a gesture and receiving motion data. The GestureDetector class is always used in companion with MotionEvent to report touch gestures.

```
MyActivity.java
1   package com.cornez.touchgesturesexperiment1;
2
3   import android.app.Activity;
4   import android.os.Bundle;
5   import android.view.GestureDetector;
6   import android.view.Menu;
```

```
7    import android.view.MenuItem;
8    import android.view.MotionEvent;
9    import android.view.View;
10   import android.widget.TextView;
```

The output, or report log, produced by this application is the sequence of callback responses triggered by a given gesture. A `GestureDetector` object is used to receive the motion data the application is expected to recognize.

Lines 11–13:   The interfaces for `GestureDetector.OnDoubleTapListener` and `GestureDetecter.OnGestureListener` are both implemented for the `MyActivity` class. The `GestureDetector.OnDoubleTapListener` interface is used to notify when a double tap or a confirmed single tap has occurred. The `GestureDetector.OnGestureListener` is a listener interface that is used to signal when a gesture occurs.

Lines 25–26:   A `GestureDetector` object, aGesture, is instantiated with a supplied gesture listener. The first parameter of the `GestureDetector` requires the application's context, the default activity. The second parameter specifies the default listener that will be invoked for all the callbacks. In addition, an `onDoubleTapListener` is set to a default listener that will be called for double-tap related gestures.

```
MyActivity.java (continued)
11   public class MyActivity extends Activity implements
12         GestureDetector.OnDoubleTapListener,
13         GestureDetector.OnGestureListener {
14
15      private GestureDetector aGesture;
16      private TextView mTouchLog;
17
18      @Override
19      protected void onCreate(Bundle savedInstanceState) {
20          super.onCreate(savedInstanceState);
21          setContentView(R.layout.activity_my);
22
23          mTouchLog = (TextView) findViewById(R.id.textView2);
24
25          aGesture = new GestureDetector(this, this);
26          aGesture.setOnDoubleTapListener(this);
27      }
```

Lines 32–36:   The `onTouchEvent()` method is called when a touchscreen event occurs that is not handled by the "clear" button or the scroll element of the `TextView`. Once this method is triggered, it produces text output indicating that a touch event has occurred. It should be noted that the default implementation of `onTouch-Event()` always returns a false value. A return of true indicates the motion event has been consumed.

Line 35:   The statement, `return aGesture.onTouchEvent (event)` is used to analyze a given motion event and trigger the appropriate callbacks supplied by the `GestureDetector. OnGestureListener`.

MyActivity.java (*continued*)

```
28      public void clearLog(View view) {
29          mTouchLog.setText(R.string.empty);
30      }
31
32      @Override
33      public boolean onTouchEvent(MotionEvent event) {
34          mTouchLog.append("\n\n------- touch event ------");
35          return aGesture.onTouchEvent(event);
        }
```

This application relies on the `OnGestureListener` to signal the occurrence of a gesture. By implementing the `GestureDetector.OnGestureListener` interface, we are required to provide a collection of methods to catch the gestures defined by this interface. For each triggered gesture, text is displayed that describes the specific touch event that has occurred.

The `MotionEvent` object that is passed as a parameter to each callback method sometimes represents the touch event that started the gesture recognition. It is also possible that the `MotionEvent` object will represent the last event that completed the gesture. For example, a single-tap event is recognized when a single-tap confirmed completes the gesture.

The `GestureDectector` class will handle all of the deciphering details for determining the kind of motion the `MotionEvent` object represents. For example:

1. The `onDown()` method will be called when a tap occurs with the down motion event that triggered it.

2. The `onLongPress()` method will be called when a long pressing motion occurs with the initial down motion event that triggered it.

3. The `onSingleTapUp()` method will be called when a tap occurs. The event will not be completed until an up motion event occurs.

4. The `onShowPress()` method will be called when the user has performed a down motion event but has not moved a finger or performed an up MotionEvent.

```
     MyActivity.java (continued)
36   @Override
37       public void onLongPress(MotionEvent event) {
38           mTouchLog.append("\nonLongPress touch event");
39       }
40
41       @Override
42       public void onShowPress(MotionEvent event) {
43           mTouchLog.append("\nonShowPress touch event");
44       }
45
46       @Override
47       public boolean onDown(MotionEvent event) {
48           mTouchLog.append("\nonDown Touch event");
49           return false;
50       }
51
52       @Override
53       public boolean onScroll(MotionEvent e1, MotionEvent e2,
54                               float distanceX, float distanceY) {
55           mTouchLog.append("\nonScroll: distanceX is " +
56                   distanceX + ", distanceY is " + distanceY);
57           return true;
58       }
59
60       @Override
61       public boolean onFling(MotionEvent event1, MotionEvent event2,
62                               float velocityX, float velocityY) {
63           mTouchLog.append("\nonFling: velocityX is " + velocityX + ", " +
64                   "velocityY is " + velocityY);
65           return true;
66       }
67
68       @Override
69       public boolean onSingleTapUp(MotionEvent event) {
70           mTouchLog.append("\nonSingleTapUp touch event");
71           return false;
72       }
73
74       @Override
75       public boolean onDoubleTap(MotionEvent event) {
76           mTouchLog.append("\nonDoubleTapUp touch event");
77           return false;
78       }
79
80       @Override
81       public boolean onDoubleTapEvent(MotionEvent event) {
82           mTouchLog.append("\nonDoubleTapUp touch event");
83           return true;
84       }
```

```
85
86         @Override
87         public boolean onSingleTapConfirmed(MotionEvent event) {
88             mTouchLog.append("\nonSingleTapConfirmed");
89             return true;
90         }
91
92
93         @Override
94         public boolean onCreateOptionsMenu(Menu menu) {
95             // Inflate the menu;
96             // this adds items to the action bar if it is present.
97             getMenuInflater().inflate(R.menu.my, menu);
98             return true;
99         }
100
101        @Override
102        public boolean onOptionsItemSelected(MenuItem item) {
103            // Handle action bar item clicks here. The action bar will
104            // automatically handle clicks on the Home/Up button, so long
105            // as you specify a parent activity in AndroidManifest.xml.
106            int id = item.getItemId();
107            if (id == R.id.action_settings) {
108                return true;
109            }
110            return super.onOptionsItemSelected(item);
111        }
```

Figure 7-5 shows the application being tested with a fling gesture. A minimum of three touch events will occur with a fling. Each fling gesture is accompanied by a series of scroll events. A fling gesture will not be completed until the onFling() method has been called.

■ 7.5 The MotionEvent Class

For simple gesture handling, the GestureDetector class allows basic detections for common gestures.

For example, this basic form of gesture detection listens for all touch events and provides a generic response. This type of gesture detection is suitable for applications that require simple gestures; however, the GestureDetector class is not designed to handle complicated gestures.

A more sophisticated form of gesture detection is to register an OnTouchListener event handler to a specific View, such as a graphic object on stage that can be dragged. In this case, notification is required whenever there is a touch event on that View object.

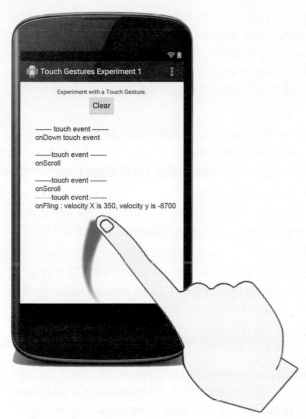

FIGURE 7-5 The Touch Experiment application is shown after a fling gesture is produced.

To provide touch event notification, the `onTouchEvent()` method can be overridden for an `Activity` or touchable `View`. In this way, an instance of `MotionEvent` can detect specific user gestures on a given object. This type of gesture detection provides more control for game applications and applications that require a high degree of interactivity.

A `MotionEvent` object describes movement in terms of an action code and a set of axis values. The action code specifies the state change that occurred, such as a finger moving up or down on the touchscreen. The axis values of a `MotionEvent` object describe the x, y position of the contact point and movement properties, such as velocity.

For example, when the user first touches the screen, the system delivers a touch event to the appropriate `View` that has been touched. This event contains the action code ACTION_DOWN and a set of axis values that include the x, y coordinates of the location on the screen. In addition, information about the pressure, size, and orientation of the contact area is produced by the event.

Most Android devices are able to report multiple movement traces at the same time. For example, multitouch screens emit one movement trace for each finger. The individual fingers generate movement trace information as motion events.

The `MotionEvent` class provides a collection of methods to query the position and other properties of fingers used in a gesture. Several methods provided by this class are as follows.

`getX():`	Returns the *x*-axis coordinate value at the finger's location on the screen.
`getY():`	Returns the *y*-axis coordinate value at the finger's location on the screen.
`getDownTime():`	Returns the time when the user initially pressed down to begin a series of events. The time is returned in milliseconds.
`getPrecisionX():`	Returns the precision of the *X* coordinate. This value can be multiplied by `getX()` to find the actual hardware value of the *X* coordinate.
`getAction():`	Returns the type of action being performed by the user, such as `ACTION_DOWN`.

Each finger in a multitouch screen can be identified by a unique id, called a pointer id. The order in which an individual finger appears within a motion event is undefined. However, the pointer id of a finger is guaranteed to remain constant as long as the finger remains active on the touchscreen. The method `getPointerId()` can be used to obtain the pointer id of a finger that will be traced across all subsequent motion events in a gesture.

For interactive optimization, motion events with `ACTION_MOVE` may batch together multiple movement samples within a single object. Consider the code segment below. The `play()` method receives a `MotionEvent` object and displays current and past information.

The coordinate location of active fingers used in a gesture are accessed using `getX()` and `getY()`. Previous coordinate positions in a gesture are accessed using `getHistoricalX()` and `getHistoricalY()`. The coordinates are "historical" only insofar as they are older than the current coordinates in a given batch.

```
1   void play(MotionEvent motionEvent) {
2       final int historySize = motionEvent.getHistorySize();
3       final int fingerCount = ev.getPointerCount();
4
5       for (int h = 0; h < historySize; h++) {
6           display(motionEvent.getHistoricalEventTime(h));
7           for (int p = 0; p < fingerCount; p++) {
```

```
 8              display(motionEvent.getPointerId(p),
 9                      motionEvent.getHistoricalX(p, h),
10                      motionEvent.getHistoricalY(p, h));
11          }
12      }
13      display(motionEvent.getEventTime());
14      for (int p = 0; p < pointerCount; p++) {
15          display(motionEvent.getPointerId(p),
16                  motionEvent.getX(p),
17                  motionEvent.getY(p));
18      }
19  }
```

Touch events can also be handled in a `ViewGroup` that has multiple `View` elements that are targets for different touch events. The `onInterceptTouch-Event()` method can be used to ensure that either the child `View` or the parent `ViewGroup` will correctly receive an intended touch event. This method receives a `MotionEvent` and returns a true or false. Once implemented, it will be called automatically to intercept touchscreen motion events detected on the surface of a `ViewGroup` and then dispatched to the intended `View`. By returning a true, the `MotionEvent` will be intercepted and will not be passed on to the child `View`. In this way, the parent `ViewGroup` will receive a touch event before its child `View`. By returning a false, the `MotionEvent` will travel down the view hierarchy to a child target, which will handle the event on its own `onTouchEvent()` method.

■ Lab Example 7-2: Touch Experiment 2: Drawn Primitive Shapes with Touch Feedback

This lab exercise experiments with primitive shapes that will be made to respond to touch events. Although `GestureDetector` is useful for simple gestures, it is not an appropriate tool for detecting gestures associated with a specific object on stage. In this lab, we will explore the use of a `Canvas` element as a custom `View`, which supports touch interactions. As shown in Figure 7-6, when a touch event occurs on the `View`, the specified gesture will be unmasked and processed by drawing on the canvas.

Part 1: Application Structure and Setup

The settings for the application are as follows:

- Application Name: Touch Gestures Experiment 2
- Project Name: TouchGesturesExperiment2
- Package Name: `com.cornez.touchgesturesexperiment2`

ACTION_UP   ACTION_DOWN   ACTION_MOVE

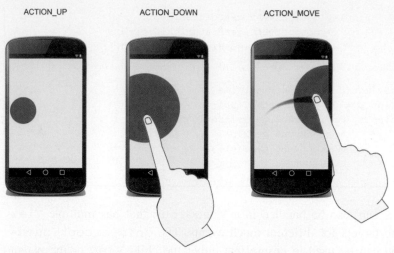

▌ FIGURE 7-6 An experiment for touch gestures associated with a View.

- Android Form: Phone and Tablet
- Minimum SDK: API 18: Android 4.3 (Jelly Bean)
- Target SDK: API 21: Android 5.0 (Lollipop)
- Compile with: API 21: Android 5.0 (Lollipop)
- Activity Name: `MyActivity`

The project structure for the application is shown in Figure 7-7. This structure contains three Java source files. The activity for the class is `MyActivity`. The `Circle` class models the graphic circle that will be drawn in various sizes and locations on the screen. This application will not use an XML layout.

▌ FIGURE 7-7 The project structure for the Touch Gestures Experiment 2 application.

Part 2: The Application Activity

The default activity, `MyActivity`, is configured with a `GameView` object containing a drawing surface. The default layout is not utilized in this application. Instead, a `View` object, one containing a drawing surface, is constructed programmatically.

Lines 19–20: The activity content is set to an explicit view, `gameView`. `gameView` is a custom `View` and will be placed directly into the activity's view hierarchy. The `GameView` class allows us to draw on the Canvas object. This class will contain the mechanism for drawing to the screen.

Line 21: A background `Thread` is used to update the canvas at delayed intervals of 200 milliseconds, producing animated movement.

Lines 24–38: The `Runnable` implementation for the thread contains a loop for adding messages to the `MessageQueue`, producing continuous movement as simple gestures are processed.

Lines 39–43: `threadHandler` is the `Handler` associated with the `MessageQueue`.

```
MyActivity.java
1   package com.cornez.touchgesturesexperiment2;
2
3   import android.app.Activity;
4   import android.os.Bundle;
5   import android.os.Handler;
6   import android.view.Menu;
7   import android.view.MenuItem;
8
9   public class MyActivity extends Activity {
10
11      GameView gameView;
12      private Thread mThread;
13
14      @Override
15      protected void onCreate(Bundle savedInstanceState) {
16          super.onCreate(savedInstanceState);
17
18          gameView = new GameView(this);
19          setContentView(gameView);
20
21          mThread = new Thread(actionRun);
22      }
23
24      private Runnable actionRun = new Runnable() {
25          private static final int DELAY = 200;
26
```

```
27          public void run() {
28              try {
29                  while (true) {
30                      Thread.sleep(DELAY);
31                      threadHandler.sendEmptyMessage(0);
32                  }
33              } catch (InterruptedException e) {
34                  e.printStackTrace();
35              }
36          }
37      };
38
39      public Handler threadHandler = new Handler() {
40          public void handleMessage(android.os.Message msg) {
41              gameView.update();
42          }
43      };
44
45      @Override
46      protected void onResume() {
47          mThread.start();
48          super.onResume();
49      }
50
51      @Override
52      protected void onPause() {
53          finish();
54          super.onPause();
55      }
56
57      @Override
58      protected void onDestroy() {
59          finish();
60          super.onDestroy();
61      }
62
63      @Override
64      public boolean onCreateOptionsMenu(Menu menu) {
65          // Inflate the menu.
66          getMenuInflater().inflate(R.menu.my, menu);
67          return true;
68      }
69
70      @Override
71      public boolean onOptionsItemSelected(MenuItem item) {
72          // Handle action bar item clicks here. The action bar will
73          // automatically handle clicks on the Home/Up button, so long
74          // as you specify a parent activity in AndroidManifest.xml.
75          int id = item.getItemId();
```

```
76          if (id == R.id.action_settings) {
77              return true,
78          }
79          return super.onOptionsItemSelected(item);
80      }
81  }
```

Part 3: onTouchEvent() and the GameView Class

As illustrated in previous chapters, a simple way to employ a Canvas object for drawing is to override the onDraw() method of a View object. Conveniently, this method has a single parameter: the Canvas object.

When a touch event occurs on the GameView, the specified gesture is unmasked and processed by drawing on the canvas. When the touch action is identified in onTouchEvent(), one of three responses are triggered, as shown in Figure 7-6. The onDraw() method is used to clear the canvas and paint a circle with a specified radius at an x, y location on the screen.

An important aspect of touch event handling involves being able to identify the type of action the user performed. We can obtain this information by making a call to the getActionMasked() method of the MotionEvent object, which was passed through to the onTouch() callback method. In this application, we detect the basic finger movements: press, lift, and move. The radius and the x, y location of the graphic circle will be altered to respond to these basic touch gestures.

The changing visual display of this application illustrates the appeal of touch-screen feedback. The user will have a sense of how the application operates based on the behavior of the drawn circle. Many Android UI elements support touch feedback that includes visual changes to components to indicate responsiveness to the user. For example, (1) a single tap on an application icon button causes the button to dim slightly, indicating that it is actionable; or (2) dragging an icon may diminish it in size, helping the user understand that dragging relocates the item.

The Java code for GameView is shown as follows:

Lines 52–65:   A touch gesture is distilled into a motion event containing an action code that specifies the state change, such as a finger going down, up, or moving. Specifically,

MotionEvent.ACTION_DOWN

MotionEvent.ACTION_UP

MotionEvent.ACTION_MOVE

Once the action code is triggered, the set of axis values are returned. The axis values describe the finger position and other movement properties. When using the emulator, the mouse cursor will substitute for a finger pointer.

```
GameView.java
1  package com.cornez.touchgesturesexperiment2;
2
3  import android.content.Context;
4  import android.graphics.Canvas;
5  import android.graphics.Color;
6  import android.graphics.Paint;
7  import android.view.MotionEvent;
8  import android.view.View;
9
10 public class GameView extends View {
11
12     private Paint paint;
13     private Circle mCircle;
14
15     public GameView(Context context) {
16         super(context);
17
18         //CREATE A CIRCLE AND SET THE PAINT, RADIUS AND X, Y LOCATION
19         mCircle = new Circle();
20
21         paint = new Paint(Paint.ANTI_ALIAS_FLAG);
22         paint.setColor(Color.rgb(126, 79, 43));
23         mCircle.setPaint(paint);
24
25         mCircle.setRadius(100);
26         mCircle.setX(400);
27         mCircle.setY(300);
28     }
29
30     @Override
31     protected void onDraw(Canvas canvas) {
32
33         //TASK 1: FILL THE BACKGROUND OF THE CANVAS
34         canvas.drawRGB(248, 232, 198);
35
36         //TASK 2: DRAW THE CIRCLE
37         canvas.drawCircle(mCircle.getX(), mCircle.getY(),
38                 mCircle.getRadius(), mCircle.getPaint());
39
40     }
41
42     public void update() {
43
44         invalidate();
45     }
46
47     @Override
48     public boolean onTouchEvent(MotionEvent event) {
49         //TASK 1:  IDENTIFY THE TOUCH ACTION BEING PERFORMED
```

```
50          int touchAction = event.getActionMasked();
51
52          //TASK 2:  RESPOND TO TWO POSSIBLE TOUCH EVENTS
53          switch (touchAction) {
54              case MotionEvent.ACTION_DOWN:
55                  mCircle.setRadius(300);
56                  break;
57              case MotionEvent.ACTION_UP:
58                  mCircle.setRadius(75);
59                  break;
60              case MotionEvent.ACTION_MOVE:
61                  mCircle.setRadius(300);
62                  mCircle.setX((int) event.getX());
63                  mCircle.setY((int) event.getY());
64                  break;
65          }
66
67          //TASK 3: INVALIDATE THE  VIEW
68          invalidate();
69
70          //TASK 4: RETURNS A TRUE AFTER HANDLING THE TOUCH ACTION EVENT
71          return true;
72      }
73 }
```

Part 4: The `Circle` Class

The `Circle` class provides the attributes for the graphic circle that appears on the canvas. These include the Paint to describe style and color, the radius, and the *x*, *y* location of the graphic on the screen. The Java code for `Circle` is shown as follows:

Circle.java
```
1  package com.cornez.touchgesturesexperiment2;
2
3  import android.graphics.Paint;
4
5  public class Circle {
6
7
8      private Paint mPaint;
9      private int mRadius;
10     private int mX;
11     private int mY;
12
13     public void setPaint(Paint paint) {
14         mPaint = paint;
15     }
```

```
16     public Paint getPaint() {
17         return mPaint;
18     }
19
20     public void setRadius(int radius) {
21         mRadius = radius;
22     }
23     public int getRadius() {
24         return  mRadius;
25     }
26
27     public void setX(int x) {
28         mX = x;
29     }
30     public int getX() {
31         return  mX;
32     }
33     public void setY(int y) {
34         mY = y;
35     }
36     public int getY() {
37         return  mY;
38     }
39 }
```

■ Lab Example 7-3: Bee Chases Finger Movement and the Motion Event

This lab example provides an animated game context for exploring the basic motion events for ACTION_UP, ACTION_DOWN, and ACTION_MOVE. Motion events describe movements in terms of an action code, as well as a set of axis values. The objective of this lab is to use action codes to specify the state change that occurs when the user's finger goes down, up, or moves. We will use axis value feedback from these actions that describe the finger position.

Part 1: Conceptual Design

When the application is first launched, the user sees a bee hovering just above a flower, located in the upper left-hand corner of the screen, as shown in Figure 7-8. As the user places a finger directly on the screen, the bee moves toward the finger in a proportional easing motion. If the user moves the finger around the touchscreen while maintaining contact, the bee chases the finger. Once the user lifts the finger from the screen, the bee returns to the flower.

FIGURE 7-8 The bee chases after the finger.

Part 2: Application Structure and Setup

The settings for the application are as follows:

- Application Name: Bee Finds Finger
- Project Name: BeeFindsFinger
- Package Name: `com.cornez.beefindsfinger`
- Android Form: Phone and Tablet
- Minimum SDK: API 18: Android 4.3 (Jelly Bean)
- Target SDK: API 21: Android 5.0 (Lollipop)
- Compile with: API 21: Android 5.0 (Lollipop)
- Activity Name: `MyActivity`
- Layout Name: `activity_my`

The application uses three Java files. The bee and the flower are modeled by separate classes: `Bee` and `Flower`. A single activity for the application serves as the controller. The application involves three drawable elements: the bee, the flower, and the background. As shown in the project structure in Figure 7-9, the bee and flower drawables are referenced as layout files in `res/layout`.

▌FIGURE 7-9 The Bee Finds Finger application project structure.

The `AndroidManifest.xml` file sets the orientation of the screen to a locked portrait mode. In addition, a fullscreen is utilized with the titlebar removed. The XML code for `AndroidManifest` is shown as follows:

```
AndroidManifest.xml
1   <?xml version="1.0" encoding="utf-8"?>
2   <manifest xmlns:android="http://schemas.android.com/apk/res/android"
3       package="com.cornez.beefindsfinger" >
4
5       <application
6           android:allowBackup="true"
7           android:icon="@drawable/ic_launcher"
8           android:label="@string/app_name"
9           android:theme=
10              "@android:style/Theme.Holo.NoActionBar.Fullscreen">
11
12          <activity
13              android:name=".MyActivity"
14              android:screenOrientation="portrait"
15              android:label="@string/app_name" >
16              <intent-filter>
```

```
17                  <action
18                      android:name="android.intent.action.MAIN" />
19
20                  <category
21                      android:name="android.intent.category.LAUNCHER" />
22              </intent-filter>
23          </activity>
24      </application>
25
26  </manifest>
```

The string resources that the application uses provide the image descriptions, specifically "Bee" and "Flower." These descriptions, defined on Lines 8–9, will be used in layout XML files for the application.

```
strings.xml
1   <?xml version="1.0" encoding="utf-8"?>
2   <resources>
3
4       <string name="app_name">Bee Finds Finger</string>
5       <string name="hello_world">Hello world!</string>
6       <string name="action_settings">Settings</string>
7
8       <string name="bee">Bee</string>
9       <string name="flower">Flower</string>
10
11  </resources>
```

Part 3: The User Interface

The visual elements, the bee and flower, are programmatically placed onto the screen. Each of these drawable components will be defined as `ImageView` Layout files in `res/layout`. The graphical layout design for `bee_image.xml` and `flower_image.xml` are shown in Figures 7-10 and 7-11, respectively.

ImageView – @drawable/bee

▌ FIGURE 7-10 The Bee is built as an XML Layout with an `ImageView`.

bee_image.xml

```
1  <?xml version="1.0" encoding="utf-8"?>
2  <ImageView xmlns:android="http://schemas.android.com/apk/res/android"
3      android:layout_width="match_parent"
4      android:layout_height="match_parent"
5      android:src="@drawable/bee"
6      android:contentDescription="@string/bee">
7
8  </ImageView>
```

FIGURE 7-11 The Flower is built as an XML Layout with an `ImageView`.

Flower_image.xml

```
1  <?xml version="1.0" encoding="utf-8"?>
2  <ImageView xmlns:android="http://schemas.android.com/apk/res/android"
3      android:layout_width="match_parent"
4      android:layout_height="match_parent"
5      android:src="@drawable/flower">
6
7  </ImageView>
```

FIGURE 7-12 The layout design shown in the Graphical Layout Editor.

The main activity for the application, `activity_my.xml`, uses a `Relative-Layout` as the root view, as shown in Figure 7-12. The coordinate system specified by the `RelativeLayout` places the $x = 0$, $y = 0$ point at the top left-hand corner of the layout.

The background of the root view is set to the `background` drawable. This allows all other `ImageViews` to be layered on top of the root view. The XML code for `activity_my.xml` is shown as follows:

activity_my.xml

```
1    <RelativeLayout
2    xmlns:android="http://schemas.android.com/apk/res/android"
3        xmlns:tools="http://schemas.android.com/tools"
4        android:layout_width="match_parent"
5        android:layout_height="match_parent"
6        android:id="@+id/relativeLayout"
7        tools:context=".MyActivity"
8        android:background="@drawable/background">
9
10   </RelativeLayout>
```

Part 4: Source Code for Application

The `Bee` class stores the *x, y* location of the bee graphic that appears on the screen. In addition, an easing velocity, the proportional movement, is computed in the `move()` method. The Java code for the `Bee` class is shown as follows:

Bee.java

```
1    package com.cornez.beefindsfinger;
2
3    public class Bee {
4        private int mX;
5        private int mY;
6        private int mVelocity;
7
8        public void setVelocity(int velocity){
9            mVelocity = velocity;
10       }
11       public int getVelocity(){
12           return mVelocity;
13       }
14
15       public void setX(int x){
16           mX = x;
17       }
18       public void setY(int y){
```

```
19            mY = y;
20        }
21        public int getX(){
22            return mX;
23        }
24        public int getY(){
25            return mY;
26        }
27        public void move(int destinationX, int destinationY){
28            int distX = destinationX - mX;
29            int distY = destinationY -  mY;
30            mX += distX / mVelocity;
31            mY += distY / mVelocity;
32        }
33    }
```

The flower graphic remains stationary in this application. The bee graphic is guided back to the flower when no touch activity takes place on the screen. The attributes for the Flower class provide a seek location for the bee and consist of an *x*, *y* point on the screen. The Java code for the Flower class appears as follows:

Flower.java
```
1    package com.cornez.beefindsfinger;
2
3    public class Flower {
4        private int mX;
5        private int mY;
6
7        public int getX(){
8            return mX;
9        }
10       public void setX(int x){
11           mX = x;
12       }
13       public int getY(){
14           return mY;
15       }
16       public void setY(int y){
17           mY = y;
18       }
19   }
```

MyActivity is the single activity that the application uses. The onCreate() method performs the visual initialization by preparing the game window and inflating the bee and flower graphic elements. In addition, game objects are instantiated.

```
MyActivity.java
 1   package com.cornez.beefindsfinger;
 2
 3   import android.app.Activity;
 4   import android.content.Context;
 5   import android.os.Bundle;
 6   import android.os.Handler;
 7   import android.view.LayoutInflater;
 8   import android.view.Menu;
 9   import android.view.MenuItem;
10   import android.view.MotionEvent;
11   import android.view.Window;
12   import android.view.WindowManager;
13   import android.widget.ImageView;
14   import android.widget.RelativeLayout;
15
16
17   public class MyActivity extends Activity {
18
19       //ACTIVITY WORK IS SPLIT INTO TWO THREADS:
20       //          CALCULATING BEE MOVEMENT - BACKGROUND
21       //          POSITIONING THE BEE      - UI THREAD
22       private Thread calculateThread;
23
24       private RelativeLayout mainLayout;
25       private ImageView beeImageView;
26       private ImageView flowerImageView;
27
28       private Flower mFlower;
29       private Bee mBee;
30
31       private int xLocation;
32       private int yLocation;
33
34       @Override
35       protected void onCreate(Bundle savedInstanceState) {
36           super.onCreate(savedInstanceState);
37
38           //TASK 1: WINDOW PROPERTIES ARE SET
39           //THIS ANDROID WINDOW WILL NOT FEATURE A TITLE
40           requestWindowFeature(Window.FEATURE_NO_TITLE);
41           getWindow().setFlags(
42                   WindowManager.LayoutParams.FLAG_FULLSCREEN,
43                   WindowManager.LayoutParams.FLAG_FULLSCREEN);
44
45           //TASK 2: SET THE LAYOUT VIEW
46           setContentView(R.layout.activity_my);
47           mainLayout = (RelativeLayout) findViewById(R.id.relativeLayout);
```

```
48
49          //TASK 3: INSTANTIATE THE FLOWER AND BEE
50          xLocation = 200;
51          yLocation = 200;
52          addFlower();
53          buildBee();
54
55          //TASK 4: INSTANTIATE THE BACKGROUND THREAD
56          calculateThread = new Thread(calculateAction);
57      }
```

The bee and flower graphic elements are layered onto the screen so that the bee sits below the flower layer.

MyActivity.java (*continued*)

```
58   private void addFlower() {
59
60          //TASK 1: CREATE A LAYOUT INFLATER
61          LayoutInflater layoutInflater;
62          layoutInflater = (LayoutInflater)
63              getSystemService(Context.LAYOUT_INFLATER_SERVICE);
64
65          //TASK 2: SPECIFY FLOWER POSITION
66          int initialXPosition = xLocation;
67          int initialYPosition = yLocation;
68
69          mFlower = new Flower();
70          mFlower.setX(initialXPosition);
71          mFlower.setY(initialYPosition);
72
73          //TASK 3: ADD THE FLOWER
74          flowerImageView = (ImageView)
75              layoutInflater.inflate(R.layout.flower_image, null);
76          flowerImageView.setX((float) mFlower.getX());
77          flowerImageView.setY((float) mFlower.getY() + 50);
78          mainLayout.addView(flowerImageView, 0);
79      }
80
81   private void buildBee() {
82
83          //TASK 1: CREATE A LAYOUT INFLATER TO
84          //        ADD VISUAL VIEWS TO THE LAYOUT
85          LayoutInflater layoutInflater;
86          layoutInflater = (LayoutInflater)
87              getSystemService(Context.LAYOUT_INFLATER_SERVICE);
88
89          //TASK 2: SPECIFY BEE ATTRIBUTES
90          int initialXPosition = xLocation;
91          int initialYPosition = yLocation;
```

```
92          int proportionalVelocity = 10;
93          mBee = new Bee();
94          mBee.setX(initialXPosition);
95          mBee.setY(initialYPosition);
96          mBee.setVelocity(proportionalVelocity);
97
98          //TASK 3: ADD THE BEE
99          beeImageView = (ImageView)
100                   layoutInflater.inflate(R.layout.bee_image, null);
101          beeImageView.setX((float) mBee.getX());
102          beeImageView.setY((float) mBee.getY());
103          mainLayout.addView(beeImageView, 0);
104      }
```

The animated movement of the bee is executed with the support of two threads. A background thread performs the computations associated with movment. The UI thread performs the updates to the `ImageView` holding the bee graphic.

MyActivity.java (*continued*)

```
105      @Override
106      protected void onResume() {
107          calculateThread.start();
108          super.onResume();
109      }
110
111      @Override
112      protected void onPause() {
113          finish();
114          super.onPause();
115      }
116
117      @Override
118      protected void onDestroy() {
119          finish();
120          super.onDestroy();
121      }
122
123
124      //****************** RUNNABLE ********************
125      private Runnable calculateAction = new Runnable() {
126          private static final int DELAY = 200;
127
128          public void run() {
129              try {
130                  while (true) {
131                      mBee.move(xLocation, yLocation);
132                      Thread.sleep(DELAY);
133                      threadHandler.sendEmptyMessage(0);
134                  }
```

```
135                } catch (InterruptedException e) {
136                    e.printStackTrace();
137                }
138            }
139        };
140
141        //*** HANDLER FOR UPDATING BEE BETWEEN SLEEP DELAYS ****
142        public Handler threadHandler = new Handler() {
143            public void handleMessage(android.os.Message msg) {
144                //SET THE BEE AT THE CORRECT XY LOCATION
145                beeImageView.setX((float) mBee.getX());
146                beeImageView.setY((float) mBee.getY());
147            }
148        };
```

The touch events that control the bee movement are implemented in onTouch-Event(). In this application, the onTouchEvent() is automatically called when a **screen touch** event has occurred. The getActionMasked() method returns the specific action that was performed.

The first handled touch action is ACTION_DOWN. The user's finger is stationary at the first touch. The location of the finger is used to reposition the bee. In a response to ACTION_MOVE, the bee graphic is moved over the extent of the screen as it traces the finger motion.

MyActivity.java (*continued*)

```
149        @Override
150        public boolean onTouchEvent(MotionEvent event) {
151            //TASK 1:   IDENTIFY THE TOUCH ACTION BEING PERFORMED
152            int touchAction = event.getActionMasked();
153
154            //TASK 2:   RESPOND TO POSSIBLE TOUCH EVENTS
155            switch (touchAction) {
156                // BEE FINDS A MOTIONLESS FINGER
157                case MotionEvent.ACTION_DOWN:
158                    xLocation = (int) event.getX();
159                    yLocation = (int) event.getY();
160                    break;
161                // BEE RETURNS TO THE FLOWER WHEN THE FINGER IS REMOVED
162                case MotionEvent.ACTION_UP:
163                    xLocation = mFlower.getX();
164                    yLocation = mFlower.getY();
165                    break;
166                // BEE FOLLOWS A MOVING FINGER
167                case MotionEvent.ACTION_MOVE:
168                    xLocation = (int) event.getX();
169                    yLocation = (int) event.getY();
170            }
171
```

```
172        //TASK 3: RETURNS A TRUE AFTER HANDLING THE TOUCH ACTION EVENT
173        return true;
174    }
175
176    @Override
177    public boolean onCreateOptionsMenu(Menu menu) {
178        // Inflate the menu.
179        getMenuInflater().inflate(R.menu.my, menu);
180        return true;
181    }
182
183    @Override
184    public boolean onOptionsItemSelected(MenuItem item) {
185        // Handle action bar item clicks here. The action bar will
186        // automatically handle clicks on the Home/Up button, so long
187        // as you specify a parent activity in AndroidManifest.xml.
188        int id = item.getItemId();
189        if (id == R.id.action_settings) {
190            return true;
191        }
192        return super.onOptionsItemSelected(item);
193    }
194 }
```

■ 7.6 The Drag-and-Drop Gesture

In human–computer interactions, drag-and-drop is the action of tapping on a virtual object and dragging it to a different location. This gesture is broadly used in graphical user interfaces; it is intuitive, efficient, and has a low learning curve. Drag-and-drop is a gesture that is most often associated with methods of data transfer. On an Android device, this gesture involves the use of a single finger to select an object, dragging this object over a desired drop target, and dropping it. This form of gesture interaction is an elegant, and frequently required, action sequence for many applications.

In a general sense, drag-and-drop is a gesture that can be used to invoke an action or create an association between two objects. This gesture assumes that a drag source and a drop target exist. In this manner, a user drags a drag source and drops it into a drop target.

The ability to reposition graphic images and text on a screen is a basic functionality of smart devices. Drag-and-drop is an important touch gesture because it increases the usability of an application by making it easy to position elements around the screen. As all Android device users know firsthand, the particular actions performed during a drag-and-drop are application-specific and are often determined by context. For example, dragging a selected graphic from one location to another might move the graphic by default. In another context, however, dragging and dropping a graphic may copy the element or perhaps an attribute of the element.

Using a drag-and-drop gesture provides an easier means to visualize or determine specific moves. Imagine dropping puzzle pieces on a puzzle board rather than visualizing the *x* and *y* coordinates as text. Although the Android framework for drag-and-drop is primarily designed for data movement, it is also possible to use it for other actions. The drag-and-drop features provided by the SDK are designed to be flexible and customizable to support a variety of drag-and-drop scenarios. For example, it is possible to create an application that mixes colors when the user drags a color icon over another icon. In this chapter, we focus on data movement, but it would be possible to use the discussed concepts for other types of actions.

The Android framework for drag-and-drop includes a drag event class, drag listeners, and helper methods and classes.

Source and target containers must be created to hold the `View` elements that will be dragged and eventually dropped. As Figure 7-13 shows, a basic drag-and-drop design relies on at least two `Views`, which serve as containers. The first `View` is a source container from which the dragged chess piece object originates. The second `View` is a target container, which receives the dropped chess piece. In this example, the drag source and drop target is a graphic image of a chess piece and is also a `View`

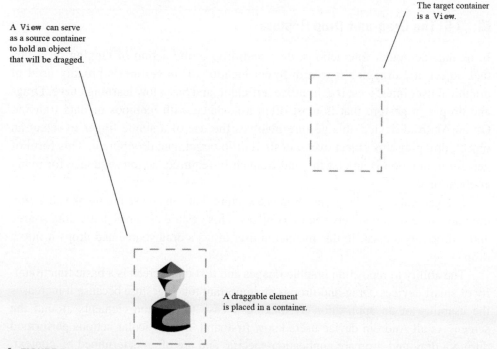

The target container
is a `View`.

A `View` can serve
as a source container
to hold an object
that will be dragged.

A draggable element
is placed in a container.

❚ FIGURE 7-13 Source and target containers for a chess piece to be dragged.

itself. The most common objects manipulated through drag-and-drop operations are graphic images and text. In Android, any `View` object is eligible for drag-and-drop.

All elements that are the intended moveable objects in a drag-and-drop process must be registered with an appropriate listener event. A touch listener, `setOnTouchListener()`, must be attached to each draggable `View` in a given application. This will register a callback to be invoked when an explicit touch event is sent to this draggable `View` object.

A view container that functions as a source or target container must be registered with an explicit "on drag" listener event. In the chess piece example shown in Figure 7-13, the target and source containers are registered with a `setOnDragListener()`. This listener event triggers a drag event callback when a drag is being dispatched to an explicit view.

For each draggable object, a touch listener can be implemented to respond to the triggered drag-and-drop registered event. This implementation allows the application to detect when a user touches a draggable object and then responds to that touch event.

A user first initiates a drag-and-drop process by pressing a finger down on the screen, usually a `LongPress`, over a `View` object. A `startDrag()` method is automatically called for the associated `View`, and the system sends a drag event with the action type `ACTION_DRAG_STARTED` to the drag event listeners for all `View` objects in the current layout.

During a drag-and-drop operation, the system provides a separate image that the user drags. For data movement, this image represents a copy of the object being dragged. This mechanism makes it clear to the user that an object is in the process of being dragged and has not yet been placed in its final target location. This dragged image is called a drag shadow because it is a shadow version of itself, as shown in Figure 7-14. A drag shadow, created using `DragShadowBuilder`, can be customized.

As a drag shadow intersects the bounding box of a target container, the system sends one or more drag events to the `View` object's drag event listener. Registered listeners can alter the appearance of a given `View` object to indicate that the listener can accept a drop event. Once the user releases the drag shadow within the bounding box of a `View` container that is designed to accept the object, the system sends an `ACTION_DROP` event and an `ACTION_DRAG_ENDED` event to indicate the drag operation has ended. The listener is expected to return `true` if the drop is successful.

Drag-and-drop operations support an event-driven model. A number of different actions are used for monitoring the entire drag-and-drop process. In a typical drag-and-drop flow, it is necessary to consider the originating source location, the draggable data element, and a target drop location. Both the drag source and the drop target use a standard set of drag-event data to handle drag-and-drop operations. Table 7-2 summarizes the standard drag-and-drop event data by action type.

Consider the following segment of code that illustrates the drag component of a drag-and-drop operation. This segment of code assumes the existence of a custom

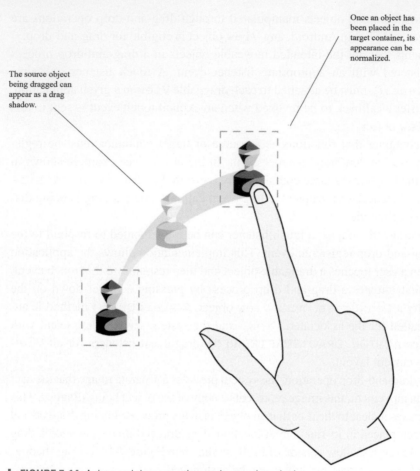

The source object being dragged can appear as a drag shadow.

Once an object has been placed in the target container, its appearance can be normalized.

❙ FIGURE 7-14 A drag-and-drop operation produces a drag shadow.

class containing the implemention of an `OnTouchListener` to set the drag-and-drop process in motion. An `ACTION_DOWN` Motion Event triggers the `onTouch()` for the detection of a drag-drop operation. A touch will be treated as the beginning of a drag operation with the intention that a chess piece, residing in a source container, will be dragged from that container.

Once it is determined that an `ACTION_DOWN` event has occurred, a listener will perform a set of basic tasks before returning true, indicating that the listener has consumed the event, or false.

1. A `DragShadowBuilder` object is created using the chess piece being dragged.

2. From the clipboard framework, a clip data element is created to use in the `startDrag()` method. To implement a drop of an object, the application must correctly interpret the data for its use. In this example, the data will be an empty string.

3. The `startDrag()` method is called for the chess piece being dragged.

TABLE 7-2 The drag-and-drop event data shown by action type

Action Type	Description
ACTION_DRAG_STARTED	The event listener for a draggable `View` object receives this action once `startDrag()` has been called. At this point, a drag shadow is generated.
ACTION_DRAG_ENTERED	The event listener for a `View` object receives this action when the drag shadow of the `View` has just entered the bounding box of the target container into which it is being dragged. This is the first event action type the listener receives when the drag shadow enters the bounding box.
ACTION_DRAG_LOCATION	A `View` object's drag event listener receives this event action type following the `ACTION_DRAG_ENTERED` event while the drag shadow is still within the bounding box of a target container.
ACTION_DRAG_EXITED	This action specifies that the user has moved the drag shadow outside the bounding box of a possible target container. The event listener for a `View` object receives this action type following an `ACTION_DRAG_ENTERED` and an `ACTION_DRAG_LOCATION` event.
ACTION_DROP	The event listener for a `View` object receives this event action when the user releases the drag shadow over a registered target container. This action type is sent only to a View object's listener if the listener returned true in response to the `ACTION_DRAG_STARTED` drag event.
ACTION_DRAG_ENDED	This action specifies that a drag-and-drop operation has ended. The event listener for a `View` object receives this action when the system has called an end to the drop. This action type is not necessarily preceded by an `ACTION_DROP` event. For example, if the system sends an `ACTION_DROP`, receiving the `ACTION_DRAG_ENDED` action type does not imply that the drop operation succeeded. The listener can call `getResult()` to get the value that was returned in response to `ACTION_DROP`. If an `ACTION_DROP` event was not sent, then `getResult()` returns false.

The original chess piece can be hidden by calling `setVisibility()`. This leaves the `DragShadowBuilder` object visible, indicating that the drag has started.

```
 1    if (motionevent.getAction() == MotionEvent.ACTION_DOWN) {
 2
 3        //TASK 1: INTERPRET THE DRAG DATA
 4        ClipData data = ClipData.newPlainText("", "");
 5
 6        //TASK 2: CREATE A DRAG SHADOW
 7        DragShadowBuilder shadowBuilder = new
 8            View.DragShadowBuilder(chessPiece);
 9
10        //TASK 3: CALL A METHOD TO START THE DRAG
11        chessPiece.startDrag(data, shadowBuilder, chessPiece, 0);
12
13        //TASK 4: HIDE THE ORIGINAL IMAGE
14        chessPiece.setVisibility(View.INVISIBLE);
15
16        return true;
17    } else {
18        return false;
19    }
```

When a drag ends, an ACTION_DRAG_ENDED event is sent to all drag listeners. The call to `getResult()` supplies information about the specific drag operation for a given drag event. Once the `DragEvent.ACTION_DRAG_ENDED` action has signaled a conclusion to a drag-drop operation, the appearance of a dropped `View` should return to its original state. The following segment of code illustrates the drop component of the drag-and-drop operation. The objective of this code is to process the actual drop of the chess piece. In this example, the chess piece was made visible again. Recall that it was hidden from view during the drag process so that the user would view only the drag shadow during the drag-drop operation.

All views that received an ACTION_DRAG_STARTED event will receive the AC-TION_DRAG_ENDED event when the drag ends. If the user releases the drag shadow on a target container that can accept a drop, the system automatically sends an AC-TION_DROP event to the View object's drag event listener. A call to `getResult()` provides the results of the operation. The return value of `getResult()` depends on what happens after the user releases the drag shadow. This method returns valid data only if the action type is ACTION_DRAG_ENDED. For example, a false will be returned if no ACTION_DROP is sent. This can happen when the user releases the drag shadow over an area outside of the application. In this case, the system sends out an ACTION_DRAG_ENDED for the drag-and-drop operation, but it does not send an ACTION_DROP.

The call to `getLocalState()` returns the local state sent to the system as part of the call to `startDrag()`. This call is used to provide local information about a specific drag-and-drop operation. For example, it can be used to indicate whether the drag-and-drop operation is a copy or a move.

```
1  case DragEvent.ACTION_DRAG_ENDED:
2      if (!(event.getResult())){
3          View chessPiece = (View) event.getLocalState();
4          chessPiece.setVisibility(View.VISIBLE);
5      }
```

■ Lab Example 7-4: Drag-and-Drop Closet Stylist

The objective of this lab is to demonstrate how to create a drag-and-drop scenario in a simple application that allows users to build a style by dragging and dropping hair-styles, dresses, and shoes onto a mannequin. When first launching this application, the user will see two wigs, two dresses, two pairs of shoes, and a mannequin named Catherine, as shown in Figure 7-15.

I FIGURE 7-15 The StylistApp relies on drag-and-drop operations.

Part 1: The Application Structure

The settings for the application are as follows:

- Application Name: Catherine Styist
- Project Name: CatherineStylist
- Package Name: `com.cornez.catherinestylist`
- Android Form: Phone and Tablet
- Minimum SDK: API 18: Android 4.3 (Jelly Bean)
- Target SDK: API 21: Android 5.0 (Lollipop)
- Compile with: API 21: Android 5.0 (Lollipop)
- Activity Name: `MyActivity`
- Layout Name: `activity_my`

The structure of the application, as shown in Figure 7-16, is driven primarily by the graphic images representing the articles of clothing, wigs, and the mannequin. All

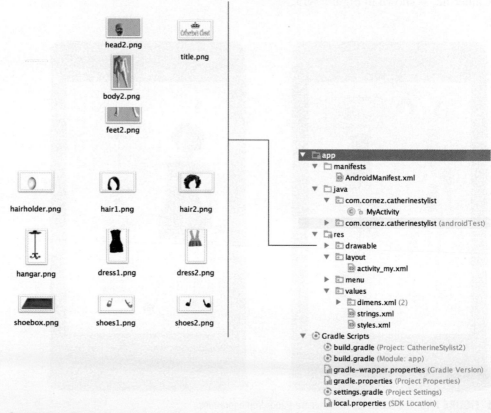

| FIGURE 7-16 The structure of the Catherine Stylist application.

of these elements are stored in the drawable resource folder. In addition, the application is simplified by the use of a single activity.

The manifest for the application is configured without a titlebar, utilizing a fullscreen, and set to portrait mode. The XML code for the manifest file is shown as follows:

```
AndroidManifest.xml
1   <?xml version="1.0" encoding="utf-8"?>
2   <manifest xmlns:android="http://schemas.android.com/apk/res/android"
3       package="com.cornez.catherinestylist" >
4
5       <application
6           android:allowBackup="true"
7           android:icon="@drawable/ic_launcher"
8           android:label="@string/app_name"
9           android:theme=
10              "@android:style/Theme.Light.NoTitleBar.Fullscreen"  >
11          <activity
12              android:name=".MyActivity"
13              android:screenOrientation="portrait"
14              android:label="@string/app_name" >
15              <intent-filter>
16                  <action android:name="android.intent.action.MAIN" />
17
18                  <category
19                      android:name="android.intent.category.LAUNCHER" />
20              </intent-filter>
21          </activity>
22      </application>
23
24  </manifest>
```

Part 2: The User Interface as a Layout XML File

The design of the interface for the application's activity relies on a `RelativeLayout` root tag that stores a collection of `LinearLayout` containers. The hierarchical structure for the layout file, `activity_my.xml`, is shown in Figure 7-17. The `LinearLayout` Views are ideal for storing single `ImageView` objects, such as hairstyles and clothing items. These `LinearLayout` elements will serve as source and target containers for `View` elements that will be dragged and dropped by the user.

The following `activity`, `_my.xml` code, performs the intricate arrangement of the draggable `Views` and the locaton of the source and target containers. It is necessary to control the Views that will be dropped into containers. For example, the user will not be permitted to place a pair of shoes on the mannequin's head, which is designated as a container solely for the purpose of holding a wig.

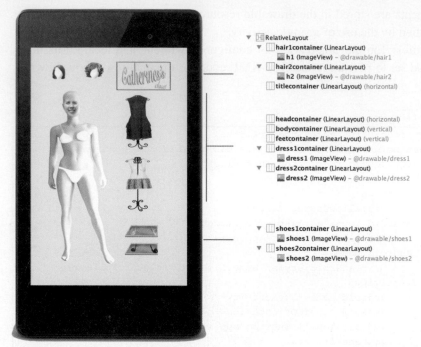

FIGURE 7-17 The interface design for `activity_my.xml` of the Stylist application.

When the application first launches, the graphics representing the wigs are placed in the hair containers. These containers are the intial source containers and will be identified by `hair1container` and `hair2container`.

```
activity_my.xml
1    <RelativeLayout
2    xmlns:android="http://schemas.android.com/apk/res/android"
3        xmlns:tools="http://schemas.android.com/tools"
4        android:layout_width="match_parent"
5        android:layout_height="match_parent"
6        tools:context=".MyActivity"
7        android:gravity="center_vertical|center_horizontal"
8        android:background="#bec2c3">
9
10        <!-- THE HAIRSTYLES -->
11        <LinearLayout
12            android:id="@+id/hair1container"
13            android:layout_width="wrap_content"
14            android:layout_height="wrap_content"
15            android:layout_alignParentLeft="true"
16            android:layout_alignParentTop="true"
17            android:background="@drawable/hairholder" >
18
19            <ImageView
20                android:id="@+id/h1"
```

```
21         android:layout_width="wrap_content"
22         android:layout_height="wrap_content"
23         android:src="@drawable/hair1"
24         android:contentDescription="@string/hair" />
25    </LinearLayout>
26    <LinearLayout
27        android:id="@+id/hair2container"
28        android:layout_width="wrap_content"
29        android:layout_height="wrap_content"
30        android:layout_alignParentTop="true"
31        android:layout_toRightOf="@+id/hair1container"
32        android:background="@drawable/hairholder" >
33        <ImageView
34            android:id="@+id/h2"
35            android:layout_width="wrap_content"
36            android:layout_height="wrap_content"
37            android:src="@drawable/hair2"
38            android:contentDescription="@string/hair"/>
39    </LinearLayout>
40    <!-- THE TITLE IMAGE -->
41    <LinearLayout
42        android:id="@+id/titlecontainer"
43        android:layout_width="wrap_content"
44        android:layout_height="wrap_content"
45        android:layout_alignParentTop="true"
46        android:layout_toRightOf="@+id/hair2container"
47        android:background="@drawable/title"
48        android:orientation="horizontal">
49    </LinearLayout>
```

The mannequin is designed as a set of three target containers for dropping hair, a dress, and a pair of shoes. The background of these containers holds the mannequin's head, body, and feet graphic elements. Each of the containers is represented by a `LinearLayout` and is identified by the names `headcontainer`, `bodycontainer`, and `feetcontainer`.

activity_my.xml (*continued*)

```
50        <!-- THE MANNEQUIN -->
51        <LinearLayout
52            android:id="@+id/headcontainer"
53            android:layout_width="wrap_content"
54            android:layout_height="wrap_content"
55            android:layout_alignParentLeft="true"
56            android:layout_below="@+id/hair1container"
57            android:layout_marginTop="5dp"
58            android:background="@drawable/head"
59            android:orientation="horizontal">
60        </LinearLayout>
61        <LinearLayout
```

```
62          android:id="@+id/bodycontainer"
63          android:layout_width="wrap_content"
64          android:layout_height="wrap_content"
65          android:layout_alignParentLeft="true"
66          android:layout_below="@+id/headcontainer"
67          android:background="@drawable/body"
68          android:orientation="vertical">
69      </LinearLayout>
70      <LinearLayout
71          android:id="@+id/feetcontainer"
72          android:layout_width="wrap_content"
73          android:layout_height="wrap_content"
74          android:layout_alignParentLeft="true"
75          android:layout_below="@+id/bodycontainer"
76          android:background="@drawable/feet"
77          android:orientation="vertical">
78      </LinearLayout>
```

The clothing items for the application are two dresses. For visual interest, the dress graphics are placed into LinearLayout containers with an image of a hanger as a background. The ImageView elements stored in the containers are identified as dress1 and dress2. The containers with hanger backgrounds are dress1container and dress2container.

The shoe items are initially stored in the containers named shoes1container and shoes2container.

activity_my.xml (*continued*)

```
79          <!-- THE DRESSES -->
80          <LinearLayout
81              android:id="@+id/dress1container"
82              android:layout_width="wrap_content"
83              android:layout_height="wrap_content"
84              android:layout_below="@+id/titlecontainer"
85              android:layout_marginTop="15dp"
86              android:layout_marginLeft="30dp"
87              android:layout_toRightOf="@+id/hair2container"
88              android:background="@drawable/hangar"
89              android:gravity="center_horizontal">
90              <ImageView
91                  android:id="@+id/dress1"
92                  android:layout_width="wrap_content"
93                  android:layout_height="wrap_content"
94                  android:src="@drawable/dress1"
95                  android:contentDescription="@string/dress"/>
96          </LinearLayout>
97
98          <LinearLayout
99              android:id="@+id/dress2container"
```

```
100            android:layout_width="wrap_content"
101            android:layout_height="wrap_content"
102            android:layout_alignLeft="@+id/dress1container"
103            android:layout_below="@+id/dress1container"
104            android:background="@drawable/hangar" >
105
106            <ImageView
107                android:id="@+id/dress2"
108                android:layout_width="wrap_content"
109                android:layout_height="wrap_content"
110                android:src="@drawable/dress2"
111                android:contentDescription="@string/shoes"/>
112        </LinearLayout>
113
114
115        <!-- THE SHOES -->
116        <LinearLayout
117            android:id="@+id/shoes1container"
118            android:layout_width="wrap_content"
119            android:layout_height="wrap_content"
120            android:layout_alignLeft="@+id/dress2container"
121            android:layout_below="@+id/dress2container"
122            android:layout_marginTop="20dp"
123            android:background="@drawable/shoebox" >
124
125            <ImageView
126                android:id="@+id/shoes1"
127                android:layout_width="wrap_content"
128                android:layout_height="wrap_content"
129                android:src="@drawable/shoes1"
130                android:contentDescription="@string/shoes"/>
131        </LinearLayout>
132
133        <LinearLayout
134            android:id="@+id/shoes2container"
135            android:layout_width="wrap_content"
136            android:layout_height="wrap_content"
137            android:layout_alignLeft="@+id/shoes1container"
138            android:layout_below="@+id/shoes1container"
139            android:layout_marginTop="10dp"
140            android:background="@drawable/shoebox" >
141
142            <ImageView
143                android:id="@+id/shoes2"
144                android:layout_width="wrap_content"
145                android:layout_height="wrap_content"
146                android:src="@drawable/shoes2"
147                android:contentDescription="@string/shoes"/>
148        </LinearLayout>
149
150  </RelativeLayout>
```

Part 3: Source Code for Application

MyActivity is the controller for the application, as well as the single source file used by the application. All drag-and-drop operations will be implemented in this document.

The main code objects for this application are the containers for the clothing and style items, as well as the containers for mannequin drop sites. The application requires the detection of illegal drops. In addition, limits need to be applied to control and restrict the area in which an item can be dropped. If the user attempts to drop a view that results in an illegal move, the View will appear to snap back to its original position.

Error detection will occur for all instances where the user attempts to place an inappropriate article of clothing on the mannequin. For example, shoes are inappropriate headwear, at least for this application. All errors will be handled with a snap-back method. In addition, the user will be informed as to why the attempted drag-and-drop operation failed to produce the intended.

The Java code for MyActivity is shown as follows:

Lines 19–30:   All style elements are ImageViews, and all containers are Lin-earLayouts. All containers are instantiated as LinearLay-out objects. In addition, the ImageView objects for wigs, dresses, and shoes are declared.

```
MyActivity.java
 1   package com.cornez.catherinestylist;
 2
 3   import android.app.Activity;
 4   import android.content.ClipData;
 5   import android.os.Bundle;
 6   import android.view.DragEvent;
 7   import android.view.Menu;
 8   import android.view.MenuItem;
 9   import android.view.MotionEvent;
10   import android.view.View;
11   import android.view.ViewGroup;
12   import android.widget.ImageView;
13   import android.widget.LinearLayout;
14   import android.widget.Toast;
15
16
17   public class MyActivity extends Activity {
18
19       // MANNEQUIN CONTAINERS
20       private LinearLayout headContainer, bodyContainer, feetContainer;
21
22       // HAIR IMAGES AND CONTAINERS
23       private ImageView hair1, hair2;
```

```
24      private ImageView dress1, dress2;
25      private ImageView shoes1, shoes2;
26
27      // CONTAINERS
28      private LinearLayout hairContainer1, hairContainer2;
29      private LinearLayout dressContainer1, dressContainer2;
30      private LinearLayout shoeContainer1, shoeContainer2;
31
32      @Override
33      protected void onCreate(Bundle savedInstanceState) {
34          super.onCreate(savedInstanceState);
35          setContentView(R.layout.activity_my);
36
37          //REFERENCE THE STYLE ELEMENTS AND THE CONTAINERS
38          getMannequin();
39          getHairStyles();
40          getDressStyles();
41          getShoeSyles();
42      }
43
44
45      void getMannequin() {
46          // IDENTIFY THE MANNEQUIN ELEMENTS
47          headContainer = (LinearLayout) findViewById(R.id.headcontainer);
48          bodyContainer = (LinearLayout) findViewById(R.id.bodycontainer);
49          feetContainer = (LinearLayout) findViewById(R.id.feetcontainer);
50
51          // REGISTER MANNEQUIN LISTENER EVENTS
52          headContainer.setOnDragListener(new ChoiceDragListener());
53          bodyContainer.setOnDragListener(new ChoiceDragListener());
54          feetContainer.setOnDragListener(new ChoiceDragListener());
55      }
```

All style elements, including the source and target containers, are referenced. In addition, all listener events, one for each individual container, are registered.

setOnTouchListener() is used to register a listener event on a style image that is draggable. The setOnDragListener() registers a drag event listener callback for the containers. The ChoiceTouchListener class is implemented for performing the drag-and-drop operation.

The makeAToast() method, located on Lines 116–118, notifies the user of unsuitable drag-and-drops.

MyActivity.java (*continued*)

```
56      void getMannequin() {
57          // IDENTIFY THE MANNEQUIN ELEMENTS
58          headContainer = (LinearLayout) findViewById(R.id.headcontainer);
59          bodyContainer = (LinearLayout) findViewById(R.id.bodycontainer);
60          feetContainer = (LinearLayout) findViewById(R.id.feetcontainer);
```

```
61
62          // REGISTER MANNEQUIN LISTENER EVENTS
63          headContainer.setOnDragListener(new ChoiceDragListener());
64          bodyContainer.setOnDragListener(new ChoiceDragListener());
65          feetContainer.setOnDragListener(new ChoiceDragListener());
66      }
67
68      void getHairStyles() {
69          // IDENTIFY THE HAIR ELEMENTS
70          hair1 = (ImageView) findViewById(R.id.h1);
71          hair2 = (ImageView) findViewById(R.id.h2);
72          hairContainer1 = (LinearLayout)
73                  findViewById(R.id.hair1container);
74          hairContainer2 = (LinearLayout)
75                  findViewById(R.id.hair2container);
76
77          // REGISTER HAIR LISTENER EVENTS
78          hair1.setOnTouchListener(new ChoiceTouchListener());
79          hair2.setOnTouchListener(new ChoiceTouchListener());
80          hairContainer1.setOnDragListener(new ChoiceDragListener());
81          hairContainer2.setOnDragListener(new ChoiceDragListener());
82      }
83
84      void getDressStyles() {
85          // IDENTIFY THE DRESS ELEMENTS
86          dress1 = (ImageView) findViewById(R.id.dress1);
87          dress2 = (ImageView) findViewById(R.id.dress2);
88          dressContainer1 = (LinearLayout)
89                          findViewById(R.id.dress1container);
90          dressContainer2 = (LinearLayout)
91                          findViewById(R.id.dress2container);
92
93          // REGISTER DRESS LISTENER EVENTS
94          dress1.setOnTouchListener(new ChoiceTouchListener());
95          dress2.setOnTouchListener(new ChoiceTouchListener());
96          dressContainer1.setOnDragListener(new ChoiceDragListener());
97          dressContainer2.setOnDragListener(new ChoiceDragListener());
98      }
99
100     void getShoeSyles() {
101         // IDENTIFY THE SHOE ELEMENTS
102         shoes1 = (ImageView) findViewById(R.id.shoes1);
103         shoes2 = (ImageView) findViewById(R.id.shoes2);
104         shoeContainer1 = (LinearLayout)
105                         findViewById(R.id.shoes1container);
106         shoeContainer2 = (LinearLayout)
107                         findViewById(R.id.shoes2container);
108
109         // REGISTER SHOE LISTENER EVENTS
110         shoes1.setOnTouchListener(new ChoiceTouchListener());
```

```
111        shoes2.setOnTouchListener(new ChoiceTouchListener());
112        shoeContainer1.setOnDragListener(new ChoiceDragListener());
113        shoeContainer2.setOnDragListener(new ChoiceDragListener());
114    }
115
116    void makeAToast(String message) {
117        Toast.makeText(this, message, Toast.LENGTH_LONG).show();
118    }
```

Lines 119–135:   The `ChoiceTouchListener` class is implemented using `View.OnTouchListener` The `OnTouchListener` interface for the `onTouch` callback is invoked each time a touch event occurs for a registered `View`.

The user begins the drag process with a simple touch gesture, in this case an `ACTION_DOWN`. In response to this touch gesture, a `ClipData` object is created for the element being dragged. As part of the `ClipData` object, metadata can be stored in a `ClipDescription` object within a `ClipData` object. For an operation that involves data movement, the supplied arguments can be strings containing tag and label information, or they can be an actual object. The `ClipData` object used in this instance does not require specific information from the `ImageView`; hence, null strings will be supplied for the arguments.

Lines 137–231:   During the drag operation, the system dispatches drag events to the drag event listeners of the View objects in the current layout. The listeners will react by calling `getAction()` to access the action type. At the start of a drag operation, this method will return `ACTION_DRAG_STARTED`.

The two action responses required for this simplified application are `ACTION_DRAG_ENDED` and `ACTION_DROP`. Immediately after the user releases the drag shadow, the system sends a drag event to all of the drag event listeners in the application. The action type specified by this drag event is `ACTION_DRAG_ENDED`. This will conclude the drag-and-drop operation.

In this application, the detection of an illegal drop results in the item snapping back to its original location. An illegal drop resets the `View` to its default appearance. This is a visual indication that the operation is over and that the user did not successfully perform a drag-and-drop.

A larger version of the articles of clothing and the wigs are placed on the mannequin. This means that once the items are successfully dragged to the mannequin or back to the closet, the item needs to be rescaled. The swapItems () method performs this task.

MyActivity.java (*continued*)

```java
119      private final class ChoiceTouchListener implements
120                              View.OnTouchListener {
121         public boolean onTouch(View view, MotionEvent motionevent) {
122             if (motionevent.getAction() == MotionEvent.ACTION_DOWN) {
123                 ClipData data = ClipData.newPlainText("", "");
124                 View.DragShadowBuilder shadowBuilder = new
125                                 View.DragShadowBuilder(view);
126                 view.startDrag(data, shadowBuilder, view, 0);
127
128                 // MAKE THE CLOSET ITEM INVISIBLE DURING THE DRAG
129                 view.setVisibility(View.INVISIBLE);
130                 return true;
131             } else {
132                 return false;
133             }
134         }
135     }
136
137      private class ChoiceDragListener implements View.OnDragListener {
138
139         public boolean onDrag(View destinationV, DragEvent e) {
140             // IDENTIFY ELEMENTS BEING DRAGGED AND DROPPED
141             View draggedV = (View) e.getLocalState();
142             ViewGroup parentSourceV = (ViewGroup) draggedV.getParent();
143             LinearLayout container = (LinearLayout) destinationV;
144
145
146             switch (e.getAction()) {
147                 case DragEvent.ACTION_DRAG_STARTED:
148                     break;
149                 case DragEvent.ACTION_DRAG_ENTERED:
150                     break;
151                 case DragEvent.ACTION_DRAG_EXITED:
152                     break;
153                 case DragEvent.ACTION_DRAG_ENDED:
154                     draggedV.setVisibility(View.VISIBLE);
155                     break;
156                 case DragEvent.ACTION_DROP:
```

```
157            if (container.getChildCount() < 1) {
158                // ITEMS MOVED TO THE MANNEQUIN
159                if (container.equals(feetContainer)) {
160                    if (draggedV.equals(shoes1) ||
161                        draggedV.equals(shoes2))
162                        swapItems(parentSourceV, draggedV,
163                                    container, 2.0f);
164                    else {
165                        draggedV.setVisibility(View.VISIBLE);
166                    }
167                } else if (container.equals(bodyContainer)) {
168                    if (draggedV.equals(dress1) ||
169                        draggedV.equals(dress2))
170                        swapItems(parentSourceV, draggedV,
171                                    container, 2.0f);
172                    else {
173                        draggedV.setVisibility(View.VISIBLE);
174                    }
175                } else if (container.equals(headContainer)) {
176                    if (draggedV.equals(hair1) ||
177                        draggedV.equals(hair2))
178                        swapItems(parentSourceV, draggedV,
179                                    container, 2.0f);
180                    else {
181                        makeAToast("Illegal style.");
182                        draggedV.setVisibility(View.VISIBLE);
183                    }
184                }
185                // ITEMS RETURNED TO THEIR STORAGE LOCATION
186                else if (container.equals(shoeContainer1)
187                        || container.equals(shoeContainer2)) {
188                    if (draggedV.equals(shoes1) ||
189                        draggedV.equals(shoes2))
190                        swapItems(parentSourceV, draggedV,
191                                    container, 1.0f);
192                    else
193                        draggedV.setVisibility(View.VISIBLE);
194                } else if (container.equals(hairContainer1)
195                        || container.equals(hairContainer2)) {
196                    if (draggedV.equals(hair1) ||
197                        draggedV.equals(hair2))
198                        swapItems(parentSourceV, draggedV,
199                        container, 1.0f);
200                    else
201                        draggedV.setVisibility(View.VISIBLE);
202                } else if (container.equals(dressContainer1)
203                        || container.equals(dressContainer2)) {
204                    if (draggedV.equals(dress1) ||
205                        draggedV.equals(dress2))
```

```
206                                      swapItems(parentSourceV, draggedV,
207                                      container, 1.0f);
208                              else
209                                      draggedV.setVisibility(View.VISIBLE);
210                          }
211                      }
212                      break;
213
214              default:
215                  break;
216          }
217          return true;
218      }
219  }
220
221  void swapItems(ViewGroup parentSourceV, View draggedV,
222                  LinearLayout container, float scale) {
223      parentSourceV.removeView(draggedV);
224      container.addView(draggedV);
225      draggedV.setPivotX(0);
226      draggedV.setPivotY(0);
227      draggedV.setScaleX(scale);
228      draggedV.setScaleY(scale);
229
230      draggedV.setVisibility(View.VISIBLE);
231  }
232
233  @Override
234  public boolean onCreateOptionsMenu(Menu menu) {
235      // Inflate the menu.
236      getMenuInflater().inflate(R.menu.my, menu);
237      return true;
238  }
239
240  @Override
241  public boolean onOptionsItemSelected(MenuItem item) {
242      // Handle action bar item clicks here. The action bar will
243      // automatically handle clicks on the Home/Up button, so long
244      // as you specify a parent activity in AndroidManifest.xml.
245      int id = item.getItemId();
246      if (id == R.id.action_settings) {
247          return true;
248      }
249      return super.onOptionsItemSelected(item);
250  }
251 }
```

■ 7.7 Fling Gesture

A fling is a core touchscreen gesture that is also known as a swipe. Specifically, a fling is a quick swiping movement of a finger across a touchscreen. A fling can be performed in any direction and can cover a range of distances. For example, a fling can be a small flick of the finger that produces a simple and common behavior, such as flipping between the pages of an e-book. A fling can also be a great swiping motion that covers a large portion of the touchscreen. This more powerful gesture is often used in game applications, as well as in common desktop applications for basic behavior, such as a fast scrolling up and down a page. For this usage, the velocity of the fling can be computed to determine a data component, such as how far a page is able to scroll.

Fling gestures have been used since the early days of smartphones to make navigation easier and more efficient, making it a very natural way to browse content. As a core gesture, a fling is a common component for interactions in game applications, partly because it can easily remove user interface clutter on a content screen. For example, an application that features action bar tabs can utilize a fling gesture to navigate between different views. Many applications are implemented with a sideswiping menu, allowing users to fling the view to the right to reveal navigation elements. This technique can make a content-focused application easier to navigate by requiring a fewer number of touch gestures.

A fling begins when the finger first makes contact with the touchscreen, and it ends when the finger leaves the touchscreen. A motion can be interpreted that is either downward, upward, to the left, or to the right. As a touch event, a fling can be intercepted in an Activity or View by overriding the `onTouchEvent()` callback. Processing can be performed on these events to determine if a gesture has occurred.

As with other gestures, the MotionEvent object can be used to report a fling event. The motion events will describe the fling movement in terms of an action code and a set of axis values describing movement properties. Consider the following code segment. At the start of a fling gesture, the user touches the screen and the system delivers a touch event to the appropriate View with the action code ACTION_DOWN and a set of axis values that include the x, y coordinates of the touch. If the user then removes their finger after performing a fling, a second set of coordinates are delivered by the system.

In the code segment below, `x1` and `y1` represent the first set of coordinates, and `x2` and `y2` represent the second set. When `y2` is less than `y1`, a fling from the bottom of the screen to the top has just occurred. If `x2` is less than `x1`, then a fling from left to right has just occurred.

As an alternative to an onTouchEvent(), the View.OnTouchListener object can be attached to a View object for an explicit fling behavior. In the following code segment,

```
1
2      public boolean onTouchEvent(MotionEvent touchevent) {
3        switch (touchevent.getActionMasked(touchevent)){
4          case MotionEvent.ACTION_DOWN:
5            x1 = touchevent.getX();
6            y1 = touchevent.getY();
7            break;
8          case MotionEvent.ACTION_UP:
9            x2 = touchevent.getX();
10           y2 = touchevent.getY();
11       }
12       return false;
13     }
```

an OnTouchListener object is used to interact with the carrot ImageView using a touch gesture.

For common gestures, such as `onFling`, Android provides the `Gesture-Detector` class that can be used in tandem with the `onTouchEvent` callback

```
1
2    ImageView carrot = findViewById(R.id.carrot);
3    carrot.setOnTouchListener(new OnTouchListener() {
4        public boolean onTouch(View view, MotionEvent event) {
5            /*
6             .
7             . Respond to touch events
8             .
9            return true;
10       }
11   });
```

method. An application Activity can implement the `GestureDetector.OnGes-tureListener` interface to identify when a specific touch event has occurred. Once these events are received, they can be handed off to the overridden `onTouchEvent` callback.

In the following code segment, `MyActivity` implements the `GestureDe-tector`. A gesture detector, `mGesture`, is instantiated with the application context and an implementation of `GestureDetector.OnGestureListener`. The first argument refers to the application context, and the second is the listener invoked for all of the callbacks, which must not be null.

```
1   public class MyActivity extends Activity implements
2           GestureDetector.OnGestureListener,
3           GestureDetector.OnDoubleTapListener{
4
5           private GestureDetector mGesture;
6
7
8       @Override
9       public void onCreate(Bundle savedInstanceState) {
10          super.onCreate(savedInstanceState);
11          setContentView(R.layout.activity_my);
12
13
14          mGesture = new GestureDetector(this,this);
15      }
16
17      @Override
18      public boolean onTouchEvent(MotionEvent event) {
19          return mGesture.onTouchEvent(event);
20      }
21
22      @Override
23      public void onFling(,MotionEvent event1, MotionEvent event2) {
24          .
25          .
26          .
27
28      }
```

■ Lab Example 7-5: Fling and the Predator-and-Prey Game

This lab example explores a turn-based predator-and-prey game, "Escape the Catcher," that requires fling interactions to move the butterfly on the board.

Part 1: Conceptual Design

"Escape the Catcher" is a board game based on a simplified concept of the predator vs. prey relationship. The game consists of a board organized by rows and columns. At the start of a game, the board contains a collection of obstacles, an exit, and two characters representing the predator and prey. Figure 7-18 shows the game in mid-play. The butterfly is the prey and the catcher is the enemy predator. The user of the application will play the role of the butterfly. The objective of the player is to escape the predator. The blocks represent wooden obstacles blocking a pathway.

The player (user) is first to take a turn. Using a fling gesture, the player can move the butterfly up, down, left, or right on the game board as long as there are no obstacles in the way. Once the player has taken a turn, the enemy predator will compute the next move.

To win the game, the user must navigate the butterfly around the board obstacles, avoid colliding with the enemy, and successfully exit through the single opening on the board. When it is the enemy's turn, the catcher will actively hunt down the butterfly. If a collision occurs between the enemy and the butterfly, the game is over and the player is defeated.

❙ FIGURE 7-18 The user moves the butterfly with a swiping motion.

Part 2: Application Structure and Setup

The settings for the application are as follows:

- Application Name: Escape the Catcher
- Project Name: EscapetheCatcher
- Package Name: `com.cornez.escapethecatcher`
- Android Form: Phone and Tablet
- Minimum SDK: API 18: Android 4.3 (Jelly Bean)
- Target SDK: API 21: Android 5.0 (Lollipop)
- Compile with: API 21: Android 5.0 (Lollipop)
- Activity Name: `MyActivity`
- Layout Name: `activity_my`

The application launcher is set to the Android default `ic_launcher.png` file. Five graphic elements representing the application backdrop, obstacles, prey, enemy, and exit are added as PNG files to the drawable directory.

The structure of the complete application is shown in Figure 7-19. The Java source files consist of classes that model the butterfly and the enemy, the logic codes for the game board, and the application Activity, `MyActivity`.

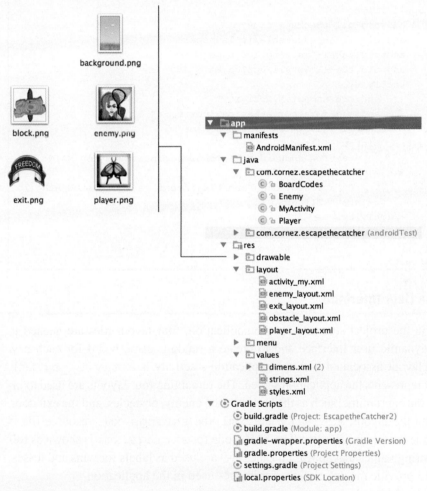

FIGURE 7-19 The project structure for the "Escape the Catcher" application.

Three XML layout files needed for this application are used to hold the graphic objects for the enemy, the player, and the obstacles blocking the path to the exit. In addition to these containers, a main activity layout is used to store all the elements in a relativeLayout root View.

The screen settings are indicated in the `AndroidManifest` file. A fullscreen is utilized and the titlebar is removed. The screen orientation is locked in portrait mode. The XML code for `AndroidManifest` is shown as follows:

AndroidManifest.xml

```
1   <?xml version="1.0" encoding="utf-8"?>
2   <manifest xmlns:android="http://schemas.android.com/apk/res/android"
3       package="com.cornez.escapethecatcher" >
4
5       <application
6           android:allowBackup="true"
7           android:icon="@drawable/ic_launcher"
8           android:label="@string/app_name"
9           android:theme="@style/AppTheme" >
10          <activity
11              android:name=".MyActivity"
12              android:screenOrientation="portrait"
13              android:label="@string/app_name" >
14              <intent-filter>
15                  <action android:name="android.intent.action.MAIN" />
16                  <category
17                      android:name="android.intent.category.LAUNCHER" />
18              </intent-filter>
19          </activity>
20      </application>
21
22  </manifest>
```

Part 3: The User Interface

As shown in the project structure for the application, four layout files are needed to support a dynamic user interface and to create a random game board for each new game. The layout associated with the application's activity is `activity_my.xml`. This layout represents the application screen. The remaining four layouts are used to inflate views during runtime, such as the butterfly, the enemy, obstacles, and the exit door.

To build the layout, `activity_my.xml`, the `strings.xml` resource file is used to define the labels and titles. The XML code for `strings.xml` is shown as follows. The string values that appear on Lines 8–9 are used as labels for wins and losses. Lines 10–13 provide the descriptions for images used in the application.

strings.xml

```
1   <?xml version="1.0" encoding="utf-8"?>
2   <resources>
3
4       <string name="app_name">Escape the Catcher</string>
5       <string name="hello_world">Hello world!</string>
```

```
6        <string name="action_settings">Settings</string>
7
8        <string name="win">Wins:</string>
9        <string name="losses">Losses:</string>
10       <string name="obstacle">Obstacle</string>
11       <string name="player">Player - Butterfly Prey</string>
12       <string name="enemy">Enemy - Butterfly Catcher</string>
13       <string name="exit">Exit</string>
14
15   </resources>
```

▌ FIGURE 7-20 The layout design for activity_my.xml.

The user interface for the activity's content is `activity_my.xml`. As shown in Figure 7-20, this layout is designed with a `RelativeLayout` root tag, identified as `relativeLayout`. This identifier name is used to reference the layout from within `MyActivity`. As a `RelativeLayout`, the *x, y* coordinate system will reference 0, 0 at the upper-left corner of the screen. This coordinate system is used in the arrangement of visual elements that will be dynamically added to the board during runtime.

The XML code for `activity_my.xml` is shown as follows. For visual appeal, the drawable file named `background.png` is applied to the background of the root `View`. Two `TextView` elements are added to provide the win-and-loss game results.

```
activity_my.xml
1   <RelativeLayout
2   xmlns:android="http://schemas.android.com/apk/res/android"
3       xmlns:tools="http://schemas.android.com/tools"
4       android:id="@+id/relativeLayout"
5       android:layout_width="match_parent"
6       android:layout_height="match_parent"
7       android:background="@drawable/background"
8       tools:context=".MyActivity">
9
10
11      <TextView
12          android:id="@+id/lossesTextView"
13          android:layout_width="wrap_content"
14          android:layout_height="wrap_content"
15          android:layout_alignParentBottom="true"
16          android:layout_centerHorizontal="true"
17          android:layout_marginBottom="50dp"
18          android:text="@string/losses"
19          android:textAppearance="?android:attr/textAppearanceLarge"
20          android:textSize="40sp" />
21
22      <TextView
23          android:id="@+id/winsTextView"
24          android:layout_width="wrap_content"
25          android:layout_height="wrap_content"
26          android:layout_above="@+id/lossesTextView"
27          android:layout_centerHorizontal="true"
28          android:text="@string/win"
29          android:textSize="40sp" />
30  </RelativeLayout>
```

The game board for the application is populated with obstacles, an exit banner, and game players once the application launches. To inflate these graphic elements, each display object type is modeled as a layout file with an `ImageView` specified as the root element. The XML code for the player, the enemy, the obstacle, and the exit layouts are shown as follows:

```
player_layout.xml
1   <?xml version="1.0" encoding="utf-8"?>
2   <ImageView xmlns:android="http://schemas.android.com/apk/res/android"
3       android:layout_width="match_parent"
4       android:layout_height="match_parent"
5       android:src="@drawable/player"
6       android:contentDescription="@string/player">
7
8   </ImageView>
```

```
enemy_layout.xml
1   <?xml version="1.0" encoding="utf-8"?>
2   <ImageView xmlns:android="http://schemas.android.com/apk/res/android"
3       android:layout_width="match_parent"
4       android:layout_height="match_parent"
5       android:src="@drawable/enemy"
6       android:contentDescription="@string/enemy">
7
8   </ImageView>
```

```
obstacle_layout.xml
1   <?xml version="1.0" encoding="utf-8"?>
2   <ImageView xmlns:android="http://schemas.android.com/apk/res/android"
3       android:layout_width="match_parent"
4       android:layout_height="match_parent"
5       android:src="@drawable/block"
6       android:contentDescription="@string/obstacle">
7
8   </ImageView>
```

```
exit_layout.xml
1   <?xml version="1.0" encoding="utf-8"?>
2   <ImageView xmlns:android="http://schemas.android.com/apk/res/android"
3       android:layout_width="match_parent"
4       android:layout_height="match_parent"
5       android:src="@drawable/exit"
6       android:contentDescription="@string/exit">
7
8   </ImageView>
```

Part 4: The Logic Board

To control the placement and movement of the player and the enemy, the game algorithm depends on a logic board. As shown in Figure 7-21, this logic board is constructed as an array consisting of eight rows and five columns. Each cell of the array holds a code indicating the presence of an obstacle, an exit door, or a nonexisting element. Code 1 is used to indicate the presence of an obstacle. Code 2 indicates a cell is empty. An empty cell means the player and the enemy can freely move in this unblocked location. Code 3 indicates an exit door, represented by an exit banner graphic.

The algorithm for the application relies on board codes for logical positioning, manuevering, and computing the moves made by the player and the enemy.

The designated board codes are also used to arrange specific visual objects on the screen, such as the obstacles and the exit banner. At the start of every game, MyActivity implements a game board. The codes stored on the game board are defined in the Java class BoardCodes as follows:

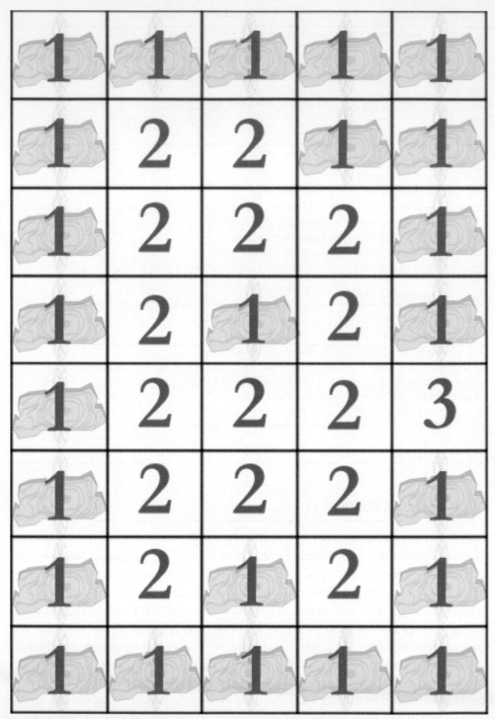

FIGURE 7-21 The Butterfly application is a turn-based board game that uses coded blocks.

```
BoardCodes.java
1   package com.cornez.escapethecatcher;
2
3   public class BoardCodes {
4       final static int isOBSTACLE = 1;
5       final  static int isEMPTY = 2;
6       final static int isHOME = 3;
7
8   }
```

Part 5: The Player and Enemy

The movements of the player and the enemy are governed by the codes assigned to the cells on the game board. If an obstacle exists on the board, the player and enemy are not allowed to move into that board's cell location.

When it is the user's turn to make a move on the board and a fling gesture is detected by the application, the player's ability to move right, left, up, or down is verified prior to moving the butterfly into the new position on the board. If it is established there are no obstacles barring the indicated move, the ImageView will be updated within MyActivity; otherwise the turn is consumed.

The Java code for the Player class is shown as follows:

```
Player.java
1   package com.cornez.escapethecatcher;
2
3   public class Player {
4       private int mRow;
5       private int mCol;
6
7       public void move(int[][] gameBoard, String button) {
8
9           if (button.equals("RIGHT")) {
10              if (gameBoard[mRow][mCol + 1] != BoardCodes.isOBSTACLE) {
11                  mCol++;
12              }
13          } else if (button.equals("LEFT")) {
14              if (gameBoard[mRow][mCol - 1] != BoardCodes.isOBSTACLE)
15                  mCol--;
16          } else if (button.equals("UP")) {
17              if (gameBoard[mRow - 1][mCol] != BoardCodes.isOBSTACLE) {
18                  mRow--;
19              }
20          } else if (button.equals("DOWN")) {
21              if (gameBoard[mRow + 1][mCol] != BoardCodes.isOBSTACLE) {
22                  mRow++;
23              }
24          }
25      }
```

```
26
27    public void setRow(int row) {
28        mRow = row;
29    }
30
31    public int getRow() {
32        return mRow;
33    }
34
35    public void setCol(int col) {
36        mCol = col;
37    }
38
39    public int getCol() {
40        return mCol;
41    }
42
43 }
```

The enemy will behave as a predator. For example, its movements are based on typical predator/prey logic rules. The Java code for the Enemy class is shown as follows:

Lines 8–22:   The move() method utilizes the codes assigned to the game board and simple predator capture rules to determine the best positioning to attack its prey on the game board.

Enemy.java

```
1   package com.cornez.escapethecatcher;
2
3   public class Enemy {
4
5       private int mRow;
6       private int mCol;
7
8       public void move(int[][] gameBoard, int preyCol, int preyRow) {
9           if (mCol < preyCol && gameBoard[mRow][mCol + 1] ==
10              BoardCodes.isEMPTY) {
11              mCol++;
12          } else if (mCol > preyCol && gameBoard[mRow][mCol - 1]
13                  == BoardCodes.isEMPTY) {
14              mCol--;
15          } else if (mRow < preyRow && gameBoard[mRow + 1][mCol]
16                  == BoardCodes.isEMPTY) {
17              mRow++;
18          } else if (mRow > preyRow && gameBoard[mRow - 1][mCol]
19                  == BoardCodes.isEMPTY) {
20              mRow--;
21          }
```

```
22        }
23
24        public void setRow(int row) {
25            mRow = row;
26        }
27
28        public int getRow() {
29            return mRow;
30        }
31
32        public void setCol(int col) {
33            mCol = col;
34        }
35
36        public int getCol() {
37            return mCol;
38        }
39    }
```

Part 6: The Game Controller

MyActivity will serve as the game controller for the application. Its objective is to initialize the game elements, update the UI display objects on the screen, determine when a game has concluded, and detect fling gestures, which are required for the user to move the butterfly. For this simplified version of the game, the enemy will always be positioned in the second row, fourth column of the game board. The player (butterfly) will be positioned in the first row, first column.

The Java code for MyActivity is shown as follows:

Lines 20–22:	MyActivity is implemented with the GestureDetector interface. To implement a listener for notification when a confirmed single tap occurs, the OnDoubleTapListener is also implemented.
Lines 32–41:	To simplify the game for demonstration in this lab example, a fixed logic gameboard is constructed. The final board will appear similar to the one shown in Figure 7-21.
Lines 100–125:	The visual elements on the logic board are added. Obstacle ImageViews will be inflated and arranged on the logic gameboard in the appropriately coded cells. The exit banner graphic is placed on the screen.
Lines 126–139:	The Enemy ImageView is inflated and placed on the screen, using the arrangement specified by the logic gameboard.
Lines 140–154:	The Player ImageView is inflated and arranged on the screen.

```
MyActivity.java
1    package com.cornez.escapethecatcher;
2
3    import android.app.Activity;
4    import android.content.Context;
5    import android.os.Bundle;
6    import android.util.DisplayMetrics;
7    import android.util.Log;
8    import android.view.GestureDetector;
9    import android.view.LayoutInflater;
10   import android.view.Menu;
11   import android.view.MenuItem;
12   import android.view.MotionEvent;
13   import android.widget.ImageView;
14   import android.widget.RelativeLayout;
15   import android.widget.TextView;
16
17   import java.util.ArrayList;
18
19
20   public class MyActivity extends Activity implements
21           GestureDetector.OnDoubleTapListener,
22           GestureDetector.OnGestureListener {
23
24       private GestureDetector aGesture;
25
26
27       //BOARD INFORMATION
28       final int SQUARE = 130;
29       final int OFFSET = 70;
30       final int COLUMNS = 8;
31       final int ROWS = 8;
32       final int gameBoard[][] = {
33               {1,1,1,1,1,1,1,1},
34               {1,2,2,1,2,1,2,1},
35               {1,2,2,2,2,2,2,1},
36               {1,2,1,2,2,2,2,1},
37               {1,2,2,2,2,1,2,1},
38               {1,2,2,2,2,2,2,3},
39               {1,2,1,2,2,2,2,1},
40               {1,1,1,1,1,1,1,1}
41       };
42
43       //VISUAL OBJECTS ARE ORGANIZED IN AN ARRAYLIST
44       private ArrayList<ImageView> visualObjects;
45       Player player;
46       Enemy enemy;
47
48       //LAYOUT AND INTERACTIVE INFORMATION
49       private RelativeLayout relativeLayout;
```

```java
50      private ImageView enemyIMG;
51      private ImageView playerIMG;
52      private ImageView obstacleIMG;
53      private ImageView exitIMG;
54      private int exitRow;
55      private int exitCol;
56
57      //  WINS AND LOSSES
58      private int wins;
59      private int losses;
60      private TextView winsTextView;
61      private TextView lossesTextView;
62
63      private LayoutInflater layoutInflater;
64
65
66
67      @Override
68      protected void onCreate(Bundle savedInstanceState) {
69          super.onCreate(savedInstanceState);
70
71          //TASK 1: SET THE LAYOUT CONTENT FOR THE ACTIVITY
72          setContentView(R.layout.activity_my);
73
74          //TASK 2: REFERENCE THE ACTIVITY LAYOUT AND TEXTVIEWS
75          relativeLayout = (RelativeLayout)
76              findViewById(R.id.relativeLayout);
77          winsTextView = (TextView) findViewById(R.id.winsTextView);
78          lossesTextView = (TextView) findViewById(R.id.lossesTextView);
79
80          //TASK 3: INSTANTIATE THE LAYOUT INFLATER
81
82          layoutInflater = (LayoutInflater)
83              getSystemService(Context.LAYOUT_INFLATER_SERVICE);
84
85          //TASK 4: BUILD THE LOGIC BOARD AND CONSTRUCT THE GAME
86          visualObjects = new ArrayList <ImageView>();
87          buildLogicBoard();
88          createEnemy();
89          createPlayer();
90          wins = 0;
91          losses = 0;
92          winsTextView.setText("Wins: " + wins);
93          lossesTextView.setText("Losses: " + losses);
94
95          //TASK 5: INSTANTIATE A GESTURE DETECTOR
96          aGesture = new GestureDetector(this, this);
97          aGesture.setOnDoubleTapListener(this);
98      }
99
```

```
100     private void buildLogicBoard() {
101         for (int row = 0; row < ROWS; row++){
102             for (int col = 0; col < COLUMNS; col++) {
103                 if (gameBoard[row][col] == BoardCodes.isOBSTACLE){
104                     obstacleIMG = (ImageView)
105                         layoutInflater.inflate(R.layout.obstacle_layout,
106                         null);
107                     obstacleIMG.setX(col * SQUARE + OFFSET);
108                     obstacleIMG.setY(row * SQUARE + OFFSET);
109                     relativeLayout.addView(obstacleIMG,0);
110                     visualObjects.add(obstacleIMG);
111                 }
112                 else if (gameBoard[row][col] == BoardCodes.isHOME){
113                     exitIMG = (ImageView)
114                         layoutInflater.inflate(R.layout.exit_layout,
115                         null);
116                     exitIMG.setX(col * SQUARE + OFFSET);
117                     exitIMG.setY(row * SQUARE + OFFSET);
118                     relativeLayout.addView(exitIMG,0);
119                     visualObjects.add(exitIMG);
120                     exitRow = 5;
121                     exitCol = 7;
122                 }
123             }
124         }
125     }
126     private void createEnemy() {
127         int row = 2;
128         int col = 4;
129         enemyIMG = (ImageView)
130             layoutInflater.inflate(R.layout.enemy_layout, null);
131         enemyIMG.setX(col * SQUARE + OFFSET);
132         enemyIMG.setY(row * SQUARE + OFFSET);
133         relativeLayout.addView(enemyIMG,0);
134
135         enemy = new Enemy ();
136         enemy.setRow(row);
137         enemy.setCol(col);
138         visualObjects.add(enemyIMG);
139     }
140     private void createPlayer() {
141         int row = 1;
142         int col = 1;
143
144         playerIMG = (ImageView)
145             layoutInflater.inflate(R.layout.player_layout, null);
146         playerIMG.setX(col * SQUARE + OFFSET);
147         playerIMG.setY(row * SQUARE + OFFSET);
148         relativeLayout.addView(playerIMG,0);
```

```
149
150        player = new Player ();
151        player.setRow(row);
152        player.setCol(col);
153        visualObjects.add(playerIMG);
154    }
```

Lines 156–164:   A motion event is analyzed. If it is applicable, it will trigger the appropriate callbacks supplied by the `GestureDetector.OnGestureListener` interface. The `onFling()` callback is the only game gesture the application is required to respond to. When a fling is detected, `movePlayer()` is called and passed the fling velocity along the *x*- and *y*-axis.

Lines 198–238:   The velocity of the finger movement along the *x* and *y*-axis determines the fling direction. Threshold values of 2500 and −2500 are used in this example. Based on the experiments performed in Lab Example 7-1, this value is enough to indicate both a feeble and strong direction of a given fling.

Lines 240–254:   Once the player has either successfully escaped the enemy or been captured, a new game will begin. The screen is cleared for a new arrangement of visual elements.

`MyActivity.java` (*continued*)

```java
155    @Override
156    public boolean onTouchEvent(MotionEvent event) {
157        return aGesture.onTouchEvent(event);
158    }
159    @Override
160    public boolean onFling(MotionEvent event1, MotionEvent event2,
161                           float velocityX, float velocityY) {
162        movePlayer(velocityX, velocityY);
163        return true;
164    }
165    @Override
166    public void onLongPress(MotionEvent event) {
167    }
168    @Override
169    public void onShowPress(MotionEvent event) {
170    }
171    @Override
172    public boolean onDown(MotionEvent event) {
173        return false;
174    }
```

```
175    @Override
176    public boolean onScroll(MotionEvent e1, MotionEvent e2,
177                            float distanceX, float distanceY) {
178        return true;
179    }
180    @Override
181    public boolean onSingleTapUp(MotionEvent event) {
182        return false;
183    }
184    @Override
185    public boolean onDoubleTap(MotionEvent event) {
186        return false;
187    }
188    @Override
189    public boolean onDoubleTapEvent(MotionEvent event) {
190        return true;
191    }
192    @Override
193    public boolean onSingleTapConfirmed(MotionEvent event) {
194        return true;
195    }
196
197
198    private void movePlayer(float velocityX, float velocityY) {
199        String direction = "undetectable";
200
201        //TASK 1: MOVE THE PLAYER IN THE FLING DIRECTION
202        if (velocityX > 2500) {
203            direction = "RIGHT";
204        } else if (velocityX < -2500) {
205            direction = "LEFT";
206        } else if (velocityY > 2500) {
207            direction = "DOWN";
208        } else if (velocityY < -2500) {
209            direction = "UP";
210        }
211
212        if (!direction.contains("undetectable")) {
213            player.move(gameBoard, direction);
214            playerIMG.setX(player.getCol() * SQUARE + OFFSET);
215            playerIMG.setY(player.getRow() * SQUARE + OFFSET);
216            Log.v("Player movement", "row=" + player.getCol()
217                    + " col=" + player.getRow());
218
219            //TASK 2: IT IS NOW THE ENEMY'S TURN. MOVE THE ENEMY
220            enemy.move(gameBoard, player.getCol(), player.getRow());
221            enemyIMG.setX(enemy.getCol() * SQUARE + OFFSET);
222            enemyIMG.setY(enemy.getRow() * SQUARE + OFFSET);
223        }
224
```

```
225         //TASK 2: CHECK IF THE GAME IS OVER
226         //  CHECK IF ENEMY CATCHES PLAYER
227         if (enemy.getCol() == player.getCol() &&
228             enemy.getRow() == player.getRow()) {
229             losses++;
230             lossesTextView.setText("Losses: " + losses);
231             startNewGame();
232         } else if (exitRow == player.getRow() &&
233                     exitCol == player.getCol()) {
234             wins++;
235             winsTextView.setText("Wins: " + wins);
236             startNewGame();
237         }
238     }
239
240     private void startNewGame() {
241         //TASK 1:  CLEAR THE BOARD AND REMOVE PLAYERS
242         int howMany = visualObjects.size();
243         for (int i = 0; i < howMany; i++) {
244             ImageView visualObj = visualObjects.get(i);
245             relativeLayout.removeView(visualObj);
246         }
247         visualObjects.clear();
248
249         //TASK 2:  REBUILD THE  BOARD
250         buildLogicBoard();
251
252         //TASK 3:  ADD THE PLAYERS
253         createEnemy();
254         createPlayer();
255     }
256
257     @Override
258     public boolean onCreateOptionsMenu(Menu menu) {
259         // Inflate the menu;.
260         getMenuInflater().inflate(R.menu.my, menu);
261         return true;
262     }
263
264     @Override
265     public boolean onOptionsItemSelected(MenuItem item) {
266         // Handle action bar item clicks here. The action bar will
267         // automatically handle clicks on the Home/Up button, so long
268         // as you specify a parent activity in AndroidManifest.xml.
269         int id = item.getItemId();
270         if (id == R.id.action_settings) {
271             return true;
272         }
273         return super.onOptionsItemSelected(item);
274     }
275 }
```

■ 7.8 Fling Velocity

Well-designed user interfaces are often made interactive by allowing elements to respond to user input in a way that closely resembles a real-world action. For example, a user may fling an object in a game to produce movement. The resulting momentum will take into account the *x*, *y* coordinates of the object and the velocity of the gesture. In addition, the object in motion may slow down gradually, as dictated by the implementation of the application. In a typical game, the behavior of the moving object is subject to the physics of the game world being implemented.

In a given fling gesture, an `onFling` motion event notification occurs with an initial `ACTION_DOWN` `MotionEvent`, followed by an `ACTION_MOVE` `MotionEvent`, and ends with an `ACTION_UP` `MotionEvent`. As illustrated in "Escape the Catcher" game of Lab Example 7-5, a fling is based more on movement than on simple contact.

Tracking the movement in a fling gesture requires the start and end positions of the finger, as well as the velocity of the movement across the touchscreen. The direction of a fling can be determined by the *x* and *y* coordinates captured by the `ACTION_DOWN` and `ACTION_UP` `MotionEvents` and the resulting velocities.

Consider the following segment of code that implements `onFling()`. The `MotionEvent` `e1` contains the *x*, *y* coordinates captured by the `MotionEvent` that started the fling gesture. The `MotionEvent` `e2` contains the *x*, *y* coordinates captured by the `MotionEvent` that triggered the onFling gesture. The distance of the gesture is measured as the distance between these two points. The velocities are measured in pixels per second along the specified axis.

```
1    public boolean onFling(MotionEvent e1, MotionEvent e2,
2                       float velocityX, float velocityY) {
3
4        final float xDistance = Math.abs(e1.getX() - e2.getX());
5        final float yDistance = Math.abs(e1.getY() - e2.getY());
6
7        velocityX = Math.abs(velocityX);
8        velocityY = Math.abs(velocityY);
9
10       if(velocityX > 30 && xDistance > 30){
11          //LEFT FLING: RIGHT TO LEFT
12          if(e1.getX() > e2.getX())
13             . . .
14          else
15          //RIGHT FLING: LEFT TO RIGHT
16             . . .
17       }
18       else if(velocityY > 30 && yDistance > 30){
19          //UPWARD FLING: BOTTOM TO TOP
```

```
20        if(el.getY() > e2.getY())
21            . . .
22        else
23          //DOWNWARD FLING: TOP TO BOTTOM
24            . . .
25      }
26    return result;
27  }
```

VelocityTracker is an Android helper class for tracking the velocity of touch events, including the implementation of a fling. In applications such as games, a fling is a movment-based gesture that produces behavior based on the distance and direction a finger travels with a gesture. The VelocityTracker class is designed to simplify velocity calculations in movement-based gestures.

Lines 10–11:   The obtain() method is used to retrieve a new instance of a VelocityTracker once tracking needs to be performed. If the VelocityTracker object is currently null, a new one is retrieved to watch the velocity of a motion.

Line 12–13:   The established VelocityTracker is reset back to its initial state for new tracking.

Line 14:   The addMovement() method is used to add the triggered MotionEvents to the velocity tracker.

Lines 18–22:   While the movement-based gesture is being tracked, the computeCurrentVelocity() method can be used to retrieve the velocity of a moving finger. getXVelocity() is used to return the last computed *x* velocity. Both the getXVelocity() and getYVelocity() methods must be called after an immediate call to computeCurrentVelocity().

```
1    private VelocityTracker mVelocityTracker = null;
2    private int velocityX, velocity;
3
4    @Override
5    public boolean onTouchEvent(MotionEvent event) {
6        int index = event.getActionIndex();
7        int action = event.getActionMasked();
8
9        switch(action) {
10            case MotionEvent.ACTION_DOWN:
11                if(mVelocityTracker == null)
12                    mVelocityTracker = VelocityTracker.obtain();
13                else
14                    mVelocityTracker.clear();
```

```
14              mVelocityTracker.addMovement(event);
15              break;
16
17          case MotionEvent.ACTION_MOVE:
18              mVelocityTracker.addMovement(event);
19              mVelocityTracker.computeCurrentVelocity(1000);
20              mVelocityTracker.computeCurrentVelocity(1000);
21              float velocityX = mVelocityTracker.getXVelocity(1000);
22              float velocityY = mVelocityTracker.getYVelocity(1000);
23              break;
24          case MotionEvent.ACTION_UP:
25          }
26      return true;
27  }
```

■ Lab Example 7-6: Fling Velocities Billiard Ball

The Billiard Ball lab example explores momentum produced by a fling gesture. Using a quick fling movement, the user can set the billiard ball in motion, as shown in Figure 7-22. The magnitude of the resulting velocity is directly proportional to the force of the fling.

Given the force applied to the ball, there are several values that will be computed in this experimental application. The first is the initial velocity of the ball that results from the fling. Once the ball has been assigned a fling velocity that sets it in motion, the force of friction acts on the ball as it begins to move. The velocity will continually be updated, as friction is applied to the momentum of the ball until it eventually comes to a stop. How far the ball moves depends on its initial velocity. When the ball encounters the wall of the table at the edge of the touchscreen, a collision will be detected and the velocity of the ball will be updated.

Part 1: Application Structure and Setup

The settings for the application are as follows:

- Application Name: Billiard Ball
- Project Name: BilliardBall
- Package Name: com.cornez.billiardball
- Android Form: Phone and Tablet
- Minimum SDK: API 18: Android 4.3 (Jelly Bean)
- Target SDK: API 21: Android 5.0 (Lollipop)

- Compile with: API 21: Android 5.0 (Lollipop)
- Activity Name: `MyActivity`
- Layout Name: `activity_my`

The project structure for the application is shown in Figure 7-23. Two drawable PNG files are added to the drawable directories: (1) the billiard ball, `ball.png`, and (2) the billiard table.

The Java source files for the Billiard Ball application are minimal: `Ball` and `MyActivity`. The `Ball` class is used to model the billiard ball with which the user interacts. The single activity of the application is `MyActivity`, the controller for UI operations and gesture detection.

The UI interface layout associated with `MyActivity` is `activity_my.xml`. `activity_my.xml` and `ball_layout.xml` are both required by the Activity.

The screen orientation for the Billiard Ball experiment is locked into portrait mode. The XML code for the AndroidManifest is shown as follows:

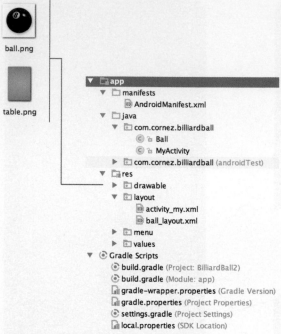

ball.png

table.png

▼ 🗀 app
  ▼ 🗀 manifests
       📄 AndroidManifest.xml
  ▼ 🗀 java
    ▼ 🗀 com.cornez.billiardball
         © 🔒 Ball
         © 🔒 MyActivity
    ▶ 🗀 com.cornez.billiardball (androidTest)
  ▼ 🗀 res
    ▶ 🗀 drawable
    ▼ 🗀 layout
         📄 activity_my.xml
         📄 ball_layout.xml
    ▶ 🗀 menu
    ▶ 🗀 values
▼ ⚙ Gradle Scripts
     ⚙ build.gradle (Project: BilliardBall2)
     ⚙ build.gradle (Module: app)
     🔧 gradle-wrapper.properties (Gradle Version)
     🔧 gradle.properties (Project Properties)
     ⚙ settings.gradle (Project Settings)
     🔧 local.properties (SDK Location)

❚ FIGURE 7-23 The Billiard Ball project structure.

```
AndroidManifest.xml
1   <?xml version="1.0" encoding="utf-8"?>
2   <manifest xmlns:android="http://schemas.android.com/apk/res/android"
3       package="com.cornez.billiardball" >
4
5       <application
6           android:allowBackup="true"
7           android:icon="@drawable/ic_launcher"
8           android:label="@string/app_name"
9           android:theme="@style/AppTheme" >
10          <activity
11              android:name=".MyActivity"
12              android:screenOrientation="portrait"
13              android:label="@string/app_name" >
14              <intent-filter>
15                  <action android:name="android.intent.action.MAIN" />
16
17                  <category
18                      android:name="android.intent.category.LAUNCHER" />
19              </intent-filter>
20          </activity>
21      </application>
22
23  </manifest>
```

Part 2: The User Interface

frameLayout

▌ **FIGURE 7-24** A FrameLayout is used as a container in activity_my.xml.

The Billiard Ball experiment is a movement-based application that is designed to display a single item. A `FrameLayout` root `View` is useful for blocking out an area on the screen to hold a single child view. The layout design for `activity_my.xml` is shown in Figure 7-24. The single element is a container, the `FrameLayout` root `View`. This container holds the billiard ball, which will be added programmatically in the application's activity. For visual appeal, the background of the root `View` is set to the `background.png` drawable.

The XML code for `activity_my.xml` is shown as follows. Line 5 sets the identifier name for the container as `frameLayout`.

```
activity_my.xml
1  <FrameLayout xmlns:android="http://schemas.android.com/apk/res/android"
2      xmlns:tools="http://schemas.android.com/tools"
3      android:layout_width="match_parent"
4      android:layout_height="match_parent"
5      android:id="@+id/frameLayout"
6      tools:context=".MyActivity"
7      android:background="@drawable/table">
8
9  </FrameLayout>
```

ImageView – @drawable/ball

FIGURE 7-25 ball_layout.xml uses an ImageView as its root element.

The ball drawable will be added to the screen content programmatically. For this purpose, the drawable is implemented as a layout file, `ball_layout.xml`, with an `ImageView` root element. The design of this file is illustrated in Figure 7-25. The XML code for `ball_layout.xml` is shown as follows:

ball_layout.xml

```
1  <?xml version="1.0" encoding="utf-8"?>
2  <ImageView xmlns:android="http://schemas.android.com/apk/res/android"
3      android:layout_width="match_parent"
4      android:layout_height="match_parent"
5      android:src="@drawable/ball"
6      android:contentDescription="@string/app_name">
7
8  </ImageView>
```

Part 3: Ball Class

The billiard ball is modeled by `Ball.java`. Its behavior is based on velocity, radius, and the boundaries that define collisions. As shown in Figure 7-26, the velocity vector for a moving ball has an x and a y component.

The class attributes for collisions have been simplified for this experiment. For example, when the ball collides with a wall, it simply reverses direction while maintaining its momentum. The friction, or linear damping, to slow the ball down is stored as a constant value, 0.93.

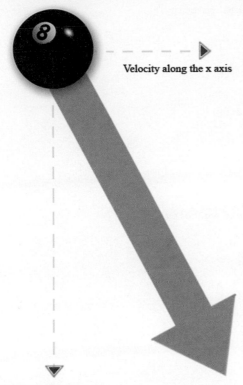

Velocity along the x axis

Velocity along the y axis.

▌ FIGURE 7-26 The velocity vector of a billiard ball.

The Java code for the `Ball` class is shown as follows:

```
Ball.java
1   package com.cornez.billiardball;
2
3
4   public class Ball {
5       private int mX;
6       private int mY;
7       private int mRadius;
8       private double mVelocityX;
9       private double mVelocityY;
10      private int left, right, top, bottom;
11
12      private int REVERSE = -1;
13      private double FRICTION = .93;
14
```

```
15    public void setVelocityX(double velocity){
16        mVelocityX = velocity;
17    }
18    public double getVelocityX(){
19        return mVelocityX;
20    }
21
22    public void setRadius(int radius){
23        mRadius = radius;
24    }
25    public int getRadius(){
26        return mRadius;
27    }
28
29    public void setVelocityY(double velocity){
30        mVelocityY = velocity;
31    }
32    public double getVelocityY(){
33        return mVelocityY;
34    }
35
36    public void setX(int x){
37        mX = x;
38    }
39    public int getX(){
40        return mX;
41    }
42    public void setY(int y){
43        mY = y;
44    }
45
46    public int getY(){
47        return mY;
48    }
49    public void move(){
50        //MOVE BALL
51        mX +=  mVelocityX;
52        mY +=  mVelocityY;
53
54        //SLOW THE BALL DOWN BY APPLYING FRICTION
55        mVelocityX *= FRICTION;
56        mVelocityY *= FRICTION;
57        if (Math.abs(mVelocityX) < 1){
58            mVelocityX = 0;
59        }
60        if (Math.abs(mVelocityY) < 1){
61            mVelocityY = 0;
62        }
```

```
63
64            //CHECK FOR COLLISIONS
65            checkCollision();
66        }
67        public void setCollisionBoundaries(int l, int r, int t, int b){
68            left = l + mRadius;
69            right = r - mRadius;
70            top = t + mRadius;
71            bottom = b - mRadius;
72        }
73
74        private void checkCollision() {
75            if (mX < left){
76                mX = left;
77                mVelocityX *= REVERSE;
78            }
79            else if (mX > right){
80                mX = right;
81                mVelocityX *= REVERSE;
82            }
83
84            if (mY < top){
85                mY = top;
86                mVelocityY *= REVERSE;
87            }
88            else if (mY > bottom){
89                mY = bottom;
90                mVelocityY *= REVERSE;
91            }
92        }
93    }
```

Part 4: MyActivity

The activity for the application implements a GestureDetector to detect flings. A background thread is used to perform the animation calculations, and the main UI thread updates the position of the billiard ball at paused intervals.

The Java code for MyActivity is shown as follows. The onTouchEvent() is called when a touch event occurs. The onFling() callback is triggered when it is determined the user performs a fling gesture. The calculated velocity of the fling along the x- and y-axis is supplied to this callback method. The billiard ball is set in motion when its velocity is assigned the fling velocity in pixels per second. The constant, ADJUST, is used to finely tune the speed of the ball. This value is set to .025 of the supplied pixels per second.

MyActivity.java

```java
1    package com.cornez.billiardball;
2
3    import android.app.Activity;
4    import android.content.Context;
5    import android.os.Bundle;
6    import android.os.Handler;
7    import android.util.DisplayMetrics;
8    import android.view.GestureDetector;
9    import android.view.LayoutInflater;
10   import android.view.Menu;
11   import android.view.MenuItem;
12   import android.view.MotionEvent;
13   import android.view.Window;
14   import android.view.WindowManager;
15   import android.widget.FrameLayout;
16   import android.widget.ImageView;
17
18   public class MyActivity extends Activity implements
19                   GestureDetector.OnGestureListener {
20
21       private GestureDetector aGesture;
22
23       //ANIMATION IS SPLIT INTO TWO THREADS:
24       //      BACKGROUND THREAD: BILLIARD MOVEMENT
25       //      UI THREAD        : VIEW UPDATE
26       private FrameLayout mainLayout;
27       private Thread calculateThread;
28
29       private ImageView ballImageView;
30       private Ball mBall;
31
32       @Override
33       protected void onCreate(Bundle savedInstanceState) {
34           super.onCreate(savedInstanceState);
35
36           //TASK 1: WINDOW PROPERTIES ARE SET
37           //THIS ANDROID WINDOW WILL NOT FEATURE A TITLE
38           requestWindowFeature(Window.FEATURE_NO_TITLE);
39           getWindow().setFlags(
40                   WindowManager.LayoutParams.FLAG_FULLSCREEN,
41                   WindowManager.LayoutParams.FLAG_FULLSCREEN);
42
43           //TASK 2: SET COORDINATE SYSTEM OFFSET
44           DisplayMetrics metrics = new DisplayMetrics();
45           getWindowManager().getDefaultDisplay().getMetrics(metrics);
46           int windowWidth = metrics.widthPixels;
47           int windowHeight = metrics.heightPixels;
48
```

```
49      //TASK 3: SET THE LAYOUT VIEW
50      setContentView(R.layout.activity_my);
51      mainLayout = (FrameLayout) findViewById(R.id.frameLayout);
52
53      //TASK 4: INSTANTIATE A BILLIARD BALL
54      buildBall(windowWidth, windowHeight);
55
56      aGesture = new GestureDetector(this, this);
57
58      //TASK 4: INSTANTIATE THE BACKGROUND THREAD
59      calculateThread = new Thread(calculateAction);
60  }
61
62  private void buildBall(int windowWidth, int windowHeight) {
63
64      //TASK 1: CREATE A LAYOUT INFLATER TO ADD VIEWS TO THE LAYOUT
65      LayoutInflater layoutInflater;
66      layoutInflater = (LayoutInflater)
67              getSystemService(Context.LAYOUT_INFLATER_SERVICE);
68
69      //TASK 2: SPECIFY BILLIARD BALL ATTRIBUTES
70      int initialXPosition = (int) (-200);
71      int initialYPosition = (int) (200);
72
73      mBall = new Ball();
74      mBall.setX(initialXPosition);
75      mBall.setY(initialYPosition);
76      mBall.setVelocityX(0);
77      mBall.setVelocityY(0);
78      mBall.setRadius(120);
79      mBall.setCollisionBoundaries(-windowWidth / 2,
80              windowWidth / 2, -windowHeight / 2, windowHeight / 2);
81
82      //TASK 3: ADD THE BALL TO THE LAYOUT
83      ballImageView = (ImageView)
84              layoutInflater.inflate(R.layout.ball_layout, null);
85      ballImageView.setScaleX((float) .3);
86      ballImageView.setScaleY((float) .3);
87      ballImageView.setX((float) mBall.getX());
88      ballImageView.setY((float) mBall.getY());
89      mainLayout.addView(ballImageView, 0);
90  }
91
92
93  //*************** RUNNABLE *********************
94  private Runnable calculateAction = new Runnable() {
95      private static final int DELAY = 50;
96
```

```
97          public void run() {
98              try {
99                  while (true) {
100                     mBall.move();
101                     Thread.sleep(DELAY);
102                     threadHandler.sendEmptyMessage(0);
103                 }
104             } catch (InterruptedException e) {
105             }
106         }
107     };
108
109     //****** HANDLER FOR UPDATING THE UI VIEW  ******
110     public Handler threadHandler = new Handler() {
111         public void handleMessage(android.os.Message msg) {
112             //SET THE BEE AT THE CORRECT XY LOCATION
113             ballImageView.setX((float) mBall.getX());
114             ballImageView.setY((float) mBall.getY());
115         }
116     };
117
118     @Override
119     protected void onResume() {
120         calculateThread.start();
121         super.onResume();
122     }
123
124     @Override
125     protected void onPause() {
126         finish();
127         super.onPause();
128     }
129
130     @Override
131     protected void onDestroy() {
132         finish();
133         super.onDestroy();
134     }
135
136     //**********************TOUCH GESTURES**********************
137
138     @Override
139     public boolean onTouchEvent(MotionEvent event) {
140         return aGesture.onTouchEvent(event);
141     }
142     @Override
143     public boolean onFling(MotionEvent event1, MotionEvent event2,
144                         float velocityX, float velocityY) {
145
```

```
146          final float ADJUST = 0.025f;
147          mBall.setVelocityX((int) velocityX * ADJUST);
148          mBall.setVelocityY((int) velocityY * ADJUST);
149          return true;
150      }
151
152      @Override
153      public void onLongPress(MotionEvent event) {
154      }
155
156      @Override
157      public void onShowPress(MotionEvent event) {
158      }
159
160      @Override
161      public boolean onDown(MotionEvent event) {
162          return false;
163      }
164
165      @Override
166      public boolean onScroll(MotionEvent e1, MotionEvent e2,
167                              float distanceX, float distanceY) {
168          return true;
169      }
170
171      @Override
172      public boolean onSingleTapUp(MotionEvent event) {
173          return false;
174      }
175
176      @Override
177      public boolean onCreateOptionsMenu(Menu menu) {
178          // Inflate the menu;
179          getMenuInflater().inflate(R.menu.my, menu);
180          return true;
181      }
182
183      @Override
184      public boolean onOptionsItemSelected(MenuItem item) {
185          // Handle action bar item clicks here. The action bar will
186          // automatically handle clicks on the Home/Up button, so long
187          // as you specify a parent activity in AndroidManifest.xml.
188          int id = item.getItemId();
189          if (id == R.id.action_settings) {
190              return true;
191          }
192          return super.onOptionsItemSelected(item);
193      }
194 }
```

■ 7.9 Multitouch Gestures

Most Android devices possess the ability to respond to multiple consecutive touches. The most common multitouch gestures are pinch and zoom, also referred to as pinch and spread. A pinch gesture involves two fingers placed on the screen. The finger positions, and the distance between them, are recorded. When the fingers are lifted from the screen, the distance separating them is recorded. If the second recorded distance is less than the first distance, the gesture is recognized as a pinch. A spread gesture is similar to a pinch gesture in that it also records the start and end distance between the fingers on the touchscreen. If the second recorded distance is greater than the first, it is a spread gesture.

In a single-touch gesture, a `MotionEvent` object is passed to the `onTouch()` callback method. The `MotionEvent` object contains information about the specific touch gesture, such as the location of the touch within the view and the type of action performed. In a multitouch gesture, the `MotionEvent` object supplies information about the multiple pointers that constitute the multitouch gesture. Each finger placed on the screen in a multitouch gesture is referred to as a pointer by the Android framework. Each pointer is referenced by an index value and assigned an ID. The current number of pointers in a gesture can be obtained from the `getPointerCount()` method for a given MotionEvent object. In addition, the assigned ID for a pointer can be obtained from the MotionEvent `getPointerID()` method. In the following code segment, the number of pointers and the first pointer, at index zero, is obtained when a touch event occurs.

```
1   public Boolean onTouchEvent (MotionEvent motionEvent) {
2       int pointerCount = motionEvent.getPointerCount();
3       int pointerID = motionEvent.getPointerID(0);
4       return true;
5   }
```

Multitouch gestures begin with an `ACTION_DOWN` `MotionEvent`. This occurs when the first pointer in the gesture touches the screen. This first pointer is the primary pointer of the gesture. The index for the primary pointer is always at index 0 in the list of active pointers. When additional pointers in the gesture are placed on the touchscreen, an `ACTION_POINTER_DOWN` occurs. `getActionIndex()` will return the index value for a pointer that triggered the `MotionEvent`.

A multitouch gesture ends when both pointers in the gesture are removed from the touchscreen. `ACTION_POINTER_UP` occurs when the secondary pointer goes up and `ACTION_UP` occurs when the last pointer leaves the touchscreen.

Consider the following sequence of pointer `MotionEvents` for a multitouch gesture that involves two pointers.

Pointer 1 (primary pointer) goes down: ACTION_DOWN.

Pointer 2 (secondary pointer) goes down: ACTION_POINTER_DOWN.

Both pointers move: `ACTION_MOVE.`

Pointer 2 (secondary pointer) goes up: `ACTION_POINTER_UP.`

Pointer 1 (primary pointer) goes up: `ACTION_UP.`

A touch gesture will generate a stream of `MotionEvents` before the pointer or pointers are lifted up from the touchscreen. An application may need to track individual touches over multiple touch events.

Consider the following segment of code that handles multiple pointers directly in a multitouch gesture. The objective of the code is to track two-finger pointers as they travel around the screen. As shown in Figure 7-27, the primary pointer is tracked by

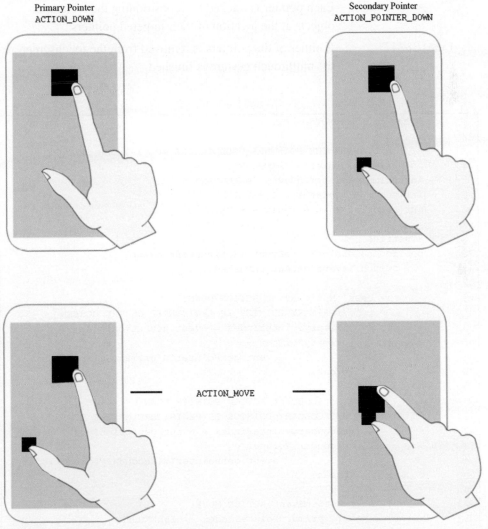

I FIGURE 7-27 The primary and secondary pointers in a multitouch gesture.

a large black rectangle. The primary pointer represents the first pointer placed on the screen. The secondary pointer is tracked by a smaller black rectangle.

Lines 13–25:   As the primary and secondary fingers are placed on the touchscreen, their pointer identifiers are accessed using their pointer data index. These identifiers provide the actual pointer number associated with the MotionEvent data, accounting for individual pointers going up and down from the start of the gesture.

Lines 27–36:   Once the ACTION_MOVE MotionEvent is triggered, a pointer index is used to find its *x*, *y* location on the screen. Each pointer is tracked by repositioning the rectangle objects at the location of their targeted pointers.

Lines 38–47:   If either of the pointers is removed from the touchscreen, the multitouch gesture is finished.

```
1       final int IsREMOVED= -1;
2
3        // INITIALIZE THE POINTERS USED IN THE MULTI-TOUCH GESTURE
4       int primaryPointer = IsREMOVED;
5       int primaryPointerIndex = IsREMOVED;
6       int secondaryPointer = IsREMOVED;
7       int secondaryPointerIndex = IsREMOVED;
8
9       @Override
10      public boolean onTouchEvent (MotionEvent event){
11          switch (event.getActionMasked()){
12
13          case  MotionEvent.ACTION_DOWN:
14              //PRIMARY POINTER IS REGISTERED ON THE SCREEN
15              primaryPointerIndex = event.getActionIndex();
16              primaryPointer =
17                      event.getPointerId(primaryPointerIndex);
18              break;
19
20          case MotionEvent.ACTION_POINTER_DOWN:
21              //SECONDARY POINTER IS REGISTERED ON THE SCREEN
22              secondaryPointerIndex = event.getActionIndex();
23              secondaryPointer =
24                      event.getPointerId(secondaryPointerIndex);
25              break;
26
27          case MotionEvent.ACTION_MOVE:
28              if (primaryPointerIndex != IsREMOVED){
29                  android1.setX(event.getX(primaryPointerIndex));
```

```
30                     android1.setY(event.getY(primaryPointerIndex));
31                  }
32                  if (secondaryPointerIndex != IsREMOVED){
33                     android2.setX(event.getX(secondaryPointerIndex));
34                     android2.setY(event.getY(secondaryPointerIndex));
35                  }
36                  break;
37
38           case MotionEvent.ACTION_POINTER_UP:
39                  primaryPointerIndex = IsREMOVED;
40                  secondaryPointerIndex = IsREMOVED;
41                  break;
42
43           case MotionEvent.ACTION_UP:
44                  primaryPointerIndex = IsREMOVED;
45                  secondaryPointerIndex = IsREMOVED;
46           }
47           return true;
48      }
```

■ Lab Example 7-7: Photo Zoom, Pinch, and Move Experiment

This lab is a touch experiment application that explores the implementation of the zoom and pinch multitouch gestures. Zoom and pinch are standard gestures that Android application users expect to use on photographs and other UI screens. As an experiment for gesture recognition, the application is limited to a single photograph. When the application is launched, the photograph shown in Figure 7-28 will appear on the screen. The user can zoom, pinch, or adjust the location of the image on the screen.

Part 1: Application Structure and Setup

The settings for the application are as follows:

- Application Name: Touch Gestures Experiment 3
- Project Name: TouchGesturesExperiment3
- Package Name: `com.cornez.touchgesturesexperiment3`
- Android Form: Phone and Tablet
- Minimum SDK: API 18: Android 4.3 (Jelly Bean)
- Target SDK: API 21: Android 5.0 (Lollipop)
- Compile with: API 21: Android 5.0 (Lollipop)
- Activity Name: `MyActivity`

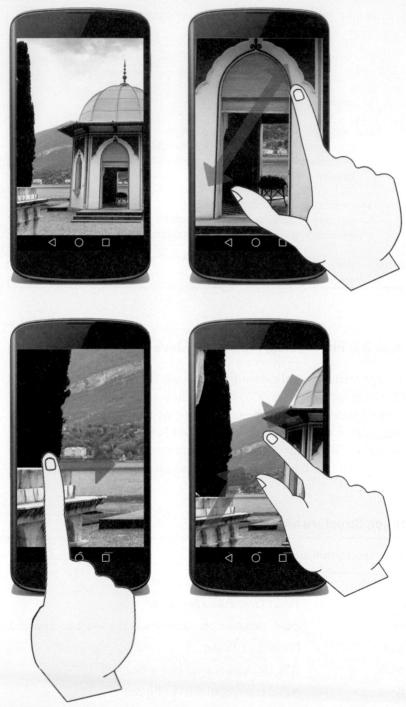

▌FIGURE 7-28 The Touch Gestures Experiment 3 application illustrates multitouch gestures.

The project structure for the application is shown in Figure 7-29. The single photograph, a drawable PNG file, is stored in the drawable directories. The Java source files for the multitouch experiment are `MyActivity` and `ZoomImageView`. A UI interface layout will not be built as an XML file for this application.

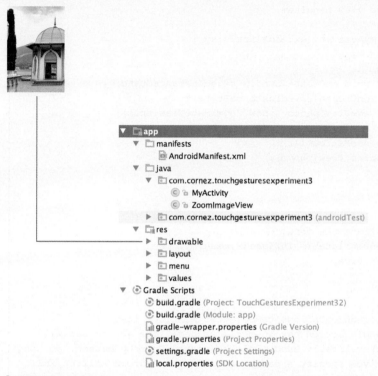

| FIGURE 7-29 The Touch Gestures Experiment 3 application project structure.

Part 2: `MyActivity.java`

The objective of `MyActivity` is to place the photo on the screen. This photo is set as the content `View` associated with the activity of the application. The Java code for `MyActivity` is shown as follows:

Lines 13–14:	The `ZoomImageView` class is a subclass of an `ImageView`. The `photo` object is instantiated and its content is set to the photograph in the drawable directory.
Line 15:	The maximum scale amount for the `ImageView` is initialized to the value 3.0.
Line 16:	The content for `MyActivity` is set to the `ZoomImageView` object, `photo`.

```
MyActivity.java
1   package com.cornez.touchgesturesexperiment3;
2
3   import android.app.Activity;
4   import android.os.Bundle;
5   import android.view.Menu;
6   import android.view.MenuItem;
7
8   public class MyActivity extends Activity {
9
10      @Override
11      protected void onCreate(Bundle savedInstanceState) {
12          super.onCreate(savedInstanceState);
13          ZoomImageView photo = new ZoomImageView(this);
14          photo.setImageResource(R.drawable.photo);
15          photo.setMaxZoom(4f);
16          setContentView(photo);
17      }
18
19      @Override
20      public boolean onCreateOptionsMenu(Menu menu) {
21          // Inflate the menu.
22          getMenuInflater().inflate(R.menu.my, menu);
23          return true;
24      }
25
26      @Override
27      public boolean onOptionsItemSelected(MenuItem item) {
28          // Handle action bar item clicks here. The action bar will
29          // automatically handle clicks on the Home/Up button, so long
30          // as you specify a parent activity in AndroidManifest.xml.
31          int id = item.getItemId();
32          if (id == R.id.action_settings) {
33              return true;
34          }
35          return super.onOptionsItemSelected(item);
36      }
37  }
```

Part 3: `ZoomImageView`—Implementing the Multitouch Gesture

The `ZoomImageView` detects the multitouch gesture this application uses. User activities are categorized by three codes: 0, 1, and 2. When the user is not performing an activity, the activity mode is set to 0, or NONE. If the user is performing a single pointer gesture that is identified as moving the photo, the activity mode is set to 1, or MOVE. Finally, when the user is performing a multitouch gesture that is defined as a zoom—or its reverse, a pinch—the activity mode is set to 2, or ZOOM.

Lines 24–25:	To specify the amount the user can zoom, the values of the minScale and maxScale are set. maxScale was also set in MyActivity.
Lines 52–84:	To support the scaling of the photo, a ScaleGesture-Detector is used with a supplied listener. To simplify it even further, ScaleGestureDetector extends SimpleOnScaleGestureListener to listen for a subset of scaling-related events. The methods required by the interface are used to respond to the beginning of a scaling gesture and the scaling events for a gesture in progress.
Lines 86–131:	The touch events are implemented. A zoom or pinch produces an increase or reduction in the image size based on the distance between the two pointers, current and last. Once the ACTION_POINTER_UP is triggered, movement and zoom/pinch operations will end with mode variable set to NONE.
Lines 134–214:	Matrix transformations scale and move the photo object intact to a new location.

ZoomImageView.java

```
1    package com.cornez.touchgesturesexperiment3;
2
3    import android.content.Context;
4    import android.graphics.Matrix;
5    import android.graphics.PointF;
6    import android.graphics.drawable.Drawable;
7    import android.view.MotionEvent;
8    import android.view.ScaleGestureDetector;
9    import android.widget.ImageView;
10
11   public class ZoomImageView extends ImageView{
12
13       // ACTION CODES FOR USER MODE
14       static final int NONE = 0;  //NO ACTIVITY
15       static final int MOVE = 1;  //MOVING THE PHOTO
16       static final int ZOOM = 2;  //ZOOMING OR PINCHING THE PHOTO
17       int mode = NONE;
18
19       private Matrix matrix;
20
21       // ZOOM ATTRIBUTES
22       private PointF last = new PointF();
23       private PointF start = new PointF();
24       private float minScale = 1f;
```

```
25      private float maxScale = 3f;
26      private float[] m;
27
28      private int viewWidth;
29      private int viewHeight;
30      private static final int CLICK = 3;
31      private float saveScale = 1f;
32      private float origWidth;
33      private float origHeight;
34
35      private ScaleGestureDetector mScaleDetector;
36
37      public ZoomImageView(Context context) {
38          super(context);
39
40          mScaleDetector = new ScaleGestureDetector(context,
41                                          new ScaleListener());
42          matrix = new Matrix();
43          m = new float[9];
44          setImageMatrix(matrix);
45          setScaleType(ScaleType.MATRIX);
46      }
47
48      public void setMaxZoom(float x) {
49          maxScale = x;
50      }
51
52      private class ScaleListener extends
53                      ScaleGestureDetector.SimpleOnScaleGestureListener {
54          @Override
55          public boolean onScaleBegin(ScaleGestureDetector detector) {
56              mode = ZOOM;
57              return true;
58          }
59
60          @Override
61          public boolean onScale(ScaleGestureDetector detector) {
62              float mScaleFactor = detector.getScaleFactor();
63              float origScale = saveScale;
64              saveScale *= mScaleFactor;
65              if (saveScale > maxScale) {
66                  saveScale = maxScale;
67                  mScaleFactor = maxScale / origScale;
68              } else if (saveScale < minScale) {
69                  saveScale = minScale;
70                  mScaleFactor = minScale / origScale;
71              }
72
```

```
 73            if (origWidth * saveScale <= viewWidth ||
 74                origHeight * saveScale <= viewHeight)
 75                matrix.postScale(mScaleFactor, mScaleFactor,
 76                                viewWidth / 2, viewHeight / 2);
 77            else
 78                matrix.postScale(mScaleFactor, mScaleFactor,
 79                            detector.getFocusX(), detector.getFocusY());
 80
 81            fixTrans();
 82            return true;
 83        }
 84    }
 85
 86    //************* onTouchEvent *************************
 87    @Override
 88    public boolean onTouchEvent(MotionEvent event) {
 89        mScaleDetector.onTouchEvent(event);
 90        PointF current = new PointF(event.getX(), event.getY());
 91
 92        switch (event.getAction()) {
 93            case MotionEvent.ACTION_DOWN:
 94                last.set(current);
 95                start.set(last);
 96                mode = MOVE;
 97                break;
 98
 99            case MotionEvent.ACTION_MOVE:
100                if (mode == MOVE) {
101                    float distanceX = current.x - last.x;
102                    float distanceY = current.y - last.y;
103                    float fixTransX = getFixDragTrans(distanceX,
104                                viewWidth, origWidth * saveScale);
105                    float fixTransY = getFixDragTrans(distanceY,
106                                viewHeight, origHeight * saveScale);
107                    matrix.postTranslate(fixTransX, fixTransY);
108                    fixTrans();
109                    last.set(current.x, current.y);
110                }
111                break;
112
113            case MotionEvent.ACTION_UP:
114                mode = NONE;
115                int xDiff = (int) Math.abs(current.x - start.x);
116                int yDiff = (int) Math.abs(current.y - start.y);
117                if (xDiff < CLICK && yDiff < CLICK)
118                    performClick();
119                break;
120
```

```
121             case MotionEvent.ACTION_POINTER_UP:
122                 mode = NONE;
123                 break;
124         }
125         //SET THE IMAGE AND INVALIDATE THE COMPLETE VIEW
126         setImageMatrix(matrix);
127         invalidate();
128
129         //RETURN A TRUE TO INDICATE THE EVENT WAS HANDLED
130         return true;
131     }
132
133
134     //************** Matrix Translations ***************
135     void fixTrans() {
136         matrix.getValues(m);
137         float transX = m[Matrix.MTRANS_X];
138         float transY = m[Matrix.MTRANS_Y];
139
140         float fixTransX = getFixTrans(transX, viewWidth,
141                                       origWidth * saveScale);
142         float fixTransY = getFixTrans(transY, viewHeight,
143                                       origHeight * saveScale);
144
145         if (fixTransX != 0 || fixTransY != 0)
146             matrix.postTranslate(fixTransX, fixTransY);
147     }
148
149     float getFixTrans(float trans, float viewSize, float contentSize) {
150         float minTrans, maxTrans;
151
152         if (contentSize <= viewSize) {
153             minTrans = 0;
154             maxTrans = viewSize - contentSize;
155         } else {
156             minTrans = viewSize - contentSize;
157             maxTrans = 0;
158         }
159
160         if (trans < minTrans)
161             return -trans + minTrans;
162         if (trans > maxTrans)
163             return -trans + maxTrans;
164         return 0;
165     }
166
167     float getFixDragTrans(float delta, float viewSize,
168                           float contentSize) {
```

```
169            if (contentSize <= viewSize) {
170                return 0;
171            }
172            return delta;
173        }
174
175        @Override
176        protected void onMeasure(int widthMeasureSpec,
177                                 int heightMeasureSpec) {
178            super.onMeasure(widthMeasureSpec, heightMeasureSpec);
179            viewWidth = MeasureSpec.getSize(widthMeasureSpec);
180            viewHeight = MeasureSpec.getSize(heightMeasureSpec);
181
182            if (saveScale == 1) {
183                //TASK 2: SCALE THE IMAGE TO FIT THE SCREEN
184                float scale;
185
186                Drawable drawable = getDrawable();
187                if (drawable == null || drawable.getIntrinsicWidth() == 0
188                                      || drawable.getIntrinsicHeight() == 0)
189                    return;
190                int bmWidth = drawable.getIntrinsicWidth();
191                int bmHeight = drawable.getIntrinsicHeight();
192
193                float scaleX = (float) viewWidth / (float) bmWidth;
194                float scaleY = (float) viewHeight / (float) bmHeight;
195                scale = Math.min(scaleX, scaleY);
196                matrix.setScale(scale, scale);
197
198                // TASK 3: PLACE THE IMAGE IN THE CENTER OF THE SCREEN
199                float centerX = (float) viewWidth
200                                        - (scale * (float) bmWidth);
201                float centerY = (float) viewHeight
202                                        - (scale * (float) bmHeight);
203                centerX /= (float) 2;
204                centerY /= (float) 2;
205
206
207                matrix.postTranslate(centerX, centerY);
208
209                origWidth = viewWidth - 2 * centerX;
210                origHeight = viewHeight - 2 * centerY;
211                setImageMatrix(matrix);
212            }
213            fixTrans();
214        }
215 }
```

■ Exercises

7.1   List eight basic touch gestures.

7.2   When is an `onTouchEvent()` method triggered?

7.3   Briefly describe three action codes supported by the `MotionEvent` class.

7.4   Describe the usage of the `GestureDetector` class. What are its limits?

7.5   List and describe the callback methods contained in the `GestureDetector` class.

7.6   The `MotionEvent` class provides a collection of methods to query the position and other properties of fingers in a gesture. Name and describe five of these methods.

7.7   Outline the implementation of a drag-and-drop gesture.

7.8   Describe the purpose of `DragShadowBuilder`. How can a drag shadow be customized?

7.9   Write a segment of code that determines the direction of a fling gesture.

7.10 Write a segment of code that determines the velocity of a fling gesture.

7.11 Outline the sequence of `MotionEvents` for a multitouch gesture that involves two pointers.

8 Sensors and Camera

Chapter Objectives

In this chapter you will:

- Understand Motion Sensors, Environmental Sensors, and Positional Sensors.
- Learn how to acquire measurement data from a sensor.
- Explore the SensorEvent class and SensorEventListener interface.
- Create applications using the accelerometer.
- Learn to utilize the built-in camera application.

■ 8.1 Sensors and Mobile Devices

Android devices come with a varied set of embedded sensors; collectively, these sensors enable the creation of applications across a wide range of domains, such as gaming, healthcare, social networks, safety, environmental monitoring, and transportation. A sensor is simply a device that measures a physical quantity (e.g., the tilt of a device, or sudden movement) and converts it into a signal that an application can interpret. Android users typically experience sensors by means of touchscreens, accelerometers, gyroscopes, cameras, and GPS. For example, an accelerometer often enhances a camera-based application by helping to determine whether the user is holding the device in a landscape or portrait view. The application can then use that information to automatically reorient the display or correctly orient captured photos on the device during viewing.

Sensors allow incorporation of different input methods to improve user interface design and application functionality. Android application developers should consider alternative forms of user input when designing an application. It is particularly useful to explore opportunities in adaptability and the formation of new kinds of user interfaces during the design phase. For example, users of gaming apps may benefit from gesture-based control, such as tilting the device as an input method. Gesture-based game applications can provide challenging and engaging experiences, with increasing levels of skill required related to mastery of the sensor-software interface.

For individuals with physical limitations, being able to control a mobile device with the flick of a wrist or a simple turning motion can provide enhanced access to app features, such as editing or typing text, that would otherwise not be available. Innovations in gesture control are particularly appropriate for applications designed for use on wearable devices. For example, a user with disabilities could rely on sensors to navigate through onscreen icons by a simple turn of the head.

■ 8.2 Android Sensors

Most Android devices have multiple built-in sensors. These sensors supply raw data from three general categories: motion, environmental conditions, and the orientation of the device. Measurements are often provided with a relatively high degree of precision and accuracy, making them useful for monitoring device movement and positioning within three dimensions and also changes in the ambient environment near a device.

8.2.1 Motion Sensors

Users generate motion events when they move, shake, or tilt a device. An application can interpret motion in two basic ways: (1) Movement can be the result of direct user input, such as the user tilting the device to steer a moving object in a game, and (2) motion can also be detected as feedback from the physical environment, such as a device being present in a car that is moving. Hardware sensors, such as accelerometers and gyroscopes, detect motion events. Although accelerometers and gyroscopes are similar in purpose, they measure different things.

The general purpose of an accelerometer is to measure the force of acceleration, whether gravity or movement has caused the acceleration. The accelerometer is commonplace in existing applications for detecting a device's orientation. Because gravity is applying a constant acceleration toward the Earth, the Android platform can determine which way is down, based on the accelerometer. Figure 8-1 illustrates changes in orientation of a stationary device. Android's built-in three-axis accelerometer is often used to manage context-aware elements in an application, such as controlling game interfaces, performing power management, shuffling music, performing "undo" actions, and enabling pedometers.

The gyroscope measures the rate of rotation around three axes. Also called angular rate sensors, gyroscopes measure how quickly an object rotates, allowing a device to measure and maintain orientation. Gyroscopic sensors can monitor device positions, orientation, direction, angular motion, and rotation. When applied to an application, a gyroscopic sensor commonly performs gesture-recognition functions.

Gyroscopes are the only inertial sensors that provide accurate, latency-free measurement of rotations without being affected by external forces, including magnetic, gravitational, or other environmental factors. Figure 8-2 illustrates how the rotations, which are measured in radians, behave along the three axes: x (pitch), y (roll), and z (yaw). Pitch,

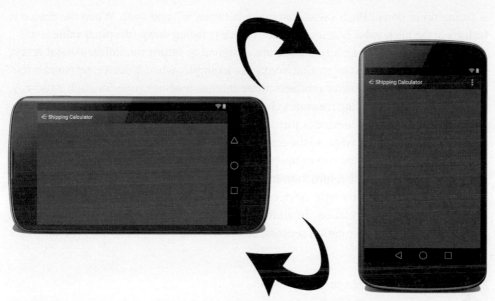

FIGURE 8-1 The Accelerometer can gauge the orientation of a stationary device.

roll, and yaw motions are transformations from world to body frame with motions performed relative to body-frame axes. Yaw, the rotation angle around the world-frame z-axis, is required to determine whether the device is facing north, south, east, or west. It takes values between π and $-\pi$, with 0 representing north and $\pi/2$ representing east. Pitch, the rotation angle around the world-frame x-axis, can be used to determine whether the device

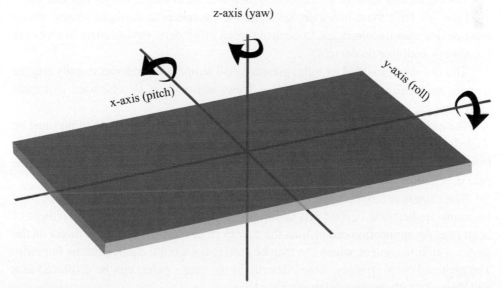

FIGURE 8-2 A gyroscope will return rate-of-rotation data for the three coordinate axes.

is facing up or down. Pitch values can range between $\pi/2$ and $-\pi/2$. When the device is facing up, the pitch value is zero; when the device is facing down, the pitch value is $\pi/2$.

The accelerometer and gyroscope are designed to return multidimensional arrays of sensor values for a given motion event. For example, when a device registers a motion event, the accelerometer produces three motion readings, one for each axis: x, y, and z. Each motion reading measures changes in velocity over time along a linear path. This means that when a device is tilted upwards, it is being pitched with the top edge rising above the bottom edge, so the sensor reads a negative y value. Rolling the device to the right, so the left side comes up, produces a reading that shows positive x values.

The gyroscope will return rate-of-rotation data for the three coordinate axes. When combined into a single device, the accelerator and gyroscope can create a powerful array of information. In addition, software-based sensors, such as gravity, linear acceleration, and rotation sensors, can derive their data from the accelerometer and gyroscope.

8.2.2 Environmental Sensors

Android devices may contain a range of environmental sensors that make the device aware of the world around it. Environmental sensors measure specific environmental parameters, such as ambient air temperature and pressure, illumination, and humidity. It should be noted that very few devices have dedicated ambient temperature sensors. An application can compute the temperature based on the temperature of the device's internal electronics or battery, which is similar to the ambient temperature of a device that has been on standby. Most often, an application uses a weather service content provider to supply ambient temperature.

Environmental sensors are hardware-based and are available only if a device manufacturer has built them into a device. With the exception of the light sensor, which most device manufacturers use to control screen brightness, environment sensors are not always available on devices.

The raw data provided by light, pressure, and temperature sensors usually require no calibration, filtering, or modification. These sensors can also be used alongside each other.

For example, dew point is the temperature at which a given volume of air must be cooled, at constant barometric pressure, for water vapor to condense into water. Data from a device's humidity sensor and temperature sensor can be used in tandem to compute dew point.

The camera is also classified as an environmental sensor. The camera can be used for many applications beyond just taking photographs. Consider the measurement of heart rate. An application can instruct the user to place the tip of an index finger on the device's built-in camera, which can then be used to track color changes in the fingertip. The captured color changes, linked directly to the user's pulse, can be displayed as a real-time chart illustrating the user's heartbeat.

8.2.3 Positional Sensors

A magnetometer, such as a geomagnetic field sensor, is built into most Android devices. This type of sensor is used to determine the position of a device. A proximity sensor, also prevalent in devices, is used to determine how close an object is to the device, specifically to the face of the device. Proximity data are particularly important when creating applications that must determine when a device is being held close to a user's face, such as during a phone call.

Positional sensors are useful for determining a device's physical position in the world's frame of reference, such as computing the device's position relative to the magnetic North Pole. These sensors are often used in tandem with motion sensors. For example, the geomagnetic field sensor can be used in combination with the accelerometer to determine a device's horizontal compass reading. Positional sensors are not typically used to monitor device movement or motion, such as shake, tilt, or thrust.

8.3 Working with Sensors

In addition to the sensors mentioned previously, Android also relies on software-based sensors. Software-based sensors imitate hardware-based sensors by deriving their data from one or more of the embedded physical sensors. For example, linear acceleration measures acceleration along a single axis. This software-based sensor requires raw data derived from the accelerometer.

Few Android-powered devices have every type of sensor. Most devices include an accelerometer and a magnetometer, but fewer devices have barometers or thermometers. It is also not uncommon for a device to have more than one sensor of a given type, such as the inclusion of two gravity sensors, each one with a different range. Table 8-1 summarizes a set of common sensors that are supported by the Android platform. The `getSensorList()` method lists all of the available sensors in a particular device.

To acquire measurement data from a sensor, a `SensorManager` object is required. Once instantiated, this object can be used to specify an instance of a physical sensor. Consider the following segment of code. The object `mSensorManager` is used to access both hardware-based and software-based sensors.

Lines 2–5:   The `Sensor` class is used to create an instance of a specific sensor. This class provides various methods that let you determine a sensor's capabilities.

Lines 10–11:   `SensorManager` is used to access the device's sensors. An instance of the sensor service is created.

Lines 13–18:   The `SensorManager` object is used to get instances of specific sensors. This class also provides several sensor constants that are used to report sensor accuracy, set data acquisition rates,

TABLE 8-1 Android Sensors

Sensor	Identifier Name and Description
Accelerometer	`TYPE_ACCELEROMETER` Measures the acceleration force in m/s^2 that is applied to a device on all three physical axes (x, y, and z), including the force of gravity. Useful for motion detection, such as shaking and tilting.
Ambient temperature	`TYPE_AMBIENT_TEMPERATURE` Measures the ambient room temperature in degrees Celcius. Commonly used for monitoring air temperatures.
Gravity	`TYPE_GRAVITY` Measures the force of gravity in m/s^2 that is applied to a device on all three physical axes (x, y, and z). This sensor is similar to an accelerometer. However, unlike an accelerometer, which is a hardware sensor, the gravity sensor can be software- or hardware-based.
Gyroscope	`TYPE_GYROSCOPE` Measures a device's rate of rotation in rad/s around each of the three physical axes. This hardware sensor detects rotation, such as spinning and turning.
Light	`TYPE_LIGHT` Measures the ambient light level and is used to control screen brightness.
Linear acceleration	`TYPE_LINEAR_ACCLERATION` Measures the acceleration force in m/s^2 that is applied to a device. This sensor can be used to monitor acceleration along a single axis.
Magnetic field	`TYPE_MAGNETIC_FIELD` Measures the ambient geomagnetic field and is required for creating applications that need a compass.
Pressure	`TYPE_PRESSURE` Measures the ambient air pressure and is useful in monitoring air pressure changes.
Proximity	`TYPE_ACCELEROMETER` Measures the proximity of an object relative to the device. This sensor is often used to determine the position of a person's ear to a mobile phone during a call.
Relative humidity	`TYPE_RELATIVE_HUMIDITY` Measures the relative ambient humidity (in percent).
Rotation vector	`TYPE_ACCELEROMETER` Measures the orientation of a device using a rotation vector.
Step detector	`TYPE_STEP_DETECTOR` The step detector analyzes accelerometer input to recognize when the user has taken a step. An event can be triggered with each step.
Step counter	`TYPE_STEP_COUNTER` The step counter tracks the number of steps taken by the user. An event is triggered with each change in the step count.

and calibrate sensors. A reference to a constant value provides access to different types of sensors. For example:

```
int     Sensor.TYPE_GYROSCOPE
int     Sensor.TYPE_MAGNETIC_FIELD
int     Sensor.TYPE_ACCELEROMETER
```

```
1   private SensorManager mSensorManager;
2   private Sensor mPressure;
3   private Sensor mGravity;
4   private Sensor mMagneticField;
5   private Sensor mRotationVector;
6
7   .
8   .
9   .
10  mSensorManager = (SensorManager)
11      getSystemService(Context.SENSOR_SERVICE);
12
13  mPressure = mSensorManager.getDefaultSensor(Sensor.TYPE_PRESSURE);
14  mGravity = mSensorManager.getDefaultSensor(Sensor.TYPE_GRAVITY);
15  mMagneticField =
16      mSensorManager.getDefaultSensor(Sensor.TYPE_MAGNETIC_FIELD);
17  mRotationVector =
18      mSensorManager.getDefaultSensor(Sensor.TYPE_ROTATION_VECTOR);
```

The SensorManager class provides various methods for accessing and listing sensors. It is also used for registering and unregistering sensor event listeners.

The SensorEvent class is used by the system to create a sensor event object, which provides information about a sensor event. The SensorEventListener interface uses two callback methods that receive notifications (sensor events) when sensor values change or when sensor accuracy changes. A SensorEvent object includes the following information:

1. Raw sensor data
2. Type of sensor that generated the event
3. Accuracy of the data
4. Time-stamp for the event

In the segment of code shown below, PlayActivity is an Activity that implements a SensorEventListener interface. A SensorManager object is used to access the gyroscope sensor. A listener event for the gyroscope sensor is registered in the activity's onResume() callback. It is unregistered in the onPause() callback. It is considered good practice to unregister sensor listeners when they are no longer needed.

Two abstract methods are implemented in SensorEventListener: on-AccuracyChanged() and onSensorChanged(). If the gyroscope's accuracy changes, the onAccuracyChanged() method will be called. If the gyroscope reports a new value, the onSensorChanged() method will be called. The onSensor-Changed() callback method typically handles incoming sensor data.

```
1   public class PlayActivity extends Activity implements
2           SensorEventListener {
3
4       private SensorManager mSensorManager;
5       private Sensor mGyroscope;
6
7       public PlayActivity () {
8           mSensorManager =
9               (SensorManager)getSystemService(SENSOR_SERVICE);
10          mGyroscope =
11              mSensorManager.getDefaultSensor(Sensor.TYPE_GYROSCOPE);
12      }
13
14      protected void onResume() {
15          super.onResume();
16          mSensorManager.registerListener(this, mGyroscope,
17              SensorManager.SENSOR_DELAY_NORMAL);
18      }
19
20      protected void onPause() {
21          super.onPause();
22          mSensorManager.unregisterListener(this);
23      }
24
25      public void onAccuracyChanged(Sensor sensor, int accuracy) {
26      }
27
28      public void onSensorChanged(SensorEvent event) {
29      }
30  }
```

Not all sensors are present in every device. It is considered good practice to verify the existence of a sensor before attempting to use it. To identify the sensors that are on a device, a SensorManager object is first used to reference the sensor service. getSensorList() can then be called by that object to return a list of sensors on a device. In the code segment below, the constant TYPE_ALL is used to specify every sensor on the device.

```
1   SensorManager mSensorManager;
2   List <Sensor> deviceSensors;
3
4   mSensorManager = (SensorManager)getSystemService(SENSOR_SERVICE);
5   deviceSensors = mSensorManager.getSensorList(Sensor.TYPE_ALL);
```

To determine the existence of a specific type of sensor, the method get-DefaultSensor() can be called for verification. In the code segment below, get-DefaultSensor() is passed the type constant for the gyroscope sensor. If a device has more than one sensor of a given type, one of the sensors must be designated as the default sensor. If a default sensor does not exist for a given type of sensor, the method call returns null, which means the device does not have that type of sensor.

```
1  SensorManager mSensorManager;
2  mSensorManager = (SensorManager)getSystemService(SENSOR_SERVICE);
3  if (mSensorManager.getDefaultSensor(Sensor.TYPE_GYROSCOPE) != null){
4      // The device has a gyroscope.
5  }
6  else {
7    // The device does not have a gyroscope
8  }
```

Android device manufacturers have flexibility in how they construct their mobile devices. No specific requirements exist for the configuration of sensors in an Android-powered device; this means that attributes and capabilities of sensors are not uniform across all devices. The ability to determine sensor characteristics is often useful for an application, which may require different behavior based on sensor capabilities.

The code segment below uses method calls to get specific information about an existing sensor; for example, getPower() can be used to obtain the sensor's power requirements. getMaxumumRange() can determine a sensor's resolution and maximum range of measurement. The getMinDelay() method, called on Line 9, is useful for obtaining the rate at which a sensor can acquire raw data. The method will return an integer value representing the minimum time interval (in microseconds) the sensor can use to sense data. A sensor that returns a nonzero value for the getMinDelay() method is a streaming sensor. Streaming sensors can sense data at regular intervals. A nonstreaming sensor reports data only when there is a change in the parameters it is sensing.

Additional method calls, such as those found on Lines 11 and 12, can be used to determine a version number or whether a particular vendor has supplied the embedded sensor.

```
1  SensorManager mSensorManager;
2  Sensor mGyroscope;
3
4  mSensorManager = (SensorManager)getSystemService(SENSOR_SERVICE);
5  mGyroscope = mSensorManager.getDefaultSensor(Sensor.TYPE_GYROSCOPE);
6
7  float maxRange = mGyroscope.getMaximumRange();
8  float power = mGyroscope.getPower();
```

```
9    float minDelay = mGyroscope.getMinDelay();
10
11   String vendorName = mGyroscope.getVendor();
12   int versionNumber = mGyroscope.getVersion();
```

■ 8.4 Coordinate System

The coordinate system of an Android device is defined relative to the screen of the device in its default orientation. For example, the default mode of an Android mobile phone is typically the portrait orientation. As shown in Figure 8-3, the x-axis runs in the direction of the short side of the screen. The y-axis runs in the direction of the long side of the screen, and the z-axis points out of the screen.

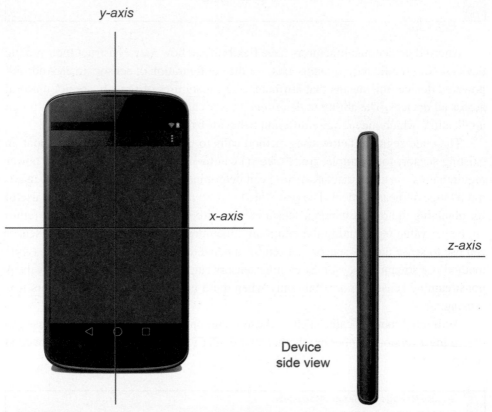

| FIGURE 8-3 The coordinate system for an Android phone.

The natural orientation for many tablet devices is landscape, rather than portrait mode. It is important that an application does not assume that a device's default orientation will always be portrait. Consider an accelerometer on an Android phone with a default portrait orientation. In this system, coordinates behind the screen have negative z-axis values. These axes for the device will not be swapped when the device's screen orientation changes. The sensor's coordinate system will not change as the device moves.

The coordinate system of the world, the inertial frame of reference, defines the x-axis as the cross-product of the y-axis with the z-axis. The y-axis is tangential to the ground and points toward the North Pole. The z-axis points perpendicular to the ground toward the sky.

These two coordinate systems are aligned when the mobile phone is sitting perfectly flat on a table with the screen facing up and pointing north. In this orientation, the accelerometer, which measures acceleration in meters/seconds^2 for each axis, will produce the results: 0, 0, 9.8. These values are the acceleration measurements applied to the phone minus the force of gravity. The force of gravity is 9.8 meters/seconds^2, defined by the constant `SensorManager.GRAVITY_EARTH`.

values[0]: Acceleration minus the force of gravity on the x-axis

values[1]: Acceleration minus the force of gravity on the y-axis

values[2]: Acceleration minus the force of gravity on the z-axis

This means that when the device lies flat on a table and is pushed on its left side toward the right, the x acceleration value is positive. When the device lies flat on a table, the acceleration value is `+9.8`, which corresponds to the acceleration of the device (`0 m/s`^{2}) minus the force of gravity (`-9.8 m/s`^{2}).

When the device lies flat on a table, face-up, with an acceleration of (`A m/s`^{2}), the acceleration value is equal to (`A+9.8`) which corresponds to the acceleration of the device (`+A m/s`^{2}) minus the force of gravity (`-9.8 m/s`^{2}). Table 8-2 shows the axes values read from the sensor corresponding to several positions of the device.

TABLE 8-2 Accelerator axes readings

	Orientation	X value	Y value	Z value
	Default Portrait	0	9.8 m/s^2	0
	Landscape	9.8 m/s^2	0	0

(continues)

TABLE 8-2 Accelerator axes readings (continued)

	Orientation	X value	Y value	Z value
	Reverse Portrait	0	-9.8 m/s^2	0
	Reverse Landscape	-9.8 m/s^2	0	0
	Face Up	0	0	9.8 m/s^2
	Face Down	0	0	-9.8 m/s^2

■ Lab Example 8-1: Experiment with Tilt Input: Roaming Ball

The market for mobile gaming often dominates other gaming platforms. As different control interfaces emerge, mobile game developers can consider multiple input options, including tilt as an input method. Tilt-detection is as simple as detecting which accelerometer axis is experiencing the most force from gravity. This lab example explores the use of the accelerometer to move a ball around the screen. More specifically, it illustrates how rotations, along the axes of the device, can be detected and used to control onscreen action. Accelerometer-based tilt input is supported on a variety of mobile games and is frequently used as a means of user input, most notably used in apps where tilting and rotating the device can control game play.

It should be noted that it is not possible to test sensor code on an emulator because an Android virtual device cannot emulate sensors. This lab example, as well as the remaining lab examples in this chapter, must be tested on a physical device.

Part 1: The Design

When the application first launches, the user is presented with a ball positioned at a specific x, y location on the screen. Three text fields are used to display the x-, y-, and z-axis readings from the accelerometer. As the user tilts and rotates the device, the text fields are updated to show the current accelerometer readings. In addition, the ball moves in accordance with the tilt and roll of the device, as shown in Figure 8-4. The ball is not allowed to roll offscreen, and it is constrained by the virtual boundaries of the screen.

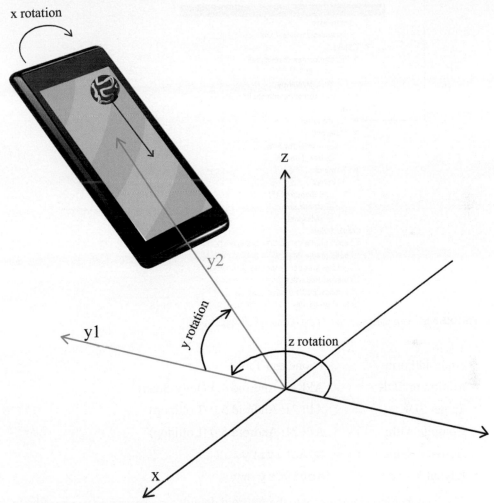

❙ FIGURE 8-4 Tilt and pitch input for the Roaming Ball Application.

Part 2: Application Structure and Setup

The settings for the application are as follows:

- Application Name: Roaming Ball
- Project Name: RoamingBall
- Package Name: `com.cornez.roamingball`

FIGURE 8-5 The project structure of the Roaming Ball application.

- Android Form: Phone and Tablet
- Minimum SDK: API 18: Android 4.3 (Jelly Bean)
- Target SDK: API 21: Android 5.0 (Lollipop)
- Compile with: API 21: Android 5.0 (Lollipop)
- Activity Name: `MyActivity`
- Layout Name: `activity_my`

The launcher icon remains set to the Android default `ic_launcher.png` file. In addition to this graphic element, the background.png and ball.png have been added to the drawable directory. The complete structure for the application is shown in Figure 8-5. Given that this exercise is a simple experiment, a single activity, `MyActivity`, is used for the implementation of the accelerometer response, the thread mechanism, and control of the onscreen action. The `Ball` class, located in the Java source directory, is the data model for the ball located on the screen.

It is often a good idea to declare `<uses-feature>` elements for all of the features that an application requires. Declared `<uses-feature>` elements are informational only, which means that the Android system itself does not check for matching feature support on the device before installing an application. Services such as Google Play, however, may check the application's `<uses-feature>` declarations as part of handling or interacting with the application.

Although the `<uses-feature>` element is activated only for devices running API Level 4 or higher, it is recommended that this element be included for all applications. Devices running older versions of the platform will ignore the element. To signal that your application uses or requires a hardware feature, declare each value in an `android:name` attribute in a separate `<uses-feature>` element. The following sensors can be specified:

```
android.hardware.sensor.accelerometer

android.hardware.sensor.barometer

android.hardware.sensor.compass

android.hardware.sensor.gyroscope

android.hardware.sensor.light

android.hardware.sensor.proximity

android.hardware.sensor.stepcounter

android.hardware.sensor.stepdetector
```

The code listing for `AndroidManifest.xml` is shown as follows:

```
AndroidManifest.xml
1   <?xml version="1.0" encoding="utf-8"?>
2   <manifest xmlns:android="http://schemas.android.com/apk/res/android"
3       package="com.cornez.roamingball" >
4
5       <uses-feature android:name="android.hardware.sensor.accelerometer"
6           android:required="true" />
7
8       <application
9           android:allowBackup="true"
10          android:icon="@drawable/ic_launcher"
11          android:label="@string/app_name"
12          android:theme=
13              "@android:style/Theme.Holo.Light.NoActionBar.Fullscreen"
14          >
15
16          <activity
17              android:name=".MyActivity"
18              android:screenOrientation="portrait"
19              android:label="@string/app_name" >
20
```

```
21          <intent-filter>
22              <action android:name="android.intent.action.MAIN" />
23
24          <category
25              android:name="android.intent.category.LAUNCHER" />
26          </intent-filter>
27       </activity>
28    </application>
29
30 </manifest>
```

Part 3: The User Interface

The user interface consists of a RelativeLayout that is used to store the image of the ball and text fields for the *x*-, *y*-, and *z*-axis accelerometer readings. strings.xml contains labels for the text fields and the content description for the ball image. The code listing for this file is shown as follows:

strings.xml

```
1  <?xml version="1.0" encoding="utf-8"?>
2  <resources>
3
4      <string name="app_name">Roaming Ball</string>
5      <string name="hello_world">Hello world!</string>
6      <string name="action_settings">Settings</string>
7
8      <string name="ball_item">Ball Item</string>
9      <string name="x_axis">x-axis :</string>
10     <string name="y_axis">y-axis :</string>
11     <string name="z_axis">z-axis :</string>
12
13 </resources>
```

The layout file for the application is activity_my.xml. The graphical design for this layout is shown in Figure 8-6. The RelativeLayout root element is given an identifier name, @+id/relativeLayout, so that it may be referenced within the application's main activity when adding an image of the ball during run-time. The TextViews in activity_my.xml are used for labels and output text fields. The accelerometer measurements along the three axes will be displayed in the TextViews: textView2 (*x*-axis), textView4 (*y*-axis), and textView6 (*z*-axis). The XML code listing for activity_my.xml is shown as follows:

activity_my.xml

```
1  <RelativeLayout
2  xmlns:android="http://schemas.android.com/apk/res/android"
3      xmlns:tools="http://schemas.android.com/tools"
```

```
 4          android:layout_width="match_parent"
 5          android:layout_height="match_parent"
 6          android:id="@+id/relativeLayout"
 7          tools:context=".MyActivity"
 8          android:background="@drawable/background">
 9
10          <!-- X-AXIS LABEL AND OUTPUT TEXT FIELD -->
11          <TextView
12              android:layout_width="wrap_content"
13              android:layout_height="wrap_content"
14              android:textAppearance="?android:attr/textAppearanceLarge"
15              android:text="@string/x_axis"
16              android:id="@+id/textView1"
17              android:layout_alignParentTop="true"
18              android:layout_alignParentStart="true"
19              android:layout_marginLeft="40dp"
20              android:layout_marginTop="112dp" />
21
22          <TextView
23              android:layout_width="wrap_content"
24              android:layout_height="wrap_content"
25              android:textAppearance="?android:attr/textAppearanceLarge"
26              android:text="0"
27              android:id="@+id/textView2"
28              android:layout_alignBottom="@+id/textView1"
29              android:layout_toEndOf="@+id/textView1" />
30
31          <!-- Y-AXIS LABEL AND OUTPUT TEXT FIELD -->
32          <TextView
33              android:layout_width="wrap_content"
34              android:layout_height="wrap_content"
35              android:textAppearance="?android:attr/textAppearanceLarge"
36              android:text="@string/y_axis"
37              android:id="@+id/textView3"
38              android:layout_below="@+id/textView1"
39              android:layout_alignStart="@+id/textView1"
40              android:layout_marginTop="40dp" />
41
42          <TextView
43              android:layout_width="wrap_content"
44              android:layout_height="wrap_content"
45              android:textAppearance="?android:attr/textAppearanceLarge"
46              android:text="0"
47              android:id="@+id/textView4"
48              android:layout_alignBottom="@+id/textView3"
49              android:layout_toEndOf="@+id/textView1" />
50
51          <!-- Z-AXIS LABEL AND OUTPUT TEXT FIELD -->
52          <TextView
53              android:layout_width="wrap_content"
```

```
54              android:layout_height="wrap_content"
55              android:textAppearance="?android:attr/textAppearanceLarge"
56              android:text="@string/z_axis"
57              android:id="@+id/textView5"
58              android:layout_below="@+id/textView3"
59              android:layout_alignStart="@+id/textView1"
60              android:layout_marginTop="40dp" />
61
62          <TextView
63              android:layout_width="wrap_content"
64              android:layout_height="wrap_content"
65              android:textAppearance="?android:attr/textAppearanceLarge"
66              android:text="0"
67              android:id="@+id/textView6"
68              android:layout_alignBottom="@+id/textView5"
69              android:layout_toEndOf="@+id/textView5" />
70      </RelativeLayout>
```

▼ ⊞ relativeLayout
    Ab **textView1** – @string/x_axis
    Ab **textView2** – @string/zero
    Ab **textView3** – @string/y_axis
    Ab **textView4** – @string/zero
    Ab **textView5** – @string/z_axis
    Ab **textView6** – @string/zero

❙ FIGURE 8-6 The layout design for `activity_my.xml`.

The image of the ball is stored in an independent XML layout file, `ball_item.xml`. This allows the ball to be added to the screen during runtime. `ball_item.xml`, shown in Figure 8-7, requires an `ImageView` root element. The code listing for this layout file is shown as follows. Note that a content description is supplied to the root element on Line 6.

```
ball_item.xml
1   <?xml version="1.0" encoding="utf-8"?>
2   <ImageView xmlns:android="http://schemas.android.com/apk/res/android"
3       android:layout_width="match_parent"
4       android:layout_height="match_parent"
5       android:src="@drawable/ball"
6       android:contentDescription="@string/ball_item">
7
8   </ImageView>
```

ImageView – @drawable/ball

FIGURE 8-7 The layout design for `ball_item.xml`.

Part 4: Source Code for Application

The data model for the ball requires data members for representing an x, y position on the screen, the width of the ball, and its current velocity along the x- and y-axis. The Java code listing for the `Ball` class is as follows:

```
Ball.java
1   package com.cornez.roamingball;
2
3   public class Ball {
4
```

```
5        private float mX;
6        private float mY;
7        private int mWidth;
8        private float mVelocityX;
9        private float mVelocityY;
10
11       public void setX(float x){
12           mX = x;
13       }
14       public float getX(){
15           return mX;
16       }
17
18       public void setY(float y){
19           mY = y;
20       }
21       public float getY(){
22           return mY;
23       }
24
25       public void setWidth(int width){
26           mWidth = width;
27       }
28       public int getWidth(){
29           return mWidth;
30       }
31       public void setVelocityX(float velocityX){
32           mVelocityX = velocityX;
33       }
34       public float getVelocityX(){
35           return mVelocityX;
36       }
37       public void setVelocityY(float velocityY) {
38           mVelocityY = velocityY;
39       }
40       public float getVelocityY(){
41           return mVelocityY;
42       }
43   }
```

The SensorEventListener is implemented to monitor raw accelerometer data. Android will invoke the two callback methods onAccuracyChanged() and onSensorChanged() when the sensor's accuracy changes and when the sensor reports a new value. Lines 1–139 of MyActivity.java are shown as follows:

Lines 100–113:   onResume() and onPause() callback methods are used to register and unregister the accelerator event listener. Failing to unregister a sensor can drain the battery. Sensors can have substantial power requirements and can use up battery power quickly. The system will not disable sensors automatically when the screen turns off.

Lines 102–103: The default data delay, SENSOR_DELAY_NORMAL, is specified when the accelerometer sensor listener is registered. The data delay is used to control the interval at which sensor events are sent to the application via the onSensorChanged() callback method. The default data delay is suitable for monitoring typical screen orientation changes and uses a delay of 200,000 microseconds. It is possible to specify other data delays, such as:

SENSOR_DELAY_GAME   20,000 microsecond delay

SENSOR_DELAY_UI   60,000 microsecond delay

SENSOR_DELAY_FASTEST   0 microsecond delay

It is also possible to specify the delay as a value in microseconds. Using a larger delay imposes a lower load on the processor and therefore uses less power.

When you register a sensor with the registerListener() method, be sure you choose a delivery rate that is suitable for your application or use case. Sensors can provide data at very high rates. Allowing the system to send extra data that you do not need wastes system resources and uses battery power.

Lines 128–129: Once a sensor has registered a new value, the measurement readings are applied to the ball's velocity data members. sensorEvent.values[0] and sensorEvent.values[0] refer to the accelerometer reading along the *x*-axis and *y*-axis. In the remaining lines of the onSensorChanged() callback method, the text fields are updated with accelerometer feedback.

MyActivity.java

```
1   package com.cornez.roamingball;
2
3   import android.app.Activity;
4   import android.content.Context;
5   import android.content.pm.ActivityInfo;
6   import android.content.res.Configuration;
7   import android.hardware.Sensor;
8   import android.hardware.SensorEvent;
9   import android.hardware.SensorEventListener;
10  import android.hardware.SensorManager;
```

```
11   import android.os.Bundle;
12   import android.os.Handler;
13   import android.util.DisplayMetrics;
14   import android.view.LayoutInflater;
15   import android.view.Menu;
16   import android.view.MenuItem;
17   import android.widget.ImageView;
18   import android.widget.RelativeLayout;
19   import android.widget.TextView;
20
21
22   public class MyActivity extends Activity
23                            implements SensorEventListener {
24
25       private SensorManager sensorManager;
26       private Sensor sensorAccelerometer;
27
28       private LayoutInflater layoutInflater;
29       private RelativeLayout mainLayout;
30       private ImageView ballImage;
31       private Ball mBall;
32
33       private Thread movementThread;
34
35       static int TOP;
36       static int BOTTOM;
37       static int LEFT;
38       static int RIGHT;
39
40       private TextView x_axis;
41       private TextView y_axis;
42       private TextView z_axis;
43
44
45       @Override
46       protected void onCreate(Bundle savedInstanceState) {
47           super.onCreate(savedInstanceState);
48           setContentView(R.layout.activity_my);
49
50           // SET THE REFERENCES TO THE LAYOUTS
51           mainLayout = (RelativeLayout) findViewById(R.id.relativeLayout);
52           x_axis = (TextView) findViewById(R.id.textView2);
53           y_axis = (TextView) findViewById(R.id.textView4);
54           z_axis = (TextView) findViewById(R.id.textView6);
55
56           // ADD THE BALL AND INITIALIZE MOVEMENT SETTINGS
57           mBall = new Ball();
58           initializeBall();
59           layoutInflater = (LayoutInflater)
60               getSystemService(Context.LAYOUT_INFLATER_SERVICE);
```

```
61          ballImage = (ImageView)
62              layoutInflater.inflate(R.layout.ball_item,null);
63          ballImage.setX(50.0f);
64          ballImage.setY(50.0f);
65          mainLayout.addView(ballImage, 0);
66
67
68          // REGISTER THE SENSOR MANAGER
69          sensorManager = (SensorManager)
70              getSystemService(Context.SENSOR_SERVICE);
71          sensorAccelerometer =
72              sensorManager.getDefaultSensor(Sensor.TYPE_ACCELEROMETER);
73
74          // IMPLEMENT THE MOVEMENT THREAD
75          movementThread = new Thread(BallMovement);
76      }
77
78      private void initializeBall() {
79          //COMPUTE THE WIDTH AND HEIGHT OF THE DEVICE
80          DisplayMetrics metrics =
81              this.getResources().getDisplayMetrics();
82          int screenWidth = metrics.widthPixels;
83          int screenHeight = metrics.heightPixels;
84
85          //CONFIGURE THE ROAMING BALL
86          mBall.setX(50.0f);
87          mBall.setY(50.0f);
88          mBall.setWidth(225);
89
90          mBall.setVelocityX(0.0f);
91          mBall.setVelocityY(0.0f);
92
93          TOP = 0;
94          BOTTOM = screenHeight - mBall.getWidth();
95          LEFT = 0;
96          RIGHT = screenWidth - mBall.getWidth();
97      }
98
99      // REGISTER THE SENSOR LISTENER
100     protected void onResume() {
101         super.onResume();
102         sensorManager.registerListener(this, sensorAccelerometer,
103             SensorManager.SENSOR_DELAY_NORMAL);
104
105         //START THE THREAD
106         movementThread.start();
107     }
108
109     // UNREGISTER THE LISTENER
110     protected void onPause() {
```

```
111          super.onPause();
112          sensorManager.unregisterListener(this, sensorAccelerometer);
113      }
114
115      protected void onStop() {
116          super.onStop();
117          finish();
118      }
119
120      @Override
121      public void onDestroy(){
122          finish();
123          super.onDestroy();
124      }
125
126      public void onSensorChanged(SensorEvent sensorEvent) {
127
128          if (sensorEvent.sensor.getType() == Sensor.TYPE_ACCELEROMETER) {
129              mBall.setVelocityX(sensorEvent.values[0]);
130              mBall.setVelocityY(sensorEvent.values[1]);
131
132              x_axis.setText(" " + sensorEvent.values[0]);
133              y_axis.setText(" " + sensorEvent.values[1]);
134              z_axis.setText(" " + sensorEvent.values[2]);
135          }
136      }
137
138      public void onAccuracyChanged(Sensor arg0, int arg1) {
139      }
```

Lines 140–172:   BallMovement, on Lines 140–171 will determine the new ball location by computing it using a separate thread.

Lines 174–180:   threadHandler is associated with movementThread, specifically the Runnable BallMovement. This handler updates the ball's location on the screen.

MyActivity.java (*continued*)

```
140  // UPDATES THE BALL POSITION CONTINUOUSLY
141      private Runnable BallMovement = new Runnable() {
142          private static final int DELAY = 20;
143
144          public void run() {
145              try {
146                  while (true) {
147                      mBall.setX(mBall.getX() - mBall.getVelocityX());
148                      mBall.setY(mBall.getY() + mBall.getVelocityY());
149
```

```
150                     // CHECK FOR COLLISIONS
151                     if (mBall.getY() < TOP)
152                         mBall.setY(TOP);
153                     else   if (mBall.getY() > BOTTOM)
154                         mBall.setY(BOTTOM);
155
156                     if (mBall.getX() < LEFT)
157                         mBall.setX(LEFT);
158                     else if (mBall.getX() > RIGHT)
159                         mBall.setX(RIGHT);
160
161
162                     //DELAY BETWEEN ANIMATIONS
163                     Thread.sleep(DELAY);
164
165                     //HANDLE THE RELOCATION OF THE VIEW (IMAGEVIEW)
166                     threadHandler.sendEmptyMessage(0);
167                 }
168             } catch (InterruptedException e) {
169                 e.printStackTrace();
170             }
171         }
172     };
173
174     public Handler threadHandler = new Handler() {
175         public void handleMessage(android.os.Message msg) {
176             //HANDLE THE RELOCATION OF THE IMAGEVIEW
177             ballImage.setX(mBall.getX());
178             ballImage.setY(mBall.getY());
179         }
180     };
181
182
183     // @Override
184     // Stops the user from changing the Orientation.
185     // If the user rotates the device it will not
186     // change to the landscape orientation.
187     public void onConfigurationChanged(Configuration newConfig) {
188         // TODO Auto-generated method stub
189         super.onConfigurationChanged(newConfig);
190         setRequestedOrientation(
191             ActivityInfo.SCREEN_ORIENTATION_PORTRAIT);
192     }
193
194     @Override
195     public boolean onCreateOptionsMenu(Menu menu) {
196         // Inflate the menu.
197         getMenuInflater().inflate(R.menu.my, menu);
198         return true;
199     }
```

```
200
201     @Override
202     public boolean onOptionsItemSelected(MenuItem item) {
203         // Handle action bar item clicks here. The action bar will
204         // automatically handle clicks on the Home/Up button, so long
205         // as you specify a parent activity in AndroidManifest.xml.
206         int id = item.getItemId();
207         if (id == R.id.action_settings) {
208             return true;
209         }
210         return super.onOptionsItemSelected(item);
211     }
212 }
```

■ 8.5 Accelerometer and Force

Force is an occurrence that is related to acceleration. Newton's Second Law of Motion gives us an exact relationship between force, mass, and acceleration, which is expressed in the mathematical equation:

$$Force = Mass * Acceleration$$

Accelerometers are a natural choice for supplying information about the force applied to a device. Given a fixed mass, an Android device will experience an increase in force when the acceleration of the device is increased. When the accelerometer measures a zero force, the device is either still or moving at a constant speed. When the acceleration of the device is increased, such as a quick jerk of the hand, the accelerometer registers an increase in force. A decrease in movement is negative acceleration, or deceleration.

The accelerometer can efficiently report the combined effect of gravity. For example, to interpret certain gestures, such as an intended shake in the device, it may be necessary to remove the impact of gravity from the accelerometer readings and consider only acceleration engendered by the gesture.

The accelerometer is actually made up of three accelerometers, one for each axis: x, y, and z. Each one measures changes in velocity over time along a linear path. Combining all three accelerometers lets you detect accelerated force in any direction. While acceleration is a vector quantity, g-force is often expressed as a scalar, with positive g-forces pointing upward (indicating upward acceleration), and negative g-forces pointing downward.

Detecting the forces applied to a device requires the collection of accelerated movement on all three axes. This movement is measured in meters per second squared (the SI unit). The linear acceleration can be converted into a g-force measurement by neutralizing gravity, which is supplied by the constant SensorManager.GRAVITY_EARTH.

To compute a directionless g-force measurement, the Pythagorean theorem can be applied to the different acceleration axes readings.

Detecting force from the accelerometer is an important information source in healthcare applications, such as an application that monitors and detects when an elderly person has fallen down.

■ Lab Example 8-2: Shake Experiment and the Magic Answer App

The Magic Answer application in this lab example explores the use of a shake gesture. A shake gesture requires an accelerometer and monitoring directionless force. As a gesture, a single shake is a movement that involves two specific elements: a shake action followed by a period of rest. To register as a shake gesture, the computed force of the shake action must measure above a declared threshold. Declaring a threshold allows the app to distinguish between an intended vigorous shake and an accidental movement of the device.

Part 1: The Design

The Magic Answer application is similar in design to the popular toy, Magic Eight Ball. This application will be used to predict the answer to a "yes" or "no" question supplied by the user. When the user launches the application, a fixed layout appears that contains an `EditText` for input, a soft keyboard, and a `TextView` for output. The user enters the question and shakes the device to obtain a magic answer, as shown in Figure 8-8. The answer is generated randomly from a set of stored XML string values. Using the activity/rest/threshold model, the application can significantly reduce the possibility of responding to accidental or unwanted shaking.

Part 2: Application Structure and Setup

The settings for the application are as follows:

- Application Name: Shake Experiment
- Project Name: ShakeExperiment
- Package Name: `com.cornez.shakeexperiment`
- Android Form: Phone and Tablet
- Minimum SDK: API 18: Android 4.3 (Jelly Bean)
- Target SDK: API 21: Android 5.0 (Lollipop)
- Compile with: API 21: Android 5.0 (Lollipop)
- Activity Name: `MyActivity`
- Layout Name: `activity_my`

I FIGURE 8-8 Magic Answer application supplies an answer when the user shakes the device.

The Drawable folder contains the Android default launch icon, as well as the background image, `background.png`. The layout `activity_my.xml` is used for the user interface, featuring text fields for input and output. Three Java source files are required for this app. `ShakeDetector` is the implementation of the shake gesture. `MagicAnswer` is the data model for magic answers to the user's questions. `MyActivity` serves as the controller, acting as the intermediary between the layout elements, the shake events, and magic answers. The final project structure for this application is shown in Figure 8-9.

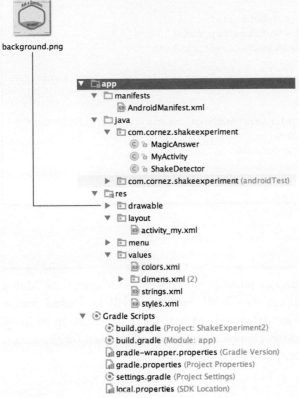

background.png

│ ▼ ☐ app
│   ▼ ☐ manifests
│   ☐ AndroidManifest.xml
│   ▼ ☐ java
│   ▼ ☐ com.cornez.shakeexperiment
│   ⓒ ☐ MagicAnswer
│   ⓒ ☐ MyActivity
│   ⓒ ☐ ShakeDetector
│   ▶ ☐ com.cornez.shakeexperiment (androidTest)
│   ▼ ☐ res
└─────▶ ☐ drawable
│   ▼ ☐ layout
│   ☐ activity_my.xml
│   ▶ ☐ menu
│   ▼ ☐ values
│   ☐ colors.xml
│   ▶ ☐ dimens.xml (2)
│   ☐ strings.xml
│   ☐ styles.xml
▼ ⊙ Gradle Scripts
   ⊙ build.gradle (Project: ShakeExperiment2)
   ⊙ build.gradle (Module: app)
   ☐ gradle-wrapper.properties (Gradle Version)
   ☐ gradle.properties (Project Properties)
   ⊙ settings.gradle (Project Settings)
   ☐ local.properties (SDK Location)

❙ FIGURE 8-9 The project structure of the Magic Answer application.

The accelerometer is required hardware for this application. This is specified in the `<uses-feature>`, Lines 10–12, in the `AndroidManifest.xml` file. The XML code listing for this file is as follows:

```
AndroidManifest.xml
1    <?xml version="1.0" encoding="utf-8"?>
2    <manifest xmlns:android="http://schemas.android.com/apk/res/android"
3        package="com.cornez.shakeexperiment" >
4
5        <application
6            android:allowBackup="true"
7            android:icon="@drawable/ic_launcher"
8            android:label="@string/app_name"
9            android:theme="@style/AppTheme" >
10           <uses-feature
11               android:name="android.hardware.sensor.accelerometer"
12               android:required="true" />
13
```

```
14          <activity
15              android:name=".MyActivity"
16              android:label="@string/app_name"
17              android:screenOrientation="portrait" >
18              <intent-filter>
19                  <action android:name="android.intent.action.MAIN" />
20
21                  <category
22                      android:name="android.intent.category.LAUNCHER" />
23              </intent-filter>
24          </activity>
25      </application>
26
27  </manifest>
```

Part 3: Resources

The `strings.xml` is used to declare possible answers to users' questions. Magic answers, stored in a `<string-array>` XML structure, will be loaded into a `MagicAnswer.class` data object when the application is launched. In addition to `strings.xml`, `color.xml` is created to define the color used for the screen design. Both XML code listings are as follows:

strings.xml
```
1   <?xml version="1.0" encoding="utf-8"?>
2   <resources>
3
4       <string name="app_name">Shake Experiment</string>
5       <string name="hello_world">Hello world!</string>
6       <string name="action_settings">Settings</string>
7
8       <!-- LABELS -->
9       <string name="enter_request">Enter your question here.</string>
10      <string name="answer">Shake your device to see the \n
11                  answer to your question.</string>
12
13      <!-- POSSIBLE MAGIC ANSWERS -->
14      <string-array name="magic_answer_list">
15          <item>Cannot say at this time.</item>
16          <item>It is not possible.</item>
17          <item>Have some sausages and ask again.</item>
18          <item>Do not know.</item>
19          <item>No no and no.</item>
20          <item>Sure, it is always possible.</item>
21          <item>Eventually.</item>
```

```
22          <item>Perhaps, if the year was 1930.</item>
23          <item>Just assume a yes and see what happens.</item>
24          <item>Put it out of your mind.</item>
25      </string-array>
26
27  </resources>
```

`colors.xml` declares a yellow color that matches the background and is used to give the application a more polished look.

```
colors.xml
1  <?xml version="1.0" encoding="utf-8"?>
2  <resources>
3      <color name="yellow">#EEE8AC</color>
4  </resources>
```

Part 4: The User Interface

The interface for the application requires two text elements: (1) an `EditText` for the user to input the question, and (2) a `TextView` to display the magic answer supplied once the user has shaken the device. Figure 8-10 shows the design and

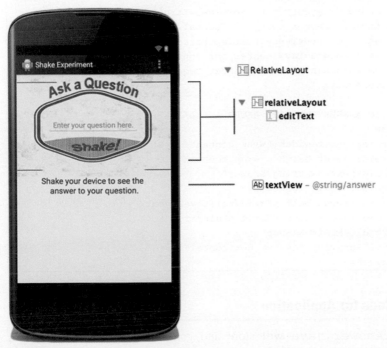

I FIGURE 8-10 The user interface for `activity_my.xml`.

hierarchical structure of Views comprising the layout. The XML code listing for
activity_my.xml is written as follows:

```
activity_my.xml
1   <RelativeLayout
2   xmlns:android="http://schemas.android.com/apk/res/android"
3       xmlns:tools="http://schemas.android.com/tools"
4       android:layout_width="fill_parent"
5       android:layout_height="fill_parent"
6       tools:context=".MyActivity"
7       android:background="@color/yellow">
8
9       <!-- USER ENTERED QUESTION -->
10      <RelativeLayout
11          android:layout_width="fill_parent"
12          android:layout_height="wrap_content"
13          android:layout_alignParentTop="true"
14          android:layout_centerHorizontal="true"
15          android:background="@drawable/background"
16          android:id="@+id/relativeLayout">
17
18          <EditText
19              android:layout_width="wrap_content"
20              android:layout_height="wrap_content"
21              android:id="@+id/editText"
22              android:layout_centerVertical="true"
23              android:layout_centerHorizontal="true"
24              android:inputType="textCapCharacters|textMultiLine"
25              android:gravity="center_horizontal"
26              android:hint="@string/enter_request" />
27      </RelativeLayout>
28
29      <!-- MAGIC ANSWER SUPPLIED AFTER A SHAKE -->
30      <TextView
31          android:layout_width="wrap_content"
32          android:layout_height="wrap_content"
33          android:text="@string/answer"
34          android:id="@+id/textView"
35          android:layout_below="@+id/relativeLayout"
36          android:layout_centerHorizontal="true"
37          android:textSize="20sp"
38          android:gravity="center_horizontal" />
39  </RelativeLayout>
```

Part 5: Source Code for Application

The class MagicAnswer.java will store and generate magic answers. When
instantiated, a MagicAnswer object will collect all answers defined in the array named magic_answer_list declared within strings.xml. The method

getRandomAnswer() will generate a random response when called upon by a shake gesture. The Java source code for MagicAnswer.java appears as follows:

```
MagicAnswer.java
1   package com.cornez.shakeexperiment;
2
3   import android.content.Context;
4
5   public class MagicAnswer {
6       private String[] allAnswers;
7
8       public MagicAnswer(Context context) {
9           //COLLECT ALL THE POSSIBLE ANSWERS FROM THE ARRAY
10          allAnswers =
11              context.getResources().getStringArray(
12              R.array.magic_answer_list);
13      }
14
15      public String getRandomAnswer() {
16          int i = (int) Math.ceil(Math.random() * (allAnswers.length-1));
17          return allAnswers[i];
18      }
19  }
```

The objective of ShakeDetector.java is to listen for a sensor event and determine whether a valid shake gesture has occurred. The user must shake the device fairly vigorously to produce a magic answer. A simple movement of the device or a small accidental rotation should not register as a shake. We must implement controls to be sure the user is shaking the device on purpose. The ShakeDetector.java class is written as follows:

Line 8:   The ShakeDetector.java class implements SensorEventListener.

Lines 13–14:   To trigger a new magic answer, the computed force of acceleration must be greater than a specified threshold level. In addition, the time between acceleration events must be within a fixed time. This will prevent the occurrence of accidental or constant shaking.

Lines 25–66:   The logic for a shake detection will be implemented in the onSensorChanged() method. This method is called every time a new acceleration value is available.

Lines 30–33:   G-force can be used to register as a shake. A shake gesture uses the accelerometer to detect movement in three directions:

Left to right:	values[0]
Top to bottom:	values[1]
Forward to backward:	values[2]

Lines 35–39:   All input vectors automatically include the Earth's gravitation forces. The position of the device in three-dimensional space is irrelevant. In addition, it is unknown which of the vectors (*x*, *y*, or *z*) is affected by the Earth's gravity. Therefore, gravitational effects can be neutralized. In this way, the app can respond to an intended shake.

Lines 41–47:   Rather than finding the main direction of the shake, the directionless g-force of the device's movement can be computed.

Lines 50–63:   A shake is detected if the computed g-force is bigger than the force threshold and a significant amount of time has elapsed since the last acceleration change.

Sensor data can change at a high rate, which means the system may call the onSensorChanged() method quite often. As a best practice, you should perform work within the onSensorChanged() method as efficiently as possible.

```
ShakeDetector.java
1    package com.cornez.shakeexperiment;
2
3    import android.hardware.Sensor;
4    import android.hardware.SensorEvent;
5    import android.hardware.SensorEventListener;
6    import android.hardware.SensorManager;
7
8    public class ShakeDetector implements SensorEventListener {
9
10
11       private long mTimeOfLastShake;
12
13       private static final float SHAKE_THRESHOLD_GRAVITY = 22.0f;
14       private static final int SHAKE_TIME_LAPSE = 500;   //IN MILLISECONDS
15
16
17       // OnShakeListener THAT WILL BE NOTIFIED WHEN A SHAKE IS DETECTED
18       private OnShakeListener mShakeListener;
19
20       // CONSTRUCTOR SETS THE SHAKE LISTENER
21       public ShakeDetector(OnShakeListener shakeListener) {
22          mShakeListener = shakeListener;
23       }
24
25       @Override
26       public void onSensorChanged(SensorEvent sensorEvent) {
```

```
27
28        if (sensorEvent.sensor.getType() == Sensor.TYPE_ACCELEROMETER) {
29
30            //TASK 1: COLLECT SENSOR VALUES ON ALL THREE AXIS
31            float x = sensorEvent.values[0];
32            float y = sensorEvent.values[1];
33            float z = sensorEvent.values[2];
34
35            //TASK 2: CONVERT EACH ACCELEROMETER MEASUREMENT INTO
36            //   A G-FORCE MEASUREMENT BY SUBTRACTING GRAVITY_EARTH.
37            float gForceX = x - SensorManager.GRAVITY_EARTH;
38            float gForceY = y - SensorManager.GRAVITY_EARTH;
39            float gForceZ = z - SensorManager.GRAVITY_EARTH;
40
41            //TASK 3: COMPUTE  G-FORCE AS A DIRECTIONLESS MEASUREMENT
42            // NOTE: G-FORCE WILL BE APPROXIMATELY 1 WHEN
43            //        THERE IS NO SHAKING MOVEMENT.
44            double value = Math.pow(gForceX, 2.0) +
45                           Math.pow(gForceY, 2.0) +
46                           Math.pow(gForceZ, 2.0);
47            float gForce = (float) Math.sqrt(value);
48
49
50            //TASK 4: DETERMINE IF THE G-FORCE IS ENOUGH TO
51            //REGISTER AS A SHAKE
52            if (gForce > SHAKE_THRESHOLD_GRAVITY) {
53                //IGNORE CONTINUOUS SHAKES -
54                //    CHECK THAT 500 MILLISECONDS HAVE LAPSED
55                final long now = System.currentTimeMillis();
56                if (mTimeOfLastShake + SHAKE_TIME_LAPSE > now) {
57                    return;
58                }
59                mTimeOfLastShake = now;
60
61                //THE LISTENER REGISTERED A SHAKE
62                mShakeListener.onShake();
63            }
64        }
65    }
66
67    @Override
68    public void onAccuracyChanged(Sensor sensor, int accuracy) {
69    }
70
71    public interface OnShakeListener {
72        public void onShake();
73    }
74 }
```

MyActivity.java is the only Activity of this basic application. It serves as the controller for the application and is used to register and unregister the sensor listeners and interact with the user. The Java code listing appears as follows:

Lines 60–65:   It is important to disable sensors when you do not need them (such as onPause()); otherwise you will drain your battery very fast. Be sure to unregister a sensor's listener when you are finished using the sensor or when the sensor activity pauses. If a sensor listener is registered and its activity is paused, the sensor will continue to acquire data and to use battery resources unless you unregister the sensor. The following code shows how to use the onPause() method to unregister a listener:

```
MyActivity.java
 1   package com.cornez.shakeexperiment;
 2
 3   import android.app.Activity;
 4   import android.content.Context;
 5   import android.hardware.Sensor;
 6   import android.hardware.SensorManager;
 7   import android.os.Bundle;
 8   import android.view.Menu;
 9   import android.view.MenuItem;
10   import android.widget.EditText;
11   import android.widget.TextView;
12
13   public class MyActivity extends Activity  {
14       private SensorManager mSensorManager;
15       private Sensor mSensorAccelerometer;
16       private ShakeDetector mShakeDetector;
17
18       MagicAnswer mMagicAnswer;
19       private TextView mAnswerTV;
20       private EditText mQuestionET;
21
22       @Override
23       protected void onCreate(Bundle savedInstanceState) {
24           super.onCreate(savedInstanceState);
25           setContentView(R.layout.activity_my);
26
27           // TASK 1: SET THE REFERENCES TO THE LAYOUT ELEMENTS
28           mQuestionET = (EditText) findViewById(R.id.editText);
29           mAnswerTV = (TextView) findViewById(R.id.textView);
30           mMagicAnswer = new MagicAnswer (MyActivity.this);
31
32           // TASK 2: REGISTER THE SENSOR MANAGER AND
33           //         SETUP THE SHAKE DETECTION
34           mSensorManager = (SensorManager)
```

```
35           getSystemService(Context.SENSOR_SERVICE);
36       mSensorAccelerometer =
37           mSensorManager.getDefaultSensor(Sensor.TYPE_ACCELEROMETER);
38       mShakeDetector = new ShakeDetector(new
39           ShakeDetector.OnShakeListener() {
40           @Override
41           public void onShake() {
42               displayMagicAnswer();
43           }
44       });
45
46   }
47
48   private void displayMagicAnswer(){
49       String magicAnswer = mMagicAnswer.getRandomAnswer();
50       mAnswerTV.setText(magicAnswer);
51   }
52
53   @Override
54   protected void onResume() {
55       super.onResume();
56       mSensorManager.registerListener(mShakeDetector,
57           mSensorAccelerometer, SensorManager.SENSOR_DELAY_UI);
58   }
59
60   @Override
61   protected void onPause() {
62       mSensorManager.unregisterListener(mShakeDetector,
63           mSensorAccelerometer);
64       super.onPause();
65   }
66
67   @Override
68   public boolean onCreateOptionsMenu(Menu menu) {
69       // Inflate the menu.
70       getMenuInflater().inflate(R.menu.my, menu);
71       return true;
72   }
73
74   @Override
75   public boolean onOptionsItemSelected(MenuItem item) {
76       // Handle action bar item clicks here. The action bar will
77       // automatically handle clicks on the Home/Up button, so long
78       // as you specify a parent activity in AndroidManifest.xml.
79       int id = item.getItemId();
80       if (id == R.id.action_settings) {
81           return true;
82       }
83       return super.onOptionsItemSelected(item);
84   }
85 }
```

■ 8.6 Sensor Batching

Android offers sensor batching for the development of fitness and health applications. Hardware sensor batching is a technique that is designed to reduce the power consumed by sensors commonly used in fitness, location tracking, and monitoring service applications. Sensor batching allows hardware sensors to collect and deliver sensor-related data more efficiently in batches, rather than individually.

For example, consider an accelerometer-driven application, used for healthcare purposes, to track a user's physical activity level. Assume that this application is designed to measure activity level as the number of steps the person takes. To detect steps, the application must capture readings from the accelerometer and distinguish the step pattern. Such an application ideally should run in the background, counting steps and tracking location. These tasks require that a process must remain in an active state, which can cause the battery life to lose power at a faster rate. With the release of Android 4.4, the use of sensor batching has reduced the impact of an active state process. Sensor batching provides optimization to decrease power consumed by ongoing sensor activities. When a sensor is in batch mode, the application processor is prevented from waking up to receive each event. Instead, these events can be grouped and processed together.

Collecting and delivering sensor events efficiently within batches, rather than individually as they are typically detected, lets the application processor remain in a low-power idle state until batches are delivered. It is possible to request batched events from any sensor using a standard event listener, as well as control the interval at which batches are received.

Sensor batching is ideal for low-power, long-running tasks, particularly for fitness and healthcare detection that requires efficient continuous monitoring, even while the screen is off and the system is asleep.

At the time of this writing in early 2015, sensor batching is not currently available on all Android devices.

8.6.1 Step Counter and Step Detector

Physical activity tracking is required for pedometer-type applications. Pedometer applications are generally designed to focus on step counting, but they can often be customized to consider other activities, such as running and stair climbing. To monitor physical activity accurately, such an application should be able to detect different types of activity.

Many Android mobile devices have been equipped with sensors that can be used to collect data for activity classification. To create a physical activity classification model, data are often required from several sensors, including the camera and GPS.

A simple approach to detecting and classifying physical activity requires the use of accelerometer data along with two activity classification sensors: the step detector and step counter.

The step detector can recognize when a user takes a step and then triggers an event as a result. By analyzing accelerometer input, this sensor can detect an individual step movement. Following each recognized step, it delivers an event with a value of 1.0 and a time-stamp, indicating when the step occurred. The constant TYPE_STEP_DETECTOR is used to specify the step detector.

The step counter, identified by the constant TYPE_STEP_COUNTER, can track the total number of steps taken since the last device reboot. It triggers an event for each detected step and adds to the accumulated number of steps since the sensor was first registered by the application. Step functionality, logic, and management are built into the platform and underlying hardware. This means there is no need to maintain your own detection algorithms in your application.

In the following segment of code, the sensor manager is used to access the sensors for a pedometer application. It should be noted that a TYPE_STEP_COUNTER event will occur with a higher latency than an event from a TYPE_STEP_DETECTOR. This is because the TYPE_STEP_COUNTER algorithm requires more processing to eliminate false positives. In this way, the TYPE_STEP_COUNTER may be slower to deliver events, but its results are often more accurate.

```
1    // REGISTER THE SENSOR MANAGER
2    sensorManager = (SensorManager)
3        getSystemService(Context.SENSOR_SERVICE);
4    sensorAccelerometer =
5        sensorManager.getDefaultSensor(Sensor.TYPE_ACCELEROMETER);
6
7    stepCounterSensor =
8        sensorManager.getDefaultSensor(Sensor.TYPE_STEP_COUNTER);
9    stepDetectorSensor =
10       sensorManager.getDefaultSensor(Sensor.TYPE_STEP_DETECTOR);
11
12   //SENSOR VERIFICATION
13   if (stepCounterSensor == null){
14       Toast.makeText(this, "This device does not contain the
15           appropriate step sensor.", Toast.LENGTH_LONG).show();
16   }
```

In this segment of code, a listener is registered for the step counter sensor in batch mode. If the maximum delay is set to zero, events will be delivered in a continuous mode without batching. In addition, the initial step counter value can be reset.

```
1    // REGISTER THE SENSOR LISTENER
2    final boolean batchMode = sensorManager.registerListener(
3        sensorListener,
4        stepCounterSensor,
5        SensorManager.SENSOR_DELAY_NORMAL,
6        maximumDelay);
7
```

In the following code segment, `onSensorChanged()` is used to detect a step action.

```
1    public void onSensorChanged(SensorEvent event) {
2        Sensor sensor = event.sensor;
3        float[] values = event.values;
4        int value = -1;
5
6        if (values.length > 0) {
7            value = (int) values[0];
8        }
9
10       if (sensor.getType() == Sensor.TYPE_STEP_COUNTER) {
11           stepDetectorTV.setText("Step Counter Detected : " + value);
12       } else if (sensor.getType() == Sensor.TYPE_STEP_DETECTOR) {
13           stepDetectorTV.setText("Step Detector Detected : " + value);
14       }
15   }
```

■ 8.7 Composite Sensors

Android devices typically come equipped with three embedded sensors: a magnetometer, an accelerometer, and a gyroscope. These three sensors are base sensors and work independently of one another. Activating one of these sensors does not deactivate or reduce the rate of another base sensor.

Base sensors can be used in tandem to give developers flexibility in the creation of composite sensor types. When monitoring a physical environment, base sensors are often used jointly to create sensors that are finely tuned to an application's needs. For example, when determining the direction a device is facing, an interface can rely on raw data provided by both an accelerometer and a magnetometer. This composite sensor feedback will determine a device's position relative to the world's frame of reference, as opposed to the application's frame of reference.

Examples of composite sensor types include a game rotation vector sensor and geomagnetic rotation sensor. A composite game rotation vector relies on the underlying accelerometer and gyroscope base sensors. A geomagnetic rotation vector relies on the accelerometer and magnetometer. Table 8-3 shows a collection of composite sensors.

■ Lab Example 8-3: Geomagnetic Rotation—Compass

This lab example implements a geomagnetic rotation vector for measuring the orientation of an Android device relative to a north, south, east, and west direction. The completed application is a compass app, as shown in Figure 8-11.

TABLE 8-3 Composite Sensors

Game rotation vector	Measures the orientation of the device relative to the East-North-Up coordinates frame. Base class: accelerometer and gyroscope.
Geomagnetic rotation vector	This sensor is similar to game rotation vector; however, it is continuously powered and consumes a very low amount of battery compared with the game rotation vector (accelerometer and gyroscope). Game rotation vector is more sensitive than the geomagnetic rotation vector and is triggered by games, which receive 3-D tilt data as input. Base class: accelerometer and magnetometer.
Gravity	Measures the direction and magnitude of gravity in the device's coordinates. Units are m/s². The coordinate system is the same as is used for the acceleration sensor. When the device is at rest, the output of the gravity sensor should be identical to that of the accelerometer. Base class: accelerometer and gyroscope.
Linear acceleration	Indicates the linear acceleration of the device, not including gravity. The output is `TYPE_ACCELERATION` value minus `TYPE_GRAVITY` value. Base class: accelerometer, magnetometer, and gyroscope.
Step counter	A time-stamp is used to indicate when a step has occurred. This corresponds to when the foot hits the ground, generating a high variation in acceleration. Base class: accelerometer.
Step detector	Both the step detector and the step counter will detect when the user is walking, running, and climbing up the stairs. The Step counter and detector events are not triggered when the user is biking or driving. Base class: accelerometer.

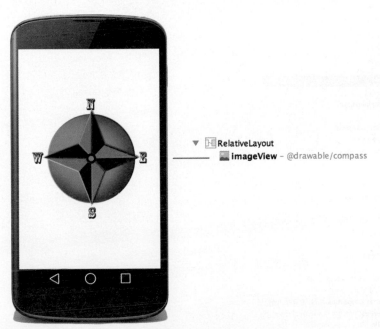

FIGURE 8-11 The layout structure for input_layout.xml.

Part 1: Application Structure and Setup

The settings for the application are as follows:

- Application Name: Compass
- Project Name: Compass
- Package Name: `com.cornez.compass`
- Android Form: Phone and Tablet
- Minimum SDK: API 18: Android 4.3 (Jelly Bean)
- Target SDK: API 21: Android 5.0 (Lollipop)
- Compile with: API 21: Android 5.0 (Lollipop)
- Activity Name: `MyActivity`
- Layout Name: `activity_my`

The launcher icon for this application is set to the Android default ic_launcher.png file. An additional PNG file, the compass image, has been added to the `res/drawable` directories.

The final project structure, shown in Figure 8-12, contains a single Activity and its associated layout XML user interface.

FIGURE 8-12 Project structure for the Compass application.

A geomagnetic rotation vector sensor is a composite sensor that will be defined by the accelerometer in tandem with the magnetometer. The application specifies each feature in a separate <uses-feature> element within the AndroidManifest file.

Lines 5 and 6 indicate that the application will use motion readings from an accelerometer and directional readings from a magnetometer (compass) on the device. In addition, a portrait screen orientation is set for the application.

```
AndroidManifest.xml
1   <?xml version="1.0" encoding="utf-8"?>
2   <manifest xmlns:android="http://schemas.android.com/apk/res/android"
3       package="com.cornez.compass" >
4
5       <uses-feature android:name="android.hardware.sensor.accelerometer"/>
6       <uses-feature android:name="android.hardware.sensor.compass"/>
7
8       <application
9           android:allowBackup="true"
10          android:icon="@drawable/ic_launcher"
11          android:label="@string/app_name"
12          android:theme="@android:style/Theme.Light.NoTitleBar" >
13          <activity
14              android:name=".MyActivity"
15              android:screenOrientation="portrait"
16              android:label="@string/app_name" >
17              <intent-filter>
18                  <action android:name="android.intent.action.MAIN" />
19
20                  <category
21                      android:name="android.intent.category.LAUNCHER" />
22              </intent-filter>
23          </activity>
24      </application>
25
26  </manifest>
```

Part 2: The User Interface

In addition to the default strings used in the application, strings.xml contains a description of the compass image that will be displayed to the user. The complete strings.xml file appears as follows:

```
strings.xml
1   <?xml version="1.0" encoding="utf-8"?>
2   <resources>
3
4       <string name="app_name">Compass</string>
5       <string name="hello_world">Hello world!</string>
6       <string name="action_settings">Settings</string>
```

```
 7
 8        <string name="compass_image">Compass Image</string>
 9
10   </resources>
```

The layout XML file associated with the launched activity, `activity_my.xml`, is designed to display a compass that will rotate as the user alters the direction. The layout design is shown in Figure 8-11 and the XML code appears as follows. The compass image is stored in the `ImageView` named imageView and is placed in the center of the screen.

activity_my.xml
```
 1   <RelativeLayout
 2   xmlns:android="http://schemas.android.com/apk/res/android"
 3       xmlns:tools="http://schemas.android.com/tools"
 4       android:layout_width="match_parent"
 5       android:layout_height="match_parent"
 6       android:paddingLeft="@dimen/activity_horizontal_margin"
 7       android:paddingRight="@dimen/activity_horizontal_margin"
 8       android:paddingTop="@dimen/activity_vertical_margin"
 9       android:paddingBottom="@dimen/activity_vertical_margin"
10       tools:context=".MyActivity">
11
12
13       <ImageView
14           android:layout_width="wrap_content"
15           android:layout_height="wrap_content"
16           android:id="@+id/imageView"
17           android:layout_centerVertical="true"
18           android:layout_centerHorizontal="true"
19           android:src="@drawable/compass"
20           android:contentDescription="@string/compass_image" />
21   </RelativeLayout>
```

Part 3: Source Code for Application

All the source code for the application is placed in `MyActivity.java`. This class implements a `SensorEventListener`.

Line 20:   The compass image is declared. This image will be rotated when the sensor event listener indicates a change in orientation.

Line 23:   The compass angle is recorded in degrees. This variable is declared as a float data-type.

Lines 30–31:   The device's sensor data will be collected and stored in the arrays `accelerometer` and `geomagnetic`.

Lines 44–47:   The two sensors, `sensorAccelerometer` and `sensorMagnetometer`, are assigned.

```
MyActivity.java
1   package com.cornez.compass;
2
3   import android.app.Activity;
4   import android.content.Context;
5   import android.hardware.Sensor;
6   import android.hardware.SensorEvent;
7   import android.hardware.SensorEventListener;
8   import android.hardware.SensorManager;
9   import android.os.Bundle;
10  import android.view.Menu;
11  import android.view.MenuItem;
12  import android.view.animation.Animation;
13  import android.view.animation.RotateAnimation;
14  import android.widget.ImageView;
15
16
17  public class MyActivity extends Activity implements SensorEventListener{
18
19      // COMPASS IMAGE ON SCREEN
20      private ImageView compassImage;
21
22      // RECORD THE COMPASS ANGLE IN DEGREES
23      private float currentDegree = 0.0f;
24
25      // SENSOR MANAGER AND THE SENSORS THAT WILL BE MONITORED
26      private SensorManager mSensorManager;
27      private Sensor sensorAccelerometer;
28      private Sensor sensorMagnetometer;
29
30      private float[]accelerometer;
31      private float[] geomagnetic;
32
33      @Override
34      protected void onCreate(Bundle savedInstanceState) {
35          super.onCreate(savedInstanceState);
36          setContentView(R.layout.activity_my);
37
38          // REFERENCE THE COMPASS IMAGE ON THE LAYOUT
39          compassImage = (ImageView) findViewById(R.id.imageView);
40
41          // INITIALIZE THE SENSOR CAPABILITIES
42          mSensorManager = (SensorManager)
43                  getSystemService(Context.SENSOR_SERVICE);
44          sensorAccelerometer = mSensorManager
45                  .getDefaultSensor(Sensor.TYPE_ACCELEROMETER);
46          sensorMagnetometer = mSensorManager
47                  .getDefaultSensor(Sensor.TYPE_MAGNETIC_FIELD);
48
49      }
```

onResume() is overridden to register the listeners for both accelerometer and magnetometer sensors. onPause() unregisters the listeners to save battery life.

```
MyActivity.java (continued)
50        @Override
51        protected void onResume() {
52            super.onResume();
53            //SENSOR_DELAY_GAME IS THE ONLY ONE THAT WORKS
54            mSensorManager.registerListener(this, sensorAccelerometer,
55                    SensorManager.SENSOR_DELAY_GAME);
56            mSensorManager.registerListener(this, sensorMagnetometer,
57                    SensorManager.SENSOR_DELAY_GAME);
58
59        }
60
61        @Override
62        protected void onPause() {
63            super.onPause();
64            mSensorManager.unregisterListener(this);
65        }
```

When the registered listener triggers an onSensorChanged event, data are collected from the two base sensors, accelerometer and geomagnetic. The length and contents of the values array depend on a sensor type.

Line 73: Data values for the accelerometer are collected along the three axes in SI units.

Line 76: Magnetic field data values for the Sensor.TYPE_MAGNETIC_FIELD are collected along three axes in micro-Tesla units.

Lines 79–91: The rotation of the compass is computed using the inclination matrix (i) and the rotation matrix (r), provided by the method call getRotationMatrix(). A vector from the device coordinate system is transformed to the world's coordinate system.

Lines 86–88: If the rotation of the device has been altered, the rotation matrix (r) is used to compute the device's new orientation.

Line 91: The orientation change will be determined along the *x*-axis, as shown in Figure 8-13.

Lines 94–98: An animation is produced to control the rotation of the compass. Rotation will occur in reverse, from the current degree to –degree.

Lines 100–108: The duration of the animation is set, and the animation is applied. Once the animation is complete, the angle of the compass orientation is recorded.

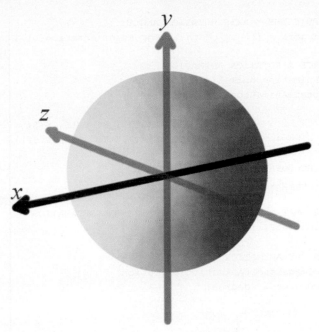

▌ FIGURE 8-13 The orientation change will be determined along the *x*-axis.

```
MyActivity.java (continued)
66      @Override
67      public void onSensorChanged(SensorEvent event) {
68          //ROTATION ANIMATION IS SET FOR 1000 MILLISECONDS
69          final int DELAY = 1000;
70
71          //COLLECT DATA FROM AN ACCELEROMETER DRIVEN EVENT
72          if (event.sensor.getType() == Sensor.TYPE_ACCELEROMETER)
73              accelerometer= event.values;
74          //COLLECT DATA FROM A MAGNETOMETER DRIVEN EVENT
75          if (event.sensor.getType() == Sensor.TYPE_MAGNETIC_FIELD)
76              geomagnetic = event.values;
77
78          //CHECK IF BOTH SENSORS CAUSED THE EVENT
79          if (accelerometer != null && geomagnetic != null) {
80              float r[] = new float[9];
81              float i[] = new float[9];
82              boolean foundRotation = SensorManager.getRotationMatrix(
83                      r, i, accelerometer,geomagnetic);
84
85              //ROTATION HAS OCCURRED
86              if (foundRotation) {
87                  float orientation[] = new float[3];
88                  SensorManager.getOrientation(r, orientation);
89
```

```
90                    // COMPUTE THE X-AXIS ROTATION ANGLE
91                    float degree = (float) Math.toDegrees(orientation[0]);
92
93                    // CREATE A ROTATION ANIMATION
94                    RotateAnimation animation = new
95                        RotateAnimation(currentDegree,
96                                    -degree,
97                                    Animation.RELATIVE_TO_SELF, 0.5f,
98                                    Animation.RELATIVE_TO_SELF, 0.5f);
99
100                   //SET THE DURATION OF THE ANIMATION
101                   animation.setDuration(DELAY);
102
103                   //SET ANIMATION AFTER THE END OF THE TRANSFORMATION
104                   animation.setFillAfter(true);
105
106                   //BEGIN THE ANIMATION
107                   compassImage.startAnimation(animation);
108                   currentDegree = -degree;
109               }
110           }
111       }
112
113       @Override
114       public void onAccuracyChanged(Sensor sensor, int accuracy) {
115       }
116
117
118       @Override
119       public boolean onCreateOptionsMenu(Menu menu) {
120           // Inflate the menu.
121           getMenuInflater().inflate(R.menu.my, menu);
122           return true;
123       }
124
125       @Override
126       public boolean onOptionsItemSelected(MenuItem item) {
127           // Handle action bar item clicks here. The action bar will
128           // automatically handle clicks on the Home/Up button, so long
129           // as you specify a parent activity in AndroidManifest.xml.
130           int id = item.getItemId();
131           if (id == R.id.action_settings) {
132               return true;
133           }
134           return super.onOptionsItemSelected(item);
135       }
136   }
```

■ 8.8 Camera

The camera sensor is one of the most frequently used sensors on an Android device. Even though the camera is ubiquitous on mobile devices, not all Android devices contain a camera, even though this was a requirement at one time. The necessity of a camera on a device was relaxed when Android began to be used on set-top boxes. Set-top boxes are devices that allow users to listen to music, view content, and play games on their television sets.

To prevent an application that requires a camera from being installed on devices that do not feature a camera component, a <uses-feature> tag should be placed in the AndroidManifest file. This will allow Google Play to filter the appropriate devices. The android.hardware.camera feature is shown in the code line below:

```
1      <uses-feature android:name="android.hardware.camera" />
```

In addition to providing Google Play with the ability to filter out devices that do not meet an application's sensor requirements, it is also important to check the availability of the camera within an activity that uses a camera feature. The existence of camera components can be verified by using `PackageManager`. Android devices often come equipped with multiple cameras. For example, a back-facing camera is most often used for taking typical photographs. A front-facing camera may also be available on a device because strategically it is highly suitable for making video calls. The availability of camera features can be identified with three constants:

FEATURE_CAMERA_ANY:	The device has at least one camera or can support an external camera being connected to it.
FEATURE_CAMERA:	The device has a camera facing away from the screen. This is also referred to as a rear-facing camera.
FEATURE_CAMERA_FRONT:	The device has a front-facing camera.

The following segment of code illustrates the use of a `PackageManager` and a `Toast` to indicate which camera features are available. `PackageManager` is used to retrieve information related to the application packages that are currently installed on a device.

```
1   PackageManager packageManager = this.getPackageManager();
2
3   //CHECK FOR ANY CAMERA
4   boolean hasAnyCamera = packageManager.hasSystemFeature(
5       PackageManager.FEATURE_CAMERA_ANY);
6   if (hasAnyCamera == true) {
```

```
7      Toast.makeText(this, "Any camera exists.",Toast.LENGTH_SHORT).show();
8   }else {
9      Toast.makeText(this, "No camera exists.", Toast.LENGTH_SHORT).show();
10  }
11
12  //CHECK FOR A FRONT FACING CAMERA
13  boolean hasFrontCamera = packageManager.hasSystemFeature(
14      PackageManager.FEATURE_CAMERA_FRONT);
15  if (hasFrontCamera == true) {
16     Toast.makeText(this, "Front camera exists."
17         Toast.LENGTH_SHORT).show();
18  }else {
19     Toast.makeText(this, "No front camera.", Toast.LENGTH_SHORT).show();
20  }
21
22  //CHECK FOR A REAR FACING CAMERA
23  boolean hasRearCamera =
24  packageManager.hasSystemFeature(PackageManager.FEATURE_CAMERA);
25  if (hasRearCamera == true) {
26     Toast.makeText(this, "Rear camera exists.",
27         Toast.LENGTH_SHORT).show();
28  } else {
29     Toast.makeText(this, "No rear camera.", Toast.LENGTH_SHORT).show();
30  }
```

Camera sensors use arrays with millions of tiny light photosites to record a single image. Compared to other sensors, the incorporation of a camera sensor into an application requires the collection of a large amount of data. Before developing an application that uses a camera, the requirements for photo capturing and storage should be considered.

Captured photographs and video can be stored in various ways. For example, an application can allow or prohibit other applications from accessing the captured images or video. If the application is required to store its captured photographs or video in external storage, then writing to external storage requires special permission. Permission for writing to external storage can be set using a <uses-permission> tag in the AndroidManifest.xml file, as shown on Lines 1 and 2 below. When recording video, a <uses-permission> must also be set to record the audio element of the video. This is shown on Lines 4 and 5.

```
1       <uses-permission
2           android:name="android.permission.WRITE_EXTERNAL_STORAGE" />
3
4       <uses-permission
5           android:name="android.permission.RECORD_AUDIO" />
```

Two general options are available to developers when creating an application that requires capturing photos or video. Choosing the appropriate option depends upon how much camera flexibility is necessary for the application. For example, if the application requires limited camera control, the preferred option is to utilize the device's built-in camera application. If integrating photos is only a small part of your application, one of the device's installed camera applications can be used. The built-in camera application can be launched, using an explicit intent, and the resulting images can be stored for specific use by the current application or made available to other applications. Most Android-powered devices have at least one built-in camera.

In special cases, full camera integration and specialized control is required by an application. In these circumstances, a custom camera interface must be built. It should be noted that creating a customized camera user interface with special features is beyond the scope of this introductory textbook.

8.8.1 The Built-in Camera Application

Using a device's built-in camera requires the camera application to be launched from an application's activity. An `Intent` needs to be invoked to activate the external camera application, and the captured photograph or video can be accessed when focus is returned to the calling activity.

To access a captured image or video recording from a camera activity, the camera intent must be initiated using the `startActivityForResult()` call. As opposed to using `startActivity()` to initiate the intent, the call to `start ActivityForResult()` allows the activity to not only start the camera application, but also to receive the captured photo as a result. The captured photo can be accessed in the `onActivityResult()` callback.

The following segment of code illustrates how such an `Intent` is created and used to capture a photograph. The device's camera application requests an image capture using `MediaStore.ACTION_IMAGE_CAPTURE`. `MediaStore` is a media provider that contains metadata for all available media on both internal and external storage devices. On Line 4, a path where the photograph will be stored is specified.

The `startActivityForResult()` method, on Line 7, starts the `Intent` that launches the camera application. The second argument in the `startActivity ForResult()` call is a request code that can be used to set a specific request, which can also be used to identify the action that took place. The request code in the code segment below is specfied as `CAMERA_CAPTURE_PHOTO_REQUEST_CODE`. This will be used to indicate that the camera will take a simple photograph.

The `resolveActivity()` method will return the activity class name that should execute the intent. This ensures that the intent can be safely handled by an activity.

```
1   Intent takePhotoIntent= new Intent(MediaStore.ACTION_IMAGE_CAPTURE);
2
3   fileUri = getOutputMediaFileUri(MEDIA_TYPE_IMAGE);
4   intent.putExtra(MediaStore.EXTRA_OUTPUT, fileUri);
5
```

```
6    if (takePhotoIntent.resolveActivity(getPackageManager()) != null) {
7        startActivityForResult(takePhotoIntent,
8                            CAMERA_CAPTURE_PHOTO_REQUEST_CODE);
9    }
```

Once the built-in camera application has been launched from an activity and the user has completed the intended task of capturing video or a photograph, the user can exit the external camera application. Upon exiting the camera app, focus will be returned to the calling activity. Since the camera was launched using `startActivityForResult()`, the Android system will automatically call the activity's `onActivityResult(int requestCod,int resultCode, Intent data)` method upon return. The original `requestCode` supplied to `startActivityForResult()` is also returned, making it easy to identify the specific request of the intent. For example, a `requestCode` can be used to identify whether the result is from a request to capture an image, such as `CAMERA_ CAPTURE_PHOTO_REQUEST_CODE`, or a request to capture a video.

The `resultCode` parameter in `onActivityResult()` specifies the general outcome of the operation. For example, if the resultCode returns RESULT_OK, then the camera successfully captured a photo or video. A value of RESULT_CANCELED means the user backed out of the camera operation, or the camera failed to take a photo or record video for some reason.

The `Intent data` is used to return result data to the caller. The `data` parameter, on Line 3, carries the result data from the camera. Applications included with the Android platform offer their own APIs that you can count on for specific result data, where various data can be attached to Intent "extras." The Camera app encodes and returns the captured photo as a Bitmap in the "data" extra, which is delivered to `onActivityResult()`.

The following segment of code illustrates the retrieval of a photograph captured by the camera app. Line 12 places this bitmap in an `ImageView`.

```
1    @Override
2    protected void onActivityResult(int requestCode,
3                                int resultCode, Intent data) {
4
5        //CHECK IF THE ACTIVITY REQUEST WAS TO CAPTURE AN IMAGE
6        if (requestCode == REQUEST_IMAGE_CAPTURE) {
7
8            // CHECK THAT USER HAS SUCCESSFULLY CAPTURED A PHOTO
9            if (resultCode == RESULT_OK) {
10               Bundle extras = data.getExtras();
11               Bitmap imageBitmap = (Bitmap) extras.get("data");
12               mImageView.setImageBitmap(imageBitmap);
13           }
```

```
14
15          // CHECK THAT USER HAS CANCELLED THE CAMERA CAPTURE
16          else if (resultCode == RESULT_CANCELED) {
17              Toast.makeText(getApplicationContext(),
18                      "User cancelled photo capture", Toast.LENGTH_SHORT)
19                      .show();
20          }
21
22          // CHECK THAT FAILED TO CAPTURE THE PHOTO
23          else {
24              Toast.makeText(getApplicationContext(),
25                      " Failed to capture photo", Toast.LENGTH_SHORT)
26                      .show();
27          }
28      }
```

BitmapFactory creates the imageBitmap object from various sources, including files, streams, and byte-arrays. Managing multiple full-sized images can be tricky with limited memory. If you find your application running out of memory after displaying just a few images, you can dramatically reduce the amount of dynamic heap used by expanding the JPEG into a memory array that is already scaled to match the size of the destination view. The following example method demonstrates this technique.

The method inSampleSize() requests the decoder to subsample the original image. If set to a value > 1, this method returns a smaller image to save memory. The sample size is the number of pixels in either dimension that correspond to a single pixel in the decoded bitmap. For example, inSampleSize == 4 returns an image that is 1/4 the width/height of the original, and 1/16 the number of pixels. Any value <= 1 is treated the same as 1. Note that the decoder uses a final value based on powers of 2; any other value will be rounded down to the nearest power of 2.

```
1       // Get the dimensions of the bitmap
2       BitmapFactory.Options mOptions = new BitmapFactory.Options();
3
4       // Determine how much to scale down the image
5       mOptions.inSampleSize = mSize;
6
7       Bitmap bitmap = BitmapFactory.decodeFile(mCurrentPhotoPath, mOptions);
```

Once a photograph or video recording is captured, it should be saved on the device in the public external storage slot so that it may be accessible to other applications. The proper directory for shared photos is provided by getExternalStoragePublicDirectory(), with the DIRECTORY_PICTURES argument. This directory is shared among all applications. To read to and write from this location requires WRITE_EXTERNAL_STORAGE permission. The permission allows both reading and writing. If the photos taken by your app need to remain private to your application, you can instead use the directory provided by getExternalFilesDir(). In this case, the media scanner cannot access these files because they are private to your app.

The instructions in Lines 3–17 will create a fully qualified file name containing a time stamp, prefix, suffix, and directory.

```
1     private File createImageFile () throws IOException {
2
3         //TASK 1: CREATE A TIMESTAMP
4         String timeStamp = new SimpleDateFormat("yyyyMMdd_HHmmss",
5                 Locale.getDefault()).format(new Date());
6
7         //TASK 2: CONSTRUCT THE PREFIX
8         String imageFileName = JPEG_FILE_PREFIX + timeStamp + "_";
9         File album = Environment.getExternalStoragePublicDirectory(
10                Environment.DIRECTORY_PICTURES);
11
12        //TASK 3: GENERATE A FILE WITH A PREFIX AND SUFFIX
13        File imageFile = File.createTempFile(
14                    imageFileName,          /* prefix */
15                    JPEG_FILE_SUFFIX,       /* suffix */
16                    album                   /* directory */
17        );
18        return imageFile;
19    }
```

Adding a captured photograph to a Media Provider's database makes it available in the Android Gallery application. This means that other applications will have access to it. This is performed using an Intent of type ACTION_MEDIA_SCANNER_SCAN_FILE.

The code segment shown below illustrates how a full-size photo is added to a specified album in the device's photo gallery. This photo gallery relies on the Media Provider's database, making it available in the Android Gallery application and to other apps. The path to the file will be contained in the mCurrentPhotoPath field, shown on Line 7.

If you choose to save media content to the directory provided by getExternalFilesDir(), the media scanner cannot access the files because they are private to your app.

```
1     //TASK 1: CREATE AN INTENT - REQUEST THE MEDIA SCANNER TO
2     //        SCAN A FILE AND  ADD IT TO THE MEDIA DATABASE
3     Intent mediaScanIntent = new
4             Intent(Intent.ACTION_MEDIA_SCANNER_SCAN_FILE);
5
```

```
6     //TASK 2: A FILE ENTITY IDENTIFIED BY A PATHNAME
7     File f = new File(mCurrentPhotoPath);
8
9     //TASK 3: A UNIFORM RESOURCE IDENTIFIER IS CREATED
10    //          TO IDENTIFY THE FILE RESOURCE.
11    Uri contentUri = Uri.fromFile(f);
12
13    //TASK 4: THE DATA FOR THE INTENT IS SET TO contentUri.
14    mediaScanIntent.setData(contentUri);
15    this.sendBroadcast(mediaScanIntent);
```

■ Lab Example 8-4: Basic Camera

This lab example explores the usage of the built-in camera application for capturing photos. The application design, as shown in Figure 8-14, allows the user to launch the camera application by tapping the button labeled "Take a Photo." Once the camera application launches, the user can take a photograph, which will be displayed as a small preview. The user then has the option of storing the photo in an album in the photo gallery.

Part 1: Application Structure and Setup

The Basic Camera application does not provide any special features and is just meant to take advantage of the built-in camera application. It is designed to work on phones and tablets running Android 4.4+ KitKat.

The settings for the application are as follows:

- Application Name: Basic Camera
- Project Name: BasicCamera
- Package Name: com.cornez.basiccamera
- Android Form: Phone and Tablet
- Minimum SDK: API 18: Android 4.3 (Jelly Bean)
- Target SDK: API 21: Android 5.0 (Lollipop)
- Compile with: API 21: Android 5.0 (Lollipop)
- Activity Name: MyActivity
- Layout Name: activity_my

The final project structure for the Basic Camera is shown in Figure 8-15.

The orientation of the screen will be locked into portrait mode, which will be done in the AndroidManifest.xml file. To ensure proper device compatibility, it is important to add the <uses-feature> declaration, which describes the camera hardware as

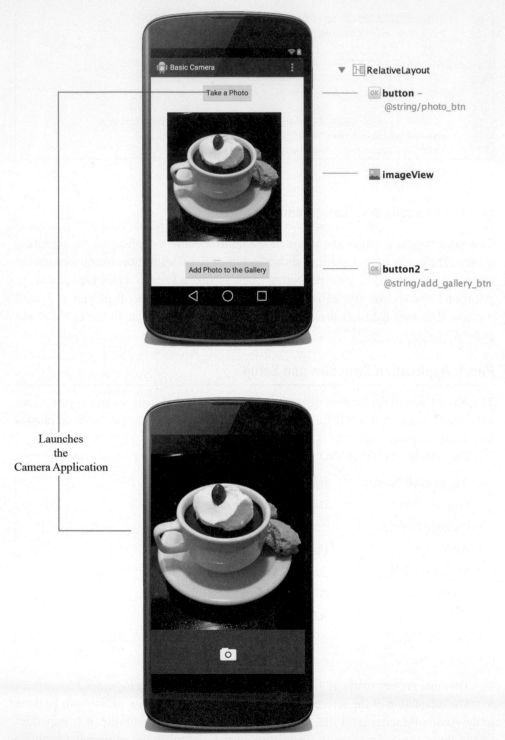

FIGURE 8-14 The Basic Camera application uses the built-in camera.

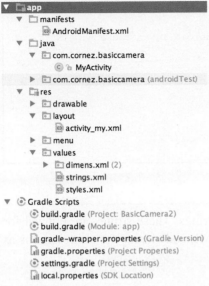

| FIGURE 8-15 Project structure for the Basic Camera application.

a device feature for this application. The `required` attribute on Line 7 specifies the camera hardware as a requirement. When declaring a camera hardware feature, a set of permissions must also be set to access the camera API. Requesting the permission grants your application access to the appropriate hardware and software. Permission is set to allow writing to external storage, which allows captured photographs to be saved.

```
AndroidManifest.xml

1   <?xml version="1.0" encoding="utf-8"?>
2   <manifest xmlns:android="http://schemas.android.com/apk/res/android"
3       package="com.cornez.basiccamera" >
4
5       <uses-feature
6           android:name="android.hardware.camera"
7           android:required="true"/>
8       <uses-permission
9           android:name="android.permission.WRITE_EXTERNAL_STORAGE"/>
10      <uses-permission
11          android:name="android.permission.CAMERA"/>
12
13      <application
14          android:allowBackup="true"
15          android:icon="@drawable/ic_launcher"
16          android:label="@string/app_name"
17          android:theme="@style/AppTheme" >
18          <activity
19              android:name=".MyActivity"
20              android:screenOrientation="portrait"
```

```
21              android:label="@string/app_name" >
22          <intent-filter>
23              <action android:name="android.intent.action.MAIN" />
24
25              <category
26                  android:name="android.intent.category.LAUNCHER" />
27          </intent-filter>
28      </activity>
29  </application>
30
31 </manifest>
```

Part 2: The User Interface

The values for this application are limited to strings. These strings are utilized for the buttons in the application's interface. The XML code listing for strings.xml is as follows:

```
strings.xml
1  <?xml version="1.0" encoding="utf-8"?>
2  <resources>
3
4      <string name="app_name">Basic Camera</string>
5      <string name="hello_world">Hello world!</string>
6      <string name="action_settings">Settings</string>
7
8      <string name="photo_btn">Take a Photo</string>
9      <string name="photo_preview">Photo Preview</string>
10     <string name="add_gallery_btn">Add Photo to the Gallery</string>
11
12 </resources>
```

The application uses a single-user interface screen. The layout file `activity_my.xml` is associated with the activity `MyActivity.java`. The UI requirements include a button to launch the built-in camera application, an ImageView to display a preview of the photograph taken by the camera application, and a button to allow storage of the just-taken photo in an album so the user can access and manage it on the device. The XML code listing for the user interface is as follows:

```
activity_my.xml
1  <RelativeLayout
2  xmlns:android="http://schemas.android.com/apk/res/android"
3      xmlns:tools="http://schemas.android.com/tools"
4      android:layout_width="match_parent"
5      android:layout_height="match_parent"
6      android:paddingLeft="@dimen/activity_horizontal_margin"
7      android:paddingRight="@dimen/activity_horizontal_margin"
```

```
8      android:paddingTop="@dimen/activity_vertical_margin"
9      android:paddingBottom="@dimen/activity_vertical_margin"
10     tools:context=".MyActivity">
11
12
13     <Button
14         android:layout_width="wrap_content"
15         android:layout_height="wrap_content"
16         android:text="@string/photo_btn"
17         android:id="@+id/button"
18         android:layout_alignParentTop="true"
19         android:layout_centerHorizontal="true"
20         android:onClick="takePhoto"/>
21
22     <ImageView
23         android:layout_width="fill_parent"
24         android:layout_height="wrap_content"
25         android:id="@+id/imageView"
26         android:layout_below="@+id/button"
27         android:layout_centerHorizontal="true"
28         android:layout_marginTop="5dp"
29         android:contentDescription="@string/photo_preview" />
30
31     <Button
32         android:layout_width="wrap_content"
33         android:layout_height="wrap_content"
34         android:text="@string/add_gallery_btn"
35         android:id="@+id/button2"
36         android:layout_alignParentBottom="true"
37         android:layout_centerHorizontal="true"
38         android:onClick="addPhotoToGallery"/>
39 </RelativeLayout>
```

Part 3: Source Code for Application

MyActivity.java contains the complete source code for the application. It should be noted that the activity must check the camera's availability at runtime by calling hasSystemFeature(PackageManager.FEATURE_CAMERA). In order to save space and simplify the lab, this task is not performed in this lab example. The listing for this file appears as follows:

Lines 51–76:   The takePhoto() method is the onClick handler that is activated when the user decides to take a photograph. A camera intent is constructed to make a request to capture a photo through an existing camera application. Once the built-in camera app has launched and the photograph has been taken, control is returned back to our application.

Lines 54–55:   An Intent to launch the default camera activity is created. This intent requests an image using the intent type `MediaStore.ACTION_IMAGE_CAPTURE`. This specified action requests an image from the built-in camera application. For an Intent action that requests a video from the built-in camera application, the intent type would be specified as `MediaStore.ACTION_VIDEO_CAPTURE`.

Line 58:   The resulting photo is temporarily stored in a file identified by a pathname. This file is set up in Lines 78–84.

Lines 65–66:   Using a camera intent to capture an image requires extra information. In this example, a `Uri` object is used to store the requested photograph.

Lines 69–70:   The `startActivityForResult()` method executes the camera intent. The request code specified by this intent is `CAMERA_CAPTURE_IMAGE_REQUEST_CODE`. Once the built-in camera application launches, the user can take a photograph. The method `onActivityResult()`, located on Lines 86–107, receives the callback and the data from this camera intent.

MyActivity.java

```
1   package com.cornez.basiccamera;
2
3   import android.app.Activity;
4
5   import android.content.Intent;
6   import android.graphics.Bitmap;
7   import android.graphics.BitmapFactory;
8   import android.net.Uri;
9   import android.os.Bundle;
10  import android.os.Environment;
11  import android.provider.MediaStore;
12  import android.view.Menu;
13  import android.view.MenuItem;
14  import android.view.View;
15  import android.widget.ImageView;
16  import android.widget.Toast;
17  import java.io.File;
18  import java.io.IOException;
19  import java.text.SimpleDateFormat;
20  import java.util.Date;
21  import java.util.Locale;
22
23
24  public class MyActivity extends Activity {
25
```

```
26     //ACTIVITY REQUEST CODE
27     private static final int CAMERA_CAPTURE_IMAGE_REQUEST_CODE = 1;
28
29     //DIRECTORY NAME TO STORE CAPTURED PHOTOGRAPHS
30     private static final String IMAGE_DIRECTORY_NAME = "mycamera";
31
32     //FILE URL TO STORE THE PHOTOGRAPH FOR RESTORATION
33     private Uri fileUri;
34
35     private ImageView photoPreview;
36     private String mCurrentPhotoPath;
37
38     private static final String JPEG_FILE_PREFIX = "IMG_";
39     private static final String JPEG_FILE_SUFFIX = ".jpg";
40
41
42     @Override
43     protected void onCreate(Bundle savedInstanceState) {
44         super.onCreate(savedInstanceState);
45         setContentView(R.layout.activity_my);
46
47         //SET REFERENCES TO THE IMAGE VIEW FOR THE PHOTO PREVIEW
48         photoPreview = (ImageView) findViewById(R.id.imageView);
49     }
50
51     public void takePhoto(View view) {
52
53         //COMPOSE A CAMERA INTENT
54         Intent takePhotoIntent = new Intent
55                 (MediaStore.ACTION_IMAGE_CAPTURE);
56
57         // A FILE WILL BE USED TO SETUP PATHNAME INFO FOR THE PHOTO
58         File f = null;
59
60         try {
61             //CREATE THE IMAGE FILE FOR THE PHOTO INTENT
62             f = setUpPhotoFile();
63
64             // EXTENDED DATA - PATHNAME - IS ADDED TO THE INTENT
65             takePhotoIntent.putExtra(MediaStore.EXTRA_OUTPUT,
66                 Uri.fromFile(f));
67
68             //START THE PHOTO CAPTURE INTENT
69             startActivityForResult(takePhotoIntent,
70                 CAMERA_CAPTURE_IMAGE_REQUEST_CODE);
71         } catch (IOException e) {
72             e.printStackTrace();
73             f = null;
74             mCurrentPhotoPath = null;
75         }
```

```
76          }
77
78          private File setUpPhotoFile() throws IOException {
79              File f = createImageFile();
80
81              //STORE THE ABSOLUTE PATH OF THIS FILE
82              mCurrentPhotoPath = f.getAbsolutePath();
83              return f;
84          }
```

Lines 88–108:   It is important to get the image back from the camera application. The Android camera application encodes the photo in the return `Intent` delivered to `onActivityResult()` as a small `Bitmap` in the extras, within the data key. Once the built-in camera application has executed and a photo has successfully been taken, the photograph is intercepted within the `onActivityResult()` method. The image intercepted from the `data` parameter is useful as a thumbnail, but it is not a full-sized image.

Line 88:   The `requestCode` returns either an image or a video. The image request code specified in this example application is `CAMERA_CAPTURE_IMAGE_REQUEST_CODE`.

Line 89:   When the camera application exits, the `resultCode` specifies whether the existing activity resulted in a canceled operation. If the results from the camera intent are okay, the results can be retrieved. The `resultCode` parameter provides information that identifies when the user has successfully captured a photo, canceled the image capture, or if the camera app has failed.

Lines 92–96:   A small preview of the photograph is constructed. Memory can be an issue when viewing captured photographs; therefore, it is usually a good idea to prescale the target bitmap into which the image file is decoded.

The method call `inSampleSize()` requests a decoder to subsample the original image, returning a smaller image. The sample size is the number of pixels in either dimension that correspond to a single pixel in the decoded bitmap. For example, `inSampleSize == 4` returns, an image that is one-quarter the width and height of the original.

The camera application will save a full-size photo if a filename is provided. A captured photo is often saved on the device in public external storage so that it is accessible by other applications.

Line 97:   The content of the `ImageView` named `photoPreview` is set to `bitmap`.

Lines 109–117:   An image file is created. The name of the file is constructed as a unique name using a time-stamp combined with a prefix, suffix, and an album name within the photo gallery.

Lines 119–129:   An album directory named "`mycamera`," declared as a constant in Line 30, is created, unless one already exists. This album name is placed in the top-level public external storage directory. At this location, users are allowed to manage their own files. `getExternalStoragePublicDirectory()` provides a directory of shared photos.

Lines 131–144:   `addPhotoToGallery()`is the onclick handler for the "Add Photo to Gallery" button. Photographs or video files can be added to a device's gallery by using a broadcast intent. In this example, the intent operation requests the media scanner to scan the image file and add it to the media database.

```
MyActivity.java (continued)
85       @Override
86       protected void onActivityResult(int requestCode,
87                                    int resultCode, Intent data) {
88           if (requestCode == CAMERA_CAPTURE_IMAGE_REQUEST_CODE) {
89               if (resultCode == Activity.RESULT_OK) {
90                   //CONSTRUCT A PREVIEW OF THE PHOTO
91                   // PLACE THE PHOTO IN THE IMAGE VIEW
92                   BitmapFactory.Options mOptions = new
93                       BitmapFactory.Options();
94                   mOptions.inSampleSize = 4;
95                   Bitmap bitmap = BitmapFactory.decodeFile
96                       (mCurrentPhotoPath, mOptions);
97                   photoPreview.setImageBitmap(bitmap);
98
99               } else if (resultCode == Activity.RESULT_CANCELED) {
100                  Toast.makeText(this, "Image capture canceled",
101                      Toast.LENGTH_LONG).show();
102              } else {
103                  Toast.makeText(this, "Image capture failed",
104                      Toast.LENGTH_LONG).show();
105              }
106          }
107      }
108
109      private File createImageFile () throws IOException {
110          String timeStamp = new SimpleDateFormat("yyyyMMdd_HHmmss",
111              Locale.getDefault()).format(new Date());
```

```
112         String imageFileName = JPEG_FILE_PREFIX + timeStamp + "_";
113         File album = getAlbumDir();
114         File imageFile = File.createTempFile(imageFileName,
115             JPEG_FILE_SUFFIX, album);
116         return imageFile;
117     }
118
119     private File getAlbumDir() {
120         File albumDir =  new
121             File(Environment.getExternalStoragePublicDirectory(
122             Environment.DIRECTORY_PICTURES), IMAGE_DIRECTORY_NAME);
123
124         if (albumDir == null){
125             Toast.makeText(this, "Failed to create a directory",
126                 Toast.LENGTH_LONG).show();
127         }
128         return albumDir;
129     }
130
131     public void addPhotoToGallery (View view){
132         if (mCurrentPhotoPath != null) {
133             Intent mediaScanIntent = new
134               Intent("android.intent.action.MEDIA_SCANNER_SCAN_FILE");
135
136             File f = new File(mCurrentPhotoPath);
137             Uri contentUri = Uri.fromFile(f);
138             mediaScanIntent.setData(contentUri);
139             this.sendBroadcast(mediaScanIntent);
140
141             //CLEAR OUT THE PATH FOR THE NEXT PHOTO
142             mCurrentPhotoPath = null;
143         }
144     }
145
146     @Override
147     protected void onSaveInstanceState(Bundle outState) {
148         super.onSaveInstanceState(outState);
149         //SAVE THE FILE URL IN A BUNDLE TO BE RESTORED
150         outState.putParcelable("file_uri", fileUri);
151     }
152
153
154     @Override
155     protected void onRestoreInstanceState(Bundle savedInstanceState) {
156         super.onRestoreInstanceState(savedInstanceState);
157
158         // GRAB THE SAVED FILE FROM THE STORED BUNDLE AND RESTORE IT
159         fileUri = savedInstanceState.getParcelable("file_uri");
```

```
160        }
161
162
163        @Override
164        public boolean onCreateOptionsMenu(Menu menu) {
165            // Inflate the menu.
166            getMenuInflater().inflate(R.menu.my, menu);
167            return true;
168        }
169
170        @Override
171        public boolean onOptionsItemSelected(MenuItem item) {
172            // Handle action bar item clicks here. The action bar will
173            // automatically handle clicks on the Home/Up button, so long
174            // as you specify a parent activity in AndroidManifest.xml.
175            int id = item.getItemId();
176            if (id == R.id.action_settings) {
177                return true;
178            }
179            return super.onOptionsItemSelected(item);
180        }
181
182 }
```

■ 8.9 Manipulating Photos

When creating applications that integrate built-in camera hardware, the resulting images may need to be edited or manipulated in some fashion. For example, users may be allowed to apply style filters to a captured image, or an application may require that an image be reconstructed with effects based on photography techniques.

A digital image is a two-dimensional array of pixels, each pixel containing a numeric value indicating variations of color. Traditional cameras on an Android device are engineered with filters that detect light that masks each pixel for only a single color: red, green, or blue. Editing an image, such as applying a filter, requires editing this pixel information.

A captured image can be manipulated by altering pixels, which store four values (red, green, blue, and alpha), with effects such as brightness, darkness, and grayscale or color conversions. Each of these values is stored in one byte of memory, with 0 representing no intensity and 255 representing full intensity. For example, a red value of 0 is no red at all, and a red value of 255 has the maximum amount of red. All of the colors that we can make in a picture are made up of combinations of red, green, and blue values, and each of those pixels sits at a specific (x, y) location in the photo.

The following color chips show several RGB examples.

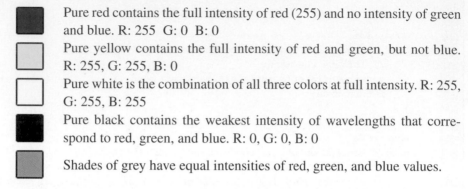

Pure red contains the full intensity of red (255) and no intensity of green and blue. R: 255 G: 0 B: 0

Pure yellow contains the full intensity of red and green, but not blue. R: 255, G: 255, B: 0

Pure white is the combination of all three colors at full intensity. R: 255, G: 255, B: 255

Pure black contains the weakest intensity of wavelengths that correspond to red, green, and blue. R: 0, G: 0, B: 0

Shades of grey have equal intensities of red, green, and blue values.

Figure 8-16 shows a collection of photographs. The original photograph, located in the upper-left corner, was manipulated in three ways. The first manipulation produced a yellow filter by maintaining the original intensities for red and green, and reducing the blue intensity by 50 percent. A pink filter was achieved by maintaining the

❙ FIGURE 8-16 Photographs with added filters.

original color intensities, with the exception of green, which is reduced by 50%. The final photograph was manipulated by reducing both red and green values.

```
1    //ELIMINATE RED
2    redVal = 0;
3
4    //REDUCE GREEN BY 25%
5    greenVal -= greenVal * .25;
6
7    //INCREASE BLUE BY 10%
8    blueVal += blueValue * .1;
9
10   //APPLY NEW COLOR VALUES
11   bmp.setPixel(x, y, color);
```

The Android Bitmap class, android.graphics.bitmap, is used for handling images, as shown in the previous lab example. The following segment of code illustrates how a color filter can be applied to a bitmap. The bitmap result of this code, shown in Figure 8-17, has been manipulated by swapping color values.

FIGURE 8-17 A photograph with swapped blue, red, and green values.

Lines 1–3:   A drawable bitmap is instantiated and populated with the image stored within an ImageView, `photoPreview`. You can instantiate a bitmap in many ways; in this example, we are editing a bitmap of an image from the imageView.

Line 5:   `getBitmap()` is called to retrieve the bitmap from the `BitmapDrawable` object and assign it to `bmp`.

Lines 6–7:   A mutable bitmap object is instantiated with the same width and height as `bmp`. The bitmap configuration is set to match the original bitmap.

Lines 9–10:   The Bitmap object, `bmp`, is processed pixel by pixel.

Line 11:   getPixel () returns the color values at the specified *x*, *y* pixel location.

Lines 12–14:   Each color value for the red, green, and blue components is retrieved using `Color.red(p)`, `Color.green(p)`, and `Color.blue(p)`, where p is the pixel.

Lines 16–18:   Color values are swapped. Red will acquire the blue value, blue will acquire the green value, and green will acquire the red value.

Line 20:   `setPixel()` is called to write the specified color into the editedBmt object at the given *x*, *y* coordinate.

Line 24:   The content of the `ImageView`, `photoPreview`, is replaced with `editedBmp`.

```
1   private void manipulatePhotoImageView() {
2        BitmapDrawable abmp = (BitmapDrawable)
3                             photoPreview.getDrawable();
4
5        Bitmap bmp = abmp.getBitmap();
6        Bitmap editedBmp = Bitmap.createBitmap(bmp.getWidth(),
7                            bmp.getHeight(), bmp.getConfig());
8
9        for (int x = 0; x < bmp.getWidth(); x++) {
10            for (int y = 0; y < bmp.getHeight(); y++){
11                int p = bmp.getPixel (x, y);
12                int r = Color.red(p);
13                int g = Color.green(p);
14                int b = Color.blue(p);
15
16                int red = (int) (b);
17                int blue = (int) (g);
18                int green = (int) (r);
19
20                editedBmp.setPixel (x, y, Color.argb(Color.alpha(p),
21                                    red, green, blue));
22            }
23        }
24        photoPreview.setImageBitmap(editedBmp);
25
26    }
```

The `Bitmap` class provides a set of methods for handling the management and transformation of raw bitmaps decoded by the camera. The following is a list of the more common methods:

copy ():   This method is used to copy a bitmap's pixels into a new bitmap. It requires the original bitmap configuration as an argument and a Boolean value indicating whether the bitmap is mutable.

`createBitmap():`	There are multiple methods for creating a bitmap. At its most basic, `createBitmap()` returns an immutable bitmap from a source bitmap. The new bitmap may be the same object as source, or a copy may have been made. It is initialized with the same density as the original bitmap. A mutable bitmap can also be generated by createBitmap(). It is also possible to create a mutable bitmap, which requires a display structure, `DisplayMetrics`, to describe the initial density of the bitmap. In addition, a width and height can be specified along with an array of color values to apply to corresponding pixels.
`extractAlpha():`	Returns a new bitmap that captures the alpha values of the original bitmap.
`getDensity():`	Returns the density, the scaling factor, of a given bitmap. It is also possible to set the density of a bitmap using `setDensity()`.
`getRowBytes():`	Returns the number of bytes between rows of the native bitmap pixels.

The simplest level adjustment that can be made to an image is to negate the image. In basic terms, this means converting white to black and black to white. For color bitmaps, this means adjusting colors by converting them to their complementary color. For example, the complement of red is cyan. The following segment of code illustrates the negating of color in a captured photograph, as shown in Figure 8-18.

FIGURE 8-18 A photograph with its color negated.

As each pixel is processed, the complement of the existing color values are produced by subtracting the red, green, and blue components from 255, the maximum intensity. For example, white will appear when the red component is 255, the green component is 255, and the blue component is 255. Black is produced when white is subtracted from 255, resulting in red: 0, green: 0, and blue: 0.

```
1    BitmapDrawable drawableBmp = (BitmapDrawable)
2                    photoPreview.getDrawable();
3
4
5    Bitmap bmp = drawableBmp.getBitmap();
6    Bitmap invertedBmp = Bitmap.createBitmap(bmp.getWidth(),
7                    bmp.getHeight(), bmp.getConfig());
8
9    for (int x = 0; x < bmp.getWidth(); x++) {
10       for (int y = 0; y < bmp.getHeight(); y++){
11           //GRAB A PIXEL
12           int p = bmp.getPixel (x, y);
13
14           //COMPUTE NEGATIVE RGB
15           int negativeRed = 255 - Color.red(p);
16           int negativeGreen = 255 - Color.green(p);
17           int negativeBlue = 255 - Color.blue(p);
18
19           //SET THE INVERTED RGB VALUES FOR THE PIXEL
20           invertedBmp.setPixel (x, y, Color.argb(Color.alpha(p),
21                             negativeRed,
22                             negativeGreen,
23                             negativeBlue));
24       }
25    }
26
27    //DISPLAY THE INVERTED BITMAP
28    photoPreview.setImageBitmap(invertedBmp);
```

■ Lab Example 8-5: ASCII Camera Conversion Application

ASCII art consists of images pieced together from characters defined by the ASCII Standard Character Set. An ASCII Camera Converson application is a tool for converting captured photographs to ASCII art.

This lab example explores the creation of an ASCII conversion program that quantifies the grayscale value of each pixel in a photograph captured by the camera. A black and white text component will be created to contain assigned ASCII text characters that approximate the grayscale value. The application will generate a complete representation of a given photograph as a TextView containing a collection of characters, as shown in Figure 8-19.

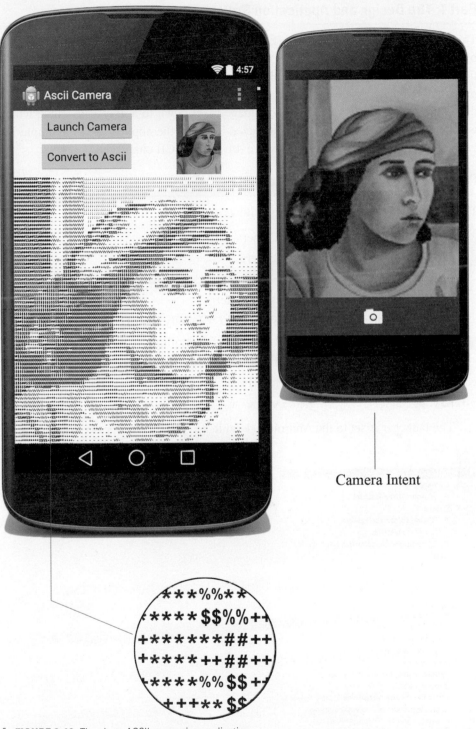

Camera Intent

FIGURE 8-19 The photo ASCII conversion application.

Part 1: The Design and Application Structure

This application is designed to work with images, specifically photographs captured by the built-in camera, defined by pixel data. The ASCII art generated by this application uses a monospace font, where all characters are identical in width. Courier is the most popular monospace font, and is used in this lab exercise. The application produces the ASCII art by sampling each image pixel down to a grayscale value, which is then assigned a specific ASCII character. To keep the application as a simple lab exercise, the application uses only twelve different ASCII characters.

Part 2: Application Structure and Setup

The settings for the application are as follows:

- Application Name: Ascii Camera
- Project Name: AsciiCamera
- Package Name: `com.cornez.asciicamera`
- Android Form: Phone and Tablet
- Minimum SDK: API 18: Android 4.3 (Jelly Bean)
- Target SDK: API 21: Android 5.0 (Lollipop)
- Compile with: API 21: Android 5.0 (Lollipop)
- Activity Name: `MyActivity`
- Layout Name: `activity_my`

The launcher is set to the Android's default `ic_launcher.png` file.

❚ FIGURE 8-20 Project structure for the photo ASCII conversion application.

The structure for this application is simplified with a single Activity and no drawable images, as shown in Figure 8-20. The orientation of the screen is locked into portrait mode, as shown in the following `AndroidManifest.xml` file.

Lines 6–12:   The `<uses-permission>` and `<uses-feature>` tags for the camera hardware and external storage are shown.

AndroidManifest.xml

```
1   <?xml version="1.0" encoding="utf-8"?>
2   <manifest
3       xmlns:android="http://schemas.android.com/apk/res/android"
4       package="com.cornez.asciicamera" >
5
6       <uses-permission
7           android:name="android.permission.CAMERA"/>
8       <uses-permission
9           android:name="android.permission.WRITE_EXTERNAL_STORAGE"/>
10      <uses-feature
11          android:name="android.hardware.Camera"
12          android:required="true" />
13
14      <application
15          android:allowBackup="true"
16          android:icon="@drawable/ic_launcher"
17          android:label="@string/app_name"
18          android:theme="@style/AppTheme" >
19          <activity
20              android:name=".MyActivity"
21              android:screenOrientation="portrait"
22              android:label="@string/app_name" >
23              <intent-filter>
24                  <action android:name="android.intent.action.MAIN" />
25
26                  <category
27                      android:name="android.intent.category.LAUNCHER" />
28              </intent-filter>
29          </activity>
30      </application>
31
32  </manifest>
```

Part 3: The String Resources

The `strings.xml` file is the only resource requirement for the application. This file supplies the text labels for the UI buttons.

strings.xml

```
1   <?xml version="1.0" encoding="utf-8"?>
2   <resources>
3
```

```
4        <string name="app_name">Photo to Ascii</string>
5        <string name="hello_world">Hello world!</string>
6
7        <string name="camera">Launch Camera</string>
8        <string name="convert_ascii">Convert to Ascii</string>
9        <string name="thumbnail">Photo Thumbnail</string>
10
11   </resources>
```

Part 4: The User Interface

The layout design for the application is shown in Figure 8-21. `activity_my.xml` uses a `RelativeLayout` as the root tag. The UI components consist of a button to launch the built-in-camera, a small thumbnail view to see the returned camera photograph, and a button to perform the ASCII conversion. In addition, a `TextView` element is used to store and display the generated ASCII characters.

To appear as a small thumbnail view, a photograph is resized to a lower resolution, while maintaining its aspect ratio. As shown in Figure 8-21, the thumbnail view will be stored in the `ImageView` named `imageView1`.

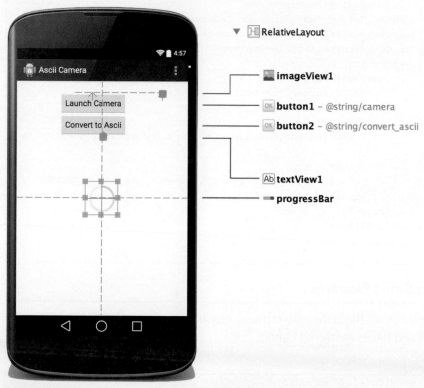

❙ FIGURE 8-21 `activity_my.xml` layout structure.

Lines 12–21: The first button on the layout is used to launch the Camera application. This button, identified by `button1`, is registered with an `onClick` event to be handled by `toCamera()`.

Lines 23–31: The second button on the layout is used to convert a captured photograph into ASCII artwork. This button is identified by `button2`. Its `onClick` event handler is `toAsciiConversion()`.

Lines 33–40: The `ImageView` identified by `imageView1` will be used to display a reduced-size version of the captured photograph: a thumbnail.

Lines 42–50: The generated ASCII artwork is a text element that contains ASCII text characters. This string of characters, once generated, will be displayed in the TextView element named `textView1`. The typeface attribute is set to monospace. Most ASCII art is rendered using a monospace font, where characters each occupy the same amount of horizontal space. This differs from variable-width fonts, where the characters vary in size from one another, as do spacings between the characters.

Lines 52–58: While the application is processing the photograph and generating the ASCII artwork, a progress bar will appear. This provides the user with rudimentary feedback about the conversion progress; that is, it is an indication that a process is occurring.

```
activity_my.xml
1   <RelativeLayout
2   xmlns:android="http://schemas.android.com/apk/res/android"
3       xmlns:tools="http://schemas.android.com/tools"
4       android:layout_width="match_parent"
5       android:layout_height="match_parent"
6       android:paddingLeft="@dimen/activity_horizontal_margin"
7       android:paddingRight="@dimen/activity_horizontal_margin"
8       android:paddingTop="@dimen/activity_vertical_margin"
9       android:paddingBottom="@dimen/activity_vertical_margin"
10      tools:context=".MyActivity">
11
12      <Button
13          android:id="@+id/button1"
14          android:layout_width="wrap_content"
15          android:layout_height="wrap_content"
16          android:layout_alignParentLeft="true"
17          android:layout_alignParentTop="true"
18          android:layout_marginLeft="80dp"
19          android:layout_marginTop="10dp"
```

```
20        android:text="@string/camera"
21        android:onClick="toCamera"/>
22
23    <Button
24        android:id="@+id/button2"
25        android:layout_width="wrap_content"
26        android:layout_height="wrap_content"
27        android:layout_alignParentLeft="true"
28        android:layout_below="@+id/button1"
29        android:layout_marginLeft="80dp"
30        android:text="@string/convert_ascii"
31        android:onClick="toAsciiConversion" />
32
33    <ImageView
34        android:id="@+id/imageView1"
35        android:layout_width="wrap_content"
36        android:layout_height="wrap_content"
37        android:layout_marginStart="80dp"
38        android:layout_toEndOf="@+id/button2"
39        android:contentDescription="@string/thumbnail"
40        android:layout_alignTop="@+id/button1" />
41
42    <TextView
43        android:id="@+id/textView1"
44        android:layout_width="wrap_content"
45        android:layout_height="wrap_content"
46        android:layout_below="@+id/button2"
47        android:layout_centerHorizontal="true"
48        android:text=""
49        android:textSize="5sp"
50        android:typeface="monospace" />
51
52    <ProgressBar
53        style="?android:attr/progressBarStyleLarge"
54        android:layout_width="wrap_content"
55        android:layout_height="wrap_content"
56        android:id="@+id/progressBar"
57        android:layout_centerVertical="true"
58        android:layout_centerHorizontal="true" />
59
60 </RelativeLayout>
```

Part 5: Source Code for Application

The conversion feature of the application requires images captured by the built-in camera. The photo image pixel data are analyzed in pairs of pixels. This means that every other pixel within the photograph is analyzed and then represented by an ASCII character. It is crucial that the original photograph be resized to a lower resolution. If the resolution of the JPEG image is maintained at its original size, the resulting text may have far too many rows and columns of characters to fit on a small-screen device.

Lines 33–34:	A request code for capturing an image by the camera is defined as a constant. This request code will be used by the `Intent` that launches the camera application.
Lines 37–41:	The two objects identified by `photoCaptured` and `asciiImage` will store the photograph and the corresponding ASCII art image. The TextView, located in the activity's layout, is referenced by `asciiImage`. The application buttons will be references so that they can be disabled at processing time.
Lines 52–54:	References to the layout UI components are set for later management by the application.
Line 57:	Until the camera takes a photograph, an ASCII conversion is not allowed. This button is disabled.
Line 60:	The progress bar is used solely for the purpose of notifying the user that an ASCII conversion process is taking place. This UI component will be set directly before and after the conversion. At the launch of the application, the progress bar must be hidden.
Lines 64–68:	The `onClick` event handler `toCamera()` creates an Intent to launch the external camera application with an intent action `ACTION_IMAGE_CAPTURE`. The request code, named `CAPTURE_IMAGE_ACTIVITY_REQUEST_CODE`, will be used to identify that the camera captured an image.
Lines 73–99:	A call to `onActivityResult()` is automatically made when the camera application exists. The requestCode is used to identify that a photograph was taken, and the resultCode provides acknowledgment that a photograph was successfully captured.

MyActivity.java

```
1   package com.cornez.asciicamera;
2
3   import android.app.Activity;
4   import android.content.Context;
5   import android.content.Intent;
6   import android.graphics.Bitmap;
7   import android.graphics.Canvas;
8   import android.graphics.Color;
9
10  import android.os.AsyncTask;
11  import android.os.Bundle;
```

```
12    import android.os.Environment;
13    import android.provider.MediaStore;
14    import android.util.DisplayMetrics;
15    import android.view.Menu;
16    import android.view.MenuItem;
17    import android.view.View;
18    import android.widget.Button;
19    import android.widget.ImageView;
20    import android.widget.ProgressBar;
21    import android.widget.TextView;
22    import android.widget.Toast;
23
24    import java.io.File;
25    import java.io.FileNotFoundException;
26    import java.io.FileOutputStream;
27    import java.io.IOException;
28    import java.io.OutputStream;
29
30    public class MyActivity extends Activity {
31
32        //CREATE A REQUEST CODE TO REQUEST A PHOTOGRAPH
33        private static final int
34                CAPTURE_IMAGE_ACTIVITY_REQUEST_CODE = 100;
35
36        //OBJECTS USED BY THE APP
37        private Bitmap photoCaptured;
38        private TextView asciiImage;
39        private Button asciiButton;
40        private Button cameraButton;
41        private ProgressBar asciiProgressBar;
42
43        @Override
44        protected void onCreate(Bundle savedInstanceState) {
45            super.onCreate(savedInstanceState);
46            setContentView(R.layout.activity_my);
47
48            //REFERENCE THE TEXTVIEW THAT WILL HOLD THE ASCII IMAGE
49            asciiImage = (TextView) findViewById(R.id.textView1);
50
51            //REFERENCE THE APPLICATION BUTTONS AND THE PROGRESS BAR
52            cameraButton = (Button) findViewById(R.id.button1);
53            asciiButton = (Button) findViewById(R.id.button2);
54            asciiProgressBar = (ProgressBar) findViewById(R.id.progressBar);
55
56            //DISABLE THE ASCII BUTTON PRIOR TO CAPTURING A PHOTO
57            asciiButton.setEnabled(false);
58
59            //HIDE THE PROGRESS BAR
60            asciiProgressBar.setAlpha(0);
61        }
62
```

```
63    //ON CLICK EVENT HANDLER TO LAUNCH THE CAMERA
64    public void toCamera(View view) {
65        Intent intent = new Intent(MediaStore.ACTION_IMAGE_CAPTURE);
66        startActivityForResult(intent,
67                        CAPTURE_IMAGE_ACTIVITY_REQUEST_CODE);
68    }
69
70    // CALLED ONCE THE CAMERA HAS LAUNCHED AND
71    // A PHOTOGRAPH HAS BEEN TAKEN
72    @Override
73    public void onActivityResult(int requestCode, int resultCode,
74                        Intent data) {
75        super.onActivityResult(requestCode, resultCode, data);
76
77        //REFERENCE THE IMAGEVIEW - LOCATED ON THE LAYOUT
78        ImageView photoPreview = (ImageView)
79                findViewById(R.id.imageView1);
80
81        //VERIFY A PHOTO WAS TAKEN
82        if (requestCode == CAPTURE_IMAGE_ACTIVITY_REQUEST_CODE) {
83            if (resultCode == Activity.RESULT_OK) {
84                //COLLECT THE PHOTOGRAPH TAKEN BY THE CAMERA
85                // AND PLACE IT IN THE IMAGE VIEW
86                Bundle extras = data.getExtras();
87                photoCaptured = (Bitmap) extras.get("data");
88                photoPreview.setImageBitmap(photoCaptured);
89                asciiButton.setEnabled(true);
90            } else if (resultCode == RESULT_CANCELED) {
91                Toast.makeText(this, "result canceled",
92                        Toast.LENGTH_LONG).show();
93            } else {
94                Toast.makeText(this, "image capture failed",
95                            Toast.LENGTH_LONG)
96                            .show();
97            }
98        }
99    }
```

Lines 101–104:   The onClick() event handler for the conver-
                  sion to ASCII button is defined. The processing of
                  the photogragh is performed in an AsyncTask.
                  PerformAsyncTask().execute() is called.

                  When loading and processing large bitmaps, an AsyncTask
                  should be used to perform the work off the main UI thread.
                  This is particularly necessary when the bitmap is accessed
                  from external storage. The AsyncTask class can execute much
                  of the processing work in a background thread and publish the
                  results back on the UI thread.

Line 109:

The ASCII artwork is built using a simple `String` object. Text characters will be added to `asciiArtWork` as each photo pixel is analyzed.

Lines 112–124:

Prior to processing the photograph, all the buttons on the application are disabled. In addition, the progress bar is made visible to the user.

Lines 129–136:

Pixels will be read from the `photoThumbnail` object. The bitmap image is scaled so that only half of its pixels will be represented by ASCII values. This will make for a faster conversion and the resulting text will be easily accommodated on a small screen. Depending on the screen size of the device, a width and height can be defined by scaling up or down.

Lines 138–187:

The ASCII artwork is built pixel by pixel.

Lines 146–151:

The color values for individual pixels from the bitmap object are normalized to find a grayscale value. The average of red, green, and blue components of color gives its gray factor.

Lines 151–180:

ASCII characters have been selected based on their brightness and weight. These characters have been assigned to represent gray values found in a typical photograph.

Line 183:

At the end of each line in a grid of pixels, a new line must be added to the ASCII artwork.

Lines 190–202:

During the postexecution of the `AsyncTask`, the ASCII artwork has been generated and the application buttons are reenabled.

Line 198:

In addition, the `asciiProgressBar` is hidden from the viewer. Finally, the generated ASCII artwork is placed in the `TextView` referenced by `asciiImage`.

```
MyActivity.java (continued)
100  //CONVERT THE IMAGE TO ASCII TEXT
101      public void toAsciiConversion(View view) {
102          //PROCESS THE PHOTOGRAPH IN AN ASYNCTASK
103          new PerformAsyncTask().execute();
104      }
105
106      private class PerformAsyncTask extends AsyncTask<Void, Void, Void> {
107
108          //DECLARE A STRING TO STORE THE COMPLETE ASCII TEXT
109          String asciiArtWork;
110
111          @Override
112          protected void onPreExecute() {
113              super.onPreExecute();
```

```
114
115        //DISABLE THE APPLICATION BUTTONS
116        cameraButton.setEnabled(false);
117        asciiButton.setEnabled(false);
118
119        //DISPLAY THE PROGRESS BAR
120        asciiProgressBar.setAlpha(1);
121
122        //CLEAR THE TEXT STRING FOR THE FINAL ARTWORK
123        asciiArtWork = "\n";
124    }
125
126    @Override
127    protected Void doInBackground(Void... params) {
128        //TASK 1: ACCESS THE PHOTOGRAPH CAPTURED BY THE CAMERA
129        Bitmap photoThumbnail = photoCaptured;
130
131        //GET THE WIDTH AND HEIGHT OF THE PREVIEW IMAGE
132        int thumbnailWidth = photoThumbnail.getWidth();
133        int thumbnailHeight = photoThumbnail.getHeight();
134
135        int scaleWidth = 2; // shrink bitmap height
136        int scaleHeight = 2; // shrink bitmap height
137
138        //GENERATE ASCII ARTWORK PIXEL BY PIXEL
139        for (int y = 0; y < thumbnailHeight / scaleHeight; y++) {
140            for (int x = 0; x < thumbnailWidth / scaleWidth; x++) {
141                // COLLECT PIXEL INFORMATION AT A SPECIFIC LOCATION
142                int pixel = photoThumbnail.getPixel(x * scaleWidth,
143                                                    y * scaleHeight);
144
145                // COLLECT THE RED, GREEN, AND BLUE VALUES
146                int redVal = Color.red(pixel);
147                int greenVal = Color.green(pixel);
148                int blueVal = Color.blue(pixel);
149
150                // COMPUTE THE GRAYSCALE VALUE
151                int grayVal = (redVal + greenVal + blueVal) / 3;
152
153                // MATCH GRAY VALUE SPECTRUMS WITH
154                // DIFFERENT ASCII CHARACTERS
155                if (grayVal < 35)
156                    asciiArtWork += "MM";
157                else if (grayVal <= 52)
158                    asciiArtWork += "$$";
159                else if (grayVal <= 69)
160                    asciiArtWork += "##";
161                else if (grayVal <= 86)
162                    asciiArtWork += "%%";
163                else if (grayVal <= 103)
164                    asciiArtWork += "**";
```

```
165                          else if (grayVal <= 120)
166                              asciiArtWork += "++";
167                          else if (grayVal <= 137)
168                              asciiArtWork += "vV";
169                          else if (grayVal <= 154)
170                              asciiArtWork += "-;";
171                          else if (grayVal <= 171)
172                              asciiArtWork += "--";
173                          else if (grayVal <= 188)
174                              asciiArtWork += ";;";
175                          else if (grayVal <= 205)
176                              asciiArtWork += "::";
177                          else if (grayVal <= 222)
178                              asciiArtWork += "..";
179                          else
180                              asciiArtWork += "  ";
181                      }
182                      // ADD A LINE BREAK AT THE END OF EACH LINE
183                      asciiArtWork += "\n";
184                  }
185
186              return null;
187          }
188
189          @Override
190          protected void onPostExecute(Void result) {
191              super.onPostExecute(result);
192
193              //ENABLE THE APPLICATION BUTTONS
194              cameraButton.setEnabled(true);
195              asciiButton.setEnabled(true);
196
197              //TURN THE PROGRESS BAR OFF - MAKE IT INVISIBLE
198              asciiProgressBar.setAlpha(0);
199
200              //DISPLAY THE ASCII ARTWORK
201              asciiImage.setText(asciiArtWork);
202          }
203      }
```

A screen snapshot can be taken of the final artwork. The following code segment loads a bitmap from the TextView storing the ASCII characters:

```
MyActivity.java (continued)
204      public void takeScreenSnapShot(){
205          //GET A BITMAP FROM THE TEXTVIEW
206          Bitmap bitmap = loadBitmapFromView(this, asciiImage);
207          String mPath = Environment.getExternalStorageDirectory() +
```

```
208                         File.separator +
209                         "screen_" +
210                         System.currentTimeMillis() + ".jpeg";
211
212         File imageFile = new File(mPath);
213         OutputStream fileOut = null;
214         try {
215             fileOut = new FileOutputStream(imageFile);
216             bitmap.compress(Bitmap.CompressFormat.JPEG, 90, fileOut);
217             fileOut.flush();
218             fileOut.close();
219         } catch (FileNotFoundException e) {
220             e.printStackTrace();
221         } catch (IOException e) {
222             e.printStackTrace();
223         }
224     }
225
226     public static Bitmap loadBitmapFromView(Context context,
227                                             View view) {
228         DisplayMetrics dm = context.getResources().getDisplayMetrics();
229         view.measure(View.MeasureSpec.makeMeasureSpec(dm.widthPixels,
230                     View.MeasureSpec.EXACTLY),
231                     View.MeasureSpec.makeMeasureSpec(dm.heightPixels,
232                     View.MeasureSpec.EXACTLY));
233         view.layout(0, 0, view.getMeasuredWidth(),
234                     view.getMeasuredHeight());
235         Bitmap returnedBitmap =
236                     Bitmap.createBitmap(view.getMeasuredWidth(),
237                     view.getMeasuredHeight(), Bitmap.Config.ARGB_8888);
238         Canvas c = new Canvas(returnedBitmap);
239         view.draw(c);
240         return returnedBitmap;
241     }
242
243     @Override
244     public boolean onCreateOptionsMenu(Menu menu) {
245         // INFLATE THE MENU
246         getMenuInflater().inflate(R.menu.my, menu);
247         return true;
248     }
249
250     @Override
251     public boolean onOptionsItemSelected(MenuItem item) {
252         // Handle action bar item clicks here. The action bar will
253         // automatically handle clicks on the Home/Up button, so long
254         // as you specify a parent activity in AndroidManifest.xml.
255         int id = item.getItemId();
256         if (id == R.id.action_settings) {
257             return true;
```

```
258        }
259        return super.onOptionsItemSelected(item);
260    }
261 }
```

■ Exercises

8.1 Describe the three categories of sensors found in an Android device.

8.2 List two motion sensors.

8.3 Explain the difference between a gyroscope and an accelerometer.

8.4 Describe three common environmental sensors found in an Android device.

8.5 Describe how `Sensor` and `SensorManager` are used to work with a device's sensors.

8.6 A `SensorEvent` object includes specific information about a sensor event. Name four elements of information included in this object.

8.7 Name the two abstract methods that must be implemented in the `Sensor-EventListener` interface.

8.8 In the code segment below, explain the use of the value stored in the variable *n*.

```
1 SensorManager mSensorManager;
2 Sensor mGyroscope;
3
4 mSensorManager = (SensorManager)getSystemService(SENSOR_SERVICE);
5 mGyroscope = mSensorManager.getDefaultSensor(Sensor.TYPE_GYROSCOPE);
6
7 String vendorName = mGyroscope.getVendor();
8 int n = mGyroscope.getVersion();
```

8.9 Briefly explain how information can be accessed about the forces applied to an Android device.

8.10 What is sensor batching and why is it useful?

8.11 Briefly explain how a Step Counter differs from a Step Detector.

8.12 Provide an example of a composite sensor. Explain how a device uses a composite sensor.

8.13 Briefly list the sensors used in a compass application that determines the direction the device is facing.

8.14 List the three constants that identify camera categories on an Android device. Briefly describe the difference between `FEATURE_CAMERA` and `FEATURE_CAMERA_FRONT`.

8.15 Name the `<uses-permission>` attributes for storing an image or photograph to external storage.

9

File Storage, Shared Preferences, and SQLite

Chapter Objectives

In this chapter you will:

- Learn about data storage methods.
- Understand use of Shared Preferences.
- Learn how to insert data using key-value pairs.
- Understand File-based Storage.
- Understand the differences between internal storage and external storage.
- Learn how to build applications using SQLite databases.

■ 9.1 Storing Data

Working with stored data is essential to Android applications. At the most rudimentary level, an application often stores information about a user's preferences in order to provide a more sophisicated level of personalization and responsiveness. For example, a user can log into and out of an application, and the application will remember the user when the application is relaunched. In addition, users expect to be able to choose settings according to their personal needs (such as specific background sounds and images) and have them automatically persist across user sessions.

Advanced Android applications are frequently data-driven and can require the management of a larger and more complex volume of data. An application can use databases and files to store structured data or information that will be made available to other applications.

Android supports multiple options for storing and accessing data. Choosing the manner in which data are stored depends upon the specific needs of the application, such as the amount of data to be stored and whether the data will be kept private within the application or made accessible to other applications.

The Android platform allows data files to be saved on the device's internal memory and on an external storage media, such as a Secure Device (SD) card. Files that are saved within the device's internal storage memory tend to be small, as opposed to external storage, which typically holds larger volume files, such as images.

Internal storage is used most often to store persistent data that can be retrieved when the user accesses the application again. The Android SDK provides SharedPreferences for the most primitive type of data storage, specifically user preferences, to enhance the user's application experience. A SharedPreferences file is stored internally and managed by the framework. By default, all data stored in internal storage are private to applications, whereas files stored in external storage can be made accessible to other applications.

A network connection or server-side storage is another data storage option on which Android applications can rely. Rather than maintaining information directly on the device, such as SharedPreference, File-Based storage, and SQLite, some applications need to send and access information through the Web and persist it on a server.

This chapter explores storage and access options for Android. This includes SharedPreferences, File-based Storage, the SQLite database, and accessing content from a data provider.

■ 9.2 Shared Preferences

The term `Shared Preferences` refers to the storage of a limited set of primitive data used to make persistent changes in an Android application. More specifically, it is a simple way to read and write key-value pairs of data. `SharedPreference` files are primarily used to store a user's personal settings and a small amount of application session data.

`SharedPreference` information is backed up in XML files in internal storage. These data are proprietary and inaccessible to outside applications. Data values can quickly be retrieved each time the application is launched or when an Activity is resumed after being paused.

`SharedPreference` data supports an intuitive and responsive experience for a user by allowing preference data values to persist automatically throughout sessions, regardless of how they end. This includes the exit of an application, a shutdown of the device, or—in a worst-case scenario—a system crash.

When a user decides to uninstall an application that relies on `SharedPreference` storage, this data will no longer persist. All `SharedPreference` information associated with the application will automatically be removed when the application is deleted.

A key-value pair is a data representation model that uses a set of key identifiers along with associated data values. This model is frequently used in hash tables and configuration files. This simple mechanism provides access to a data value or object by specifying its associated key. The `SharedPreferences` API provides a set of methods for reading and writing key-value pairs to files. This data can be made available at the Activity level or shared across all Activities within the application package. Shared Preferences supports the `String` data type and most of the Java primitive data types, such as `int`, `float`, `long`, and `boolean`.

The following code example illustrates how data values can be written to a Shared-Preferences file:

Lines 1–3:   To access a new or existing shared preferences file, the method `getSharedPreferences()` is used. It specifies the name preferences file, "MyPreferences," and its operating mode. The preferences file named MyPreferences does not yet exist and will therefore be created. The operating mode, `MODE_PRIVATE`, is used to control permissions. `MODE_PRIVATE` stores a bit value of 0, which represents the private default operation for `SharedPreferences`. This value can be stored as a constant.

The object named preferences is established as the SharedPreferences interface for accessing and modifying preference data for MyPreferences.

Line 5:   To write shared preference values to file, an `Editor` object is required. An `Editor` is an interface used for modifying values in a `SharedPreferences` object. Once an `Editor` has been instantiated, values can be set in the preferences editor.

Lines 6–10:   The methods `putString()`, `putInt()`, and `putBoolean()` will set a value in the preferences editor for a given key. Key names are strings. Values can be Strings or a Java primitive data type.

Line 12:   The call to `commit()` will perform changes back from the `SharedPreferences.Editor`.

```
1       SharedPreferences preferences =
2               getApplicationContext().getSharedPreferences(
3                   "MyPreferences", PRIVATE_MODE);
4
5       SharedPreferences.Editor editor = preferences.edit();
6
7       editor.putString(KEYNAME1, value1);
8       editor.putString(KEYNAME2, value2);
9       editor.putInt(KEYNAME3, value3);
10      editor.putBoolean(KEYNAME4, value4);
11
12      editor.commit();
```

In the following code example, values are retrieved from the `SharedPreferences` object, `preferences`. If the preference value does not exist for the specified key, a default value is returned. The default value is identified by the second argument.

```
1    preferences.getString(KEYNAME1, null);
2    preferences.getString(KEYNAME2, null);
3    preferences.getInt(KEYNAME3, 0);
4    preferences.getBoolean(KEYNAME4, false);
```

The `editor` object can mark a preference key-value pair for removal within the `SharedPreferences` file. Once the key is used to identify which key-value pair is marked for removal, `commit()` is called to perform the final changes.

```
1    editor.remove(KEYNAME1);
2    editor.remove(KEYNAME2);
3    editor.commit();
```

All key-value data sets within the shared preferences file can be easily cleared using the `clear()` method. Once `commit()` is called, the only remaining preferences will be any key-value pairs that were not defined in the `editor` object.

```
1    editor.clear();
2    editor.commit();
```

■ 9.3 File Storage—Internal and External Storage

In Android, a File-based Storage option allows data to be written to an actual file structure. This storage method requires more control regarding read-and-write permissions. For example, do you want to allow read-and-write access solely within the context of your application? Or, do you want other applications to be able to read these files as well?

Internal storage allows data to be stored directly onto the device's memory. This storage is always available, assuming there is space. External storage may not always be obtainable on a device. For example, some devices have removable external storage, such as an SD card, but others do not. This means that if an application attempts to use external storage, it must not assume it exists and should always take the precaution of checking for availability. Android devices are often designed to provide both internal storage and external storage built directly into the device. When external storage is supplied by nonremoveable means, it is technically regarded as internal to the device. It cannot be classified as internal storage, however, because it remains external to the operating system.

There are significant differences in how external and internal storage are utilized in an application. Internal storage files can be configured to be readable and writeable by the application. Typically, internal storage is utilized when processing an image, video and audio elements, and large data files. By default, files saved to internal storage arc private to the application. When the user uninstalls the application, the associated internal storage data files are removed.

External storage is publicly shared storage, which means that it can be made available to external applications. For example, a photography application can access photos from the Android photo gallery, allow the user to edit them, and resave them to the gallery, which is outside the context of the application. Unlike internal storage, once an application is uninstalled, external storage files continue to exist.

In the following code example, a `FileOutputStream` object is used to write data to a file. `FileOutputStream` is an extension of the `OutputStream` class, which writes bytes to a file.

Lines 2–3: The `fileOutput` object is used to open a file named "`myApplicationFile`." If the file does not exist, it will be created. The operating mode for this file is established as MODE_PRIVATE, which means the file is not world-writeable. For non-private data, applications should use ContentProvider to allow all other applications to have write access to the created file.

Line 6: Once data content has been written to the file, the stream is closed by calling `close()`.

```
1    try {
2        FileOutputStream fileOutput =
3                openFileOutput("myApplicationFile", MODE_PRIVATE);
4
5        fileOutput.write(dataContent.getBytes());
6        fileOutput.close();
7
8    } catch (IOException e){
9        e.printStackTrace();
10   }
```

Reading from an existing file is performed using a `FileInputStream`, as shown in the code example below. `FileInputStream` is an input stream that reads bytes from a file. It is not buffered and therefore it is advisable that callers wrap the stream with a `BufferedInputStream`.

```
1    try{
2        FileInputStream fileInput = openFileInput("myAppFile");
3        int bytes = fileInput.read();
4
5            .
6            .
7            .
```

```
 8
 9              }catch(IOException e){
10                  e.printStackTrace()
11
12          }
```

The external storage directory on a device is media/shared storage, intended to hold a relatively large amount of data that are shared across applications. Prior to using external storage, the permission WRITE_EXTERNAL_STORAGE must be set within the AndroidManifest.xml file. For Android versions KitKat and greater, read access requires the READ_EXTERNAL_STORAGE permission for applications that do not have preexisting write permission granted.

The mechanism for reading and writing to a file is the same for external storage and internal storage. However, external storage can be present on a device in various configurations. For example, external storage might be a permanent fixture on the device, or it can be available as a removeable disk. The method isExternalStorageRemovable() can be used to check if the storage device can be removed.

Before data are written to or read from external storage, it is important to check whether the storage is available. The method getExternalStorageDirectory() will return the primary external storage directory for the device; however, this directory may not currently be accessible if it has been physically removed from the device or damaged. The method getExternalStorageState() can be called to determine the current state of the external storage for the device, or more specifically to check if the storage is available to read and write. Both of these methods can be used to notify the user with more information when an application needs access.

The following code example illustrates how the availability of external storage on a device can be tested prior to reading and writing content:

Lines 5–6:   Environment.getExternalStorageState() provides access to the variables for the external storage environment.

Lines 8–13:   MEDIA_MOUNTED indicates the external storage is present and mounted with read/write access.

Lines 14–20:   MEDIA_MOUNTED_READ_ONLY indicates a mount point with read-only access.

Lines 21–25:   There is no indication that external storage exists for either read or write access.

```
 1  public boolean isSD_Readable() {
 2
 3      boolean mExternalStorageAvailable = false;
 4      try {
```

```
5      String externalStorageState =
6              Environment.getExternalStorageState();
7
8      if (Environment.MEDIA_MOUNTED.equals(externalStorageState)) {
9          mExternalStorageAvailable = true;
10         Toast.makeText(getApplicationContext(),
11                 "External storage card is readable and writable.",
12                 Toast.LENGTH_SHORT).show();
13     }
14     else if (Environment.MEDIA_MOUNTED_READ_ONLY.equals(
15             externalStorageState)) {
16         mExternalStorageAvailable = true;
17         Toast.makeText(getApplicationContext(),
18                 "External storage card is readable.",
19                 Toast.LENGTH_SHORT).show();
20     }
21     else {
22         Toast.makeText(getApplicationContext(),
23                 "External storage is NOT available.",
24                 Toast.LENGTH_SHORT).show();
25                 mExternalStorageAvailable = false;
26     }
27 } catch (Exception e) {
28     e.printStackTrace();
29 }
30
31 return mExternalStorageAvailable;
32 }
```

■ 9.4 Android Database with SQLite

Many Android applications require the storage of complex data structured as a relational database. For example, a bird-watching application may allow users to keep track of details and the specific locations of birds they have viewed. To store intricately structured data, a database is essential.

SQLite provides the foundation for managing private and embedded databases in an Android application. The Android SDK includes the SQLite software library that implements the SQL (Structured Query Language) database engine. This library is used for defining the database structure and adding and managing the database content as required by the application. The Android SDK also includes an SQLite database tool for explicit database debugging purposes.

As a condensed version of SQL, SQLite supports the standard SQL syntax and database transactions. Although SQLite is not a full-featured database, it supports a large set of the SQL standard and is sufficient for Android developers needing a simple database engine to plug into their applications. The advantage of using SQLite for

Android development is its compact code footprint and efficient use of memory, even for large projects with complex data structures. It is meant for serious applications; however, it is not suitable for large databases or applications that produce a large volume of transactions.

SQLite is a complete relational database engine, which means that an Android application can access content using high-level queries. In this environment, a database is implemented as a largely self-contained file. For example, a database file stores all the contents of the database and contains indices, triggers, and any metadata needed by SQLite. It requires minimal support from external libraries or from the Android operating system. The implementation of a database file will be accessible by name to any class in the application, but not outside the application.

SQLite differs from conventional database systems in that it does not require a server. This means that data can be easily read from and written to a file without requiring server interprocess communication. No additional programs or components are required for SQLite to run. SQLite is imported into an application as a library, android. database.sqlite.SQLiteDatabase. All database operations are handled by the application using methods provided by the SQLite library.

An SQLite database file is a collection of data organized in a table. The SQLite database table is structured by a set of rows and columns. A row represents a single record, the implicitly structured data entry in the table. A column represents a data field, an attribute of a data record. A field is a single item that exists at the intersection between one row and one column.

The possible data types for an individual field of data consist of NULL, INTEGER, REAL, TEXT, and BLOB. BLOB is a data type used to store a large array of binary data (bytes). SQLite does not provide specific data storage classes for values that need to be represented as Boolean, date, or time. Instead, these values can be stored as an INTEGER or TEXT. For example, a Boolean value can be stored as an INTEGER data type with 0 for false and 1 for true. Dates and times have a more complicated format and can therefore be stored as TEXT values. A string arrangement can be configured, such as "YYYY-MM-DD HH:MM:SS.SSS," to represent a specific time/date format.

Consider the construction of a database table required to store information about individual students. Defining a database table structure means specifying field names, assigning data types, and applying various constraints on fields. The `students'` table will be defined to hold the following fields: `_id`, `name`, `gender`, `year_born`, and `gpa`. The `id` field represents the primary key for the table. SQLite will produce an error when an attempt is made to insert a table row with an `id` value that already exists. The formal declaration of how the database is organized is called the schema.

Table 9-1 shows an outline for the `students'` database table schema as follows. An AUTOINCREMENT key will be used to create a value for the `id` field automatically when a new row is inserted without a specific id value. The UNIQUE key

TABLE 9-1 Students' Database Table Schema

Table: students		
Column Names	**Data Type**	**Key**
_id	INTEGER	PRIMARY KEY AUTOINCREMENT
name	TEXT	UNIQUE NOT NULL
gender	TEXT	
year_born	INTEGER	NOT NULL
gpa	REAL	

attribute can be used to prohibit duplicate values from being inserted into a given table column. The 'NOT NULL' key will prohibit empty values from being inserted into a table column.

SQLite statements are divided into two categories: data definition language (DDL) and data manipulation language (DML). DDL statements are used to build and modify the structure of a database table. DML is used to query and update data. The following DDL statement is used to create the students' database table. CREATE is used to create the table and define its structure, which includes field names, assigned data types, and key constraints.

```
1   -- SQL for creating the students table
2
3   CREATE TABLE students(
4                   _id INTEGER PRIMARY KEY,
5                   name TEXT UNIQUE NOT NULL,
6                   gender TEXT,
7                   year_born INTEGER
8                   gpa REAL
9   );
```

The SQLite INSERT INTO statement is used to add new rows of data into a table in the database. The code example below illustrates two methods used for INSERT. The set of statements will create seven records in the students' database table.

Lines 1–6:   When values for all columns within a record will be added, it is not necessary to specify the column identifier names. The INSERT statements shown within these lines will supply column values in sequence.

Lines 9–10:   When inserting a row containing values for a select set of columns, the VALUES keyword is required in an INSERT statement. The INSERT statement shown in this example will omit the _id column. The _id column is defined as INTEGER PRIMARY KEY. Such columns are auto-incremented in SQLite.

```
1   INSERT INTO students VALUES(1, 'Bill Jones', 'M', 1999, 3.4);
2   INSERT INTO students VALUES(2, 'John Chavez', 'M', 2001, 3.7);
3   INSERT INTO students VALUES(3, 'Carol Wan', 'F', 2002, 3.3);
4   INSERT INTO students VALUES(4, 'Liz Til', 'F', 2001, 3.5);
5   INSERT INTO students VALUES(5, 'Bon Bon', 'M', 2000, 3.6);
6   INSERT INTO students VALUES(6, 'Frank Seep', 'M', 2002, 4.0);
7
8
9   INSERT INTO students (name, gender, year, gpa) VALUES ('Elise Jack',
10  'F', 2000, 3.7);
```

The SELECT statement is used to query data from a database table. In the following code example, the SELECT statement uses the asterisk symbol in its syntax to include all column table values in the table.

```
1   SELECT * FROM students;
```

The results of the above statement will select all the records in the table, as shown by the following record listing.

_id	Name	Gender	Year	GPA
1	Bill Jones	M	1999	3.4
2	John Chavez	M	2001	3.7
3	Carol Wan	F	2002	3.3
4	Liz Til	F	2001	3.5
5	Bon Bon	M	2000	3.6
6	Frank Seep	M	2002	4.0
7	Elise Jack	F	2000	3.7

A limited set of column values can be accessed in a SELECT statement. In the SELECT statement shown below, the column values stored in name and gender will be fetched.

```
1   SELECT name, gender FROM students;
```

The results of the above statement will be the following record listing:

Name	Gender
Bill Jones	M
John Chavez	M
Carol Wan	F
Liz Til	F
Bon Bon	M
Frank Seep	M
Elise Jack	F

A WHERE clause can be added to a SELECT statement to restrict records being fetched. In the SELECT statement shown below, only records that meet the criteria specified by gender = 'F' will be selected.

```
1   SELECT name, gender FROM students WHERE gender = 'F';
```

The results of the above statement will be the following record listing:

Name	Gender
Carol Wan	F
Liz Til	F
Elise Jack	F

The DELETE statement is used to delete data from a table. The SQLite instruction shown below uses the WHERE clause with DELETE to eliminate the row containing the value 1 for _id.

```
1   DELETE FROM students WHERE _id=1;
```

The UPDATE statement is used to modify data within a table record. The SQLite instruction shown below uses the SET keyword to specify the column value to be altered and the WHERE keyword to identify the specific record to be changed.

```
1   UPDATE students SET name = 'Elise Jicky' WHERE _id=7;
```

■ 9.5 SQLiteOpenHelper

The Android SDK provides a set of classes for working with SQLite databases. One important class is SQLiteOpenHelper, which is essential for the creation and management of database content, as well as database versioning.

In an Android SQLite application, SQLiteOpenHelper must be subclassed. In addition, it must contain the implementation of onCreate() and onUpgrade(). The objective of onCreate() is to assume the responsibility for creating the database and opening it, or just opening it if it already exists. The purpose of onUpgrade() is to perform an upgrade of the database if necessary.

The onCreate() method is called when the database is created for the first time. The code segment below illustrates the construction of a database table named myTable. On Lines 2–9, the schema for myTable is built with seven attributes, including the unique identifier, KEY_ID. Each of the column names is stored as a string. For example, KEY_ID is used to hold the string "_id." The underscore in _id is a common convention for a primary key and will be used in this text.

On Line 11, the execSQL() method is used to execute a direct SQL statement. This SQL statement is stored as a text string, instruction, which was assembled on Lines 2–9.

It is considered good practice to create each database table in a separate class within the onCreate() and onUpdate() methods.

```
1   public void onCreate (SQLiteDatabase database){
2        String instruction = "CREATE TABLE " + "myTable" + "("
3              + KEY_ID + " INTEGER PRIMARY KEY, "
4              + KEY_COLUMN1 + " REAL, "
5              + KEY_COLUMN2 + " TEXT, "
6              + KEY_COLUMN3 + " REAL, "
7              + KEY_COLUMN4 + " TEXT, "
8              + KEY_COLUMN5 + " TEXT,
9              + KEY_COLUMN6 + " INTEGER" + ")";
10
11        database.execSQL (instruction);
12   }
```

SQLiteOpenHelper uses the methods getReadableDatabase() and getWriteableDatabase() to provide access to an SQLiteDatabase object. The database object will allow access in read or write mode.

There are several methods for inserting data into a table. A common method is to construct the content of a table record using a ContentValues object. The following code segment illustrates how a table record can be written to a database in writeable mode. A ContentValues object named values is first instantiated. Initially, it will consist of no content. Key-value pairs can be added to the ContentValues object using the put() method. Once all table column values have been added, the ContentValues object, which represents a record, can be inserted into the database. Line 16 shows the complete set of values added to the table using an insert() method. The close() method releases the reference to the table object in writeable mode and closes the object.

```
1        public void addRecord(DB_Record record) {
2            SQLiteDatabase db = this.getWritableDatabase();
3            ContentValues values = new ContentValues();
4
5            //ADD KEY-VALUE PAIR INFORMATION
6            values.put(KEY_ID, record.id());
7            values.put(KEY_COLUMN1, record.getColumn1());
8            values.put(KEY_COLUMN2, record.getColumn2());
9            values.put(KEY_COLUMN3, record.getColumn3());
10           values.put(KEY_COLUMN4, record.getColumn4());
11           values.put(KEY_COLUMN5, record.getColumn5());
12           values.put(KEY_COLUMN6, record.getColumn6());
```

```
13
14              // INSERT THE ROW IN THE TABLE
15              db.insert(DATABASE_TABLE, null, values);
16
17              // CLOSE THE DATABASE CONNECTION
18              db.close();
19          }
```

A second approach to inserting a record into a database table is to construct an SQLite INSERT statement and then execute it. In the code example below, the INSERT statement is stored in the string named insertStm. This statement is constructed on Lines 5–18. The execSQL() method will execute the string that stores the SQL statement.

When inserting a row into a database table, developers often prefer the use of ContentValues. The main reason is that it returns a −1 when an error has occurred. The execSQL() method is a void method and unable to provide feedback.

```
1       public void addRecord(DB_Record record) {
2           SQLiteDatabase db = this.getWritableDatabase();
3           SQLiteDatabase db = getWritableDatabase();
4
5           String insertStm = "INSERT or replace INTO " + TABLE_NAME +   "("
6                   + KEY_COLUMN1 +", "
7                   + KEY_COLUMN2 + ", "
8                   + KEY_COLUMN3 +", "
9                   + KEY_COLUMN4 +", "
10                  + KEY_COLUMN5 +", "
11                  + KEY_COLUMN6 + ") " +
12                  "VALUES('"
13                  + record.getColumn1() + "','"
14                  + record.getColumn2() + "','"
15                  + record.getColumn3() + "','"
16                  + record.getColumn4() + "','"
17                  + record.getColumn5() + "','"
18                  + record.getColumn6() +"')" ;
19          db.execSQL(insertStm);
20
21          // CLOSE THE DATABASE CONNECTION
22          db.close();
23      }
```

Database queries can be created using the rawQuery() or query() method. As shown in the following example, rawQuery() executes an SQL instruction and returns a result set produced by the query. This instruction is assembled as a string value.

The code shown on Lines 3–4 is used to illustrate how a Cursor object can provide read-write access to the result set of records returned by the query. The Cursor object is first positioned at the first record in the result set and then sequentially moves to subsequent records.

```
1          SQLiteDatabase database = this.getReadableDatabase();
2
3      Cursor cursor =
4          database.rawQuery("SELECT * FROM " + DATABASE_TABLE, null);
5
6      //COLLECT EACH ROW IN THE TABLE
7      if (cursor.moveToFirst()){
8          do {
9
10            .
11            .
12            .
13
14         } while (cursor.moveToNext());
15     }
```

The query() method, shown in the code below, will query a given table and return a Cursor object over the result set. Filtering, ordering, and limits can be set directly from the arguments. Note that the second argument of the query() method is used to supply a list of the columns that will be returned in the result set.

```
1          SQLiteDatabase database = this.getReadableDatabase();
2
3      Cursor cursor = db.query(DATABASE_TABLE, new String[]{
4          KEY_COLUMN1,
5          KEY_COLUMN2,
6          KEY_COLUMN3,
7          KEY_COLUMN4,
8          KEY_COLUMN1 =5},
9          KEY_COLUMN1 + "=?", new
10         String[]{String.valueOf(value)},null,null,null,null);
11
12     //COLLECT EACH ROW IN THE TABLE
13     if (cursor.moveToFirst()){
14         do {
15
16            .
17            .
18            .
19
20         } while (cursor.moveToNext());
21     }
```

■ Lab Example 9-1: SQLite Database Experiment ToDo Today Application

The application built in this lab example is a database experiment that will evolve into a full application in Lab Example 9-2. The application, ToDo Today, is inspired by to-do lists and allows users to build and manage a list of tasks that need to be completed. In this version of ToDo Today, users can create a short-term task list: tasks that can be completed in a single day. For example, the user can build a task list in the morning and check off tasks as they are successfully completed by the end of the day. On the following day, the previous day's tasks are cleared away and a new set of tasks is placed on the list. Figure 9-1 shows such a list.

FIGURE 9-1 To-do tasks that can be completed in a single day.

This lab example is a first look at the use of SQLite for storing, managing, and accessing data in an application. ToDo Today requires structured data that will be embedded into the application. The objective of this lab example is to build a database and explore SQLite's transactional statements.

Part 1: The Design

An SQLite database is stored as a single file. This file will contain a database table consisting of columns that form the schema of the table, as well as rows that store the data values. The name of the database file will be toDo_Today.

The toDo_Today database will contain a single table, toDo_Items, for storing each task item entered by the user.

The schema for the database table will use the INTEGER and TEXT data types. The primary key, the unique identifier for each task item in the database table, will be stored as an INTEGER and will be specified by the identifier _id.

A ToDo task description is stored in the column named description. Once a user has specified that a task has been completed, this action will be denoted by a value in the table column named is_done. The column labeled is_done is meant to store a Boolean value, true or false. SQLite does not have a separate Boolean storage class. Instead, Boolean values must be stored as integers 0 (false) and 1 (true).

The complete database schema for the ToDo Today application is shown as follows:

Database: toDo_Today Table: toDo_Items		
Column Names	Data Type	Key
_id	INTEGER	Primary Key
description	TEXT	
is_done	INTEGER	

Part 2: Application Structure and Setup

The settings for the application are as follows:

- Application Name: ToDo Today
- Project Name: ToDoToday
- Package Name: com.cornez.tododay
- Android Form: Phone and Tablet
- Minimum SDK: API 18: Android 4.3 (Jelly Bean)
- Target SDK: API 21: Android 5.0 (Lollipop)
- Compile with: API 21: Android 5.0 (Lollipop)
- Activity Name: MainActivity
- Layout Name: activity_main

The project structure for the application is shown in Figure 9-2. This structure contains three Java source files. The activity for the class is MainActivity. The ToDo_Item class models a single ToDo item placed on the list. DBHelper will provide the database management support. As an experimental application, this project will not use an XML layout.

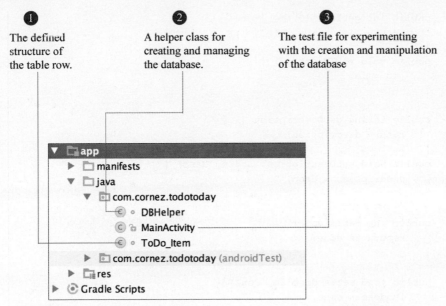

I FIGURE 9-2 The ToDo Today application project structure.

Part 3: The `ToDo_Item` class

The `ToDo_Item` class provides the data attributes for each task on the list. These include the description of the task and the completion status: `is_done`. The Java code for `ToDo_Item` is shown as follows:

```
ToDo_Item.java
 1   package com.cornez.todotoday;
 2
 3   class ToDo_Item {
 4
 5       //MEMBER ATTRIBUTES
 6       private int _id;
 7       private String description;
 8       private int is_done;
 9
10       public ToDo_Item() {
11       }
12
13       public ToDo_Item(int id, String desc, int done) {
14           _id = id;
15           description = desc;
16           is_done = done;
17       }
18
```

```
19      public int getId() {
20          return _id;
21      }
22      public void setId(int id) {
23          _id = id;
24      }
25
26      public String getDescription () {
27          return description;
26      }
27      public void setDescription (String desc) {
28          description = desc;
29      }
30
31      public int getIs_done() {
32          return is_done;
33      }
34
35      public void setIs_done(int done) {
36          is_done = done;
37      }
38
39  }
```

Part 4: The `DBHelper` Class

By default, SQLite on Android does not have a management interface. `DBHelper.java` will be written to build and manage the `toDo_Today` database. This Java class will provide methods for handling all database operations: create, read, update, and delete.

Line 6:   `SQLiteDatabase` is the base class for working with an SQLite database.

Line 7:   `SQLiteOpenHelper` is a helper base class that will support the database creation and version management.

Line 11:   `DBHelper` is a subclass of `SQLiteOpenHelper`. It will override the implementation of `onCreate()` and `onUpgrade()`. Additionally, this class will provide database operations for adding, editing, deleting, and reporting records in the database.

Line 14:   The first version number of the database must begin at 1. The version number will be used to upgrade the database if the schema has been updated.

Lines 31–38: `onCreate()` is called when the database is created for the first time. The creation of the database and the database table is performed with the execution of a single SQL statement.

Lines 41–46:   Alterations to a database are performed by `onUpgrade()`. A database is upgraded when the schema is altered. This includes adding new tables, removing existing tables, or changing column data types. The method, `onUpgrade()`, is inherited from `SQLiteOpenHelper` class and therefore must be overridden. This method is invoked when the version number specified in the constructor of the class changes. When a database is altered, a new version number must be supplied to the constructor of the class.

DBHelper.java

```
1   package com.cornez.todotoday;
2
3   import android.content.ContentValues;
4   import android.content.Context;
5   import android.database.Cursor;
6   import android.database.sqlite.SQLiteDatabase;
7   import android.database.sqlite.SQLiteOpenHelper;
8
9   import java.util.ArrayList;
10
11  class DBHelper extends SQLiteOpenHelper {
12
13      //TASK 1: DEFINE THE DATABASE AND TABLE
14      private static final int DATABASE_VERSION = 1;
15      private static final String DATABASE_NAME = "toDo_Today";
16      private static final String DATABASE_TABLE = "toDo_Items";
17
18
19      //TASK 2: DEFINE THE COLUMN NAMES FOR THE TABLE
20      private static final String KEY_TASK_ID = "_id";
21      private static final String KEY_DESCRIPTION = "description";
22      private static final String KEY_IS_DONE = "is_done";
23
24      private int taskCount;  //COUNTS THE NUMBER OF TASKS ON THE LIST
25
26      public DBHelper (Context context){
27          super (context, DATABASE_NAME, null, DATABASE_VERSION);
28      }
29
30      @Override
31      public void onCreate (SQLiteDatabase database){
32          String sqlStatement = "CREATE TABLE " + DATABASE_TABLE + "("
33                  + KEY_TASK_ID + " INTEGER PRIMARY KEY, "
34                  + KEY_DESCRIPTION + " TEXT, "
35                  + KEY_IS_DONE + " INTEGER" + ")";
36          database.execSQL (sqlStatement);
37          taskCount = 0;
38      }
```

```
39
40        @Override
41        public void onUpgrade(SQLiteDatabase database,
42                              int oldVersion,
43                              int newVersion) {
44          database.execSQL("DROP TABLE IF EXISTS " + DATABASE_TABLE);
45          onCreate(database);
46        }
```

SQLiteDatabase provides methods for accessing database content. Database operations, such as adding new data elements and deleting data records, can be performed using these access methods.

Line 51:	The database is opened for writing. Once opened, the database is cached. getWritableDatabase() must be called each time prior to writing to the database.
Line 52:	An empty set of content values is created. Key-value pairs will be added to this ContentValue object, which will eventually be inserted into the database.
Lines 54–63:	The ToDo task information is added to the ContentValue object.
Line 66:	A data row is inserted into the database table. The insert () method specifies the database table and the ContentValue object of the data row.
	The null value in the insert method call is used to represent a nullColumnHack value. By default, SQL does not allow the insertion of a completely empty row. However, if nullColumnHack specifies a column name, the parameter can be used to explicitly insert null content.
Line 69:	Once the writing activity has concluded, the method close() is called.
Lines 80–83:	During an editTaskItem process, the method update() is called to update the data content of a record in the database. This method is provided with the name of the database table, a new set of content values, and a whereClause. The whereClause is just the string value that specified the location of the record.
Lines 90–95:	A Cursor provides read-write access to the result set returned by a database query.
Lines 101–105:	The Cursor object is used to return the value of the requested columns. These columns are specified as indices [0], [1], and [2].

Lines 129–142:   A Cursor object is used to collect each row in the table. The cursor is positioned on the first row by calling
moveToFirst().

```
DBHelper.java (continued)
47      //********** DATABASE OPERATIONS:  ADD, EDIT, DELETE
48
49        //ADD A ToDo TASK TO THE DATABASE
50      public void addToDoItem(ToDo_Item task) {
51          SQLiteDatabase db = this.getWritableDatabase();
52          ContentValues values = new ContentValues();
53
54          taskCount++;
55          //ADD KEY-VALUE PAIR INFORMATION FOR THE TASK DESCRIPTION
56          values.put(KEY_TASK_ID, taskCount);
57
58          //ADD KEY-VALUE PAIR INFORMATION FOR THE TASK DESCRIPTION
59          values.put(KEY_DESCRIPTION, task.getDescription()); // task name
60
61          //ADD KEY-VALUE PAIR INFORMATION FOR IS_DONE
62          //  0- NOT DONE, 1 - IS DONE
63          values.put(KEY_IS_DONE, task.getIs_done());
64
65          // INSERT THE ROW IN THE TABLE
66          db.insert(DATABASE_TABLE, null, values);
67
68          // CLOSE THE DATABASE CONNECTION
69          db.close();
70      }
71
72        // EDIT A TODO TASK IN THE DATABASE
73      public void editTaskItem(ToDo_Item task){
74          SQLiteDatabase db = this.getWritableDatabase();
75          ContentValues values = new ContentValues();
76
77          values.put(KEY_DESCRIPTION, task.getDescription());
78          values.put(KEY_IS_DONE, task.getIs_done());
79
80          db.update(DATABASE_TABLE, values, KEY_TASK_ID + " = ?",
81                  new String[]{
82                          String.valueOf(task.getId())
83                  });
84          db.close();
85      }
86
87        // RETURN A SPECIFIC TODO TASK IN THE DATABASE
88      public ToDo_Item getToDo_Task(int id) {
89          SQLiteDatabase db = this.getReadableDatabase();
90          Cursor cursor = db.query(
```

```
91              DATABASE_TABLE,
92              new String[]{KEY_TASK_ID, KEY_DESCRIPTION, KEY_IS_DONE},
93              KEY_TASK_ID + "=?",
94              new String[]{String.valueOf(id)},
95              null, null, null, null );
96
97      if (cursor != null)
98          cursor.moveToFirst();
99
100     ToDo_Item task = new ToDo_Item(
101             cursor.getInt(0),
102             cursor.getString(1),
103             cursor.getInt(2));
104     db.close();
105     return task;
106 }
107
108  // DELETE A SPECIFIC TODO TASK FROM THE DATABASE
109 public void deleteTaskItem (ToDo_Item task){
110     SQLiteDatabase database = this.getReadableDatabase();
111
112     // DELETE THE TABLE ROW
113     database.delete(DATABASE_TABLE, KEY_TASK_ID + " = ?",
114             new String[]
115                     {String.valueOf(task.getId())});
116     database.close();
117 }
118
119 public int getTaskCount() {
120     return taskCount;
121 }
122
123  //ADD A TODO TASK TO THE DATABASE
124 public ArrayList<ToDo_Item> getAllTaskItems() {
125     ArrayList<ToDo_Item> taskList = new ArrayList<ToDo_Item>();
126     String queryList = "SELECT * FROM " + DATABASE_TABLE;
127
128     SQLiteDatabase database = this.getReadableDatabase();
129     Cursor cursor = database.rawQuery(queryList, null);
130
131     //COLLECT EACH ROW IN THE TABLE
132     if (cursor.moveToFirst()){
133         do {
134             ToDo_Item task = new ToDo_Item();
135             task.setId(cursor.getInt(0));
136             task.setDescription(cursor.getString(1));
137             task.setIs_done(cursor.getInt(2));
138
139             //ADD TO THE QUERY LIST
140             taskList.add(task);
```

```
141            } while (cursor.moveToNext());
142        }
143        return taskList;
144    }
145 }
```

Part 5: `MainActivity` Class

`MyActivity` is the controller for the application, as well as the test file that performs the database experiments. These experiments will consist of the following:

Experiment 1:   Create the database structure. Add the following five ToDo task items to the database and display the records in the LogCat window.

	_id	description	is_done
1	1	Read Hamlet	true
2	2	Study for exam	false
3	3	Call Andy and Sam	true
4	4	Create newsletter	true
5	5	Buy a dog	false

Experiment 2:   Modify the first record of the database. Replace "Read Hamlet" with "Read newspaper."

Experiment 3:   Display the second record of the database in the LogCat window.

Experiment 4:   Delete the "Buy a dog" record from the database. Display all the records in the LogCat window.

The Java code for `MyActivity` is shown as follows:

MainActivity.java

```
1  package com.cornez.todotoday;
2
3  import android.app.Activity;
4  import android.os.Bundle;
5  import android.util.Log;
6  import java.util.ArrayList;
7
8  public class MainActivity extends Activity {
9
10     @Override
11     protected void onCreate(Bundle savedInstanceState) {
12         super.onCreate(savedInstanceState);
13         setContentView(R.layout.activity_main);
```

```
14
15          //EXPERIMENT 1: CREATE THE DATABASE
16
17          DBHelper database = new DBHelper(this);
18
19          //              ADD FIVE TASK ITEMS TO THE DATABASE
20          database.addToDoItem(new ToDo_Item(
21                  1, "Read Hamlet", 1));
22          database.addToDoItem(new ToDo_Item(
23                  2, "Study for exam", 1));
24          database.addToDoItem(new ToDo_Item(
25                  3, "Call Andy and Sam", 0));
26          database.addToDoItem(new ToDo_Item(
27                  4, "Create newsletter", 1));
28          database.addToDoItem(new ToDo_Item(
29                  5, "Buy a dog", 0));
30
31          //              DISPLAY ALL THE TASK ITEMS IN THE TABLE
32          String taskItemList = "\n";
33          ArrayList<ToDo_Item> taskList = database.getAllTaskItems();
34          for (int i = 0; i < database.getTaskCount(); i++) {
35              ToDo_Item task = taskList.get(i);
36              taskItemList += "\n" + task.getDescription() + "\t" +
37                      task.getIs_done();
38          }
39          Log.v("DATABASE RECORDS", taskItemList);
40
41          // EXPERIMENT 2: MODIFY A RECORD
42          database.editTaskItem(new ToDo_Item(
43                  1, "Read newspaper", 1));
44
45          //EXPERIMENT 3: DISPLAY A SPECIFIC RECORD
46          ToDo_Item anItem = database.getToDo_Task(2);
47          Log.v("DATABASE RECORDS", anItem.getDescription());
48
49          //EXPERIMENT 4: DELETE A RECORD
50          database.deleteTaskItem(new ToDo_Item(
51                  15, "Buy a dog", 0));
52
53          //              DISPLAY ALL THE TASK ITEMS IN THE TABLE
54          taskItemList = "\n";
55          taskList = database.getAllTaskItems();
56          for (int i = 0; i < database.getTaskCount(); i++) {
57              ToDo_Item task = taskList.get(i);
58              taskItemList += "\n" + task.getDescription() + "\t" +
59                      task.getIs_done();
60          }
61          Log.v("DATABASE RECORDS", taskItemList);
62      }
63
64 }
```

The output produced by a test run of the application is shown in Figure 9-3.

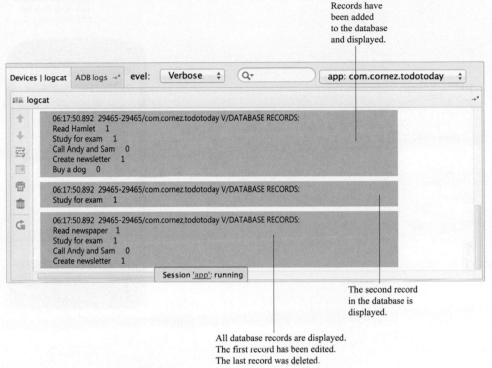

Records have
been added
to the database
and displayed.

The second record
in the database is
displayed.

All database records are displayed.
The first record has been edited.
The last record was deleted.

❙ FIGURE 9-3 The result sets produced by a test run of the database experiment.

◼ 9.6 Adapters and AdapterViews

An Adapter object is a mechanism that binds a data source, such as a database, to an AdapterView. An AdapterView is a container widget that is populated by a data source, determined by an Adapter. Common AdapterViews are ListViews, GridViews, and Spinners.

Figure 9-4 illustrates the process of populating an AdapterView with items from a data source. The data source in this example is a database containing cities in California. The individual items from the data source are converted into a View and then added to and displayed inside the AdapterView. The AdapterView in this example is a ListView.

In this manner, the Adapter object behaves as an intermediary between the data source and the AdapterView layout. The Adapter retrieves the data from the data source and dynamically adds it to the AdapterView.

A ListView is often at the heart of data-driven applications. A ListView is an AdapterView that provides a simple approach for an application to display a scrolling list of records. These records can be displayed with a default format, using a built-in style, or customized extensively.

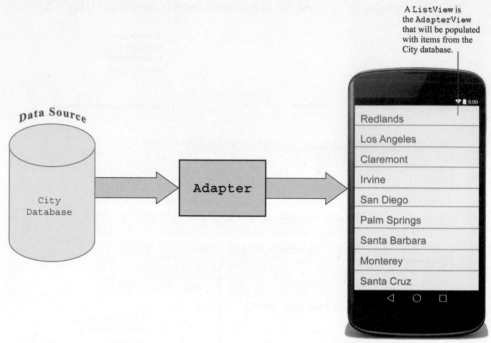

A `ListView` is the `AdapterView` that will be populated with items from the City database.

Data Source

City Database

Adapter

Redlands
Los Angeles
Claremont
Irvine
San Diego
Palm Springs
Santa Barbara
Monterey
Santa Cruz

┃ FIGURE 9-4 An `Adapter` object binds a data source to an `AdapterView`.

As an `AdapterView`, a `ListView` object requires an `Adapter` to provide it with data. A `ListView` consists of a collection of sequential items. As shown in Figure 9-5, each item is a visual representation of a data record in a list. Each record item is placed into an independent `View`. The `View` elements on the left are shown as default views defined by a resource file. The items on the right are designed with a simplified custom layout.

When a `ListView` is populated with many records, a fast-scrolling feature can be enabled and customized to help the user better navigate the list of data. For example, when scrolling through long lists, an index can be displayed indicating the location currently being viewed within the layout.

Consider the example shown in Figure 9-6. An `AdapterView` is populated with data collected from a data source. The `AdapterView` in this example is a `ListView`. The data source is a `String` array holding the names of dessert items. An `ArrayAdapter` is the object mechanism that performs the task of filling the `ListView` with a `View` object for each dessert item. In addition, the dessert `View` objects are made clickable to display general facts, such as name and index value, in a `Toast` popup.

FIGURE 9-5 A List can be a default format or a custom-built layout.

FIGURE 9-6 An AdapterView is populated from data.

The following Java code shows the creation of the Adapter and the `setOn-ItemClickListener()` assignment to each of the dessert items in the list.

Task 1:	A `ListView` UI component has been placed on the layout associated with this `Activity`. It is referenced by `adapterView`.
Task 2:	The data source is an array, `dessertData`. Each dessert item is stored in the array as a string element.
Task 3:	An `Adapter` object is defined and provided with information, such as the name of the `AdapterView` it will populate, the name of the `View` element that will hold an individual item object, and the data source.
	It should be noted that there are two types of Adapters: `ArrayAdapter` and `CursorAdapter`. In this example, an `ArrayAdapter` is used because it configures well with arrays and ArrayLists. The `CursorAdapter` can be used when binding data from a private SQLite database.
	A layout resource will be used to instantiate the `View` objects that will populate the `ListView`. For example, the string "cake" will reside in a `View` layout that will be added to the `ListView`. In this example, the layout named `record_item.xml` has been designed to hold a TextView, which will eventually store the name of a dessert. The id of the `TextView` has been set to `R.id.dessert`. The last argument, on Line 21, identifies the data source, `dessertData`.
Task 4:	The adapter is assigned to the `ListView` object by calling the method `setAdapter()`. The `ListView` object is now populated with data from the specified data source. At this point, all of the desserts will appear in the `ListView`.
Task 5:	Click listeners are applied to each of the items stored in the `ListView`. `AdapterView` is a view whose children are determined by an `Adapter`.

```
MainActivity.java
1    public class MainActivity extends ActionBarActivity {
2        ListView adapterView;
3
4        @Override
5        protected void onCreate(Bundle savedInstanceState) {
6            super.onCreate(savedInstanceState);
7            setContentView(R.layout.activity_main);
8
```

```
 9      //TASK 1: REFERENCE THE LISTVIEW ELEMENT IN THE LAYOUT
10      adapterView = (ListView) findViewById(R.id. adapterView);
11
12      //TASK 2: ITEM VALUES THAT WILL BE PLACED IN THE ADAPTERVIEW
13      String [] dessertData = {"cake", "pie", "ice cream",
14                      "licorice", "fudge", "cookie"};
15
16      //TASK 3: DEFINE AN ADAPTER
17      ArrayAdapter<String> adapter = new
18                      ArrayAdapter<String>(this,
19                      R.layout.record_item,
20                      R.id.dessert,
21                      dessertData);
22
23      //TASK 4: ASSIGN AN ADAPTER TO THE LISTVIEW
24      adapterView.setAdapter(adapter);
25
26      //TASK 5: SET CLICK LISTENERS FOR EACH ITEM
27      adapterView.setOnItemClickListener(new
28              AdapterView.OnItemClickListener() {
29          @Override
30          public void onItemClick(AdapterView<?> parent,
31                                  View view,
32                                  int position, long id) {
33              int index = position;
34              String itemName = (String)
35                      adapterView.getItemAtPosition(position);
36
37              // DISPLAY INFORMATION ABOUT EACH ITEM CLICKED
38              Toast.makeText(getApplicationContext(), "Item "
39                      + index " is " + itemName,
40                      Toast.LENGTH_SHORT).show();
41          }
42      });
43  }
```

■ Lab Example 9-2: ToDo Today—The Complete Application

This lab example presents the complete ToDo Today application. As with the previous version of the application from Lab Example 9-1, the SQLite datatabase table toDo_Items will be used, along with the DBHelper class for creating and managing the data content. The main features added to this version of the application will be the user interface and the mechanism for listing the interactive items on the screen. The objective of this lab example is to explore the link between SQLite data files, Adapters, and AdapterViews.

Part 1: The Design

The user interface for the application, TODO Today II, will allow the user to add ToDo items to a scrollable list of items one at a time. An ADD ToDo ITEM button will display the entered item at the bottom of the list seen on the screen. In addition, this item will be added as a row to the database table.

Figure 9-7 shows the application after five ToDo items have been added to the database. Each ToDo item is displayed alongside a checkbox. Users will use the checkbox to indicate whether a task has been completed. A second button, CLEAR ALL To-DoS, will allow the user to clear all stored records in the database. Because the list on the screen is linked directly to the database table, its scrollable content will be deleted.

▌FIGURE 9-7 The ToDo Today II application.

Part 2: Application Structure and Setup

The settings for the application are as follows:

- Application Name: ToDo Today II
- Project Name: ToDoTodayII
- Package Name: `com.cornez.todotodayii`

- Android Form: Phone and Tablet
- Minimum SDK: API 18: Android 4.3 (Jelly Bean)
- Target SDK: API 21: Android 5.0 (Lollipop)
- Compile with: API 21: Android 5.0 (Lollipop)
- Activity Name: `MainActivity`
- Layout Name: `activity_main`

The structure for the final application is shown in Figure 9-8. In addition to the `ToDo_Item` class, the `DBHelper` class, and the `MainActivity`, a layout file characterizing a single `View` of the ToDo item will be required. The layout file named `todo_item.xml` will be used to embody this View. As an interactive list item, it will provide the checkbox UI component.

| FIGURE 9-8 Final project structure for ToDo Today II application.

A portrait orientation of the screen is specified in `AndroidManifest.xml`. The single activity of the application is specified on Lines 10 through 20. The complete XML for `AndroidManifest.xml` is shown as follows:

```
AndroidManifest.xml
1   <?xml version="1.0" encoding="utf-8"?>
2   <manifest xmlns:android="http://schemas.android.com/apk/res/android"
3       package="com.cornez.todotodayii" >
4
```

```
5      <application
6          android:allowBackup="true"
7          android:icon="@drawable/ic_launcher"
8          android:label="@string/app_name"
9          android:theme="@style/AppTheme" >
10         <activity
11             android:screenOrientation="portrait"
12             android:name=".MainActivity"
13             android:label="@string/app_name" >
14             <intent-filter>
15                 <action android:name="android.intent.action.MAIN" />
16
17                 <category
18                     android:name="android.intent.category.LAUNCHER" />
19             </intent-filter>
20         </activity>
21     </application>
22
23 </manifest>
```

Part 3: The User Interface

The ToDo Today II application uses values from the `strings.xml` file to store static button labels used by the layout associated with `MainActivity`. Color resources are defined to visually partition the screen and make the application easier to navigate. The XML code for these two files is shown as follows:

colors.xml

```
1  <?xml version="1.0" encoding="utf-8"?>
2  <resources>
3      <color name="yellow">#fffffba1</color>
4      <color name="aqua">#B3CAB5</color>
5      <color name="cream">#c2d5da</color>
6      <color name="dark_aqua">#9fb3a0</color>
7
8  </resources>
```

strings.xml

```
1  <?xml version="1.0" encoding="utf-8"?>
2  <resources>
3
4      <string name="app_name">TODO Today II</string>
5      <string name="hello_world">Hello world!</string>
6      <string name="action_settings">Settings</string>
7
```

```
8          <string name="add">Add TODO Item</string>
9          <string name="task">Enter TODO Item</string>
10         <string name="delete">Clear all TODOs</string>
11         <string name="desc">Description</string>
12
13
14    </resources>
```

The user interface for the application is `activity_main.xml`. This layout file places UI objects relative to each other on the screen within a `RelativeLayout` root element. Within this root element are two main containers: `RelativeLayout` and `ListView`. The hierarchical layout structure is shown in Figure 9-9.

The controls for the application are placed in the `RelativeLayout`, named `relativeLayout1`. This consists of an `EditText` for ToDo item entries and buttons for adding and removing items.

The second container in the user interface is a `ListView`, named `listView1`. This component is the `AdapterView` that will be linked to the database table.

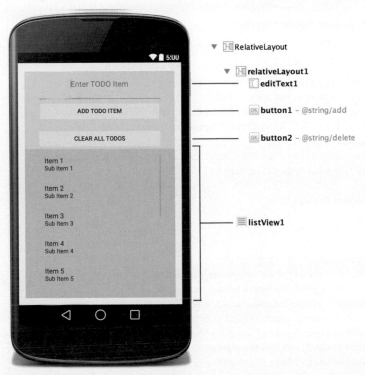

❚ FIGURE 9-9 The layout structure for `activity_main.xml`.

The two buttons, located in the relativeLayout1 container, are assigned `onClick` event handlers. The complete XML code for `activity_main.xml` is shown as follows:

```
activity_main.xml
1   <RelativeLayout
2   xmlns:android="http://schemas.android.com/apk/res/android"
3       xmlns:tools="http://schemas.android.com/tools"
4       android:layout_width="match_parent"
5       android:layout_height="match_parent"
6       android:paddingLeft="@dimen/activity_horizontal_margin"
7       android:paddingRight="@dimen/activity_horizontal_margin"
8       android:paddingTop="@dimen/activity_vertical_margin"
9       android:paddingBottom="@dimen/activity_vertical_margin"
10      tools:context=".MainActivity">
11
12      <RelativeLayout
13          android:id="@+id/relativeLayout1"
14          android:layout_width="wrap_content"
15          android:layout_height="wrap_content"
16          android:layout_marginTop="4dp"
17          android:background="@color/aqua"
18          android:paddingLeft="30dp"
19          android:paddingRight="30dp" >
20
21          <EditText
22              android:id="@+id/editText1"
23              android:layout_width="match_parent"
24              android:layout_height="70dp"
25              android:layout_alignParentLeft="true"
26              android:layout_alignParentTop="true"
27              android:ems="10"
28              android:gravity="center_horizontal|center_vertical"
29              android:hint="@string/task" >
30
31              <requestFocus />
32          </EditText>
33
34          <Button
35              android:id="@+id/button1"
36              android:layout_width="match_parent"
37              android:layout_height="wrap_content"
38              android:layout_below="@+id/editText1"
39              android:layout_centerHorizontal="true"
40              android:layout_marginRight="5dp"
41              android:onClick="addTaskNow"
42              android:text="@string/add" />
43
```

```
44          <Button
45              android:id="@+id/button2"
46              android:layout_width="match_parent"
47              android:layout_height="wrap_content"
48              android:layout_below="@+id/button1"
49              android:layout_centerHorizontal="true"
50              android:onClick="clearTasks"
51              android:text="@string/delete" />
52
53      </RelativeLayout>
54
55      <ListView
56          android:id="@+id/listView1"
57          android:layout_width="match_parent"
58          android:layout_height="wrap_content"
59          android:layout_alignParentLeft="true"
60          android:layout_below="@+id/relativeLayout1"
61          android:background="@color/dark_aqua"
62          android:paddingBottom="4dp"
63          android:paddingLeft="30dp"
64          android:paddingRight="30dp"
65          android:paddingTop="10dp" >
66
67      </ListView>
68
69
70  </RelativeLayout>
```

Part 4: A Single Table Record Layout: `todo_item.xml`

ToDo items are added to the scrollable `ListView` by inflating a `View`. This `View` will be defined by the layout `todo_item.xml`. This `View` will be displayed as the item in the list.

To simplify the construction of this layout, a simple `CheckBox` widget will be used for both the text element of the ToDo item and the checkbox. The layout structure for `todo_item.xml` is shown in Figure 9-10.

The complete XML code for `todo_item.xml` is shown as follows. The `CheckBox` identifier, `chkStatus`, will be used to update the database automatically when an `onClick()` event occurs on the checkbox.

todo_item.xml
```
1   <?xml version="1.0" encoding="utf-8"?>
2   <RelativeLayout
3   xmlns:android="http://schemas.android.com/apk/res/android"
4       android:layout_width="match_parent"
5       android:layout_height="match_parent">
```

```
 6
 7        <CheckBox
 8            android:id="@+id/chkStatus"
 9            android:layout_width="match_parent"
10            android:layout_height="wrap_content"
11            android:background="@color/yellow"
12            android:focusable="false"
13            android:focusableInTouchMode="false"
14            android:padding="10dp"
15            android:textSize="20sp" />
16
17    </RelativeLayout>
```

FIGURE 9-10 The `todo_item.xml` layout design for a single ToDo item.

Part 5: Revised Version of `DBHelper.java`

The `DBHelper` class will perform similarly to the class designed for the first version of the application. The database table will be contructed using the following schema. In this schema, the _id column will be typeset as `INTEGER PRIMARY KEY AUTOINCREMENT`.

Database table: toDo_Items	
Column Names	Data Type
_id	INTEGER PRIMARY KEY AUTOINCREMENT
description	TEXT
is_done	INTEGER

The database operation for adding an individual record to the database table will remain relatively the same as the previous version.

Lines 77–101: The method getAllTasks() will be used by the main activity of the application to collect the list of ToDo tasks. A List-Adapter can maintain the data backing this list and produce a view to display that data set.

The two new methods added to the class are clearAll() and updateTask().

Lines 103–109: The method clearAll() performs two tasks. First, the items located on the List structure are cleared. Second, the complete set of records in the database is cleared.

Line 107: The database is made available for writing.

Line 108: The delete() method is called to delete rows from the database table. By passing a null value to the WHERE class, indicated by the second parameter, all rows will be deleted.

Lines 112–122: The updateTask() method uses ContentValues to add a row of data to the database table.

```
DBHelper.java
1   package com.cornez.todotodayii;
2
3
4   import android.content.ContentValues;
5   import android.content.Context;
6   import android.database.Cursor;
7   import android.database.sqlite.SQLiteDatabase;
8   import android.database.sqlite.SQLiteOpenHelper;
9
10  import java.util.ArrayList;
11  import java.util.List;
12
13  public class DBHelper extends SQLiteOpenHelper {
14      //TASK 1: DEFINE THE DATABASE AND TABLE
15      private static final int DATABASE_VERSION = 1;
```

```
16    private static final String DATABASE_NAME = "toDo_Today";
17    private static final String DATABASE_TABLE = "toDo_Items";
18
19
20    //TASK 2: DEFINE THE COLUMN NAMES FOR THE TABLE
21    private static final String KEY_TASK_ID = "_id";
22    private static final String KEY_DESCRIPTION = "description";
23    private static final String KEY_IS_DONE = "is_done";
24
25    private int taskCount;
26
27    public DBHelper (Context context){
28        super (context, DATABASE_NAME, null, DATABASE_VERSION);
29    }
30
31
32    @Override
33    public void onCreate(SQLiteDatabase db) {
34
35        String table =
36          "CREATE TABLE " + DATABASE_TABLE + "("
37              + KEY_TASK_ID + " INTEGER PRIMARY KEY AUTOINCREMENT, "
38              + KEY_DESCRIPTION + " TEXT, "
39              + KEY_IS_DONE + " INTEGER" + ")";
40
41        db.execSQL(table);
42    }
43
44    @Override
45    public void onUpgrade(SQLiteDatabase database,
46                          int oldVersion,
47                          int newVersion) {
48        // DROP OLDER TABLE IF EXISTS
49        database.execSQL("DROP TABLE IF EXISTS " + DATABASE_TABLE);
50
51        // CREATE TABLE AGAIN
52        onCreate(database);
53    }
54
55
56    //********** DATABASE OPERATIONS:  ADD, EDIT, DELETE
57    // Adding new task
58    public void addToDoItem(ToDo_Item task) {
59        SQLiteDatabase db = this.getWritableDatabase();
60        ContentValues values = new ContentValues();
61
62        //ADD KEY-VALUE PAIR INFORMATION FOR THE TASK DESCRIPTION
63      values.put(KEY_DESCRIPTION, task.getDescription()); // task name
64
```

```
65          //ADD KEY-VALUE PAIR INFORMATION FOR
66          //IS_DONE VALUE: 0- NOT DONE, 1 - IS DONE
67          values.put(KEY_IS_DONE, task.getIs_done());
68
69          // INSERT THE ROW IN THE TABLE
70          db.insert(DATABASE_TABLE, null, values);
71          taskCount++;
72
73          // CLOSE THE DATABASE CONNECTION
74          db.close();
75      }
76
77      public List<ToDo_Item> getAllTasks() {
78
79          //GET ALL THE TASK ITEMS ON THE LIST
80          List<ToDo_Item> todoList = new ArrayList<ToDo_Item>();
81
82          //SELECT ALL QUERY FROM THE TABLE
83          String selectQuery = "SELECT  * FROM " + DATABASE_TABLE;
84
85          SQLiteDatabase db = this.getWritableDatabase();
86          Cursor cursor = db.rawQuery(selectQuery, null);
87
88          // LOOP THROUGH THE TODO TASKS
89          if (cursor.moveToFirst()) {
90              do {
91                  ToDo_Item task = new ToDo_Item();
92                  task.setId(cursor.getInt(0));
93                  task.setDescription(cursor.getString(1));
94                  task.setIs_done(cursor.getInt(2));
95                  todoList.add(task);
96              } while (cursor.moveToNext());
97          }
98
99          // RETURN THE LIST OF TASKS FROM THE TABLE
100         return todoList;
101     }
102
103     public void clearAll(List<ToDo_Item> list) {
104         //GET ALL THE LIST TASK ITEMS AND CLEAR THEM
105         list.clear();
106
107         SQLiteDatabase db = this.getWritableDatabase();
108         db.delete(DATABASE_TABLE, null, new String[]{});
109         db.close();
110     }
111
112     public void updateTask(ToDo_Item task) {
113         // UPDATE RECORD
```

```
114            SQLiteDatabase db = this.getWritableDatabase();
115            ContentValues values = new ContentValues();
116
117            values.put(KEY_DESCRIPTION, task.getDescription());
118            values.put(KEY_IS_DONE, task.getIs_done());
119
120            db.update(DATABASE_TABLE, values, KEY_TASK_ID + " = ?",
121                    new String[]{String.valueOf(task.getId())});
122            db.close();
123        }
124
125    }
```

Part 6: The `Activity` for the Application

`MainActivity` serves as the controller of the application. It will regulate the flow of data between the elements in the layout and the data content stored in the database, and it will respond to user actions.

A custom `Adapter` class, `MyAdapter`, will be used to populate the user interface screen layout with data from the database. `MyAdapter` is written as an extension of the `ArrayAdapter`.

The Java code for `MainActivity` is shown below:

Lines 28–39:   The `onCreate()` callback method will perform three tasks. The first task is to launch the layout containing the `EditText`, add and clear buttons, and the scrollable `ListView`, used to store the ToDo data content. The second task will establish the reference to the input element, allowing the user to input the ToDo item.

    The final task performed by `onCreate()` is the setup of the initial database.

Lines 41–48:   The `onResume()` callback method will populate the ListView with ToDo task items, gathered from the database. An Adapter object, instantiated from MyAdapter, is defined and given the name of the `AdapterView` it will populate with data. This adapter is assigned to the listTask object, the ListView UI placed on the layout.

Lines 50–70:   The `onClick` event registered to the ADD button is implemented in addTaskNow(). The description of the ToDo task is collected from the `EditText` referenced by `myTask`. If an empty error has not occurred, the task is added to the database. The `adapter` object is used to add the item to the `ListView`.

The call to `notifyDataSetChanged()` will notify any attached observers that data has been changed in the database. This means that any `AdapterView` displaying the data set can refresh itself.

Lines 72–76:   The CLEAR button, located on the layout, will trigger the `onClick` event handler `clearTasks()`. All ToDo tasks are deleted from the database. The call to `notifyDataSet-Changed()` will notify the attached `AdapterView` that data has been changed and it can reflect the changes in the `ListView` display.

Lines 78–87:   The `MyAdapter()` class is a custom `ArrayAdapter`. This class provides a resource id to reference the layout named `todo_item.xml`. The constructor parameters consist of the current context, the resource ID for the layout file containing the ToDo item, and the `ListView`. The layout will be used for instantiating views containing data. The final parameter object representing the `ListView` will display the collection of ToDo items.

Lines 89–136:   The `getView()` method defines and inflates individual ToDo items to be displayed in the ListView. Each of these inflated views is registered as clickable. This allows the user to specify the status of the ToDo task. If the user has completed a ToDo task, a check symbol will appear in the checkbox.

When an `onClick()` event is triggered for a ToDo item, the database helper object will update the data stored in the database.

```
MainActivity.java
1   package com.cornez.todotodayii;
2
3   import android.app.Activity;
4   import android.content.Context;
5   import android.os.Bundle;
6   import android.view.LayoutInflater;
7   import android.view.Menu;
8   import android.view.MenuItem;
9   import android.view.View;
10  import android.view.ViewGroup;
11  import android.widget.ArrayAdapter;
12  import android.widget.CheckBox;
13  import android.widget.EditText;
14  import android.widget.ListView;
15  import android.widget.Toast;
16
```

```java
17   import java.util.ArrayList;
18   import java.util.List;
19
20   public class MainActivity extends Activity {
21
22       protected DBHelper mDBHelper;
23       private List<ToDo_Item> list;
24       private MyAdapter adapt;
25       private EditText myTask;
26
27       @Override
28       protected void onCreate(Bundle savedInstanceState) {
29           super.onCreate(savedInstanceState);
30           // TASK 1: LAUNCH THE LAYOUT REPRESENTING THE MAIN ACTIVITY
31           setContentView(R.layout.activity_main);
32
33           // TASK 2: ESTABLISH REFERENCES TO THE UI
34           //         ELEMENTS LOCATED ON THE LAYOUT
35           myTask = (EditText) findViewById(R.id.editText1);
36
37           // TASK 3: SET UP THE DATABASE
38           mDBHelper = new DBHelper(this);
39       }
40
41       @Override
42       protected void onResume(){
43           super.onResume();
44           list = mDBHelper.getAllTasks();
45           adapt = new MyAdapter(this, R.layout.todo_item, list);
46           ListView listTask = (ListView) findViewById(R.id.listView1);
47           listTask.setAdapter(adapt);
48       }
49
50       //BUTTON CLICK EVENT FOR ADDING A TODO TASK
51       public void addTaskNow(View view) {
52           String s = myTask.getText().toString();
53           if (s.isEmpty()) {
54               Toast.makeText(getApplicationContext(),
55                       "A TODO task must be entered.",
56                       Toast.LENGTH_SHORT).show();
57           } else {
58
59               //BUILD A NEW TASK ITEM AND ADD IT TO THE DATABASE
60               ToDo_Item task = new ToDo_Item(s, 0);
61               mDBHelper.addToDoItem(task);
62
63               // CLEAR OUT THE TASK EDITVIEW
64               myTask.setText("");
65
66               // ADD THE TASK AND SET A NOTIFICATION OF CHANGES
67               adapt.add(task);
```

```
68              adapt.notifyDataSetChanged();
69          }
70      }
71
72      //BUTTON CLICK EVENT FOR DELETING ALL TODO TASKS
73      public void clearTasks(View view) {
74          mDBHelper.clearAll(list);
75          adapt.notifyDataSetChanged();
76      }
77
78      //******************* ADAPTER ******************************
79      private class MyAdapter extends ArrayAdapter<ToDo_Item> {
80          Context context;
81          List<ToDo_Item> taskList = new ArrayList<ToDo_Item>();
82
83          public MyAdapter(Context c, int rId, List<ToDo_Item> objects) {
84              super(c, rId, objects);
85              taskList = objects;
86              context = c;
87          }
88
89      //**************** TODO TASK ITEM VIEW *********************
90          /**
91           * THIS METHOD DEFINES THE TODO ITEM THAT WILL BE PLACED
92           * INSIDE THE LIST VIEW.
93           *
94           * THE CHECKBOX STATE IS THE IS_DONE STATUS OF THE TODO TASK
95           * AND THE CHECKBOX TEXT IS THE TODO_ITEM TASK DESCRIPTION.
96           */
97
98          @Override
99          public View getView(int position,
100                         View convertView,
101                         ViewGroup parent) {
102
103             CheckBox isDoneChBx = null;
104             if (convertView == null) {
105                 LayoutInflater inflater = (LayoutInflater) context
106                     .getSystemService(Context.LAYOUT_INFLATER_SERVICE);
107
108                 convertView = inflater.inflate(R.layout.todo_item,
109                         parent, false);
110                 isDoneChBx = (CheckBox)
111                         convertView.findViewById(R.id.chkStatus);
112                 convertView.setTag(isDoneChBx);
113
114                 isDoneChBx.setOnClickListener(
115                         new View.OnClickListener() {
116
117                     @Override
118                     public void onClick(View view) {
```

```
119                         CheckBox cb = (CheckBox) view;
120                         ToDo_Item changeTask = (ToDo_Item) cb.getTag();
121                         changeTask.setIs_done(
122                                 cb.isChecked() == true ? 1 : 0);
123                         mDBHelper.updateTask(changeTask);
124                     }
125                 });
126             } else {
127                 isDoneChBx = (CheckBox) convertView.getTag();
128             }
129             ToDo_Item current = taskList.get(position);
130             isDoneChBx.setText(current.getDescription());
131             isDoneChBx.setChecked(
132                     current.getIs_done() == 1 ? true : false);
133             isDoneChBx.setTag(current);
134             return convertView;
135         }
136     }
137
138     @Override
139     public boolean onCreateOptionsMenu(Menu menu) {
140         // Inflate the menu.
141         getMenuInflater().inflate(R.menu.menu_main, menu);
142         return true;
143     }
144
145     @Override
146     public boolean onOptionsItemSelected(MenuItem item) {
147         // Handle action bar item clicks here. The action bar will
148         // automatically handle clicks on the Home/Up button, so long
149         // as you specify a parent activity in AndroidManifest.xml.
150         int id = item.getItemId();
151
152         //noinspection SimplifiableIfStatement
153         if (id == R.id.action_settings) {
154             return true;
155         }
156
157         return super.onOptionsItemSelected(item);
158     }
159 }
```

■ Lab Example 9-3: Pet Contacts

Applications that store and manage contact information can help organizations, businesses, and the general user to work with customers, members, and other people. The Pet Contacts application, as shown in Figure 9-11, is a simplified look at how to incorporate database elements, along with data collected from externally stored files.

Part 1: The Design

Pet Contacts is designed as a veterinarian tool to record patient data. Along with information about the pet's name, health condition, and owner's phone number, an image can be added to the contact sheet. More specifically, a photo of the pet will be retrieved from the Camera/Gallery and added to the database.

The SQLite database will be designed as follows:

DATABASE NAME: DATABASE TABLE:	petManager contact
Table Column Names	**Data Type**
_id	INTEGER PRIMARY KEY AUTOINCREMENT
name	TEXT
details	TEXT
phone	TEXT
photo	TEXT

FIGURE 9-11 Pet Contacts application.

Part 2: Application Structure and Setup

The settings for the application are as follows:

- Application Name: Pet Contacts
- Project Name: PetContacts
- Package Name: `com.cornez.petcontacts`
- Android Form: Phone and Tablet
- Minimum SDK: API 18: Android 4.3 (Jelly Bean)
- Target SDK: API 21: Android 5.0 (Lollipop)
- Compile with: API 21: Android 5.0 (Lollipop)
- Activity Name: `MainActivity`
- Layout Name: `activity_main`

The launcher is set to the Android default `ic_launcher.png` file. The project structure, shown in Figure 9-12, contains three Java source files and two layout files. Pet objects are modeled by the `Pet` class. As pet contacts are displayed on the screen, they are visually constructed using the layout named `listview_item.xml`.

`MainActivity` is the controller of the application, and its associated user interface layout is `activity_main.xml`. As with previous lab examples, `DBHelper` is responsible for database management.

The `none.png` file is used as a default image when a photo is not found.

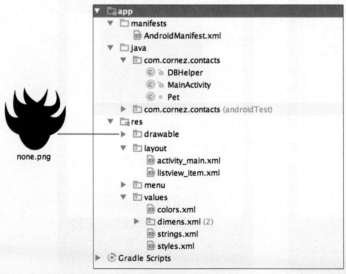

FIGURE 9-12 The project structure for the `Pet Contacts` application.

Applications that declare WRITE_EXTERNAL_STORAGE permission are implicitly granted READ_EXTERNAL_STORAGE permission. The Pet Contacts application will not require or request write permission. Because read permission is not implied using WRITE, the <uses-permission> for READ_EXTERNAL_STORAGE is specified.

The manifest file identifies `MainActivity` as the sole activity for the application. No other activities are started by this activity or will be used by the application. The orientation for the main activity is set to portrait. The complete XML code for `AndroidManifest.xml` is shown as follows:

```
AndroidManifest.xml
1   <?xml version="1.0" encoding="utf-8"?>
2   <manifest xmlns:android="http://schemas.android.com/apk/res/android"
3       package="com.cornez.petcontacts" >
4
5       <uses-permission
6           android:name="android.permission.READ_EXTERNAL_STORAGE"/>
7
8       <application
9           android:allowBackup="true"
10          android:icon="@drawable/ic_launcher"
11          android:label="@string/app_name"
12          android:theme="@style/AppTheme" >
13          <activity
14              android:name=".MainActivity"
15              android:screenOrientation="portrait"
16              android:label="@string/app_name" >
17              <intent-filter>
18                  <action android:name="android.intent.action.MAIN" />
19
20                  <category android:name="android.intent.category.LAUNCHER" />
21              </intent-filter>
22          </activity>
23      </application>
24
25  </manifest>
26
```

Part 3: The User Interface

The Pet Contacts application uses values from the `strings.xml` file to store titles and button labels used by the layout associated with `MainActivity`. The XML code for `strings.xml` and `colors.xml` is shown as follows:

```
strings.xml
 1   <?xml version="1.0" encoding="utf-8"?>
 2   <resources>
 3
 4       <string name="app_name">Pet Contacts</string>
 5       <string name="hello_world">Hello world!</string>
 6       <string name="action_settings">Settings</string>
 7
 8       <string name="my_pets">Pet Listing</string>
 9       <string name="name">Name</string>
10       <string name="details">Pet Details</string>
11       <string name="phone_number">Phone Number</string>
12       <string name="add_btn">Add Pet Contact</string>
13       <string name="enter">Pet Contact</string>
14       <string name="photo">photo of pet</string>
15
16   </resources>
```

```
colors.xml
 1   <?xml version="1.0" encoding="utf-8"?>
 2   <resources>
 3       <color name="dark_blue">#ff49546e</color>
 4       <color name="pale_blue">#ffdeffee</color>
 5       <color name="tab_color">#ff788aa2</color>
 6   </resources>
```

The user interface for the application is designed in the `activity_main.xml` layout. This layout file uses a `RelativeLayout` root element and relies on one of two possible displays identified by a `TabHost`. A `TabHost` is a container for a tabbed window View. This object holds two children: a set of tab labels that the user clicks to select a specific tab, and a FrameLayout object that displays the contents of that page.

As shown in Figure 9-13, the tab labels appear at the top of the screen. When the application is executing, the first label reads "ADD PET INFORMATION." When this tab is activated, the FrameLayout object displays the content from the Relative-Layout container named `tabInfo`. The content consists of a set of widgets for the user to enter pet information, such as a pet name, phone number of the owner, and a photo.

When the tab for VIEW ALL PETS is activated, the `FrameLayout` object displays content from the RelativeLayout container named `tabList`. The content for this tab component is a ListView that displays a scrollable list of all available pet contact information.

| FIGURE 9-13 The User Interface structure for `Pet Contacts` application.

The complete XML code for `activity_main.xml` is shown as follows:

```
activity_main.xml
1
2    <RelativeLayout
3    xmlns:android="http://schemas.android.com/apk/res/android"
4        xmlns:tools="http://schemas.android.com/tools"
5        android:layout_width="match_parent"
6        android:layout_height="match_parent"
7        tools:context=".MainActivity">
8
9        <TabHost
10           android:id="@+id/tabHost"
11           android:layout_width="fill_parent"
12           android:layout_height="fill_parent"
13           android:layout_alignParentBottom="true"
14           android:layout_marginBottom="50dp">
15
16           <RelativeLayout
17               android:layout_width="fill_parent"
18               android:layout_height="fill_parent"
19               android:orientation="vertical">
20
21               <TabWidget
22                   android:id="@android:id/tabs"
23                   android:layout_width="fill_parent"
```

```
24                    android:layout_height="wrap_content"
25                    android:background="@color/tab_color"
26                    android:showDividers="beginning|middle|end"></TabWidget>
27
28            <FrameLayout
29                    android:id="@android:id/tabcontent"
30                    android:layout_width="fill_parent"
31                    android:layout_height="fill_parent">
32
33                <RelativeLayout
34                    android:id="@+id/tabList"
35                    android:layout_width="wrap_content"
36                    android:layout_height="fill_parent">
37
38                    <TextView
39                        android:id="@+id/textView1"
40                        android:layout_width="match_parent"
41                        android:layout_height="wrap_content"
42                        android:text="@string/my_pets"
43                        android:layout_alignParentTop="true"
44                        android:layout_centerHorizontal="true"
45                        android:layout_marginTop="60dp"
46                        android:background="@color/dark_blue"
47                        android:gravity="center_horizontal"
48
49 android:textAppearance="?android:attr/textAppearanceLarge"
50                        android:textColor="@color/pale_blue"
51                        android:textSize="55sp" />
52
53                    <ListView
54                        android:id="@+id/listView"
55                        android:layout_width="fill_parent"
56                        android:layout_height="fill_parent"
57                        android:layout_alignParentEnd="true"
58                        android:layout_alignParentStart="true"
59                        android:layout_below="@+id/textView1"
60                        android:background="@android:color/white" />
61                </RelativeLayout>
62
63                <RelativeLayout
64                    android:id="@+id/tabInfo"
65                    android:layout_width="fill_parent"
66                    android:layout_height="fill_parent">
67
68                    <TextView
69                        android:id="@+id/textView2"
70                        android:layout_width="match_parent"
71                        android:layout_height="wrap_content"
72                        android:text="@string/enter"
73                        android:layout_alignParentTop="true"
74                        android:layout_centerHorizontal="true"
```

```
75                      android:layout_marginTop="60dp"
76                      android:background-"#ff49546e"
77                      android:gravity-"center_horizontal"
78
79  android:textAppearance="?android:attr/textAppearanceLarge"
80                      android:textColor="@color/pale_blue"
81                      android:textSize="55sp" />
82
83              <ImageView
84                      android:id="@+id/memberPhoto"
85                      android:layout_width="250dp"
86                      android:layout_height="250dp"
87                      android:layout_below="@+id/textView2"
88                      android:layout_centerHorizontal="true"
89                      android:layout_marginTop="20dp"
90                      android:src="@drawable/none"
91                      android:contentDescription="@string/photo" />
92
93              <EditText
94                      android:id="@+id/memberName"
95                      android:layout_width="fill_parent"
96                      android:layout_height-"wrap_content"
97                      android:layout_alignParentStart="true"
98                      android:layout_centerVertical="true"
99                      android:hint="@string/name"
100                     android:inputType="textCapWords"
101                     android:textSize="25sp" />
102
103             <EditText
104                     android:id="@+id/memberDetail"
105                     android:layout_width="fill_parent"
106                     android:layout_height="wrap_content"
107                     android:layout_alignParentStart="true"
108
109                     android:layout_below="@+id/memberName"
110                     android:hint="@string/details"
111                     android:inputType=
112                         "textMultiLine|textCapSentences"
113                     android:textSize="25sp" />
114
115             <EditText
116                     android:id="@+id/memberPhoneNumber"
117                     android:layout_width="fill_parent"
118                     android:layout_height="wrap_content"
119                     android:layout_alignParentStart="true"
120                     android:layout_below="@+id/memberDetail"
121                     android:hint="@string/phone_number"
122                     android:inputType="phone"
123                     android:textSize="25sp" />
124
125             <Button
```

```
126                              android:id="@+id/addBTN"
127                              android:layout_width="wrap_content"
128                              android:layout_height="wrap_content"
129                              android:layout_below="@+id/memberPhoneNumber"
130                              android:layout_centerHorizontal="true"
131                              android:enabled="false"
132                              android:text="@string/add_btn"
133                              android:textSize="25sp" />
134
135                  </RelativeLayout>
136
137
138
139              </FrameLayout>
140
141          </RelativeLayout>
142      </TabHost>
143
144  </RelativeLayout>
```

Part 4: The `listview_item` Layout

Each pet contact record is added to the scrollable `ListView` by inflating a `listView_item.xml` for each record added to the list of contacts.

The construction of this layout is shown in Figure 9-14. The `LinearLayout` root element simplifies the structure, which contains an `ImageView` and a nested

❙ FIGURE 9-14 Pet contact record appears as a layout using `listview_item.xml`.

LinearLayout. This design allows the photo of a pet to appear on the left side of the record and the name, details, and phone number for the pet's owner to appear on the right.

The XML code for `listview_item.xml` is as follows:

```
listview_item.xml
1   <?xml version="1.0" encoding="utf-8"?>
2   <LinearLayout xmlns:android="http://schemas.android.com/apk/res/android"
3       android:layout_width="match_parent"
4       android:layout_height="match_parent">
5       <ImageView
6           android:layout_width="200dp"
7           android:layout_height="200dp"
8           android:id="@+id/memberPhoto"
9           android:contentDescription="@string/app_name"
10          android:padding="30dp"
11          android:paddingLeft="30dp"
12          android:paddingTop="30dp"
13          android:paddingRight="30dp"
14          android:paddingBottom="30dp" />
15
16      <LinearLayout
17          android:orientation="vertical"
18          android:layout_width="fill_parent"
19          android:layout_height="fill_parent">
20
21
22          <TextView
23              android:layout_width="wrap_content"
24              android:layout_height="wrap_content"
25              android:text="@string/name"
26              android:id="@+id/textViewName"
27              android:textSize="30sp"/>
28
29          <TextView
30              android:layout_width="wrap_content"
31              android:layout_height="wrap_content"
32              android:text="@string/details"
33              android:id="@+id/textViewDetail"
34              android:textSize="20sp"/>
35
36          <TextView
37              android:layout_width="wrap_content"
38              android:layout_height="wrap_content"
39              android:text="@string/phone_number"
40              android:id="@+id/textViewPhone"
41              android:textSize="20sp"/>
42      </LinearLayout>
43
44
45  </LinearLayout>
```

Part 5: The `Pet` Data Model

The `Pet` class is used to model a pet object. This class corresponds with the columns in the SQLite database table. The photo for the pet is stored as a uniform resource identifier, URI.

```
Pet.java
1    package com.cornez.petcontacts;
2
3
4    import android.net.Uri;
5
6    class Pet {
7        private int _id;
8        private String name;
9        private String detail;
10       private String phone;
11       private Uri photoURI;
12
13       public Pet(int id, String nm, String det, String ph, Uri iURI){
14           _id = id;
15           name = nm;
16           detail = det;
17           phone = ph;
18           photoURI = iURI;
19       }
20       public int getId(){
21           return _id;
22       }
23
24       public String getName(){
25           return name;
26       }
27
28       public String getDetails(){
29           return detail;
30       }
31
32       public String getPhone(){
33           return phone;
34       }
35
36       public Uri getPhotoURI(){
37           return photoURI;
38       }
39
40   }
```

Part 6: The `DBHelper` for the Application

The database table will be contructed using the schema identified in Part 1 of this lab example. In this schema, the _id column will be typeset as INTEGER PRIMARY KEY AUTOINCREMENT. The Java code for DBHelper is shown as follows:

```
DBHelper.java
1   package com.cornez.petcontacts;
2
3   import android.content.ContentValues;
4   import android.content.Context;
5   import android.database.Cursor;
6   import android.database.sqlite.SQLiteDatabase;
7   import android.database.sqlite.SQLiteOpenHelper;
8   import android.net.Uri;
9
10  import java.util.ArrayList;
11  import java.util.List;
12
13
14  public class DBHelper extends SQLiteOpenHelper {
15      private static final int DATABASE_VERSION = 1;
16      private static final String DATABASE_NAME = "petManager";
17      private static final String TABLE_NAME = "contacts";
18      private static final String KEY_ID = "_id";
19      private static final String KEY_NAME = "name";
20      private static final String KEY_DETAIL = "detail";
21      private static final String KEY_PHONE = "phone";
22      private static final String KEY_IMAGEURI = "imageUri";
23
24      public DBHelper(Context context){
25          super(context,DATABASE_NAME, null, DATABASE_VERSION);
26      }
27
28      @Override
29      public void onCreate(SQLiteDatabase db){
30          db.execSQL("CREATE TABLE " + TABLE_NAME + "("
31                  + KEY_ID + " INTEGER PRIMARY KEY AUTOINCREMENT,"
32                  + KEY_NAME + " TEXT,"
33                  + KEY_DETAIL + " TEXT,"
34                  + KEY_PHONE + " TEXT,"
35                  + KEY_IMAGEURI + " TEXT)" );
36      }
37
38      @Override
39      public void onUpgrade(SQLiteDatabase db,
40                          int oldVersion,
```

```
41                                      int newVersion){
42          db.execSQL("DROP TABLE IF EXISTS "+ TABLE_NAME);
43          onCreate(db);
44      }
45
46      public void createContact(Pet pet){
47          SQLiteDatabase db = getWritableDatabase();
48
49          String insert = "INSERT or replace INTO " + TABLE_NAME +   "("
50                  + KEY_NAME +", "
51                  + KEY_DETAIL + ", "
52                  + KEY_PHONE +", "
53                  + KEY_IMAGEURI + ") " +
54                  "VALUES('"
55                  + pet.getName() + "','"
56                  + pet.getDetails() + "','"
57                  + pet.getPhone() + "','"
58                  + pet.getPhotoURI() +"')" ;
59          db.execSQL(insert);
60          db.close();
61      }
62
63
64
65      public Pet getContact(int id){
66          SQLiteDatabase db = getReadableDatabase();
67
68          Cursor cursor = db.query(TABLE_NAME, new String[]{
69                  KEY_ID, KEY_NAME, KEY_DETAIL, KEY_PHONE,
70                  KEY_IMAGEURI}, KEY_ID + "=?",
71                  new String[]{String.valueOf(id)},null,null,null,null);
72
73          if(cursor!=null){
74              cursor.moveToFirst();
75          }
76          Pet pet = new Pet(Integer.parseInt(
77              cursor.getString(0)),
78              cursor.getString(1),
79              cursor.getString(2),
80              cursor.getString(3),
81              Uri.parse(cursor.getString(4)));
82          db.close();
83          cursor.close();
84
85          return pet;
86      }
87
88
89      public void deleteContact(Pet pet){
90          SQLiteDatabase db = getWritableDatabase();
```

```
91          db.delete(TABLE_NAME,
92                  KEY_ID + "=?",
93                  new String[]{String.valueOf(pet.getId())});
94          db.close();
95      }
96
97      public int getContactsCount(){
98          SQLiteDatabase db = getReadableDatabase();
99          Cursor cursor = db.rawQuery("SELECT * FROM "+ TABLE_NAME, null);
100         int count = cursor.getCount();
101         db.close();
102         cursor.close();
103
104         return count;
105     }
106
107
108     public int updateContact(Pet pet){
109         SQLiteDatabase db = getWritableDatabase();
110
111         ContentValues values = new ContentValues();
112         values.put(KEY_NAME, pet.getName());
113         values.put(KEY_DETAIL, pet.getDetails());
114         values.put(KEY_PHONE, pet.getPhone());
115         values.put(KEY_IMAGEURI, pet.getPhotoURI().toString());
116
117         int rowsAffected = db.update(
118                 TABLE_NAME,
119                 values,
120                 KEY_ID +
121                 "=?", new String[] {String.valueOf(pet.getId())});
122         db.close();
123
124         return rowsAffected;
125     }
126
127     public List<Pet> getAllContacts(){
128         List<Pet> allPets = new ArrayList<Pet>();
129
130         SQLiteDatabase db = getWritableDatabase();
131         Cursor cursor = db.rawQuery("SELECT * FROM "+ TABLE_NAME, null);
132
133         if(cursor.moveToFirst()){
134
135             do{
136                 allPets.add(new Pet(Integer.parseInt(
137                 cursor.getString(0)),
138                 cursor.getString(1),
139                 cursor.getString(2),
140                 cursor.getString(3),
```

```
141                      Uri.parse(cursor.getString(5))));
142              }
143              while(cursor.moveToNext());
144          }
145          cursor.close();
146          db.close();
147
148          return allPets;
149      }
150
151  }
```

Part 7: The Application Controller–`MainActivity`

`MainActivity` serves as the controller of the application. It allows the user to choose one of two tab activities: (1) add a new pet contact to the database, or (2) list all the pet contacts in the database.

An `ArrayAdapter` will be used to populate the list of contacts displayed when the VIEW ALL PETS tab is active.

The Java code for `MainActivity` is shown as follows:

Lines 45–46:   A default image will be assigned to pet contacts that do not have a photograph. The none.png drawable is located by its path:

android.resource://com.cornez.petcontacts/drawable/none.png

Line 57:   A `TabHost` container for the tabbed window view is declared. The content for its action tabs will be set in the `onCreate()` callback method.

```
MainActivity.java
 1   package com.cornez.petcontacts;
 2
 3   import android.app.Activity;
 4   import android.content.Intent;
 5   import android.graphics.drawable.Drawable;
 6   import android.net.Uri;
 7   import android.os.Bundle;
 8   import android.text.Editable;
 9   import android.text.TextWatcher;
10   import android.view.ContextMenu;
11   import android.view.Menu;
12   import android.view.MenuItem;
13   import android.view.View;
14   import android.view.ViewGroup;
15   import android.widget.AdapterView;
```

```
16   import android.widget.ArrayAdapter;
17   import android.widget.Button;
18   import android.widget.EditText;
19   import android.widget.ImageView;
20   import android.widget.ListView;
21   import android.widget.TabHost;
22   import android.widget.TextView;
23   import android.widget.Toast;
24
25   import java.util.ArrayList;
26   import java.util.List;
27
28
29   public class MainActivity extends Activity {
30
31       //DATABASE AND ADAPTER OBJECTS
32       DBHelper dbHelper;
33       ArrayAdapter<Pet> arrayAdapter;
34
35       //SINGLE RECORD INFORMATION IN A LISTVIEW
36       List<Pet> PetArrayList = new ArrayList<Pet>();
37
38       //PET CONTACT DATA ENTRY SCREEN
39       Button addContactBTN;
40       ImageView inputPhotoId;
41       EditText inputPetName;
42       EditText inputPetDetails;
43       EditText inputPhoneNumber;
44       Drawable noPetImage;
45       Uri defaultImage = Uri.parse("android.resource:
46                       //com.cornez.petcontacts/drawable/none.png");
47
48       Boolean newEntry = true;
49
50       //PET LISTING SCREEN
51       ListView petListView;
52       ImageView listViewPhoto;
53       TextView listViewName;
54       TextView listViewDetails;
55       TextView listViewPhone;
56
57       TabHost tabHost;
58       int contactIndex;
```

The `onCreate()` callback method will perform the initialization for the application. This includes instantiating a DBHelper object to establish the database schema, inflating the activity's user interface layout, referencing widgets in the UI, and installing the action tabs.

Lines 68–74:   The widgets for the tab container to ADD PET INFORMATION are referenced.

Lines 75:   The widget for the tab container to VIEW ALL PETS is referenced. This widget is a ListView that will display the records stored in the database.

Lines 79–91:   A simple approach to allowing the user to delete a contact is to register a context menu for the items in a ListView. The context menu simplifies a navigation system by appearing only when the user performs a long-click gesture (a click followed by a hold).

The method call registerForContextMenu() will register a context menu to be shown for the given pet contact element. This method will set the View.OnCreateContext-MenuListener on the view to this activity, so onCreate-ContextMenu(ContextMenu, View, ContextMenu-Info) will be called when it is time to show the context menu.

The specific pet contact is identified by an index position, shown on Line 88.

Lines 94–96:   The TabHost container is located on the activity_main.xml layout. setup() is called before adding tab information.

Lines 97–101: The action tab for ADD PET INFORMATION is initialized. Each tag is assigned the information as follows:

1. Tab indicator: Specified by its initial label.

2. Tab content: Specified by the id of the View.

3. Tab tag spec: A tag name. For example, "information" is the tag name used for the ADD PET INFORMATION tag.

Lines 103–106: The action tab for VIEW ALL PETS is initialized.

```
MainActivity.java (continued)
59      @Override
60      protected void onCreate(Bundle savedInstanceState) {
61          super.onCreate(savedInstanceState);
62          setContentView(R.layout.activity_main);
63
64          // TASK 1: SET UP THE DATABASE
65          dbHelper = new DBHelper(getApplicationContext());
66
67          // TASK 2: REFERENCE INPUT UI COMPONENTS FROM THE LAYOUT
68          addContactBTN = (Button) findViewById(R.id.addBTN);
69          inputPetName = (EditText) findViewById(R.id.memberName);
70          inputPetDetails = (EditText) findViewById(R.id.memberDetail);
```

```
71      inputPhoneNumber = (EditText)
72              findViewById(R.id.memberPhoneNumber);
73      inputPhotoId = (ImageView) findViewById(R.id.memberPhoto);
74      noPetImage = inputPhotoId.getDrawable();
75      petListView = (ListView) findViewById(R.id.listView);
76
77
78      //TASK 3: DELETE PET CONTACT
79      registerForContextMenu(petListView);
80      petListView.setOnItemLongClickListener(
81              new AdapterView.OnItemLongClickListener() {
82                  @Override
83                  public boolean onItemLongClick(
84                      AdapterView<?> parent,
85                      View view,
86                      int position,
87                      long id) {
88                    contactIndex = position;
89                    return false;
90                  }
91              });
92
93      // TASK 4: CREATE ACTION TABS: ADD PET INFORMATION
94      tabHost = (TabHost) findViewById(R.id.tabHost);
95
96      tabHost.setup();
97      TabHost.TabSpec tabSpec =
98                  tabHost.newTabSpec("add pet information");
99      tabSpec.setContent(R.id.tabInfo);
100     tabSpec.setIndicator("add pet information");
101     tabHost.addTab(tabSpec);
102
103     tabSpec = tabHost.newTabSpec("view all pets");
104     tabSpec.setContent(R.id.tabList);
105     tabSpec.setIndicator("view all pets");
106     tabHost.addTab(tabSpec);
107
108     // TASK 5: A PET CAN BE ADDED ONCE USER HAS ENTERED A NAME
109     inputPetName.addTextChangedListener(new TextWatcher() {
110         @Override
111         public void beforeTextChanged(CharSequence s,
112                                         int start,
113                                         int count,
114                                         int after) {
115         }
116
117         @Override
118         public void onTextChanged(CharSequence s,
119                             int start, int before, int count) {
120             addContactBTN.setEnabled(String.valueOf(
121                 inputPetName.getText()).trim().length() > 0);
```

```
122              }
123
124              @Override
125              public void afterTextChanged(Editable s) {
126
127              }
128          });
129
130          // TASK 6: LISTENER EVENTS FOR PHOTO SELECTION AND BUTTON
131          inputPhotoId.setOnClickListener(getPhotoFromGallery);
132          addContactBTN.setOnClickListener(recordPetInformation);
133
134          //TASK 7: POPULATE THE DATABASE
135          if (dbHelper.getContactsCount() != 0)
136              PetArrayList.addAll(dbHelper.getAllContacts());
137
138          populateList();
139      }
```

Lines 142–154:   An `OnClickListener` callback is defined: `getPhoto-FromGallery`. This callback is invoked when the `Image-View` representing a photo of the pet is clicked. An `Intent` is used to launch an activity to select a photo image from the gallery. By calling the method `setType()`, an explicit intent is created to return an image.
Note: The `onActivityResult()` method on Lines 232–242 will return a photo selected from the photo gallery.

Lines 157–189:   An `OnClickListener` callback is defined: `record-PetInformation`. When this callback is triggered, a pet contact record is added to the database and displayed in the ListView on the screen. If the contact already exists, an error message is displayed as a Toast pop-up.

```
MainActivity.java (continued)
140     //******* ACTIVATE AN INTENT
141     //******* TO CHOOSE A PHOTO FROM THE PHOTO GALLERY
142     private final View.OnClickListener getPhotoFromGallery =
143             new View.OnClickListener() {
144
145                 public void onClick(View v) {
146                     Intent intent = new Intent();
147                     intent.setType("image/*");
148                     intent.setAction(Intent.ACTION_GET_CONTENT);
149
150                     startActivityForResult(
151                             Intent.createChooser(intent,
```

```
152                                        "Select Contact Image"), 1);
153                 }
154         };
155
156     //*********** ADD PET RECORD TO THE DATABASE *******
157     private final View.OnClickListener recordPetInformation =
158             new View.OnClickListener() {
159
160             public void onClick(View v) {
161                 Pet contact = new Pet(
162                         dbHelper.getContactsCount(),
163                         String.valueOf(
164                             inputPetName.getText().toString()),
165                         String.valueOf(
166                             inputPetDetails.getText().toString()),
167                         String.valueOf(
168                             inputPhoneNumber.getText().toString()),
169                         defaultImage);
170
171                 if (!contactExists(contact)) {
172                     dbHelper.createContact(contact);
173                     PetArrayList.add(contact);
174                     arrayAdapter.notifyDataSetChanged();
175                     Toast.makeText(getApplicationContext(),
176                             inputPetName.getText().toString()
177                                     + " has been added.",
178                             Toast.LENGTH_SHORT).show();
179                     newEntry = true;
180                     onResume();
181                     return;
182                 }
183                 Toast.makeText(getApplicationContext(),
184                         String.valueOf(inputPetName.getText())
185                                 + "has already been added."
186                                 + "Use another name",
187                         Toast.LENGTH_LONG).show();
188             }
189         };
```

Lines 192–202: onCreateContextMenu() is called when a context menu for the pet contact View is about to be shown. Context menu attributes, such as an icon and header title are set. A single menu item, DELETE (Delete Contact), is placed on the context menu.

Lines 204–211: onContextItemSelected() is called when an item in a context menu is selected. In this simple application, only one item was added to the context menu, DELETE.

The index of the record to be deleted is identified and the row is removed from the database table. The `ArrayAdapter` calls its member method `notifyDataSetChanged()` to notify the attached `ListView` that the underlying data has been changed and should refresh itself.

```
MainActivity.java (continued)
190  //*************CONTEXT MENU : DELETE A PET
191
192      public void onCreateContextMenu(
193                          ContextMenu menu,
194                          View view,
195                          ContextMenu.ContextMenuInfo menuInfo) {
196
197          super.onCreateContextMenu(menu, view, menuInfo);
198
199          menu.setHeaderIcon(R.drawable.ic_launcher);
200          menu.setHeaderTitle("Contact ...");
201          menu.add(Menu.NONE, 1, Menu.NONE, "Delete Contact");
202      }
203
204      public boolean onContextItemSelected(MenuItem item) {
205                  dbHelper.deleteContact(
206                      PetArrayList.get(contactIndex));
207                  PetArrayList.remove(contactIndex);
208                  arrayAdapter.notifyDataSetChanged();
209
210          return super.onContextItemSelected(item);
211      }
212
213      private boolean contactExists(Pet member) {
214          String first = member.getPhone();
215          int contactCount = PetArrayList.size();
216
217          for (int i = 0; i < contactCount; i++) {
218              if (first.compareToIgnoreCase(
219                  PetArrayList.get(i).getPhone()) == 0)
220                  return true;
221          }
222          return false;
223      }
```

Lines 238–241:   `populateList()` is called to bind the data associated with the `ArrayAdapter` to the `ListView`.

Lines 243–275:   The `ContactListAdapter()` class is a custom `ArrayAdapter`. This class provides a resource id to reference the layout named `listview_item.xml`.

The constructor parameters consist of the current context, the layout resource ID for a pet contact item, and the ListView. The pet contact item layout will be used when instantiating layout views containing contact data.

```
MainActivity.java (continued)
224
225        // INTENT RETURNS A PHOTO SELECTED FROM THE PHOTO GALLERY
226        public void onActivityResult(int reqCode,
227                                     int resCode,
228                                     Intent data) {
229            if (resCode == RESULT_OK) {
230                if (reqCode == 1) {
231                    newEntry = false;
232                    defaultImage = data.getData();
233                    inputPhotoId.setImageURI(data.getData());
234                }
235            }
236        }
237
238        private void populateList() {
239            arrayAdapter = new ContactListAdapter();
240            petListView.setAdapter(arrayAdapter);
241        }
242
243        private class ContactListAdapter extends ArrayAdapter<Pet> {
244            public ContactListAdapter() {
245                super(getApplicationContext(),
246                        R.layout.listview_item, PetArrayList);
247            }
248
249            @Override
250            public View getView(int position,
251                                View view,
252                                ViewGroup parent) {
253                if (view == null)
254                    view = getLayoutInflater().inflate(
255                            R.layout.listview_item, parent, false);
256
257                Pet currentContact = PetArrayList.get(position);
258
259                listViewName = (TextView)
260                        view.findViewById(R.id.textViewName);
261                listViewDetails = (TextView)
262                        view.findViewById(R.id.textViewDetail);
263                listViewPhone = (TextView)
264                        view.findViewById(R.id.textViewPhone);
265                listViewPhoto = (ImageView)
```

```
266                            view.findViewById(R.id.memberPhoto);
267
268                listViewName.setText(currentContact.getName());
269                listViewDetails.setText(currentContact.getDetails());
270                listViewPhone.setText(currentContact.getPhone());
271                listViewPhoto.setImageURI(currentContact.getPhotoURI());
272
273                return view;
274            }
275        }
276
277        @Override
278        public void onResume() {
279            super.onResume();
280            //CLEAR OUT PET INFORMATION IF IT IS A NEW ENTRY
281            if (newEntry) {
282                inputPetName.setText("");
283                inputPetDetails.setText("");
284                inputPhoneNumber.setText("");
285                inputPhotoId.setImageDrawable(noPetImage);
286            }
287
288        }
289
290        @Override
291        public boolean onCreateOptionsMenu(Menu menu) {
292            // Inflate the menu.
293            getMenuInflater().inflate(R.menu.menu_main, menu);
294            return true;
295        }
296
297        @Override
298        public boolean onOptionsItemSelected(MenuItem item) {
299            // Handle action bar item clicks here. The action bar will
300            // automatically handle clicks on the Home/Up button, so long
301            // as you specify a parent activity in AndroidManifest.xml.
302            int id = item.getItemId();
303
304            //noinspection SimplifiableIfStatement
305            if (id == R.id.action_settings) {
306                return true;
307            }
308
309            return super.onOptionsItemSelected(item);
310        }
311    }
```

■ Exercises

9.1 Briefly describe three scenarios for data storage suitable for SharedPreferences.

9.2 Briefly describe what can happen when information entered by a user is not persisted.

9.3 Briefly describe the characteristics of the following storage options.
   a. SharedPreferences
   b. File-based Storage
   c. SQLite

9.4 What type of data storage would you choose for saving your favorite recipes?
   a. SharedPreferences
   b. File-based Storage
   c. SQLite

9.5 True or False. Files saved into external storage can be configured for deletion or long-term storage on a device when the application is removed.

9.6 True or False. An SD card is always available as external storage on an Android device.

9.7 True or False. Data saved to internal storage will be available after an application is uninstalled from a device.

9.8 True or False. Internal storage is always available, assuming there is space.

9.9 True or False. By default, files saved to internal storage cannot be viewed by other applications.

9.10 Which of the following primitive data types is not supported by SharedPreferences?
   a. Int
   b. Double
   c. Float
   d. Boolean

9.11 Which of the following data types is not supported by SQLite?
   a. TEXT
   b. REAL
   c. BLOB
   d. DATE

9.12   Which SQLite data type can be used to store a date or time value?
   a. INTEGER

   b. REAL

   c. TEXT

   d. All of the above

9.13   When an image data is stored in SQLite, what value type will typically be used?
   a. REAL

   b. BLOB

   c. DATE

9.14   True or False. SharedPreferences support many collections of key-value pairs.

9.15   Which of the following is not an operation in SQLite?
   a. LOCATE

   b. SELECT

   c. UPDATE

Index